PRAISE FOR NEUROTR

"*NeuroTribes* is a sweeping and penetrating history . . . presented with -ing reading; it will change how you think of autism, and it belongs alo a Claiborne Park, on the bookshelf of anyone interested in autism and t

—from the foreword by Oliver Sacks, auth gs

"*NeuroTribes* is beautifully told, humanizing, important. It has earned its enthusiastic forew ; it has found its place on the shelf next to *Far from the Tree*, Andrew Solomon's landmark appreciation of neurological differences. At its heart is a plea for the world to make accommodations for those with autism, not the other way around, and for researchers and the public alike to focus on getting them the services they need."

—*New York Times Book Review*

"*NeuroTribes* is remarkable . . . Silberman has done something unique: He's taken the dense and detailed history of autism and turned the story into a genuine page-turner. The book is sure to stir considerable discussion."

—John Elder Robison, neurodiversity scholar in residence at the College of William & Mary and author of *Look Me in the Eye*

"A lively, readable book . . . To read *NeuroTribes* is to realize how much autistic people have enriched the scope of human knowledge and diversity, and how impoverished the world would be without them." —*San Francisco Chronicle*

"The monks who inscribed beautiful manuscripts during the Middle Ages, Cavendish (an 18th century scientist who explained electricity), and many of the geeks in Silicon Valley are all on the autism spectrum. Silberman reviews the history of autism treatments from horrible blaming of parents to the modern positive neurodiversity movement. Essential reading." —Temple Grandin, author of *Thinking in Pictures* and *The Autistic Brain*

"Required reading for every parent, teacher, therapist, and person who wants to know more about autism."

—Parents.com

"Epic and often shocking . . . Everyone with an interest in the history of science and medicine—how it has failed us, surprised us and benefited us—should read this book." —*Chicago Tribune*

"The best book you can read to understand autism." —Gizmodo

"This gripping and heroic tale is a brilliant addition to the history of autism."

—Uta Frith, professor emeritus of cognitive development at University College, London

"It is a beautifully written and thoughtfully crafted book, a historical tour of autism, richly populated with fascinating and engaging characters, and a rallying call to respect difference." —*Science*

"Silberman's discovery, which he writes about in . . . *NeuroTribes: The Legacy of Autism and the Future of Neurodiversity*, is not trifling. Not only does it cast serious doubt on the notion that Kanner's discovery was completely independent of Asperger. Of perhaps greater importance, it may help resuscitate the reputation of Asperger—a man whose prescient ideas were long ignored." —*The Atlantic*

"Explores in fascinating, near-encyclopedic depth how autism has evolved . . . a gripping narrative written with journalistic verve." —*The Guardian*

"Steve Silberman reveals the untold history of autism: from persecution to parent blaming; from *Rain Man* to vaccines; of doctors for whom professional ego trumped compassion; of forgotten heroes like Hans Asperger, unfairly tainted by Nazi links. It ends on an optimistic note, with autistics reclaiming the narrative and defining autism on their terms—more difference than disability and an essential part of the human condition. Highly recommended for anyone with an interest in autism or Asperger's, or simply a fascination with what makes us tick."

—Benison O'Reilly, coauthor of *The Australian Autism Handbook*

"Few other books on the subject provide such a rich amalgam of social history and contemporary reportage."

—*Financial Times*

"Silberman's sweeping history is always sensitive and builds a persuasive argument that the ability to think differently is useful, necessary even, for the success of the modern world." —*New Scientist*

"An essential resource. My own copy is already dog-eared." —*Nature*

"A well-researched, readable report on the treatment of autism that explores its history and proposes significant changes for its future . . . In the foreword, Oliver Sacks writes that this 'sweeping and penetrating history . . . is fascinating reading' that 'will change how you think of autism.' No argument with that assessment." —*Kirkus Reviews*

NeuroTribes

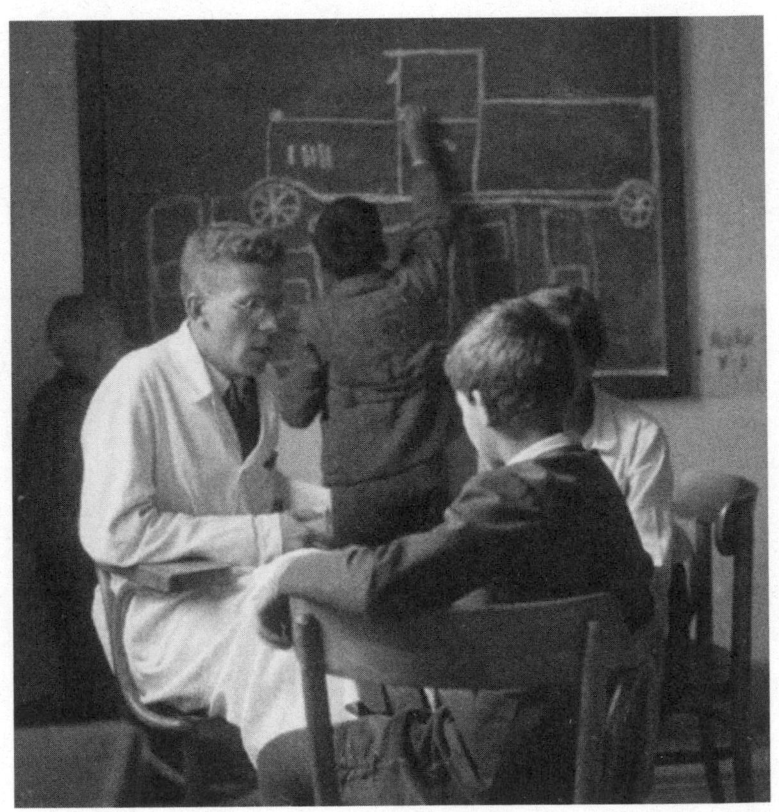

Hans Asperger and children at the University of Vienna, 1930s.

NeuroTribes

THE LEGACY OF AUTISM AND THE FUTURE OF NEURODIVERSITY

Steve Silberman

AVERY
an imprint of Penguin Random House
New York

AVERY
an imprint of Penguin Random House LLC
375 Hudson Street
New York, New York 10014

A portion of the introduction, "Beyond the Geek Syndrome," appeared in a different form in *Wired* magazine.
Photograph of Dr. Hans Asperger is courtesy of Dr. Maria Asperger Felder.
Originally published in hardcover by Avery, 2015

The Library of Congress has catalogued the hardcover edition as follows:

Silberman, Steve.
Neurotribes : the legacy of autism and the future of neurodiversity / Steve Silberman.
p. cm.
ISBN 978-1-58333-467-6
1. Autism. 2. Autistic people. 3. Neurobehavioral disorders. 4. Neuropsychology. I. Title.
RC553.A88S54 2015 2015006545
616.85'882—dc23

ISBN 978-0-399-18561-8 (paperback)

Printed in the United States of America
1 3 5 7 9 10 8 6 4 2

Book design by Meighan Cavanaugh

For Keith Karraker

Contents

Foreword

BY OLIVER SACKS

I first met Steve Silberman in 2001. He was a young journalist then, assigned to do a profile of me before the publication of my memoir *Uncle Tungsten.* He quickly gained my confidence, and I was to spend many hours talking with him, going with him to London, where I grew up, and introducing him to many of my friends and colleagues. Steve always dug deeper, asked more penetrating questions. He thought about things and made connections.

Around that time, he developed an interest in the growing "epidemic" of autism and Asperger's syndrome. He had been intrigued when I wrote about Temple Grandin and the savant artist Stephen Wiltshire in *An Anthropologist on Mars*, and now he set out to talk to researchers, physicians and therapists, parents of autistic children, and—most importantly—autistic people themselves. I know of no one else who has spent so much time simply listening, trying to understand what it is like to be autistic. Steve's journalistic instincts and skills led him to do a tremendous amount of research, illuminating as no one has before the history of Leo Kanner and Hans Asperger and their clinics, as well as those who followed. He has portrayed the remarkable shifting of attitudes toward autism and Asperger's over the past few decades.

NeuroTribes is a sweeping and penetrating history of all this, presented with a rare sympathy and sensitivity. It is fascinating reading; it will change how you think of autism, and it belongs alongside the works of Temple Grandin and Clara Claiborne Park, on the bookshelf of anyone interested in autism and the workings of the human brain.

NeuroTribes

Introduction: Beyond the Geek Syndrome

There is more than one way to do it.

—LARRY WALL

On a bright May morning in 2000, I was standing on the deck of a ship churning toward Alaska's Inside Passage with more than a hundred computer programmers. The glittering towers of Vancouver receded behind us as we slipped under the Lions Gate Bridge heading out to the Salish Sea. The occasion was the first "Geek Cruise"—an entrepreneur's bid to replace technology conferences in lifeless convention centers with oceangoing trips to exotic destinations. I booked passage on the ship, a Holland America liner called the *Volendam*, to cover the maiden voyage for *Wired* magazine.

Of the many legendary coders on board, the uncontested geek star was Larry Wall, creator of Perl, one of the first and most widely used open-source programming languages in the world. Thousands of websites we rely on daily—including Amazon, Craigslist, and the Internet Movie Database—would never have gotten off the ground without Perl, the beloved "Swiss Army chainsaw" of harried systems administrators everywhere.

To an unusual and colorful extent, the language is an expression of the mind of its author, a boyishly handsome former linguist with a Yosemite Sam mustache. Sections of the code open with epigrams from Larry's favorite literary trilogy, *The Lord of the Rings*, such as "a fair jaw-cracker dwarf-language must be." All sorts of goofy backronyms have been invented to explain the name (including "Pathologically Eclectic Rubbish Lister"), but Larry says that he derived it from the parable of the "pearl of great price" in the Gospel of Matthew. He told me that he wanted the code to be like Jesus in its own humble way: "Free, life-changing, and available to everyone." One often-used command is called *bless*.

But the secret of Perl's versatility is that it's also an expression of the minds of Larry's far-flung network of collaborators: the global community of Perl "hackers." The code is designed to encourage programmers to develop their own style and everyone is invited to help improve it; the official motto of this community is "There is more than one way to do it."

In this way, the culture of Perl has become a thriving digital meritocracy in which ideas are judged on their usefulness and originality rather than on personal charisma or clout. These values of flexibility, democracy, and openness have enabled the code to become ubiquitous—the "duct tape that holds the Internet together," as Perl hackers say. As the *Volendam* steered into open water, I watched with admiration as my fellow passengers pulled Ethernet cables, routers, and other networking paraphernalia out of their bags to upgrade the ship's communication systems. Instead of dozing in chaise longues by the pool, my nerdy shipmates were eager to figure out how things work and help make them work better. By midweek, they persuaded the captain to give them a tour of the engine room.

Each evening as our ship climbed toward the Arctic Circle, Larry made a dramatic entrance to the ship's dining hall on the arm of his wife, Gloria, sporting a ruffled shirt and neon tuxedo. He wore a different color tuxedo each night, in a retina-scorching array of lime, orange, sky blue, and mustard made possible by a going-out-of-business sale in his hometown. Belying the stereotype of hard-core coders as dull and awkward conversationalists, Larry and my other companions at the Wizards' Table displayed a striking gift for puns, wordplay, and teasing banter. One night, the topic of conversation was theoretical physics; the next, it was the gliding tones of Cantonese opera, followed by thoughts on why so many coders and mathematicians are also chess players and musicians. The tireless curiosity of these middle-aged wizards gave them an endearingly youthful quality, as if they'd found ways of turning teenage quests for arcane knowledge into rewarding careers. On weekends, they coded recreationally, spinning off side projects that lay the foundations of new technologies and startups.

After a few days on the ship, I came to feel that my fellow passengers were not just a group of IT experts who happened to use the same tools. They were more like a tribe of digital natives with their own history, rituals, ethics, forms of play, and oral lore. While the central focus of their lives was the work they did in solitude, they clearly enjoyed being with others who are on the same frequency. They were a convivial society of loners.

Their medieval predecessors might have spent their days copying manuscripts, keeping musical instruments in tune, weaving, or trying to transmute base metals into gold. Their equivalents in the mid-twentieth century aimed telescopes at the stars, built radios from mail-order kits, or blew up beakers in the garage. In the past forty years, some members of this tribe have migrated from the margins of society to the mainstream and currently work at companies with names like Facebook, Apple, and Google. Along the way, they have refashioned pop culture in their own image; now it's cool to be obsessed with dinosaurs, periodic tables, and *Doctor Who*—at any age. The kids formerly ridiculed as nerds and brainiacs have grown up to become the architects of our future.

WHEN THE *VOLENDAM* ARRIVED in Glacier Bay, at the midpoint of our journey, we drifted through a natural cathedral of ice with the engines switched off. The thunder of glaciers calving a few hundred yards away ricocheted across the deck. At three a.m., the sun barely dipped toward the horizon before rising again.

Just before the ship arrived back in Vancouver, I asked Larry if I could do a follow-up interview at his home in Silicon Valley. "That's fine," he said, "but I should tell you, my wife and I have an autistic daughter." I took note of his remark but didn't think much about it. Everything I knew about autism I had learned from *Rain Man*, the 1988 film in which Dustin Hoffman played a savant named Raymond Babbitt who could memorize phone books and count toothpicks at a glance. He was certainly a memorable character, but the chances of meeting such a person in real life seemed slim. As far as I knew, autism was a rare and exotic neurological disorder, and savants like Raymond were even rarer than that.

Larry was genial and forthcoming during our interview as he explained how Perl was born as a top secret project at the National Security Agency. His boss asked him to design a software tool for configuring two sets of computers remotely, one on the East Coast and one on the West. But Larry—who once wrote that the three great virtues of programmers are their laziness, impatience, and hubris—was loath to spend a month coding a widget that could be used for only a single task. Instead, he crafted Perl and slipped a tape containing the source code into his pocket before walking out the door.

As I chatted with Larry about his illustrious invention, a bulb lit up on the wall behind us. He had replaced the chime on his clothes dryer with an unobtrusive bulb because the little *ding!* at the end of each cycle disconcerted him. Such tinkering seemed par for the course for a man whose code made it possible for a Perl hacker named Bruce Winter to automate all the devices in his house and have his e-mail read to him over the phone—in 1998. It didn't occur to me until much later that Larry's keen sensitivity to sound might provide a link between his daughter's condition and the tribe of industrious hermits who invented the modern digital world.

A few months later, I started working on a profile of one of the most highly regarded female technologists in Silicon Valley, an entrepreneur named Judy Estrin. As a graduate student at Stanford in the 1970s, she helped Vint Cerf develop the TCP/IP protocols that form the backbone of the Internet. Judy went on to a successful career, launching startups in the male-dominated tech industry. To fill out Judy's personal story, I reached out to her brother-in-law Marnin Kligfeld, and asked him if I could interview him at home. "Sure," he said, "but just so you know, we have an autistic daughter."

That certainly seemed like an odd coincidence—*two* technically accomplished families in the Valley whose children had a rare neurological disorder? The next day, I was telling a friend at a neighborhood café about this curious synchronicity. Suddenly, a trim, dark-haired young woman at the next table blurted out, "I'm a special-education teacher. Do you realize what's going on? There is an epidemic of autism in Silicon Valley. *Something terrible is happening to our children.*"

Her words were chilling. Could they be true?

I STARTED READING every news story about autism I could find and downloading journal articles by the score. It soon became clear that the mysterious rise in diagnoses was not restricted to Silicon Valley. The same thing was happening all over the world.

To put the rising numbers in context, I familiarized myself with the basic time line of autism history, learning the story of how this baffling condition was first discovered in 1943 by a child psychiatrist named Leo Kanner, who noticed that eleven of his young patients seemed to inhabit private worlds, ignoring the people around them. They could amuse themselves for hours with little rituals like spinning pot lids on the floor, but they were panicked by the smallest changes in their environments, such as a chair or favorite toy being moved from its usual place without their knowledge. Some of these children were unable to speak, while others only repeated things they heard said around them or spoke of themselves detachedly in the third person. Claiming that their condition differed "markedly and uniquely" from anything previously reported in the clinical literature, Kanner named their condition *autism*—from the Greek word for self, *autos*—because they seemed happiest in isolation.

Then a year later, in an apparent synchronicity, a Viennese clinician named Hans Asperger discovered four young patients of his own who seemed strangely out of touch with other people, including their own parents. Unlike Kanner's young patients in Baltimore, these children spoke in elaborate flowery sentences while displaying precocious abilities in science and math. Asperger affectionately compared them to little professors. He also called their condition autism, though it's still a matter of dispute if what he saw in his clinic was the same syndrome that Kanner described.

For decades, estimates of the prevalence of autism had remained stable at just four or five children in ten thousand. But that number had started to snowball in the 1980s and 1990s, raising the frightening possibility that a generation of children was in the grips of an epidemic of unknown origin. After telling my editor about the frightening thing that the teacher in the café said about what was happening in Silicon Valley—the heart of *Wired*'s tech-savvy readership—I got permission to pursue this intriguing lead.

My research was facilitated by the fact that our apartment in San Francisco is located just down the hill from the University of California, which boasts one of the best medical libraries in the country. I became a regular browser in the stacks, poring through articles on epidemiology, pediatrics, psychology, genetics, toxicology, and other relevant subjects. Meanwhile, my shelves at home filled up with books like Clara Claiborne Park's *The Siege*, Oliver Sacks's *An Anthropologist on Mars*, and Temple Grandin's *Thinking in Pictures*. Each offered a view of the diverse world of autism from a unique vantage point.

The Siege, published in 1967, was the first book-length account of raising an autistic child by a loving and devoted parent. In a dark age when psychiatrists falsely blamed "refrigerator mothers" for causing their children's autism by providing them with inadequate nurturing, Park offered a candid portrait of life with her young daughter Jessy (called Elly in the book), who would sit by herself for hours, sifting sand through her fingers. With the meticulous eye of an explorer mapping uncharted territory, Park chronicled each small thing that Jessy learned to do in her first years, usually with great effort—only to apparently unlearn it shortly thereafter.

> Lying in bed in the leisurely mornings the summer she was two, I listened to her pronounce her name. "El-ly," she said. "El-ly"—laughing, chuckling, over and over again. The sounds, even the consonants, were exquisitely clear. I'm glad I got the chance to hear her. For a month or so she said it. Then she ceased completely. It was two years at least until she spoke her name again.

Sacks's books examined autism from the point of view of a compassionate clinician, embodying the tradition of astute observers like Jean-Martin Charcot, the founder of modern neurology, and Alexander Luria, who wrote case histories of his patients so full of insight into the human condition that they read like novels. In nuanced portraits of autistic people like artist Stephen Wiltshire and industrial designer Temple Grandin, Sacks cast light on the challenges that they face in their day-to-day lives while paying tribute to the ways they bring the strengths of their atypical minds to their work. "No two people with autism are the same: its precise form or expression is different in every case," he wrote. "Moreover, there may be a most intricate (and potentially creative) interaction between the autistic traits and the other qualities of the individual. So, while a single glance may suffice for clinical diagnosis, if we hope to understand the autistic individual, nothing less than a total biography will do."

Thinking in Pictures was such a biography written from the inside. Grandin, who didn't learn to speak until she was four, was initially misdiagnosed with brain damage—a common occurrence in the days when autism was still widely unknown even among medical professionals. Encouraged by her mother, Eustacia Cutler, and a supportive high school science teacher named Bill Carlock, Grandin developed her instinctive kinship with animals into a set of practical skills that enabled her to succeed in the demanding job of designing facilities for the livestock industry. Instead of the usual inspirational fable about an extraordinary person "triumphing" over a tragic medical condition, *Thinking in Pictures* was the story of how Grandin had come to regard her autism as both a disability and a gift—as "different, not less."

Then my real reporting began. I interviewed an eleven-year-old boy named Nick who told me that he was building an imaginary universe on his computer. Chubby, rosy-cheeked, and precociously articulate, he informed me that he had already mapped out his first planet: an anvil-shaped world called Denthaim that was home to gnomes, gods, and a three-gendered race called the *kiman*. As he told me about the civilization he was creating on his desktop, he gazed up at the ceiling, humming fragments of a melody over and over. The music of his speech was pitched high, alternately poetic and pedantic, as if the soul of an Oxford don had been awkwardly reincarnated in the body of a boy. "I'm thinking of making magic a form of quantum physics, but I haven't decided yet, actually," he said. I liked him immediately.

But Nick's mother broke down in tears as she told me that he didn't have a single friend his own age. She recalled one terrible day when his classmates bribed him to wear a ridiculous outfit to school. Because autistic people struggle to make sense of social signals in real time, Nick didn't realize that his schoolmates were setting him up for humiliation. I wondered what would become of this bright, imaginative, trusting boy as he got older and his peers became obsessed with social status and dating.

Other parents shared the ingenious strategies they developed to help their children learn to cope with a world full of unavoidable changes and surprises. A family event like a first trip on an airplane required months of careful planning and preparation. Marnin told me about the steps that he and his wife, Margo, an internist in the Bay Area, took to help their daughter Leah feel comfortable on her first visit to a new dentist. "We took pictures of the dentist's office and the staff, and drove her past the office several times," he said. "Our dentist scheduled us for the end of the day, when there were no other patients, and set goals with us. The goal of the first session was to have my daughter sit in the chair. The second session was so she could rehearse the steps involved in treatment without actually doing them. The dentist gave all of his equipment special names for her. Throughout this process, we used a large mirror so she could see exactly what was being done, and to ensure that there were no surprises."

Like many parents, Marnin and Margo had become amateur autism researchers themselves, devoting hours of their precious alone time each week to poring through the latest studies and evaluating therapies that might be of help to Leah. I learned that it was not unusual for parents whose finances were already strained by the cost of behavioral interventions to have to walk away from careers they loved to effectively become case managers for their children, fielding teams of behavioral therapists while going into battle with school boards, regional centers, and insurance companies to ensure that their children got the education and services they deserve.

One of the hardest things about having a child with autism, parents told me, was struggling to maintain hope in the face of dire predictions from doctors, school administrators, and other professionals who were supposed to be on their side. When Leah was diagnosed, an autism specialist told Marnin, "There is very little difference between your daughter and an animal. We have no idea what she will be able to do in the future." (At twenty-five, Leah is a bright, engaging, and affectionate young woman who remembers the names of every teacher and fellow student in her classes—going all the way back to preschool—and sings along with her favorite songs in perfect pitch.) In some ways, things hadn't changed much since the era when Clara Claiborne Park and Eustacia Cutler were told to put their daughters in institutions and move on with their lives.

To get to the bottom of what was happening in Silicon Valley, I asked Ron Huff of the California Department of Developmental Services to isolate the data from the agency's regional centers in Santa Clara County from the data in other areas of the state. He confirmed that there was a disproportionately high demand for autism services in the cradle of the technology industry.

By the time I wrote my article, the notion that high-tech hot spots like Silicon Valley and Route 128 outside Boston were havens for brilliant, socially awkward programmers and engineers was becoming a cliché in popular culture. It was a familiar joke in the industry that many hard-core coders in IT strongholds like Intel, Adobe, and Silicon Graphics—coming to work early, leaving late, sucking down Big Gulps in their cubicles—were residing somewhere in Asperger's domain. Kathryn Stewart, director of the Orion Academy, a high school for autistic kids in Moraga, California, said that she called Asperger's syndrome "the engineers' disorder." In his popular novel *Microserfs*, Douglas Coupland quipped, "I think all tech people are slightly autistic."

One possible explanation for a surge of autism in tech-centric communities like the Valley, UCLA neurogeneticist Dan Geschwind suggested to me, was that the culture of these places had opened up social possibilities for men and women on the spectrum that had never before existed in history. A speech-language pathologist named Michelle Garcia Winner told me that many parents in her practice became aware of their own autistic traits only in the wake of their child's diagnosis. Temple Grandin observed in *Thinking in Pictures*, "Marriages work out best when two people with autism marry or when a person marries a handicapped or eccentric spouse . . . They are attracted because their intellects work on a similar wavelength."

Attraction between people with similar genetic traits is called assortative mating. In 1997, cognitive psychologist Simon Baron-Cohen found that the fathers and grandfathers of children with autism were more likely to be engineers. Could assortative mating between men and women carrying the genes for autism be responsible for the rising number of diagnoses in the Valley?

My story exploring that hypothesis, "The Geek Syndrome," was published in the December issue of *Wired* in 2001. The world was still reeling from the horror of the attacks on the World Trade Center and the Pentagon on September 11, but e-mail started pouring into my inbox even before the magazine officially hit the newsstands. I heard from parents who said that the article helped them feel less isolated from other parents facing the same challenges with their own children; from clinicians who saw the same dynamic at work in their own high-tech communities; and from readers who had been struggling in social situations for most of their lives without knowing why. This flood of responses was both inspiring and humbling.

I have a twelve-year-old son. He takes accelerated math and science courses. His hobby is memorizing facts and figures about civil and military aircraft dating back to WWI. He's always had a fascination with clocks and watches. As you may have guessed, he has Asperger's syndrome. I've always asked myself, "Why is my son the way he is?" No one has been able to give me a possible answer until I read your article. You see, my husband is an engineer. After reading your article, it felt like the pieces were falling into place . . .

Your article sheds light on my original computer mentor. He could play four games of chess simultaneously and best all four opponents. He always knows what the total cost of the grocery shopping will be, including sales tax, before he enters the checkout line. But his son has trouble making eye contact . . .

When I was five years old, I was taking my electronic toys apart to see how they worked. (I also attempted to put them back together, with mixed results.) I have always been a voracious reader. I was reading college-level physics books bought at garage sales in the second grade. I used to annoy my father to no end wanting to build scale models of nuclear reactors, submarines, trains, anything you could think of. I have only had very small groups of close friends. I always considered that odd but never knew how to go about correcting it. Quite frankly, I find most people quite annoying and illogical—probably another common Asperger trait. :)

> It is so important that the general public and the hiring companies understand this group of people. Many will fall through the cracks due to their "odd" behaviors. Many have so much to contribute if given the chance.

Thankfully I received only a few e-mails like this one:

> Like many people, I'm starting to get fed up with the multiplication of psychological disorders such as attention deficit disorder and Asperger's syndrome. In the old days, if you didn't pay attention in class, you got whacked, and that usually did the trick for many youngsters.

I also got a call from a supervisor at Microsoft who told me, "All of my top debuggers have Asperger syndrome. They can hold hundreds of lines of code in their head as a visual image. They look for the flaws in the pattern, and that's where the bugs are."

At a conference a few months after my article came out, the grandmother of a young girl asked me to sign a copy of my article that had been photocopied so many times that I could barely make out the text.

Years passed, and I still got e-mail about "The Geek Syndrome" nearly every week. As time went on, though, I became convinced that by focusing on the dynamics of autism in one highly specialized community, I had missed a larger and more important story.

"THE ULTIMATE HACK FOR a team of Silicon Valley programmers," I wrote in 2001, "may turn out to be cracking the genetic code that makes them so good at what they do." The first decade of the new century was a time of hope for many families, as parents told me they felt optimistic that science was on the verge of finally unraveling the mystery of their children's condition. At the same time, nearly every public discussion of autism was dominated by a rancorous debate about vaccines, based on the controversial findings of a gastroenterologist in England named Andrew Wakefield who claimed to have uncovered a potential link between the measles, mumps, and rubella vaccine (commonly known as the MMR) and a form of regression that he dubbed "autistic enterocolitis."

Parents seeking advice about raising their newly diagnosed children wandered into a minefield of conflicting information about the safety of routine childhood inoculations and the potential role of heavy metals like mercury (contained in trace amounts in vaccine preservatives like thimerosal) in contributing to their children's developmental delays. As fears of a vast conspiracy between Big Pharma and corrupt government officials to cover up the effects of a global wave of vaccine injury circulated on the newly emerging Internet, vaccination uptake rates worldwide began to fall, raising the specter of a resurgence of plagues like pertussis that formerly killed tens of thousands of children a year. The official explanation for the soaring prevalence estimates was that the diagnostic criteria for autism had been gradually broadened over the years. But if that was the case, why were the criteria so inappropriately narrow in the first place? How could a formerly rare and obscure syndrome that was allegedly rooted in genetics suddenly seem to be everywhere at once?

Driven by the public outcry about the rising numbers, autism research—long neglected by funding agencies like the National Institutes of Health (NIH) precisely because the condition was believed to be so rare—was on the threshold of a golden age. Between 2000 and 2011, NIH grants in the field climbed each year by an average of $51 million, including a $1 billion boost in 2006 from the Combating Autism Act. Private funding groups like the Simons Foundation also pitched in, pushing the total investment in autism research to its highest levels in history. In 2011, Autism Speaks, the largest autism fund-raising organization in the world, announced a $50 million team effort with the Beijing Genomics Institute to map the whole genomes of ten thousand individuals from families with two or more autistic children. The organization's vice president of scientific affairs, Andy

Shih, promised that the project would generate "a transformative level of information."

By the end of the decade, it was clear that the scientists had done just what they had been paid to do. Molecular biologists had identified more than a thousand candidate genes and hundreds of de novo mutations associated with autism. They had also come to a greater understanding of epigenetics, the science of factors that mediate interactions between genes and the environment. The list of suspected environmental triggers for autism seemed to grow longer every day, encompassing dozens of chemicals in common use, prompting *Forbes* science writer Emily Willingham, the mother of an autistic son, to write a blog post with the headline, "This Just In . . . Being Alive Linked to Autism." Yet for families like Willingham's, the long-promised transformative moment that would improve the quality of their children's lives somehow never arrived.

The authors of a major study published in *Nature* admitted that even the most common genetic factors brought to light in their research were found in less than 1 percent of the children in their sample. "Most individuals with autism are probably genetically quite unique," said Stephen Scherer of the Hospital for Sick Children in Toronto. UCLA neurogeneticist Stanley Nelson added, "If you had 100 kids with autism, you could have 100 different genetic causes." A wry saying popular in the autistic community, "If you meet one person with autism, you've met one person with autism," turns out to be true even for molecular biologists.

In 2010, I spoke to one of the fathers I'd interviewed nine years earlier. He told me that he was no longer worrying about what had caused his daughter's autism. Instead, he was concerned about her future. She was about to "age out" of the modest level of services that the state of California provided to the family. Despite years of behavioral therapy, her skills had not developed to the point where he and his wife felt confident that she would ever be able to live on her own. "The question that keeps me up at night," he said, "is what will happen to our beloved daughter when we die?"

With the Centers for Disease Control (CDC) currently estimating that one in sixty-eight school-aged children in America are on the autism spectrum, millions of families will be facing sleepless nights in the coming decades. Many autistic adults are not exercising the strengths of their atypical minds at companies like Apple and Google—instead, a disproportionate number are unemployed and struggling to get by on disability payments. Two decades after the passage of the Individuals with Disabilities Education Act (IDEA), parents still routinely find themselves having to sue their local school boards to obtain an appropriate classroom placement for their son or daughter. Furthermore, very little of the money raised by advocacy organizations like Autism Speaks addresses the day-to-day needs of autistic people and their families. By focusing primarily on funding searches for potential causes and risk factors, these organizations reinforce the idea that autism is a historical anomaly—a distinctive problem of modern times that could be solved by a discovery that seems perpetually just around the corner.

As the mainstream world had a long argument about vaccines, newly diagnosed adults were engaged in a very different conversation about the difficulties of navigating and surviving in a world not built for them. By sharing the stories of their lives, they discovered that many of the challenges they face daily are not "symptoms" of their autism, but hardships imposed by a society that refuses to make basic accommodations for people with cognitive disabilities as it does for people with physical disabilities such as blindness and deafness.

A seemingly simple question began to formulate in my mind: After seventy years of research on autism, why do we still seem to know so little about it?

To FIND THE ANSWER to that question for this book, I decided to start my reporting at the very beginning, even before Kanner's and Asperger's allegedly independent discoveries of autism in the 1940s. By taking nothing for granted, I learned that the standard time line of autism history—its creation myth, so to speak—is fundamentally flawed in ways that render autistic people in previous generations harder to see. Until these inaccuracies in the time line are corrected, they will continue to hamper our ability to make wise choices about the kinds of research and societal accommodations that would be most beneficial to autistic people and their families.

One of the most promising developments since the publication of "The Geek Syndrome" has been the emergence of the concept of *neurodiversity*: the notion that conditions like autism, dyslexia, and attention-deficit/hyperactivity disorder (ADHD) should be regarded as naturally occurring cognitive variations with distinctive strengths that have contributed to the evolution of technology and culture rather than mere checklists of deficits and dysfunctions. Though the spectrum model of autism and the concept of neurodiversity are widely believed to be products of our postmodern world, they turn out to be very old ideas, proposed by Hans Asperger in his first public lecture on autism in 1938.

The idea of neurodiversity has inspired the creation of a rapidly growing civil rights movement based on the simple idea that the most astute interpreters of autistic behavior are autistic people themselves rather than their parents or doctors. In 2007, a woman named Amanda (now Amelia) Baggs posted an extraordinary video to YouTube called "In My Language" that has already been viewed more than a million times after being picked up by major media outlets like CNN and the *New York Times*. At first, the camera follows Baggs—who finds using spoken language difficult but can type 120 words a minute—as she presses her face into a book, rubs her fingers across her keyboard, flaps her hands, hums to herself, and bobs a Slinky up and down. A clinician would likely say that she is exhibiting self-stimulating behavior, one of the classic signs of autism. But in the second part of the video, "A Translation," Baggs makes clear that she is not sharing these intimate glimpses of her life as a plea for pity. Her intent is more subversive: celebrating the joy of her existence on her own terms. "My language is not about designing words or even visual symbols for people to interpret," she explains. "It is about being in a constant conversation with every aspect of my environment, reacting physically to all parts of my surroundings. Far from being purposeless, the way that I move is an ongoing response to what is around me." Her words are articulated by a text-to-speech program, as if a machine itself is speaking, yet few clips on YouTube offer a glimpse into a mind so profoundly humane.

Another impetus for writing this book was attending Autreat, an annual retreat organized by autistic people for autistic people, in a social environment carefully constructed to eliminate sources of sensory overload and anxiety while maximizing opportunities for people on the spectrum to simply relax, enjoy being themselves, and make connections with one another. My conversations at Autreat—some mediated by keyboards or other devices for augmenting communication—taught me more about the day-to-day realities of being autistic than reading a hundred case histories would. They also offered me the chance to be in the neurological minority for the first time in my life, which illuminated some of the challenges that autistic people face in a society not built for them, while disabusing me of pernicious stereotypes such as the idea that autistic people lack humor and creative imagination. After just four days in autismland, the mainstream world seemed like a constant sensory assault.

The notion that the cure for the most disabling aspects of autism will never be found in a pill, but in supportive communities, is one that parents have been coming to on their own for generations. In her last book, *Exiting Nirvana*, Clara Claiborne Park described how her neighbors helped her daughter build a life of happiness and fulfillment in Williamstown, Massachusetts, where Jessy still lives now, years after her mother's death. At fifty-five, she continues to work in the mailroom at Williams College while painting luminous, meticulously precise images of the world as she sees it, as she has done since her high school art teacher encouraged her to take up a brush forty years ago.

"That society has opened up a place for Jessy is what, more than anything else, has made it possible for her to live in, and even contribute to, the community she was born in," Park wrote in 2001. "I can write these words with a faith in a future I'll never see."

Steve Silberman
San Francisco
August 2010–2015

One

THE WIZARD OF CLAPHAM COMMON

As an experimenter he did not accept nature as given, but adapted it to respond to his questions.

—Christa Jungnickel and Russell McCormmach, *Cavendish: The Experimental Life*

Every evening in the last years of the eighteenth century, at precisely the same hour, a solitary figure stepped forth from the most unusual house on Clapham Common to take his nightly constitutional. To avoid the prying eyes of his neighbors, he stuck to the middle of the road, never hailing those who recognized him or touching his hat to acknowledge passersby. Dressed in fussy clothes that had last been in fashion decades earlier, he walked with a distinctive slouching gait, his left hand held behind his back. His route, like his departure time, never varied. He would proceed down Dragmire Lane to Nightingale Lane and walk for another mile, past quiet town houses and rows of oak and hawthorn trees, until he arrived at Wandsworth Common. Then he would walk back the way he came.

He had made only one revision to this itinerary in a quarter of a century, after attracting the attention of two women who planted themselves at a corner where they were likely to catch sight of him. Spotting them from some distance away, he abruptly launched himself in the perpendicular direction, making an undignified but effective escape through the muck of a freshly plowed field. After that, he scheduled his walks after dusk, when he was least likely to be seen.

He guarded his precious solitude within the boundaries of his estate as rigorously as he did outside them, communicating with his household staff in notes left on a hall table. A maid wielding a broom once made the error of surprising him in a stairwell, and his swift response was to order the construction of a second set of steps at the rear of the residence to prevent such an incident from ever happening again.

His neighbors in this rustic London suburb knew little about his solitary labor in the shed beside his house that would one day make his name immortal. There were rumors going around Clapham that he was some sort of wizard. Admittedly, the most striking feature of his estate did not help to dispel those rumors. From a little hillock in the yard, an eighty-foot pole projected into the sky, like a ship's mast rising from dry land.

By declining to sit for a formal portrait—usually a de rigueur concession for a man of his station—he nearly managed to block out the inquisitive gazes of historians from the future. The sole image of Henry Cavendish captured in his lifetime shows an aristocratic-looking man in a frock coat, frilled shirt-wrists, and white stockings, wearing a knocker-tailed periwig under a black three-cornered hat. This was a defiantly unchic style of dress even in the late 1700s, and he wore the same outfit every day of his adult life. Each year, when his coat—always the same shade of gray-green or violet—was on the verge of fading, he would prompt his tailor to sew up another one, identical to the first.

He was equally consistent in his dining habits. Though his personal fortune could have afforded him an ever-changing banquet of exotic delicacies shipped in from the farthest reaches of the empire, he subsisted for decades on the same humble dish at nearly every meal: leg of mutton. Once a week, when he took supper with his colleagues at the Royal Society Club, he invariably sat in the same chair, after hanging his hat and coat from a peg that may as well have had a plaque beside it engraved with his name.

That's how a sly young draftsman named William Alexander finally succeeded in capturing his portrait—by acting like the Georgian equivalent of a paparazzo. After talking his way into the club, Alexander parked himself unobtrusively in a corner of the room and sketched Cavendish's hat and coat dangling from the inevitable peg. At a subsequent meal, he drew his subject's face as he prepared to tuck into his dish of mutton. Then the artist combined the two images, yielding a composite portrait of the complete man.

Cavendish's inflexible routines and unvarying timetables were no more subject to amendment than the tides in Portsmouth harbor. On one rare occasion when he invited four Royal Society colleagues to dine with him in Clapham, a cook boldly ventured to suggest that a leg of mutton would hardly provide an adequate repast for five men. He replied, with characteristic terseness, "Well, then, get two."

DESPITE HIS ECCENTRIC COUTURE and the strange totem rising from his backyard, Henry Cavendish was not a wizard. He was, in eighteenth-century terms, a natural philosopher, or what we now call a scientist. (The word *scientist* wasn't coined until the nineteenth century, when it was proposed as a counterpart to *artist* by oceanographer and poet William Whewell.) He was not only one of the most ingenious natural philosophers who ever lived, he was one of the first true scientists in the modern sense.

His tireless explorations ranged across an entire university's worth of disciplines, encompassing chemistry, math, physics, astronomy, metallurgy, meteorology, pharmacy, and a few fields that he pioneered on his own. In an age when data-mining the Lord's creation was not yet regarded as a legitimate profession but more like an enlightened hobby, he defined the scope, conduct, and ambition of the scientific method for centuries to come.

The first surviving account of his work in the lab, a sheaf of papers dated 1764, details his study of arsenic and its metamorphosis into an off-white powder called "arsenical salt," now known as potassium arsenate. Like most of his peers, Cavendish mistakenly believed that the hidden agent of this transformation was phlogiston, an element akin to fire. By understanding this element, he hoped to discover a key to many types of chemical reactions. The phlogiston hypothesis turned out to be bunk—and he quickly abandoned it—but his observations in the lab were so astute that he anticipated the synthesis of potassium arsenate by ten years, using a simpler method than the man usually given credit for that discovery, pharmacist Carl Wilhelm Scheele. Unlike Scheele, however, Cavendish neglected to issue the equivalent of a press release, so he got none of the credit—while Scheele became famous by popularizing an inferior method of synthesis.

Cavendish's next major breakthroughs were in the study of the atmosphere. A late bloomer in the journals compared to his peers, he didn't even submit his first paper for publication until age thirty-five, chronicling his discovery of an unstable gas he called "inflammable air"—the element now known as hydrogen, the basic building block of the universe. He then determined the composition of water by using a spark of electricity to combine this new gas and "dephlogisticated" air—oxygen. When he removed the nitrogen and oxygen from a flask in his lab, he noticed that a tiny bubble of a third gas remained. In that bubble was the element argon, which wouldn't be officially discovered for another hundred years.

Scores of equally bold experiments followed. Cavendish analyzed the mathematics of musical intervals, formulated the theory of electrical potential, and was the first scientist to realize that a solution's electrical conductivity varies with its concentration. He proposed that a long-tailed fish called the torpedo was able to generate its own current like a living battery, and then proved it by sculpting an artificial fish in his lab out of shoe leather, pewter plates, glass tubes, and sheepskin and hooking it up to Leyden jars, creating a perfect simulation of the fish's electrical organs.

In 1769, lightning struck the steeple of the church of San Nazaro in Brescia, an ancient Roman city built at the foot of the Alps. The massive high-voltage pulse was conducted through the walls of the sanctuary to the basement, where the Venetian army had inconveniently stored one hundred tons of gunpowder. The resulting blast killed three thousand people, knocking one-sixth of the city flat. To prevent a similar fate from befalling the British army's powder cache in its arsenal at Purfleet, the Royal Society appointed Lord Henry to the "lightning committee" assigned to studying ways of insulating it. Among the foreign dignitaries who came along on that trip was a natural philosopher from the thirteen colonies who knew a thing or two about electricity himself—Benjamin Franklin.

The lightning committee devised a crafty plan, based on Cavendish's prescient theories of electricity, to surround a warehouse with metal rods, tipped with copper conductors, to draw impertinent discharges away from the unstable powder. While his paper on electrical theory was dismissed as too abstruse during his lifetime, two years after his death, a Royal Society historian declared it "the most rigid and satisfactory explanation of the phenomena of electricity . . . beyond dispute, the most important treatise on the subject that has ever been published."

Cavendish submitted only a fraction of his work to the Royal Society journal, *Philosophical Transactions*. But he was an exhaustive chronicler of his own research, churning out an endless stream of carefully annotated tables, charts, graphs, and notebooks that only a small circle of his colleagues ever saw. He prized the open and egalitarian sharing of data but felt no compulsion to take credit for his discoveries. He preferred to avoid competition and controversy, and simply wanted to perform his experiments in peace.

As a result, the formula that describes the flow of electrical current as a function of resistance is known as Ohm's law rather than Cavendish's law, though he anticipated the Bavarian physicist by a century. Likewise, a law describing electrostatic interaction between charged particles—the foundation of modern electromagnetic theory—is synonymous with the name of French physicist Charles Augustin de Coulomb, though Cavendish thought of it first. His seminal discovery that water is not a monolithic element but composed of hydrogen and oxygen is usually attributed to Antoine Lavoisier. Once again, Cavendish had figured this out earlier but neglected to make a fuss about it—unlike the grandiose Lavoisier, who invited members of the Royal Academy to assist him in a public demonstration. Thus it is Lavoisier, rather than Cavendish, who is hailed as the father of modern chemistry, though his experimental methods made that revolution possible.

Cavendish may have dressed like a man from the past, but he lived like one from the future. If he had been born three centuries later, he would have been hailed as a visionary "maker"—a hacker who isn't afraid to get his hands dirty in a machine shop.

II

To say that Cavendish's distaste for hype and self-promotion extended to his personal life would be an understatement. The statesman Lord Henry Brougham observed in 1845 that his taciturn colleague "uttered fewer words in the course of his life than any man who lived to fourscore years, not at all excepting the monks of La Trappe."

The source of this apparent shyness was social anxiety so intense that it nearly immobilized him in certain situations. Brougham described his face as "intelligent and mild, though, from the nervous irritation which he seemed to feel, the expression could hardly be called calm." At weekly gatherings of his colleagues hosted by Royal Society president Joseph Banks, he would pause outside on the stoop, hesitant to knock on the door, until the arrival or departure of another guest virtually forced him to go in.

On one such occasion, he was introduced to a fan from Austria who regaled him with fulsome praise. Cavendish stood silent, eyes downcast, until he spotted an opening in the crowd, at which point he bolted from the room and leapt into his carriage, which carried him directly home. His anxiety may have been exacerbated by the fact that the intonations of his voice struck others as odd and displeasing—"squeaking," according to the chemist Humphry Davy, who said that he seemed "even to articulate with difficulty." Another colleague described him uttering a "shrill cry" at Royal

Society meetings as he "shuffled quickly from room to room" to avoid being directly engaged. Cavendish was particularly discomfited if anyone tried to catch his eye.

It is not true, however, that he wanted to remove himself entirely from the company of his peers; he just wanted to stand off to the side, soaking everything in. Two scientists conversing on a topic of interest at the Royal Society's Monday Club might notice a hunched figure in a gray-green coat lurking in the shadows, listening intently. Eager to solicit his appraisal of their work, his fellow natural philosophers devised a devious but effective method of drawing him into an exchange.

"The way to talk to Cavendish is never to look at him," said astronomer Francis Wollaston, "but to talk as it were into a vacancy, and then it is not unlikely but you may set him going." Once he was set going, it turned out that he had plenty to say. "If he speaks to you, continue the conversation," Wollaston advised. "He is full of information, particularly as to chemistry."

One of the few people that Lord Henry welcomed into the innermost precincts of his life was Charles Blagden, a young scientist he met through the Royal Society who was similar to him in several important ways. He was relentlessly curious, was scrupulous in the conduct of his experiments, and had an indelible memory for facts. But Blagden was also an avid reader, linguist, and conversationalist who maintained a thriving correspondence with researchers and explorers all over the world. "It is scarcely possible that any philosophical discoveries can be made in England," he once bragged, "without coming to my knowledge by one channel or another."

Together, the two men forged a mutually indispensable alliance. Cavendish became Blagden's human Google, answering any query that came up in his own work. The elder scientist's guiding hand was visible in six of the ten papers that Blagden published in *Philosophical Transactions*. In return, the reclusive lord was able to keep up with the state of his art without having to schmooze his way through the eighteenth-century equivalent of

TED conferences. Through Blagden, his life was richly interwoven with the lives and work of a global community of thinkers who were kept at a safe and comfortable distance.

III

Partly owing to Cavendish's great wealth, his preference for solitude was often confused with arrogance, selfishness, or disdain. A fellow scientist once described him as "the coldest and most indifferent of mortals," while others characterized him as insensitive, blind to the emotions of others, or mean. But he was not a nasty or vindictive man; he simply had no idea how to conduct himself in public. After a conversation with Blagden about the Monday Club, Cavendish explained his behavior by saying that some men lack "certain feelings," declining to be any more specific than that. In his diary, Blagden sympathetically described his mentor as a man of "no affections" who nonetheless "always meant well."

The most probing glimpse into the soul of this elusive genius was provided by the chemist George Wilson, who wrote the first full-length biography of Cavendish in 1851 based on accounts by his contemporaries. Appraising his subject's seeming lack of interest in anything but science, Wilson painted Cavendish's emotional life as a series of negations: "He did not love; he did not hate; he did not hope; he did not fear . . . His brain seems to have been but a calculating engine . . . He was not a Poet, a Priest, or a Prophet, but only a cold, clear intelligence, raying down pure white light, which brightened everything on which it fell, but warmed nothing."

Wilson also recognized, however, that Cavendish's reserve made it possible for him to conduct his research with such single-minded intensity. He was not self-absorbed; he was the opposite. He was wholly engaged in his study of nature, which provided its own form of communion—if not with the souls of other people, then with the hidden forces behind the visible face of things.

> Wisely, therefore, he dwelt apart, and bidding the world farewell, took the self-imposed vows of a Scientific Anchorite, and, like the Monks of old, shut himself up within his cell. It was a kingdom sufficient for him, and from its narrow window he saw as much of the Universe as he cared to see.

The kingdom of natural philosophy that Cavendish built on Clapham Common was surely more than "sufficient"—it would have been an extraordinary resource for a scientist in any century. The colleagues invited to join him for a dish of mutton must have seen something amazing: a house transformed into a vast apparatus for interrogating the mysteries of existence.

The first thing a visitor arriving by carriage from London would have noticed was that eighty-foot pole aimed at the sky, supported by huge struts near the base. Contrary to local rumors, it was not an instrument of divination but a towering mount for one of Cavendish's telescopes. Upon renting the estate in 1785, he immediately sketched out a design for this impressive piece of equipment, a crucial adjunct to his plan to convert the upper floor of the house into an astral observatory, complete with a transit room for recording the positions of stars as they traversed the meridian.

He turned the downstairs drawing room into a lab, installing a furnace, crucible, and fume hood, and stocking it with hundreds of beakers, flasks, pipes, and balances. In an adjoining room, he built a forge. Cavendish's passion for precision was manifest in the astonishing variety of measuring instruments—barometers, clocks, sundials, compasses, and rain gauges—arrayed throughout the house and grounds. When he took a road trip with Blagden (never for a mere vacation, but, say, to visit a factory to take notes on the production of iron), he affixed a primitive odometer called a "way-wiser" to the wheels of his carriage, so they would know precisely how many miles they had traveled. He also brought along a thermometer to take the temperature of any wells they happened to pass.

As a young inductee in the Royal Society, Cavendish was appalled to learn that the thermometers of his day could differ in their readings of the boiling point of water by two or three degrees. To the roster of his servants in Clapham, he added a dedicated instrument maker. His cabinets were filled with custom-made rulers, scales, triangles, maps, and other measuring devices fashioned of wood and brass. A scaffolding outside the house served as a mount for meteorological instruments. No potential source of data on the estate was wasted—not the wind, the rain, the passages of sunlight through the garden, nor the weight of damp air collecting in the branches of the oaks that stood around the house like sentinels.

Even the front yard was pressed into the service of his quantifying muse. The lawn, according to Wilson, "was invaded by a wooden stage, from which access could be had to a large tree, to the top of which Cavendish, in the course of his astronomical, meteorological, electrical, or other researches occasionally ascended." Six years after his death, when the last of his gear went on auction after being thoroughly picked over by his colleagues, eleven telescopes and forty-four thermometers were still available.

The contents of a lab cabinet cannot provide an inventory of a man's emotional life. But in this way too, Cavendish stayed out of view. No revealing diary entries, telling admissions, or confessions of unrequited yearning have come to light in his letters, which are predictably focused on science and the minutiae of his mundane affairs. Humphry Davy—a Byronically charismatic figure whose lectures drew standing-room-only crowds—clearly wanted to forge a friendship with the man he regarded as a mentor, but anything beyond a working relationship was perpetually out of reach. "He gave me once some bits of platinum, for my experiments, and came to see my results on the decomposition of the alkalis," Davy recalled. "But he encouraged no intimacy with anyone." After Cavendish's death, he told Wilson that he considered Cavendish "a great man, with extraordinary singularities."

Yet the life of a tree-climbing scientist can hardly be considered barren or bereft of fulfillment. He transformed his whole environment into a playground for his keenly focused senses and intellect. Charles Darwin once described his own brain as a machine for churning out hypotheses. Cavendish's was an engine for generating finely calibrated distinctions: *this, but not that.* His analysis of a single substance could yield volumes of rhapsodic description. His modern-day biographers, Christa Jungnickel and Russell McCormmach, wrote in *Cavendish: The Experimental Life*:

> By smell, he distinguished between the various acids and their products. He felt and observed textures: dry, hard, thin jelly, gluey, thick, stiff mud, lump. With colors, he made the greatest number of distinctions: milky, cloudy, yellow, pale straw, reddish yellow, pale madeira, red, reddish-brown, dirty red, green, bluish green, pearl color, blue, and transparent, turgid, and muddy. No poet paid greater attention to his sensations than Cavendish did to his.

One house-sized laboratory alone turned out to be insufficient to meet his research needs. He also turned a handsome three-story brick residence at No. 11 Bedford Square in London into a private library worthy of his alma mater, Cambridge. Contrary to the notion that he was an ungenerous man, Cavendish made his library's holdings freely available to fellow scholars. Visitors were furnished with a catalog, an on-site librarian to help them navigate the stacks, and a ledger for keeping track of checked-out items. (He dutifully entered the books he took home himself into the ledger.) Decorated all in green like its founder's beloved coat—with jade curtains, jade slipcovers, and fireplace screens of emerald silk—the library even boasted a prototype copier machine designed by James Watt. Etchings of the moon's surface were featured on the walls, like an exhibit from the twentieth century. There was even a special "museum" hall where he showed off his beloved collection of rare minerals.

Predictably, what was not on offer at No. 11 was an audience with the proprietor himself. Prospective borrowers were instructed not to disturb Cavendish if they caught sight of him browsing in the stacks and to promptly hasten home with their selections. Obviously he wasn't much for people, as another socially inept genius, Albert Einstein, observed about himself.

But to describe Cavendish as a man of no affections, or a passionless man, also misses the mark. His life was devoted to one single, all-consuming passion: the slow and patient increase of the sum of human knowledge. His mind was like a mirror held up to nature, unclouded by bias, rationalization, lust, jealousy, competition, pettiness, rancor, ego, and faith. As Wilson put it:

> His theory of the universe seems to have been, that it consisted *solely* of a multitude of objects which could be weighed, numbered, and measured; and the vocation to which he considered himself called was, to weigh, number, and measure as many of these objects as his allotted three-score years and ten would permit.

The virtuoso act of measurement that inscribed his name indelibly into history is now known simply as the Cavendish experiment. Its goal was as lofty as the apparatus it required was simple. Using four lead spheres, some rods, and a length of wire, he built a device to measure the density of Earth. The key to its cunning design—conceived in rudimentary form by geologist John Michell, who died before he could perform the experiment himself—was the correspondence between the mass of an object and its gravitational force.

Two of the spheres weighed 350 pounds, while the others were comparatively light at 1.6 pounds each. By attaching the lighter spheres to the ends of a wooden rod suspended on a wire, mounting the heavier spheres a few inches away, and setting the rod in motion like a pendulum, Cavendish contrived to gauge the torque of the wire as it oscillated. This, he hoped, would enable him to calculate the magnitude of the force acting on the spheres using Newton's law of universal gravitation and thus determine the density of the planet. It was an ambitious scheme, and Newton himself was doubtful that it could be successful. The attraction between the spheres, he predicted, would be so minute that it would be swamped by the tidal attraction of Earth's mass.

Newton was correct that the attraction between the spheres was very slight (just one part in 10 compared to Earth's gravity), but he underestimated what a man like Cavendish could pull off through sheer dogged persistence. First he built a stand-alone shed in his backyard to isolate the delicate oscillations of the mechanism from stray drafts and vibrations. Then he sealed the apparatus itself in a mahogany box and rigged up a system of pulleys so he could set the pendulum going without touching it. To calculate the forces acting on the spheres, he installed telescopes at both ends of the box, focusing them on vernier scales inside the chamber that enabled him to calculate the wire's torque to within 0.01 inch.

Working solo, he began his rounds of measurement at the height of summer on August 5, 1797. (He was sixty-six years old by that point.) Over and over, he set the pendulums swinging, took his position at the telescopes, and recorded his observations in a notebook. For months, he diligently applied himself to this single task, finally wrapping up his epic series of trials in May.

Ironically, Cavendish made a minor error of addition in his report for *Philosophical Transactions*, throwing off his published results by a fraction of a percent. But the figure he came up with was so close to the actual density of Earth that no researcher could best it for another hundred years. As a side benefit, his experiment indirectly provided the first estimate of the gravitational constant, known among physicists as "Big G," which also turned out to be astonishingly accurate. Cavendish's experiment is now recognized as the inaugural moment of modern physics, laying the groundwork for centuries of breakthroughs to come, including Einstein's theories of relativity.

It was also his last major foray in science. On February 24, 1810, Cavendish succumbed to an inflammation of the colon with no panic or drama, leaving the lion's share of his fortune to his nephew, George. Even in dying, he guarded the solitude that had enabled him to accomplish so much. His final instructions to his servants were to summon his young heir only after he had drawn his last breath and to leave him alone so that he could spend his final moments in peace.

A few days after Cavendish's death, Blagden paid tribute to his mentor by describing him as a "true anchor" who could "always depend on knowing what was right for him." It was a fitting eulogy for a man who lived completely on his own terms but benefited everyone by doing so.

The great house in Clapham is gone now, replaced in 1905 by rows of brick villas. Nightingale Lane is home to young entrepreneurs who take the Northern Line to central London each morning, breezing past kebab shops and chippies while chattering away on their smartphones—the perpetually humming, information-rich, intimately interconnected world that Cavendish made possible by serving his quantifying muse in solitude.

His last experiment brought him more fame after death than he ever sought in his lifetime. For decades after his interment in the family crypt in the All Saints' Church north of London, mothers would pause reverently before his yard, point to his abandoned shed, and tell their children, "On this spot, a man named Henry Cavendish weighed the world."

IV

The extraordinary singularities of this solitary pioneer were a source of perpetual puzzlement and frustration to his colleagues. In his diary, Wilson alluded to "talk about Mr. Cavendish, & explanation of character." But the theories proposed to explain his eccentricities over the years have often felt provisional or incomplete, as if some crucial data point was missing.

The word invoked most often to make sense of his behavior is *shy*. His contemporaries described him as "excessively shy," "peculiarly shy," even "shy and bashful to a degree bordering on disease." But mere shyness doesn't explain the overall oddity of his conduct, such as his adherence to rigid timetables, his insistence on wearing only one outfit for decades, and his habit of listening obliquely to conversations rather than talking face-to-face. The introduction of Jungnickel and McCormmach's magisterial biography is titled "The Problem of Cavendish," as if the man himself was one of the knotty conundrums that he spent his life trying to solve. In a follow-up book, McCormmach confessed that he had not yet laid the enigma to rest:

> These many years later, I still look for a fuller understanding, which I equate with explanation . . . Without an understanding of Cavendish's behavior, he appears simply strange, an object of curiosity at best, of moral judgment at worst, drawing pity or scorn. To leave him that way unnecessarily is a shame. He was an outstanding scientist, and one of the most baffling personalities in the history of science. A fuller understanding of him benefits both his biography and the history of science.

A famous story made the rounds that Cavendish once saw his fellow philosophers clustered around a window, where he thought they were looking at the moon. But after "bustling up to them in his odd way," he realized they were admiring a beautiful woman, and turned away saying "Pshaw!" With little more evidence than this and his run-in with the maid, some of his peers ventured to suggest that he had a pathological fear of women. But the Duchess Georgiana of Devonshire, who had a keen interest in chemistry, was one of the few people whom he regularly kept abreast of his experiments.

Psychoanalytically minded pundits have speculated that Cavendish may have been traumatized as a child by the death of his mother, Lady Anne de Grey. But she died before his second birthday, and his brother, Frederick, grew up to become an affable extrovert. As Wilson put it:

> Hundreds of youths have been . . . motherless, as Cavendish was, and have, nevertheless, grown-up to be warmhearted, generous, and even enthusiastic men. Frederick Cavendish was exposed to the same influences as his brother Henry, but became, notwithstanding, an exceedingly cheerful, genial, and benevolent, though somewhat eccentric man. The peculiarities, indeed, of a character like Henry Cavendish's, must be referred much more to original conformation, than to anything else.

A thoroughgoing appraisal of his "original conformation" would require a detailed accounting of his psychological development, but records of his early years are scant. Blagden said that Cavendish's preference for solitude had been established at a very young age: "His habits had, from early life, been secluded." One of the few things known about his childhood is that his entry into Hackney Academy, a private boarding school north of London, was delayed for four years; the standard age of enrollment was seven, but he was homeschooled by tutors until he was eleven, a style of education that had fallen out of favor among upper-class families decades earlier.

Some historians have proposed that Henry didn't get along with his father, Lord Charles, a prominent Whig and noted natural philosopher himself. But Charles—the Royal Society's resident expert on thermometers—showed every sign of being lovingly devoted to his son. When Henry was a boy, Charles invited him to conduct measurements of Earth's magnetic field in the garden of the house they shared for thirty years on Great Marlborough Street in London. After Henry returned from Cambridge, his father built him a lab so that his life's work could begin in earnest. Charles surrounded him with potential mentors by hosting Royal Society dinners, channeling his son's intellect into science, which became the one true love of his life. Finally, his last gift to him—a sizable fortune—enabled Henry to live for the rest of his life in a private world that was perfectly suited to his needs.

Cavendish was clearly an extraordinary man, fortunate enough to be born to a family of extraordinary means. If his father had been a brakeman or a miner, one of the greatest scientists in history might have ended up on a ward at the Bethlem Royal Hospital (commonly known as "Bedlam"), enduring the regimen of cold baths in vogue for the treatment of "withdrawn" patients at the time.

Few Nobel laureates of either gender have much resembled the Renaissance ideal of the *Uomo Universale*—the suave and supremely well-rounded human being equally accomplished in the rigors of the lab, the aesthetics of the atelier, and the art of scintillating conversation. Instead, they have tended to be persnickety oddballs in ill-tailored suits, sensible dresses, and rumpled cardigans, ruling deep domains of expertise with slide rules and unwavering commitments to accuracy. In many ways, the father of modern physics and the awkward prodigy who helped lead the field into the quantum era were kindred spirits born two centuries apart.

V

Raised in humbler circumstances than his posh Georgian predecessor, Paul Dirac grew up in Bristol, the son of a librarian and a tyrannically strict French teacher. His classmates remembered him as a tall, quiet, "un-English-looking" boy in unfashionable knickerbockers who virtually lived in the library, maintaining a "monomaniacal focus" on science while seeking refuge from his father's pedantry in adventure novels and comic books.

His uncanny aptitude for math showed itself early. A teacher once sent young Dirac home with a set of problems designed to keep him occupied all evening and was shocked when he had solved them by the afternoon. Even as a boy, he preferred a life of contemplation to the hurly-burly of the schoolyard. When he was nine, his teachers at the Bishop Road School awarded him with a telling prize: a copy of Daniel Defoe's *Robinson Crusoe*, the fictional autobiography of a castaway marooned for twenty-eight years on a remote island.

Lacking an aristocratic father to introduce him to potential mentors in science, Dirac trained at a technical school to become an electrical engineer. In his first year, he distinguished himself so highly that Cambridge offered him a scholarship to its prestigious math program. At St. John's College, his diffidence and taciturnity became "the stuff of legend," writes Graham Farmelo in a biography of the physicist called *The Strangest Man*. The newly matriculated Dirac would sit stiffly in the dining hall, hesitant to ask the person eating beside him to pass the salt, and greeting every question posed to him with blank silence or a stark yes or no. Incapable of bluffing his way through the protocols of polite conduct, he came across as cold, rude, disinterested, or uncaring, though he didn't intend to.

A classmate once tried to break the ice with him by casually remarking,

"It's a bit rainy, isn't it?" Dirac's strictly empirical response was to march over to the window, peer out, return to his chair, and reply, "It is not now raining." Inspired by his extreme verbal parsimony, his fellow students at St. John's invented a unit of measurement for the number of words that a person might utter in conversation, christening the minimum rate one "Dirac"—one word per hour. But like Cavendish lurking in the shadows at the Monday Club, he would often eavesdrop inconspicuously as his peers swapped stories.

Oblivious to contemporary modes of dress, Dirac wore cheap, unstylish suits in all weathers until they were threadbare, even after securing a generous salary as the Lucasian Chair of Mathematics at Cambridge (the position later held by Stephen Hawking). His mother practically had to beg him to buy a winter coat so she could stop fretting about his health. Though he seemed impervious to freezing temperatures, he was acutely sensitive to sounds—particularly the din of barking dogs, which were permanently banned from his household. Dirac's motor skills were notoriously poor; a classmate described his method of wielding a cricket bat as "peculiarly inept." Yet he was as devoted as Cavendish was to taking long walks on a regimented timetable, holding his hands behind his back as he efficiently ticked off the miles in his "metronomic" stride.

In an era when physicists like Einstein and Max Planck were fêted as international heroes in the press, Dirac had no interest in being a public figure. He routinely turned down honorary degrees because he felt they should be rewarded strictly on merit, and he refused an offer of knighthood because he didn't want strangers chummily referring to him as "Sir Paul" rather than "Mr. Dirac." Upon winning the Nobel in physics with Erwin Schrödinger in 1933, he told a reporter from a Swedish newspaper, "My work has no practical significance."

His life path diverged from Cavendish's in at least one important way: he married a bubbly Hungarian extrovert named Margit Wigner—nicknamed "Manci"—who urged him to supplement his pop-culture diet of comic books and Mickey Mouse cartoons with novels and an occasional foray to the ballet. (As Farmelo puts it, "He had wed his anti-particle.")

The newlyweds honeymooned in Brighton, where the love-struck groom rigged up a camera with a string so he could click the shutter himself. In one shot, the gawky physicist reclines beside his bride on the beach, attired in his usual three-piece suit, with a thicket of pencils sprouting from his pocket. "You have made a wonderful alteration to my life. You have made me human," Dirac gushed shortly after the wedding. This turned out to be an ongoing job. When Manci complained that he habitually ignored her questions, he pasted her queries into a spreadsheet and filled it in with his replies.

As a theoretical physicist, Dirac didn't need a lab to do his work; all he needed was a pencil, because his most finely calibrated instrument was his mind's eye. When he was young, a teacher told him that she felt he was cogitating not in words but in "another medium of forms and figures." He once described his own thoughts as essentially "geometrical." While visiting an art gallery in Copenhagen, he turned to fellow Nobel laureate Niels Bohr and said that he liked a certain painting because "the degree of inaccuracy is the same all over." He told journalists who asked him to make sketches of his highly abstract concepts for their readers that they would melt away like "snowflakes" if he tried.

The breakthrough that assured him of his own eponymous place in history is known as the Dirac equation. Worked out on scraps of paper at a schoolboy's desk in his sparsely furnished room at St. John's in a few months in 1927, his formula bridged a seemingly impassable gulf in physics by reconciling quantum mechanics and Einstein's special relativity in a single concise line of variables. His equation also implied the existence of a previously unsuspected form of particle—antimatter—three years before a scientist named Carl Anderson glimpsed the ghostly arcs of positrons passing through a lead plate in his lab.

Dirac made only one major miscalculation in the course of his career: underestimating the practical applicability of his work. The relationships between matter and energy that he described made possible the development of semiconductors, transistors, integrated circuits, computers, handheld devices, and the other innovations in microelectronics that ushered in the digital age. By capturing the ephemeral snowflakes in his mind in the universal language of mathematics, this man who found communication so arduous made it much easier for everyone else to communicate.

But even in a field in which absentminded professors are the rule rather than the exception, Dirac's colleagues were left unsettled and confused by his behavior. Einstein confessed, "I have trouble with Dirac. This balancing on the dizzying path between genius and madness is awful." Bohr claimed that Dirac was "the strangest man" he had ever met, furnishing Farmelo with a title for his biography. Like Cavendish, he was a walking riddle to everyone who crossed his path.

VI

It's hard to imagine the state of the modern world if these two remarkable scientists had never lived. Many aspects of life that we currently take for granted might never have been invented. Both men may have wondered at times if they had accidentally been born on the wrong planet, among chatty, well-intentioned creatures who wasted precious time trying to impress, flatter, outwit, and seduce each other. But their atypical minds were uncannily suited to the work they were born to do. They lived their lives in ways that were as precise, ritualized, and methodical as their experiments.

In 2001, neurologist Oliver Sacks proposed that he had uncovered the elusive solution to the problem of Cavendish in a condition that had fascinated him for decades. Writing for his peers in the journal *Neurology*, he observed that accounts of the reclusive lord's seemingly inexplicable idiosyncrasies—his "striking literalness and directness of mind, extreme single-mindedness, [and] passion for calculation and quantitative exactitude . . . coupled with a virtual incomprehension of social behaviors and human relationships"—closely resembled descriptions of adults with a type of autism called Asperger's syndrome, first described in America in the 1994 edition of the *Diagnostic and Statistical Manual of Mental Disorders*. Sacks also pointed out, however, that it was precisely these qualities that made Cavendish such a brilliant and prolific researcher. His singularities were inextricable from his genius.

When Sacks made this provocative suggestion, it was hard to remember an era when autism wasn't a frequent topic of conversation, even among people who had no personal connection to the subject. But enormous changes had taken place in an astonishingly short time. Just fifteen years earlier, mothers of autistic children often had to gently correct neighbors who thought they'd said their son or daughter was "artistic." The few pediatricians, psychiatrists, and teachers who read about the obscure condition in a textbook could safely assume that they would get through their entire careers without having to diagnose a single case. Sacks himself had played a role in this sea change by making the distinctive traits of autism recognizable to his colleagues in his sensitive portrayals of artist Stephen Wiltshire, the "calculating twins" George and Charles Finn, and industrial designer Temple Grandin in *An Anthropologist on Mars* and *The Man Who Mistook His Wife for a Hat.* He also served as an advisor to Dustin Hoffman when he developed the role of Raymond Babbitt for *Rain Man*, which provided audiences worldwide with their first glimpse of an adult identified as autistic.

By the time the burly British-born neurologist turned his diagnostic eye on the father of modern physics, the formerly obscure condition was well on its way to becoming a national obsession. Parsing the faintest signs of gaze aversion and self-stimulatory rocking in nerdy celebrities like Bill Gates had become a kind of hipster parlor game, while the increasingly convenient phrase "on the spectrum" telegraphed a whole constellation of quirks and eccentricities. At the outset of his article on Cavendish, however, Sacks stated firmly that he was not just jumping on the bandwagon of retrodiagnosing famous geeks from history with a trendy disorder. "There has been some tendency recently to claim Einstein, Wittgenstein, Bartok, and others as exemplars of autism," he wrote, dismissing the justifications for these claims as "very thin at best." But in the case of Cavendish, he found the evidence for an Asperger's diagnosis "almost overwhelming."

Dirac biographer Graham Farmelo came to a similar conclusion after a process of cautiously weighing the alternatives. "Nearly all" of the Dirac stories that physicists have been telling each other for years, he wrote in *The Strangest Man*, "might also be called 'autism stories.'" He says that he had no intention of venturing a diagnosis when he began researching the great man's biography. "Only after talking with about thirty people who knew Dirac very well (including two members of his close family) did I conclude that his behavior was so singular that I needed to say something about it," he told me. "My conclusion was that he very clearly passed every criterion for autistic behavior."

Physicist Freeman Dyson took Farmelo to task in the *New York Review of Books* for his speculative diagnosis of a man his wife found "friendly and amusing" when she went for a walk with him in Princeton. "Autism was until recently a rare disease, characterized by mental disorders that made the patient incapable of a normal life," he wrote. "The main symptom was a failure to achieve or understand social relationships with other human beings. If Dirac was autistic, then the word 'autism' must have a different meaning."

He had the right to be skeptical. By then the word *autism had* acquired a different meaning than the one that he was used to. But this radical reframing of the diagnosis had been negotiated in niche journals and closed-door meetings of subcommittees at the American Psychiatric Association, far from public view. The effects of these momentous decisions were still rippling outward to a world unprepared to make sense of them.

One thing is certain: if the Wizard of Clapham Common had managed to construct a time machine in his backyard, beaming himself directly to the waiting room of child psychiatrist Leo Kanner after his announcement of the discovery of autism in 1943, the brusque, cigar-puffing clinician would have sent him down the hall to another clinic. Adults weren't on Kanner's radar at all until much later, and the notion that his young patients might grow up to become physicists or chemists would have seemed absurdly optimistic. A more likely prognosis was a lifetime of custodial care in a state hospital: Raymond Babbitt's fate in *Rain Man*.

Even now, few people outside a small circle of cognitive psychologists know that the adoption of the spectrum model of autism by the psychiatric establishment in the 1980s represented a decisive defeat for the father of the diagnosis. For decades, Kanner maintained that his syndrome was monolithic by definition, limited to childhood, and vanishingly rare. The notion of an influential economist like Tyler Cowen touting the virtues of having an "autistic cognitive style," a Hollywood star like Daryl Hannah coming out in midlife about her diagnosis, or a Fields Medal–winning mathematician like Richard Borcherds musing about his autistic traits in the press would have seemed irresponsible to him, if not downright delusional. (Even comedian Jerry Seinfeld eventually got into the act, telling *Nightly News* host Brian Williams, "On a very drawn-out scale, I think I'm on the spectrum. Basic social engagement is really a struggle. But I don't see it as dysfunctional. I just think of it as an alternate mind-set.") To Kanner, autism was not merely an eccentric cognitive style or an alternate mind-set. It was a tragic form of childhood psychosis, akin to schizophrenia, caused by inadequate parenting. It was certainly nothing to be proud of.

The architect of the spectrum model was the mother of an autistic child herself, a British psychiatrist named Lorna Wing. Kanner would have instantly recognized her daughter Susie as a member of his rare tribe, but Wing well understood the challenges faced by families of children who had been excluded from a diagnosis on his terms. By overturning his conception of autism as a rare, inevitably devastating, and homogeneous disorder, she made it possible for tens of thousands of children, teenagers, and adults to gain access to the educational placements and social services they deserved, for the first time in history.

But Wing's quiet victory over the clinician who had dominated the field for more than forty years had unanticipated consequences. One was the emergence of gifted autistic adults like Temple Grandin into public life. As they began to articulate their experiences of growing up, they found commonalities that challenged even many of Wing's long-held assumptions about autism, such as the notion that people like her daughter lack empathy. Instead of seeing themselves as psychotic or intrinsically disordered, they came to take pride in their eccentricities, learning to see their minds as "different, not less," as Grandin put it.

Another unintended effect of the adoption of the spectrum model, however, was the reaction of concerned parents to a steep rise in estimates of autism prevalence all over the world. Few children diagnosed under Wing's new criteria seemed destined to become reclusive Nobel laureates, socially awkward Hollywood stars, or the next Bill Gates. Many of them struggled to acquire simple spoken language and rudimentary self-care skills and were prone to seizures and outbursts of self-injurious behavior. Even growing up to become the real-life equivalent of Raymond Babbitt (who was invariably described as a rare and extraordinarily capable "savant," though he was judged incapable of surviving outside of an asylum) seemed out of reach for many kids, particularly in the first difficult years of their lives.

And while the scope and understanding of the diagnosis changed drastically, the attitudes of many clinicians and educators were still catching up. Autism was widely considered a universally devastating condition, and parents were routinely told to prepare themselves for the inevitable day when their son or daughter would have to be shipped off to an institution.

In the shadow of the rising numbers, stories began to circulate on the Internet about babies that seemed to be developing normally until they received a routine immunization for measles, mumps, diphtheria, or whooping cough. Parents described the light going out of their children's eyes at the moment the needle punctured their skin, followed by violent convulsions, piercing cries, fever, and the sudden onset of severe digestive disturbances. Rumors of a new and terrifying form of autism, marked by dramatic regression, raced through online forums. Parents referred to their sons and daughters as having been kidnapped, as if a thief—dressed in a pediatrician's white coat—had stolen them away in the night. Meanwhile, public health officials, caught off guard by the soaring prevalence estimates, and alarmed by the growing number of parents deciding to opt their children out of mandatory vaccination programs, tried to tamp down panic with cautious, qualified terms of art like *broadened diagnostic criteria, heightened public awareness*, and *improved case finding*. To a worried mother searching her son or daughter's face for a telltale failure of eye contact, they may as well have been speaking Latin.

Parents of children born in the last decade of the twentieth century had to make their way forward through a maze of conflicting information. Was autism a congenital and incurable developmental disorder rooted in the complexities of the human genome, or the toxic by-product of a corrupt medical establishment driven to seek profit at all costs? Should they invest their energy in fighting daily battles with local school boards, insurance companies, and other byzantine bureaucracies, or pursue the myriad avenues to "recovery" for their children, touted by groups like Defeat Autism Now! and Talk About Curing Autism?

The parents in these groups were often caricatured as poorly informed, anti-science "denialists," but they were generally better acquainted with the state of autism research than the outsiders presuming to judge them. They obsessively tracked the latest developments in the field on electronic mailing lists and websites. They virtually transformed their homes into labs, keeping meticulous records of their children's responses to the most promising alternative treatments. They believed that the fate of their children's health was too important to be left to the alleged experts who had betrayed and misled families like theirs for decades. Motivated by the determination to relieve their children's suffering, they became amateur researchers themselves, like the solitary man who calculated the density of the earth in his backyard with the help of his global network of correspondents.

Two

THE BOY WHO LOVES GREEN STRAWS

In a room on a high ridge overlooking the Santa Cruz Mountains in California, Leo Rosa is waking up. The sun breaks through a bank of coastal fog, filling his window with streaks of orange and crimson. A cherubic eleven-year-old with hazel eyes under a tuft of russet curls, he climbs out of bed to give his father a hug.

Leo's father, Craig, produces science videos for KQED, a public TV station in San Francisco. Shannon Rosa is a blogger, editor, and software consultant. Each morning, they take turns helping their son get ready for school. The first thing that Leo does each day is read a list of icons taped to his door, which Shannon made for him by downloading and laminating clip art from the Internet. This list—his "visual schedule"—is written in a pictorial language that is easier for his mind to absorb than words. An image of a boy putting on his shoes prompts Leo to get dressed, followed by the likeness of a toothbrush, and then an icon of a boy making his bed.

Leo's visual schedule parses the sprawling unpredictability of an eleven-year-old's life into a series of discrete and manageable events. This helps him regulate his anxiety, which is a challenge for people on the spectrum at every age. Physical traces of his struggle to channel the unruly energy flowing through him are visible throughout the Rosa household, but only if you know just where to look. The white posts along the railing on the second floor are freshly painted, because Leo splintered them one day, enjoying the soothing feeling of deep pressure as he wedged himself between the railing and the wall. There are thin cracks in the lid of an antique camphorwood chest at the foot of Craig and Shannon's bed, because the chest made a perfect launching pad for experimental flights toward their mattress.

The Rosas have adapted their lives and their living space to create as safe and comfortable an environment for Leo as possible. The location of the house—on a cul-de-sac at the brushy summit of a barely paved mountain road in an unincorporated area of Redwood City—is far enough away from traffic that they don't have to worry too much if Leo slips out the door on an unscheduled outing. The layout of the building—a two-story ranch house with a floor-to-ceiling space at the center, which the Rosas keep clear of furniture—enables Leo to pace furiously in circles, jump up and down, or propel himself across the floor on his scooter board without bashing into walls or sharp edges. When nothing else but an hour of intense, pounding physical activity will do, there's a trampoline in the backyard. (Friends in the city have made similar accommodations for their kids by getting creative with inexpensive beanbags and trapezes.)

The open-plan arrangement of the house also lets the Rosas keep a watchful eye on their son and enables him to know where they are. Lying next to Craig in bed at night, Shannon can listen to the sounds that Leo is making in his room next door. If she hears him softly singing himself to sleep, she knows he's okay.

A FRAMED SHEET OF paper by the front door is titled "Questions to Ask Leo." Shannon designed this list—*What is your name? How old are you? What is your address? What is your big sister's name? What is your little sister's name?*—to serve two purposes: to encourage shy visitors to initiate conversations with her son, and to help Leo learn to verbalize things that he knows but isn't always able to communicate. Leo can understand many of the phrases that his parents say to him (in clinical terms, he has good receptive language), but expressive speech does not come easily.

On a good day, Leo might say about forty words, mostly nouns. "Pizza for dinner," he'll say brightly. "Costco." Some days, Leo hardly says anything at all, though no one could accuse him of being unexpressive. He has his own versatile lexicon of nonverbal sounds, song fragments, and catchphrases that he uses to communicate with the people he knows and trusts.

When Leo is happy, he bursts out in riffs of scat singing, making up little melodies as he goes. When he's basically content but feeling restless, he makes a sound like *tikka, tikka, tikka*. If he's more anxious than that, he makes a sound like Jimmy Durante: "*Atch-cha-cha!*" A sudden burst of happiness can inspire Leo to whirl his arms around and gallop in circles shouting, "*Whoop! Whoop! Whoop!*" When he's tired, he makes a soft keening noise. And when Leo is hungry, he just sobs his heart out. After visiting an aquarium in Seattle with his family, he added the chirps of a beluga whale to his repertoire of echolalia (the term of art for the way that autistic people sample the speech they hear around them and repurpose it for their own use).

When Leo is in the car with his mother and doesn't know where they're going, he might say, "We're *not* going to pick up Kianna"—the name of a girl in preschool that he carpooled with many years ago. When he really wants to climb something but knows he's not supposed to (though in truth he may have climbed it already), he'll announce: "*No climbing!*" When Leo is so angry that he wants to push somebody but also wants to demonstrate to his mother that he has good self-control, he'll say: "Don't want to push."

And when Shannon is driving past his favorite doughnut shop, he'll steel himself against disappointment by saying something that she muttered under her breath a long time ago: "We're not going to get any fucking doughnuts today." Shannon doesn't use that kind of language casually in front of her two daughters, Zelly and India. But the moment that she heard Leo echo that phrase, she realized that her son is always listening, even when he seems to be off in his own world.

In a cluttered room down the hall, Leo's sisters are also getting ready for the day. Zelly (short for Gisela, the name of Craig's aunt) already has the poised, self-possessed air of the thoughtful young woman she's becoming at thirteen. In a family of brazen eccentrics, she's taken on the job of being the "normal" one. India, who is five years younger, exudes her own potent brand of charisma, but it's more antic and subversive, with mischief and drama perpetually brewing in her bright green eyes behind thick glasses. While Zelly is generally reserved, India will walk right up to a stranger in a restaurant and say, "My, what a pretty dress you have!" She instinctively knows how to make herself the center of attention and work a crowd. As the Rosa girls will readily inform you, they're getting a little too old to sleep in the same room. "My sister is a total PITA," India whispers when we're alone, using the family-friendly acronym for *pain in the ass.* But five minutes later, she and Zelly are doing gymnastics on the floor together. Their yearning for more personal space is trumped by their fierce loyalty to their brother.

While eating breakfast with his sisters in the kitchen, Leo suddenly jumps down from his chair as an alarming expression—between terror and exhilaration—takes possession of his face. He bolts for the door but his father doesn't flinch; instead, Craig calls after him in his softest voice, "Where ya goin', buddy?"

Leo immediately sits down again and resumes eating as if nothing had happened. His first spoonful of yogurt this morning contains a crushed tablet of Risperdal, an atypical antipsychotic developed for the treatment of schizophrenia in adults. His parents don't like the idea of giving him this powerful drug, but for now, it seems to be helping him get a handle on his most distressing behavior, which is teasing and bullying India. Leo has never quite forgiven her for being an unexpected intrusion into a world that he was just getting used to himself. (On the day that Shannon brought India home from the hospital, his response was to march up to his mother and announce, "Bye-bye baby!") One of the downsides of the drug is that it amplifies Leo's already considerable appetite. His uncanny ability to snatch food from distant plates has earned him a family nickname: the Cobra. When Shannon brings bowls of oatmeal to the table, India quietly slides hers out of Cobra range and mutters under her breath, "This is mine."

Smells of coffee and toast waft through the kitchen. Leo starts banging his bowl against the counter, but India doesn't even look up. Sitting at the table in a frilly white dress and sparkly slippers ("I like shiny things," she whispers, "I'm a magpie!") India looks like a miniature princess from a grander civilization, accepting the hospitality of common folk who are doing the best they can.

Suddenly Leo jumps up from the table again and says to his father, "Green straw?" It is not yet time for his first green straw of the day, but he will get one before the school bus pulls into the driveway—one of tens of thousands of wide, bright green Starbucks straws that Leo has used over the years for the purpose of stimming (self-stimulation), one of the things that autistic people do to regulate their anxiety. They also clearly enjoy it. When nonautistic people do it, it's called fidgeting and it's rarely considered pathological.

A red straw from Burger King can occasionally fit the bill, or a blue one from Peet's. Clear straws from Costco just don't cut it. But a green straw from Starbucks is Leo's Platonic stim. If Shannon allowed him to do so, he would take a green straw to bed with him, or even better, a pair—one between his lips and the other in his toes. He would stim in the bath, on the toilet, and jumping on the trampoline.

Leo's fascination with straws is a wonder to behold. First, he tears the coveted object free of its paper wrapper; then he wets his lips and starts nibbling along its length, palpating the stiff plastic to pliability; finally, he masticates it to a supple L-shaped curve. All the while, he's twiddling the far end in his fingers, making it dance with a finesse that would be considered virtuosic if he was performing sleight-of-hand tricks. Watching Leo's Ritual of Straws is like seeing one of W. C. Fields's vaudeville routines with a hat and cane run at hyperspeed.

The Rosas let their son indulge in his passion for green straws within certain limits. But Shannon quickly realized that jamming a few extras into her purse at the mall would never result in enough to meet his needs. She did what she often does now when she's coping with some aspect of Leo's behavior that proves unexpectedly difficult to manage: she turned to her online posse. She put the word out on her blog that she was looking for volunteers for a grassroots effort dubbed L.U.S.T.—the League of Unrepentant Straw Thieves.

> The agents of L.U.S.T. are dedicated and sneaky. They keep Leo well supplied with contraband. They are experts at slipping out of restaurants with a fully paid bill (and generous tip) to distract from the extra straws in their pockets. L.U.S.T. agents have no problem hopping into the car with me and Leo—even on a Thanksgiving evening—and cruising the Starbucks stall in a local grocery store for a few pieces of The Good Stuff, because they know that those straws might make the difference between a successful and an explosive dinner.

The covert forces of L.U.S.T. descended on the espresso bars and drive-throughs of the South Bay en masse. Owners of local Starbucks franchises may have wondered why an apparently inexplicable run on Frappuccinos was not reflected in the day's total at the register. One particularly hip barista allowed Shannon to liberate a fistful of the primo green from her corporate overlords in Seattle out of a stock closet.

Operation L.U.S.T. was a triumphant success. Leo got what he needed, and having an abundant stash of the Good Stuff around the house inspired him to an unprecedented flood of expressive language. Admittedly, this language was very focused: "New straw! New GREEN straw! I want a new straw! Mommy, I want a new straw, PLEASE! Mommy! MOMMY!" By working with Leo's home-program supervisor, Shannon learned that it was possible to strike a balance with her son by reassuring him that his green-straw jones would be gratified at regular intervals. An L-shaped icon was promptly incorporated into Leo's visual schedule.

A few years ago, Shannon pulled the family minivan up to the entrance of Zelly's summer camp, when Leo, with his usual exquisite timing, made it known that he had to pee. There were no bathrooms in the vicinity, so Shannon escorted her son behind a convenient bush and urged him to do his business as India and her pal Katie pretended not to watch. She assured the girls that peeing on school grounds was tolerated under certain circumstances, and even kind of cool. "Sometimes, when you're a boy, it's great," she said. "You can pee in bushes all over the world!"

"And sometimes, when you're a girl, you have a brother with autism," India shot back. "And then your whole world changes."

II

Raising Leo has transformed the Rosas' world in ways that they couldn't have imagined. One of the most common misconceptions about autism is that it drives families apart. (It's a pernicious myth perpetuated by the media: divorce rates are no higher for families like the Rosas.) But helping Leo become the best Leo he can be has brought the family closer, binding them into a tight circle of love and support around their boy. When Zelly was ten, she wrote a poem:

Leo
My brother
Leo is different
Yet I love him
still. Hits, grabs elbows,
chews on straws. I
cope with all of this
For I am his big sister.

The day-to-day effort of ensuring that Leo gets the respect and support he deserves has also brought the Rosas closer to other families. Many of their friends are either parents of kids with developmental disabilities, on the autism spectrum themselves, or both. These friends don't flinch when Leo bursts out of line at the museum to beat his chest and howl like Tarzan, and they don't cast withering looks in Shannon's direction when he has a meltdown at the mall. They understand why, in movie theaters, she and Leo always sit in the last row of seats close to the door.

These friends speak the initiated language of special-needs parenting—an alphabet soup of acronyms like *OT* (occupational therapist) and *SLP* (speech-language pathologist), and nouns that have evolved into verbs, like *tantrumming* and *toileting*. They know how to work effectively with teachers to put together an IEP, an individualized education program—a plan outlining a set of learning goals for a single child. Until Congress passed the Education for All Handicapped Children Act in 1975 (renamed the Individuals with Disabilities Education Act in 1990), kids with all sorts of disabilities were routinely denied access to an education. Children with autism were particularly vulnerable to institutionalized prejudice because most psychologists believed they were incapable even of rote learning. This theory was debunked in the 1970s, but subtler forms of discrimination persist. Several couples in the Rosas' social circle have been forced to sue their local school boards to obtain the education for their kids legally mandated by IDEA.

But raising Leo has required the Rosas to modify some daydreams they had when they were young. When Shannon was in her twenties, producing digital atlases at Electronic Arts and the Learning Company—the perfect job for a self-professed "cartography geek"—she used to fantasize about immersing herself in foreign cultures and exotic climes with a boyfriend who wouldn't want to laze around the pool while she went scuba diving through the Chandelier Caves. Paying tens of thousands of dollars a year for Leo's behavioral therapy, which was not covered by Craig's health insurance until recently, made some destinations seem even farther away. But the Rosas decided early on that they would not stop going to museums, movies, and restaurants because they have an exuberant boy who occasionally feels like he needs to tear his clothes off. They've let their friends know that they're eager to be invited along on family activities—even if they need to make arrangements, even if they have to slip out the back door at some point, even if they occasionally have to say no.

The waiters at their favorite Indian restaurant in Redwood City know that bringing a steaming plate of naan (Leo's favorite) to their table with dispatch is a good idea. At the café where Craig and Shannon have been enjoying breakfast on Saturday mornings together since before their kids were born, the staff encourages Leo to practice his social communication by asking him, "How are you?" and really listening when he answers. The owners of a local bakery never let the Rosas apologize for Leo's shouting when the buttery aroma of croissants fresh out of the oven launches him into a paroxysm of joy. They just shrug and say, "That's what kids are like."

AT THE END OF a long day in the editing suite at KQED, Craig settles onto the couch beside Leo to watch Hayao Miyazaki's enchanting animated tale *My Neighbor Totoro*. It's not the first time they've seen the film together, or even the five hundredth: nearly every night for the past decade, Leo has concluded his activities for the day by saying, "*Totoro!*"

That's Craig's cue to boot up his old VHS machine and join Leo on the couch. A few years ago, Disney bought the rights to the film and released a DVD version with dubbing that was more faithful to the original Japanese dialogue. Inevitably, Leo deemed the new version unacceptable, so the Rosas have held on to their ancient VHS deck as the technology around it evolved into a home theater that would have seemed like science fiction when the film came out in 1988.

"If you have to get hooked on something, at least this film is pretty good," Craig chuckles good-naturedly as his son is transfixed by the scenes they've watched together thousands of times. To stay engaged, Craig tries to notice one previously unseen detail each night that slipped past him before.

But the film has also turned out to be a valuable tool for aiding his son's language development. When Leo was younger, if he was introduced to someone new, he would cry out, "It's Mei!" like the little girl announcing her arrival in the film. Then he started making comments that aren't in the film, like saying "Chopping broccoli" during a cooking scene. Now when his mother walks into the kitchen, he'll announce that it's time for chopping broccoli. What began as a mere echo evolved into a scripted interaction, and then the script became Leo's way of engaging the world.

Tonight's *Totoro* rerun is brief because Leo is sleepy after a day at the Morgan Autism Center, the school in San José where he attends small classes led by teachers who are deeply devoted to their work. He jumps off the couch and says, "Upstairs!" Craig replies, "What's upstairs, bud?" Leo chirps, "Bed!" The exchange is so familiar that it unfolds with the comforting rhythms of a litany. And off they go.

A few years ago, Shannon was interviewed on the radio with an autism expert from a local medical school. When the microphones were shut off, the psychologist looked at her quizzically and said, "You sure look *happy* for the mother of an autistic kid." (This was news to Shannon, who characterizes herself as grumpy.) She and her husband do seem generally content these days, but reaching this point of equanimity was not easy. They earned it over the course of a long journey that included many detours and heartbreaking reversals, along with miles of pushing onward in the dark toward an uncertain destination.

III

For the first few months after he was born, Leo seemed like a typically developing baby, if an exceptionally cheerful one. He nursed normally, slept regularly, and frequently made eye contact with the people around him. Often, for no apparent reason, he would start giggling. Like a seed sprouting where no one could see it, Leo's difference was initially invisible. His diagnosis was the product of a slow and careful accretion of observations and intuitions—like his parents' gradual process of falling in love.

Craig and Shannon met in the late 1980s through a mutual friend at the

University of California in Los Angeles. Craig was a gregarious soccer player and performance-art geek who grew up on a heady brew of science fiction, *Omni* magazine, and New Wave rock and roll. Shannon was the intriguingly remote Goth girl with purple hair, fishnet stockings, and monkey boots who made sandwiches at the dorm deli. A couple of years passed before they even had a conversation.

During this time, Shannon left behind a troubled relationship by applying to an exchange program at another school to study geography. To get as far away from the memories of that relationship as possible, she chose a school that was on a different West Coast entirely: the former Gold Coast of Africa. Enrolling at the University of Ghana, Shannon immersed herself in the local culture, spending hours browsing in dressmakers' stalls at the local bazaar, where you could take bolts of outrageously colorful fabric (batik, Dutch Wax, tie-dye) to a tailor who would design a one-of-a-kind outfit to your specifications in a day or two. She was immediately seduced by the aromatic local cuisine: sticky balls of *fufu* pounded in a mortar with fiery groundnut stew; fermented *kenkey* dumplings steamed in banana leaves, like a Ghanaian version of sourdough; and chewy, caramelized *kelewele*—plantains—fried with spices that don't even have names in America.

In a society that values good-natured teasing, Shannon discovered the joys of ribbing without malice. She was ridiculed for speaking only English, while her classmates spoke three or more Ghanaian languages. If she aced an exam, her professor would tell her classmates, "Well, the woman has beat you again." Even a guy on crutches who had survived a polio epidemic wasn't immune to the abuse: his classmates would say, "Can't you move along any faster?" (And he would kid them right back.) Shannon was amazed to see disability treated as just a natural part of life, without the usual displays of pity and pompous solemnity. "I loved being in a completely different reality where all my usual touchstones were gone," she recalls. "Everything was new and different, and different was good."

Upon returning to Los Angeles, Shannon crossed paths with her future husband again at a Valentine's Day dinner, but he ended up asking one of her friends out on a date instead. Not to be daunted, she started bombarding

Craig with notes and flowers signed by a secret admirer. After weeks of playing cat and mouse, she sealed the deal by sending him an original comic book featuring an imaginary version of herself browsing through personals ads until she found one describing the perfect man, who bore an uncanny resemblance to Craig. He responded by arriving at the deli unannounced with a bouquet of flowers. They were married in 1995.

ZELLY'S BIRTH WAS not easy. After an episode of premature labor, Shannon was confined to her bed for weeks. And the first few months of motherhood were rough going, because Zelly didn't take naturally to breastfeeding, unlike the infants nursing blissfully in the pages of *Mothering* magazine. Shannon became a self-milking machine, up every two hours all night long, pumping, bottling, and sterilizing.

But then her daughter got in the groove. Suddenly, being a mom was everything it was advertised to be. Zelly settled into being such a happy, well-behaved infant that she became what Shannon calls a "decoy baby"—the kind that tricks other young couples into thinking that having kids is a cinch.

Shannon's pregnancy with Leo was uneventful compared with her experience with Zelly. His delivery in the hospital, with help from Craig and a doula, went smoothly. On November 9, 2000, when her son Leonel (named after Craig's great-uncle, a guitar virtuoso from Portugal) poked his glistening head into the world for the first time, Shannon greeted him by saying, "Hey, Leo, how are you? It's so great to see you. *Welcome!*"

Leo got the hang of dining au naturel right away. Shannon started to feel so confident in her mothering abilities that she could even help take care of other people's babies. But how could any couple deal with having more than two? When did they have time to read fantasy novels or take long showers?

Her son began sitting up on his own at seven months, right on schedule. A month later, he crawled, and he took his first tentative steps four months after that—all within the range of typical development. It wasn't until Leo's first birthday that the Rosas noticed anything unusual about him. He started taking his favorite toys and sliding them from one place on the floor to another, over and over again. He didn't even seem all that interested in playing with them—just in transferring the toys back and forth, like some sort of private ceremony.

As Leo started exploring the house in earnest, he mapped out a preferred route through the living room that he stuck to like a pilgrim following the Stations of the Cross. He touched the same chairs and tables in exactly the same places every time he crossed the room, and he invariably concluded this sequence by hurling himself down on the couch. At first, Craig and Shannon thought his little ritual was cute; they dubbed it Leo's Circuit. But eventually, "watching him do it so many times in a row got a little uncomfortable," Craig says.

Midway through his second year, the Rosas took a family vacation in Sonoma with a friend who was also a pediatrician. Leo quickly plotted out a new circuit for himself in the guesthouse. The pediatrician friend observed him making his rounds—*touch*, *run*, *touch*, *run*, *touch*, *run*, *flop*—and tried calling out his name, but Leo just ignored him and kept on going. "At his age, he should be paying more attention," Craig's friend told him privately. "You might want to have that checked out."

THE FIRST THING THAT the Rosas checked was their son's hearing, because he'd had several ear infections in the previous months. The testing had to be cut short because Leo couldn't abide anyone poking around in his ears, but his hearing turned out to be fine after all. The doctor prescribed an antibiotic called Augmentin to prevent future infections. But Leo's overall trajectory was deviating further and further from those of typical children. Shannon's efforts to potty-train him were unsuccessful, though she kept on trying for years.

Leo had spoken his first words—*dada* and *ball*—when he was ten months old. But then he just stopped saying them, as if the first green shoots of his language had withered into silence. One by one, his other milestones started falling by the wayside. The Rosas' pediatrician assured them that Leo's tardiness in hitting these marks didn't mean anything serious. He was a sunny, affectionate little bear who loved to be snuggled and tickled, and *kids with autism just aren't like that,* the pediatrician insisted.

"Plus, Leo looks me in the eyes," the doctor added, intending to settle the matter. Clearly, their son was no Rain Man in the making. Yet there was something unmistakably, undeniably *different* about Leo, which became more obvious every day. In the months to follow, there would be many more appointments, more tests, more car trips, more interviews, and more evaluations by professionals.

"Using hand pulling, grunting, and jargoning to get needs met," a clinician noted in Leo's chart. (Gradually, the Rosas were slipping into the domain of initiated language.) "Therapist called his name throughout the session and Leo rarely gave a response," wrote another. A third noted that it seemed to take Leo fifteen minutes to even notice that she was sitting there.

The Rosas cast a wide net to figure out what was going on with their little bear. He had always been a picky if enthusiastic eater. His diet consisted almost exclusively of peanut butter and jelly sandwiches, bananas, guacamole, Goldfish crackers, and Veggie Booty popcorn snacks despite Shannon's attempts to get him to diversify. He began suffering from frequent episodes of diarrhea and vomiting. Shannon took Leo to an allergy specialist, who tested him for sensitivities to soy, corn, egg white, peanuts, milk, mold, cat dander, dog dander, local trees, local bushes, and dust mites. All the tests came back negative.

Meanwhile, his private ceremonies were becoming more elaborate. Rather than fetching a toy himself, he would tap his mother's elbow to prompt her to get it for him. He was mesmerized by patterns in the sidewalk, but the sound of two people singing together—like his sisters, who love to sing—made him fly into a rage. He would investigate unfamiliar objects by inserting them into his mouth; if Shannon gave him a slice of orange, he would rub it all over his lips and eyelids. He was also developing a curious fascination with straws, which he would press against his upper lip over and over.

By then, the A-word was starting to crop up regularly in his evaluations. The director at a regional center told Craig and Shannon that if their son were older, he would immediately diagnose him as either autistic or "mentally retarded." There was no longer any room for denial.

Shannon felt devastated, in part because she likes to think of herself as a highly capable person. "Helping, fixing, signing off, pressing Send, checking that box, and moving on to the next task is what keeps me fulfilled and happy," she says. But Leo's autism was something that she didn't know how to fix. After years of being a sound sleeper, she found herself staring at the ceiling at three a.m., night after night. Running errands in her car, she would suddenly have to pull over, because the rules of the road no longer made sense.

Seeking information on the Internet for parents coping with a child's diagnosis, she came across an article by *Salon* writer Scot Sea, who said that his experience with his own autistic daughter helped him understand why a California man named Delfin Bartolome had shot his son and then himself.

"The odor has finally made its way down the hall. When you see the balled-up pants and diaper on the floor, you know you are too late," Sea began ominously. "A bright red smear across the door, the molding, the wall. Turn the corner and the bedroom is a crime scene. An ax murder? In fact, it is only your daughter at her worst." He described a scene worthy of a slasher movie: "Splashes of blood glistening like paint, black clots, yellow-brown feces, and a 3-foot-in-diameter pond of vomit that your daughter stands in the middle of . . . hands dripping, face marked like a cannibal."

Parents in previous eras were spared these horrors, he explained, because "idiot" children were promptly "tossed down the well or thumped against the fence post." For "educated" families in more recent times, he added, at least there was a way out—institutionalization. But now, desperate parents had to find their own ways out, as Bartolome had been forced to do with a handgun when he ran out of options. This was the harsh reality of raising a child with autism, according to Sea. (He neglected to mention that weeks before the shooting, Bartolome—described by his relatives as a loving and devoted father—had been laid off just before retirement, shunting him into a series of temporary jobs and putting his son's future care at risk.)

Shannon felt herself becoming physically ill while reading Sea's article. Was this her family's future?

IV

SHANNON'S SKILLS AS A freelance researcher kicked into high gear. She spent hours online, in bookstores, in libraries, and talking with other parents, searching for any scrap of information she could use to help her son.

Two books in particular made deep impressions on her: Catherine Maurice's *Let Me Hear Your Voice: A Family's Triumph over Autism*, and *Understanding the Mystery of Autism and Pervasive Developmental Disorder: A Mother's Story of Research and Recovery* by Karyn Seroussi. Both promoted the notion that autistic children could be brought to the point of recovery while offering different road maps for getting there. "These books told me the only news I wanted to hear," Shannon says. "That my son could be made normal again."

Maurice's book focused on applied behavior analysis (ABA), a form of behavior modification based on the animal-learning theories of B. F. Skinner and pioneered as an early intervention for autism in the 1960s by psychologist Ivar Lovaas at the University of California in Los Angeles. In the first chapters of the book, the author's two-year-old daughter, Anne-Marie, is trapped in a swirling vortex of regression, like a time lapse of development in reverse. After losing the few words she had learned to speak months earlier, Anne-Marie seemed to retreat into a hermetic existence, solitary and unreachable.

> Her activities were becoming stranger, more bizarre. I watched her, feeling very close to panic, as she repetitively sorted through puzzle pieces, then held them up two by two, always at right angles to each other, and stared at them. Oh please baby. Please don't do that. Why are you doing that?

Anne-Marie's increasingly autistic behavior filled Catherine and her husband, Marc, with a sense of doom, as if they were watching their daughter being devoured by a monster in front of their eyes. "We were racing against the days," Catherine wrote, "racing to find some way of halting her inexorable progression backwards." Grieving for the little girl she felt she was losing, Catherine fell to her knees and prayed. "Please make the diagnosis be wrong. Please make her not be autistic," she cried. "Lord, make it not be. Give me back my baby girl. Give her back to me. Don't let this happen. Stop it. Give her back!"

Willing to try nearly anything, Catherine and Marc explored a number of interventions in vogue at the time, including one called *holding therapy* based on ornithologist Nikolaas Tinbergen's observations of birds. The Dutch animal-behavior expert—who had no previous experience working with children—insisted that autism was caused by "upsetting experiences in early childhood" and "very serious" parents rather than by genetics or other factors. "We are not *blaming* these unfortunate parents," he declared upon receiving the Nobel Prize in medicine in 1973. "The parents of autists deserve as much compassion, and may be as much in need of help, as the autists themselves."

Holding therapy required mothers to "tame" their children by hugging them for an hour each day—by force, if necessary—while gazing intently into their eyes and confessing their innermost feelings. The goal of this process was an emotional breakthrough called "resolution," which Tinbergen promoted as a "new hope" for parents—a "cure" for their children. Catherine sought out a prominent practitioner of holding therapy named Martha Welch, who touted a 50 percent recovery rate among her clients.

When pressed to provide evidence of the therapy's effectiveness, Welch chided her for being obsessed with "numbers and statistics." In one of her training videos, a mother lies on top of her autistic daughter in bed, telling her how angry she is because her daughter doesn't listen.

"How does that make you feel?" the mother says.

"I can't *breathe*!" her daughter groans.

"Well, I don't care about that right now," the mother snaps back. "You're not going to get up until we resolve this."

Seeking insight from an expert who blamed you for inadvertently causing your child's autism was a common double bind for parents, but a key element of the appeal of holding therapy for Catherine was the fact that Welch seemed to empathize with her anguish. By contrast, ABA was strictly empirical: the child was rewarded with M&Ms, sips of apple juice, and phrases like "Good job!" for doing things like making eye contact and sitting at a table, and punished with a loud "NO!" for hand flapping and stimming. Against Welch's advice, the Maurices also engaged the services of a young ABA therapist named Bridget Taylor who proffered no psychological theories of autism and declined to make any promises of miraculous recovery. "I've never seen it," she bluntly told Catherine—despite the fact that Lovaas himself claimed that nearly half of the children enrolled in his most immersive program had achieved "normal" functioning. Though Catherine initially doubted ABA, which seemed robotic and mechanical compared to Welch's emphasis on emotional "rebonding," Taylor eventually became like a member of the family, arriving every weekday afternoon to work patiently with their daughter.

In the months that followed, Anne-Marie became more alert and engaged, and Catherine wrote that she seemed to enjoy the "highly predictable, stable, structured environment" provided by Taylor during their sessions. She eventually felt betrayed by Welch, who pressured her into providing a testimonial to the BBC for a broadcast that attributed her daughter's progress to an hour a week of holding therapy. When the program aired, families all over Europe clamored to find holding therapists for their own children, and Catherine felt partially responsible for misleading them. In ABA, however, the Maurices felt they had found an authentic reason for hope. They threw themselves into the role of being Anne-Marie's co-therapists with the fervor of religious converts. The slightest signs of autistic behavior were no longer tolerated. "Day by day we grew more relentlessly demanding of her," Catherine wrote. "No gazing into space, no teeth grinding, no playing with her hands, no manneristic touching of surfaces, no *anything* that looked autistic."

As Anne-Marie's behavior became more "normal," Catherine admitted that there was no way of knowing what was responsible—holding therapy, ABA, or her own maturation process. But gradually, the proto-language she had seemingly lost began flooding back: *Ba-ba* (bye-bye), *ju* (juice), *ka* (cookie). By the end of the book, Anne-Marie is four, and her doctor declares her "clearly no longer autistic." Driving home from the evaluation, Christine turns to Marc and whispers, "God has answered our prayers."

After finishing the book, Shannon enrolled Leo in an intensive schedule of speech therapy, occupational therapy, and ABA sessions. This program cost the Rosas several thousand dollars a month, which they were able to afford only with help from Craig's parents. But they felt that there was no time to waste. The prevailing belief among autism clinicians was that if kids like Leo missed a narrow developmental window in which their brains were still amenable to rewiring by experience (a process that is now known to last a lifetime), they would never reach the goal of becoming, as Lovaas had put it, indistinguishable from their peers.

If Catherine Maurice sought a cure for autism by modifying her child's behavior—working from the outside in—Karyn Seroussi's *Understanding the Mystery of Autism and Pervasive Developmental Disorder* tells the story of a mother pursuing the same goal by working from the inside out.

The book opens in an emergency room, where the author's eighteen-month-old son, Miles, is trembling with a 106-degree fever. The previous morning, the boy received his eighteen-month shot of diphtheria-pertussis-tetanus (DPT) vaccine. Are the two events related? The doctor doesn't know. Miles had a similarly terrifying episode after his first DPT, and another after his MMR, the routine childhood inoculation against measles, mumps, and rubella. A month later, a psychologist gives him a preliminary diagnosis of autism spectrum disorder based on his delays in acquiring language. To Seroussi, the dreaded word *autism* conjures up one thing: the image of "a profoundly disturbed child rocking in a corner." The diagnosis is subsequently confirmed by a formal evaluation.

It didn't exactly come out of the blue. Miles had always been a more remote and solitary child than his sister, Laura. Each morning, she would climb into her parents' bed to cuddle, but Miles wasn't the cuddling type. After scraping his knee on the playground, he would run up to his mother for comfort, but then turn away when she tried to hug him. Instead of just playing with his toys, he seemed to "systematically experiment" with them, Seroussi observed, as if he took after his father, Alan, a brilliant research chemist who didn't know how to behave in social situations. On the night that Alan proposed to Karyn, he took her hand and said, "I can teach you all about the world, and you can teach me how to live in it."

Karyn goes to the local library and finds only two books about autism on the shelves: one by a doctor about his son who "likes to eat with his fingers," which terrifies her. The other is *Let Me Hear Your Voice*. She enrolls Miles in an intensive ABA program. But she doesn't stop there. Talking with her mother-in-law, she learns that Alan, too, exhibited severe developmental delays when he was a baby. He would sit silently in his crib, turning the same toy over and over or lining his Matchbox cars up in rows. There had even been speculation that he was intellectually disabled, which clearly wasn't true. These speculations ended when his mother stopped letting him drink milk, one of only two foods he was willing to eat (the other was applesauce) on the advice of a doctor who feared he was becoming anemic. Soon after that, Alan spontaneously began walking and talking.

Seroussi embarked on a path to curing her son known as biomedical intervention, developed by a network of parents, clinicians, and practitioners of alternative medicine under the guidance of one of the most trusted experts in the autism parents' community, Navy psychologist Bernard Rimland. The foundation of this approach is the so-called GFCF diet, a strict regimen free of any traces of gluten and casein, two proteins commonly found in wheat and dairy products. Rimland believed that vaccines like the DPT and the MMR leave some children unable to adequately digest these proteins, while rendering the walls of their intestines abnormally permeable ("leaky gut syndrome"). The undigested proteins are then carried by the bloodstream to the brain, where they wreak havoc with normal development. Along with the GFCF diet, Seroussi employed an aggressive program of high-dose vitamins, minerals, enzymes, and supplements developed by Rimland's Defeat Autism Now! (DAN!) network.

Seroussi framed the battle against her son's autism in biblical terms, as a primordial showdown between good and evil. "The shadow of the beast has fallen over my home, and my doorway has been darkened by its dreaded countenance," she writes. "Miles will be a father someday, and there is a good chance that he will have to fear for his own children. By that time, I need to know that the beast has been slain." Like *Let Me Hear Your Voice*, the book ends on a triumphant note. A member of the DAN! network tells Seroussi, "There is not a trace of autism left in that boy."

In his introduction to Seroussi's book, Rimland proclaimed that she had found "what all parents hope for: a cure for her son." With his endorsement, the notion that autistic children could be cured by making changes in their diet sent ripples of hope through the parent community at a time when the fear of a worldwide epidemic caused by vaccines was reaching its peak.

After reading Seroussi's book, Shannon decided that Leo's days of munching on gluten-rich Goldfish crackers and sugary PB & J sandwiches were over. To share her own account of recovering her son, she launched a blog called "The Adventures of Leelo the Soon-to-Be-Not Autistic Boy and His Potty-Mouthed Mom."

Through a Yahoo group for mothers of kids with special needs, Shannon found a DAN! doctor in nearby Los Altos. His walls were plastered with testimonials from dozens of grateful mothers and fathers paying tribute to the effectiveness of his therapies for autism, Lyme disease, mold exposure, fatigue, and a host of other conditions. His treatment protocols included some that Craig and Shannon had never heard of, such as infrared therapy. But they felt reassured that his practice was not some shady, fly-by-night operation. It was a huge, bustling office in a modern medical complex on the main street of town.

The doctor—a boyish Indian man in his forties with earnest, knowing eyes and a reassuringly competent manner—was optimistic about Leo's potential for a cure. He had seen "hundreds of kids" like him recover in his own practice, he said. The old view of autism as an untreatable condition, he added, was being replaced by a new science of hope based on an emerging understanding of autism as a reversible disruption of multiple systems in the body—the systems targeted by the DAN! protocol.

Each child on the spectrum is different, requiring an individualized treatment strategy, he said. But certain steps were fundamental: a healthier diet and the elimination of problem foods; detection and treatment of undiagnosed allergies; megadose vitamin and mineral supplementation; antifungals and probiotics to create a healthier environment in the intestines; antioxidants to reduce oxidative stress, which affects everything from gut permeability to neurotransmitter synthesis; and, finally, a whole-body purge of heavy metals like mercury and aluminum, which had been identified by DAN! practitioners as playing key roles in impairing brain function in autistic kids. It was all a little overwhelming to the Rosas, but it made sense: a robust, aggressive, full-spectrum approach for their spectrum kid. Here, at last, was the promise of a happier future for Leo and his family.

"Let's start with some tests," the doctor offered. "We can run some lab checks on Leo's blood and hair and concretely measure for the presence of mercury, antibodies, antigens, and other imbalances. Then we can try some changes in his diet. Even if we don't see huge results, you'll end up with a healthier kid." That sounded like a no-lose proposition, but then the conversation took a more sobering turn. "Of course, if the tests show that Leo's carrying a lot of mercury, we'll have to start thinking about chelation."

As science geeks, the Rosas knew a thing or two about chelation, the process of removing heavy metals from the body employed after industrial accidents. During World War I (dubbed by some historians "the chemists' war") the Germans started using poisonous gases like chlorine as airborne messengers of death that killed in a particularly gruesome fashion. Allied soldiers caught in trenches without their gas masks were often found dead with clenched fists, blue faces, and blackened lips. But then a British research team discovered that certain compounds could bind with the toxic gas, which then enabled the body to flush it out in urine. These compounds were christened *chelating* agents, from the Greek word for "claw," which described their pincerlike action as they "grabbed" the toxic molecules out of the bloodstream and sequestered them for excretion. Over the years, alt-med practitioners have touted chelation for a wide range of ailments, including heart disease and ovarian cancer.

On a tour of the office, the Rosas saw the chelation clinic, whose walls were covered with letters from parents describing the ways that this process had benefited their kids. Craig told himself that he would do some Web searching at home to find out more about chelation and catch up in general with the state of autism research. The most attractive thing about the biomedical approach for the Rosas was its ethic of empowerment in the face of a medical establishment that had few practical suggestions to offer for raising kids like their son. "We saw other parents getting proactive, taking charge, and trying to do something good for their children," Craig says.

Soon, samples of Leo's blood, hair, stool, and urine were dispatched to a network of labs for analysis, including Doctor's Data in Illinois and the Great Plains Laboratory in Kansas, which acted as central testing hubs for the whole DAN! network. Unlike most conventional medical testing outfits, these labs provide not only quantified results directly to doctors but printouts for patients with interpretive commentary and suggested baseline "reference ranges" for individual tests. The Great Plains Laboratory, for example, suggested that children with "abnormal" levels of peptides in their urine be put on the GFCF diet and be tested for food allergies.

The overall effect was to reinforce the notion that definitive links between food allergies, heavy metals, and autism have been established, though these links were in fact still purely speculative. A disclaimer at the bottom of the page acknowledged that the peptide test "has not been cleared or approved by the U.S. Food and Drug Administration," but cheerfully noted that "the FDA has determined that such clearance or approval is not necessary."

The results of Leo's tests, impressively illustrated with brightly colored bars and graphs, were not encouraging. "It's just as I thought," the doctor said solemnly, before leading Craig and Shannon through the lists and charts and laying out a game plan for their son's recovery.

The allergist who had tested Leo months earlier hadn't turned up any red flags, but the DAN! network of labs—apparently more attuned to the problems of kids on the spectrum—seemed much more thorough. Leo turned out to be extremely "reactive" to peanuts and soy, highly allergic to gluten and rye, and moderately sensitive to lentils, oats, and wheat. No wonder her son had been battling diarrhea for years, Shannon thought.

The lab results also indicated that the massive quantities of sugar in his favorite strawberry jelly (no other kind would do) had triggered an explosion of yeast in his intestines at the expense of healthy gut flora. The consequences of yeast overgrowth could include chronic inattention (*check*), bedwetting (*check*), bellyaches (*check*), anger and aggression (*check*), sugar cravings (*check*), stimming (*check*), plateaus in skill development (*check*), climbing and jumping off objects (*check*), inability to potty-train (*check*), inappropriate laughter (*check*), inexplicable bouts of crying (*check*), and picky eating (*check*)—as it happened, many of the same clinical manifestations of autism itself. Leo was a classic case of *Candida* gone wild, the doctor explained. He was being poisoned by his beloved PB & J sandwiches.

Furthermore, he added, Leo's inflammatory and immunological markers were extremely high as his body rebelled against this toxic onslaught:

nearly off the charts, judging from the ominous black bars on his charts. His level of an antibody called immunoglobulin A—which plays a critical role in the layer of intestinal mucus that is one of the body's first lines of defense—was fifteen times the reference range cited by the lab. Leo's GI tract was evidently pumping out heroic quantities of antibodies in a futile effort to repel a hellstorm of allergens and pathogens.

Leo's heavy-metal profile was also extremely problematic in the doctor's view. The lab report on his hair sample indicated that his body was shedding high levels of aluminum, which can cause a buildup of ammonia in cells, resulting in a disruption of DNA metabolism and protein synthesis. The test also showed elevated levels of boron, which is often a tip-off to the lurking presence of blatantly neurotoxic elements like mercury, cadmium, and lead. The doctor told Craig and Shannon that they should seriously consider chelation to kick-start their son's recovery process—and sooner rather than later.

In the meantime, the Rosas could make many changes to improve their son's quality of life immediately. Step one was to eradicate even trace amounts of gluten and casein from his diet, as described in Seroussi's book. (Leo's tests didn't indicate any acute reactivity to casein, but the doctor warned Craig and Shannon that not all of his sensitivities would show up on the tests.) His allergen assessment came with a detailed chart describing an elaborate elimination and rotation diet deemed appropriate for a kid with his reactivity profile. (Glancing down the list, Shannon tried to suppress her doubts about convincing a boy who subsisted on Goldfish and Veggie Booty to start scarfing down oysters, grapefruit, herring, and kidney beans.) His penchant for eating the same meals day after day could no longer be indulged, the doctor said, because continuous exposure to single foods could engender new sensitivities.

He reassured the Rosas that while they prepared Leo for chelation, they could undertake a number of other treatments to help correct his systemic imbalances. One such therapy, called BioSET, was devised by a chiropractor as a way of clearing "dissonant" energy blockages from the body using enzyme therapy, acupressure, homeopathy, and chiropractic. This was especially important for people with chronic conditions like autism, BioSET's inventor claimed, because their systems become "chaotic," leaving "vital organ systems, which rely on proteins, carbohydrates and fatty acids for their proper functioning . . . effectively undernourished."

Leo's doctor happened to know of a skilled BioSET practitioner who had an office just down the block and said that he would provide the Rosas with a referral. He also furnished them with a list of vitamin and mineral supplements that he offered to sell them directly from his office. This one-stop-shopping approach is common in the biomed community. The founder of the Great Plains Laboratory, for example, also runs a supplement company called New Beginnings Nutritionals that specializes in products with names like BrainChild, Spectrum Support II, and Bio-Chelat. If Great Plains tests show deficiencies in certain minerals, supplies of the relevant supplements are just a click away. The New Beginnings website also features a video clip of a mother named Lori Knowles who tells the story of her son Daniel's recovery from autism, which she attributes to his GFCF diet, chelation, and an extensive supplement program. (A voiceover briefly mentions that the boy also had years of intensive ABA and speech therapy.) "The dream of the child you had just goes up in a puff of smoke" after an autism diagnosis, Knowles says. But since Daniel's recovery, "he looks and acts just like any normal boy," she adds proudly, before the camera cuts to a scene of him immersed in a video game. Knowles is the general manager of New Beginnings.

The Rosas walked out of the doctor's office reeling but resolved—*out* with the gluten-infested Goldfish, the hyperallergenic peanut butter, and the yeast-producing jellies; *in* with the rice bread, almond butter, GFCF pancake mix, cod liver oil, K-Mag Aspartate, probiotics, CoQ10, B-12, zinc, selenium, digestive enzymes, glutathione cream, folic acid, antifungals, and immune-boosting mushroom extract. The monthly bill for these foods and supplements was enormous, on top of the thousands that the Rosas paid each month for ABA and other therapies. But they saw these expenses as crucial investments in Leo's future.

The popularity of biomedical treatments for autism mirrored the general rise of interest in so-called complementary and alternative medicine in recent decades. By the first years of the twenty-first century, the trade in high-dose vitamins and supplements had become an economic powerhouse, with annual sales topping $33 billion. Americans now consult their homeopaths, naturopaths, herbalists, acupuncturists, chiropractors, and Reiki workers more often than they see their primary care physicians. Up to three quarters of all autistic children in the United States receive some form of alternative treatment, with dietary interventions often beginning even before their diagnosis.

Soon after visiting the doctor in Los Altos, Shannon was holding her wriggling son in her lap as a BioSET therapist cleared energy blocks from his meridians by applying an electrical current along his spine. The therapist promised that when these blockages were removed, Leo's sensitivities to dozens of problem foods would be reduced—but they had to be eliminated one at a time, at a cost of $70 per session. None of this would have been possible without more help from Craig's parents. When Craig told his father, Marty, about Leo's treatment regimen, Marty asked to see some of the medical literature they were reading that supported it. Craig sent him a list of websites. After poring through them, Marty told his son quietly, "This is not the science that I learned in med school."

But that was precisely the point. After studying autism for decades, mainstream medicine had failed to come up with a gold standard of treatment. Usually, the next step of receiving a difficult diagnosis from your doctor is the moment she gives you a reassuring look and says, "But here's what we can do. Here are the next steps we can take." For the parents of kids like Leo, that moment never seemed to come. Within the biomed community, however, there were dozens of next steps you could take.

One of the first things that Shannon and Craig decided to do was to stop vaccinating their children. Having lived in Ghana, where she saw the terrible human cost of the great pandemics with her own eyes, Shannon felt conflicted about turning her back on what she had previously thought of as the signature triumph of public health in the twentieth century. But watching Leo struggle to express himself and learn basic life skills, she was determined not to inflict the same fate on her other kids. She agreed to give birth to India in the hospital only after extracting assurance from her doula that no one would try to immunize her newborn without her permission.

When Shannon's mother asked her if she was worried that her next child might turn out to be autistic too, she put on a brave face, but she broke down sobbing alone in the car afterward. As Leo went through one of his cycles of particularly difficult behavior, she wrote a journal entry to her daughter in utero:

> Trying to be optimistic. Little nugget, I am pleased that you are here. We are 8½ weeks along, you and I. Let's stick it out. I will breastfeed you until kindergarten, and will keep you away from all those nasty vaccines. You will be perfect.

She also launched a war against mandatory vaccination on her blog. In the face of an incendiary public debate about vaccines sparked by gastroenterologist Andrew Wakefield's controversial claims that the MMR was driving a worldwide epidemic of a "leaky gut" condition he called autistic enterocolitis, media outlets tried to provide a fair and balanced view. When *People* magazine ran an article called "Desperate Measures" that quoted antivaccine activist Lyn Redwood alongside a doctor who treated a boy who died of the measles—while pointing out that rates of diagnosis were still climbing in Sweden, where thimerosal had been removed from vaccines in 1993—Shannon tore the author apart online for "fearmongering and misinformation."

After India was born, the Rosas' pediatrician pushed back on Shannon's plan to either exempt her kids from immunization or have the MMR shots be administered individually. But she held her ground and he eventually kicked the family out of his practice. Shannon also enrolled India in a study of the siblings of autistic children at UC Davis's MIND Institute. She later found a female pediatrician who told her that she would be willing to let her follow any modified vaccine schedule that the institute suggested.

V

Trading his PB & J sandwiches for GFCF pancakes without syrup made Leo a sad boy. He responded to his new regime by howling at the kitchen table as Shannon daydreamed about spiriting him away to a mountain aerie where he would eat only foods on the approved list. She consoled herself with the knowledge that for a child who ate a drastically limited menu by choice, he was now eating a much healthier diet, and his chronic diarrhea had finally stopped. Leo also occasionally surprised his mother by gulping down potions she never thought he'd tolerate, like cocktails of cod liver oil blended with watered-down pear juice. Now it was the sweetest thing he was allowed to consume.

Like generations of autism parents before her, Shannon became a minute observer of her son's behavior, filling notebooks and charts with his reactions to every tweak in his recovery program, hunting for elusive threads of causation in a dense web of correlations. She plotted Leo's pills, elixirs, capsules, creams, and shots on a grid—an impressive twenty-five items at that point.

Leo's doctor was happy with an apparent decrease in his hyperactivity but warned the Rosas that if they didn't begin at least oral chelation soon to flush the mercury from his brain, he could end up permanently impaired. To go this route, however, Leo would have to start loading up on supplements, because the chelation process leaches out essential minerals with the heavy metals. The problem was that Leo's BioSET practitioner had detected sensitivities to several of his supplements, which would have to be dealt with first—in twice-weekly sessions—before he could begin ramping up on minerals.

Shannon's to-do list kept getting longer and longer, not even counting the many hours a week that were required to coordinate her son's speech and OT sessions, which she often had to cancel or cut short to accommodate Leo's BioSET schedule. She couldn't believe how much *work* taking care of an autistic child could be—but if it resulted in his recovery, she told herself, it would all be worth it.

During one of Leo's BioSET treatments, Shannon happened to glance at a photograph on the therapist's desk and remembered that the doctor up the street had the identical photo of the same boy on his own desk. It turned out that the doctor and the therapist were a couple, and the boy in the picture was their son. But the doctor hadn't said a word about their relationship when he made his referral, and the therapist hadn't mentioned it either. It was a tidy little arrangement they had, referring clients to each other for expensive treatments that Leo seemed to need more of all the time if he wasn't going to face a lifetime of disability. For her son's sake, Shannon tried to put this awkward thought out of her mind.

A FEW MONTHS LATER, the Rosas returned to the doctor's office in Los Altos for another round of lab results and consultations. Unfortunately, the new batch of printouts showed that the *Candida* in Leo's gut was more rampant than ever, along with thriving colonies of *Lactobacillus*, gamma and beta *Streptococci*, and an infestation of non-lactose-fermenting *E. coli*. As a result, the doctor said, Leo's GI tract was seriously inflamed, which would require a new round of probiotics and enzymes. Now his almond butter—a poor substitute for his preferred PB, but better than nothing—also had to go.

And there was more bad news. The latest hair test showed that Leo's body was now excreting *low* levels of mercury. The doctor explained that this meant that the neurotoxins were building up in his system again, threatening to reverse all the progress he'd made in the past year. This development made Leo an urgent candidate for IV chelation, which the doctor said he would be happy to provide in the back room.

Craig had been trying to set aside his doubts about chelation for months. "I spent a long time trying to get to the root of this research," he says. "It *sounded* like science: polymorphisms, environmental triggers, oxidative stress, molecules passing through the blood-brain barrier, glutathione, methylation, and the constant through-line of mercury detoxification. I read these reports and thought, 'My God, I've got to figure this out.'"

The vaccination issue was particularly confusing for Craig, because he'd been reading a new batch of studies challenging the validity of Wakefield's paper and the mercury/autism hypothesis in general. A study in Japan found that rates of autism diagnosis continued to rise steeply even after the combination MMR was replaced by single vaccines. Another study in Hong Kong found that mercury levels in the bloodstreams of kids with autism were not significantly higher than those in typical children.

Even overlooking the fact that the link between mercury exposure and autism was still unproven, it was impossible to tell from reading Leo's lab reports if the levels detected by the tests were truly dangerous or even significantly elevated from normal background exposure. Since the labs also specified the alleged baseline levels, it was easy for parents to assume that any level above that was evidence of toxicity—an assumption actively encouraged by DAN! doctors.

Meanwhile, rates of measles infection were spiking in England, Ireland, Wales, the United States, Italy, and other countries. In a few years, MMR coverage in some parts of London would fall to 50 percent, from a high of 92 percent just before Wakefield made headlines with his paper. Measles would eventually be declared endemic again in England for the first time in years, with 1,348 cases recorded in 2008, up from a mere 56 cases in 1998. One in ten of these children was sick enough to require hospitalization.

Still, Leo was *their* child, and the Rosas had to do what was best for him. Craig told his father that they were considering intravenous chelation on the advice of their doctor and sent him a paper outlining the DAN! consensus on heavy-metal toxicity. Marty replied with a lengthy letter in which he expressed his concerns. "To imply that there are similar symptoms between mercury poisoning and autism may be true, but that does not necessarily mean that they are the same," he wrote. "Many of the physicians in the symposium have autistic children. I think that these folks may be somewhat biased and willing to grasp at something that looks possible, NOW! This is totally understandable, as we all hope that there is magic treatment that will heal our little boy, Leo. However, after reading many more scientific papers, I am not encouraged that we can put our hopes on chelation and food supplements."

He added that, as a health care professional, he was unnerved by the sheer number of disclaimers in the DAN! report. These ranged from an admission that "the theories and medical models on which these therapies are based are not universally accepted," to the fact that "no well-controlled outcome studies have yet been performed," to the sobering note that the therapies described "may potentially make some autistic children significantly worse." Marty concluded his letter by saying that he felt the risks to Leo were too high.

Craig and Shannon kept reading encouraging stories online about kids who had recovered to the point of losing their diagnosis, but their son's trajectory seemed to be much more uneven. At times, he took encouraging steps forward, but those advances seemed more related to progress in his other therapies than whatever supplements had been added to his list that month. On other days, Leo seemed to take three steps back.

With so many interventions going on simultaneously, it was difficult for them to accurately gauge the effectiveness of any single one. Only by going over her records carefully was Shannon able to determine that the abrupt cessation of Leo's diarrhea was related not to the changes in his diet but to stopping the antibiotic that he'd been taking for ear infections. But she plowed on, terrified of missing the window when biomedical interventions could make a significant impact on his future.

VI

One thing became clear: Leo's new regime was making him miserable. He had always seemed to look forward to mealtimes with his family, but now he dragged himself to the table with a disconsolate look on his face. Sometimes he just started throwing his food on the floor. There was one way, however, that his diet accelerated his acquisition of expressive language: he started begging Shannon for specific foods that she didn't even know he knew the names of, like yogurt and watermelon.

He had always been an exceptionally cheerful boy, even with the many practical challenges he faced daily. Now he seemed to be in a continuous state of rebellion against the hourly swallowing of pills, the endless fussing over the contents of his diapers, and the nightly administration of a vitamin B-12 shot. He looked as exhausted as his parents felt.

On the Rosas' next pilgrimage to Los Altos, the doctor inevitably brought up chelation. But this time Craig challenged him. "Wait a second," he told the doctor. "You're telling me that the recommended course of action for a low reading of mercury toxicity is chelation?" "Yes," the doctor replied. "And the recommended course of action for high mercury toxicity is chelation?" The doctor nodded yes again. Finally Craig asked him, "Is there *any* sort of outcome that would contraindicate chelation?" And the doctor said, "No."

At that point, Craig and Shannon said, "Thank you very much," walked out of the doctor's office, and never went back to Los Altos to see him again.

Leo was nowhere close to recovery, but he was thriving in his own ways. He made a deep connection with his ABA therapist, Fiona, a sunny Australian redhead with a no-nonsense manner both sweet and firm. For twenty-five hours a week, she worked with him on mastering simple tasks like greeting people if they walked into a room, correctly naming the parts of his body (he was up to twenty-one), and being able to dress and undress himself. Instead of aiming to extinguish Leo's autistic behaviors, as the Maurices' therapist had done, Fiona focused on teaching him skills that would enable him to care for himself and express his desires and preferences more effectively.

The beginning of autonomy is being able to communicate *yes* and *no*, something that Leo had been unable to do months earlier. Now if he wanted to go out to the backyard, he would ask his mother or father to open the door. He could also make simple requests like "I want to sit on bean bag," "Watch Tubbies," and "Give me hat." This language was also a gateway to more reciprocal social interaction. Now Leo said "my turn" when it was his time to play with a toy, and yielded the toy when he heard another child say that. He could also marshal his attention on a task for up to fifteen minutes at a stretch—an accomplishment for any kid his age.

Leo would still occasionally bail on an activity by vaulting headfirst onto the couch, galloping across the room, or bursting into song. But Fiona appreciated and encouraged his natural exuberance, as did Shannon. If he got frustrated and lashed out at Fiona, she would respond with kindness and redirection by telling him what he could do instead. If he became overwhelmed, she'd let him do a less stressful activity so he could blow off steam and try again later. Within this supportive framework, Leo made progress quickly, mastering dozens of tasks in a short time.

None of this was easy. Each day required a new steep learning curve for Leo and his family. But raising him was not the soul-shattering nightmare that the writer of the *Salon* article, and dozens like it, had predicted. It was more like a series of practical challenges, such as knowing what to look for in an occupational therapist, finding a school for Leo that focused at least as much on discovering his strengths as on managing his behavior, and learning to walk proudly when people gave the Rosas the side-eye in public. One thing that didn't seem to help was dwelling on the cause of his autism or pitying him as the hapless victim of a Big Pharma conspiracy.

Then Shannon read a book that inspired her to start thinking differently about Leo and her own fate as his mother. *Making Peace with Autism* was

Susan Senator's story of raising her autistic son, Nat, and his two brothers, Max and Ben, with her husband, Ned, a software programmer. With candor and compassion, Susan described the day-by-day, practical steps that she and her husband took to cope with their son's behavior, nurture his intelligence, and fight for his right to an education. There was no whitewashing: she described dark periods when she and Ned were in "siege mode" because their son seemed so intent on behaving in destructive ways. But by working together, they found ways to adapt to Nat's behavior—often having to improvise, because there seemed to be no good guidebooks for raising a child like him.

To prepare Nat for holiday dinners with relatives and other family outings, Susan started making what she called "crisis storybooks," illustrated with pictures cut out from magazines, so she could offer him detailed previews of what was to come—like Leo's visual schedule. These storybooks proved to be a stunning success. At Christmas dinner with Ned's family, Nat looked around the table and said approvingly, "Christians!"

The book promoted no theories of autism causation and promised no astonishing recovery. The climax of the story was quite different: in the middle of one of Nat's inexplicable storms of laughter, Susan realized that, even in his most difficult moments, he was trying to communicate with her. "He was looking at me warmly," she wrote. "Now my throat was burning—this had cracked me wide open. *Oh my God. He really does it to connect with us. Just doesn't know how, other than to annoy us.*"

Her insight proved to be a pivotal moment for the whole family: "My epiphany about Nat's laughter would mark a profound, positive change in how we dealt with Nat *and* how he responded to us." Instead of being the story of a family's triumph over autism, Susan's book was an account of taking the first steps of a lifelong journey of discovery with her son. "We help Nat become the best he can be, and in the process, he makes us who we are," she wrote. "We cannot be typical, we cannot be normal. But this is certain: We are OK."

Making Peace with Autism marked a turning point in the Rosas' story too. "It was the first autism parenting book I encountered that was both practical and positive," Shannon recalls. "Susan wasn't selling a cure, a miracle, or anything, really, except the need to let other families know they weren't alone, and to offer them advice grounded in personal experience to smooth their paths. It was the first time I encountered an autism parent who was in acceptance mode rather than in martyr mode or resignation mode. The book helped me realize that autism would always be a part of who my son is." Instead of referring to him as *low functioning*, *severely affected*, or *profoundly impaired*—the standard clinical terms for kids like him—Shannon started calling Leo her "high-octane boy" so that she wasn't constantly defining him in terms of his deficits.

Both sets of grandparents told Shannon they were relieved to see her stop treating her son "like a science experiment," she says, and family outings were certainly easier to manage once she no longer had to bring along a trunk full of special foods and supplements. As Susan's family had done for Nat, the Rosas began improvising creative ways of making connections with Leo and meeting his needs. But abandoning the hope of his recovery also came at a cost. Friends who had cheered on Shannon's efforts to cure her "soon-to-be-nonautistic boy" turned chilly. Readers of her blog accused her of jeopardizing Leo's future by giving up on him too quickly. The Rosas soon felt isolated again, venturing with their son into unmapped territory.

MANY OF THEIR PEERS were moving in the opposite direction, flocking to conferences where presenters touted the amazing curative properties of camel milk, bleach enemas, and home hyperbaric chambers, conveniently available from the vendors lining the hallways. Nearly all of the emerging online forums for parents of newly diagnosed children were dominated by concerns about mercury and vaccines; those who expressed skepticism that the combination MMR was responsible for triggering a global autism epidemic were accused of "having their heads in the sand" and "shilling for Big Pharma." Beleaguered parents dubbed these endlessly looping arguments the Autism Wars.

Then Shannon came across a blog by a classics professor named Kristina

Chew, whose son Charlie was Leo's age and like him in many ways. As a baby, he spent hours alone watching sunbeams migrate across the floor and leafing through picture books. If these reveries were interrupted, Charlie would start battering his head with his hands and burst out screaming. But he was also an athletic and tirelessly energetic boy who loved swimming, biking, and other outdoor activities. The verdict on him from other parents generally ran along the lines of "He's a handful."

When Charlie was diagnosed just after his second birthday, Kristina and her husband, James Fisher, tried everything they could to avert the tragic future predicted for him. They purged all traces of wheat and dairy from his diet, pored through books like *Biological Treatments for Autism and PDD* and *Children with Starving Brains*, ordered test kits from DAN!-affiliated labs, stocked up on supplements and megavitamins, started him on a regimen of antifungals, and took him to a healer on Staten Island who claimed that he could redirect the flow of Charlie's cerebrospinal fluid by massaging the bones of his skull.

After three years of intensive therapies, on top of forty hours a week of ABA, Charlie was still essentially nonverbal and unable to care for himself. One day it occurred to Kristina that the DAN! practitioner she was seeing seemed to have little interest in even meeting her son—all she wanted to talk about was expanding her list of treatments. "I realized that I wasn't thinking so much about what Charlie needed as what I thought I had to do as a parent," Kristina wrote on her blog. "I had an image of what Charlie 'should' be. I wasn't keeping my eyes focused on the real boy in front of me. I realized that the 'autism wars' were inside of me."

Like Susan, she decided that her efforts would be better applied to fighting for her son's education. This task proved to be even more daunting than pursuing his recovery. Kristina and her family had to move eight times in ten years—leaving behind a tenured position at St. Peter's University in Jersey City, where she had built up a thriving classics department—to find the right school for him. But what made it even harder was that there seemed to be so little information available about raising kids on the spectrum that didn't view their autism as the principal problem to be surmounted, rather than tackling the practical barriers that stood in the way of fulfilling their potential.

What had parents done in the past to ensure that their children got the help and resources that they needed? What happened to kids like Charlie and Leo when they grew up? Were they all institutionalized like Raymond Babbitt? How did they end up sharing the spectrum with chatty software engineers and eccentric scientists like Temple Grandin? Even prominent experts in the field struggled to answer these basic questions. Whole chapters of autism history seemed to be . . . *missing* somehow.

As a result, more than half a century after Leo Kanner announced his discovery of a "unique 'syndrome,' heretofore unreported" among the young patients in his Baltimore clinic, parents like Shannon, Susan, and Kristina found themselves in Year Zero, trying to cobble together hopeful futures for their children out of scraps gleaned from regional-center brochures and threads on Yahoo mailing lists, with few visible role models of autism in maturity available to help them make wise choices. Actress and model Jenny McCarthy, who became the public face of an army of "mother warriors" by publishing a trio of bestsellers about "saving" her son Evan from autism with chelation, probiotics, and other treatments, insisted that "there weren't any" autistic adults in the past. "It's all now."

In the shadow of the rising numbers, making peace with autism—by viewing it as a lifelong disability that deserves support, rather than as a disease of children that can be cured—seemed like a new and radical idea. In fact, it was the oldest idea in autism research. But it had been forgotten, along with the story of a brave clinician who tried to rescue the children in his care from the darkest social engineering experiment in human history.

Three

WHAT SISTER VIKTORINE KNEW

> Once one has learnt to pay attention to the characteristic manifestations of autism, one realizes that they are not at all rare.
>
> —Hans Asperger

Gottfried K. was nine and a half when his grandmother brought him to the Children's Clinic at the University Hospital for an examination. Tall and lanky for his age, he was a good-looking boy, with strikingly handsome brown eyes. Alas, he was so physically uncoordinated, and his facial expressions were so hard to read, that the first clinician to have a look at him—a young psychologist named Anni Weiss—assumed that he was "feeble-minded."

That wasn't the first time that had happened, Gottfried's grandmother told her. People often misjudged her grandson as slow and stupid. His cruel classmates christened him with a nickname that made her flush with rage: Gottfried the Fool. She knew that they were wrong about him, because he was so clever and earnest when his teachers called on him in class. But she had to admit that she, too, was often confused by his behavior.

At home and in the company of adults, Gottfried seemed cheerful and content, but the smallest changes in his routine discombobulated him. When he was upset, he would start fidgeting, giggling, and chattering away in a loud voice. Because he acted the same way when he was happy, it was hard for his grandmother to tell precisely how Gottfried was feeling. He was terrified of other children, which was not surprising, considering the abuse that they heaped on him. But he also seemed unusually helpless. He would often forget to brush his teeth and bathe and required adult assistance even to tie his shoes. And he had childish fears of things that most boys his age take in stride, including dogs, loud noises, clouds, and the wind.

Weiss listened carefully, taking notes. She liked Gottfried's grandmother right away, describing her as "a simple woman of sixty, good-hearted, and full of common sense." She felt warmly toward the boy too, though she could see why his grandmother was baffled by his behavior. Weiss believed her when she insisted that her grandson was not willfully mischievous or disobedient. On the contrary, he was softhearted and naïve, and felt terribly embarrassed when his failings were pointed out to him. He just seemed constitutionally incapable of behaving appropriately in public.

His grandmother had certainly brought him to the right place—perhaps the only clinic in the world where he would get the kind of care and attention he needed. Weiss looked forward to discussing this case with her colleagues, particularly a soft-spoken pediatrician who had recently joined the staff and seemed to take a special interest in gifted, sensitive children who had been cast out by their peers. His name was Hans Asperger.

In one of the few photographs of the clinic to survive to the present day, the shy doctor and a boy sit facing one another at a table, engaged in conversation. Boyish and trim in his round-rimmed glasses, Asperger is dressed more formally than his colleagues on the other side of the room, wearing a crisp collar and tie under his white doctor's coat. He had been encouraged to do his postgraduate work at the clinic by his thesis advisor, an influential specialist in the infectious diseases of children, Franz Hamburger.

The University of Vienna housed one of the most prestigious hospitals in a city renowned the world over for the quality of its health care. Vienna was the home of Sigmund Freud, the former neurologist whose theories of the psyche dominated popular views of the mind for nearly a century. It was also the city of Carl von Rokitansky, the pathologist who revolutionized medicine in the nineteenth century by systematizing the clinical analysis of symptoms while reminding his colleagues that they must always regard their patients with respect rather than seeing them merely as guinea pigs for their research.

Doctors from all over Europe flocked to the city to observe surgeries in vast operating theaters and consult with the leading experts of the day. Each September, Hamburger offered a popular course in children's diseases at the clinic, attended by pediatricians who arrived on steamships from America. Nicknamed "Red Vienna" in the years after World War I because of its proudly socialist government, anticlerical tradition, and housing projects for working families paid for by taxes on the wealthy, the vibrant Austrian capital hosted dozens of ongoing salons where physicians and scientists mingled with artists and musicians for wide-ranging discussions of politics, art, science, and philosophy.

Much of this cultural ferment originated in Vienna's lively Jewish community, which dated all the way back to the twelfth century. Gustav Mahler's music echoed from radios and concert halls, while Jewish patrons commissioned the exquisite paintings by Gustav Klimt and Egon Schiele displayed in local galleries. In the years after the First World War, one in five inhabitants of the city were Jews, as were many of the faculty members who taught at the university.

Asperger and Weiss worked on a ward at the Children's Clinic founded in 1911 by a physician, schoolteacher, and social reformer named Erwin Lazar. His approach to special education would still be considered innovative today. Instead of seeing the children in his care as flawed, broken, or sick, he believed they were suffering from neglect by a culture that had failed to provide them with teaching methods suited to their individual styles of learning. He had an uncanny knack for spotting signs of potential in every boy and girl no matter how difficult or rebellious they were alleged to be.

Lazar became adept at intuiting which career path might offer a child the best chance to live a fulfilling life while making a meaningful contribution to society. He viewed each child as embodying a particular archetype, as if the mass of humanity were organized by innate predisposition into clans or tribes, each with its own distinctive attributes. Instead of viewing the children as "patients," he saw them as future bakers, barbers, farmers, professors, and engineers. Some seemed to belong to another time, as if they were characters from the Gothic or Renaissance eras who had been transported to the twentieth century. Others seemed older or younger than their chronological ages, or of different classes or races than their parents. The devoted members of Lazar's staff were in awe of his ability to accurately assess each child's situation and sum it up in a single phrase:

> His names for the various types were always quite incisive and informed by a good sense of humor, without any disrespect toward the child. When he characterized children with one word, this was the clearest possible way of describing their particular abilities, talents, and future prospects. One instantly understood the child's problems and the way in which they were the natural consequence of his or her personality; one understood the child's conflicts and knew which side of the child's personality needed to be handled with care, what challenges he could face, and how his future path could be shaped.

By combining elements of psychology, medicine, and progressive pedagogy, Lazar developed an approach to helping each child attain his or her potential based on the nineteenth-century concept of *Heilpädagogik*, "therapeutic education." Rather than treating allegedly psychological problems in isolation, Lazar aimed to turn his clinic into a microcosm of a more humane society in which the children could learn to interact in a context of mutual respect and appreciation. Such a facility, he used to say, must never be too small: "It must give every child a chance to find a comrade like himself."

He developed these compassionate theories with a teacher and psychoanalyst named August Aichhorn, who ran a boarding school in Vienna for troubled teenagers in the years following World War I. "It had never occurred to any of us to see [the children] as delinquents or criminals from whom society had to be protected," Aichhorn wrote in a manifesto called *Wayward Youth*. "For us, they were people on whom life had imposed too great a burden, whose negative attitudes and hate of society was justified; a milieu therefore had to be created for them in which they could feel at ease." Aichhorn's notion of the therapeutic milieu proved to be widely influential, providing a blueprint for progressive institutions all over the world.

Lazar's special-education unit, known as the Heilpädagogik Station, was in keeping with a tradition of bold innovations at the hospital. The cofounder of the Children's Clinic, an immunologist named Clemens von Pirquet—who developed the modern concept of allergies—was a strong advocate for women's equality. He elevated the status of the ward maids to the level of collaborators and transformed the hospital kitchen into a laboratory for the study of nutrition, which enabled a hundred thousand starving children in the city to be fed in the years after World War I. For young patients with tuberculosis, he built a cheerful open-air pavilion on the roof. Each morning, a procession of these children would descend a winding staircase while singing choral music, on their way to classes in the hospital garden.

Asperger joined a tight-knit staff at the Heilpädagogik Station that included Weiss, psychiatrist Georg Frankl, psychologist Josef Feldner, and a nun named Sister Viktorine Zak who had a special way of working with unusual children. There was also a young physician on staff who specialized in treating gastrointestinal disorders, Erwin Jekelius. Meeting at each other's apartments for roundtable discussions several times a week, Asperger and his colleagues discussed their young patients in depth, viewing each case from as many perspectives as possible. Dispensing with Aichhorn's enthusiasm for psychoanalysis, they nourished the developing minds of their patients by engaging them with an integrated program of music, literature, nature study, drama, art, speech therapy, and athletics, coordinated by Sister Viktorine, whom Asperger praised as the "true genius" of his clinic.

Their approach to diagnosis was based on a method of intensive observation developed by Lazar. He believed that only by watching a child in course of his or her daily life—in class, at play, at the dinner table, and at rest—could the true dimensions of the child's condition be gauged. Putting children through a battery of tests, or hauling them into an examination room, was not enough. Sister Viktorine, who worked alongside Lazar before his death, used to say that it was crucial to observe the children's behavior "down to their very toes." No one mastered this intimate style of observation better than Georg Frankl, a Czech who started working at the clinic in 1927 after graduating from the university. Frankl became Asperger's chief diagnostician.

Asperger would often just sit with the children, reading poetry and stories to them from his favorite books. "I don't want to simply 'push from outside' and give instructions, observing coolly and with detachment," he said. "Rather, I want to play and talk with the child, all the while looking with open eyes both into the child and into myself, observing the emotions that arise in reaction to everything that occurs in the conversation between the two of us."

Previous accounts of life in his clinic have been based on a report published in 1991 by cognitive psychologist Uta Frith, but an overlooked paper by an American psychiatrist named Joseph Michaels, who visited the Heilpädagogik Station in the mid-1930s, provides valuable insight into the ways that Asperger's staff put their ambitious theories into practice.

Mornings began with an hour of gymnastics and exercise led by Sister Viktorine, often set to music. Then academic lessons were offered to the children. On Mondays, the clinic hosted math classes; on Tuesdays, there were courses in reading; Wednesday's focused on handwriting and composition; and there were lessons in geography and history on Thursdays. On Friday mornings, the children went for walks in the garden, and on Saturdays, they worked on arts and crafts. Afternoons were devoted to rest and play, with plenty of free time built into the schedule so the children could hang out together and pursue their own interests. After church on Sundays, they spent the afternoon organizing group games and putting on plays.

Michaels was initially baffled by the apparent lack of systematized methodology for treating the young patients. Upon making inquiries as to the psychoanalytical frameworks that guided the conduct of Asperger and his colleagues, he was told that they had "no such formulations to offer." In an era when psychology was striving to prove its empirical validity by embracing standardized tests like the Stanford-Binet intelligence scale (commonly known as the IQ test), the ward's emphasis on "looking with open eyes," as Asperger put it, seemed like a throwback to the nineteenth century, when clinicians like Jean-Martin Charcot encouraged his patients to make art. Michaels was shocked to see happy children at play, throwing a ball around, instead of sitting "fixed in numbered seats to await their turn, as we in America are accustomed to see them."

After a few days in Vienna, however, he was won over. In a report published in the *American Journal of Orthopsychiatry*, Michaels marveled, "In this 'age of technocracy' with its overemphasis on technical procedures, it is rather unusual to find a highly personal approach characterized by an appreciable absence of what are ordinarily regarded as rigid methods, apparatus, statistics, formulae and slogans." Instead, "great value is placed on intuition gained . . . while working, or better, while living with the children."

Even the standards of "normal" conduct on the ward seemed surprisingly open-ended. The criterion for classifying behavior as normal or abnormal was the challenges that it created for the individual child, not whether it strayed from an idealized template of psychological health. "Fundamentally there appears to be no special interest in the differences between normal and abnormal," Michaels wrote, "as it is felt that theoretically this is unclear, and practically it is of no great importance."

Another valuable window into the mind-set of the staff is provided by Weiss in a paper on conducting "play interviews" with children in nursery school. Play therapy was a fad in the 1930s, promoted by psychoanalysts like Hermine Hug-Hellmuth, Anna Freud, and Melanie Klein, who subjected their young patients' behavior to heavy-handed interpretations in the Freudian style. (To Klein, for example, one boy's fascination with doors and door handles was really about "the penetration of the penis into the mother's body . . . Doors and locks stood for the ways in and out of her body, while the door-handles represented the father's penis and his own.")

But Weiss took a lighter approach. Instead of setting up a strict schedule of appointments with the children, she simply made it known that she had toys available for kids who wanted to play. How each child responded to that opportunity told her a lot even before the formal interviewing sessions began.

> Some children frequently volunteered for play turns when it was obvious that they had no chance; others tended to pick the right moment for asking to be admitted. Some came from time to time to see if they could have a turn, and apparently were prepared for either alternative. They would leave again without being upset when they found that another child had come first; or else they decided to wait. Other children, however, came with nothing in mind but a wish to play, and resented finding themselves barred.

Weiss's play sessions were designed to offer the children maximum freedom of expression. An inviting assortment of building blocks, crayons and paper, clay, dolls, cooking utensils, toy cars, trucks, stuffed animals, rags, and scarves was laid out for them to choose from as they pleased. By seeing how each child acted in this situation, she was able to gauge their capacity for social adaptation, imagination, and spontaneous enjoyment. Then she would introduce a rule into each session (such as "Toys must go back in the bag after playing with them") to observe how they reacted to constraint and authority. No possibility for learning from a child's behavior was wasted.

Michaels admitted that the clinic's approach seemed like "more of an art than a science." But he recognized that the ambitions of this art went beyond the mere formulation of a diagnosis. Instead, he wrote, Asperger and his colleagues aimed at nothing less than "to determine the innate capacities of the child, the alterable components of his personality, the causes of his pathological behavior, what will best assure his personal happiness, security and social welfare, what his right place is in the family, society, what are his personal goals and ambitions, and how these can all be realized."

Even the physical layout of the Heilpädagogik Station—with comfortable chairs and tables and decorative friezes on the walls—made it clear that the ward was not intended to be a custodial institution where demoralized patients would be shut away from the eyes of polite society. It was a place where children and teenagers could rediscover the potential of their humanity.

II

On his first day at the hospital, Gottfried did nothing but cry. His tears gradually subsided, but he was still upset that he would have to stay there for a month, trapped in an unfamiliar setting with unfamiliar people. Some kids at the clinic—especially those referred by the juvenile courts—became enraged when they realized that they couldn't just walk out the door. But Gottfried's response to his predicament was unusually sober and deliberate.

Instead of throwing a tantrum, he tried to reason with the staff. He patiently explained how unhappy he was, attempting to buttress his case by informing them that his mother was ill, which meant his grandmother was home alone, and was surely at her wits' end. The upcoming Sunday was a holiday, and he was expected to walk in a procession at his church. Clearly, he should be allowed to go home immediately.

These attempts at persuasion were unsuccessful, but they cast light on the unusually logical tenor of Gottfried's mind. For a boy who often came across as immature, he could behave in surprisingly grown-up ways. He often seemed more at ease around adults than his peers, but even his interactions with the staff were strangely impersonal. If a doctor or nurse took a moment to listen to him, his face would brighten and he would become cheerful; but it didn't seem to matter to Gottfried *which* adult paid attention to him. Most of the other children, by contrast, quickly developed a passionate attachment to one staff member or another.

Gradually, Gottfried adapted to his new life on the ward. The reliable rhythms of the daily schedule seemed to comfort him. He studied it diligently, as if he were learning the local customs while exiled in a foreign land. He was at his best in class, where he beamed with pride when a teacher called on him. But given a choice between associating with other children and being alone, he would wander off by himself, unless the children were organizing a game. Then he would lobby a sympathetic adult staff member to be included in the group.

Sadly, when no adults were around, Gottfried's peers teased him as mercilessly as they did at home, particularly when they discovered that they could upset him by telling him he'd done something inappropriate. While some kids took pleasure in flouting the clinic's regulations, Gottfried seemed horrified by the idea—but then he would break the same rules inadvertently, as if they had simply slipped his mind.

GOTTFRIED'S COMPLICATED RELATIONSHIP with rules and expectations also came up during a free-association test. Weiss prepared him in the usual manner by presenting the test as a kind of game: *Just close your eyes and say whatever comes into your mind. All we're looking for is words, ordinary nouns; don't worry about forming complete sentences.*

As the boy tried to do what he thought was expected of him—slowly, haltingly, with a long pause between each answer—it became clear to Weiss that suggesting to the boy that he focus on nouns had been a mistake. He wasn't freely associating at all; instead, he was scrutinizing each word internally to verify that it was a noun before saying it out loud, and laboring with such intensity that he kept forgetting to close his eyes as she had instructed him to do. Thus his score on the test was merely average, despite the fact that he had worked much harder on it than most kids. But Weiss was too astute an observer to take Gottfried's middling score at face value. "We cannot be interested so much in the concrete result—average though it may be—as in the particular direction he gave to the test performance," she noted. "After knowing the child's way of thinking and acting, it is impossible to believe that he happened to turn in this direction by chance. We know how important laws and rules are to keep him in his psychic balance and so it seems quite natural that he is peculiarly interested in them."

She then gave the boy a series of pictures depicting the capture and training of a dancing bear, presented out of order. She asked him to think up a story that fit the pictures and put them in the appropriate sequence. Most children had fun with this test, convinced that they were being given a chance to figure out the secret of what *really* happened to the bear. But instead, Gottfried complained that he couldn't possibly sequence the pictures correctly without knowing the story first. "G. is not able to escape from his logical attitude," Weiss observed. "He can recognize the facts, but cannot invent what may lie between them. Many children younger and simpler than he can manage that much better. For them, the picture becomes vivid at once like a fairy tale and they will begin interpreting and not worry about what really is in the pictures or what they have to add to them. But for G. the picture is either real just as it is or unintelligible."

The same habit of taking things literally dictated his responses to every test that Weiss gave him. Asked to recall a short story he'd just read, he repeated the text nearly word for word, but he didn't embellish on the narrative with his own imaginative flourishes. He performed well on a handwriting test—indeed, Weiss described his orthography as "peculiarly regular"—but he became preoccupied with the rules of grammar and the fact that his sheet of paper had a crease in it. Gottfried was acutely aware of details that other children missed, but he was perpetually getting lost in the forest while fretting about individual trees.

Seeing this pattern helped Weiss understand why so many people thought he was slow and stupid at the same time that his grandmother knew he was highly intelligent. Gottfried *was* highly intelligent—but in ways that didn't register on the clinic's standardized tests. As Weiss got to know him better over the course of the month, she came to glimpse the earnest nine-year-old struggling behind the mask of indignation that he adopted to get through social situations that didn't make sense to him. Asked to compare pairs of words like *bush* and *tree* and *ladder* and *staircase*, for example, he would preface his replies with the haughty-sounding phrase "Well, good gracious." This annoyed Weiss at first, but she came to understand that Gottfried didn't mean to sound rude. Comparing ladders to staircases just seemed like a pointless exercise to him.

Gottfried was precociously smart, but he was apparently unaware of things that most kids know instinctively. He could see right through the polite façades and social games unfolding all around him, but didn't know how to play them to his own advantage.

III

Over the course of a decade, Asperger and his staff examined more than two hundred children who displayed a similarly striking cluster of social awkwardness, precocious abilities, and fascination with rules, laws, and schedules. They also saw a number of teenagers and adults who fit the same profile. The most severely disabled children had been branded as feebleminded and warehoused in asylums. Others were prodigies who were failing in school because their teachers interpreted their pedantic mannerisms and failure to obey instructions as willful insurrection. Even the most gifted of these kids found it hard to learn basic life skills like dressing, bathing, and behaving politely at the table. They also tended to be clumsy and inept at sports, which singled them out for mockery in a culture that exalted athletic vigor as a sign of spiritual health.

Many of them also struck Asperger as exceptionally beautiful, with finely chiseled, mature-looking features. But they wore grave and serious expressions, as if their constant worrying had aged them prematurely. They seemed particularly disturbed by unanticipated changes in their environment and events turning out in ways that defied their expectations. ("If something was only slightly different from the way that he had imagined it or from what he was used to," Asperger wrote of one child, "he was upset and confused and would go into long tirades.") Their behavior tended to become highly regimented—as if by doing things in a routinized manner they could ward off chaos itself.

In its most extreme forms, this rage for order took the form of repetitive, stereotypic movements, such as rocking back and forth, beating on tables and walls, fussing with a shoelace for hours, or repeating the same phrase over and over. The children would line up their toys in rows in accord with laws and patterns that were apparent only to them, and explode in tantrums if these sequences were disturbed by their parents. But they could also turn this need for repetition and symmetry into a source of pleasure. They built up huge collections of treasured objects, which could be as mundane as scraps of cotton thread or as esoteric as a supply of chemicals for a home laboratory. Asperger reported that one boy became determined to collect a thousand matchboxes, "a goal which he pursued with fanatical energy."

Some of the children were astonishingly articulate, even poetic in their speech, and acute observers of their own experience. One boy described to Asperger how he soothed his homesickness at night: "If one lays one's head on the bolster, then there is such a strange noise in the ear, and one has to lie very quietly for a long time, and that is nice." But sometimes their florid constructions outstripped the literal meaning of the words, and their delivery took on a stilted, singsong quality, as if they were declaiming in verse. They tended to launch into monologues, with one verbal tributary flooding into the next, whether the person they were talking to was really listening or not. They also had a hard time keeping their pronouns straight. One boy began speaking at a very young age but was never able to learn to use *Sie*, the polite form of address, employing the more familiar *Du* instead, which came across as presumptuous.

These children were bundles of paradoxes: precocious and childish, sophisticated and naïve, clumsy but formal, standoffish but lonely, attuned to the music of language but insensitive to the rhythm of reciprocal interaction. They were, as Asperger put it, "a particularly interesting and highly recognizable type of child." He came to believe that they were representative of a distinct syndrome that was "not at all rare" but had somehow escaped the notice of his predecessors.

In fact, a young Russian psychiatrist named Grunia Sukhareva had written about a nearly identical group of young people in Moscow two decades earlier. The focus of her work was an emerging field of psychiatry: adolescent psychosis. Sukhareva made the case that her patients had come into the world with a disorder that resembled schizophrenia but with an essential difference. While adult schizophrenics almost invariably declined, these odd young ducks often made dramatic improvements over time.

The parents of a thirteen-year boy Sukhareva called M.Sch. sensed that he was different from his siblings even as a baby. He was excruciatingly sensitive to sound and flinched at every noise in his crib. As he got older, he developed intense phobias—of the dark, of being alone, of locked doors, of monsters that seemed to be hiding everywhere—and, most of all, of other children. He was obsessed with illness, death, and coffins. If M.Sch. heard about someone who died young, instead of expressing sympathy for the deceased and their loved ones, he would sigh, "I shall not live very long."

It wasn't hard to figure out why other kids frightened him. M.Sch. walked with a noticeably odd gait, and they bullied him mercilessly for it. But he also had startlingly mature insights into his predicament. He explained to Sukhareva that his classmates "are very good at games and won't let me play. The character of the children is such that they choose the stronger ones." He may have felt that he was feeble in body, but he was not feeble in mind. He scored two years ahead of his peers on a scale of intellectual development and showed a natural aptitude for music. Introduced to the violin at age seven, he made such rapid progress that he was admitted to the famed Moscow Conservatory. But he struggled to achieve the self-discipline required to become a successful concert violinist.

Concerned for his future, his parents checked him into Sukhareva's in-patient program at the hospital. There he adopted the role of the clown, cracking vulgar jokes and chasing girls around the ward. He knew he was being naughty, but he seemed unable to stop himself. Once M.Sch. started doing something, or even thinking about something, it was almost impossible for him to switch tracks. "It often seems to me that a word is going round and round in my head, and if I do not do something or other, something will happen to me," he explained. "To start anything, I have to make lengthy preparations, and afterwards it is hard for me to stop."

Like Gottfried, he sounded more like a middle-aged fussbudget than a boy barely in his teens. Asked if he had enjoyed a book, he hemmed and hawed and said, "It seems to me that I liked the book, but I am really not sure. The principle of reading is such that one is bound to be taken in." Yet his art teacher considered him a prodigy. When he was immersed in music, he was "totally transformed," Sukhareva said, "giving the impression of a confident and sensitive musician."

Another boy, M.R., taught himself all about the War of 1812 by the time he was ten and could expound at length on the events leading up to it. But if these lengthy perorations were interrupted, he would become agitated and start all over again from the beginning. When the nanny of a third boy asked him to sit up straight at the table, he replied, "I have my principles and am pedantic, and therefore I will not do it."

A.D. was fascinated by numbers and counting. As he waited for a play to begin, he would total up the number of spectators in the theater and then dash out to the lobby to add in the latecomers. He took frequent polls of his classmates, firing off questions like "Which party got the most votes in the recent elections in England?" and "What are the best strains of rabbit?" (They cruelly nicknamed him "the talking machine.") By the time he was thirteen, he had extensive knowledge of politics in the emerging Soviet Union.

Two of Sukhareva's patients started spontaneously rapping in rhyme when they were three years old. All of them seemed to have insatiable appetites for puns, quips, and catchphrases. A boy called K.A. told his nannies that he was planning to deliver a lecture on "the nutritional value of cotton wool" and once slipped a note into his doctor's bag awarding him a membership in "the Society of Fried Dogs."

Despite their shambling exteriors, these children had rich inner lives. They shunned communal games but devoured fairy tales and fantasy books in solitude. When P.P. was three, he astonished his parents by sitting down at a piano and reproducing his favorite melodies note for note. Sukhareva described him as a sensitive child with "deep feelings for the beauty of nature" who would burst into tears at the slightest rebuke. But he had no friends other than his sister. Asked why he avoided his classmates, he replied, "The children are too noisy and disturb my thinking." At twelve, he moved through the world like a monk in a contemplative order of one.

To describe this curious syndrome, Sukhareva proposed the term *schizoid personality disorder.* She was uncertain if it had any true relationship to schizophrenia (literally, "splitting of the mind"), named by Swiss psychiatrist Eugen Bleuler fifteen years earlier. These children didn't seem to be going through any sort of disease process similar to the tragic arc of schizophrenia; they were just deeply, constitutionally different from their peers—more like one of Lazar's archetypes than patients who could ever be made well. If they found a teacher who protected them from bullies and encouraged them to cultivate their natural talents, they might thrive, though they would always remain eccentric. "All affected patients were under our observation for a number of years and all were seen to make considerable progress," Sukhareva reported. M.Sch. "had excellent achievements in music and art." M.R. "did well at school and his personality became significantly better adjusted." A.D. "made good technical progress in music," though he remained distinctly reserved.

She cautioned her colleagues that the term *schizoid* might lead to "conceptual confusion and misinterpretation" if the two conditions turned out to be completely unrelated. Her concerns proved to be well-founded.

Though Asperger was apparently unaware of Sukhareva's work, he too saw parallels between his patients' condition and schizophrenia—particularly a tendency toward what Bleuler called "autistic thinking," defined as self-centered rumination and retreat into fantasy. These children pursued their own goals tenaciously, like the boy determined to collect a thousand matchboxes, but they seemed immune to the expectations of others. "In everything these children follow their own impulses and interests," he observed, "regardless of the outside world."

Schizophrenic patients typically experience a progressive loss of contact with the social world that begins in adolescence; Asperger's patients, on the other hand, seemed to come into the world beyond the reach of interpersonal contact—though he astutely noted that this often didn't become apparent to their parents and medical professionals until they were two years old or older. As they were clearly not psychotic, Asperger coined the term *Autistischen Psychopathen* ("autistic psychopathy") to describe their condition, employing a nineteenth-century term for the hazy borderland between mental health and illness. He also employed the simpler term *Autismus* and referred to it as a "natural entity," like a field biologist describing a life-form he'd discovered flourishing in plain sight.

He pointed out that the distinctive characteristics of this natural entity were already familiar in stock characters from pop culture like the "absent-minded professor" and Count Bobby, a fictitious aristocrat who was the butt of many Austrian jokes. Crucially, Asperger also described *Autismus* as remaining "unmistakable and constant throughout the whole life-span," and said that it encompassed an astonishingly broad cross section of people, from the most gifted to the most disabled. There seemed to be nearly as many varieties of *Autismus* as there were autistic people.

> The range [of this type] encompasses all levels of ability from the highly original genius, through the weird eccentric who lives in a world of his own and achieves very little, down to the most severe, contact-disturbed,

> automaton-like mentally retarded individual . . . Autistic individuals are distinguished from each other not only by the degree of contact disturbance and the degree of intellectual ability, but also by their personality and their special interests, which are often outstandingly varied and original.

There was no doubt in Asperger's mind that autism was passed down through the family tree. "We have been able to discern related incipient traits in parents or relatives," he wrote, "in *every* single case where it was possible for us to make a closer acquaintance." But he cautioned his colleagues that it would be folly to search for a single gene responsible for such a complex range of behaviors and traits. "It is a vain hope to think there may be a clear and simple mode of inheritance," he said. "These states are undoubtedly polygenetic."

In a postgraduate thesis submitted to Hamburger in 1943, Asperger described four "prototypical cases" named Fritz V., Harro L., Ernst K., and Hellmuth L.—all boys between the ages of seven and ten. He apologized for not including a young woman in his quartet of prototypes, explaining that he had never seen a full-blown female case in his practice:

> While we have never met a girl with the fully fledged picture of autism, we have, however, seen several mothers of autistic children whose behavior had decidedly autistic features. It is difficult to explain this observation. It may be only chance that there are no autistic girls among our cases, or it could be that autistic traits in the female become evident only after puberty. We just do not know.

He went so far as to characterize *Autismus* as "an extreme variant of male intelligence," a view echoed forty years later by British psychologist Simon Baron-Cohen, who linked the development of autism to exposure to high levels of testosterone in the womb. It's more likely, though, that one of the primary factors contributing to the absence of girls in Asperger's practice was the fact that teachers and judges of the juvenile court were a major source of referrals for his clinic. The socialization of *junge Wienerinnen* to be compliant and self-effacing—to fade demurely into the background—undoubtedly led young women to work extra hard to suppress the behaviors that brought their male counterparts to the attention of the authorities. Similar dynamics would contribute to the underestimation of the prevalence of autism in women into the twenty-first century.

Asperger's choice of presenting four prototypical cases in his thesis has led many commentators (including the authors of the Asperger FAQ at the National Institutes of Health) to claim that his work in autism was based solely on observations of just four boys. But he was very clear on that point: "We want only to state briefly that over the course of ten years we have observed more than 200 children who all showed autism to a greater or lesser degree." From these observations (including Weiss's in-depth case study of Gottfried, which has been overlooked since its publication in 1935) he developed sketches of four characters as memorable as any in popular fiction.

The first boy, Fritz, a lanky scion of poets and recluses, had a precocious vocabulary and a prodigious command of math but was expelled from kindergarten after only a few days for idly strolling around in class and "demolishing the coat-racks." Harro was a short, muscular boy with a wizened face and resonant voice who tossed off deadpan observations like "I am dreadfully left-handed"—despite the fact that he was only eight years old. "Sometimes he appeared to be in deep thought," Asperger observed, "then he would draw together his brows and assume a strange, slightly funny dignity." Ernst was so perpetually overwhelmed that he looked like he had just "fallen from the sky." He maintained a running commentary on his actions, as if he were the voice-over narrator of his own life: "He had to tell others at once whatever it was that captured his attention. Some of these 'asides' were quite remarkable, not only in the sense that they were very adult in diction, but also because they showed good observation." Finally, there was poor Hellmuth, who was so chubby and ungainly that he was unable to play a game of catch in the schoolyard, standing rigidly among his peers "like a frozen giant." Yet if Hellmuth was prompted to talk about his favorite subject, poetry, he could be startlingly eloquent and original, "seemingly full of insight and superiority."

Like Cavendish standing off to the side as his colleagues conversed at the Royal Society, all four children regarded the world of people slantwise—in fleeting, peripheral glances. But Asperger determined that they took in a lot of information that way: "It is occasionally revealed that they have perceived and processed a surprisingly large amount of the world around them." This was an extraordinarily prescient insight; later clinicians nearly universally assumed that autistic children were deliberately avoiding looking people in the eye.

Like Sukhareva's patients, they often had talents that were not apparent to the casual observer. Some were capable of amazing feats of rote memory, such as knowing the names of the saints for every day of the year, or being able to recall the routes of all the streetcar lines in Vienna. Others had developed homegrown methods of rapid calculation, as if they had invented their own kind of math from scratch. Fritz, for example, taught himself about fractions without lessons. He understood the properties of negative numbers and could solve logic problems with ease. Asperger suspected that he could have performed well on intelligence tests, but he refused to cooperate. Instead, he would jump down from his chair and slap the examiner on the hand.

Harro could not only perform complex mathematical operations in his head, he was an avid reader who had a vivid and original way of talking about things. Asked to compare the words *fly* and *butterfly*, he launched into an etymological reverie: "The butterfly is colorful and the fly is black. The butterfly has big wings so that two flies could go underneath one wing. But the fly is much more skillful and can walk up the slippery glass and up the wall . . . The microscope explains how the fly can walk up the wall: just yesterday I saw it has teeny weeny claws on the feet and at the ends tiny little hooks."

But Harro was failing in school, because he was very disruptive in class, like Fritz. He would crawl around on all fours and announce that a lesson was "far too stupid" for him. He rarely did his homework, and if a teacher gave him a makeup assignment, he would sneer, "I wouldn't *dream* of doing this." He spent his days immersed in the books he loved, a stranger to the children around him.

IV

As Sukhareva had been impressed by her patients' prodigious abilities in music and art, Asperger was struck by these boys' natural aptitude for science:

> We know an autistic child who has a particular interest in the natural sciences. His observations show an unusual eye for the essential. He orders his facts into a system and forms his own theories even if they are occasionally abstruse. Hardly any of this has he heard or read, and he always refers to his own experience. There is also a child who is a "chemist." He uses all his money for experiments which often horrify his family and even steals to fund them. Some children have even more specialized interests, for instance, only experiments which create noise and smells. Another autistic boy was obsessed with poisons. He had a most unusual knowledge in this area and possessed a large collection of poisons, some quite naively concocted by himself. He came to us because he had stolen a substantial quantity of cyanide from the locked chemistry store at his school.

One boy sought refuge from neighborhood bullies by engaging in discussions with an old watchmaker who took a liking to him. Another child knew "an incredible amount about complex machinery" and bombarded adults with obscure technical questions that were "nearly impossible to fend off." This boy also had a fertile imagination and was daydreaming about rocket ships and other "fantastic inventions" long before they became a reality. This inspired Asperger to comment, "Here one observes how remote from reality autistic interests often are." But the advent of space exploration in the 1950s required him to retract that statement in favor of a suggestion that the designers of spaceships themselves were autistic.

Furthermore, Asperger recognized that his patients' blatant disregard for authority could be developed into the skepticism indispensable to any scientist. When he asked one eleven-year-old boy if he was religious, he replied, "I wouldn't like to say I'm unreligious, I just don't have any proof of God."

The pediatrician concluded that the innate gifts of these children were as central to the condition he was describing as their social difficulties. He became convinced that these boys had the potential to become innovators in their fields of interest precisely *because* they were constitutionally unable to take things on faith.

> Autistic children have the ability to see things and events around them from a new point of view, which often shows surprising maturity. This ability, which remains throughout life, can in favorable cases lead to exceptional achievements which others may never attain. Abstraction ability, for instance, is a prerequisite for scientific endeavor. Indeed, we find numerous autistic individuals among distinguished scientists.

He christened this distinctive cluster of aptitudes, skills, attitudes, and abilities *autistic intelligence*, making the bold suggestion that autistic people have played an unappreciated role in the evolution of culture:

> It seems that for success in science and art, a dash of autism is essential. For success, the necessary ingredient may be an ability to turn away from the everyday world, from the simply practical, an ability to rethink a subject with originality so as to create in new untrodden ways.

This was a significant departure from the traditional view of so-called idiot savants in psychology, which was to frame their extraordinary abilities merely as compensation for gross deficits in other areas of development.

The nineteenth-century French physician and educator Édouard Séguin, who coined the term *idiot savant*, described the striking talents of his patients in terms more befitting a malignant tumor. "Among the wealthier classes, idiocy is not only oftener aggravated by accessory diseases, but also complicated with abnormal semi-capacities or disordered instincts, which produce heterogeneous types to an almost unlimited extent," he said in 1869. "It is from this class, almost exclusively, that we have musical, mathematical, architectural, and other varieties of the *idiot savant*; the useless protrusion of a single faculty, accompanied by a woeful general impotence."

Asperger was under no illusions that his patients were all budding Beethovens or Newtons. "Unfortunately, in the majority of cases, the positive aspects of autism do not outweigh the negative ones," he acknowledged. But the mission of the Heilpädagogik Station, in keeping with Lazar's original vision, was to find individualized approaches to education that would enable these children to make the most of their innate gifts while ensuring that they had the resources to cope with the challenges of their disabilities. As Weiss put it in her case study of Gottfried:

> In the case of learning difficulties, the question is never "How well or how badly does the child learn?" but "Why does the child learn badly?" and "Which is the best teaching method for him?"

The clinic staff did not predicate the eventual success or failure of these children in society on their being cured of their autistic traits. Asperger wrote of a former patient who had done poorly in school, showed little regard for his hygiene and appearance, and seemed so unaware of other people that he failed to recognize acquaintances even when he passed them in the street. But he had been able to make the most of his abilities with the support and encouragement of his mother. Seeing that he was already fascinated by geometry at age three, she drew a triangle (a *Dreieck*, or three-cornered figure), a square (a four-cornered figure), and a pentangle (a five-cornered figure) for him in the sand. He immediately drew a line and a dot, proclaiming the line a *Zwei-eck* (a two-cornered figure) and the dot an *Ein-eck* (a one-cornered figure). Soon he was calculating cubic roots in his head.

He had barely been able to get through elementary school because of his uncouth behavior but was spared from expulsion specifically because of his abilities in math. By pleading with his teachers to give him advanced tutoring, he managed to pass the college entrance exam. In his first year at university, he became interested in theoretical astronomy. Taking nothing for granted, he quickly detected an error in one of Newton's proofs. He wrote his dissertation on the subject and eventually became an assistant professor of astronomy at a prestigious university, though Asperger described his behavior as still "extremely clumsy and gauche."

THE JOB OF THE STAFF of the Heilpädagogik Station, as Asperger saw it, was to teach these children how to put their autistic intelligence to work. He compared them to absentminded professors. Instead of treating them merely as patients, he saw them as indispensable allies in developing methods of pedagogy that would be most appropriate and effective for them.

One of his mentors in this quest was Harro, who behaved so outrageously in school. "Although the boy was aloof from things and people—or perhaps *because* of this—he had rich experiences and his own independent interests," Asperger observed. "It was possible to talk to him as to an adult, and one could really learn from him."

Among the things he learned was that trying to leverage peer pressure in the classroom didn't work with these children, because they were already alienated from their peers. Flattery was equally ineffective, as they were curiously immune to it. What kids like Harro *did* care passionately about, however, was logic. They had an innate desire—almost a compulsion—to seek out universal laws and objective principles. (Paradoxically, this could result in the appearance of impairment, as when Gottfried got distracted on the free-association test by Weiss's suggestion that he think of nouns.)

The primary motivation for learning in typical children was their emotional ("affective") identification with the teacher. But autistic children sought *learning for its own sake* in the course of pursuing their passionate interests. They didn't care how their teachers felt about them; they just wanted to know the facts. The best teachers for these children, Asperger observed, were willing to meet the children halfway, instead of insisting that they act like everybody else.

> The teacher must at all costs be calm and collected and must remain in control. He should give his instructions in a cool and objective manner, without being intrusive. A lesson with such a child may look easy and appear to run along in a calm, self-evident manner. It may even seem that the child is simply allowed to get away with everything, any teaching being merely incidental. Nothing could be further from the truth. In reality, the guidance of these children requires a high degree of effort and concentration.

He put it even more succinctly in a 1953 textbook that has never been translated into English. "In short," Asperger wrote, "the teacher has to become somehow 'autistic.'"

WHO WAS THIS MAN who identified so strongly with children who no one else wanted to deal with? Not surprisingly, Asperger had been a gifted, eccentric, solitary child himself. He was born in 1906 in the village of Hausbrunn in Lower Austria, the eldest of three boys. But his brothers died young and he became an only child. Asperger's mother, a pious and affectionate woman, doted on her surviving son. His father, by contrast, was a stern disciplinarian who hated working as an accountant—a tedious job that he felt was beneath him. Asperger attributed his own drive to excel in his studies to his father's frustration at having been too poor to go to university.

Studying the classics in elementary school, young Hans could lose himself in a book for a whole day, only realizing in a panic at night that he still had homework to do. He exasperated his peers by endlessly quoting poetry, particularly the verses of Franz Grillparzer, the wunderkind who wrote the oration read at Beethoven's funeral before a crowd of twenty thousand weeping mourners.

After his five-act satire of the upper classes in Vienna flopped, he penned his own eulogy:

As a human being, misunderstood,
as a civil servant, overlooked,
as a poet, tolerated at best,
I drag my monotonous life away.

Like a nineteenth-century Goth, Grillparzer the Miserable became a hero to Asperger the Outcast, who attributed his interest in autistic children to his youthful infatuation with the poet. (It's tempting to speculate that the relative of Fritz he described as "one of Austria's greatest poets" was Grillparzer himself.) "Reading is bound up with one's fate and destiny," Asperger mused in a radio interview in 1974. "A person finds what he needs, or, to put it another way, *it* finds *him*."

YOUNG HANS RESCUED HIMSELF from a life of tedious pedantry by falling in with a group of kindred spirits who called themselves the Wandering Scholars. One of dozens of "Catholic renewal" groups in Austria that aimed to rekindle respect for traditional Teutonic values in the years between the world wars, the Scholars would head off on monthlong treks to the wilderness to hike and read poetry aloud in the bracing Alpine air, which had the added benefit of getting them out from under the prying eyes of their Teutonic parents. Asperger met his wife-to-be, Hanna Kalmon, on one of these trips while taking field notes and honing the powers of observation that would serve him well as Lazar's successor at the

Heilpädagogik Station. Asperger called the Wandering Scholars "one of the noblest flowerings of the German spirit."

The second turning point in his early life was a dissection in biology class, when he noticed an ivory-colored bump on the crimson surface of a mouse's liver. Slicing into the bump with his scalpel, Asperger was shocked to see a long white worm wriggle out. Fascinated by the uncanny intimacy of the two creatures, he decided to devote his life to medicine. "The way that one life can live within another life," he said, "shouldn't one get to the bottom of *that*?"

After enrolling at the University of Vienna, Asperger attracted the attention of his future mentor, Franz Hamburger, a charismatic pediatrician who wrote an exposé of the role of unhygienic living conditions in the prevalence of tuberculosis among Vienna's poorest families. In this supremely capable physician, Asperger saw an embodiment of the motto of the Wandering Scholars: "To lead and to help." In 1931, Hamburger assigned his eager young protégé to the Children's Clinic, where he would work for the next two decades.

Near the end of his thesis, which was published as *Die "Autistischen Psychopathen" im Kindesalter* ("Autistic Psychopathy in Childhood") in a German journal of neurology in 1944, Asperger struck an oddly strident note:

> The example of autism shows particularly well how even abnormal personalities can be capable of development and adjustment. Possibilities of social integration which one would never have dreamt of may arise in the course of development. This knowledge determines our attitude towards complicated individuals of this and other types. It also gives us the right and the duty to speak out for these children with the whole force of our personality.

It's easy to misread this passage only as an anodyne testimonial to the value of special education. But the true meaning of these lines becomes clear only when one examines the historical and political context in which they were written. Asperger's statement was likely a last-ditch plea to his former mentor, who had gone off in a very different direction since his days as a champion of Vienna's least fortunate families.

When Asperger submitted his thesis to Hamburger in 1943, the University of Vienna was a mockery of the prestigious center of learning that it had been five years earlier. Of the nearly two hundred senior members of the medical faculty, fewer than fifty remained, and their replacements were bumbling fanatics. Asperger's colleagues, Anni Weiss and Georg Frankl, had been forced to flee the country, and many of the other former faculty were in exile, imprisoned in concentration camps, or dead of suicide. The beautiful city of Vienna had become an abattoir of surreal brutality.

Asperger was speaking out with the "force of his whole personality" for the sake of children all over Europe who had not yet been murdered by a monstrous idea of human perfectibility—an idea that his supervisors, who were fervent Nazis, had imported from America.

V

In October 1921, the National Research Council, under the auspices of the National Academy of Sciences, hosted a gala weeklong event at the American Museum of Natural History in midtown Manhattan. The State Department had been mailing out invitations for months, and eager delegates arrived at the grand edifice on Central Park West from every continent on earth.

The Second International Congress of Eugenics was intended to be much more than another celebrity-studded science conference. Backed by the moral authority of one of America's most prestigious museums and promoted in journals like *Science* and the *Scientific Monthly*, the congress was designed to be nothing less than the turning point in history when the human species seized control of its own destiny instead of trusting in the gradual process of natural selection. An icon displayed prominently on the brochures depicted a tree with roots in biology, psychiatry, politics, economics, statistics, genealogy, intelligence testing, and other fields, with the progressive-sounding slogan: "Eugenics is the self direction of human evolution."

Museum officials devoted two floors of the building to the event, temporarily changing the names of Darwin Hall and Forestry Hall to Eugenics Hall and lining them with exhibits on heredity, psychology, climate change, human migration, "institutional management of the socially inadequate," and animal husbandry. Two exhibits were devoted to contrasting *aristogenic* family lines (those that boasted evidence of specific talents) with *cacogenic* lines (those that carried specific "degenerate qualities"). A cross section of an ancient sequoia presided over the exhibit, situating the proceedings in the natural order of things. Papers were presented on "Racial Differences in Musical Ability," "Distribution and Increase of Negroes in the United States," "Inheritance of Mental Diseases," and "Some Notes on the Jewish Problem."

At one end of Eugenics Hall stood a statue of the "average young American male," with a reminder that a hundred thousand white veterans had perished in the trenches of Europe two years earlier. At the other end of the hall, another statue depicted the Platonic ideal of the athlete, composited from the physiques of the "50 strongest men at Harvard."

The recent war in Europe was much on the mind of Henry Fairfield Osborn, the museum's president, who delivered the welcoming address. The barrel-chested, blue-eyed son of a railroad magnate, he developed the theory of aristogenesis to explain long-term trends in evolution that he believed couldn't be accounted for by random mutation and the pressures of natural selection. Attempting to reconcile his deep Presbyterian faith and science, Osborn was a proponent of *conscious evolution*—the notion that God set the universe in motion to engender the birth of geniuses in genetically superior family lines. A former dean of science at Columbia University, he refused to believe that any creature as noble as *Homo sapiens* could have evolved from one as lowly as a monkey. Instead, he promoted the theory of an aristocratic predecessor called Dawn Man, based on the alleged discovery of Piltdown Man, which was later revealed to be the most successful hoax in the history of British archaeology.

Osborn began his address on an ominous note. "Europe, in patriotic self-sacrifice on both sides of the World War, has lost much of the heritage of centuries of civilization which can never be regained." As a result, he said, "in certain parts of Europe the worst elements of society have gained the ascendancy and threaten the very best." He was vague about the identity of these "worst elements" but confided that his fellow scientists were gaining a new appreciation of the "spiritual, intellectual, moral, and physical value of the Nordic race."

At the same time, he insisted that, as a man of science, he was not advocating anything as barbaric as race hatred. "In the selection of the best we should know no prejudice. We write nothing down in malice," Osborn said. It was just that "500,000 years of human evolution . . . had impressed certain distinctive virtues as well as faults on each race." Striking a pose of magnanimity, he went on, "If the Negro fails in government, he may become a fine agriculturalist or a fine mechanic." The Chinese and Japanese, meanwhile, clearly showed a cunning facility for poetry and art, particularly ceramics. The American democratic notion that "all men are born with equal rights," he cautioned, must not be confused with the "political sophistry that all men are born with equal character and the ability to govern themselves and others."

One of the most insidious forces undermining the viability of the human species, Osborn added, was the failure of governmental and religious institutions to safeguard the "monogamous" family (which he defined as "one husband, one wife") against the rampant individualism promoted by decadent art forms that exalted selfish impulses over sober self-discipline. He ended his speech by saying that it was the duty of his fellow scientists to "enlighten government in the prevention of the spread and multiplication of worthless members of society, the spread of feeblemindedness, of idiocy, and of all moral and intellectual as well as physical diseases."

These views of race and disability were not fringe science—the ranting of a deranged extremist at the academic equivalent of a Ku Klux Klan rally. They were the perspective of a broad swath of the scientific mainstream in America after World War I, backed by ongoing research in the United States and Europe funded by major foundations like the Carnegie Institution and the Rockefeller Foundation. Of the fifty-three papers presented at the conference, forty-one were the work of American scientists.

The honorary president of the congress was Alexander Graham Bell, inventor of the telephone and telegraph. Bell had his own theories about the threat that people with disabilities represented to the future of the species. His mother and wife had both been born deaf, and in 1883 he warned the National Academy of Sciences that unless the use of sign language was vigorously discouraged in schools for the deaf, society ran the risk of engendering "a race of deaf-mutes."

The word *eugenics* (which means "the good birth") was coined in 1887 by the younger half cousin of Charles Darwin, Francis Galton. A former child prodigy with a striking gift for data mining, he popularized the notion of regression toward the mean in statistical research, launched the science of forensics by discovering that each person possesses a unique set of fingerprints, and created the first weather maps. As Edwin Black described Galton in his history of eugenics in America, *War Against the Weak*:

> He joyously applied his arithmetical prowess and razor-like powers of observation to everyday life, seeking correlation. Galton distinguished himself by his ability to recognize patterns, making him an almost unique connoisseur of nature—sampling, tasting, and discerning new character in seemingly random flavors of chaos.

Darwin's son, Leonard, was the star speaker at the congress. Echoing Osborn's fulminations about the imminent decline of the republic, he warned the assembly, "The inborn qualities of civilized communities are deteriorating, and the process will inevitably lead to an all-round downward movement." To avert this catastrophe, he prescribed a tax increase on single people and childless couples while promoting childbearing as a patriotic duty for "naturally well-endowed" families. As for the hundreds of thousands of "idiots" confined to institutions, he hailed the American Stock Breeders' Association's experiments with sterilization by X-ray as a promising development, particularly since compulsory surgery tended to increase popular "prejudice" against the practice.

ON THE LAST DAY of the congress, the delegates filed onto buses for a field trip to the Eugenics Record Office in Cold Spring Harbor on Long Island. Launched in 1910, the ERO was a massively influential organization funded by the widow of Union Pacific railroad baron E. H. Harriman, the Rockefeller family, and the Carnegie Institution. Until its demise in 1939, the organization churned out hundreds of papers on such topics as "fit and unfit matings" and the care and training of the "mentally and physically defective classes." Teams of ERO investigators compiled voluminous "trait files" to tease out the role of heredity in such characteristics as woolly hair, protuberant noses, and "sinisterity" (left-handedness). They also mapped the pedigrees of such notable personages as Thomas Edison, Abraham Lincoln, Theodore Roosevelt, and Johann Sebastian Bach.

One of the institute's primary interests was congenital disorders of the psyche. Field investigators fanned out across the Eastern Seaboard, touring prisons and mental institutions and rifling through medical records in a comprehensive effort to take a census of carriers of the genetic roots of insanity, criminality, perversion, dementia, melancholia, alcoholism, stuttering, lisping, vertigo, migraine, bedwetting, sleepwalking, wanderlust, and other alleged forms of degeneracy.

Campaigns to sterilize the residents of mental asylums and prisons received a significant boost from experts who declared that people with developmental disorders were not only cognitively but *morally* impaired. Martin Barr, the chief physician at the Pennsylvania School for Feeble-Minded Children, insisted that his students suffered from "exaggerated sexual impulses" that they could not control, describing them as "mere creatures of the moment" and slaves to temptation. "Indeed they are so crooked that they are parallel to nothing," Barr declared, "and one can hardly fathom how protean are the vagaries of mental defect." Raising the specter of jails and reform schools filled with defectives waiting out their incarceration so they could return to lives of profligacy, he claimed that "idiots" and "imbeciles" were prone to becoming prostitutes, and "reproduce their kind 2 to 6 times more rapidly than do normal people." He then took aim at laws intended to shield disabled children from exploitation and abuse:

> While we have some laws for the protection of the feeble-minded we have accomplished but little to stem the tide of degeneracy, and pollution of our normal population . . . We must face the fact that the very lifeblood of the nation is being poisoned by the rapid production of mental and moral defectives, and the only thing that will dam the flood of degeneracy and insure the survival of the fittest, is abrogation of all power to procreate . . . Unconsciously innocent poisoners of a normal race, they are nevertheless its worst enemy.

Terrifying predictions of "race suicide" by clinicians like Barr exerted a decisive influence on the lay public's view of disability. By 1937, a *Fortune* poll indicated that two-thirds of the magazine's influential business readership was in favor of forcibly sterilizing mental patients.

That initiative was already well under way. In 1909, a statute had been passed in California granting public-health officials the right to forcibly castrate convicts and the residents of the California Home for the Care and Training of Feebleminded Children, located in Sonoma County. Thirty U.S. states eventually passed similar laws, and a wave of sterilizations swept through asylums and prisons coast to coast.

As influential as they were at home, American eugenicists received an even warmer welcome in Germany, where they found enthusiastic support for their ideas in another country that had recently suffered the loss of a generation of bright, physically fit young men in war. Fearing that this decimation would act like natural selection in reverse, the ambitious leaders of this proud and wounded nation undertook a plan to secure the future of their race by wiping "mental defectives" off the face of the earth forever.

VI

One day in 1920, Ewald Meltzer, director of the Katharinenhof State Home for Non-Educable Feebleminded Children in Saxony, sent out a survey to the fathers and male guardians of nearly two hundred children in his care. The survey was worded carefully, because Meltzer was unsure how parents would react to a strategy for reducing a burden on society that was swiftly gaining currency among his colleagues:

1. Would you give your consent in every circumstance to a painless shortening of your child's life, after an expert had determined him incurably imbecilic?
2. Would you give your consent only if you could no longer care for your child, for example if you were about to pass away?
3. Would you give your consent if your child were suffering serious physical and mental anguish?
4. What is your wife's opinion of questions 1–3?

After reassuring his recipients that his questions were purely theoretical, Meltzer was surprised to discover how many of them responded favorably to the idea of "painlessly shortening" their children's lives. In fact, some respondents told him that the relevant authorities should simply do whatever they thought wise, without distressing them by asking them for consent.

"It would have been better if you hadn't asked me at all, if you had just put the child to sleep," one mother replied. "I would have preferred not to have been bothered with this question," another said. "If it had been news of sudden death, we would have accepted it." Meltzer concluded that these mothers and fathers "would like to free themselves and perhaps the child as well from a burden, but they would like to do it with a clear conscience."

The results of Meltzer's survey bolstered popular support for the controversial theories of psychiatrist Alfred Hoche and penal law expert Karl Binding, who co-authored a book in 1920 called *The Liberation and Destruction of Life Unworthy of Life*. They argued that food and medical care are not everyone's birthright but are properly earned by doing productive labor. They described disabled people as *Lebensunwertes Leben* ("life unworthy of life"), calling them "useless eaters" and "human ballast" who consume precious resources without repaying their debt to society. Ending the lives of these "empty human husks"—who were not even aware of the misery that they inflicted on others—was not only a socially beneficial act, Hoche and Binder claimed, it was the most compassionate thing that could be done under the circumstances.

> Their life is absolutely pointless, but they do not regard it as being unbearable. They are a terrible, heavy burden upon their relatives and society as a whole. Their death would not create even the smallest gap—except perhaps in the feelings of their mothers or loyal nurses.

One of the organizations likely to object was the Catholic Church. But in 1927, the Roman Catholic theologian Josef Mayer provided clerical cover for Hoche and Binding by publishing a book that argued that forced sterilization of "mentally handicapped" people was entirely in accord with Catholic ethics and tradition. Inconveniently, Pope Pius XI issued an encyclical three years later condemning the practice of sterilization for other than "therapeutic uses." But the concept of "life unworthy of life" left a lasting mark on a culture struggling through a postwar depression, and the encyclical likely played a role in later persecution of Catholic clergy.

Hoche and Binder's rhetoric resonated deeply with an aspiring politician who had been convicted of high treason for launching an unsuccessful coup against the leaders of the Weimar Republic inspired by Benito Mussolini's seizure of power in Rome. Stewing in the Landsberg Fortress in Bavaria, this young man—whose name was Adolf Hitler—dreamed of leading his people to glory against the corrosive forces of liberal democracy.

Hitler referred to Landsberg as the "university" where he gave himself a crash course in eugenics. (Later, he allowed his name to be used in advertisements for Hoche and Binding's book.) His bible on the subject was *The Passing of the Great Race*, a hodgepodge of racist pseudoscience, anti-immigration rants, and archaeological poppycock by a dapper, mustachioed Yale graduate named Madison Grant. Throughout the book, Grant refers to the descendants of the Mayflower families as the real "native Americans." The thrust of his argument was that the Nordic "race" (a fictitious amalgam of Swedes, Danes, and other Northern Europeans) was rapidly becoming an endangered species, elbowed aside by "swarms" of ignorant Negroes, "servile" Orientals, and Polish Jews that had already "literally driven" whites "of the old stock . . . off the streets of New York City."

Grant concluded that Galton's strategies for encouraging men and women of the "genius-producing classes" to be fruitful and multiply would be insufficient to stem the rising tide of idiocracy. Instead, he directed his fellow eugenicists to develop more expeditious means of shoving alien usurpers and other forms of human ballast overboard:

> A rigid system of selection through the elimination of those who are weak or unfit—in other words, social failures—would solve the whole question in a century, as well as enable us to get rid of the undesirables who crowd our jails, hospitals and insane asylums . . . This is a practical, merciful and inevitable solution of the whole problem and can be applied to an ever widening circle of social discards.

This was martial music to the ears of young Hitler, who shared Grant's visceral revulsion for social failures, defectives, and weaklings, despite the fact that with his dark hair and eyes, he hardly resembled the Nordic types exalted in the book. In *Mein Kampf*, the manifesto that Hitler dictated to his deputy Rudolf Hess while incarcerated in Landsberg, the future Führer put forced sterilization at the core of his vision of a new society while framing it as a compassionate defense of the lives of children yet unborn. The state, he wrote, "must declare unfit for propagation all who are in any way visibly sick or who have inherited a disease and can therefore pass it on, and put this into actual practice . . . Those who are physically and mentally unhealthy and unworthy must not perpetuate their suffering in the body of their children."

A 1913 textbook by Géza Hoffman called *Die Rassenhygiene in den Vereinigten Staaten von Nordamerika* (*Racial Hygiene in the United States*) became the seminal guide to applied eugenics for German biology students. As the National Socialist party rose to power in the 1930s, the body of American eugenic law became the blueprint for Nazi policies to defend Nordic—rechristened "Aryan"—*Blut und Rasse* ("blood and race") from dysgenic influences.

"We will not allow ourselves to be turned into niggers," Hitler bragged to the editor of a conservative German daily in 1931. "The Nordic blood available in England, northern France and North America will eventually go with us to reorganize the world."

Unlike their American counterparts, German eugenicists did not plan to limit their efforts to asylums, prisons, and schools for the feebleminded. Instead, they aimed to carry out the implications of eugenic theory to their fullest extent in the population at large.

In July 1933, Reich Minister of the Interior Wilhelm Frick put the Law for the Prevention of Genetically Diseased Offspring into effect. Any German citizen who showed signs of schizophrenia, bipolar disorder, epilepsy, inherited blindness or deafness, Huntington's disease, or alcoholism could be forcibly sterilized. The law also mandated the creation of Genetic Health Courts that decided the outcome of individual cases and heard appeals (which were rarely granted). In 1934 alone, 84,600 cases were brought to the court, resulting in 62,400 forced sterilizations. Eventually, more than four hundred thousand men, women, and children were sterilized against their will by the Nazi regime.

Among the Austrian medical professionals who viewed the rise of Nazism with alarm was Hans Asperger himself. From April to the end of May in 1934, he took part in a practicum in Leipzig and Potsdam with child psychiatrists Hans Heinze and Paul Schröder, two of the leading eugenicists in Germany. On April 10, he wrote in his travel diary, "An entire people goes in a single direction, fanatically, with narrowed vision, certainly, but also with enthusiasm and dedication, with enormous discipline and control, with a terrible persuasiveness. Now only soldiers, soldierly thinking—ethos—Germanic paganism."

As unsettled as Asperger was by the rapid militarization of German culture, he was willing to look the other way, dispassionately appraising the clinical work of Heinze and Schröder as he would the efforts of any fellow practitioners in the field. He wrote of his experiences during the practicum, "I find the teaching not too bad. To all appearances, the overall structure fits well with our perspectives, certainly in many details . . . well-grounded structure with clear, diagnostically useful concepts. One can learn a great deal there and work well. But I also think about the efforts that Dr. Frankl puts into his diagnostics for special-needs education."

He also made an observation that was likely the first lighthearted comment about autism in history. "We have very good concepts for our own work, but we tend to express them in jargon that is understood very differently by outsiders—talk about autistic!—which makes it hard for us to pass them on to others." Soon, however, Asperger would no longer have the luxury of being able to look the other way.

Two months after Asperger returned from his practicum, agents of Hitler's Schutzstaffel burst into the Chancellery building in Vienna disguised as police officers. Panicked members of the cabinet hid themselves behind thin doors that proved no match for the SS men, who smashed through them with rifle butts as they advanced on the apartment where

Chancellor Engelbert Dolfuss had taken refuge. Simultaneously, eight Nazis took over the main radio station in the city. They shot the station manager, killed a radio actor with a hand grenade, and forced a newscaster to go on the air and declare that Dolfuss was resigning.

Meanwhile, back at the Chancellery, Hitler's men cornered Dolfuss, shot him in the head, and dumped him bleeding on a sofa, where he begged for a doctor, then for a glass of water, and finally for a priest. Dolfuss was hardly a liberal; rather, he was a proud Fascist who styled himself after Mussolini and had launched his own right-wing party called the Fatherland Front, which took as its symbol the swastika-like *Krückenkreuz*. The Italian dictator received word of Dolfuss's assassination while signing off on blueprints for a new mental hospital and delivered the bad news himself to the chancellor's pregnant widow, who was staying at his villa in Riccione with her two children.

This brazen attempt at a coup ultimately failed, but the fact that Nazis were assassinating Fascists for being insufficiently loyal to the Führer is an indication of the state of Austrian politics at the time. Dolfuss's successor, Kurt von Schuschnigg, presided over a right-wing government that became more pro-German and anti-Semitic by the day. The Nazis were also escalating their propaganda war against the residents of Austria's mental institutions. The official newspaper of the NSDAP, the Nazi party, featured full-page spreads of grinning "idiots," zombielike "lunatics," and dysmorphic babies under headlines about the "cruelty of compassion" and the blessings of forced sterilization. Posters appeared at "racial exhibits" showing strapping Aryan workers straining under the burden of scowling mental patients riding seesaws perched across their shoulders, with captions claiming that the cost of housing such patients into old age was fifty thousand reichsmarks.

At a time when belonging to NSDAP was practically obligatory at the university, Asperger did not join, according to his daughter. He may have been particularly averse to doing so because of his loyalty to the Wandering Scholars. The network of Catholic youth organizations known as the

Neuland-Bund was originally inclined to support the party but turned against them once Nazis began openly persecuting members of the Church.

Progressive youth groups like the Neuland-Bund were eventually banned in Austria, while their right-wing equivalents were assimilated into the Hitlerjugend (Hitler Youth movement), furnishing the Reich with a supply of indoctrinated soldiers. Meanwhile, both Asperger's former mentor, Franz Hamburger, and his trusted colleague at the Heilpädagogik Station, Erwin Jekelius, became fervent party members.

By 1935, when Weiss published her paper on Gottfried in the *American Journal of Orthopsychiatry*, a massive exodus from Austria was under way, prompted by new laws stripping Jews of property, jobs, and basic rights of citizenship. Jewish-owned businesses, homes, and tourist attractions all over the city were in the process of being "Aryanized" and turned over to non-Jewish owners. Signs appeared on park benches throughout the city reading *NUR FÜR ARIER* ("FOR ARYANS ONLY"), while children sang taunting songs about how the only green space left for Jews could be found in the cemetery.

Hundreds of families mobbed the Jewish emigration agency every day, desperate to get out of the country, often leaving nearly everything they owned behind. Many Jews took flight to Palestine, where their parents and grandparents had sought refuge from successive waves of pogroms. Others headed to the United States, where the liberal immigration policies that Osborn had condemned at the Second Eugenics Congress offered them a safe harbor, but only if they could provide proof of employment. The same community of pediatricians, surgeons, psychoanalysts, and specialists in other fields that had turned "Red Vienna" into a global beacon of medical expertise was under siege. Of the nearly 5,000 physicians practicing in the city, 3,200 were Jews—a legacy of the Middle Ages, when medicine was one of the few occupations that Jews were allowed to enter, because doctoring in the era of the Great Plagues was an unenviable high-risk profession.

Austria's loss was the world's gain. Anni Weiss was the first of Asperger's team to leave, arriving in America in 1934. The clinic's gifted diagnostician, Georg Frankl, took flight in 1937, emigrating to Maryland with the aid of a Jewish doctor who had left Austria years earlier. But as the NSDAP's power and influence grew, the careers of the true believers thrived. Erwin Jekelius—whose sole lasting contribution to the pediatric literature in English was coining the term *paradoxal obstipation* to describe anal leakage and intestinal inflammation caused by a plug of fecal matter stuck in the rectum—became the city's chief public-health officer at the urging of the president of the Evangelical Church Council, who was stacking the local government with officials loyal to the Reich. The venerable Society of Physicians on Frankgasse, where Freud had debuted his insights into the psyche, was purged of Jews and renamed the Viennese Medical Society.

In 1938, Asperger's mentor Hamburger gave a lecture to the society titled "National Socialism and Medicine" that left no doubts about his loyalties. It was an odd speech for a physician of his stature, more of a rant on the power of faith healing (which he called "nature healing") than to the work of "so-called scientists," as he put it. He began by telling the roomful of eminent physicians that sports and tourism did "more for health than all the doctors put together." Then he extolled the virtues of the "practical country doctor" (a ruddy Aryan, no doubt) who spread "courage and confidence" among the sick, inspiring blind, unquestioning faith among his patients. "This faith, in all cases," he said, "leads to the improvement—often even to the elimination—of the symptoms of the disease." Hitler was playing a similar role for the whole Reich, he explained. "Now we must face the fact that a single man, a non-medical man, through his superior qualities, has opened up new avenues of health for the eighty million folk of Germany."

One of these avenues was the Führer's refusal to coddle the mentally ill in "luxurious" institutions. Only an "over-intellectualized Jewish patient" would question the wisdom of his doctor's diagnosis, Hamburger pointedly added—implying that only Jews and other undesirables would challenge Hitler's diagnosis of society's ills. It was a vision of the *Reichsführer* as the

Grand Placebo, healing the *Volk* of all manner of maladies and malaises by overwhelming force of his "superior qualities." Hamburger then affirmed his support for the Law for the Prevention of Genetically Diseased Offspring, adding a word of praise for Aryan women who turned away from the "manifold amenities of life" to do their patriotic duty of bearing an annual child for the Reich. "National Socialism is the true instrument for the achievement of the health of our people," he thundered. "Under National Socialism, doctors are quite officially the *führer* of the people, called to the leadership of its health."

Inexorably, the shadow of death was falling over Asperger's little professors.

VII

On March 11, 1938, as thousands of Austrians huddled by their radios, von Schuschnigg finally resigned, declaring that his army had been instructed not to oppose the Wehrmacht troops marching across the border. The final strains of the national anthem barely had faded from the airwaves before they were replaced by another sound rising from the streets: thousands of Austrians singing the "Horst Wessel Song," the bombastic Nazi anthem that von Schuschnigg's government had explicitly banned.

Clear the streets for the brown battalions,
Clear the streets for the stormtrooper!
Millions are looking upon the swastika full of hope,
The day of freedom and of bread dawns!
Millions are looking upon the swastika full of hope,
The day of freedom and of bread dawns!

The long-awaited day of *Anschluss*—the "joining" of Austria and Germany—was at hand. Soon the former First Republic of Austria would be rechristened *Ostmark*, which meant "Eastern March." To celebrate the homecoming of the Austrian-born Führer and his troops, swastika flags and banners fluttered from balconies and windows throughout the city. Cheering Austrians lined the streets as women and children showered the incoming convoys with cigarettes.

The official organ of the Wehrmacht described the day's events like an ecstatic tent revival, tapping into the vein of Germanic paganism that Asperger had mentioned in his diary:

> Everywhere and without exception, there was invisible, spontaneous contact from heart to heart, that mysterious flow of natural connectedness: in the mountains of Tyrolia, in the Salzburg hills, in Upper Austria, on the Danube and the Inn, and then into the farthest corners of Steiermark, Kärnten, the Vienna Woods and the Burgenland. It was more than mere liking—it was love at first sight. Who among our soldiers in gray or blue will ever forget the joy looking his way from the eyes of all the Austrians who lined the streets of the cities and villages! Who will not still hear the enthusiastic shouts that everywhere received him to the end of his days?

But the seasoned British war correspondent G. E. R. Gedye saw it differently:

> As I crossed the Graben to my office, the Brown flood was sweeping through the streets. It was an indescribable witches' Sabbath—storm-troopers, lots of them barely out of the schoolroom, with cartridge-belts and carbines, the only other evidence of authority being Swastika brassards, were marching side by side with police turncoats, men and women shrieking or crying hysterically the name of their leader, embracing the police and dragging them along in the swirling stream of humanity, motor-lorries filled with storm-troopers clutching their long-concealed weapons, hooting furiously, trying to make themselves heard above the din, men and women leaping, shouting and dancing in the light of smoking torches which soon began to make an

> appearance, the air filled with a pandemonium of sound in which intermingled screams of "Down with the Jews! *Heil Hitler! Heil Hitler! Sieg Heil!*"

Gangs of civilians calling themselves *Rollkommandos* roared up to department stores and shops in the Jewish quarter, smashed doors and windows, and dumped the inventory into waiting trucks, often assisted by the police. Mobs roamed the streets, stealing whatever they saw and dragging terrified families out of their homes in their nightclothes. One particularly brutal form of humiliation dished out to the Jews was the organization of *Reibpartien* ("scrub parties"), where men and women were forced to crawl on their hands and knees with toothbrushes and buckets of corrosive acid to erase anti-*Anschluss* slogans from the pavement. Gedye saw an elderly man and woman driven down the street by a phalanx of storm troopers to scrub an offending stencil from the base of a statue. As a crowd chanted, "We have found work for the Jews at last, work for the Jews at last!" the old man patted the hand of his wife, who was silently weeping.

The Nazi medical establishment was preparing the ultimate punishment for those who threatened the Reich from within by passing their inferior qualities on to future generations. At an evening seminar for doctors hosted by the SS, Vienna neurologist Walter Birkmeyer told his colleagues, "Only the purity of our race and the health of our genes can save our people from decadence. It is our duty as fanatical followers to exterminate everything that is morbid, impure, and corruptive."

The University of Vienna was transformed into the intellectual center of an academic movement to put *Aufartung* (racial improvement) and *Rassenforschung* (racial research) at the top of the medical agenda. When the campus reopened three weeks after the *Anschluss*, the newly installed dean of medicine, anatomist Eduard Pernkopf, delivered a rousing speech to the faculty before a somber portrait of the Führer, dressed in his storm trooper's uniform and flanked by a cordon of SS men. He championed Nazism as an all-encompassing worldview that transcended medicine and science, advocated the use of "negative selection" by extinction (*Ausmerzung*), and praised Hitler as "the greatest son of our home country," concluding his lecture with a triumphant triple "*Sieg Heil!*"

The new dean wasted no time Aryanizing the most prestigious medical school in Europe. He ordered all faculty members to produce the birth certificates of their parents, grandparents, and spouses to "clarify" that they were of Aryan descent. They were also required to sign loyalty oaths to Hitler, and those who refused were forced to retire immediately. Within weeks, 80 percent of the medical faculty had been dismissed. (Among those fired from other departments were Erwin Schrödinger, who shared the 1933 Nobel Prize in physics with Paul Dirac, and the brilliant mathematician Kurt Gödel.) Swastika flags flew from the university's main building, and the few Jewish students allowed to remain were required to produce "entry permits" to walk onto campus.

Before the *Anschluss,* more than 5,000 physicians were practicing in Vienna. By that fall, less than 750 would remain. Many former professors at the university—the brightest minds of their generation—died in concentration camps. Others took their own lives. The zealots who took their places dismissed their former mentors and colleagues as "charlatans."

The Reich rewarded its loyal servants handsomely. Pernkopf was appointed president (*Rektor Magnificus*) of the university and given special dispensation to work on his magnum opus, an anatomical atlas called *Topographische Anatomie des Menschen.* This epic multivolume work featured lavish watercolor plates of each organ, bone, and blood vessel in the human body, accurate in every hue and detail. Praised by the *Journal of the American Medical Association* as "a work of art," Pernkopf's *Anatomy* became the go-to guide for surgeons all over the world who needed to brush up on their knowledge of internal organs before attempting a tricky procedure. Only in 1996, when a Jewish surgeon working with a Holocaust scholar demanded an investigation in the letters column of *JAMA*, did the medical profession admit that it had been teaching students how to become surgeons for nearly sixty years with paintings of the flayed bodies of disabled children and political prisoners.

A decree by the German minister of education ensured that Pernkopf had an adequate supply of source material for his atlas, which proved so effective that some executions had to be delayed as fresh cadavers piled up outside his dissection rooms. The sympathies of the painters who contributed to this massive effort were never in question: their signatures were festooned with swastikas and SS lightning bolts, which were discreetly airbrushed out of later editions of the atlas by the publisher.

IN THIS CLIMATE OF rabid fanaticism, on October 3, 1938, Asperger gave the first public talk on autism in history, in a lecture hall at the University Hospital. It's likely that Hamburger was in attendance, an imposing face in a sea of swastikas, and the children at the *Kinderklinik* were surely on his radar; a year earlier, the Vienna Psychiatric and Neurological Association issued a decree that "psychopaths" who could not be legally declared insane should be placed under continuous supervision as a permanent menace to society.

Asperger began by stating the obvious: "We are standing in the midst of an enormous change of our intellectual life, which has taken over all aspects of this life, not least, the area of medicine . . . Here, we are dealing with the most precious good of the nation—its health." He acknowledged that the "thorough change in our whole attitude" demanded by the Führer required medical workers to value the health of the *Volk* over the needs—and implicitly, the lives—of individual patients. "Many of the cases we deal with here are genetic disorders," he admitted. Then he paid lip service to the obligation to report such cases to the appropriate committees: "As doctors, we must take the tasks emerging in this area with our full responsibility." (After a similar statement in 1940, Asperger's trusted colleague at the clinic, Josef Feldner, advised him that such rhetoric was "a bit too Nazistic for your reputation. I would omit the thanks to the Führer.")

But then Asperger pivoted in an unexpected direction: "Today, let me not discuss the problem from the point of view of the people's health, for then we would have to discuss the laws for the prevention of diseased genetic material; instead we will address it from the point of view of the abnormal children. How much can we do for these people? That shall be our question." He then made a radical statement that might have caused his mentor to raise a disapproving eyebrow in the gallery: "Not everything that steps out of the line, and is thus 'abnormal,' must necessarily be 'inferior.'"

Asperger admitted that this assertion might "initially provoke protest." But then he did something sly: he launched into the case histories of his patients, putting his audience on reassuringly familiar turf. First he described a boy brought to the clinic by his father with a baffling set of symptoms. He had frequent and explosive tantrums and described himself as anxious and "quite melancholic." The boy's hearing was unusually acute, and he could be kept awake by the slightest sound in his room. He was also obsessed with eating sour things, and his diet was extremely limited as a result.

But there was another side to this boy, the pediatrician explained. His vocabulary and syntax were mature beyond his years, and he loved exploring philosophical questions in depth. He also had a keen eye for detecting faults in other people and himself, which indicated that he had sharp powers of observation. Asperger posed a provocative question: Were this boy's precocious abilities merely the product of "hyper-compensation," like Demosthenes, driven to become the greatest orator in Greece by his stuttering, which he conquered by learning to enunciate with a mouthful of pebbles? No, said Asperger. "We do not believe this. We claim—not on the basis of theory, but on the basis of our experiences with many children like this—that this boy's positive and negative qualities are two natural, necessary, interconnected aspects of one well-knit, harmonious personality. We could express it this way: this boy's difficulties—which particularly affect his relationships with himself and other people—are the price that he has to pay for his special gifts."

Then Asperger proposed a radical way of thinking about cognitive disabilities that was in direct opposition to the dogma of racial hygiene. "The good and bad in a person, their potential for success or failure, their aptitudes and deficits—they are mutually conditional, arising from the same source," he said. "Our therapeutic goal must be to teach the person how to bear their difficulties. Not to eliminate them for him, but to train the person to cope with special challenges with special strategies; to make the person aware not that they are ill, but that they are responsible for their lives."

Then he described a young patient who may have been the basis for his description of Harro. This boy was disruptive in class and "like a red rag to bulls" in the schoolyard. He was unable to dress himself without his mother's help and seemed so unaware of other people that Asperger's staff thought he was hard of hearing at first. But they found that even this "coarse, rough boy" had clever insights into his own behavior and expressed himself in highly creative ways when he was given the chance. All of these qualities together formed the clinical picture of autistic psychopathy, he explained. The special gifts of these children were inextricable from their impairments.

"Who among us does not recognize the autistic scientist," Asperger said, "whose clumsiness and lack of instincts have made him a familiar caricature, but who is capable of extraordinary accomplishments in a highly specialized field?" He made a plea to his colleagues to "never give up" on these children, because "strengths and capacities" might appear in them as they came of age that were not immediately apparent. By helping them live up to their full potential, his colleagues would be benefiting society as a whole—a goal even a fervent eugenicist could support.

Then Asperger made a remark that provides crucial insight into why he based his prototypical cases on his chatty little professors rather than on the more profoundly impaired children he saw in institutions. "I thought it more rewarding to choose two not too severe and thus more promising cases," he said, "and to explain, in reference to them, the path of our therapeutic approach." Unfortunately, his strategy of accentuating the positive to his Nazi superiors—shaped by the knowledge that the lives of his young patients were at stake—would contribute to widespread confusion in the coming decades.

On the basis of the four prototypical boys in Asperger's thesis, many clinicians and historians have assumed that he saw only "high-functioning" children in his practice, which ended up obscuring his most important discovery. The autism that he and his colleagues learned to recognize in prewar Vienna was "not at all rare," was found in all age groups, and had a broad range of manifestations, from the inability to speak to an enhanced capacity for focusing on a single subject of interest for an extended period of time without distractions.

In other words, it was a spectrum. Once you knew what to look for, you saw it everywhere.

THAT NIGHT, the sun sank over the deserted sidewalk cafés of Vienna, marking the beginning of Yom Kippur, the most sacred day in the Jewish calendar. For the next twenty-four hours, storm troopers and *Rollerkommandos* made brutal raids in once-thriving neighborhoods, stealing, burning, plundering, and killing.

This paroxysm of street violence turned out to be only a preview of the horror unleashed a month later on Kristallnacht, the Night of Broken Glass, when ninety-five synagogues in Vienna went up in flames, and Jewish homes, hospitals, schools, and shops were demolished with sledgehammers. In Berlin, more than thirty thousand Jews were dragged off to Dachau, Buchenwald, and other camps, most never to be seen again.

Meanwhile, Asperger's old colleague, Erwin Jekelius, was rising swiftly through the party ranks. At the end of the year, he became the director of a former rehabilitation facility for alcoholics called Am Spiegelgrund (formerly known as Am Steinhof). There, he helped Nazi officials draft a secret plan to rid the world of children like Gottfried, Fritz, and Harro that would become Hitler's blueprint for the Final Solution against the Jews. This monstrous scheme, which Jekelius and his cohorts carried out with brutal efficiency, began with the murder of a single child who had been declared an idiot by his doctors.

VIII

On February 20, 1939, a boy named Gerhard Kretschmar was born in the village of Pomssen, southeast of Leipzig, where Bach once played the organ at a funeral. The birth of a boy in rural Saxony would normally be cause for celebration, but Gerhard was born blind and intellectually disabled, with one arm and only a partial leg, and he was prone to seizures. His parents, Richard and Lena, were ardent Nazis. Richard brought his son to the University of Leipzig, where he begged the chief neurologist, Werner Catel, to "put him to sleep."

The eminent neurologist was likely to be sympathetic to the request. In his own book *Grenzsituation des Lebens* (*Extreme Situations of Life*), Catel called children like Gerhard "such monsters . . . that they are nothing but a *massa carnis*"—theologian Martin Luther's term for a heap of insensible flesh lacking a soul. But he informed the Kretschmars that he was powerless to help them, because the mercy killing of children was illegal. He hinted, however, that if Richard sent a letter directly to the Führer, he might be granted a special exemption.

The birth of Gerhard Kretschmar provided an opportunity that Hitler had been waiting for since his days in Landsberg prison. He dispatched Karl Brandt, one of his personal physicians, to Leipzig to examine the child. "If the facts given by the father were correct, I was to inform the physicians that [in Hitler's name], they could carry out euthanasia," Brandt later testified. "The important thing was that the parents should not have the impression that they were responsible for the death of the child." He also told Catel and his colleagues that if any charges were brought against them in court, the Führer would personally intervene in their favor.

The doctors in Leipzig replied that euthanasia was already standard practice on the maternity wards—it just wasn't talked about openly. While Catel conveniently went on vacation, one of his subordinates murdered the baby with an injection as the nurses took their coffee break.

That summer, another of Hitler's doctors, Theo Morel, prepared a memo detailing the financial burden on the Reich of long-term care for people with disabilities: "5,000 idiots costing 2,000 RMs [reichsmarks] each per annum = 100 million a year." (Even his math was wrong, as 5,000 × 2,000 = 10 million, not 100 million.) He stressed that this bottom line was only a fraction of the true cost to the Reich, because these "creatures" aroused horror in normal people, sapping their strength at a time when they needed to prepare for war.

In August, the Committee for the Registration of Severe Hereditary Ailments issued a decree calling for the registration of all children born with congenital abnormalities of any kind. Doctors and midwives were required to report all cases of deafness, blindness, Down syndrome, hydrocephaly, tic disorders, and other conditions to the committee. In return, they would receive a small sum for each report.

Under the pretext that Polish soldiers had made incursions into German territory, the Wehrmacht invaded Poland on September 1—the official start of World War II. A month later, Hitler signed a secret order authorizing the creation of a program called *Aktion* T-4, short for Tiergartenstrasse 4, the address of the Charitable Foundation for Curative and Institutional Care in Berlin. The aim of the program was to convert hospitals, clinics, and long-term-care institutions into factories of death for the carriers of heritable diseases and chronic disabilities. To provide legal cover for doctors and nurses who had already started murdering their patients, Hitler backdated the order by a month.

Closed-door meetings were held throughout Germany and Austria to educate medical students about child euthanasia and T-4, which primarily targeted disabled adults. Smooth adoption of these programs was facilitated by the development of a sanitized clinical lexicon to discuss formerly unspeakable acts. People with disabilities were to be referred to as *refractory therapy cases*. Laws promoting euthanasia were dubbed *negative population policies*. The act of killing was called delivering *final medical assistance*. Clinics for disabled children were christened *Kinderfachabteilungen*—"specialist children's wards."

A blizzard of official paperwork from Berlin enhanced the aura of respectability around these programs. The Reich Committee formulated questionnaires to determine which patients were candidates for final medical assistance, distributing copies by the thousands. Physicians were required to fill out a form on each patient in triplicate. These reports were reviewed by a panel of three medical experts in Berlin, who ticked a box on each form: a plus sign if the child was to die, a minus sign if the child was to be allowed to live, and a question mark for the handful of cases that required further consideration.

Based solely on these forms—and without ever seeing the children—the committee made arrangements with local health officials for young patients marked with plus signs to be transferred to *Kinderfachabteilungen*. Often what made the difference between a plus sign and a minus sign was nothing more than the score on an IQ test. Now the floodgates were open.

UNDER JEKELIUS'S GUIDANCE, Am Spiegelgrund became the primary children's killing ward for all of Austria. The institution had 640 beds when he arrived, and he added 240 more in a section of the hospital that he referred to as the Heilpädagogik Clinic, though therapeutic education was not on the agenda.

Over the next five years, Jekelius and his successors, Ernst Illing and Heinrich Gross, murdered 789 children at the facility, including 336 from the infants' ward. Most of these children had been diagnosed with feeblemindedness, epilepsy, or schizophrenia—the three diagnoses that autistic children were most likely to receive in the days before autism was an accepted diagnostic category. Nonverbal patients were favored for extermination because they created extra work for the nurses; eventually children who were "simply annoying" were added to the list.

A variety of killing methods, all equally barbaric, were employed by Jekelius's team and by medical staff in other institutions. Some children were killed with an injection of carbolic acid, and some with an excess of barbiturates; others were simply left outside, exposed to the harsh Austrian winter, until they contracted pneumonia. Parents would typically receive a note in the mail informing them that their son or daughter had died of natural causes. (The lesson of Meltzer's 1920 survey of parents had not been lost on Hitler.) Often these notes also included a bill for cremation or burial expenses.

T-4 and the child euthanasia program became fertile ground for medical research that could not have been conducted in contexts where the patient was expected to live. One doctor at the Maria Gugging Psychiatric Clinic in Vienna specialized in killing the children in his care with massive doses of electroconvulsive therapy, which had recently been introduced to psychiatry by the Italian neurologist Ugo Cerletti, who was inspired by seeing a butcher immobilize pigs with shock before slitting their throats. Often children were subjected to elaborate procedures like spinal taps or an excruciating process called pneumoencephalography, which entailed the replacement of their cranial fluids with air or helium before their brains were X-rayed and they were finally allowed to die. After the war, Gross based his career as a prominent psychiatrist and neurologist on his research on hundreds of brains harvested during the program, which were stored in jars in the cellar of Am Spiegelgrund for decades.

Another enthusiastic participant in the child euthanasia program was a psychiatrist named Hermann Pfannmüller, director of the Eglfing-Haar clinic in Munich, who led tours of his wards to educate psychiatry students about the pressing need to rid the world of these "empty human husks." He claimed to have received dozens of letters from parents who were grateful to him for putting their sons and daughters out of their misery.

His preferred method of delivering final medical assistance was to put children on his "special diet." Pfannmüller once explained the rationale behind his diet to a medical student named Ludwig Lehner, who never forgot it. "For me as a National Socialist, these creatures obviously represent only a burden for our healthy national body," the psychiatrist told Lehner. "We do not kill with poison, injections, and so forth, because that would only provide propaganda material for the foreign press . . . No, our method is, as you can see, much simpler and far more natural." He explained that his diet consisted of giving the children ever-diminishing portions of food—strictly fat-free—until they were receiving no sustenance at all. As the obese psychiatrist uttered these words, a nurse lifted a skeletal infant from its crib. "This one," Pfannmüller purred, "has two or three more days left."

More than two hundred thousand disabled children and adults were murdered during the official phases of the child euthanasia and T-4 programs, and thousands more were killed in acts of "wild euthanasia" by doctors and nurses on their own initiative. Obviously, the notion of transporting hundreds of corpses on roads that had to be kept clear for military convoys was impractical. As clinics, hospitals, and schools throughout the Reich dedicated their resources to the programs, crematoria were built next to these institutions, with conveyor belts to transport the bodies from the *Kinderfachabteilungen* to the ovens. In some institutions, improvised furnaces on wheels were employed to dispose of the corpses.

What began in secrecy inevitably became the subject of widespread rumors and gossip. Elderly people told their relatives with a knowing wink that once the feebleminded were gone, they would surely be the next "useless eaters" to go. Children became terrified of going to the doctor for any reason. When a bus pulled up to a clinic, they would say, "Here comes the murder-box again!" As mothers got wind of the fact that their children were not actually dying of natural causes, some made frantic attempts to intervene with the authorities. A nurse named Anny Wödl became frightened about the fate of her son, Alfred, who she had placed in Gugging after he failed to develop speech. (Like Gottfried's grandmother, Wödl intuited that her son was highly intelligent and "understood everything," despite the fact that he was nonverbal.) First she took a train to Berlin to make her case to the Reich Committee, but they told her that they were in favor of euthanasia and pointed her to the door.

Finally Wödl made an appointment with Jekelius to plead her son's case with him directly. "Dr. Jekelius was fully aware of what was happening," she testified at the Nuremburg Trials. "It was unambiguously clear from his remarks that he totally endorsed the entire operation against 'life unworthy of life' and that he was prepared to act as the Nazi state demanded." She begged Jekelius to at least grant her son a quick and painless death, and he promised to do that. On February 22, 1941, Alfred, six years old, perished of "pneumonia" at Am Spiegelgrund. When Wödl viewed her son's corpse, it was obvious that he had died in agony.

The most fateful of these attempted interventions concerned an older female patient with schizophrenia named Aloisia Veit. She had spent most of her life chained to an iron bed, haunted by visions of a grinning skull. One day at his office, Jekelius was told that a distinguished guest had arrived to meet him: the Führer's sister, Paula Hitler. She argued that Aloisia—who was her second cousin—should be allowed to live. It's hard to imagine Jekelius turning her down without approval from Berlin, but Paula's efforts were unsuccessful. (Undoubtedly her brother Adolf was not eager to have it known that he, too, had "cacogenic" influences in his family line.) At age forty-nine, Aloisia died in a room full of carbon monoxide at the Hartheim killing center.

Paula's passionate entreaty did, however, profoundly affect Jekelius in another way: he fell in love with her. The feeling was mutual, and Paula asked her brother for permission to marry him. But things did not go well. Shortly after she made her request, Heinrich Himmler, *Reichsführer* of the SS, had a telephone conversation with Reinhardt Heydrich, another high-ranking Nazi official praised by Hitler as "the man with an iron heart." Among the notes that Himmler scribbled on a notepad during the call were two words: "Arrest Jekelius."

After a brief stint in jail, Jekelius was drafted into the Wehrmacht and sent to the Russian front, where he was swiftly captured by Red Army soldiers and shipped off to the Lubianka prison camp in Moscow. There, he earned his final footnote in history by befriending a fellow POW who later became a patient of Viktor Frankl, the psychiatrist-author of *Man's Search for Meaning*, a memoir of surviving three years in Auschwitz, Theresienstadt, and Dachau. In a section of the book about redemption, Frankl wrote:

> Let me cite the case of Dr. J. He was the only man I ever encountered in my whole life whom I would dare call a Mephistophelean being, a satanic figure. At that time he was generally called "the mass murderer of

Steinhof" (the large mental hospital in Vienna). When the Nazis started their euthanasia program, he held all the strings in his hands and was so fanatic in the job assigned to him that he tried not to let one single psychotic individual escape the gas chamber . . .

Recently, however, I was consulted by a former Austrian diplomat who had been imprisoned behind the Iron Curtain for many years, first in Siberia and then in the famous Lubianka prison in Moscow. While I was examining him neurologically, he suddenly asked me whether I happened to know Dr. J. After my affirmative reply he continued: "I made his acquaintance in Lubianka. There he died, at about the age of forty, from cancer of the urinary bladder. Before he died, however, he showed himself to be the best comrade you can imagine! He gave consolation to everybody . . . He was the best friend I met during my long years in prison!"

This is the story of Dr. J, the "mass murderer of Steinhof." How can we dare predict the behavior of man?

IX

Though Maria Asperger-Felder's claims that her father never joined the Nazi party are credible, owing to his loyalty to the Wandering Scholars, it's unlikely that he would have been allowed to retain his position at the university without signing a loyalty oath to Hitler, given Pernkopf's 1938 decree.

But even that was not enough. Asperger found himself in what he described in a 1974 interview as "a truly dangerous situation." Twice, the Gestapo showed up at his clinic to arrest him. Both times, however, Franz Hamburger used his power as a prominent NSDAP member to intervene in his favor. By 1941, the entire medical infrastructure of Germany and Austria had been transformed into an industry of death, with only scattered pockets of resistance from figures in the Catholic Church who often paid a terrible price. Students at the University of Munich who called themselves the White Rose resistance group bravely spoke out against the Nazi regime's racial hygiene policies—inspired by a sermon by Bishop Clemens August, Graf von Galen decrying the T-4 program—and were arrested, convicted of treason by a "people's court," and beheaded.

At one point, Asperger suggested to his superiors that his little professors would make superior code breakers for the Reich. He was living in what Holocaust survivor Primo Levi called "the gray zone": the morally ambiguous position of subjects of the Reich who performed their jobs under Nazi rule, making horrific compromises and trade-offs they would never have considered under normal conditions. According to scholar Waltraud Häupl, whose sister Anne-Marie perished at Am Spiegelgrund, Asperger signed a letter of referral to Jekelius in 1941 for a little girl named Herta Schreiber who had suffered a major brain injury caused by encephalitis. In his report, Jekelius described Herta as "very affectionate" and "easily inclined to cry." Her mother, who was raising five other children at home and was sympathetic to Nazi principles, saw her daughter as a burden. In his letter, Asperger declared that "permanent placement at the Spiegelgrund seems absolutely necessary." Herta was admitted on July 1, 1941, and died there two months later, with the cause of death listed as "pneumonia."

Furthermore, another historian named Herwig Czech, whose grandfather was a Nazi, has found evidence that in 1942, Asperger—as a senior pediatrician representing the city of Vienna—served on a committee of seven doctors who decided which children were "educable" or not. In one group of 210 children, for example, the committee decided that thirty-five were incapable of learning and should be dispatched to Am Spiegelgrund.

By the time Asperger filed his thesis to Hamburger in October 1943, he clearly knew that thousands of children like Herta all over Austria and Germany had already been sent to their deaths by other colleagues working in the gray zone. Perhaps his concluding statement about "the duty to speak out for these children with the whole force of our personality" was written for the benefit of future generations. His thesis was published the following June in a journal called *Archiv für Psychiatrie und Nervenkrankheiten.*

By then, the Reich needed doctors on the front lines more than it needed them in psychiatric clinics, and Asperger was drafted into the Wehrmacht.

He first became an ambulance driver and then worked as a surgeon in a field hospital in Croatia. He maintained his correspondence with Sister Viktorine and the remaining members of his staff at the Heilpädagogik Station, continuing to participate remotely in roundtable discussions about his patients. He also jotted down his observations of Croatian culture in his ever-present pocket notebook. When his unit got lost in the mountains, he employed the orienteering skills he'd learned in the Wandering Scholars to guide them to safety by using his compass and the stars. "The fact that I was never called upon to kill anyone," he wrote in his diary, "is a great gift of fate."

THE SUMMER OF 1944 was punishing for the British and American troops trying to fight their way to Vienna. The Austrian capital was nicknamed "the Reich's air-raid shelter" because it was out of range of long-range bombers from England, and concrete *Flaktürme* formed a protective ring around the city like Sauron's towers rising from the valley of Mordor. Between the ground artillery and the crack pilots of the Luftwaffe, one in ten Allied planes was blasted out of the sky.

But the momentum of the war was at last turning decisively against Hitler. The successful invasion of Italy finally put the Reich's air-raid shelter within range of the American flotilla stationed off the coast of Foggia, and mining the Danube critically disrupted Nazi fuel lines. That fall, the Allied forces were finally able to punch through the city's defenses, though many lives were lost in the attempt.

Screaming toward the city at an altitude of twenty-five thousand feet, with hellstorms of small-caliber shells chipping away at their fuselages from below, young pilots would stack flak jackets on the floor, say a prayer, and head in to drop their lethal payloads. One day in September, while Asperger was still serving in Croatia, the University of Vienna became a target for the first time. Allied bombs rained down through the roof of the Children's Clinic, reducing the Heilpädagogik Station to rubble.

As the ceiling gave way, Sister Viktorine threw her arms around one of her boys to protect him. They were buried together.

Four

FASCINATING PECULIARITIES

Dinosaurs don't cry.

—Elaine C.

Asperger survived the war, but his concept of autism as a broad and inclusive spectrum (a "continuum," his diagnostician Georg Frankl called it) that was "not at all rare" was buried with the ashes of his clinic and the unspeakable memories of that dark time, along with his case records. A very different conception of autism took its place.

By the time Leo Rosa was diagnosed, that model of autism—invented by Leo Kanner—had prevailed for half a century, virtually unquestioned by clinicians who considered the Baltimore child psychiatrist the lone pioneer of the field of autism research. Asperger's thesis, published in German a year after Kanner's "Autistic Disturbances of Affective Contact," became a mere footnote to his landmark accomplishment. All over the world, autism was referred to simply as "Kanner's syndrome." The fact that two clinicians, working independently on both sides of the Atlantic, discovered it nearly simultaneously is still considered one of the great coincidences of twentieth-century medicine.

The annals of science are replete with episodes of multiple discovery, when a long-hidden pattern in nature suddenly reveals itself to independent investigators at the same time. Isaac Newton and Gottfried Leibniz developed calculus in parallel in the last years of the seventeenth century and then fought a bitter war of words for priority that lasted until Leibniz's death. If it weren't for astronomer August Ferdinand Möbius, those ingeniously twisted paper loops would be known as "Listing strips," after Johann Benedict Listing, who published a paper about them first. "When the time is ripe," mused mathematician Farkas Bolyai, "these things appear in different places in the manner of violets coming to light in early spring."

Kanner himself encouraged the view that Asperger's work was unworthy of serious consideration by maintaining a Sphinxlike silence about his Viennese counterpart, broken only once in his entire career. The fact that Asperger's account of autism languished in obscurity, never cited by the world's leading authority on the subject, is usually explained away by saying that in the aftermath of the atrocities committed by the Reich, clinicians in America and Europe were not eager to read papers translated from the German. Yet Kanner, as a native speaker, would not have required the services of a translator, and his other citations show him to have been intimately familiar with nearly every other paper written in the emerging field of child psychiatry during that era—in German, English, Russian, and any of the other dozen languages he spoke fluently.

In recounting the tale of his famous breakthrough to his colleagues, Kanner compared himself to the legendary Persian prince Serendip, who "went out for a stroll one day, with no particular quest in mind, and unexpectedly came upon a hoard of treasures," as he put it.

It was a good yarn, in keeping with his carefully cultivated image as a man destined from a young age to make a lasting contribution to society. But it wasn't the whole truth. Kanner's omission had grave consequences for autistic people and their families, which are still playing out today. And the one clinician in America who knew the real story wasn't apt to say anything about it in public, because he owed Kanner the ultimate debt: his life.

II

The life of Leo Kanner began in a culturally and spiritually rich, erudite, and humane world that was about to vanish. He was born Chaskel Lieb Kanner in 1896, in Klekotów, a tiny Ukrainian village near the Russian border. The mellifluous sounds of Yiddish—the beloved *mame-loshn* ("mother tongue") of the shtetls of Eastern Europe—woke him each morning, encouraged him when he acted like a *mensch* (an honorable person), rebuked him when he committed mischief, and sent him to bed at night.

When he was five, his father, Abraham, taught him Hebrew by enlisting his help in translating the Torah. As they pondered the meaning of the sacred syllables, Kanner would hear Meir, his grandfather, making tea in a giant samovar in the next room. Abraham was a shy and unworldly man who wrote meticulously cross-referenced books on Jewish law without ever intending to publish them, which Kanner affectionately referred to as his "way of playing solitaire."

Historian Adam Feinstein speculates that Abraham—who was celebrated in Klekotów for his astonishingly prodigious memory—had more than a touch of the syndrome that his son would become famous for discovering. By contrast, Kanner's mother, Klara, was a brash extrovert who openly mocked her husband's pious orthodoxy. (Her brother and sisters nicknamed her "Klara the Cossack.") Kanner claimed that she regarded his father as "a sort of mechanical toy which she thought she could wind up to go in any direction, a walking encyclopedia of knowledge which she regarded as useless but which made her bask in the glory of reflected prestige."

Despite his mixed feelings for his mother's worldly ways, Kanner was also drawn to a secular life. As a teenager, he discovered that *Lieb* is Yiddish for the Hebrew name *Aryeh*, which means "lion." So he began calling himself Leo, which sounded more modern, instead of Chaskel Lieb. At the same time, his traditional Jewish upbringing nurtured a keen sense of social justice in him. He was haunted for years by the story of an elderly deaf man with a disabled son who was shot by a sentry when they inadvertently crossed one of the ever-changing local borders without heeding the cry of "Halt!" He waged heroic battles in his imagination against Tsar Nikolai II and other corrupt Russian officials for launching vicious pogroms against the Jews.

After a business transaction went bad, the Kanners were compelled to move to Brody, the largest town in the region. There, Leo was personally exposed to anti-Semitism for the first time. One of the Polish teachers at his new school would throw open the classroom window saying, "It stinks! The Jews must be behind this." He began playing hooky to attend meetings of agnostics and other freethinkers, eager to hear their ideas for building a more humane society free of strife between competing religious sects.

After familiarizing himself with the sacred texts of Buddhism, Islam, and Protestantism, he plunged wholeheartedly into secular literature. He began reading Sherlock Holmes stories in pulp magazines and joined a neighborhood theater company that performed Shakespeare's plays in German. Developing a passion for the poetry of Goethe, he started writing poems of his own and submitting them to literary magazines. He also employed his innate talent for complex forms of wordplay, inherited from his father, to burnish his social standing by writing verses and acrostics that his friends used to woo girls. Later in his life, Kanner would say that if he had been a more successful poet, he would have died in a concentration camp.

Based on what he heard in freethinkers' meetings and his discussions with a bright and rebellious older boy, Kanner developed a personal philosophy that he considered his fundamental approach to life from then on. Most men and women, he believed, were stuck at an intermediate stage of evolution, still enslaved to the crude symbols and primitive superstitions that lurked behind the tenets of every major religion. A handful of bold visionaries, however, had managed to free themselves from the shackles of the old beliefs and were living in the liberated way that everyone would live in the future.

Kanner felt confident that he was a member of this elite group, destined to play a transformative role in society. Mindful of the poet Horace's advice that profound truths are often best disguised as jokes ("*Ridentem dicere verum quid vetat?*" or "What prevents a laughing man from telling the truth?"), he decided to make ironic quips, elaborate double entendres, and droll bon mots his personal trademark—the outward sign of his inner liberation.

Kanner also inherited his mother's adept social skills and craving for public approval. One day during a final exam in his high school—where he was the top student in his class—he got a headache so painful that he was unable to finish his essay. When he got the exam back, however, he was surprised to discover that his teacher had rated it excellent anyway, reassuring him that if he could have finished, he would have surely turned in a masterpiece. He concluded, "Obviously, there is nothing like an established reputation."

In addition to sharing his father's love for the intricacies of language, he boasted an equally prodigious memory. By the time Kanner enrolled at the University of Berlin in 1913, he had mastered Old German, Middle High German, modern German, Polish, French, Latin, Greek, Ruthenian, and a dabbling of Sanskrit, though he still spoke no English. Ignoring his grandfather's advice to become a rabbi, he set out to study medicine, continuing to write poems on the side, which he would do for the rest of his life.

Immersed in his studies, he regarded the tumultuous state of German politics from a comfortable distance. But when Austria-Hungary entered World War I in the summer of 1914, he was drafted into the army and ordered to serve in the medical corps. En route to his deployment, he stepped off the train to take a stroll in the woods and came upon the bodies of a dozen of his countrymen beside their dead horses in a clearing, slain in a surprise attack by Russian soldiers. Arriving on the front lines, he was ordered to set up a new field hospital with a jury-rigged operating table. Morphine was perpetually in short supply, and when tetanus swept through the ranks, the mortality rate was 100 percent. It was indeed a medical education, but not the one he'd had in mind. After months of being confronted with death and agony on a mass scale, he felt numb.

Then, in a moment of pure grace, everything changed. In a little village in Galicia, Kanner met Dziunia Lewin, a sweet-faced fourteen-year-old girl with long blond braids who was the daughter of his mother's cousin Chaim. Despite their six-year age difference, he was instantly smitten. He would stand in front of Dziunia's house for hours, hoping to catch a brief glimpse of her as she ran errands. "All of a sudden, on a sleety winter evening," Kanner recalled, "the world in which there were unreasonableness and pogroms and wars turned into a delightful paradise illuminated by the existence of one little girl." When he resumed his studies after the war, he wrote letters to Dziunia every day, sending her more than two thousand pages in total. With her father's blessing, he married her in 1921.

By all accounts, Kanner was on the road to a brilliant career—in cardiology. Ironically, the one merely satisfactory grade he received at the university was in a psychology course taught by one of his heroes, Karl Bonhoeffer, a pioneering neurologist. Bonhoeffer parted ways with the father of diagnostic psychiatry, Emil Kraepelin, by pointing out the deceptively seductive power of naming a condition. The problem with labels, he said, is that they seem to correspond to disease entities that live independently of the patient, like types of viruses or bacteria. But in psychiatry, labels describe constellations of behavior that can be related to any number of underlying conditions. Bonhoeffer gave Kanner only a passing grade because he misinterpreted the symptoms of a patient with tabes dorsalis, a form of neural degeneration caused by an untreated syphilis infection. It was not the last time that Kanner would be tripped up by an error of interpretation.

After earning his degree, he hung out his shingle as a general practitioner in Berlin, opening an office in the tiny apartment that he shared with his wife and their newborn daughter, Anita. He stitched up cuts, lanced boils, soothed queasy stomachs, and performed the other humble duties of a family doctor. In his unpublished memoir, he described an elderly female patient as a tiresome spinster who wasted his time by unburdening herself of her cares and woes during his examinations. "I must confess that, when I gave her a few minutes of my attention," he wrote, "I felt a bit as John D. Rockefeller may have felt when he stopped to donate a dime to a street urchin."

In a time of runaway inflation, he was clearly dreaming of grander things than consoling aging patients who could only afford to pay for his expertise with health insurance. His capacity for self-reinvention showed itself when the government issued a decree allowing dentists—traditionally low on the totem pole in German medicine—to earn a doctorate by writing a thesis. After a friend mentioned that his proposals to write on cavities and bleeding gums kept getting rejected, Kanner suggested that he collect tooth-related folklore from peasants in rural villages to frame the occupation of dentistry in the broader context of anthropology and psychology. Kanner's friend's next proposal was immediately accepted. As word got around, dentists all over the city started commissioning him to work the same magic on their own applications.

Kanner launched an unlikely business on the side that became a little gold mine for his family: a "Literary Bureau for Dentists." (Dziunia ended up doing most of the work, composing all the thesis abstracts and doing all the typing, while caring for Anita.) Seeking to raise his public profile even further, he organized public events for prominent Zionists visiting Berlin, including Albert Einstein and Sholem Aleichem. Kanner had a knack for cultivating friendships that he could turn to his social and professional advantage. He once diagnosed himself as a "collector of people."

One of the friendships he cultivated opened a door to an entirely new life. While substitute-teaching a course in electrocardiography in 1923, Kanner met a visiting American doctor named Louis Holtz who became a frequent dinner companion. Holtz regaled Leo and Dziunia with tales of his life in the United States but also confessed that he felt lonely there after the sudden death of his wife. Kanner had no burning desire to leave Germany, but the economy was in shambles, and his opportunities for advancement were limited. Even before the Nazis came to power, Jewish doctors had to work much harder than their colleagues to earn faculty positions and were only rarely allowed to become department chairs.

A month after the Beer Hall Putsch that landed Hitler in Landsberg prison, Holtz told Kanner that if he ever wanted to come to America, he would provide the guarantee of employment required by immigration officials to apply for a visa. Two weeks later, Holtz found him a position as a psychiatric assistant at the Yankton State Hospital in South Dakota, with room and board for the whole family. If he wanted to take the job, the family would be required to relocate immediately.

After consulting an encyclopedia, Kanner's cousin warned him that Yankton was an infamous "Indian trading post." This argument proved insufficiently dissuasive. A crowd of relatives and friends came down to the train station to see the Kanners off, and in Cuxhaven, they boarded the SS *Albert Ballin*, a luxury liner named after the Jewish shipping magnate who invented pleasure cruises. The ship ran into rough seas during the crossing, but Kanner felt completely at peace venturing into the unknown with his beloved wife and daughter beside him.

"The past was behind us and every knot removed us farther from it," he wrote. "Everything was drenched in beauty."

III

Kanner's serene mood was shaken upon arriving in New York City, where a son of a German colleague accompanied him for his first ride on the subway. Seeing the other passengers clenching their teeth and swiveling their jaws in a rotary motion, Kanner ventured that the poor devils had been afflicted by a tic disorder in the wake of the global epidemic of encephalitis lethargica that began in 1918. His young host gently informed him that their fellow straphangers were in the grips of another plague entirely: the craze for chewing Wrigley's gum, which had not yet caught on in Berlin. Kanner was mortified by his greenhorn error. "For many years to come," he confessed, "I was embarrassed at the thought of my diagnostic blunder."

After crossing the Great Plains by rail, Kanner discovered that the Yankton State Hospital—a sprawling institution that featured a reproduction of the Sistine Madonna in its marble lobby—was surrounded by more than fifteen hundred acres of farmland, which was used to raise pigs, corn, and dairy cattle to feed the patients. He wrote to a friend in Berlin that it was like working in a park. In the weeks to come, though, he was dismayed to find out that only one of his new colleagues—his supervisor, hospital superintendent George Adams—had any formal training in psychiatry. The nursing staff consisted of retirees seeking a productive way of passing the time, and the ward attendants were farmers' sons and daughters looking to make a little money.

The style of psychiatry practiced at the hospital seemed astonishingly primitive. Patients were diagnosed by popular vote after performing trivial tasks like counting backward from one hundred by seven and repeating tongue twisters like "truly rural" and "Methodist Episcopal." Kanner was appalled by the spectacle of his senior colleagues trying "to look erudite when they cast their vote on whether a patient 'had' *dementia praecox*, manic-depressive psychosis, paranoia, general paresis, senile, alcoholic, epileptic, or 'undiagnosed' psychosis." He concluded that the only virtue of this process was to bolster the insecure egos of the staff: "You were clever if you could distinguish unerringly between *dementia praecox* and manic-depressive psychosis, almost in the same manner that an experienced drinker can distinguish between Old Forester and Old Grand Dad."

While Kanner was making his rounds of the Stone Room—the staff's nickname for Ward M, reserved for the most intractable cases of psychosis—a farmer named Charlie Miller who had been mute, catatonic, and bedridden for years sat up and said, "Dr. Kanner, I wish to have an interview with Dr. Adams." The next morning, Miller got up out of bed and dressed himself with the help of an attendant. He spoke with Adams at length about making arrangements to ensure the financial security of his wife and children. For the next two weeks, he got up every morning, had breakfast in the dining room, and assisted the staff in caring for other patients who had been written off as hopeless. After that, just as abruptly, he refused to get out of bed again and never spoke another word until he died.

One day Kanner told a schizophrenic farmer what he assumed would be distressing news: his son had also been diagnosed with schizophrenia and would soon be joining him on the ward. But the farmer, who managed the hospital print shop and spent an hour each day in quiet meditation, was unruffled. When his son arrived at the hospital, he patiently taught him to set type. From then on, they worked side by side, seemingly content in their shared silence.

Kanner came to believe that the most astute clinical observer on staff was a disabled volunteer in the Stone Room who treated the patients respectfully as individuals. This man would spend hours just listening as they related stories about growing up and their hopes and aspirations before they were declared insane. Though he was not one of the resident "experts," he had a decisive effect on Kanner's approach to psychiatry. Instead of grilling the residents of Yankton with inane questionnaires, he began probing into his patients' family backgrounds to seek out the deep roots of their illnesses.

ON HIS FIRST Christmas Eve at the hospital, Kanner proposed that patients who were not violent should be liberated from their straitjackets and other forms of restraint. When a supervisor objected, he offered to oversee the wards himself on Christmas Day. This humane experiment was a success, and the patients were allowed to move about more freely from then on.

After reading a paper about the therapeutic value of art, he distributed paints, crayons, pencils, and paper throughout the hospital and set up a gallery in the administration building that featured rotating exhibits of patients' work. (In his own way, Kanner was bringing a touch of *Heilpädagogik* to the Great Plains.) He also invited cooks, gardeners, and ward attendants over to the house to play pinochle. This scandalized his colleagues by violating an unspoken caste system among the staff but made him new friends all over the hospital. A Czech cook began furnishing Kanner and his wife with old-world pastries and green-tomato pies, while a Polish gardener supplied them with home-brewed cherry and rhubarb wine.

Grateful that he could speak their native language, a group of Mennonite schizophrenics christened Kanner "the doctor from Germany." But he yearned to be accepted by his colleagues as just a "regular fellow," as he put it. He joined the Freemasons and took up golf, while Dziunia started calling herself June. Kanner also diligently worked on his English by poring through Book-of-the-Month Club titles, solving *New York Times* crossword puzzles, and memorizing entries in the dictionary. Though he never shed his *mitteleuropäische* accent, he acquired a formidable vocabulary, aided by his keen ear for regional dialects and idioms.

IN 1925, KANNER MADE his professional debut in the *Journal of Abnormal and Social Psychology*, publishing a "psychiatric study" of Henrik Ibsen's *Peer Gynt*. Immediately after his paper appeared, Kanner regretted writing it and vowed never again to venture into the dubious genre of psycholiterary criticism. But appearing in a major journal whetted his appetite to make more meaningful contributions to his field.

He got the opportunity to do so later that year when he saw a notice in a newspaper announcing the imminent arrival of Emil Kraepelin, who was touring North America, Cuba, and Mexico with a serologist named Felix Plaut to investigate the incidence of paresis—a form of dementia caused by untreated syphilis infection—among blacks and Native Americans in mental institutions. Discovering that Kraepelin and Plaut would be spending four days at the Asylum for Insane Indians in nearby Canton, Kanner asked Adams to wangle an invitation for them and their wives from asylum superintendent Harry Hummer.

Kraepelin and Plaut were convinced that paresis was extremely rare among blacks and Native Americans, despite the fact that rates of syphilis infection in these groups were high. (Meanwhile, syphilitic dementia was so common among institutionalized whites that it was known as "general paresis of the insane.") When Kanner informed Kraepelin that one of his patients at Yankton was an "almost full-blooded Indian" with paresis, he was fascinated and recommended that he undertake a full-scale investigation of the case.

The following year, Kanner and Adams published a paper in the *American Journal of Psychiatry* based on their study of this allegedly unusual patient. The authorial voice is unmistakably Kanner's. He reports that the incidence of paresis is so low among Native Americans that not a single case has "been heretofore reported in literature," a phrase he would echo nearly verbatim in his first paper on autism. In fact, he declares, "such a case is so rare, that it is really regarded as a curiosity, a fact that very decidedly calls for explanation."

Showing a flair for dramatic narrative, Kanner relates that the patient, a Sioux elder named Thomas Robertson, was once a proud leader of his tribe with a wife, six children, and a harem of pretty "young squaws." Now tremulous and staggering, Robertson has become a full-time floor polisher at the asylum.

By probing into Robertson's family background, Kanner discovers that he is not full-blooded Sioux; in fact, his father was a "large and powerful" Scotsman of "good breeding." Kanner boldly proposes that the reason his patient is suffering from the ravages of paresis is that syphilis was unknown in the Old World in ancient times but was already well established in the Americas, which enabled the indigenous inhabitants of the New World to evolve immunity to the most debilitating aspects of the disease. In other words, Robertson had inherited his unusual susceptibility to paresis from his father, while his full-blooded brothers and sisters were left unscathed.

Kanner's bold notion that syphilis is of New World origin has gained support in recent years from phylogenetic analyses of a family of diseases called *treponematoses*, which includes syphilis and a skin disease of children called yaws. Epidemiologists now theorize that yaws mutated into the venereal form of syphilis in the Americas and sailed back to Naples with Columbus's crew in the fifteenth century. From there, the mutated spirochetes spread across the globe.

Kanner and Adams should have stopped there, but they went on to claim that Robertson's status as a "dominant figure among the Indians" was likely a result of his infusion of Anglo-Saxon blood—a speculation uncomfortably close to the racialist theories gaining a deep foothold among their peers at the time.

There was also a tragedy unfolding at the Asylum for Insane Indians that Kanner managed to overlook. Subsequent inspections by the Institute for Government Research and a psychiatrist named Samuel Silk revealed that Hummer had quietly turned the institution into a prison for native men and women on reservations deemed troublesome by federal agents. Diagnosed as insane by Hummer without a shred of medical evidence, they were confined in shackles, chains, and straitjackets, with no possibility of parole to visit their families, often for the rest of their lives. Patients routinely ate on the floor, were locked up each night with no access to toilets, and were denied basic medical care. Hummer, the only doctor at the facility for twenty-three years, barely kept any patient records; even serious accidents and suicides were not noted. Silk described conditions at the asylum as "very much below the standard of a modern prison." Lacking any legal means to contest their confinement, most of the patients admitted to the asylum also died there, as Hummer placed ads in newspapers inviting the public to a cleaned-up area of the hospital to "come see the crazy Indians." The secretary of the interior finally shut down the institution in 1934 under a cloud of scandal.

Was the case of Thomas Robertson truly as singular as Kanner claimed? Historical sources suggest that he was stretching the truth. At a symposium on syphilis in 1902, the superintendent of the Binghamton State Hospital noted "a remarkable preponderance" of paresis in his native patients. A comprehensive assessment of the state of Native American health care by physician Anne Perkins in 1927 uncovered numerous problems that interfered with accurate data gathering in this neglected and impoverished segment of the population. Few doctors in the employ of the Bureau of Indian Affairs had any training in psychiatry, and many tribes opposed both the Wasserman blood test for syphilis and autopsy for religious or social reasons. Perkins specifically called out Hummer for his "unsatisfactory" record keeping at the Asylum for Insane Indians.

Yet Kanner's paper succeeded in putting him on the map of American psychiatry. In the case of Thomas Robertson, he found a winning formula for riveting the attention of his colleagues by writing a vivid and engaging account of a case so allegedly rare that it "demanded explanation."

IV

Now that Kanner had made his mark in a prominent journal, it embarrassed him that he had been able to obtain his medical license merely by filling out a questionnaire from the state. "I was bothered by the realization that I had come to psychiatry through a back door," he wrote. "I felt that, under the circumstances, my efforts lacked consistency and direction."

He enjoyed his life in Yankton with its quaint main street, five-and-dime, and movie house. He spent weekends playing all-night poker with his wife and the usual crew from the hospital, and during the week he would invite his daughter, now four, to visit his office. Already an observant little girl, Anita noticed that you could tell the doctors and patients apart because doctors always carried keys. When she visited her father at work, Anita would say to anyone who approached her, "Let me see your keys."

But Kanner's young wife was miserable. June was a bright, culturally savvy woman who had left her childhood friends behind in Berlin with barely any time to think about it. In her new life, she wasn't even allowed to clean her own house, because the ubiquitous ward attendants did all the washing and dusting. The family ate three meals a day at a long communal table in the doctors' dining room under the watchful eye of the director's wife, a domineering busybody who banished Anita's high chair to the Siberian end of the table. After four years, June was ready to move on. She told her husband that unless he found a new job soon, somewhere very far from South Dakota, she would move to Chicago and take Anita with her.

Then fate intervened to save the day. Kanner spotted an ad in the *American Journal of Psychiatry* for a fellowship at Johns Hopkins under the directorship of the Swiss neurologist Adolf Meyer, who was president of the American Psychiatric Association (APA). "If possible," the ad stipulated, applicants should "have a working knowledge of German and French" and "spontaneity and energy in work and capacity for independent investigation." Kanner felt he was reading an ad for himself. He requested an audience with Meyer at an upcoming APA convention in Minneapolis. At the registration desk, Kanner saw every head in the room turn as a short, nimble man with a superbly groomed goatee walked in. He picked up traces of a *mitteleuropäische* accent in the man's speech and asked a colleague if he happened to know who he was. "Why, that's Adolf Meyer!" the man replied.

The neurologist interviewed Kanner for the fellowship at length the following day and also talked to George Adams about his performance at Yankton. But no word came back from Baltimore for three months, and Kanner berated himself for not being up to snuff. He finally got a cryptic note from Meyer saying that his hesitation was that Kanner seemed "more inclined toward literary work than toward concrete occupation with specific facts." Sensing his destiny near at hand, he fired off a telegram asking Meyer if he could arrive at Johns Hopkins a month later to start the fellowship immediately.

Meyer's reply was swift and oracular: "We've been expecting you."

Arriving in Baltimore with his family, Kanner checked into a hotel, pulled out a phone book, and chose a real estate agent at random to inquire about houses for rent. "What is your persuasion?" the agent asked him. At first, Kanner didn't even understand the question. The agent casually informed him that Hebrews were not welcome in certain neighborhoods, and that some landlords outside these restricted areas preferred not to rent to them.

Kanner was stupefied. Yankton had been relatively free of anti-Semitism, probably because there were hardly any other Jews there. (A reverend had assured him that if he enrolled Anita in Sunday school, he would not try to convert her.) But in Baltimore, the same discrimination he'd fled in Germany was right out in the open.

He discovered that the city he thought of as a lighthouse of democracy—the home of freethinkers like H. L. Mencken—was also segregated by race. Black children were excluded from many public schools, and their families were barred from theaters, department stores, restaurants, hotels, swimming pools, and churches. Yet the locals simply took this state of things for granted—"as if it were as natural a phenomenon as the rising and setting of the sun," as Kanner put it. Even his new employers were not immune to this insidious disease. The faculty of the Johns Hopkins department of psychiatry was strictly white for years, though many of the patients treated there were black.

But Kanner thrived under Meyer's firm guiding hand, in part because he had much in common with his new mentor, who had also paid his dues in America by working in an asylum in corn country. In the late 1890s, little or no psychiatric training was offered in U.S. medical schools, and most of the jobs available were strictly custodial: overseeing human warehouses filled with patients in restraints who "have lost even the memory of hope, sit in rows, too dull to know despair, watched by attendants: silent, grewsome [*sic*] machines which eat and sleep, sleep and eat," as neurologist Silas Weir Mitchell put it in a scathing indictment of his colleagues in 1894. In one such institution, Mitchell was unable to find even a stethoscope to examine his patients.

The Illinois Eastern Hospital for the Insane in Kankakee, where Meyer began working after immigrating from Zürich, was no exception. To establish a basic knowledge of the relationship between brain function and mental illness, he undertook a series of patient autopsies but gave up when he realized that it was a futile exercise in the absence of comprehensive medical records. He offered neurology classes to the staff but quit when he discovered that his students hadn't even been schooled in the elemental techniques of clinical observation. Even under these conditions, he pioneered the modern form of psychiatric history taking by having a stenographer accompany him as he made the rounds of the wards.

Meyer advanced swiftly through the ranks of his profession, taking a post as the head of the Pathology Institute of the New York State Hospitals, the biggest network of mental institutions in the country. He argued that no aspect of human behavior could be understood in isolation: neurology, genetics, family background, and social dynamics all had to be considered to properly evaluate a patient's mental state. In 1908, he was invited to oversee the newly endowed Henry Phipps Psychiatric Clinic at Johns Hopkins, which was expressly built on the Viennese model of combining teaching and practice in a single institution. As a walking embodiment of the European tradition, he became enormously influential. At one point, one in ten of the academic psychiatrists in the United States trained directly under him, launching a school of psychiatry that was dubbed Meyerian. He also introduced the field to its standard experimental subject, the albino rat. Coining the word *psychobiology*, he constantly exhorted his students to set theories aside and seek the facts.

Visiting Meyer's office for the first time on an October afternoon in 1928, Kanner was awestruck. An impeccably polite secretary invited him to wait in an adjacent library that seemed to extend for miles, with a convenient array of stepladders for retrieving volumes on the upper shelves. After twenty minutes, the secretary bowed deferentially and invited him into Meyer's inner sanctum, which was sparsely but elegantly furnished, its very air charged by the presence of the man behind the desk.

Kanner felt that he had finally arrived in his element. His new boss was a landsman who shared his fascination for linguistics, semantics, and philology, as well as his skepticism for psychoanalysis. Meyer was also a dashing and charismatic figure (described by a former student as possessing a "quiet, epic grandeur"), with eyes that could lift you up or annihilate you with a glance. Kanner was admittedly less prepossessing, with floppy ears, puffy eyes, bad teeth, and the woebegone countenance of a sad beagle, but Meyer did his best to make the young man feel at home, suggesting that he seek a rental in a neighborhood where other Johns Hopkins doctors were living. (Upon receiving his application for a house on Lake Avenue, the landlord told Kanner, "I knew you folks were Jewish right away, but I like you, and no one will raise any objection.")

The daily schedule at Phipps began with a conference in Meyer's library that unfolded with the solemnity of a holy ritual. As a stenographer readied her pads and pencils, the fellows sat down, leaving three chairs open. The eminent neurologist walked in with a resident and a resident's assistant, and the fellows rose until Meyer sat down. The reverent silence would be broken when he turned to the resident and said with his usual air of unassailable calm, "And what do we have this morning?"

Kanner learned the price of violating the sanctity of this ritual when a distinguished guest from Vienna, an associate of Freud's named Paul Schilder, joined the morning meetings for a semester. Kanner was taken aback when his hero Meyer showed deference to a man who didn't seem to know his basic neurology. After Schilder mentioned that he had treated a schizophrenic teenager with psychoanalysis because the "sex center" and "fear center" of the brain are adjacent, he could no longer contain himself. Kanner pointedly asked if people call their spouses "honey" because the sex center and the sugar center of the brain are also close together. A pained silence fell over the room, and Meyer quietly instructed the stenographer to strike Kanner's remark from the record.

On another occasion, Meyer chastised his young disciple for speaking his mind in a way that "antagonized a sector of the profession." Kanner was learning a heavy lesson: the way to get ahead in psychiatry was to hold your tongue, even when your esteemed colleagues were speaking nonsense.

When the term of Kanner's fellowship expired, Meyer worked behind the scenes to secure additional funding so his eager protégé could be retained on staff. He had a far-reaching mission in mind for him: setting up a new child-behavior clinic that would act as a bridge between the domains of pediatrics and psychiatry at Johns Hopkins. The two departments were located in adjacent buildings, and the door between them was kept locked.

By the end of Kanner's first year, no one ever thought about locking that door again.

The Behavior Clinic was located in the Harriet Lane Dispensary, a once-impressive edifice that had fallen into disrepair since 1911 when it was built as a home for invalid children. Kanner's new office was located in a former pantry in the old infectious-diseases annex, complete with a sink, a leaky ceiling, and rats that ventured up from the cellar to nibble away at his lunch. Despite these shabby quarters, he was ecstatic about his new mission. "I was free to proceed according to my own convictions and at my own pace," he wrote. "We were the shapers of our plans, methods, and practices . . . We were grateful for the one magnificent gift which outweighed everything else—the opportunity to work unhampered, to develop and pursue our curiosities, to test our theories, and at all times to be true to ourselves."

In an uncanny coincidence, the dispensary had been built to the specifications of Clemens von Pirquet, the pioneering immunologist who also designed Asperger's clinic in Vienna. Recruited from the Children's Clinic in 1908 to take the first chair of pediatrics at Johns Hopkins, he expanded the fledgling department from three beds to the formidable facility that Kanner inherited twenty years later. But a year and a half in Baltimore was enough for von Pirquet, and when he was offered another prestigious position in Vienna, he took it. In 1929, after a lengthy period of depression, he committed suicide with his wife, leaving behind a curious legacy—two buildings, on two continents, where two clinicians would claim to have discovered autism independently.

WITH MEYER'S ENCOURAGEMENT, Kanner embarked on his most ambitious project to date: writing the first textbook of child psychiatry in English. In practical terms, he was not just writing a book, he was creating a new field of medicine by drawing on elements of other disciplines, including psychiatry, pediatrics, and even a dash of *Heilpädagogik*.

The first edition of *Child Psychiatry*, published in 1935, was cast in a distinctly Meyerian mold. The essence of his mentor's approach, as Kanner framed it, was to regard the child as a whole, rather than as a jumble of symptoms and dysfunctions. His goal for the book was to set forth practical and teachable ways to help children without being constrained by the dogma of any particular school of psychiatry.

There was a poignant aspect to Kanner's act of channeling his mentor that was invisible to all but Meyer's students. Though the Swiss neurologist was a brilliant thinker, he has been virtually forgotten because he was an abstruse writer and lecturer who produced no books of his own. (Kanner graciously observed that Meyer did his best teaching with his eyes.) The young psychiatrist's gift to his mentor was to distill his tedious expostulations into clear guidelines that even lay readers could follow: "Work with the child. Work with the family. Work with the community."

Child Psychiatry was immediately hailed as "a remarkable achievement" and became a runaway best seller. The first edition alone went into five printings, followed by three revised editions translated into multiple languages. With every iteration, the text became less Meyerian and more Kannerian. Ponderous formulations like "Personality Differences Expressing Themselves in the Form of Involuntary Part-Dysfunctions" (which sounds like a Google translation from the Swiss) yielded to straightforward headings like "Intelligence," "Emotion," and "Problems of Speech and Language." It remained the last word on the subject through the 1960s and stayed in print for an astonishing sixty-seven years.

Kanner leveraged his new visibility to air opinions on hot-button issues like sex education, thumb sucking, and phobias. "How can we blame the children for being afraid of thunderstorms if mother shrieks and shivers every time she sees a flash of lightning or hears the sound of thunder? How can we blame a child for restlessness and impatience if father shows the same traits?" he declared in the *Washington Post*. He was superbly positioned to proffer advice to a generation of parents convinced by psychologists that their role was to be "virtual middle managers in what was imagined as a national child-rearing project . . . [using] tools provided by professionals," as culture critic Nicholas Sammond put it.

When behaviorist John B. Watson panicked the readers of his popular guide to childrearing by insisting, "The oldest profession in the race today is facing failure. This profession is parenthood," Kanner responded by writing a soothing, chatty book called *In Defense of Mothers.* He coyly mocked his Freudian colleagues for worshipping "the Great God of the Unconscious" while advising parents to set aside all the "mythical spooks and bugaboos which theorizing busybodies have thrown around them."

Preaching from the bully pulpit of the leading medical school in the country, he no longer had to worry about having slipped into psychiatry through a back door. Now he was on center stage.

Kanner made headlines coast-to-coast in 1937 by exposing a major scandal in Baltimore. Acting on a tip from the superintendent of a vocational center for the disabled called the Rosewood State Training School, he discovered that a local lawyer had been making a fortune by offering up the school's "feebleminded" female residents as cheap domestic help to wealthy families after obtaining writs of habeas corpus from an obliging judge.

The city's society matrons had come to regard the girls as disposable commodities, paying them little or nothing for their labor and simply dumping them on the street before taking an extended holiday. One client had fired thirteen young women in succession with no questions asked by the judge. The toll on the victims was enormous: eleven girls died, six were serving lengthy prison sentences, and twenty-nine were prostitutes, while others married alcoholic husbands who deserted them shortly thereafter. One client complained after physically abusing a girl and throwing her out of her house, "Instead of being a member of the animal kingdom, she was a vegetable."

After conducting an investigation, Kanner presented his report to the APA annual convention in May, which unleashed a frenzy of headlines.

The *New York Times* hailed the psychiatrist for revealing "The 'Slavery' of 168 Imbeciles." "Scheme to Set Morons Free to Work in Homes Charged," blared the Baltimore *Evening Sun.* "Record of Misery Traced in Freeing of Moronic Girls," echoed the *Washington Post.* The scandal gave Kanner a rare opportunity to focus the national spotlight on the vulnerability of disabled people in institutions and the pervasive lack of oversight in the mental health care system.

But that isn't what he did. Instead, he portrayed the innocent victims of this ghastly scheme as a menace to their community. Telling a *New York Times* reporter that more than a hundred children born to these girls were "obviously and uncontestably feeble-minded," he lent his moral authority to the classic narrative used to justify forced sterilization laws. "Time alone will tell," he said, "how many more feeble-minded, illegitimate, neglected children this group of released patients will in the future bestow on a Commonwealth that can do nothing but look on and pay the penalty for the indiscriminate habeas corpus release by its courts of justice."

Then Kanner ensured that the Commonwealth could do nothing to punish the offenders by refusing to release their names to the American Bar Association. He claimed that doing so would be redundant, because the judge had retired and the lawyer had been disbarred for "behavior even more unethical than that described by me" (whatever that might have been). He expressed hope that "the publicity . . . will contribute much toward precluding similar incidents in the future."

The Rosewood affair established Kanner in the public mind as a voice for the voiceless and a defender of the defenseless. But his failure to name those responsible, and his statements to the press, rendered unclear whom exactly he was defending. He maintained support for sterilization of "those intellectually or emotionally unfit to raise children" for years, though he opposed euthanasia in a public debate with prominent neurologist Foster Kennedy, who advocated killing "those hopeless ones—Nature's mistakes" that "so largely fill our mental hospitals" in an editorial in the *American Journal of Psychiatry.*

Still, Kanner's view of the lives that "mentally deficient" people were fit to lead was relentlessly grim. His main argument with Kennedy was that such people are capable of fulfilling useful roles in society:

> Sewage disposal, ditch digging, potato peeling, scrubbing of floors and other such occupations are as indispensable and essential to our way of living as science, literature and art. Cotton picking is an integral part of our textile industries. Oyster shucking is an important part of our seafood supply. Garbage collection is an essential part of our public hygiene measures.

"Do we really wish to deprive ourselves," he concluded, "of people whom we desperately need for a variety of essential occupations?"

By the fall of 1937, the Reich's eugenics machine was accelerating into high gear and the forced exodus of Jews was under way. As Hitler's henchmen rampaged through Kanner's homeland, the plight of his family members and colleagues became a matter of grave concern. With some of the best medical minds in Europe clamoring to flee the oncoming storm—including Freud himself—the modest quota of German immigrants allowed to enter the United States annually (less than twenty-six thousand) wasn't even being met, in part because the State Department instructed consular officials to deny visas to applicants who might require public assistance. Jews could obtain visas only by presenting affidavits from American citizens providing proof of future employment, as Holtz had done for Kanner.

Medical workers with non-Aryan spouses or relatives, and those judged insufficiently obedient by the Führer's regime, were also subject to expulsion. Kanner felt embittered by the willingness of U.S. officials to look the other way as an unprecedented human catastrophe took shape.

> Emma Lazarus' heartwarming words of invitation, written in 1886 and inscribed on the Statue of Liberty, were no longer applied fully to the

tired, the poor, the homeless, tempest-tossed. Sanctuary was apportioned sparingly through a narrow slit in the golden door to those fortunate enough to have found affiants in time to save their lives.

GROUPS FORMED SPECIFICALLY TO assist doctors seeking refuge in the United States, such as the National Committee for the Resettlement of Foreign Physicians, faced numerous obstacles beyond the quotas and visa requirements. Fearing competition from refugees, state medical boards erected a maze of resolutions requiring applicants for licenses to be U.S. citizens, to have degrees from American schools, or to produce extensive records of their education in Europe. Nazi-run universities simply ignored these requests. Even doctors who successfully relocated and tried to go into practice faced rumors that they were spies, sent overseas to poison their patients.

The Kanners rose to this historic challenge by doing something heroic. Starting that fall, they acted as an unofficial immigration agency for Jewish doctors, nurses, and researchers, providing them with the documentation they needed to obtain visas while helping them to find jobs. As Kanner buttonholed hospital superintendents at conferences to inquire about vacancies on staff for physicians, June networked with a local cardiologist to find in-home placements for nurses. Furthermore, Kanner convinced the Maryland medical board to liberalize its licensing requirements. In total, Leo and June rescued nearly two hundred colleagues from the Nazis while providing clinics, hospitals, and research labs across the country with an influx of superbly trained talent. Furthermore, they graciously opened their home in Baltimore to assist émigrés adapting to life in a new culture.

They also saved the lives of Kanner's brother Max, who married an Iowa girl and became a furrier, and his brother Josef, who migrated to Palestine. Tragically, his seventy-year-old mother, Klara, was dragged from her home and gassed. His brother Willy was shot to death in Poland, and his aunt and uncle were murdered in Holland. Thankfully, his sister Jenny and her family made it to safety by hiding under a truckload of coal bound for Switzerland. His old hometown of Brody had once been home to a vibrant community of ten thousand Jews and was celebrated throughout Europe as a center of learning, philosophy, art, music, and culture. After the war, only eighty-eight Jews were left alive.

Kanner was rewarded for these selfless efforts when one of the colleagues he rescued from the Nazis provided him with crucial assistance at the moment he made the breakthrough that assured him of the destiny he had always yearned for—a lasting place in the history of medicine.

V

On a September day in 1938, a lawyer named Oliver Triplett Jr. sat down in his office in Forest, Mississippi, to dictate a letter to his secretary. The letter, which ran on for thirty-three single-spaced pages, concerned his eldest child, a five-year-old boy named Donald. It was addressed to the one man in America who he hoped might be able to help him: Leo Kanner.

Oliver and his wife, Mary, were an exceptionally bright and successful couple, and their families had played prominent roles in Forest for three generations. The economy of the region was suffering through its own sequel to the Great Depression as the pine groves on which mill owners had staked their fortunes were exhausted, but the Tripletts remained financially secure. Mary's father was the chairman of the board of the Bank of Forest, and she was an impressive woman in her own right. In an era when few women had degrees, she was former president of her class at Belhaven University and taught English in a local high school. Oliver—known in Forest by his middle name, Beamon—graduated from Yale Law School with honors, was admitted to the bar of the U.S. Supreme Court, and became the town attorney. The couple lived in a cozy house on a seven-acre lot on the outskirts of downtown, with a screened-in porch and big windows overlooking a broad lawn.

Known as an intense and meticulous man, Beamon was perhaps a bit *too* hardworking. By the time his son was born, he had suffered two nervous breakdowns. He was prone to taking long walks in a kind of fugue state; when he came home, he would remember nothing and no one that he'd seen along the way. But these things were mere eccentricities compared to his son's behavior.

Donald had been a decidedly solitary and remote child from the moment he was born. The faces of his parents gazing down at him in his crib never inspired the usual cascades of happy wriggling and gurgling. Mary breast-fed him for seven months, supplementing his diet with formula, but nothing seemed to sit right in his stomach. He was clearly happiest when he was left alone and barely seemed to notice if another person entered the room. When his grandparents came over to the house, he ignored them. Even the sight of a man dressed as Santa Claus failed to impress him.

But he was also a bright boy, a prodigy in some ways. Blessed with the rare gift of absolute pitch, he could hum and sing many of his favorite tunes accurately by his first birthday. He also had an unusually retentive memory. At age two, he could count to one hundred, repeat the alphabet backward and forward, say the Lord's Prayer, recite the twenty-five questions and answers of the Presbyterian catechism, and name every U.S. president and vice president. He would amuse himself for hours with *Compton's Encyclopedia*, flipping instantly to the pictures that he liked best. He also memorized the locations of many houses in Forest, as if he were plotting a map in his head. In his letter to Kanner, Beaman observed that he "appears to be always thinking and thinking, and to get his attention almost requires one to break down a mental barrier between his inner consciousness and the outside world."

To coax him out of his shell, the Tripletts went to the trouble of finding a handsome boy at an orphanage and inviting him to stay at their house for a summer. But Donald simply ignored this unexpected addition to the family, never asking the boy a single question. His parents tried to teach him to ride a bicycle, but he became panic-stricken; they bought him a fancy Taylor Tot walker and he refused to have anything to do with it.

Finally, they installed a slide in their backyard and invited the neighborhood kids to play, thinking Donald might learn by their example. But when they sat him at the top of the slide and pushed him down, he was terrified. (The next morning he quietly slipped out of the house and slid down himself.)

Donald's sticky memory also had a downside. He tended to repeat phrases precisely as he heard them without modifying the pronouns appropriately. If he wanted a glass of milk, he would say, "Donnie, do you want your milk?" At dinner, he would tell his mother, "Say 'If you drink to there, I'll laugh and I'll smile,'" reproducing Mary's original intonations faithfully—as if he were sampling his mother's voice instead of truly understanding the meaning of her words.

Like Gottfried, Donald also had a curious attraction to rules and order. Once he learned to read, it never seemed right to him that *bite* wasn't spelled *bight*, like *light*. He would line up his toys in strict sequences and throw tantrums if anyone disrupted them. But his favorite thing to do was to set his toys spinning on the floor like tops. The sight of almost any spinning thing—even a pot lid from the kitchen—made him jump up and down in ecstasy.

The Tripletts' family doctor suggested that the cause of Donald's odd behavior was that his parents had "overstimulated" him, and he prescribed a radical change of environment. Willing to try anything that might help their son, Mary and Beamon committed him to the Mississippi Tuberculosis Sanatorium, forty miles away, for a stay of indefinite length. He was three years old.

Built by a lake, the enormous Victorian facility—a relic of the time when tuberculosis was blamed on poverty, immigrants, and overcrowded cities—must have seemed like a promising refuge for a child overwhelmed by everyday life. It was renowned for the compassionate ministrations of its nursing staff. Donald was admitted to a special ward called the preventorium, usually reserved for TB-infected patients who did not yet have the active form of the disease. In keeping with their doctor's advice, his parents visited him only twice a month. But, deprived of his familiar surroundings and routines, Donald did not fare well. He developed a new habit of nodding his head from side to side and withdrew to the point where he barely ate and sat in a fixed position for hours, "paying no attention to anything."

Gradually, he learned to adapt to this strange new environment. He started eating again and allowed himself to sit near other children. After nearly a year had passed, however, Mary and Beamon decided to take Donald home over the vigorous protests of the sanatorium director. He told them to leave him alone, saying, "It looks that now he is going to be perfectly all right."

When the Tripletts asked him to provide a detailed account of Donald's condition, he dashed off a note concluding that their son had "some glandular disease." Beside herself with grief and frustration, Mary referred to Donald as her "hopelessly insane child." At this point, the family pediatrician referred the Tripletts to Kanner, by then the most prominent child psychiatrist in the country.

He was immediately intrigued by Donald's case and fascinated by the sheer volume of information in Beamon's letter. Kanner invited the Tripletts to bring Donald to Johns Hopkins for a thorough clinical evaluation. In October, they boarded a train to see the great man in Baltimore.

AT FIRST, Kanner didn't know what to make of Donald's behavior. After giving him a preliminary exam at the Harriet Lane, he dispatched the Tripletts to the Child Study Home of Maryland, a Johns Hopkins affiliate launched that year under his supervision. Only a handful of clinicians could have made sense of Donald's condition at this point, and most of them were working in Vienna at the Heilpädagogik Station. One of them, however, had just been brought over from Austria by Kanner to become the full-time psychiatrist-pediatrician at the Child Study Home: Asperger's former diagnostician, Georg Frankl.

This crucial link between the two pioneers of autism has escaped the attention of historians until now, mostly because Kanner studiously avoided mentioning it. He never acknowledged Asperger's contributions to the field—a fact that has puzzled autism scholars for decades. His unpublished memoir, written in the 1950s, names Frankl as one of many clinicians whom he helped immigrate to America in the years leading up to the war but comes to a mysteriously abrupt end just before the breakthrough that made him famous. Kanner's colleagues maintained that he was simply unfamiliar with the parallel work unfolding in Vienna at the time, and he never corrected them.

In fact, Frankl was not the only member of Asperger's core team in Baltimore when Kanner made his momentous discovery. Upon arriving in New York City in November 1937, the former chief diagnostician of the Children's Clinic was reunited with his colleague Anni Weiss, the young psychologist who wrote the case history of Gottfried. In a poignant affirmation of life by two survivors, the couple got married a couple of weeks later. The following April, they joined Kanner's inner circle at Johns Hopkins, moving into a quaint shingled house a couple of blocks from the Child Study Home.

For two years, Kanner and Frankl hosted "mental clinics" together in nearby towns, where groups like the Children's Aid Society presented children for their evaluation before audiences of parents drawn by articles in local newspapers. Meanwhile, Weiss (now Weiss-Frankl) became an enthusiastic participant in Meyer's seminars at the Phipps and told him that she found his seminars more enlightening than anything else she'd done since leaving Austria.

Kanner may never have heard Asperger's name before hiring Frankl, but he was certainly familiar with the work of Erwin Lazar, the founder of the Children's Clinic. In a letter to Meyer in 1939, Kanner touted Frankl's "good background in pediatrics and close connection for eleven years with the Lazar Clinic in Vienna." With a staff of teachers, an occupational therapy department, and living quarters for nearly fifty infants and children, the Child Study Home was as close to the Heilpädagogik Station as America had to offer. There, Frankl employed the style of intimate observation that he had developed with his colleagues in Vienna to make autism visible to medicine for the second time.

Over the course of two weeks in October 1938, Frankl and a psychiatrist named Eugenia Cameron worked up a detailed portrait of Donald's behavior that proved indispensable to Kanner as he struggled to understand the boy's "fascinating peculiarities."

> [Donald] wandered about smiling, making stereotyped movements with his fingers, crossing them about in the air. He shook his head from side, whispering or humming the same three-note tune. He spun with great pleasure anything he could seize upon to spin. He kept throwing things on the floor, seeming to delight in the sounds they made . . .
>
> Most of his actions were repetitions carried out in exactly the same way in which they had been performed originally. If he spun a block, he must always start with the same face uppermost. When he threaded buttons, he arranged them in a certain sequence that had no pattern to it but happened to be the order used by the father when he first had shown them to Donald.

As the boy did these things, he would repeat cryptic phrases to himself like "The right one is on, the left one is off," "Through the dark clouds shining," and "Dahlia, dahlia, dahlia." At first, Kanner characterized these statements as "irrelevant utterances," but they often turned out to be more relevant than they first appeared. While drawing with crayons, Donald kept saying over and over, "Annette and Cécile make purple." Only later did Kanner figure out that he had named each of his five watercolor bottles after one of the Dionne quintuplets; the red bottle was called "Annette" and the blue bottle was "Cécile." Blended together, they made purple.

In addition to having an extraordinarily precise memory for numbers, dates, addresses, and encyclopedia entries, Donald performed better on a test of visual matching and dexterity called the Séguin form board than his typical peers. Asperger and his colleagues would have viewed the boy's superior visual skills, extraordinary memory, and precocious attempts to put the world in order as aspects of his autistic intelligence. They appreciated the fact that a boy fascinated by triangles drawn in the sand might someday grow up to become a professor of astronomy. But Kanner wasn't running a school for children with special needs. He was launching a new field of psychiatry.

As a clinician who specialized in the emotional disturbances of children, he was particularly interested in the fact that Donald seemed more engaged by inanimate objects than by his own mother, which seemed to flout the most basic instincts of the human species.

> He paid no attention to persons around him. When taken into a room, he completely disregarded the people and instantly went for objects, preferably those that could be spun. Commands or actions that could not possibly be disregarded were resented as unwelcome intrusions. But he was never angry at the interfering *person*. He angrily shoved away the hand that was in his way or the foot that stepped on one of his blocks, at one time referring to the foot on the block as "umbrella." Once the obstacle was removed, he forgot the whole affair. He gave no heed to the presence of other children but went about his favorite pastimes, walking off from the children if they were so bold as to join him.

Kanner was particularly struck by Mary and Beamon's recollections that their son had *never* responded to people in the usual ways, even as an infant. This suggested that Donald's condition was innate and inborn rather than a response to some kind of psychological trauma inflicted by his environment. In the case of "Donald T.," he recognized the outline of a major breakthrough for his field: the discovery of the first form of major psychosis that was endemic to infancy.

VI

If Frankl ever proposed the term *Autistischen Psychopathen* as a name for the boy's condition, Kanner would have likely rejected it out of hand for two reasons. The term *autism*, in the way that Eugen Bleuler originally used it, implied a gradual withdrawal into a private life of fantasy. But Donald showed no signs of having an overactive imagination, and he had not *withdrawn* from the social world; he had been born outside it. And Kanner loathed the term *psychopathy* as much as he loathed the terms *introvert*, *extrovert*, and *neurotic*, all cocktail-party buzzwords at a time when psychoanalysis was on the rise. In his book on mothers, he mockingly defined *psychopath* as "a fellow the expert does not want to be bothered with." Thus his records of the Tripletts' first visit concluded on a note of clinical uncertainty: "*?schizophrenia.*"

While this preliminary diagnosis may now seem like a shot in the dark, Kanner had many good reasons to suspect that Donald's behavior was related to schizophrenia—specifically, the early-onset form of the condition initially proposed by Sukhareva in reference to her young patients, a concept that was rapidly gaining acceptance among Kanner's colleagues.

The first account of "childhood schizophrenia" in America, published in 1933 by Howard Potter of the New York Psychiatric Institute, outlined a set of behaviors that overlapped closely with later descriptions of autism, including a "defect in emotional rapport," disturbances of language development, "diminution of affect," and "bizarre behavior with a tendency toward perseveration and stereotypy."

One boy that Potter described could have been Donald's brother. As an infant, he refused to come when his mother called, and he fretted and cried frequently, which she blamed on an ongoing ear infection. In kindergarten, he would wander around the classroom, giggling and talking to himself while ignoring the other children. He played incessantly with light switches, collected pieces of paper that he lined up in rows, and made "stereotyped motions with his hand in the air as though writing," blinking while repeating in a monotone, "Coo-koo, Coo-koo." About the only activities that engaged the boy's "indifferent attention," according to Potter, were "singing and dancing games in the gymnasium."

It soon became obvious that the patients in Potter's practice represented just the tip of an iceberg. A year before the Tripletts made their pilgrimage to Baltimore, Louise Despert of the Payne Whitney Psychiatric Clinic told the first international congress of child psychiatry in Paris about kids in her own practice whose "affective rapport with the environment" was either attenuated or "completely severed." One boy in this group, S.K., could recite more than a hundred nursery rhymes by his second birthday, though his expressive vocabulary was limited. His nursemaid would take him on daily outings to the park, where he happily amused himself, until his father was laid off and the family had to move into a cramped apartment with S.K.'s grandparents. The abrupt loss of his familiar surroundings and his outings with his beloved nursemaid triggered a dramatic regression. Unless his parents took him back to the specific place in the park where he had played every day, he would wave his fingers in the air while repeating over and over like a soothing mantra, "The boy played—the boy in the park." S.K.'s parents brought him to a neurological institute for evaluation, but his condition declined precipitously there, so they committed him to the New York Psychiatric Institute, where he developed "severe compulsions" and his estimated IQ plummeted by seventy points. At age eleven, he was already in custodial care.

By the end of the 1930s, Despert had emerged as the leading figure in the field of childhood "affect disorders" by identifying a cluster of behaviors and traits that could have been lifted directly from Asperger's files. She described children (both boys and girls) who seemed more interested in the form of words than in their communicative function; showed little regard for their parents and had no regular playmates; rifled through dictionaries and encyclopedias while they were still in diapers; were precociously fascinated by "abstract" pursuits like mathematics, archaeology, and astronomy; became "excessively preoccupied" with calendars, license plates, and telephone numbers; and exhibited "bizarre" repetitive movements and bouts of "intense, purposeless behavior." She concluded, "Schizophrenia in children is probably not so rare as it has long been thought."

Kanner was certainly aware of Despert's work and its deeper context in the history of psychiatry. The last chapter of his textbook was devoted to "pre-psychotic" children who were allegedly destined to become schizophrenic as adults. He cited Kraepelin's accounts of "quiet, shy, retiring children" who ended up living solitary lives. He described children who endlessly repeated phrases that became "detached from their original meaning" while they displayed "abnormal motions of a rhythmical character." He quoted Meyer on "unusually precocious" children with a "specially great tendency to shyness" that tended to develop "complex fixations" and "one-sided preoccupations." (Meyer believed that these children were worth the strongest therapeutic efforts that his colleagues could muster.)

From Kanner's perspective, however, the model of childhood schizophrenia that was rapidly taking hold in his field had several problems. The most obvious one was that the theory that this condition was a prodromal phase of adult psychosis was still untested. In most cases of schizophrenia, the first signs become apparent only after puberty. The notion of nursery-school-age psychotics not only challenged the time-tested arc of the natural course of the disorder, it subverted the psychodynamic theories in vogue at the time to explain its causation, which leaned heavily on the alleged role of "schizophrenogenic" mothers. Despert's case study of S.K., for example, began with an ominous reference to the boy's mother, described as an "aggressive, oversolicitous, American-born Jewish woman who dominates her husband"—a classic description of the type.

While the invention of this devouring Medusa is often ascribed to Freud, it actually marked a departure by American psychiatrists from Freud's belief that the etiology of schizophrenia was rooted in biology rather than psychology. In truth, the concept of the schizophrenogenic mother bloomed in a hothouse of cultural anxieties in the post–World War I era, when women who had been previously subservient and self-effacing began cutting their hair short, smoking cigarettes, demanding the right to vote, and taking jobs in fields like education that had been formerly reserved for men, replacing them as primary breadwinners in many families. One of the psychoanalysts who laid the groundwork of the schizophrenogenic mother concept was Harry Stack Sullivan—another prominent Meyerian at Johns Hopkins.

If Donald's condition was present at birth, however, arguing that Mary Triplett's personality had somehow played a role in it seemed doomed from the start. Kanner was also likely put off by Despert's style of clinical interpretation, which seemed designed to fit her patients into prefabricated pigeonholes. For example, she sorted her patients into categories of "acute onset," "insidious onset," and "insidious onset with an acute episode." She classified S.K. as a case of acute onset because of his dramatic regression, but it's clear that the development of his speech was atypical before that. Despert also often attributed her patients' "bizarre" movements to hallucinations but admitted that this was speculation on her part for the children under six, since they never spoke of seeing or hearing things that weren't there.

Furthermore, Despert's concept of childhood schizophrenia seemed to grow broader every year, sucking in an increasingly heterogeneous mass of patients, which was a problem with the whole field of research into allegedly schizoid children. In his textbook, Kanner quoted one clinician as saying, "If we wished, we could forms as many groups as there were individuals." That wasn't very helpful for a man striving to establish child psychiatry as a rigorously empirical field of medicine.

In April 1939, Kanner sent another child to Frankl and Cameron for evaluation: a seven-year-old girl named Elaine C. who had been diagnosed as feebleminded and possibly deaf. She was surely neither. Elaine would run out to the garage with her hands clapped over her ears when her mother cleaned house, terrified by the roar of the vacuum cleaner. She could say a handful of words by her first birthday but learned no new words after that for four years. Doctors reassured her parents that she would grow out of her eccentricities, but she did not. During a lesson in flower arranging in nursery school, she ate the leaves and drank the water.

Elaine adored animals and would sometimes get down on all fours to imitate their cries. Her mother filled her room with toy dogs and rabbits, which she treated like friends. But when she was forced to be in the proximity of other children, she moved among them "like a strange being, as one moves among the pieces of furniture of a room," Frankl and Cameron observed. Instead of joining in the games at the Child Study Home, Elaine would wander off by herself to gaze at pictures of elephants, alligators, and dinosaurs in books for hours. While seeming to disregard them, she managed to learn a lot about the other children, including their names, the colors of their eyes, and where each one slept at night. But instead of trying to make friends, she just wanted to sit in her room alone, entranced in a reverie of simple, familiar activities like drawing, stringing beads, or playing with blocks. As she did these things, she would utter aphorisms that sounded like surrealist poetry: *Butterflies live in children's stomachs, and in their panties, too. Gargoyles have milk bags. Men cut deer's leg. Dinosaurs don't cry.*

In May, the Tripletts returned to Baltimore for another visit. Donald climbed over tables, smeared food in his hair, and threw books into the toilet. But he was making significant progress at home, despite the fact that he was receiving no particular "treatment."

For the next three years, Mary kept in touch with Kanner by mail, sending him regular reports on her son's development.

> *September, 1939.* He continues to eat and to wash and dress himself only at my insistence and with my help. He is becoming resourceful, builds things with his blocks, dramatizes stories, attempts to wash the car, waters the flowers with the hose, plays store with the grocery supply, tries to cut out pictures with scissors. Numbers still have a great attraction for him. While his play is definitely improving, he has never asked questions about people and shows no interest in our conversation . . .

> *March, 1940.* The greatest improvement I notice is his awareness of things around him. He talks very much more and asks a good many questions. Not often does he voluntarily tell me of happenings at school, but if I ask leading questions, he answers them correctly. He really enters into the games with other children. One day he enlisted the family in one game he had just learned, telling each of us just exactly what to do. He feeds himself some better and is better able to do things for himself . . .

Kanner apologized to Mary that he had still not come up with a name for her son's condition. "Nobody realizes more than I do myself," he wrote, "that at no time have you or your husband been given a clear-cut and unequivocal . . . diagnostic term."

While Kanner may still have been groping for the right name, he was quickly learning to recognize the pattern. Shortly after Beamon's letter arrived from Mississippi, someone in his office asked the mother of a boy called Alfred L., who had been seen at the clinic back in 1935, for an update on her son's development. Was Frankl digging through old files, looking for similar cases that had fallen through the cracks? After seeing Donald and Elaine, Kanner invited Alfred and his mother back for a follow-up visit. The boy, who was eleven years old by then, instantly recognized the doctor who had previously examined him and started bombarding him with questions about the clinic's windows, window shades, and X-ray room. He was perturbed by the fact that each sheet of paper for recording patient histories had *Johns Hopkins Hospital* printed at the top. Didn't the doctors know where they were?

As word spread through Kanner's social circle of his interest in these unusual children, his colleague Wendell Muncie asked him to evaluate his daughter Bridget (changed to "Barbara K." in Kanner's writings to protect the Muncies' privacy). Like Donald, she had never responded warmly to people. When her parents leaned toward her crib, cooing affectionately, she didn't burble or scrunch up her shoulders in anticipation of being picked up. At eight years old, she was clearly very bright and wanted to know everything there was to know about pendulums, smokestacks, and military transports. But her psychiatrist father bemoaned the fact that she had "no competitive spirit" and showed "no desire to please her teacher." When Kanner intentionally pricked Bridget with a pin, she looked fearfully at the pin and said, "Hurt!" But she didn't seem to connect the cause of her pain with the man who held it.

KANNER DISCOVERED that Donald was not the only child in this group with a phenomenal memory. Before his second birthday, Charles N. could correctly distinguish between eighteen symphonies. When his mother put on one of his favorite records, he would announce, "Beethoven." John F. had a similar gift for recognizing melody. If his father began whistling a tune, he would promptly identify it as Mendelssohn's violin concerto. He could also recite many prayers and nursery rhymes from memory and recall the lyrics to songs in multiple languages, which made his mother very proud. But both boys had trouble keeping their pronouns straight. If a crayon snapped in half, Charles would say, "*You* had a beautiful purple crayon and now it's two pieces. Look what *you* did." Until he was four and a half, John habitually referred to himself in the second person. If his parents asked him to do something, he would ignore them. He was reluctant to wave bye-bye or play patty-cake, which he could do only clumsily.

As much as these children seemed remote and inaccessible to other people, they were keenly attuned to the smallest changes and asymmetries in their environment. John preferred to keep all doors and windows closed, and if his mother insisted on opening a door to "pierce through his obsession," he would slam it violently and break down in tears if she opened it again. When the parents of a boy named Frederick W. dared to rearrange some bric-a-brac on a bookshelf at home, he immediately returned it to its proper position. The cracks in the old ceiling of Kanner's office drove Susan T. to distraction—she kept asking over and over, "Who cracked the ceiling?" and "How did it crack itself?"

A confirmed cigar smoker, Kanner had no compunctions about puffing away in front of his young patients. But one day while he was exhaling a long plume of smoke, a boy named Joseph C. snatched the offending stogie out of his fingers and jammed it back between his lips where it "belonged."

It was as if the children were constantly generating rules about how things *should be* based on how they *were* when they happened to come across them. A walk taken along a certain route one day had to be taken the same way every time after that. A random sequence of actions—such as the flushing of a toilet and the switching off of lights before bedtime—instantly became a ritual that had to be endlessly reiterated. The most humble and ordinary day-to-day events became imbued with terrifying significance.

EVEN IN THEIR AWKWARDNESS, irritability, and intransigence, these children struck Kanner as exceptionally beautiful. He doted on their "strikingly intelligent physiognomies," as if the face is not just a window to the soul but into the wiring of the brain itself. His belief in their cognitive potential was tremendously consoling to their parents, who had usually been through years of fruitless searches for the pediatrician, psychiatrist, neurologist, or other specialist who could finally make sense of their son's or daughter's behavior. Several of these mothers and fathers were psychiatrists themselves and specifically sought out Kanner's opinion because they refused to believe that any child of theirs could be mentally retarded—a diagnosis historically associated with the working class, immigrants, and people of color.

Kanner was under no illusions that the pattern he recognized in these children was a unique product of modern times, as antivaccine activists would later claim, pointing to the development of mercury-containing fungicides and vaccine preservatives like Merthiolate in the 1920s and 1930s as the alleged source of the condition he described. As a scholar of medical history, Kanner saw references to his young patients' predecessors scattered throughout world literature, where they were often portrayed as unwitting agents of evil and malevolent forces. He quoted this seventeenth-century account by the Swiss poet Gottfried Keller as an example of how such a child might have fared in previous generations:

> This 7-year-old girl, the offspring of an aristocratic family, whose father remarried after an unhappy first matrimony, offended her "noble and godfearing" stepmother by her peculiar behavior. Worst of all, she would not join in the prayers and was panic-stricken when taken to the black-robed preacher in the dark and gloomy chapel. She avoided contact with people by hiding in closets or running away from home. The local physician had nothing to offer beyond declaring that she might be insane. She was placed in the custody of a minister known for his rigid orthodoxy. The minister, who saw in her ways the machinations of a "baneful and infernal" power, used a number of would-be therapeutic devices. He laid her on a bench and beat her with a cat-o'-nine-tails. He locked her in a dark pantry. He subjected her to a period of starvation. He clothed her in a frock of burlap. Under these circumstances, the child did not last long. She died after a few months, and everybody felt relieved. The minister was amply rewarded for his efforts.

Now instead of being starved and scourged with whips, children like this were being herded into gas chambers in Germany, while in America they were exiled to the margins of society—like Virginia S., the slender, neatly dressed eleven-year-old daughter of a psychiatrist who had been confined to a home for the feebleminded since she was five. One day, the head of the outpatient program at the Phipps, Esther Richards, watched Virginia calmly take down a box in which the pieces from two jigsaw puzzles were jumbled together. She patiently sorted out the pieces and then deftly assembled both puzzles. The school staff assured her that Virginia was mute and likely deaf, but Richards heard her humming a Christmas hymn while pasting together paper chains.

Kanner knew there must be many more children like Virginia, passing the empty hours in dayrooms and lockdown wards without anyone knowing who they really were. After seeing eight children who fit the pattern, he was ready to tell the world about his discovery.

VII

In January 1942, Ernest Harms, the editor of a new journal called *The Nervous Child*, asked Kanner if he would consider guest-editing an upcoming issue. Seeing an opportunity to position his work at the leading edge of a wave of research on affect disorders of childhood, Kanner intimated that he was on the verge of a major breakthrough. "I have followed a number of children who present a very interesting, unique and as yet unreported condition, which has both interested and fascinated me for quite some time," he said. "In fact, I eventually plan to use the material for a monographic presentation." Harms took the bait.

Kanner's claims that his patients' condition was "unique" and "unreported" were a stretch, considering the volume of papers coming out on childhood schizophrenia. In fact, just a couple of months later, Despert published a paper in the debut issue of Harms's journal describing children who were relentlessly solitary, terrified of change and novel situations, given to rigid mannerisms and rituals, fascinated by mathematics and astronomy, and gifted with prodigious memories. She even referred to their "autism" in Bleuler's sense of the term. As usual, though, her case descriptions were muddled by her assumptions that her patients were hallucinating and suffering from the initial stages of adult psychosis.

By comparison, Kanner's "Autistic Disturbances of Affective Contact," published in the June 1943 issue of *The Nervous Child*, was a paragon of clinical clarity. By interweaving Frankl's and Cameron's meticulous observations, excerpts from parents' diaries and letters, and his own reflections on his patients' behavior, he lifted the gestalt of the syndrome out of the psychoanalytic muck and made it visible as a diagnostic entity apart from the undifferentiated mass of "pre-psychotic" children. His vivid portraits of his first eleven patients would endure as the human face of autism for another half century.

In a voice so self-assured that he might have been speaking in the majestic plural, Kanner began, "Since 1938, there have come to our attention a number of children whose condition differs so markedly and uniquely from anything reported so far, that each case merits—and, I hope, will eventually receive—a detailed consideration of its fascinating peculiarities."

His literary background served him well. Like a poet or a novelist uncovering universal truths in the humble particularity of a life, Kanner allowed the clinical picture of autism to emerge from an accumulation of minutely observed details.

> He was in the habit of saying almost every day, "Don't throw the dog off the balcony." His mother recalled that she had said those words to him about a toy dog while they were still in England. At the sight of a saucepan he would invariably exclaim, "Peter-eater." The mother remembered that this particular association had begun when he was 2 years old and she happened to drop a saucepan while reciting to him the nursery rhyme about "Peter, Peter, pumpkin eater."

> Her grammar is inflexible. She uses sentences just as she has heard them, without adapting them grammatically to the situation of the moment. When she says, "Want me to draw a spider," she means, "I want you to draw a spider." She affirms by repeating a question literally, and she negates by not complying.

> Between tests, he wandered about the room examining various objects or fishing in the wastebasket without regard for the persons present. He made frequent sucking noises and occasionally kissed the dorsal surface of his hand. He became fascinated with the circle from the form board, rolling it on the desk and attempting, with occasional success, to catch it just before it rolled off.

Kanner felt it was premature at this point to propose a set of criteria for diagnosing the condition he described; he was still just trying to extract the salient aspects of his patients' behavior. To make the pattern visible to his peers, he proposed two "essential common characteristics" shared by all children with this syndrome.

The first was a will to self-isolation, present from birth, that he called *extreme autistic aloneness.*

> The outstanding, "pathognomonic," fundamental disorder is the children's *inability to relate themselves* in the ordinary way to people and situations from the beginning of life. Their parents referred to them as having always been "self-sufficient"; "like in a shell"; "happiest when left alone"; "acting as if people weren't there"; "perfectly oblivious to everything about him"; "giving the impression of silent wisdom"; "failing to develop the usual amount of social awareness"; "acting almost as hypnotized" . . .
>
> There is from the start an *extreme autistic aloneness* that, whenever possible, disregards, ignores, shuts out anything that comes to the child from the outside. Direct physical contact or such motion or noise as threatens to disrupt the aloneness is either treated "as if it weren't there" or, if this is no longer sufficient, resented painfully as distressing interference.

The second common characteristic was a fear of change and surprise, which Kanner memorably christened *an anxiously obsessive desire for the maintenance of sameness.* This desire, he theorized, reflected a deep-seated anxiety that could only be kept at bay by trying to maintain the status quo.

> Their world must seem to them to be made up of elements that, once they have been experienced in a certain setting or sequence, cannot be tolerated in any other setting or sequence; nor can the setting or se-

> quence be tolerated without all the original ingredients in the identical spatial or chronologic order.

At no point in the paper did Kanner give the syndrome a name, though it has been widely assumed that he did. At this point, he was still just trying to map a distinctive constellation of behavior. (In other words, it was the children's *behavior* that he was calling "autistic," not the children themselves.) Only in 1944, when Kanner produced a condensed version of his paper for *Pediatrics*—a journal with a much larger readership—did he christen his syndrome with the name that stuck: *early infantile autism*.

KANNER'S VIEW OF AUTISM had already diverged radically from the model that Asperger and his colleagues developed in Vienna. Because Kanner focused exclusively on the first years of childhood, adults and teenagers were out of the picture entirely. Instead of presenting his syndrome as a broad spectrum with widely varying manifestations, Kanner framed his patients as a strictly defined and monolithic group, to the point of being willing to overlook significant differences between them.

For example, he made the startling assertion that "there is no fundamental difference between the eight speaking and the three mute children." Kanner claimed that Elaine's surreal aphorisms, Alfred's persistent questions about the window shades and X-ray room, and Donald's spinning of toys on the floor were fundamentally the same thing: solipsistic forms of self-stimulation and nothing more. He presented Donald's fascination with quantities as a purely tedious exercise, pointedly putting the word *conversation* in scare quotes:

> The major part of his "conversation" consisted of questions of an obsessive nature. He was inexhaustible in bringing up variations: "How many days in a week, years in a century, hours in a day, hours in half a day, weeks in a century, centuries in half a millennium," etc., etc.; "How

many pints in a gallon, how many gallons to fill four gallons?" Sometimes he asked, "How many hours in a minute, how many days in an hour?" etc. He looked thoughtful and always wanted an answer.

Frankl's conception of autism, however, had not changed since his days at the Heilpädagogik Station. The differences between the two men's approaches were highlighted in dramatic fashion in the issue of *The Nervous Child* in which Kanner's landmark paper appeared. In a case study of his own called "Language and Affective Contact," Frankl offered an account of a boy named Karl K. that he clearly considered autistic, referring to him as having a "*lack of contact with persons* in its most extreme form." Like Anni's portrait of Gottfried, Frankl's paper—which has also been overlooked for decades—opens a rare window on the expansive Viennese view of autism that ended up being overshadowed by Kanner's more constricted model.

To draw a firm line between his syndrome and mental retardation, Kanner touted his young patients' "intelligent-looking appearance" as evidence of their "good cognitive potential"—a notion that carried more than a trace of the eugenicists' theory that high mental capacity is expressed outwardly as pleasing physical symmetry. Karl, on the other hand, had "primitive facial features" and a "dull expression," Frankl noted. The boy had also never spoken a word in his life, but he was capable of understanding language: "He came when something pleasant was offered to him; he ran away when asked to do something he did not like . . . Even when amid a crowd of people, [he] behaved like a solitary person."

When Frankl first saw Karl in a children's hospital, he was confined to a locked bed. He passed his days "in monotonous emptiness," rocking back and forth and performing other rhythmical movements, punctuated by occasional escapes onto the open ward, where he would run "with breathtaking speed," overturning carts and otherwise disrupting the routines of the staff. To gain a clearer understanding of the boy's true capabilities, Frankl visited him at home in classic *Kinderklinik* fashion. There, where

Karl "had his daily routine well established," Frankl observed that he was more relaxed and purposeful:

> There were things he wanted to do and did regularly. He had somewhere, high up on a shelf, a place where he liked to sit; he knew where he was permitted and where forbidden to climb around, where he could find some food. His mother even allowed him to leave the house unaccompanied, as he always stayed around the house, never caused damage or ran into danger.

The boy certainly displayed the two essential characteristics (autistic aloneness and elaborate ritualistic behavior) of the syndrome that Kanner introduced to the world in the same issue of *The Nervous Child.* But Kanner would have likely ruled out a diagnosis of autism in his case, because Karl also suffered from tuberous sclerosis, a genetic condition that causes tumors to grow in the brain, and Kanner considered such signs of organic brain damage disqualifying. Karl also suffered from epileptic seizures, another red flag to Kanner. Epilepsy is now considered one of the most common comorbidities in autism, affecting nearly a third of the diagnosed population.

Frankl stressed that Karl represented only one point on a continuum that stretched from children with profound intellectual disability to "astonishing" child prodigies. But his inclusive conception of autism was about to be doomed to obscurity by the man who had saved his life from the gas chambers. As the most prominent child psychiatrist in America, Kanner was in an ideal position to popularize his own view of autism through his extensive network of personal and professional connections. After the condensed version of his paper was published in *Pediatrics* and then anthologized in *The Year Book of Neurology, Psychiatry and Endocrinology*—an annual summation of research that was widely read throughout the medical profession—a reviewer for the *Quarterly Review of Biology* hailed it as the "most important" article in the field of child psychiatry that year. The reviewer happened to be Wendell Muncie, the father of Kanner's patient Barbara K.

Meanwhile, four months after Kanner published his paper, Asperger submitted his thesis on *Autistischen Psychopathen* to his advisor, Franz Hamburger. His superiors had turned their focus of their efforts from the extermination of disabled children to *die Endlösung der Judenfrage*—the annihilation of the Jews. When Asperger's thesis finally appeared in print a year later, his clinic lay in ruins.

Five

THE INVENTION OF TOXIC PARENTING

> One is struck again and again by what I should like to call a mechanization of human relationships.
>
> —Leo Kanner

By the time Kanner sat down to write "Autistic Disturbances of Affective Contact," Georg and Anni Frankl were long gone from Baltimore. They had been hoping to find permanent positions at Johns Hopkins, where their years of experience would have been a boon to his ongoing research. But it was not to be.

On December 4, 1940, Anni apologized to Meyer for being unable to continue attending his seminar, explaining that a position had failed to "materialize" for her at the university, compelling her to take a job in Washington State as a psychiatric social worker. "I am extremely sorry about that," she wrote, "because [the seminar] has taught me and would have continued to teach me more than anything else in the last few years." Meanwhile, Kanner was enlisting Meyer's help to find a position for Georg elsewhere that would pay him more than the Child Study Home could offer. The Frankls ended up teaching in the psychology department at the University of Kansas, far from the central hub of autism research that Kanner's office became in the 1950s.

As a result, Kanner was on his own as he formulated his conception of his syndrome. He credited Georg for conducting his observations of Donald and Elaine but barely mentioned him in his work again. In future accounts of his momentous discovery, he focused exclusively on the "serendipity" of the Tripletts' arrival from Forest.

With the Frankls' departure, Kanner lost more than Georg and Anni's years of perspective on his patients as living exemplars of points on a broad continuum extending into adulthood. He also lost the prescient Viennese view of the eccentricities of their parents and relatives. Where Asperger saw threads of genius and disability inextricably intertwined in his patients' family histories—testifying to the complex genetic roots of their condition and the "social value of this personality type," as he put it—Kanner saw the shadow of the sinister figure that would become infamous in popular culture as the "refrigerator mother."

He was an astute clinical observer and a persuasive writer, but in this case his errors in interpreting his patients' behavior had wide-reaching implications. By blaming parents for inadvertently causing their children's autism, Kanner made his syndrome a source of shame and stigma for families worldwide while sending autism research off in the wrong direction for decades.

For the most part, the couples beating a path to Kanner's office for second, third, or fourth opinions on their children were much like Kanner himself: upper-middle-class academics who were savvy and well connected. No less than four of the fathers of his original eleven patients were psychiatrists, including Wendell Muncie. Alfred L.'s mother was a psychologist, and his father was a chemist with a law degree who worked in the U.S. Patent Office. Frederick W.'s father was a plant pathologist, and Richard M.'s father was a professor of forestry. The mothers of these patients were equally distinguished. In an era when less than one in four women in the United States completed their college education, nine of the mothers had bachelor's or graduate degrees. Even the grandparents, aunts, and uncles of these children seemed unusually bright.

Kanner's thumbnail portrait of Frederick W.'s grandfather reads like a pitch for a Technicolor epic starring Laurence Olivier. After studying tropical medicine in England and organizing medical missions in Africa, he became an expert on manganese mining in Brazil while serving as an art museum director and dean of a medical school. Then he absconded to Europe with his novelist mistress for twenty-five years. "All but three of the families," Kanner marveled, "are represented either in *Who's Who in America* or in *American Men of Science*, or in both."

Asperger had also taken note of the fact that an unusual number of his patients' parents and relations were highly accomplished. Not only was Fritz V.'s mother descended from one of Austria's greatest poets, his great-uncle was a "brilliant" but reclusive pedagogue. In many cases, Asperger said, "the ancestors of these children have been intellectuals for several generations." No doubt influenced by Lazar's habit of predicting a child's profession, he added that if a manual laborer was found among the relatives of these patients, it was likely someone who had "missed his vocation"—like Harro's father, a painter and sculptor who was forced to make brooms and brushes for a living when the Austrian economy collapsed.

But their inherited gifts also came at a cost. Asperger described Fritz's mother as an unfashionable and habitually anxious woman, "strange and rather a loner," who had "limited intuitive social understanding." When she became overwhelmed by the practical demands of life, she would take off to her solitary refuge in the mountains for a week, leaving her husband and son to fend for themselves. One day, Asperger saw her walking her son to the clinic, holding her hands stiffly behind her back as Fritz raced around her "making mischief," each seemingly oblivious to the other. But he emphasized the fact that their shared quirks of personality gave them an emotional basis for relating to one another. "The mother knew her son through and through and understood his difficulties very well," he observed. "She tried to find similar traits in herself and in her relations and talked about this eloquently."

Kanner ended up taking a decidedly dimmer view. Theories of toxic parenting were particularly thick in the air at Johns Hopkins, where Meyer was also mentoring Theodore and Ruth Lidz, who became the two leading exponents of the schizophrenogenic mother hypothesis. The Lidzes were suspicious of women with professional ambitions; if their dreams were thwarted by motherhood, they predicted, the result would be deep hostility for the children, cloaked in an overweening concern for their welfare.

These theories had a decisive and devastating impact on Kanner's view of his patients' unusual fascinations and extraordinary memories. He found it inconceivable that these children might actually be interested in the geeky minutiae they rattled on about with such intensity and fervor. Where Asperger and his colleagues recognized a specialized form of intelligence systematically acquiring data in a confusing world, Kanner saw a desperate bid for parental affection. "To a child 2 or 3 years old," he wrote, "all these words, numbers, and poems ('questions and answers of the Presbyterian Catechism'; 'Mendelssohn's violin concerto'; the 'Twenty-third Psalm'; a French lullaby; an encyclopedia index page) could hardly have more meaning than sets of nonsense syllables to adults." He theorized that overambitious parents like the Tripletts had "stuffed" the impressionable minds of their children with useless information to cast themselves in a culturally favorable light and bolster their own egos.

One of Kanner's special gifts as a clinician was his uncanny ability to draw people out, cut through their defenses, and get them talking about the most intimate details of their lives—a skill he picked up from the disabled volunteer in the Stone Room at Yankton. "His interview with parents is remarkable for its capacity to elicit a sequential account of the vicissitudes of development," recalled Leon Eisenberg, the psychiatrist who became his chief disciple at Johns Hopkins. "A sensitive listener, he rarely interrupts. His questions are disarmingly gentle but shrewdly penetrating." As Kanner developed his theory of autism causation, he turned the detailed notes that parents had provided to him—which were so helpful in developing a clear picture of their children's development—into a weapon, citing them as a "telling illustration of parental obsessiveness."

He applied the word *obsessive* to his patients and their relatives nearly a dozen times in his paper, starting with his description of Beamon Triplett's thirty-three-page letter. But his condescending attitude toward the families in his practice went far beyond that. Casting himself as the only reliable narrator of his patients' lives, he described the mother of one boy as "supposedly a college graduate" and portrayed Alfred's mother as a woman who "liked to call herself a psychiatrist and to make 'psychiatric' diagnoses of the child." (This must have been particularly galling to Kanner, who set aside his own insecurity about calling himself a psychiatrist only after being hired by Meyer.) He described the mother of a boy called Richard M. as follows:

> His mother brought with her copious notes that indicated obsessive preoccupation with details and a tendency to read all sorts of peculiar interpretations into the child's performances. She watched (and recorded) every gesture and every "look," trying to find their specific significance and finally deciding on a particular, sometimes very farfetched explanation. She thus accumulated an account that, though very elaborate and richly illustrated, on the whole revealed more of her own version of what had happened in each instance than it told of what had actually occurred.

Virtually the only couple that escaped his condescension was Wendell Muncie and his wife, a Johns Hopkins nurse named Rachel Cary, whom he referred to as a "prominent psychiatrist" and "a well educated, kindly woman." Muncie would return the favor by giving his paper a rave review in the *Quarterly Review of Biology.*

"For the most part," Kanner concluded, "the parents, grandparents, and collaterals are persons strongly preoccupied with abstractions of a scientific, literary, or artistic nature, and limited in genuine interest in people. This much is certain . . . In the whole group, there are very few really warmhearted fathers and mothers. Even some of the happiest marriages are rather cold and formal affairs."

Thus he ended the paper that introduced his syndrome to the world on a poignant note of ambivalence. While emphasizing the likelihood that autism was innate and inborn, he left the door open to a more unsettling possibility: that these children had been pushed into mental illness by their selfish, compulsive, and emotionally frosty parents, who tried to substitute poems and symphonies and catechisms and encyclopedias for the nurturing love they were unable to provide.

FOR THE PURPOSES OF advancing the field of child psychiatry, both theories had their virtues and drawbacks. The discovery of the first form of major psychosis that was present at birth would lend unprecedented urgency to the study of prenatal and postnatal development, genetics, and neurology, all of which Kanner was eager to integrate with psychology. But it would also undercut the role that his many colleagues in the field of "child guidance" had carved out for themselves: the prevention of delinquency and mental illness in adulthood. A condition that was inborn could not be prevented—it could only be ameliorated.

Implicating parenting style in the etiology of his syndrome, on the other hand, would place child psychiatrists firmly at the center of family life, giving them a role arguably more powerful than that of parents themselves: the ability to intervene therapeutically for the sake of the child. For obvious reasons, this way of looking at the problem proved more popular with Kanner's psychoanalytically minded colleagues, for whom autism became an ideal platform for promoting their latest theories of psychic development.

Kanner's agnosticism on the matter was both strategic and inevitable given his background and training. Remaining open to all possibilities was the sensible, nondogmatic, *Meyerian* thing to do. It was also the politically expedient choice when the prevailing winds in American psychiatry were blowing in a decidedly Freudian direction, in part because so many Freudians had just washed up on America's shores after being driven out of Eastern Europe. The fact that his patients' parents would unjustly pay a heavy price if his theory about them turned out to be wrong didn't factor into his calculations. He left the question hanging, hoping to attract the attention of other researchers who would help him figure out the answer.

TRAGICALLY, HOWEVER, Kanner made another error in interpreting his data that had the effect of limiting interest in the study of autism altogether for the next four decades. In speculating on the prevalence of his syndrome, he posited that it was "rare enough," though he offered that it was "possible that some such children have been viewed as feebleminded or schizophrenic."

Considering the number of similar cases that had already come to light in the childhood schizophrenia literature, and the fact that nearly all of his patients had been previously diagnosed as feebleminded, his notion that more cases of autism would be uncovered by reevaluating children with those diagnoses was a safe bet. But his insistence that his syndrome was rare was decidedly premature. Kanner was one of very few child psychiatrists in the country at that point, and he had already seen thirteen cases that fit the pattern (the original eleven, plus two more mentioned in a footnote), and he would soon see seven more. Plus, families of limited means—who couldn't afford to make the rounds of pediatricians, psychologists, and neurologists until they were referred to a specialist like him—weren't even on his radar.

Furthermore, if his syndrome had less blatantly disabling forms—as most developmental disabilities do—Kanner would likely have missed them altogether, because he had set up his referral network at the Harriet Lane in such a way that he was guaranteed to see only the most perplexing, unmanageable, and difficult cases. After the publication of his textbook, the pediatricians at the clinic felt empowered to handle less daunting cases on their own by referring them to an extensive network of social service agencies like the Children's Aid Society, the Visiting Nurses' Association, and the Baltimore Division of Special Education. By the time Kanner saw Donald, only one in ten children examined at the Harriet Lane required consultation with a psychiatrist, and only those cases considered "too complicated" or "time-consuming" for anyone else ended up being seen by Kanner or one of his associates.

In essence, he was sitting at the apex of a pyramid designed to filter all but the most profoundly disabled children of the most well-connected families in America out of his caseload. From this rarefied perspective, it's not surprising that his syndrome seemed both exceptionally rare and strikingly monolithic. The milder cases among the two hundred children seen by Asperger in Vienna would likely have never made it to the top of his pyramid. What's more surprising is how far Kanner was willing to go to ensure that other researchers saw his syndrome as exceptionally rare and monolithic too, even after evidence to the contrary began to emerge.

II

Three months after Kanner's monograph appeared in *The Nervous Child*, he received a barbed letter from Louise Despert, who was unimpressed by his claims that the condition he described was "unique" and "heretofore unreported." Had he not been reading her papers? "It seems to me that the greatest contribution this article is making is in its thorough, accurate, and illuminating description of clinical cases," she wrote. "However, if you will permit me to say so, I object to the coining of new terminology for entities which, if not so carefully described, have been previously reported."

She had a point. Kanner had tried to finesse the potential competition by pretending that it didn't exist. The casual reference in his paper to children being "misdiagnosed" with schizophrenia was particularly egregious, since many of Despert's case descriptions overlapped so closely with his own. The sole justification for his claim to uniqueness was his notion that his syndrome was apparent "from the start"—at birth—while Despert fussed over relatively arbitrary categories of onset.

There were numerous problems on both sides of this divide. Could a boy like Despert's patient S.K.—who had only a limited expressive vocabulary, a "capacity above normal to retain words and use them in a mechanical way," and a repertoire of more than a hundred nursery rhymes that he recited from memory—really be said to have been developing in a typical way before his regression? (Despert admitted that this indicated S.K.'s "previous difficulty in adaptation.") Could Kanner legitimately assert that his syndrome was always apparent at birth when his patients were five years old on average when he first saw them?

The answer was no. By 1955, he would retract this claim, saying, "The case material has been expanded to include a number of children who reportedly developed normally through the first 18 to 20 months of life." Clearly, the boundaries between Kanner's "unique" syndrome and what other clinicians were calling childhood schizophrenia were blurrier than he tried to make them appear.

Kanner's overreach may explain why his paper gained surprisingly little traction at first. In typically grandiose fashion, he later insisted that it "immediately received the attention of the profession," but, he also admitted, "the earliest reactions to the issue did not appear in print for several years." (Other than Muncie's enthusiastic review, which omitted any mention of the fact that his daughter was part of the study.) In fact, only two papers on the subject, not written by Kanner, were published in the next decade, while the volume of childhood schizophrenia research was worthy of its own book-length annotated bibliography.

In 1946, Lauretta Bender, the chief of psychiatry at New York's Bellevue Hospital, described one hundred children diagnosed with early-onset schizophrenia who exhibited a number of behaviors that are now considered classic signs of autism, including whirling, stimming, echolalia, and an apparently total lack of awareness of other people. She characterized this condition as pervasive, affecting every aspect of the child's body and mind, including the nervous system and digestion. But she also noted that even some of the most profoundly disabled children—"underdeveloped, infantile in motor play, physically dependent, unconcerned with [their] body excreta and clothing, unsure of [their] own identity, inarticulate to the point of mutism, [and] unable to make any school or social adjustment"—were capable of remarkable displays of "accelerated creativeness" and "Picasso-like experiments" in music and art. Indeed, her accounts of childhood schizophrenia were closer to Asperger's and Frankl's descriptions of autistic psychopathy than Kanner's constricted view of his syndrome.

In an eerie preview of the autism "epidemic" to come four decades later, the prevalence of childhood schizophrenia started spiking in the mid-twentieth century. By 1954, Bender saw 850 young patients with that diagnosis at Bellevue alone, including 250 cases added to her files in the previous three years. Bellevue was not unique in this respect: from 1946 to 1961, one in seven children admitted to the Langley Porter Neuropsychiatric Institute in San Francisco were diagnosed as "psychotic," with most having a reported onset before three years of age.

Their case records contained descriptions of many types of behavior that would become part of the lore of autism, including "ritualistic" gestures, "circular movement of objects," strict dietary preferences (one child would "not eat anything but spaghetti cooked in a particular pan"), and a fascination with taking apart toys and home appliances. None of these young patients exhibited hallucinations, delusions, or the other fulminant manifestations typically associated with the word *psychotic*. For the most part, they were nonverbal children with unusual sensory sensitivities who shied away from other people.

Childhood schizophrenia researchers were well aware that the condition they were studying was not monolithic but had an astonishingly diverse range of presentations. "The concept of a *gradient* of severity of disorder, or that of a psychopathological spectrum," wrote S. A. Szurek in 1956, "is for several reasons becoming for us one which fits our experience most closely."

In fact, if Kanner's syndrome was defined too narrowly, childhood schizophrenia had the opposite problem: its boundaries were so diffuse that it included too many different types of patients. By 1958, Hilde Mosse of the Lafargue Clinic in Harlem reported that children with the diagnosis "filled state hospitals and schools for mental defectives." Childhood schizophrenia walked like a duck and quacked like a duck but was not a duck. Instead, it was the psychotic goose that suddenly seemed to be in everyone's backyard.

KANNER SAW THE WRITING on the wall early on. While continuing to insist that his syndrome was a condition sui generis, he quietly folded it into the schizophrenia section of the revised edition of his textbook in 1948. A year later, he officially waved the white flag. "Early infantile autism may . . . be looked upon as the earliest possible manifestation of childhood schizophrenia," he wrote in the *American Journal of Orthopsychiatry.* "I do not believe that there is any likelihood that early infantile autism will at any future time have to be separated from the schizophrenias."

In essence, Kanner attempted to negotiate a truce with researchers like Despert and Bender: if they would let him have his rare, narrowly defined syndrome, he would yield the rest of Szurek's "spectrum" to the ever-expanding field of childhood schizophrenia. As a career gambit, it worked. Kanner was rewarded with speakerships at schizophrenia conferences and a surge of interest in his own work. In retrospect, however, this truce had a hidden cost. From that point on, the terms *autism*, *childhood schizophrenia*, and *childhood psychosis* were used virtually interchangeably throughout the clinical literature (Kanner's 1974 anthology of writing on autism was titled *Childhood Psychosis*). This had a confounding effect on research, because virtually any sample of "psychotic" children was bound to include kids with a wide variety of heterogeneous conditions. It would also make accurate retrospective assessments of the prevalence of autism in the mid-twentieth century virtually impossible, because so many autistic children ended up hidden behind other labels.

Trying to make the best of changing trends in psychiatry, Kanner also yielded to the consensus of his colleagues on the role of parenting in autism. After Adolf Meyer's retirement in 1941, the dominance of his school of psychiatry in America—with its emphasis on seeking "the facts" of each patient's life rather than on elaborating unified theories of the psyche—was quickly eclipsed by the rise of psychoanalysis. To a generation of erudite intellectuals who had barely escaped extermination, Kanner's suggestion that the fate of these children was sealed at birth seemed nearly traitorous to the profession. If autism was rooted in disturbed family dynamics, however, there was still reason for hope.

Kanner's capitulation to his powerful peers was as swift as it was brutal to parents. By April 1948, when *Time* ran an article headlined "Frosted Children" (subtitle: "Diaper-Age Schizoids"), it was clear that he wasn't going to be a stickler about insisting that his syndrome was present at birth. Addressing his colleagues at a conference in Manhattan, Kanner blasted his patients' parents as cold perfectionists who barely had time to hug their children before rushing off to the lab or the next gallery opening. It wasn't that they meant to do their children harm, he said; it was that their idea of responsible parenting was "the mechanized service of the kind which is rendered by an over-conscientious gasoline station attendant." (*Time* reported ominously that "all but five of the mothers" of his patients "had a college degree.") He added that the reason these children had turned their backs on other people was that they sought solace in solitude after being "kept neatly in a refrigerator which didn't defrost."

The image of the refrigerator mother proved indelible in the popular imagination, but in Kanner's view, fathers were equally culpable. His eager protégé Leon Eisenberg published his own case series focused on his patients' fathers, as if bringing your son or daughter to the Harriet Lane for an evaluation was tantamount to an admission that you were mentally ill. In withering prose, he depicted a wealthy surgeon who "dealt with infected gall bladders, diseased bowels, or tumors, with little or no curiosity about the person in whom these anatomical problems were housed." Another father, he reported, read "mathematical treatises" before making love to his wife "in an inept fashion," leaving her unfulfilled and resentful. Eisenberg claimed that these characteristics recurred "with monotonous regularity" among the fathers in his practice, citing as an iconic example a man found in an upended railroad car after a derailment, fussing over his manuscript.

In 1956, Kanner and Eisenberg published a summation of their research in the previous dozen years. The paper was informed by a study of child-rearing practices on Israeli kibbutzim, where "warm and demonstrative" nursery workers took on many of the nurturing roles traditionally fulfilled by parents. The families of their autistic patients, they explained, were like kibbutzim "in reverse." The children were generally raised by their own parents, but not in a "warm, flexible, growth-promoting atmosphere." Instead, "physical needs were met mechanically and on schedule, according to the rigid precepts of naïve behaviorism applied with a vengeance." As a result, children were rewarded for "'perfect' behavior, cleverness, 'self-sufficiency,' and so on," rather than being valued simply for existing. "It may be a measure of the intellectual aptitude of these children that they were able to parrot long and resonant strings of meaningless words," they added, "but it even more clearly bespeaks the emphasis placed at home on such useless activities, which were a source of pride to the parents."

Though Kanner refrained from making recommendations about treatment, the predictable outcome of his statements was the widespread adoption of an approach to therapeutic intervention for autism that included years of psychoanalysis for the parents and removal of the children to an institution like Bellevue or Langley Porter "for their own good." The most prominent advocate of this approach—which was archly christened *parentectomy* in the press—was another émigré from Eastern Europe who had come into psychiatry through a back door.

III

"This is what your mother is like—cold and hard," said the world-renowned director of the Sonia Shankman Orthogenic School to an autistic boy in his care, pointing to a stone statue in the ornately decorated garden. The school, located at the University of Chicago, was designed to be the opposite of the kind of place where the director, Bruno Bettelheim, said that he had his first insights into autistic behavior: the concentration camps of Dachau and Buchenwald, where he was imprisoned for eleven months.

The walls of the school were covered with paintings and tapestries, which Bettelheim personally selected. The children painted their rooms whatever colors they liked and ate off fine china on tables dressed with linen—a civilized touch designed to boost their self-esteem and self-control. The doors of the clinic were kept locked, but for the purpose of excluding the outside world, rather than to keep the patients in. The mothers of patients in particular were discouraged from visiting, but the children could come and go as they pleased.

Bettelheim's role model in designing this therapeutic milieu was August Aichhorn, the same man who inspired Erwin Lazar to launch the Heilpädagogik Station in Vienna. Unlike the Children's Clinic, however, the Orthogenic School was founded on the principles and practice of psychoanalysis. The total environment of the school was designed to serve a single purpose: to enable the children to restart the process of ego development (with Bettelheim cast in the role of the collective superego), which had been arrested by toxic familial influences, with the help and guidance of the staff members, who would become their surrogate family.

The son of a lumber merchant, Bettelheim came of age in the city he thought of as "Freud's Vienna." Bettelheim first heard about psychoanalysis when he was fourteen from Otto Fenichel, an older boy who was already sitting in on Freud's seminars and would become a leading analyst. The young Bettelheim would go out of his way to walk down the steep slope of Bergasse as often as possible, because the great man himself lived at Number 19.

At first, he couldn't understand why Freud had chosen to reside on such a nondescript street in such a dreary part of Vienna. Later, Bettelheim would tell himself that the Bergasse—which began in a dusty warren of junk shops owned by poor Jews and ended high on a hill at the University of Vienna—must have struck Freud as an external representation of the journey of his life. It may not have been strictly true, but it was a story that wove meaning out of the ragged threads of experience. Such symbol-laden narratives—complete with his own embellishments—became Bettelheim's way of engaging the world.

He enrolled at the university, where he spent six years, eventually earning a doctorate without honors in art theory (not a PhD summa cum laude in psychology, as he would later claim). When his father died of syphilis in 1926, Bettelheim was forced to give up his daydreams of a life in academia and take over the family lumber and sawmill business. Four years later, he married Gina Alstadt, a bright, attractive, independent-minded young girl who found him "homely"—he was a short, nerdy man with enormous ears and thick glasses—but charming and well-spoken. Almost immediately after they moved in together, their relationship began to decline. Gina came to despise her husband's habit of reading only the first and last dozen pages of a book, and skimming a few pages in the middle, and then pontificating about it as if he had read the whole thing. She would later say that she was never in love with him.

Partly due to her feelings of dissatisfaction in her marriage, Gina entered psychoanalysis, and her husband eventually followed. (They even saw the same husband-and-wife team of analysts, Richard and Editha Sterba.) At a time when wealthy people were flying in from all over the world to spend a few months on the couch, Gina became deeply involved in the culture of psychoanalysis, taking seminars with Anna Freud while working as an unpaid teacher at a Montessori school. In 1932, Editha Sterba asked her for help in trying to find a school for an American girl named Patsy who seemed to be terribly shy. On meeting Gina, Patsy looked out at her from under her pageboy haircut with terrified eyes and a blank expression on her face, knotting her fingers compulsively. To calm her, Gina gave her some crayons and was pleasantly surprised when Patsy drew beautiful pictures of animals. She felt instantly attached to this strange, quiet, tormented little girl.

Thinking that Patsy might have some sort of serious emotional disturbance, Gina went to August Aichhorn for advice. "When you cannot decide if a child is disturbed or not, just turn to other children for an opinion," he told her. Gina found that Patsy's peers rejected her as a stranger in their midst. She had tried unsuccessfully for a long time to persuade Bettelheim to have a child, so she ended up taking Patsy into the household and treating her with the same devotion that she would have lavished on their own daughter. Under her loving care, Patsy learned to read and write and became more relaxed and sociable. Though it's unclear precisely what sort of difficulties Patsy had, Bettelheim would later claim her as his first autistic success story, taking credit for her development, though it was really his wife's doing.

On May 28, 1938, policemen acting on orders from Berlin arrived at Bettelheim's door to arrest him and put him on a train to Dachau for the crimes of being a Jew and an advocate of Austrian independence. Gina had already escaped to the United States, but her husband's visa application had gotten mired in red tape. On the train to the camp, his glasses were smashed and he was beaten in the head and stabbed with a bayonet. Upon arriving, he was given the prisoner number 15029. Another little *J* (for *Jude*) was entered in the sign-in book.

Gratuitous brutality and torture—physical and emotional—were everyday realities in the camp. Bettelheim struggled to maintain his sanity by using his powers of interpretation to make sense of the horrors he was witnessing. He interviewed his fellow inmates and listened to the stories of their lives, committing the details to memory. He took the advice of an old Communist who had managed to survive at the camp for four years and ate the disgusting soup that the Nazis ladled out for the prisoners with relish, because enjoying it was not something he had been *ordered* to do but a conscious assertion of his freedom.

He also put into practice the lessons he learned in his psychoanalysis. He closely monitored his own emotional reactions as he adapted to the camp's dehumanizing routines, and he observed the changes in the personalities of his fellow prisoners as they became progressively deranged by the surreal nature of their existence. He saw honest men become liars and strong men ground down until they were weeping hysterics. He felt that by noticing these things and deriving meaningful lessons from them instead of simply submitting to the process, he regained his pride and sense of himself as a human being.

He was particularly struck by the pitiful behavior of the emaciated prisoners known as *Muselmänner* because they would suddenly lie down on the ground like Muslims bowing to Mecca in prayer. They seemed to have lost their will to live entirely, as if they had collapsed inside themselves into a state of total numbness, listlessness, and apathy. He noted that these prisoners often died shortly after they reached this point, as if their physical deaths had been preceded by their psychological deaths. They trudged in the endless lines for food, showers, and the latrines like ghosts, barely able to place one foot in front of the other.

Then, on April 14, 1939, Bettelheim heard his number announced after morning roll call, informing him that he was to report to the administration. Though he feared that he was about to be shot, he discovered that he was to be released from the camp that day due to the efforts of relatives and influential friends who had been intensively lobbying the State Department to secure his freedom. (He later bragged that Eleanor Roosevelt herself had personally intervened in his favor, which may or may not have been true.) The SS men told him that if he didn't leave the country within a week, he would be rearrested or shot.

Bettelheim arrived in New York City by steamship in early May, where Gina informed him that their marriage was over. Within months, he moved to Chicago, where he began reinventing himself to become the man who would be known at the Orthogenic School as "Dr. B," embellishing the narrative of his own life as required. His doctorate in art theory became a doctorate in psychology—or two or three degrees in various subjects, all summa cum laude. Patsy had been his special project; over the years, she would morph into several autistic children that he had taken into his home and transformed utterly. He had been fully trained in psychoanalysis, and Freud himself had praised him as "exactly the person we need for psychoanalysis to grow and develop." (The closest he ever came to meeting Freud was walking past his house.) Meanwhile, his years of running the family sawmill were just a memory he left behind in Austria with his former identity as a schlemiel. Who would dare challenge the veracity of a concentration camp survivor?

He exerted his personal charm and his gift for strategic confabulation to be hired as the principal of the Orthogenic School, which was itself in the process of reinvention. Founded by the Rush Medical College in 1912 as a place for medical students to conduct examinations of children with "doubtful mentality," the school had allied with the University of Chicago and expanded its mission to encompass the study and treatment of children with a broad range of "adjustment difficulties"—educational, emotional, and social. The school was an ideal platform for Bettelheim to put his versions of psychoanalytic theory and ego psychology into practice and for becoming the influential figure that he had always wanted to be.

Shortly before taking the job, he published a reflection on the conduct of prisoners in Dachau and Buchenwald called "Individual and Mass Behavior in Extreme Situations." If he had framed it as a personal memoir, it would likely never have been published in a scholarly journal, so he cast it as the work of a highly trained independent researcher who happened to have shared the same living quarters as his subjects while claiming that he interviewed more than fifteen hundred prisoners to obtain his data, though this is unlikely. Widely reprinted in publications for lay readers like *Politics*, it attracted the attention and praise of a number of important figures, including Meyer Schapiro, Theodor Adorno, and Dwight D. Eisenhower.

Bettelheim described the social structure of the camps as a laboratory for a diabolical experiment in producing the ideal servile citizens of Nazi society by forcing adults to regress to primitive, infantile states:

> The prisoners developed types of behavior characteristic of infancy or early youth . . . They were forced to soil themselves. Their defecation was strictly regulated. Prisoners who needed to eliminate had to obtain the permission of the guard. It seemed as if the education to cleanliness would be once more repeated. It gave pleasure to the guards to hold the power of granting or withholding the permission to visit the latrines . . .

> The prisoners lived, like children, only in the immediate present; they lost the feeling for the sequence of time; they became unable to plan for the future or to give up immediate pleasure satisfactions to gain greater ones in the near future.

He would view the behavior of autistic children as essentially the same phenomenon on an individual scale. But where Kanner saw a refrigerator, Bettelheim saw a concentration camp, with the mother as *Kommandant*.

WITH THE POPULAR FASCINATION for psychoanalysis at its peak, Bettelheim's work at the Orthogenic School, his books like *Love Is Not Enough* and *Truants from Life*, his *echt* Viennese accent, and his paternalistic manner made him an enormously charismatic figure. In a series of articles for mainstream publications like *Parents* and *Popular Science*, he commented on a wide range of social issues, from the impact of anti-Semitism on children to schizophrenic art.

By 1956, when the Ford Foundation awarded the Orthogenic School a $342,500 grant for a five-year study of autism, he was on his way to becoming the first celebrity "shrink" in America—the psychoanalytic equivalent of Dr. Oz. Bettelheim cited Kanner's paper in his grant application, and the model of autism employed at the school was based on his 1943 case descriptions and commentary about the role of "refrigerator" parents. "We believed that autistic children were usually attractive, probably above normal intelligence, and showed not even 'soft signs' of organic damage," recalled Jacqueline Seevak Sanders, who worked as Bettelheim's assistant for fourteen years and eventually took over as director of the Orthogenic School. While many staff members quietly considered the possibility that the children did have some kind of inborn neurological difference that made them unusually vulnerable to the influences of their psychological environment, their assumption in practice was that the primary cause of autism was bad parenting, and that years of milieu therapy could produce a complete cure.

This assumption was simply not questioned, at least in public. The leading psychoanalytic theorist in America, David Rapaport, who was on the school's evaluation team, believed it; the renowned developmental psychologist Erik Erikson, who visited the school, supported it; and, perhaps most importantly, the parents who brought their children to Bettelheim (typically referred by psychoanalysts) were also convinced that "their treatment of the child had caused the problem," as Sanders put it. They also provided developmental histories that seemed to confirm that belief. It was a closed loop. Research that suggested an organic etiology—like Bender's papers on childhood schizophrenia—was simply ignored by the psychoanalysts who had eagerly rushed into the field.

For the young psychologists and counselors (many of whom were women) who were the lifeblood of the Orthogenic School and most intimately involved in the day-to-day lives of the children, it was a tremendously inspiring place to embark on a career. As Kanner had done at Yankton, Bettelheim instituted many reforms to humanize the institution he had inherited. He had the locks on the doors changed so that one key opened them all, allowing the counselors to look less like jailhouse guards with keys bristling on their belts. He took down the funereal black curtains covering the windows and replaced them with pretty drapes and swapped out the EEG machine and surgical bed for a Ping-Pong table. Children who wet their beds at night were no longer to be punished or shamed, and he personally ripped down the chart in the bathroom used to track the administration of laxatives. The design of the facility was to serve the psychological needs of the children, not the logistical convenience of the staff. Instead of institutional bunk beds, the children slept in custom-built wooden beds with matching dressers, and their own drawings were exhibited on the walls. Sanders described her time there in glowing terms echoed by many former staff members: "This was characteristic of the atmosphere of the school: brilliant minds at work on a new frontier of the greatest human significance, and with greatest hopefulness."

Richard Pollak offered a darker view of life in the school in his biography of Bettelheim, *The Creation of Dr. B*, depicting him as a despotic tyrant who struck children for minor infractions, whipped them with belts, dragged them out of the shower, and verbally humiliated them. Former student Ronald Angres, diagnosed as autistic by Bettelheim, wrote that in his twelve years at the school, he lived in terror of hearing the squeak of his crepe-soled shoes in the dorms—"in abject, animal terror."

Beyond his conduct at the school, the primary damage that Bettelheim did to a generation of autistic children and their families was spreading Kanner's theories of toxic parenting even further in pop culture than Kanner himself could have. Other than the occasional quote in *Time*, Kanner's comments were mostly confined to professional journals. But Bettelheim was everywhere by the 1960s, publishing articles in *Harper's* ("Growing Up Female"), *Redbook* ("Why Working Mothers Feel Guilty"), the *New York Times Magazine* ("Children Must Learn to Fear"), *Life* ("Why Does Man Become a Hater?"), and *Ladies' Home Journal*, where he had a regular column ("The Danger of Teaching Your Baby to Read," "Am I Ruining My Child for Life?"). He stated his elaboration of Kanner's theory in the starkest possible terms in *The Empty Fortress*, the book he developed from his progress reports to the Ford Foundation, which became a best seller. "The precipitating factor in infantile autism is the parent's wish that his child did not exist," he wrote. "Infants, if totally deserted by humans before they have developed enough to shift for themselves, will die. And if their physical care is enough for survival but they are deserted emotionally, or are pushed beyond the capacity to cope, they will become autistic."

The book was widely and enthusiastically reviewed and was many lay readers' introduction to the subject. Referring to autism as "an illness, a suicide really, of the soul," Eliot Fremont-Smith of the *New York Times* called *The Empty Fortress* "an extraordinary book" and chose it as one of the top nonfiction titles of the year. It was, in essence, Bettelheim's notice to the Ford Foundation that he had given them their money's worth. He claimed "good" or "fair" outcomes for 92 percent of the speaking children in his sample, saying "the seventeen children whose improvement we classified as 'good' can for all intents and purposes be considered 'cured.'"

Behind the bright yellow door of the Orthogenic School, however,

Bettelheim's staff knew his claims were hyperbolic at best. Sanders would later admit that Bettelheim had "exaggerated . . . so that success appeared both greater in kind and in quantity than it actually was." The treatment of their first cohort of eleven autistic children, which ended in 1958, had not even come close to anything resembling a cure. "None of them were 'successful' in that we had no hope of any of them being at any time able to live independently," she reported. "To us, this was failure, since we believed that any child admitted to the Orthogenic School had the potential to lead a full and independent life. I, and probably my coworkers, viewed the failure as mine and the staff's." But, she added, "we did not view it as evidence that we might be working with the wrong premises."

Sanders claimed to see significant improvement in some of the autistic children admitted to the school later, which must have been encouraging, considering that the average length of their twenty-four-hour immersion in an environment entirely devoted to their well-being was ten years. But when she took over as director in the 1970s, she became "very reluctant" to admit such children to the school, no longer believing that the staff "could have the same goals for them" as they did for the other students. She was heartbroken to see the children who didn't appear in Bettelheim's heroic narratives of redemption return to lockdown wards. Though the approach to treating autism at the Orthogenic School was based on a complex web of misconceptions and fabrications that caused their parents untold grief, the children were generally treated better there—at least by Bettelheim's staff—than they were in the brutal institutions that the school was intended to replace.

IV

Once a child diagnosed with autism or childhood schizophrenia was placed in a state hospital, he or she was no longer treated as a child. Instead, such children were blasted with the whole armamentarium of powerful drugs, last-ditch methods, and experimental treatments that the psychiatric establishment usually reserves for its most intractable adult psychotics.

Bender's preferred method of treatment at Bellevue was electroconvulsive therapy (ECT). Her young patients typically received twenty courses of ECT or more, which she claimed boosted their IQ, "stabilized" their electroencephalograms, improved their body image, made them "more normal" in general, and prompted complete "remission" in some cases. To supplement ECT, Bender also employed subcoma insulin shock and Metrazol, a drug that produces convulsions.

Her pharmacopeia for treating "autistic thinking" included chlorpromazine and prochlorperazine, first-generation antipsychotics that became infamous for causing an irreversible tic disorder known as the "Thorazine shuffle." She also employed Benzedrine, the classic pep pill of Beat Generation lore, which she found particularly helpful for autistic teenagers with "sexual preoccupations." She felt that another antipsychotic called reserpine was "among the best drugs" for treating children, despite a roster of side effects that included nightmares, vomiting, and suicidal ideation.

Another drug that Bender felt showed great promise was LSD, which she obtained legally from Sandoz Pharmaceuticals under the brand name Delysid. Every day for two months, she administered doses of the potent hallucinogen to fifty-four autistic children, ages six to fifteen. She reported that the drug made her patients more aware, talkative, and "reality-oriented," though she also noted an increase in their "anxious and depressive attitudes." By keeping her patients on a daily regimen of Delysid, she claimed, she was able to wean them off their usual diet of tranquilizers.

In the age before informed consent, Bender's use of these drugs and treatments was virtually unmonitored, particularly because she was the chief of psychiatry at the hospital. She wasn't even required to submit the designs of her uncontrolled trails for review by an ethics board before launching them.

One of the kids unlucky enough to become a subject of her experiments was Guy Susann, the son of the popular novelist Jacqueline Susann, author of *Valley of the Dolls*, and her husband, Irving Mansfield. For the first three years of his life, Guy was an affectionate and playful baby, but one afternoon his nanny brought him home from the park because he had begun screaming for no apparent reason. His disconsolate wailing lasted for the rest of the night and into the following day. On the advice of a pediatrician, his parents brought him to Bellevue, where Bender subjected Guy to a week of shock treatments that left him "destroyed . . . numb, with no expression, almost lifeless," Mansfield recalled in his autobiography.

The little boy never spoke another word, with a single harrowing exception. "When are you going to talk?" Guy's anguished mother asked him one day in the car. "When I'm ready," he replied.

Susann and Mansfield placed him in a residential facility, telling their A-list friends that he had been sent to specialists in Arizona for his asthma. Mansfield attributed his wife's drive to churn out potboilers like *The Love Machine* and *Once Is Not Enough* to her anxiety that they would run out of money for Guy's custodial care.

MEANWHILE, LEADING neo-Freudian analysts like Rudolf Ekstein were putting their patients on the couch for years at a time. Because the childhood schizophrenia "spectrum" was much more inclusive than Kanner's conception of his syndrome, children who displayed many traits now considered classic signs of autism but showed no delay in acquiring language often ended up with that diagnosis.

At a meeting of the American Psychiatric Association in Atlantic City in 1952, Ekstein described such a child: an eleven-year-old boy named Tommy, who told his therapists that he knew more about geology and biology than his teachers and that he had daydreams of becoming a wise and powerful five-star general commanding a fleet of spaceships. Ekstein described his capacity for interpersonal relationships as "almost absent." Dubbing him "the Space Child," he turned Tommy into a cottage industry, churning out papers on him for more than a decade.

Like Bettelheim, Ekstein was a product of the Viennese school. Growing up in the Austrian capital in the 1930s, he would talk philosophy with a friend who lived directly across from Freud's office and was thrilled to glimpse the great man's silhouette occasionally passing in front of the window. Ekstein's epic psychoanalysis of the Space Child revealed more about the degenerate state of Freud's legacy in the 1950s than it did about his patient's psyche.

Ekstein theorized that Tommy's precocious interest in science was likely the result of "early childhood intensive sexual traumata" caused by seduction by his mother or a nursemaid. He pondered the meaning of the boy's erections during sessions with a female therapist. The overarching theme of his analysis was that Tommy's fantasies of space travel represented an unconscious effort to put distance between himself and his "compulsive" parents. The inspiration for this "very intense destructive phantasying," he surmised, was Tommy's obsession with "science fiction, science fiction movies, and other similar literary productions."

For the first years of his analysis, Tommy was confined to the Southard School for emotionally disturbed children in Topeka, Kansas. Located in a Prairie-style farmhouse—with a lookout on the roof to discourage unscheduled outings—the school was affiliated with the Menninger Clinic, where Judy Garland and Marilyn Monroe spent stints in rehab. The Southard approach was sold to parents as "a mixture of Freud and friendliness," backed up with the ever-present threat of being sent to a lockdown ward. (One teenage patient named Dick was put on lockdown for three months for seeking out "the company of lower class colored people exclusively.") The first months of Tommy's analysis were devoted to assuaging his anxieties about activities like crossing the street. What this "scared little boy" really needed, Ekstein snidely observed, was a "personal policeman to protect him from the wrath of the world."

Within the walls of the bucolic facility, Tommy's science fiction fantasies only became more fantastic. At one point, he announced to his doctors that "Tommy" was no longer in the institution, having escaped to Arizona, where he was helping physicists to upgrade the design of the atom bomb. He informed his therapist that he had built a machine that enabled him to travel back in time to the moment that life began, envisioning himself as a fish that might be eaten by bigger fish if he couldn't swim away. Moving forward through time, he witnessed William the Conqueror's invasion of England and took a sightseeing tour through medieval Europe. Four centuries later, he barely avoided being tried for witchcraft.

Tommy explained that the goal of his time tripping was to intervene at critical junctures and save himself from the mysterious affliction that had resulted in his disappointing his parents. But Ekstein ventured that these fantasies enabled him "to deny his helplessness, his lonesomeness, his castration fear, his fear of being devoured, [and] his fear of dying or killing someone." When Tommy employed a phrase like "hundreds and thousands of light years," he was not really talking about science, Ekstein explained to his colleagues in Atlantic City. He was making "an allusion to psychological problems which he could not present in any other way." When Tommy shared a new set of fantasies about retiring to a farm in the country to raise dinosaurs, inviting his female therapist to come along, it was judged to be a critical breakthrough in his analysis.

After two years at the Southard School, Tommy was allowed to move to a boardinghouse, where he lived with a foster family. His newfound interest in baseball spawned a fantasy of managing an all-girl team that played "meticulously according to national baseball rules." After calculating each player's statistics for the season, he admitted to his therapists that fantasy baseball was not as exciting as waging intergalactic battles in his head. But he had decided that his fantasies must now be "logical" and "scientific" above all. He was growing up, as even Space Children are wont to do.

He enrolled at a local university and started taking courses in science. Ekstein noted that Tommy's foster family had come to their own understanding and acceptance of his behavior. He said that they were delighted to watch him develop into a mature and independent person, though his manner around them was "brusque and detached" and he "might never directly express his feelings of warmth and gratitude for their efforts." He added that they found deep gratification in "seeing Tom improve and their realization of the part they played helping him achieve these modifications."

By the time Tommy was twenty-three, he had been through 1,236 hours of psychoanalysis. With the support of his foster family, he had earned a graduate degree in physics and was teaching science courses at a local college. Ekstein described him as a "personable, shy, and somewhat tense" young man who was still obsessed with "space" (in scare quotes) and most comfortable around people who shared his obscure interests.

"Whether his achievements up to now and in years to come as well as our own advance in work with such youngsters justify the tremendous commitment of treatment and research time, we do not know," Ekstein mused. But he dismissed the notion that he had been on the wrong track all along in subjecting Tommy to a decade of psychoanalysis. "One cannot successfully treat children such as he," Ekstein concluded, "if one must constantly answer the question as to the worthwhileness of the treatment."

Tommy (who called himself "Tom" by then) told his former psychotherapist that he had a new daydream: joining the research organization that would eventually become NASA. By then, space travel was no longer just a "phantasy." It was a national obsession.

THE PSYCHIATRIC ESTABLISHMENT would eventually come up with a diagnostic label for kids like Tommy: *Asperger's syndrome.* But Asperger's work, which had never found a wide readership outside of Eastern Europe, had been virtually forgotten. Even the handful of clinicians who read his paper in the original German assumed that Kanner had somehow managed to overlook it.

Still, the gifted loners that Asperger wrote about kept popping up, like a lost tribe moving through the underbrush of psychiatry, occasionally glimpsed from the air. In 1953, two psychiatrists from Pennsylvania, J. Franklin Robinson and Louis J. Vitale, described a group of young patients with "circumscribed interest patterns" at a residential facility in Wilkes-Barre called the Children's Service Center. The fascinations of these children tended to cluster in "rather odd spots," like astronomy, chemistry, bus schedules, calendars, and maps. They had precocious vocabularies, extraordinary memories, and a passion for science and science fiction. But they had a hard time making friends their own age.

One boy named Tom became interested in chemistry in grade school, which led his father to decide that he was "hiding" in books. To encourage him to be more social, his mother started trailing him to school, where she would shout at him to be more outgoing, which only succeeded in turning him into the school pariah. At the Children's Service Center, Tom began reading up on corporate finance, nuclear physics, and botany. He took long walks through the woods to learn the names of the local plants and trees. (In Tom's case, "circumscribed" interests apparently meant being curious about nearly everything around him except for the other children, who nicknamed him "Creepy" and "Brains.")

In his first interview with one of the center's psychologists, he briefly perked up when he spotted a Bunsen burner on a shelf in the office. "Do you have a scientist's laboratory here?" Tom asked, a smile flickering over his face. The psychologist told him he must think about why his parents committed him to a residential facility. "It's supposed to be a nice school," Tom replied agreeably. The psychologist reminded him that it was not a nice school but a home for emotionally troubled youths. "That's it," the boy acknowledged, in a tone of voice described as "flat."

A psychiatrist asked another boy at the center, John, what he wanted to be when he grew up. He said he was interested in astronomy and had given a four-hour lecture on the subject in eighth grade. The psychiatrist wanted to know more about the lecture, but John explained that the science behind it was "quite difficult." John then asked the doctor to name the nine planets in the solar system. The psychiatrist was unable to do so, even after being prompted with a hint that one was named after the Greek god of the sea. John quickly became uncomfortable in the interview and began drawing spaceships. After he had been at the center for several months, a resident coordinator asked John how he was doing. "Lots of children want to play outside while I want to play inside," he said. "They know pretty much about cowboys. I know about astronomy. We could know a little about each, but that has actually never been solved." When members of the staff tried to involve John in games, he would slip off to the showers to deliver talks on "the mysteries of the planets" that were eagerly attended by the younger children. The staff considered John a conduct problem.

Robinson and Vitale noted that children like Tom and John were routinely diagnosed with schizophrenia, but they pointed out that such children "call to mind the syndrome described by Kanner under the designation of 'Early Infantile Autism,'" with certain differences. Unlike the Tripletts and the Muncies, the parents of these children felt that they were "normal babies" for the first years of their lives; only as they grew older and failed to make friends their own age (preferring to hang around adults) did their eccentricities become clear. They were capable of "good emotional responsiveness" to other people, but tended to be consumed with their special interests to the exclusion of more social activities. Robinson and Vitale made the interesting observation that the pursuit of these interests did not seem to be motivated by a craving for approval and reinforcement from others, but were driven by a feeling of "satisfaction from within the child." They enjoyed learning for its own sake, as Asperger had observed a decade earlier.

Furthermore, unlike Kanner's patients, they had no delays in acquiring language and did not speak in surreal aphorisms, opaque neologisms, or echolalic references to themselves in the third person. In fact, they tended to be precociously articulate—particularly when they were expounding on the subjects that fascinated them. ("One 13-year-old boy, after a brief acquaintance, wanted to talk about mortgages," they reported.) These children only decisively withdrew from interactions with adults at the center when they figured out that they weren't really interested in what they were saying.

In an afterword, Kanner insisted that the difference between the children Robinson and Vitale described and those with his syndrome was that "in the autistic group, the circumscribed interest has often been foisted on them by their parents." He cited a paper in a German journal on a large group of children in Tel Aviv who "were addicted to voracious reading to the exclusion of other interests and activities," and attributed their disinterest in social interaction to "maternal overprotection." It was another closed loop: if children came up with special interests on their own instead of being "stuffed" by their parents, they couldn't be truly autistic—QED.

That same year, after a particularly disheartening roundtable on childhood schizophrenia in Cleveland, Georg Frankl tried to explain to his colleagues what had been forgotten in the endless debates about clinical nomenclature and toxic parenting. In a draft for a paper he never published, "Autism in Childhood: An Attempt of an Analysis," he described a "brilliant autistic child prodigy," an adult "schizoid genius," and a child who abruptly stopped speaking when he was two, saying that "a continuum seems to stretch out" between all three cases. "We know of this continuum, and we can point out a few of its common characteristics," he said; "however, most of the research in this area is still to be done."

ANOTHER TWENTY-FIVE YEARS would pass before it could even get started. During that time, a consensus developed among autism researchers that the reason Kanner never discussed Asperger's work was that the two men had described two very different groups of children—one "high-functioning" (Asperger) and the other "low-functioning" (Kanner). Though Asperger had made clear that he had seen children (as well as adults) at all levels of ability his paper had not yet been translated into English, and the fact that he had intentionally highlighted his "most promising" cases to deflect the wrath of the Nazis was still unknown.

By 1955, however, Kanner was finally beginning to see the extent of variation in the continuum for himself by following up on his original patients. Even "low-functioning" children could grow up to become "high-functioning" adults, but only if they managed to stay out of an institution and were given a chance to develop their innate gifts—just as Asperger had predicted back in 1938.

One of Kanner's patients, Robert S., had "unquestionably" shown the characteristic signs of early infantile autism at age eight. By twenty-three, however, he had served two years in the Navy as a meteorologist, was studying musical composition, and was happily married with a son. "Some of his works have been performed by chamber orchestras," Kanner reported, kvelling like a proud father. His description of another boy could have been lifted directly from Asperger's files:

> Jay S., now almost 15 years old, presented in the lower grades considerable difficulties to his teachers, who were exceptionally understanding and accepting. He wandered about the classroom, masturbated openly, and staged temper tantrums. He learned to conform, did phenomenally well in mathematics, was sent to an accelerated school, and is now finishing the eleventh grade with top marks. He is a peculiar child, rather obese, who spends his spare time collecting maps and postage stamps and has little more to do with people than is absolutely necessary for the maintenance of a superficial relationship. He achieved a Binet IQ of not less than 150.

A third boy had earned a scholarship to Columbia, where he "excelled in mathematical physics." Tragically, his life was cut short when he was run over by a car while crossing Broadway in New York City.

Donald T. was also doing very well by that point. In 1942, the Tripletts sent him to live on a farm ten miles from their home, where he thrived under the care of a compassionate couple named Mr. and Mrs. Lewis. Three years later, Kanner took a trip from Maryland to Mississippi to visit the farm.

> I was amazed at the wisdom of the couple who took care of him . . . They made him use his preoccupation with measurements by having him dig a well and report on its depth. When he kept collecting dead birds and bugs, they gave him a spot for a "graveyard" and had him put up markers; on each he wrote a first name, a type of animal as a middle name,

> and the farmer's last name, e.g., "John Snail Lewis. Born, date unknown. Died (date on which he found the animal)." When he kept counting rows of corn over and over, they had him count the rows while plowing them . . . It was remarkable how well he handled the horse and plow and turned the horse around. It was obvious that Mr. and Mrs. Lewis were very fond of him and just as obvious that they were gently firm. He attended a country school where his peculiarities were accepted and where he made good scholastic progress.

As Asperger's team had done for their own patients, the Lewises had found ways for Donald to put his autistic intelligence to work, rather than treating his passions for counting and collecting as pathological obsessions inflicted on him by his parents. "If one factor is significantly useful, it is a sympathetic and tolerant reception by the school," Kanner concluded. "Those of our children who have improved have been extended extraordinary consideration by their teachers."

By 1958, Donald had earned a bachelor's degree in French and taken a job as a teller at a local bank, where he "meets the public real well," his mother reported. He was playing golf four or five days a week at a country club and had earned six trophies in local tournaments. He was active in an investor's club, the Jaycees, and his Presbyterian church, having served a term as president of the local Kiwanis Club. He owned two cars, enjoyed reading and listening to his record player, and played bridge (though he rarely initiated games). His mother's main complaint was that she wished she knew what her son's "inner feelings really are."

But there were also cautionary tales in Kanner's follow-ups about what could happen to a child who ended up in custodial care. Elaine C. did well for a few years in private school. Her father reported "rather amazing changes," describing her as a "tall, husky girl with clear eyes" who "speaks well on almost any subject," drawing from a "range of information" that was "really quite wide" with an "almost infallible" memory. But he was still unnerved by her "rambling" conversations ("frequently with an amusing point"), her "odd intonation," and her lack of "proper emphases" in speech, so he committed her to the Letchworth Village State School for the Epileptic and Feebleminded outside New York City. There, she rapidly declined, becoming "distractible" and "assaultive," and speaking in an "irrational manner with a flat affect." She ran through the wards naked, growling like an animal and banging her head against the walls.

Though Letchworth was promoted to families as a progressive and humane institution, behind its ivy-covered façade it was Bedlam for children. By the 1950s, when Elaine was placed there, four thousand boys and girls were crowded into joyless dormitories built for twelve hundred patients. A photograph of the residents dressed up for a Christmas play looks like a macabre tableau from the art of Edward Gorey. The gruesome conditions there were finally exposed to the public in the same TV broadcast by Geraldo Rivera in 1972 that revealed equally appalling conditions at Willowbrook, a state-run institution on Staten Island. After a public outcry, both facilities were shut down. For Elaine, it was too late. She lasted six months at Letchworth before being transferred to the Hudson Valley State Hospital, where she was fed a stew of tranquilizers, antipsychotics, and other drugs. The staff described her at age thirty-nine as unable to "participate in conversation except for the immediate needs."

A similarly tragic fate befell Virginia S., the tidy eleven-year-old in Kanner's original group. By 1970, she too had been confined to a state hospital—a former home for tuberculosis patients in Maryland—where she was warehoused on a ward for "adult retardates." The staff there reported that she could tell time and "care for her basic needs, but has to be told to do so." At least her caretakers no longer assumed that she was deaf: she could clearly understand what was being said to her and used "noises and gestures" to communicate. At forty, she spent her days assembling jigsaw puzzles, as she had done as a little girl. The staff noted that she chose "to keep to herself rather than associate with the other residents."

"One cannot help but gain the impression that State Hospital admission was tantamount to a life sentence," Kanner reasonably concluded. Even the precocious skills and abilities of his former patients withered in such settings.

> Richard M., Barbara K., Virginia S., and Charles N. (Cases 3, 5, 6, and 9), who spent most of their lives in institutional care, have all lost their luster early after their admission. Originally fighting for their aloneness and basking in the contentment that it gave them, originally alert to unwelcome changes and, in their own way, struggling for the status quo, originally astounding the observer with their phenomenal feats of memory, they yielded readily to the uninterrupted self-isolation and soon settled down in a life not too remote from a nirvana-like existence. If at all responsive to psychological testing, their IQ's dropped down to figures usually referred to as low-grade moron or imbecile.

The dramatic differences in the life courses of his patients finally led Kanner to question his belief that his syndrome was narrowly defined and monolithic. "It is well known in medicine that any illness may appear in different degrees of severity, all the way from the so-called *forme fruste* to the most fulminant manifestation," he wrote in 1971. "Does this possibly apply also to early infantile autism?"

It was a question Georg Frankl could have answered in the affirmative in 1938. But Kanner seemed resistant to ceding an inch of his authority to his Viennese counterparts, even if it meant consigning his former assistant to historical oblivion. When Kanner became the editor of a new quarterly called the *Journal of Autism and Childhood Schizophrenia* in 1971, the premiere issue featured an article by Dutch psychiatrist Dirk Arn Van Krevelen that reaffirmed his myth of serendipity:

> New discoveries are period-bound rather than time-bound; they often emerge at the same time in different geographic sections. The history of autism offers a striking example. Kanner in Baltimore published his paper on inborn disturbances of effective contact in 1943, referring to a group of patients which had come to his attention during the preceding

> 5 years. One year later, the Viennese pediatrician Asperger reported a number of children as autistic psychopaths. We can take it for granted that neither was then aware of the other's work.

A few months later, Kanner mentioned Asperger's name in print for the first and last time, in a magisterially disdainful review of a book called *The Autistic Child* by pediatrician Isaac Newton Kugelmass. For daring to credit Asperger (misspelled "Ansperger") for independently confirming Kanner's discovery, Kugelmass reaped a whirlwind from Baltimore. Calling the book a "laborious enterprise," Kanner dispatched the potential competition in a single withering sentence cast in the third person:

> The name is Asperger, and the man, at that time, could have no knowledge of Kanner's publication; instead, he independently described what he called "autistic psychopathy," which, if at all related to infantile autism, is at best a 42nd cousin which merits, and has received, serious attention from investigators.

In fact, Asperger's work was still virtually unknown in America, primarily because Kanner never mentioned it in his papers and lectures. Because the two men's conceptions of autism were so different, there was much more at stake than the usual inside-baseball priority dispute. From the top of his pyramid at the Harriet Lane, Kanner declared in 1957 that he had seen only 150 true cases of autism in his entire career, or eight patients a year, while fielding referrals from as far away as South Africa. He also told researcher Bernard Rimland that he turned away nine out of ten children referred to his office as "autistic" by other clinicians without an autism diagnosis.

In real-world terms, being locked out of a diagnosis often meant being denied access to an education, speech and occupational therapy, counseling, medication, and other forms of support. For undiagnosed adults, Kanner's insistence that autism was a disorder of early infancy meant decades of wandering in the wilderness, with no explanation for constant struggles in employment, dating, friendships, and simply navigating the chaos of daily life.

While the psychiatric establishment was debating theories of toxic parenting and childhood psychosis, however, Asperger's lost tribe was putting its autistic intelligence to work by building the foundations of a society better suited to its needs and interests. Like Henry Cavendish, they refused to accept their circumstances as given. By coming up with ways of socializing on their own terms, they sketched out a blueprint for the modern networked world.

Six

PRINCES OF THE AIR

> Write me a creature that thinks as well as a man, or better than a man, but not like a man.
>
> —John W. Campbell

The curious fascination that many autistic people have for quantifiable data, highly organized systems, and complex machines runs like a half-hidden thread through the fabric of autism research—from Asperger's teenage scientist stealing chemicals for his home experiments, to Donald T.'s preoccupation with measurement, to A.D.'s habit of calculating the number of people attending a theatrical performance. Asperger may have been the first clinician to notice that his patients' imaginations occasionally *anticipated* developments in science by decades, forcing him to amend his statement that the interests of his little professors were "remote" from real-world concerns. But his joking suggestion that the designers of spaceships themselves must be autistic also turned out to be prescient.

Tommy the Space Child was not the only member of Asperger's forgotten tribe to turn his youthful obsession with science fiction into a career in science. For many people on the spectrum in the years when they were still invisible to medicine, science fiction fandom provided a community where they finally felt like savvy natives after years of being bullied and abused by their peers for seeming naïve, awkward, and clueless. Another community that enabled autistic people to make the most of their natural strengths in the early and mid-twentieth century was amateur radio. By routing around the face-to-face interactions they found so daunting, even people who found it nearly impossible to communicate through speech were able to reach out to kindred spirits, find potential mentors, and gain the skills and confidence they needed to become productive members of society.

Amazingly, both of these communities were launched by the same man who was likely on the autism spectrum himself: a visionary entrepreneur named Hugo Gernsback, who foresaw the decentralized, intimately interconnected nature of twenty-first-century society before nearly anyone else with the help of his equally eccentric friend, the prolific inventor Nikola Tesla. Along the way, Gernsback and Tesla anticipated the development of television, online news, computerized dating services, videophones, and many other conveniences that we take for granted a century later.

Born Hugo Gernsbacher in 1884, Gernsback was the son of a Jewish wine merchant in Luxembourg. He became fascinated by electricity on his eighth birthday when the handyman on his father's estate made him a gift of an electric bell, a wet-cell battery, and a length of wire. When he hooked up the wire to the electrodes of the battery, the bell rang amid a shower of sparks; he was immediately hooked. Young Hugo sent away to Paris for some lightbulbs and battery-powered telephones and wired the family house for electricity. He also started working to improve battery design by developing dry cells with solid electrolyte cores, which had the virtue of being portable, because they didn't contain corrosive liquid that could slosh and spill. Though he was still in grade school, he had already pinpointed one of the factors holding back the widespread adoption of portable electronic devices.

Two years later, while attending technical classes at the Ecole Industrielle, he had another life-changing experience: reading a translation of a book by the American astronomer Percival Lowell called *Mars as the Abode of Life*. A provocative fusion of planetology and evolutionary theory, the book was illustrated with the eminent astronomer's own sketches. Lowell risked the ridicule of his colleagues by venturing that traces of water would someday be discovered on our rust-colored neighbor in the solar system (a prediction confirmed in 2009 by the Phoenix Mars Lander). He further theorized that intelligent life had arisen there, and that the extreme conditions on the planet—its vast Saharas of dust with seasonal concentrations of ice at the poles—had practically required the natives to develop a sophisticated system of aqueducts controlled by a global data infrastructure to provide them with drinkable water year-round.

Lowell speculated that the cross-hatching of lines on the planet's surface first spotted by Giovanni Schiaparelli in 1877 (which looked "to have been laid down by rule and compass," as the Italian astronomer put it) was an intricate system of canals connecting a network of artificial oases where the inhabitants of the planet had sought shelter from the desiccating Martian winds. He then declared that these crafty creatures were likely "of an order whose acquaintance was worth the making"—*if* we could develop the technological know-how to communicate with them. The book had a decisive, even devastating impact on the future entrepreneur. As historian Sam Moskowitz put it:

> The concept that intelligent life might exist on other worlds had never occurred to young Hugo . . . he lapsed into delirium, raving about strange creatures, fantastic cities, and masterly engineered canals of Mars for two full days and nights while the doctor remained in almost constant attendance. The direction of Hugo Gernsback's future thinking was greatly conditioned by that experience. He was never to be content with the accumulated scientific knowledge of his day. Now he was to search the libraries for books that opened up imaginative vistas beyond the scientific knowledge of the period.

While refining his battery designs, Gernsbacher immersed himself in gripping adventure tales by Jules Verne and H. G. Wells. At thirteen, the precocious boy installed an intercom system in a local Carmelite convent. Such an amenity was unheard-of in most private homes at the time, much less in nunneries; he was awarded a special dispensation from Pope Leo XIII to visit the sisters once a year so he could keep his system in good working order, along with a certificate from the Mother Superior praising him as a "budding electrician."

Despite this early recognition from his elders, Gernsbacher felt like an outsider in society. At seventeen, he wrote a sixty-thousand-word novel called *Ein Pechvogel* (basically, "A Jinxed Person" or "A Schlemiel") about a hapless, unworldly boy whose obsessive tinkering—which included an attempt to use solar energy to roast coffee beans—constantly got him in trouble.

But he also learned in a very dramatic way that he could employ his specialized knowledge to get *out* of trouble. One icy-cold winter's day when his parents were on vacation, he was exploring an empty cellar when a gust of wind blew the door shut behind him. The only window in the cellar was open but barred from the outside, putting him in danger of freezing to death. Fortunately, he had brought along a lantern powered by two dry-cell batteries. He extracted a thin copper wire from the lantern and used it to short-circuit the cells, making the wire white-hot. He then touched it to a piece of paper, which burst into flames. Then he used the smoldering paper to start a fire of scrap wood and burned down the cellar door so he could make his escape. Science!

After Gernsbacher's father died in 1903, the quaint charms of old Luxembourg couldn't hold him for very long. He borrowed $100 from the family fortune and boarded a steamship from Hamburg to Hoboken, drawn to the United States by the wit of Mark Twain, the martial music of John Philip Sousa, and the notion that America was a place where an industrious young inventor could reinvent himself. Upon disembarking, he spent $20 of the $100 in his wallet on a silk hat so he would look appropriately distinguished and ordered a stack of business cards billing himself as "Huck" Gernsback after the hero of Twain's picaresque odyssey down the Mississippi River. To obtain parts for his battery business, he launched a venture called the Electro Importing Company, the first mail-order supplier for home electronics buffs in the country. At age nineteen, he was already managing two startups.

In addition to his technical prowess, Gernsback was also a genius at marketing. Instead of dumping the contents of Electro Importing's vast catalog onto the market as a jumble of geeky gadgets, Gernsback framed them as hip accessories for a twentieth-century lifestyle based on scientific discovery and excitement. "This machine will give you more amusement than anything you have ever had," promised an ad for an electrostatic generator. "Charges leyden jars, fires powder, works Wireless Stations, raises a person's hair, etc." This kind of branding proved to be catnip for nerdy outcasts, who became heroic young "experimenters" in the pages of his catalogs.

Opening a retail store at the bustling intersection of Wall Street and Broadway, Gernsback displayed a precocious knack for salesmanship by offering ten-cent crystal detectors that could pick up any radio signals in the area. Soon he was selling a thousand a day and could barely keep up with the demand.

These simple semiconductor devices were only an enticement—a "come-along"—for the real product: the first radio transmitter and receiver kit designed for amateurs, the Telimco Wireless Telegraph. (A Telimco now resides at the Henry Ford Museum in Dearborn, Michigan.) The company reps, dressed dapperly in high, stiff collars and derby hats, were so adept at getting young stockbrokers on their lunch breaks excited about wireless—price for the whole outfit, $7.50, instead of the $50,000 cost of a standard commercial rig—that the mayor of New York banned the exhibitions that drew huge crowds to the shop. A policeman burst into Gernsback's office on Park Place one day to investigate a complaint that his company was flogging a device that couldn't possibly work at the advertised price. A simple demonstration was enough to avert legal action, but the cop remained skeptical. "I still think you're fakers," he snarled, glancing suspiciously around the room. "Your ad says it's a wireless set. Then what are all these wires for?"

The first version of the Telimco was relatively primitive, though it was still the most advanced radio available to amateurs at the time. It enabled an amateur radio operator (commonly known as a "ham") to transmit and receive snippets of Morse code (no voice signals yet) over a range of a mile.

But the notion of communicating at a distance, with no visible connection, was so magical that Gernsback's kits flew off the shelves, not only at his shop but also at department stores like Macy's, Gimbels, and Marshall Field's. "We feel sure," he exulted in an early catalog, "that every wide-awake American boy and every young man will feel the necessity of procuring one of these outfits, because he fully realizes that wireless telegraphy will play a very important role in the business world in the immediate future." This future was getting more immediate every day, Gernsback believed, precisely because amateur demand was now helping to drive the development of the technology. Within a year, the Telimco would transmit and receive voice signals as well as dots and dashes.

As Gernsback became wealthy, he cultivated the air of a bon vivant, packaging himself as adroitly as he packaged his crystal sets by dressing in bespoke suits and silk ties. But he inevitably struck people as odd, rude, self-centered, and even callous. On train trips to Chicago to pick up parts for his company, he would stop off in Cleveland to visit his seven-year-old cousin, Hildegarde. The entrepreneur would terrify the girl by launching into windy soliloquies about a society in which domed cities in orbit, robot doctors, and retirement colonies on Mars were commonplace. (Meanwhile, horse-drawn carts were still plying the streets outside.) If a ringing telephone interrupted him in midreverie, he would raise an admonishing finger and say to his cousin in his bristling Germanic accent, "Hildegarde, *fix your hair.* It won't be long before the caller can see your face over the wires."

II

The incident with the skeptical policeman stuck in Gernsback's craw for a long time. "It rankled me that there could be such ignorance in regard to science," he told an audience of hams and engineers in Michigan fifty years later. "I vowed to change the situation if I could." He came up with a plan to educate the next generation of scientists in a way that would also give him a powerful vehicle for promoting his business. He would launch the first magazine for ham radio operators.

To open the bright red and orange cover of *Modern Electrics*, which appeared on newsstands in 1908, was to enter a world where the marvels of the future could be soldered together in a garage from off-the-shelf parts (available, of course, from the Electro Importing Company). More staid publications like *Scientific American* targeted scientists and inventors by running news blips from the U.S. Patent Office, but Gernsback pitched his magazine to a much broader readership of aspiring boy geniuses and weekend tinkerers. Its motto—"The Electrical Magazine for Everybody"—anticipated Apple's populist tagline for the Macintosh, "Computing for the rest of us," by eighty years. Like Steve Jobs, Gernsback didn't just dominate markets; he invented them.

With a curious amalgam of whiz-bang enthusiasm and *mitteleuropäische* sophistication, *Modern Electrics* embraced a wide range of innovations beyond amateur radio, featuring articles, editorials, and special issues on airships, electronic photography, radiotelegraphy, model railroading, and a proto-Internet scheme for "typewriting by wire."

The December 1909 issue was devoted to a technology then still in its experimental infancy: television. Gernsback's international network of correspondents also tackled such far-out subjects as the potential for harnessing tides and sunlight as limitless sources of power, and investigating whether radio signals affected the navigational abilities of homing pigeons.

The magazine also ran a monthly photo contest for the subscriber who built the coolest wireless rig, making membership in a clued-in community part of the "product" that Gernsback was selling. It was the perfect approach for the kind of reader who was likely to be tinkering with electrostatic generators and Leyden jars alone in his basement rather than out carousing with his friends.

THE FOLLOWING APRIL, Gernsback took the magazine in a bold new direction—from merely speculating about the technology of the future to imagining it out of whole cloth. The cryptic string of characters on the cover—*Ralph 124C 41+*—marked the editor in chief's debut as a novelist. Standing on the shoulders of his heroes Wells and Verne, he inaugurated a genre of popular storytelling that blended hard science and speculative fiction, with a strong emphasis on gadgetry. He christened this genre "scientifiction," even taking out a patent on the awkward term, which was quickly superseded by "science fiction."

Ralph 124C 41+ anticipated a broad swath of technological marvels, including TV, radar, fluorescent lighting, stainless steel, videophones, night baseball games, speech-to-text software, and continuously updated news. (It also predicted the development of aspects of the future that haven't arrived yet, including wireless power transmission, a "Menograph" to transcribe thoughts, and electronic weather control.) Its wonky title was Gernsback's orthographic pun on his idea of the author of scientifiction as a cultural prophet: "One to foresee for more than one."

If his prophecies were unusually accurate, it was because he befriended someone already living in the future: Nikola Tesla, the brilliant Serbian inventor whose wireless experiments preceded those of the "father of radio," Guglielmo Marconi. A former lab assistant of Thomas Edison's, Tesla did trailblazing research in an astonishing array of fields, including robotics, home lighting, X-rays, proto-transistors, remote control, and alternating current. Tesla even predicted the chilling face of twenty-first-century warfare—semiautonomous drones, which he called Telautomata.

"When wireless is perfectly applied, the whole earth will be converted into a huge brain," Tesla told an interviewer in 1926. "We shall be able to communicate with one another instantly, irrespective of distance. Not only this, but through television and telephony we shall see and hear one another as perfectly as though we were face to face, despite intervening distances of thousands of miles; and the instruments through which we shall be able to do this will be amazingly simple compared with our present telephone. A man will be able to carry one in his vest pocket. We shall be able to witness and hear events—the inauguration of a President, the playing of a World Series game, the havoc of an earthquake or the terror of a battle—

just as though we were present." Gernsback, who was twenty-eight years younger, became Tesla's most prominent advocate. The first theme issue of *Modern Electrics* was wholly devoted to his work.

Whatever Tesla was, the word *typical* didn't describe him. Eccentric genius ran in his family: his mother was an expert weaver from a long line of inventors who designed her own sewing tools. His older brother was a child prodigy who died when Tesla spooked the horse he was riding, causing lifelong feelings of guilt. The future inventor suffered from a "peculiar affliction" as a boy that would likely now be diagnosed as epilepsy, marked by visions of "strong flashes of light" and elaborate hallucinations. Like Asperger's little professors, he could be honest to a fault, as when his two elderly aunts asked him to choose which one was prettier and he replied that one was "not as ugly as the other." He felt compelled to calculate the precise volume of coffee cups, soup bowls, and morsels of food at the table, and counted the exact number of steps he took when he went out for a walk. (Like Cavendish and Dirac, he developed the habit of taking extended perambulations on a rigid timetable, covering eight to ten miles every day in Manhattan.) As a teenager, Tesla developed rigid habits and aversions, along with a fascination for certain shapes. The mere sight of a pearl made him feel ill, but the glittering of objects with flat surfaces mesmerized him.

He embarked on his career as an inventor when he discovered that he could visualize theoretical machines in minute detail and even set them running in his mind, tweaking his design as parts wore out. "I needed no models, drawings, or experiments," Tesla recalled in his memoir, which was published by Gernsback. "I could picture them all as real . . . It is absolutely immaterial to me whether I run my turbine in thought or test it in my shop. I even note if it is out of balance. There is no difference whatever, the results are the same." (Temple Grandin's account of her own design process is virtually identical: "Before I attempt any construction, I test-run the equipment in my imagination. I visualize my designs being used in every possible situation, with different sizes and breeds of cattle and in different weather conditions. Doing this enables me to correct mistakes before construction.") Together, the inventor and editor forged a mutually beneficial alliance.

But as prescient as Gernsback was about technology, spinning out a believable love story was beyond his powers. Throughout *Ralph 124C 41+*, the eponymous hero (not coincidentally, a reclusive "great American inventor") and his muse, a Swiss ham radio operator named Alice 212B423, address one another as if they're reading from technical manuals, complete with an abundance of brand names and calculations carried to several decimal places. "Both the Power mast and the Communico mast were blown down the same day, and I was left without any means of communication whatsoever," Alice informs Ralph when they meet by chance owing to the equivalent of a Skype glitch. Ralph then rescues Alice by remotely directing his microwave beams to melt an onrushing avalanche. *Vive l'amour!*

Though Gernsback's own attempts to write fiction were invariably clunky and stiff, he was brilliant at fostering the formation of communities of shared interest. He began publishing his subscribers' names, radio call numbers, and addresses in a wireless registry that appeared at the back of *Modern Electrics*, and in three years, his circulation base soared from eight thousand to fifty-two thousand. By creating a decentralized network of radio enthusiasts who could get in touch with one another directly over the airwaves or by mail, he provided his magazines and gadgets with an ever-expanding market. This community would also prove indispensable once federal bureaucrats began making moves to regulate the airwaves in favor of military communications and commercial broadcasters.

In the mid-1920s, Gernsback turned his full attention to growing the market for science fiction. He started running ads announcing the launch of a new publication devoted to the genre to be called *Amazing Stories*. He also came up with a reliable formula for making his new publication popular with his target demographic, with lurid cover art depicting avenging aliens, marauding robots, giant insects, and scantily clad women perpetually at their mercy. *Amazing Stories* represented not just the emergence of a form of popular literature but the dawn of a new sensibility, embodied by coolly rational, sardonic, tech-savvy heroes of the type later to be played with consummate flair by Harrison Ford and Patrick Stewart (and all too rarely by strong women like Sigourney Weaver and Kate Mulgrew). The bold tagline—"Extravagant Fiction Today, Cold Fact Tomorrow"—practically dared its readers to build labs in their garages and help invent the marvelous future.

Within a decade, bookstore shelves and drugstore racks all over the United States and Europe were bulging with knockoff titles like *Air Wonder Stories*, *Science Wonder Quarterly*, and *Astounding Stories of Super-Science*. Printed on coarse, untrimmed wood-pulp pages, these affordable gateways to awe and mystery (cover price, ten cents) became collectively known as *the pulps*.

THE CONTEMPORARY CULTURE OF fandom in America—the whole thriving multiverse of Trekkers, Whovians, Twihards, and Potterheads—had its humble beginnings in the letters-to-the-editor column of *Amazing Stories*. There, Gernsback carried on the tradition of his wireless registry by printing his readers' names and addresses along with their letters. The exchanges in this column were often more sophisticated than the stories around them. There was more fervent discussion of Einstein's theory of relativity in the letters column of *Amazing Stories* than in mainstream science journals.

Soon pulp fans everywhere started compiling networks of pen pals, which led to the formation of organizations like the Science Correspondents Club in Chicago and the Scienceers, a group of New York City teens who met in the Harlem apartment of its first president, an African American space buff named Warren Fitzgerald, encouraged by one of Gernsback's editors. Using early methods of duplication like mimeography and hectography, these groups churned out their own hand-stapled publications with names like *The Comet* and *The Planet*—the first "fanzines" in history.

Pulp devotees did not invent the word *fan* (derived from the Latin *fanaticus*, "possessed by divine madness"), but they established the first fandom in the modern sense, with its own elaborate customs, art forms, specialized jargon, conventions, and absurdly bombastic internecine warfare. (Sam Moskowitz's 1954 chronicle of the early days of fandom, *The Immortal Storm*, inspired one critic to quip, "If read directly after a history of World War II, it does not seem like an anticlimax.") This fractious and fertile milieu nurtured the careers of many writers who went on to mainstream fame, including film critic Roger Ebert and screenwriter Leigh Brackett, celebrated for her work on *The Big Sleep*, *The Long Goodbye*, and *The Empire Strikes Back*. Other fans became science fiction immortals themselves, including Ray Bradbury, Isaac Asimov, Frederick Pohl, and Ursula K. LeGuin.

Most importantly, magazines like *Amazing Stories* and *Weird Tales* fired up the imaginations of those who turned the extravagant visions of their favorite authors into cold fact. The original members of the British Interplanetary Society, founded in 1933 to promote space exploration, were avid readers of the pulps. Arthur C. Clarke observed in 1948 that many American scientists were also fervent fans, and that "aeronautics would never have reached the stage it has now if it wasn't for science fiction, which has done much to break down the psychological barriers that retard our progress." Clarke himself circulated copies of *Thrilling Wonder Stories*, another title on Gernsback's ever-expanding roster, at the Cavendish Laboratory in Cambridge.

Darko Suvin, a leading scholar of the genre, described the subversive impulse at the heart of science fiction as an expression of "cognitive estrangement" from the mainstream. Fandom tapped into a deep yearning to rise above the circumstances of humdrum existence and become part of something noble, deeply informed, and not widely understood. The thrill of being part of something that few people could appreciate was particularly keen for those who had spent their lives being ridiculed. No one could make you a fan—or prevent you from being one—but yourself, and no one could judge you but your peers of choice: your fellow "fen." Early fans indulged these newfound feelings of confidence and superiority to the hilt, referring to the clueless nonfans who ran the world as "mundanes."

Unlike cult followings based on sports teams or rock stars, science fiction fandom was rooted in an essentially solitary activity: reading. Traits typically viewed as pathological or pathetic in the mainstream (like obsessing over trivia while accumulating vast hoards of treasured ephemera) were rewarded in the community as signs of "trufan" commitment. Fandom offered what every homesick space child yearned for: membership in an elite society of loners united by their belief in the future. For those who had felt like exiles their whole lives, forced to live among strangers, becoming a fan was like finally coming home.

III

As an editor, Gernsback was primarily a hardware man. He favored galactic potboilers crammed with fantastic gizmos, cunning contraptions, and diabolical engines of mayhem (death rays were a perennial favorite). Subtler masters of the art later ridiculed his school of the genre—in which technology took precedence over psychology, and plot and character were secondary to product placement—as "gadget fiction." Reading it, one learned a lot about the tools of the future but very little about the people who used them. Nuances of interpersonal interaction were irrelevant, women existed as hapless props to be rescued, and heroes were monastically chaste. The real protagonist of scientifiction was science itself, conquering the dark forces of irrationality and ignorance.

You could thumb through a dozen of Gernsback's titles at the drugstore and not discover that there was a Great Depression or Dust Bowl going on. When a reader objected to *Wonder Stories* publishing translations from the German as Hitler rose to power, Gernsback (or one of his editors) sniffed that the magazine remained "perfectly neutral" on the subject: "What the leader of Germany does to or for the Germans is for the Germans to think about."

In 1940, a Canadian defense specialist named A. E. van Vogt published a serial called *Slan* in *Astounding Science Fiction* that raised the bar for the whole genre by taking the theme of cognitive estrangement to the next level, helping to inaugurate what historians call the golden age of science fiction.

Published in three parts, it was the story of a race of humanoids—the "Slans" of the title—who had been genetically engineered to handle the accelerated pace of mechanized civilization. This race of elegant mutants was the creation of a twenty-first-century biologist named Samuel Lann, who began his project by experimenting on his own children. The conceptual breakthrough of *Slan* was portraying "normal" human beings not as saviors but as the enemy.

As the story opens, the book's genetically modified protagonist, Jommy Cross, and his kind are being hunted to extinction in the decaying streets of a sprawling megacity called Centropolis. Jommy's mother is forced to sacrifice her own life so that Jommy may live; with the help of a crafty old homeless woman, the boy takes shelter in an underground society surviving in the nooks and crannies of the urban landscape.

Reprinted as a stand-alone novel after World War II, *Slan* caused a sensation. Its tropes echo through later generations of science fiction: the political machinations in *Dune*, *Star Trek*'s half-Betazoid counselor Deanna Troi, the hunt for rogue replicants in *Blade Runner*, the mutant superpowers of the X-Men. For first-generation fans, *Slan* had special resonance, because they saw a reflection of their own predicament in this tale of superintelligent, supersensitive, and profoundly misunderstood mutants struggling to survive in a world not built for them. No one carried this notion further than one of the most outrageous fans that ever lived, a renegade space child named Claude Degler.

Degler's background, like every other aspect of his life, was shrouded in the mists of his own hyperbole. According to a dossier compiled by the first historian of fandom, a lawyer named Jack Speer, Degler was born in Missouri in 1920. Shortly thereafter, his father left the family, and young

Claude and his mother moved to Indiana. Like Gernsback, he was obsessed with electricity at a very young age and plunged into science fiction like a fish rediscovering the sea. He immersed himself in the pulps and signed up for the Buck Rogers Club—an early attempt to commercialize fandom that offered "ray repellent" rings in boxes of Cream of Wheat—but the neighborhood kids only taunted him for being such a nerd.

Precociously bright, Degler made the honor roll in high school, but when he was fifteen his anxiety, depression, and violent outbursts—exacerbated by constant bullying—resulted in his expulsion. His mother was advised to enroll him in a school for the feebleminded, but she refused. After he set fire to a county prosecutor's toolshed in 1936, however, she committed him to the Eastern Indiana Hospital for the Insane. The following year, his doctors issued a certificate mandating his forced sterilization, as he was likely to father "mentally incompetent" or "socially inadequate" children. Instead of going under the knife, Degler somehow got himself furloughed against his doctors' orders.

Then he read *Slan*. The book had an electrifying effect on Degler, and suddenly his true destiny became clear. He and his fellow fen were "star-begotten" mutants trapped behind enemy lines. Science fiction fandom was no mere diversion for daydreaming teenagers and egghead professors; it was the first stirrings of a geek uprising against the mundanes who had oppressed them for so long. He came up with a rallying cry that spread through fandom like a viral meme: "Fans are Slans!"

Degler set off on an epic coast-to-coast hitchhiking trip to raise the consciousness of his fellow "Cosmen" and "Coswomen," mining science club mailing lists for names of potential members of a vast network that he dubbed the Cosmic Circle. In 1941, he showed up in Denver at one of the first science fiction conventions, delivering a speech that he claimed had been written by Martians. He couch-surfed his way from Los Angeles to New York, designating fans to become officers of organizations like the Circle of Aztor, the Valdosta Philosophers, the Cosmic Thinkers, the Rose City Science Circle, the Florida Cosmos Society, the Dixie Fantasy Federation, the Empire State Slans, and the Muncie Mutants.

He also advocated the formation of all-fan households called *Slan shacks*, where his comrades could pursue their passions with minimal interference from pesky mundanes, and championed the launch of a Cosmic Camp in the Ozarks where virile Cosmen and fecund Coswomen could breed the next generation of genetically superior humanoids, complete with its own "laboratory-library" for housing vast collections of ephemera. "Fight to make the world safe for science fiction!" Degler cried in a fanzine called *Voice of the Imagi-Nation*, one of a dizzying array of publications that he contributed to in the 1940s.

His Cosmic Camp never got off the ground, but the first Slan shack—touted as "a fannish island in a sea of mundania"—was founded in Battle Creek, Michigan, in 1943. "Our planning included a fanzine room where all occupants would share access to a mimeo, and apartments with northern light for the artists," recalled Dalvan Coger, a former resident. Fans arrived from everywhere—by car, train, bus, and thumb—to savor "the feeling of closeness, of being able to be open in our ideas, that we as fans could express most easily in each other's company." A sign over the front door read simply, "Civilization."

Slan shacks with names like Oblique House, the Epicentre, Station X, the Ivory Birdbath, Prime Base, and Tendril Towers popped up all over the United States and the United Kingdom. A scheme was hatched to transform a whole city block of Los Angeles into a full-fledged Slan Center, complete with prefab housing units, hydroponic farms, and communal publishing facilities. Degler claimed that the owner of a large ranch in Arizona had granted the Cosmic Circle permission to initiate rocketry experiments there after the war, so that his star-begotten cohorts could get down to the business of turning extravagant fiction into cold fact. Ambitious projects like this, he promised, were just the beginning of a new intergalactic society: "Our children shall inherit not only this earth—but this universe! Today we carry 22 states, tomorrow, nine planets!"

Alas, the Los Angeles Slan Center never came to fruition. Degler himself proved to be fandom's most ephemeral shooting star, falling out of favor with his fellow fen when it became obvious that many of the organizations in the Cosmic Circle existed only in the universe of his brain. Even the slogan "Fans are Slans!" was eventually ridiculed as a self-parodic joke—a caricature of fandom at its most messianic and overwrought.

But there was more than a grain of truth in Degler's insistence that science fiction fans were mutants struggling to survive in the margins of a society that did not understand them. A significant minority of his fellow fen—including Gernsback—would likely have been eligible for a diagnosis of Asperger's syndrome had one been available, says prominent science fiction historian Gary Westfahl. For people on the autism spectrum before it had a name, he explains, the alternate universes of science fiction may have felt less alien than the baffling sea of mundania in which they found themselves marooned.

> Looking back at the science fiction of the 1930s pulp magazines, filled with lonely adventurers on solitary quests to distant planets and the far future, one can easily see how these stories would appeal to those young men (and some young women), then regarded only as "reclusive" or "eccentric," who we would now classify as undiagnosed cases of Asperger's Syndrome . . . to a teenager in the 1930s with Asperger's Syndrome, a story about an astronaut encountering aliens on Mars might have had an air of comforting familiarity, in contrast to stories set in the bizarre, inexplicable, and thoroughly socialized worlds of Andy Hardy and the Bobbsey Twins.

The colorful cast of characters in Harry Warner's *All Our Yesterdays*, an eyewitness account of nascent fandom, includes many fans, both male and female, who are described as "hermits," "extremely introverted," lacking in social graces, gifted but awkward, and focused on "fanac" ("fan activity") with a single-minded intensity that could easily be considered obsessive. In the 1940s, Jack Speer speculated that most fans were "handicapped" in some way that made it difficult for them to thrive in the mainstream world.

Many fans were also ham radio operators, and there was significant crossover between the two subcultures. If real Slans had existed in the early twentieth century, you might have expected to find them poring through Gernsback's catalogs, trying to piece together the technology of a more advanced civilization out of whatever crude equipment was available, like Mr. Spock assembling a communicator out of vacuum tubes in Edith Keeler's basement in a celebrated episode of the original *Star Trek* series.

The future couldn't arrive fast enough: a significant number of first-generation fans with keen interests in science and engineering ended up working in menial jobs because of their limited social skills. "Fans today can't imagine the threadbare existence of many fans of the 1930s and early '40s, riding the boxcars to Worldcons or rummaging through the trash behind hotels to recover copies of *Amazing Stories* discarded by departing patrons," wrote historian David B. Williams. "There's a reason fans were greyhound-thin in those days—food cost money."

Both amateur radio and science fiction fandom offered ways of gaining social recognition outside traditional channels. There was even a fannish word for the thrill of being respected by your peers for your contributions to the community: *egoboo.* For people who found open-ended conversations daunting, the byzantine customs and rituals of fandom furnished reassuring scripts for interaction. The elaborate jargon developed by fans in the early days (which one critic called "an addiction to obscure lingo for its own sake") was practically its own dialect and acted as a verbal force field that kept clueless mundanes at bay.

Obviously, fandom was a community that was unusually accepting of individual quirks and differences. The term *fanzine* was coined in 1940 by a deaf fan named Louis Russell Chauvenet, who was also a tournament-winning chess player and a computer technician for the Defense Department. Another fan who became a star writing for Gernsback, David Keller, was diagnosed as feebleminded as a child and spoke a private language understood only by his sister until he was six years old. One of Degler's companions on the road was a physically disabled man named Jim Kepner, who became one of the first openly gay journalists, encouraged by "reading and conjecturing about worlds in which customs might differ from ours." He went from obsessively hoarding issues of *Amazing Stories* and *Galaxy* to hunting down newsletters from pioneering gay groups like the Mattachine Society and the Daughters of Bilitis. Kepner's personal library now forms the core of ONE, the largest archive of gay history in the world, housed at the University of Southern California.

Gernsback biographer Gary Westfahl believes that it's "reasonable to assume" that the influential editor and entrepreneur was an undiagnosed Aspergian. His peers regarded him as an unsociable figure who remained coolly distant from the communities he created. The people he counted as friends tended to be prominent scientists, influential politicians, and other notable figures with whom he corresponded by mail; historian James Gunn observed in *Alternate Worlds* that he was "a strange mixture of personal reserve and aggressive salesmanship."

After Gernsback's first two marriages ended in divorce, he decided that the whole messy business of matrimony was crying out for a high-tech solution. To launch this massive undertaking, a team of scientists would first need to interview thousands of couples applying for marriage licenses to interrogate them about every aspect of their lives: their health histories, their aptitudes for music and art, the texture of their hair and skin, their favorite smells, the presence of hereditary diseases in their family lines, and a hundred other "vital aspects." Then his army of researchers would deploy an arsenal of diagnostic instruments (including electrocardiographs and lie detectors) to arrive at each person's "S.Q."—their Sexual Quotient. Once the fate of these initial couplings was ascertained, algorithms to maximize the chances of success would be fed into a computer. From that point on, fickle Cupid would yield to the unassailable objectivity of Big Data.

Gernsback was equally unsentimental about enforcing his editorial directives. "Short lines are easier to read than long ones," he advised potential contributors to his magazines. "This is due to a well-known optical law." His rejection slips listed thirty mistakes commonly made by writers, with a tick box next to each one including "plot stale" and "material offensive to moral standards." He demanded that all scientific theory in stories he published be verifiable—an insistence on literal accuracy dubbed "the Gernsback Delusion" by his stable of authors. He even applied this law to comics in the Sunday paper, fuming if he spotted an astronaut clad in an imperfectly sealed space suit.

Acutely sensitive to sound, he would withdraw to his sumptuously appointed "think room" in his West End Avenue penthouse to visualize the shape of things to come in uninterrupted silence and solitude. When he ventured out in public, he carried himself with "an air of ducal authority," holding forth in drafty perorations on his favorite subjects like "Bismarck directing the Congress of Berlin," noted a journalist who profiled him in *Life* magazine. He was equally imperious in exercising his dietary preferences. Arriving at one of the restaurants where he ate religiously (Delmonico's was a favorite), he would pop in a monocle and scrutinize the offerings du jour like a surgeon conducting a biopsy. He never hesitated to send a dish back to the kitchen that had been served on a plate he deemed insufficiently warmed, and he once dismissed three bottles of wine in one sitting. David Keller, who joined him for lunch at the Astor Hotel, recalled that the multimillionaire methodically ticked off the price of every item they ate, including the iced coffee (eighty-five cents).

Each weekday morning at precisely 8:30, he would arrive at his immaculate offices on West Fourteenth Street, doused in his favorite scent of toilet water and looking as though he were "carrying the world on his shoulders," a local store owner recalled. His telephone, desk set, thermos bottle, and office walls were all tinted the same shade of green (à la Cavendish's Bedford Street library), and at periodic intervals throughout the day, the dapper bow-tied editor would blow across his desk to keep it clear of offending soot. After Tesla died in 1943—impoverished and emaciated in his room at the Hotel New Yorker with a "do not disturb" sign permanently affixed to his door—Gernsback mounted his death mask in the corner of his office as a macabre tribute.

Though Gernsback's career as an inventor was overshadowed by his Serbian mentor's (whose wasn't?), he earned more than eighty patents in his lifetime, encompassing a range of innovations including the first walkie-talkie, one of the first bone-conduction hearing aids, a design for TV glasses (complete with a tiny aerial), and a submersible Ferris wheel.

But his most blatantly autistic creation was a contraption for reducing distracting sensory input in noisy offices called "the Isolator." The July 1925 issue of *Science and Invention* featured a surreal illustration of the editor modeling his creation, looking like a deep-sea diver in a particularly cumbersome helmet, complete with a private air supply furnished by a nearby tank. So the wearer could focus on a single line of text at a time, there were two slits drilled in the helmet. With "outside noises being eliminated," the caption advised, "the worker can concentrate with ease on the subject at hand."

Though his Isolator never caught on, Gernsback's amateur radio network turned out to be a boon for those most likely to yearn for such a device. One ham alone in a garage with a spark transmitter was a nerd—but a network of hams was a force to be reckoned with. By chaining stations together in relays, a Chicago amateur could "work" his equivalent in Christchurch, passing messages around the globe. Planet Earth suddenly became a very small and convivial place for a ham in a room with a couple of dry cells, a spark transmitter, a "cat's whisker" receiver, and a headset.

Wireless was not for everyone, Gernsback acknowledged—the learning curve was too steep for poor dullards who lacked what he called a "radio mind." A boy with such a mind (and it was nearly always a boy in his imagination, though not in reality) didn't have the same compulsion to waste time in foolish pursuits that other boys did; instead, he practically had to be forced to leave the house.

During World War II, the British spy agency MI8 secretly recruited a crew of teenage wireless operators (prohibited from discussing their activities even with their families) to intercept coded messages from the Nazis. By forwarding these transmissions to the crack team of code breakers at Bletchley Park led by the computer pioneer Alan Turing, these young hams enabled the Allies to accurately predict the movements of the German and Italian forces. Asperger's prediction that the little professors in his clinic could one day aid in the war effort had been prescient, but it was the Allies who reaped the benefits.

With the rise of wireless, the scattered members of his tribe finally had a way to become a collective force in the public sphere. Ham radio was an activity that rewarded fascination with apparatus, systems, and complex machines, and amateurs with keen memorization abilities had an advantage, because all hams in the United States were required to learn Morse code to earn their FCC licenses until 1990. With parts available by mail at reasonable prices from Gernsback and his competitors, it was an affordable hobby that could be pursued in solitude. Hams who struggled with spoken language could avoid talking altogether by communicating in code. (A photograph of an early gathering of hams shows two men sitting across a table from one another, communicating by tapping out dots and dashes on milk bottles with spoons.) But those who enjoyed gabbing away could "chew the rag" with other hams for hours, employing a lexicon as witty and ritualized as the jargon of fandom. The culture of wireless was also a strict meritocracy where no one cared about what you looked like or how gracefully you deported yourself in public. If you knew how to set up a rig and keep it running, you were welcome to join the party.

The bible of hams was a book called *Calling CQ* by an amateur named Clinton DeSoto. (The title was the phrase hams have used since the days of Marconi to invite any operator within earshot to reply.) His description of the ethos of amateur radio laid out a blueprint for a new kind of community that was ideally suited to mentoring gifted, socially awkward young people.

> The neophyte does not metamorphose easily into the full-fledged amateur. But when he does leave his chrysalis a new world is opened up to him. First he gets a new name—his radio call letters. Thenceforth he has a new identity—even a new personality and new social status. He is not known by the company he keeps nor by the clothes he wears, but by the signal he emits. He enters a new world whose qualifications for success are within his reach. Without a pedigree, a chauffeur, or an old master decorating his living room, he can become a prince—of the air.

One of the radio-minded boys who answered DeSoto's call—and would later be diagnosed with Asperger's syndrome—was Robert Hedin, who received the Rensselaer Medal as the outstanding math and science student in high school but never fit in with his peers. He was drawn to amateur radio, he says, because it offered "an opportunity for people who are less sociable to socialize with others in a nonthreatening way." It also furnished ways of receiving recognition for skills that came naturally to him, with global competitions for activities like "DXing" (making new contacts in foreign countries) and designing transmission equipment and antennas. The only body language involved was your "fist"—the term of art for how quickly and accurately you could input your keystrokes.

Wireless also offered ways into the job market for people who couldn't depend on their ability to charm interviewers or cultivate networks of in-person contacts. Using a transmitter he'd built himself, Hedin had a chance encounter over the airwaves with the chief engineer of a local TV station, who said that he'd be willing to hire him if he obtained his FCC license within six months. (The station's engineering department had already been thoroughly infiltrated by hams.) Hedin borrowed a guidebook from the public library, holed up in his ham shack, and earned his First Class Radiotelephone License within six months. He worked behind the scenes in broadcast television for the rest of his life.

After discovering that he and his sons were on the spectrum, Hedin joined the Global and Regional Asperger Syndrome Partnership (GRASP), one of the largest support groups for people with autism in the United States. Looking back, he feels certain that a number of hams he knew in the course of fifty-five years of surfing the airwaves would have qualified for a diagnosis.

The society of hams also enabled shy introverts to study the protocols of personal engagement from a comfortable distance. "Through amateur radio . . . I've learned so much about communication between people. I've had the opportunity to observe and participate in the giving and getting process, which is what communication is all about," recalled Lenore Jensen, who co-founded the Young Ladies' Radio League in 1939 to encourage more women to join the conversation. By interacting with other hams over the airwaves, she learned to conduct herself in social situations gracefully and went on to become an actress celebrated for her performances in *The Beverly Hillbillies*, *General Hospital*, and *Father Knows Best*.

For some autistic people, the attraction of wireless was more strictly technical. They simply wanted to get their hands on the gadgets that fascinated them. The first word that a ham named Mark Goodman ever spoke, at age four, was *ra-yo—radio*. He found the soothing tones emanating from the console in the living room less intimidating than the voices of grown-ups. "That sonorous hulk of varnished wood," he recalled, "became my constant companion." Assembling a crystal radio kit that his uncle gave him for Christmas encouraged him to tackle more complicated projects, which gave him a sense of purpose in a world he experienced as "largely chaotic, bewildering, [and] often indifferent."

Goodman spent hours in the local library studying technical manuals and started making pilgrimages to radio supply stores in nearby San Francisco. Eventually he was able to restore a broken console to good working order. This boosted his confidence and had an unexpected side effect: he became emotionally invested in the stories he heard on the radio.

> Sometimes I tuned in episodes crafted for those my age from serials about Tom Mix, Jack Armstrong, and Superman, which until then I'd almost never listened to. I lay back, suffused with rare contentment, eyes closed, absorbed by the sounds emanating from the hunk of wood, iron, paper, wires, glass and whatever else it took to convert radio waves back into spoken words and music that played into my imagination. It was magic, those sounds originating hundreds or thousands of miles away, all delivered to my ears via a vibrating cone of stiff, black paper.

As gratifying as these experiences were, they couldn't save Goodman from having a rough time in school at a time when the signs of autism were not widely recognized. Picked on by a sadistic teacher, he took refuge in reading "gobs of science-fiction . . . finding myself more at home on impossibly remote, imaginary worlds than the alien world I was strapped to." When he was twelve, his mother took him to Stanford for an evaluation, but the psychiatrist told her that he would eventually grow out of his problems relating to other people.

Finding a copy of *Calling CQ* in the school library, Goodman was thrilled by the story of a young ham named Walter Stiles who became a hero after a tragic flood in Pennsylvania. One night during a heavy rainstorm, Stiles picked up a weak signal from an operator near Renovo, Pennsylvania, calling "QRR"—the equivalent of SOS. He transcribed the rest of the operator's message describing a town already underwater, with more than two thousand people in immediate need of rescue and/or medical attention. "AIRPLANE LANDING IMPOSSIBLE COMMA DROP BY PARACHUTE," the desperate transmission concluded, and then the signal failed. After alerting the Red Cross, Stiles and a group of friends set off for Renovo with a truck full of medical supplies, food, and a waterproof transmitter; finding the bridges washed out, they carted their equipment for miles to the site of the disaster. There, Stiles manned his telegraph key for forty-eight hours, relaying messages to the outside world through chains of other amateurs.

Reading about the adventures of these young heroes, Goodman became determined to join their ranks. Soon he had built his own rig and earned his FCC license. But communicating by wireless could not provide all of the support and guidance he needed. He would spend the next several decades flunking out of school, losing jobs, going in and out of psychiatric institutions, and struggling to survive on disability.

He eventually sought help from more than twenty psychiatrists, psychologists, and therapists, but until the scope of the autism diagnosis was broadened to include adults, they couldn't make sense of the challenges he was facing. Finally, at age seventy, Goodman was able to get the diagnosis and access to services he needed. Joining a support group for adults run by the Asperger's Association of New England, he says, was "like coming ashore after a life of bobbing up and down in a sea that seemed to stretch to infinity in all directions."

IV

Gernsback died in 1967 as many of his predictions were coming true. TV—which made its public debut in 1928, in an experimental broadcast hosted by Gernsback's radio station WRNY—was ubiquitous, and 172 spacecraft left the earth's surface that year alone. By then, a new generation of visionaries raised on do-it-yourself electronics and pulp science fiction was laying the groundwork for a global network that would make the wireless revolution look quaint.

The modern digital age began at the Massachusetts Institute of Technology (MIT) in the late 1950s, where a mathematician and engineer named John McCarthy offered the first undergraduate course in computer programming. Instead of seeing the hulking mainframes of the day as glorified adding machines, he pondered ways of programming them so they could act in creative ways, learn to adapt to their environments, be linked in complex networks, and evolve to become smarter on their own. To describe this dynamic vision of computing, he coined the term *artificial intelligence* (AI).

A bearish man with thick black glasses, an unruly beard, and a crew cut that aspired to Mohawkhood, McCarthy was a legendary eccentric on a campus full of eccentrics. He had a habit of furiously pacing while thinking; if he was asked a question, he might just walk away without saying good-bye, only to reappear several days later with an answer as if the conversation had never been interrupted. If his colleagues wanted him to read a paper, instead of bringing it to his office where it would inevitably get lost, they would leave a copy on their own desk, and as McCarthy perambulated around the building, he would eventually stroll in, pick it up, and march off to read it, usually without uttering a word.

In *Scientific Temperaments*, writer Philip Hilts described his first encounter with McCarthy as unnerving:

> His greeting consisted of an expectant stare. No words at all. Discourse by his visitor brought from McCarthy a set of mumbles, which slowly

increased in volume and clarity, like the sound of a man emerging from a cave. Only when his mind reached the surface was something similar to normal conversation possible. His colleagues confirmed this: that John McCarthy's mind is a vehicle streamlined for rapid passage through the fluid of thought, capable of maneuvering with little outside friction. But in the open social terrain, his streamlined concentration becomes awkward and unwieldy.

McCarthy was equally ungainly in physical space, admitting to "an accumulated lack of success" in his PE classes at college. But he didn't let that stop him from taking up mountain climbing, sailing, and piloting private planes. A fellow pilot recalled McCarthy coaching himself aloud through each step of a final approach—"prop feathered . . . mixture full rich . . . airspeed check . . . okay, now we'll do this"—only to realize that he had already landed and the plane was racing along the airstrip.

But his life's work was never in doubt. When he was eight years old, McCarthy decided that he wanted to be a scientist, spurred on by Gernsbackian how-to guides like *Electricity for Boys*. His mother was a suffragette and his father was a union organizer and a member of the Communist party; their idealism would infuse his hope for computers as facilitators of democracy at a time when many left-wingers had a visceral distrust of technology. In high school, McCarthy taught himself calculus from college textbooks. At fifteen, he enrolled at the California Institute of Technology. There, he began thinking about designing machines that could simulate the human acquisition of knowledge, an interest he pursued further in his graduate work at Princeton.

In addition to his groundbreaking work on artificial intelligence, McCarthy was instrumental in developing the concept of time-sharing, which allowed multiple users to gain access to centralized computing resources through a distributed network of terminals. He advocated installing a terminal in every home, convinced that someday it would be commonplace for people to use them to read instantly updated news, order books by their favorite authors, buy plane tickets and reserve hotel rooms, edit documents remotely, and determine the efficacy of medical treatments by reading patient reviews. While this vision of information as a centralized utility, like water or power, was eventually overshadowed by the invention of personal computers and mobile devices, it survives in the vast networks of servers ("the cloud") that make the Web possible.

One of the main hangouts for his students at MIT was the Tech Model Railroad Club in Building 20, a temporary plywood facility built to aid the war effort that had been taken over by geeks thrilled to discover a building on campus where they could saw holes in the floor without prompting concern. The ranks of TMRC were divided between the artsy club members who worked on the layout (a picturesque replica of small-town America) and the habitually unwashed, Coke-guzzling, Chinese-takeout-eating obsessives who ran the fantastically elaborate apparatus that made the whole thing go. The complex tangle of wires, switches, and relays under the layout—scavenged out of parts from a local electronic-surplus store—was known as "the System," and the crew that managed it was called the Signals and Power Committee (SPC).

Building 20 was nicknamed "the Magical Incubator," and the particular brand of magic incubating there in the late 1950s was hacker culture. In the lexicon of TMRC, a "good hack" was some feat of technical virtuosity undertaken for pure pleasure rather than necessity, like programming a mainframe the size of a dozen refrigerators to play a song. As hard-core fans of science fiction, ham radio, and Japanese monster movies, MIT's protohackers were addicted to obscure lingo for its own sake, and jargon coined by the SPC (such as *mung*, *kluge*, *cruft*, and *foo*) proliferated widely through computer culture for the next several decades. Between marathon hands-on sessions to improve the System, McCarthy's students devised the first program that enabled a computer to play chess well—a good hack indeed.

McCarthy's most lasting contribution to his field was Lisp, a high-level programming language that enabled AI researchers to represent an unprecedented range of real-world events in their code. Unlike most programming languages of its vintage (with the sole exception of Fortran), it is still in wide use. But McCarthy was ready for a change in the early 1960s; when Stanford offered him a full professorship, he took it. He sold his house in Cambridge to two young Harvard professors promoting a tool for hacking the operating system of the human brain: LSD. Timothy Leary and Richard Alpert turned the alcove of McCarthy's old library (which contained equal parts of "science, fiction, and science fiction") into a rabbit hole that went down to a trip room lined with pillows, black lights, and psychedelic art.

McCarthy thrived in the hothouse of innovative ideas and technology that would soon be dubbed Silicon Valley, launching the famed Stanford Artificial Intelligence Laboratory (SAIL). By the early 1980s, he was already living in the future he foresaw a decade earlier. By typing in a few commands on the terminal on his desk, he could fetch his e-mail, listen to the radio, revise and spell-check a paper on a remote server, play chess or Go, print out a document in Elvish (he wrote an unpublished sequel to *The Lord of the Rings* that was sympathetic to the orcs), run searches on stories moving over the Associated Press wire, or fetch an up-to-date list of restaurant recommendations (called "YUMYUM") from programmers all over the world. His online .sig (signature) file and the license plate cover on his car featured the datacentric motto "Do the arithmetic or be doomed to talk nonsense."

Was McCarthy on the spectrum? He certainly displayed many of the classic features of Asperger's syndrome: his brusqueness, his single-minded focus to the point of seeming rude, his physical clumsiness, and his habit of coaching himself aloud when under stress. He also had many clearly positive traits that Asperger associated with autism: a fascination with logic and complex machines, a gift for puns and aphorisms, an uncompromising personal ethic, and the ability to solve problems from angles that his more socially oriented colleagues missed. But McCarthy would have had no need to seek out a diagnosis, because he was able to carve out a niche in an emerging field that was perfectly suited to his strengths while being tolerant—indeed, appreciative—of his many eccentricities.

His labs at MIT and Stanford were elaborate playgrounds for his extraordinary mind, as Cavendish's estate on Clapham Common was for his own. They also became magnets for other scruffy geniuses who were equally committed to the vision of a world empowered by access to computing—including two young members of a group called the Homebrew Computer Club named Steve Jobs and Steve Wozniak, who would go on to become the founders of Apple.

The culture of Silicon Valley began adapting to the presence of a high concentration of people with autistic traits even before the term *Asperger's syndrome* was invented. In 1984, a therapist named Jean Hollands wrote a popular self-help book for women called *The Silicon Syndrome* about navigating what she called "high-tech relationships." She described a distinctive breed of intensely driven "sci-tech" men who loved to tinker with machines, were slow to pick up on emotional cues, had few if any close friends outside their professional circles, approached life in rigorously logical and literal fashion like Mr. Spock, and tried to address problems in intimate relationships by "seeking data." (Holland confessed that her husband—a proud sci-tech man himself—viewed her as a member of an "alien culture.")

When the book was published, Hollands received sympathetic letters from the wives of engineers, coders, and math and physics professors all over the world. François Mitterrand, the president of France, visited her office in Mountain View with his wife, Danielle, to express his urgent concern that French couples might face the same challenges if computers became popular in Europe. There was no mention of autism in the book, but ten years later Hollands could have swapped the term *Asperger's syndrome* for *silicon syndrome* and barely changed another word in the text.

Ultimately, the future of computing belonged not to the Big Iron mainframes and networks of "dumb terminals" that McCarthy loved but to the smart little machines that the members of the Homebrew Computer Club were soldering together in their garages. The task of claiming the power of the computing for the many remained to be done by Internet pioneers like Vint Cerf and Tim Berners-Lee—and an engineer with autistic traits who launched the first social network for the people in a record store in Berkeley.

V

Lee Felsenstein had engineering in his blood. His grandfather, William T. Price, made a fortune by shrinking the design of diesel engines so they could fit into trains and trucks. At Cornell, Price was described by his classmates as a combination of Sherlock Holmes and A. J. Raffles, the gentleman thief created as the anti–Sherlock Holmes by Conan Doyle's brother-in-law, E. W. Hornung. After graduation, he embarked on a bike tour of Europe, returning just a couple of days before his wedding. Price was confused that his fiancée was upset; hadn't he come back in time as he said he would?

Like McCarthy, Felsenstein was also a Red Diaper Baby: his parents were members of the Communist party in the 1950s, and his father, Jacob, was a commercial artist who always made sure that there were plenty of art supplies around for his three children. In third grade, Lee would sketch exhaust pipes and compressors while coming up with schemes for redesigning automobiles to reduce air pollution. When a teacher accused him of daydreaming in class, he replied, "I'm not daydreaming, I'm inventing."

When he was eleven, Felsenstein inherited a half-assembled crystal radio kit from his older brother, strung up an antenna, and got it working. His first sight of a computer—a UNIVAC clacking away behind glass at the Franklin Institute Science Museum in Philadelphia—was so entrancing that he became a member of the museum so he could hang out near the machine all day.

Then a friend of his father's gave him a precious gift: a correspondence course in radio and TV repair that came complete with a voltmeter, an oscilloscope, and other apparatus that Felsenstein thought he'd never be able to afford, along with lessons on managing your own business. He started making house calls in the neighborhood to fix broken TVs as his basement filled up with glowing tubes and busted consoles, which he cannibalized for his experiments. He began to think of the basement as a holy sanctuary—his own personal monastery of technology. One night, he had a dream of being enmeshed in a luminous web of interconnected devices that were all working perfectly. He ended up running the UNIVAC exhibit at the institute in the summer between high school and college.

Felsenstein was also inspired by his father's work of organizing a neighborhood council to reform the zoning laws. When civil rights activists in the South began conducting sit-ins at lunch counters to protest segregation, he picketed a Woolworth's to show his support. Enrolling at the University of California at Berkeley, he joined the anti–Vietnam War movement, which was just getting off the ground. The administration eventually clamped down on students staffing information tables at Bancroft and Telegraph Avenues, claiming that on-campus political activities were restricted to membership in the Democratic and Republican clubs. When campus police arrested a civil rights activist for refusing to show his ID, three thousand enraged students surrounded the car and prevented it from moving for thirty-six hours until the charges were dropped.

In December 1964, students demanded that the administration negotiate its regulation of on-campus political activities, conducting a sit-in at Sproul Hall. The leader of the emerging Free Speech Movement (FSM), Mario Savio, delivered a speech to the crowd that was so passionate it became a rallying cry for antiwar protesters worldwide: "There's a time when the operation of the machine becomes so odious, makes you so sick at heart, that you can't take part. You can't even passively take part. And you've got to put your bodies upon the gears and upon the wheels . . . upon the levers, upon all the apparatus, and you've got to make it stop." That night, nearly eight hundred students were carted off to jail. The resulting furor nearly shut down the university.

The Free Speech Movement adopted Felsenstein, then nineteen, as its geek-in-residence. (Knowing how to run a mimeograph machine clinched the job.) One night, a group of students burst through the door shouting that police had surrounded the campus in preparation for another wave of mass arrests. One of the organizers turned to Felsenstein and said, "Quick, build us a police radio!" He knew that it wouldn't be that simple, but the moment was a revelation for Felsenstein. "I realized that I had made a mistake about my position in society. Up to that point, I was waiting for orders from highly intelligent people who knew much more than I did about politics, sociology, and other subjects," he says. "But then I realized that these people had no clue about what was actually possible with technology. That was my job: knowing what was possible and saying, 'Well, you can't have that, but you could have this instead.' So instead of waiting for orders, I started defining what was technologically possible."

The telephones at FSM headquarters became the nerve center for the emerging counterculture in Berkeley, but the organization's filing system was very inefficient. If someone called up and offered to fix activists' cars for free, a note would get tacked up on a wall that was already cluttered with similar notes. Felsenstein felt that there had to be a better way. He also observed that the role of leafleting on campus was changing. In 1964, when distributing leaflets was forbidden, a student passing them out would talk to each person who received one and inform them about the relevant issues. By 1967, however, they had become a crude broadcast medium. FSM activists would simply paste leaflets on walls in eye-catching patterns and hope that passersby would stop to read them.

It occurred to Felsenstein that if the counterculture was serious about building a new society that was not based on mass consumption and vacuous spectacle, it would have to design new forms of media that empowered individuals and local communities instead of relying on old broadcast models. The decentralized, user-driven future of computing was already taking shape in his mind.

FELSENSTEIN DIDN'T KNOW YET that he was autistic. As far as the psychiatric establishment was concerned, people like him didn't exist. He just knew that his girlfriends often complained that he didn't respond appropriately in social situations and that he never felt at home among people. By 1968, the stress of being an undiagnosed autistic in the middle of a cultural revolution had taken a heavy toll. After a crash into major depression, Felsenstein dropped out of Berkeley, commenced psychotherapy, and took a job at Ampex as a junior engineer.

By reading manuals, he taught himself the state of the art of programming at the time: punching holes in paper tape that corresponded to individual bits and feeding the tape into a reader that sent commands to a computer. There was no operating system and no software—just spools of perforated tape. Felsenstein describes the first time he successfully programmed a computer to type the letter *A* as a "transcendent experience."

While he was at Ampex, a researcher from Stanford named Doug Engelbart gave a presentation at a conference in San Francisco that would go down in history as "the Mother of All Demos." Engelbart and McCarthy worked on opposite sides of campus and represented opposite sides of a philosophical divide. While McCarthy wanted to design machines that were powerful enough to replace human intelligence, Engelbart wanted to figure out ways of using computers to augment it. Over the course of ninety minutes, Engelbart set forth the fundamental elements of the modern digital age in a single seamless package: graphical user interfaces, multiple window displays, mouse-driven navigation, word processing, hypertext linking, videoconferencing, and real-time collaboration. The concepts in Engelbart's presentation—refined by the work of Alan Kay and others at Xerox PARC—inspired Steve Jobs to build the Macintosh, the first personal computer (PC) designed for a mass market.

Meanwhile, the counterculture of the Bay Area was also evolving, though technologically it was still stuck in the precomputer era, depending on classified ads in underground newspapers, bulletin boards, telephone switchboards, and the post office for community organizing. It disturbed Felsenstein that valuable information was perpetually getting lost: if someone compiled a list of essential names or a box of helpful index cards and then went off to India to find a guru, the data he or she had accumulated tended to go astray. It occurred to him that computer networks could perform many of the functions of personal filing systems but much faster and better—and they didn't forget anything.

Felsenstein was also fascinated by social critic Ivan Illich's notion of promoting the use of tools that would facilitate "conviviality"—one of many aspects of social interaction that Felsenstein had always found difficult and confusing. With two fellow programmers named Efrem Lipkin and Mark Szpakowski, he began exploring ways of augmenting the community switchboards that had sprung up in subcultural hot spots like Berkeley and the Haight-Ashbury in San Francisco. The biggest practical obstacle to this noble undertaking was finding an affordable computer that was sufficiently powerful to do the job. That problem was solved when a programmer at a bustling commune in San Francisco called Project One wangled the long-term lease of an SDS 940 (retail cost: $300,000) from the Transamerica Corporation. This mighty machine—which was twenty-four feet long and required a fleet of air conditioners to stay cool—already had a storied history. It was the first computer designed to support McCarthy's time-sharing scheme directly. It was also the computer Engelbart had used to power the Mother of All Demos. It was a chunk of hardware with unusually good karma.

The hacker subculture incubated at MIT was thriving in places like SAIL, Xerox PARC, and the now legendary garages of Cupertino and San José. Soon *Whole Earth Catalog* impresario Stewart Brand would unleash this subculture on the unsuspecting inhabitants of Greater Mundania with the ultimate endorsement in *Rolling Stone*: "Computers are coming to the people. That's good news, maybe the best since psychedelics." The focus of the article was Spacewar, the seminal computer game developed in 1961 by four of McCarthy's students high on the fumes of pulp science fiction. But one of the most compelling things about the game, Brand noticed, was the insidious way that it turned a glorified number cruncher into a "communication device between humans."

For people who struggled to express themselves in face-to-face situations like Felsenstein (and people who were incapable of speech altogether), computer networks held the potential for not just "augmenting" communication but making it possible, period—minus the stuff that normally made conversation so arduous, such as eye contact, body language, tone, and the necessity of making a good impression.

The practical constraints of communicating online also required many aspects of social interaction that are normally implicit to be made explicit. Emoticons like :-)—originally proposed by Lisp hacker Scott Fahlman in 1982—were like social captioning for people who have trouble parsing sarcasm and innuendo.

With the help of Lipkin and Szpakowski, Felsenstein created the first electronic bulletin board in history, called Community Memory. On August 8, 1973, the first wide-open door to cyberspace was installed at the top of a staircase at Leopold's Records on Telegraph Avenue in Berkeley.

This portal to the digital future wasn't much to look at: it was basically an overgrown typewriter (an ASR-33 teletype, designed for the Navy) in a cardboard box that Felsenstein lined with foam to muffle the clatter of the hammers, with a vinyl window on top and two holes in front with Velcro flaps (like cat doors) to enable access to the keys. As each person came up the stairs, someone from the commune whose job it was to keep the teletype from getting jammed (which happened constantly anyway) would invite them to sit down and use it.

The mission of Community Memory, as its founders explained in a flyer, was "a process whereby technological tools, like computers, are used by the people themselves to shape their own lives and communities in sane and liberating ways . . . We invite your participation and suggestions." They dubbed the nascent network (which trickled across the Bay at a measly ten characters a second, via an Oakland telephone exchange that could make a free all-day call to San Francisco) an "information flea market."

The surprising answer to the question of who might be interested in such a resource was nearly everyone who ambled up the stairs. Because the terminal was located beneath a nonvirtual bulletin board (the kind with pushpins), many early postings to Community Memory were along the lines of "fusion-loving bass player seeks guitarist who digs ragas." But soon all manner of users were logging on to exchange a myriad of items and services. A poet offered sample poems, while other users solicited lifts to

Los Angeles; at one point, a Nubian goat was put up for sale. Some users posted ASCII art, and one posited a question that has vexed Bay Area residents for decades: "Where can I get a decent bagel?" (A baker replied by offering to provide free bagel-baking lessons.) Others held forth on Vietnam, gay liberation, and the energy crisis. Instead of merely being a computerized bulletin board, the network quickly became "a snapshot of the whole community," Felsenstein says.

Inevitably, the first public social network also gave birth to the first online troll: a wag who called himself "Dr. Benway" (the name of a drug-addicted surgeon in the novels of William Burroughs) who peppered the ongoing dialogues with Grateful Dead references and droll non sequiturs like "sensuous keystrokes forbidden" and "personal attendance required: send no replica." The identity of this mysterious pioneer of online snark was never uncovered.

Alas, without a sustainable economic model, the Project One commune was finally unable to support the considerable cost of maintaining the SDS 940. But as the prototype of a tool for promoting conviviality, Community Memory was a smashing success. Its popularity was particularly gratifying to Felsenstein, because a feeling of belonging to a community was precisely the thing that had always eluded him—even in the counterculture that was supposed to offer it to those who had never fit in anywhere else.

"As a kid, I had a feeling that I was ensconced in some sort of alcove, behind a wall, and that the street was *out there*," Felsenstein recalls. "I could see everyone else walking around engaging in life, but I couldn't go out there. So what I was doing with Community Memory was trying to expand the alcove." He moved on to other projects, including designing the Osborne 1—the first truly portable personal computer, introduced three years before the Macintosh. But he continued to struggle with depression and an inability to read other people's intentions despite years of psychotherapy.

Finally, in the 1990s, Felsenstein heard about Asperger's syndrome and recognized not only himself in the description but other members of his family. There was his illustrious grandfather William Price, the gifted inventor who was a perpetual puzzlement to his wife. Price's daughter, Caroline, never graduated from college but became one of the leading experts on bookbinding and restoration in New York City. In his interactions with her, Felsenstein found her opaque and emotionally distant. Her son Chris, who was Felsenstein's age, always seemed odd, speaking in an overly emphatic manner and staring in an unnerving way. At fifty, Chris earned a PhD in physics, though he was still unable to hold a job for long because he had a hard time getting along with people. He was finally diagnosed with Asperger's in the 1990s and suggested that Felsenstein also pursue an evaluation. Reading about autism online, Felsenstein came to think of his Asperger's as more than just a set of deficits, but as his "edge"—the edge he inherited from grandfather, which he has put to work in his career in technology for forty years.

The text-based nature of online interaction eventually provided the foundation for something that Leo Kanner couldn't have imagined: the birth of the autistic community. But two things had to happen first. Kanner's notion that autism was a rare form of childhood psychosis would have to be permanently laid to rest. Then, as Asperger's lost tribe finally emerged from the shadows, autistic people would have to overturn the notion that they were the victims of a global epidemic.

Seven

FIGHTING THE MONSTER

> That my child, therefore, may have some small share in creating this new light, I tell her story.
>
> —Pearl S. Buck, *The Child Who Never Grew*

Fittingly, the man who consigned the theory of toxic parenting to the dustbin of history was the loving father of an autistic boy himself: a warm, garrulous, obsessively curious Navy psychologist named Bernard Rimland. By writing a book called *Infantile Autism* as a self-taught outsider in the field, he firmly established autism as an inborn condition based in genetics and neurology rather than the complexities of the developing psyche.

The book's unexpected popularity inspired Rimland to launch the National Society for Autistic Children, which helped end decades of shame and isolation for families like his, and lobbied for legislation based on the principle that all children have the right to an education, including those with developmental disabilities. By crowdsourcing the search for effective autism treatments, he gave the parents in his network a sense of hope and progress at a time when research in the field was at a virtual standstill because the condition was still believed to be so rare. In many ways, his work set the stage for the rediscovery of Asperger's lost tribe and the current surge of interest in autism research.

Ironically, Rimland bitterly opposed the notion of autism as a continuum at first, like his hero, Leo Kanner. Faced with the likelihood of children like his son, Mark, being doomed to spend their lives in institutions, he forged an alliance with a psychologist named Ole Ivar Lovaas to find ways of training them to become "indistinguishable from their peers," as Lovaas put it. With the help of his parents' network, he also pursued innovative methods of treating the most debilitating features of autism with special diets, megavitamin supplements, and alternative medicines.

The controversial theories that Rimland developed—such as his notion that the allegedly unified condition called autism is composed of many distinct subtypes—anticipated major shifts in mainstream science by decades. But by promoting the hope that children like Mark could be fully "recovered" from autism with biomedical treatments, Rimland ended up diverting the energy and focus of the parents' movement he helped create into an endless quest for a cure.

BERNARD RIMLAND WAS BORN in Cleveland in 1928, the son of Russian parents who emigrated after World War I. Though he was raised in the Orthodox Jewish tradition, he grew up to become a fiercely independent thinker. He was not strictly observant, but his path in life was deeply informed by the traditional Talmudic concept of *tikkun olam*—the healing and reparation of a fractured world. When he was twelve, his father took a metalworking job with a defense contractor called Convair in California. The family relocated from northern Ohio to a San Diego neighborhood called Kensington, a cozy hamlet of palm trees and Mission-style houses with a quaint main street, an Art Deco movie house, and a thriving Jewish community.

"Cleveland had been muggy and dirty," Rimland recalled. "I got here and said, 'this is heaven. I'm never leaving.'" He never really did. Seven decades later, his storefront office on Adams Avenue—now the headquarters of a group called the Autism Research Institute (ARI), dedicated to carrying on his work—is still there.

Defying his parents' disdain for higher education (he and his sister Rose were told that college was strictly for "children of the rich"), Rimland enrolled at San Diego State University. In his junior year, he became interested in psychometrics, the quantitative measurement of human aptitude and intelligence. Its nuts-and-bolts, data-driven methodology—"how one determines what is true, or what might be true," as Rimland put it—was infinitely more fascinating to him than the speculations about the unconscious that occupied most of his peers at the time. He got his bachelor's degree in experimental psychology in 1950 and earned his master's degree a year later.

Then he met Gloria Alf, a spunky, blue-eyed Jewish girl from the neighborhood who loved to go down to the park and watch world-class badminton players tune up their game for the international championships, held every year in San Diego. Gloria's older brother, Eddie, was a popular jock around town. He had so many friends that one night when he was cramming for an exam, he asked his sister to stand guard at his door and take down the names of everyone who came by to see him. When a friend named Bernie dropped by with his badminton racket, Gloria refused to let him in. With characteristic tenacity, Rimland pushed past her and jogged up the stairs as Gloria tried to pull him down. Eddie chided her for failing in her guard duty when they arrived at his door. "But who's going to come with me while I restring my racket?" Rimland groaned. Impressed by his chutzpah, Gloria volunteered to go with him, which turned into their first date. Before heading east to Penn State to earn his doctorate, Bernie married Gloria in a local synagogue.

They felt homesick for the West Coast, but then, in a happy turn of events, the Navy launched a personnel lab at Point Loma around the same time that Rimland was completing his degree. The newlyweds returned to San Diego, and Rimland became the director of research at the new naval base. With dreams of raising a family of their own, the young couple bought a modest home a short walk from San Diego State College. Because they didn't care whether they had a boy or a girl, they painted the second bedroom, destined to be the nursery, yellow. Their son, Mark, was born in the spring of 1956.

In the maternity ward, Rimland was third in line at the viewing window. The young fathers in front of him kvelled effusively, though their newborns seemed hardly more aware of their surroundings than rag dolls. But Mark seemed different: he was "looking around wide-eyed, just as though he could talk. I was very proud of that," Rimland recalled. "I thought, 'Gee, what a precocious-looking little guy.'"

Mark turned out to be more than precociously alert; he could also be precociously loud, as Gloria discovered even before she took him home from the hospital. Amid the squalling of the other infants, she could hear Mark's piercing wail all the way down the hall. She gleefully told her husband—a formidable swimmer in his youth—that their son had inherited his lungs.

In the months to come, however, Mark's keening cry would become the never-ending soundtrack to the Rimlands' life. Their newborn hardly ever seemed to stop screaming, other than the rare moments when he passed out from sheer exhaustion. Picking Mark up to cradle him only seemed to upset him more, and he would cry so violently that Gloria could barely nurse him, and he would explode in a rage at the smallest deviation from the daily routine. If Gloria dared to shampoo her hair, he would cry until it dried and looked the same again. When summer arrived, the Rimlands opened their back door so the coastal breezes could sweep the house, but as the weather turned cool again, they had to leave the door open or their son would howl implacably for hours. The neighbors complained about the racket so many times that the Rimlands became friends with the local cops, who expressed relief that Mark was not their own child.

Eventually, Gloria decided to time her son's caterwauling to see how long it would go on. By the time Mark was a year old, he was crying twelve hours a day. "We thought we were really living," Gloria said. "That was so wonderful—only twelve hours!"

Then Mark started to hurt himself. He would bang his forehead against the wall so hard that he bore a perpetual bruise above his eyes. With his powerful little arms, he strained against the cage of his crib until it splintered. When he wasn't screeching or thrashing around, he would gaze off into space, rocking back and forth, as if in a perpetual daydream. The only thing that seemed to divert him from his misery was the sound of machines. The drone of the vacuum cleaner mesmerized him.

Gloria came to feel like a prisoner in her own house. On a good day, she might eke out enough alone time to brush her teeth. Paradise, she thought, would be having the liberty to take a shower. Desperate for a couple of hours to herself, she accepted her housekeeper's generous offer to babysit Mark. It was such a rare opportunity that she jumped into her car and started driving around town, getting out to gaze absently into shop windows. (She had forgotten to bring her purse.) Though she had long wished for such a chance to escape, she felt "like a fish out of water." When she returned home, she found her son and her housekeeper together on the floor, sobbing. Gloria never asked the woman for help again.

Yet Rimland's premonition in the maternity ward that his son would turn out to be a prodigy also seemed to come true. Mark was just eight months old when he started blurting out phrases like "Come on, let's play ball!" which made his sports-loving father swell with pride. Gradually, Rimland realized that his son was just repeating the phrases that he heard around him. He would refer to both his grandfather and grandmother as "Grandpa." One night before her husband got home from the office, Gloria held Mark up to a window and said, "It's all dark outside, honey." *It's-all-dark-honey* became his all-purpose synonym for *window* for months.

The family pediatrician, who had been in practice for thirty-five years, was at a loss to diagnose Mark's condition. Rimland used to brag that he had skipped his undergraduate coursework in psychology because he instantly knew that psychometrics was for him, but his expertise in devising aptitude tests was of no help in understanding his son. He and Gloria seemed to be on their own.

Mark's echolalia proved to be the key that unlocked the mystery of his condition. Hearing her son recite radio jingles in a monotone voice one day, Gloria remembered reading in college about some exotic disorder that made kids compulsively repeat nursery rhymes. Luckily, her old textbooks were stashed out in the garage. Bernie and Gloria tore open a cardboard box and finally had a name for their son's condition: *early infantile autism*. Now at least they knew what they were dealing with.

THE RIMLANDS BEGAN MEETING twice a week with a psychotherapist who promised to unravel the deep-seated emotional issues that were surely at the root of Mark's problems. "Tell me, why do you hate your son?" he would ask them over and over again. He advised them to commit him to an institution and move on.

But Bernie and Gloria had no intention of abandoning their son. Despite all their difficulty in raising him, they adored him and just wanted him to be a happy baby. The notion that they had somehow brought about his condition by callously ignoring his feelings seemed absurd. They spent nearly every waking moment doting on Mark while trying to find practical ways of relieving his distress.

Pushing Mark in a carriage around the neighborhood seemed to soothe him, particularly when they rolled over places in the sidewalk that were bumpy and uneven. To simulate the jiggling produced by the rough pavement, Rimland taped a yardstick to the floor so he could push Mark's cradle back and forth over it. Gloria's response to Mark's loud protests when she changed out of a certain dress was to order a closetful of identical dresses from Sears for her mother, her mother-in-law, and herself. She would do whatever was required to help him feel content.

Though the Rimlands were highly sociable people, they gradually found themselves almost completely isolated. One night they were halfway through a rare dinner out with another couple when the wife turned to Gloria and said, "You know, you just don't seem like that kind of person—the terrible kind of person that would cause all those problems for your son." Bernie and Gloria never spoke to them again.

Then their daughter, Helen, was born. To their relief, she turned out to be an affectionate and cuddly baby. If Bernie and Gloria were so disturbed that they had hobbled their son's mind in the cradle, why had their daughter been spared? They became determined to discover what the experts had overlooked.

When Rimland was a boy, his mother used to tell him a cautionary tale about his uncle who was a genius in math. During World War I, he came upon a crowd of German soldiers heaping abuse upon an elderly Jew. When he stepped in to defend the man, the soldiers beat him savagely and left him to bleed to death on the sidewalk. His mother would tell him this horrific story to teach him not to stick his nose in other people's business. Instead, however, young Bernie thought of his uncle as a hero. Now he would wage an epic battle to rescue his son from the mysterious forces that were tormenting him.

II

Rimland's research resources in the San Diego area were limited. There were no medical schools in town and no books on autism in the local libraries. Luckily, his job required him to take frequent trips across the country, visiting naval bases to evaluate their personnel-testing programs. (He would eventually publish more than forty reports and journal articles on psychometrics.) In his off-duty time on the road, he began scouring medical school libraries for any scrap of information that might shed light on his son's condition.

This quest became an all-consuming obsession. "You really would have had to see it yourself to know how little was known about autism back then, and what little was out there was speculation," Gloria recalls. "Bernard wanted to read every word that had been written on the subject." In the early 1960s, this was still a realistic goal. But the information he sought was scattered in thousands of separate collections. Copying machines were just coming into wide use, so Rimland began requesting photocopies and books by interlibrary loan. Much of the clinical literature on the subject wasn't written in English, so he organized a team of Navy translators to help him mine the international journals. He also made trips to Washington to pore over rare volumes housed in the National Library of Medicine.

When the Navy sent him to New Orleans, he declined his colleagues' invitations to bars and strip clubs and went instead to the Tulane University Medical Library, where he talked a kindly guard into letting him read papers in the locked library overnight. When her husband returned from Louisiana, Gloria was shocked at how gaunt he looked. Rimland told her that he hadn't eaten anything all weekend but chicken soup from a vending machine.

In his college days, he had been able to avoid taking notes during lectures, relying instead on his photographic memory. But this was different: "This was war. I envisioned autism as a powerful monster that had seized my child. I could afford no errors."

In addition to reading everything that he could on the subject, Rimland went straight to the father of the diagnosis, writing a letter to Kanner in 1959 describing his son's behavior and announcing his intention to write a paper on the subject. The following year, he told Kanner, "I have been continuing my study of the disease at the very intensive rate, and I now have developed a theory which, to me, accounts with surprising consistency for most of what is known." He also mentioned that he had been experimenting by giving his son a new drug called Deaner, promoted with ads in medical journals as a "psychic energizer" for problem children.

It soon became clear to Rimland that his project would require much more than several months of research. He sent frequent updates to Kanner in the coming years informing him about Mark's progress. The tone of these updates was solicitous and self-deprecating, in the manner of an earnest disciple addressing the master; often his letters referred to papers that he had recently sent to Kanner's office, hoping to hear his reaction. Though Kanner had been the originator of the refrigerator-parenting theory, Rimland flattered him relentlessly. "Only Churchill comes to mind," he wrote, "when I think of writers whose word-choice and rhetoric demonstrate similar mastery of subject matter and expression." Kanner's replies were usually brief and to the point.

Mark's development during this period was so rapid that it surprised and delighted Rimland. He told Kanner: "We feel that there is real progress. He is using a little speech now—just fragments in a high piping voice. He is naming pictures in books for the first time, and there is progress in toilet training. His disposition is vastly improved. Where before, on returning from work it was common to hear him screaming in part of an hour-long tantrum, I now often find him opening the door for me with a smile." Because it was widely believed that autistic children were incapable of learning—a misconception largely caused by their being warehoused in institutions for the "feebleminded," where education was not on the agenda—Rimland assumed that his experimental treatment was responsible for Mark's improvement: "We think it is mostly due to Deaner," he informed Kanner. He even canceled plans to bring Mark to Minneapolis for an evaluation by Kanner, "since Mark's taking of Deaner has resulted in such striking improvement that additional diagnosis of autism might be difficult."

After five years of research, Rimland had filled enough notebooks and index cards to open a medical library himself. He began compiling his observations into a monograph that he planned to call "Kanner's Syndrome of Apparent Autism." As the paper got longer and longer, he started mimeographing it and sending it out to experienced researchers in the field for comments and criticism. He was well aware that he was venturing beyond his realm of expertise.

Rimland was beginning to find his day job with the Navy—supplemented by teaching courses on abnormal psychology at local colleges—a bit dull by comparison. His moonlighting as an autism researcher took him far beyond the domain of personnel testing and number crunching, enabling him to explore the frontiers of emerging fields like genetics, neurophysiology, biochemistry, and medical anthropology. Truly understanding his son's condition would require input from experts in a dozen disciplines. "A wise man once observed that if you study an object of nature intently enough, if you focus upon it long enough with all your powers of concentration and attention," he wrote, "there comes a point at which the macrocosm behind the object is suddenly revealed—in somewhat the way in which the vista beyond a keyhole is magnified if one purposely advances his eye toward it."

Gloria tried to persuade her husband to turn his ever-growing mountain of notes into a book rather than a mere paper in a journal. But the chances of Rimland's manuscript being picked up by a major publisher were slim, because he had no relevant credentials in the field. Editors willing to take a chance on a book about a rare psychiatric disorder by a nonexpert were few and far between. But then Rimland heard that a highly respected imprint called Appleton-Century-Crofts was hosting the first in a series of annual awards for a distinguished manuscript in psychology. The submissions were to be judged by a panel of editors blindly: they wouldn't know the author's name until the winner had already been selected on the strength of the writing alone. Rimland submitted his manuscript, and a few months later the judges unanimously awarded him the first Century Psychology Series Award, which came with a $1,500 honorarium and a favorable publishing contract. Rimland's *Infantile Autism: The Syndrome and Its Implications for a Neural Theory of Behavior* was published in 1964, featuring an introduction by Kanner himself.

Kanner spent the first half of his introduction asserting his own supremacy as the preeminent authority in the field. After relating his usual account of his serendipitous discovery, he complained that his concept of early infantile autism ("I could not think of a better name," he added) had been applied so broadly that "the term was used as a pseudodiagnostic wastebasket for a variety of unrelated conditions." He concluded by characterizing Rimland as a "passer-by" in the autism field that had "tarried . . . by the roadside" long enough to write a book worthy of "respectfully sober scrutiny."

It was a gem of finely calibrated praise by an entrenched authority unwilling to cede an inch of his turf to an industrious upstart. Nevertheless, Rimland was thrilled by his mentor's introduction and humble about his own accomplishment. "This is a working paper," he wrote in the preface. "If it isn't, I don't know when it stopped being one."

He needn't have been so modest. After decades of confusion, Rimland's book finally put the science of autism back on the right track by arguing persuasively that it was an inborn "perceptual disability" rather than a form of psychosis caused by childhood trauma. By debunking neo-Freudians like Bettelheim, Rimland liberated parents from a soul-crushing burden of guilt while rendering the rationale for protecting children by putting them in institutions "for their own good" obsolete. He also demonstrated a more nuanced understanding of the special talents and abilities of these children than Kanner had done, granting them an independent existence outside the usual accounting of deficits and dysfunctions. "It is interesting to conjecture that the silent, unreachable autistic child," he wrote, "may indeed be 'lost in thought'—reliving an experience in minute detail, hearing music long since forgotten or perhaps never heard by others, or playing games with numbers or objects manipulatable only in the recesses of his brain."

He even occasionally allowed himself to take the perspective of the children that he was writing about, as when he described "the fatigue and frustration experienced by the disturbed child in trying to deal with his environment when he was not cognitively equipped to do so . . . Imagine the child's reaction to the futility of living in an incomprehensible world run by what must appear to him to be demanding, ritualistic, arbitrary and inconsistent psychotics—us!"

Undoubtedly, one of the reasons that Kanner was willing to write an introduction to the book was that Rimland went notably easy on him and Eisenberg for originating the theory of toxic parenting, shifting most of the blame to Bettelheim. He said only that Kanner and Eisenberg had "subscribed" to the notion of psychogenic causation, as if they were innocent bystanders. Thus Bettelheim would go down in history as the primary source of the theory, though he had been virtually parroting Kanner and Eisenberg while adding his own misogynistic flourishes.

III

Rimland's comprehensive review of the literature enabled him to become conversant with ideas that wouldn't be widely circulated in the field for decades. At one point in the book, he even referred to Asperger's syndrome (without explaining it), though the concept was still virtually unknown outside of Eastern Europe.

The crux of the book was that autism is primarily a product of genetic inheritance rather than family dynamics, which dozens of studies would confirm in the coming years. But Rimland also presciently suggested that in some cases the syndrome was caused by unknown environmental factors acting upon a genetic predisposition. He speculated that parents who tend to be gifted in certain fields pass this vulnerability down to their children along with the genetic factors for high intelligence. Thus, autism represented a potential for genius that had been derailed somewhere along the line—"brightness gone awry," as Rimland put it. "We must give serious consideration to the hypothesis that an infant's road to high intelligence lies along a knife-edged path," he wrote, "and the higher the potential intelligence, the steeper and more precarious the slope."

The seeds of this idea were present from the start in Asperger's descriptions of his patients' parents as brilliant eccentrics, but despite Rimland's team of translators, his paper wasn't cited in the book's comprehensive bibliography—another sign of how thoroughly erased it had been from history. The notion of a link between autism and high intelligence was also implicit in Kanner's claims that his patients' parents were highly educated. By unbundling the "brightness gone awry" hypothesis from the theory of refrigerator parenting, Rimland was no doubt intending to do his mentor a favor.

This hypothesis would fall into disrepute in the 1970s as studies by Michael Rutter and others proved that autism does not discriminate by IQ or educational level and is equally prevalent across all socioeconomic strata. Yet even in the face of this evidence, neither Kanner nor Rimland ever disavowed the theory, claiming that their clinical experience had consistently shown it to be true. One of the reasons Rimland was so resistant to the idea of a spectrum is that he was convinced that only true cases of Kanner's syndrome were linked to the potential for genius. "The conclusion I reached then, and by which I stand today," he wrote in 1994, "is that Kanner's finding is irrefutable if, but only if, one uses the strict and limited definition of autism insisted upon by him."

Clues that Rimland may have been on to something have been popping up ever since. In 2003, Kathrin Hippler at the University of Vienna undertook a study of the case records of patients diagnosed by Asperger after the war; she found a significantly higher number of fathers working in the technical professions—particularly electrical engineering—than the fathers of a control group. Researchers at the University of Edinburgh discovered in 2015 that genes associated with austism are also associated with higher levels of cognitive ability—particularly problem-solving tasks requiring nonverbal, hands-on intelligence. The flaw in Rimland's idea may have been his attempt to link autism to general intelligence—which is notoriously difficult to measure in autistic people anyway—rather than to a specific set of aptitudes.

Though Rimland never identified himself in the book as the father of an autistic child, he was unstinting in chronicling the ravaging effects of misguided autism theories on families like his own. "If autism is solely determined by organic factors," he writes, "there is no need for the parents of these children to suffer the shame, guilt, inconvenience, financial expense, and marital discord which so often accompany the assumption of psychogenic etiology." He describes families having to take their child "from clinic to clinic in the hope of finding someone who understands the disease." For parents who couldn't afford to undertake this kind of doctor shopping, it was undoubtedly even harder, which is reflected in the continuing underdiagnosis of autism in minority communities to the present day.

The most outdated aspect of the book is Rimland's unquestioning faith in Kanner's narrow definition of autism. At various points, it seems like he's trying to outdo even his mentor by coming up with more and more inventive ways of excluding children from the diagnosis. Rimland describes autistic children as "almost invariably in excellent health, beautiful and well formed, and usually of dark complexion" (as opposed to those with childhood schizophrenia, whom he portrays as having blond hair and blue eyes, translucent skin, a receding chin, and "an almost foetus-like appearance"). He marvels at their "excellent, and in fact, often extraordinary motor ability . . . with regard to both gross body movement and finger dexterity," and claims they enjoy a remarkable "freedom from allergies, asthma, metabolic disturbances, and skin problems."

In keeping with Kanner's model, he also lists a multitude of other disqualifying factors, including signs of regression, seizures, abnormal EEG readings, pale skin, a "dull, retarded" appearance, "soft doughy" muscle tone, absence of savant skills, visible anxiety and confusion, the presence of mental illness in the family tree, spinning in place, and toe-walking. The latter two behaviors were particularly curious choices, since a number of Kanner's patients exhibited them, and they are now considered telltale signs of autism.

But Rimland would brook no interlopers in his mentor's walled garden. He even apologized to the reader in advance: "It may be that some of the cases the present writer cites in this book to illustrate the phenomena of autism may in fact be instances where only some of the symptoms are shared with infantile autism, although an attempt to guard against this sort of error has been made." In Rimland's view, true cases of Kanner's syndrome were about as scarce as true Scotsmen.

BUT RIMLAND HAD ANOTHER good reason for wanting the diagnosis to be strictly defined. He nurtured the hope that autism would turn out to be a glitch in a single metabolic pathway that could be averted with a dietary intervention, like another genetic condition called phenylketonuria, or PKU.

When Rimland first read Pearl S. Buck's touching memoir of raising her daughter, Carol, *The Child Who Never Grew*, he thought it was a story about autism. Moments after Carol was born, Buck turned to a nurse and said, "Doesn't she look very wise for her age?" Even as a baby, Carol seemed to go into ecstasy when her mother played symphonies on the phonograph. But by the time she was three, it was obvious that she was losing ground, and she would explode in angry rages. The tale of PKU's discovery became a template for Rimland, who wrote his book, in part, in an attempt to make history repeat itself.

In the 1920s, a young couple in Oslo named Harry and Borgny Egeland had their first child—a daughter, Liv. Like Carol Buck and Mark Rimland, she had an aura of precocious wisdom, but by the time she was three she had still never spoken a word. The family pediatrician assured the Egelands that their daughter was perfectly healthy and would talk on her own schedule. Then the couple had a son named Dag. At first, he was a spunky and alert baby, but gradually he seemed to lose all interest in the world around him.

Then Borgny happened to notice an odd, musty odor emanating from her children's diapers. She began to wonder if this odor might be related to their failure to thrive. The Egelands took their children to doctor after doctor and finally brought Dag down to the University Hospital in Oslo for an extensive round of tests. But they revealed nothing. Desperate for any sort of help, Borgny called on healers, herbalists, and psychics who brewed up teas for the children, concocted healing baths, and sought the source of their malady in visions. Then Harry remembered that one of his professors at dental school, Asbørn Følling, was a specialist in metabolic diseases. Borgny asked her sister, who knew Følling socially, to ask him about the smell in her children's urine, and he agreed to run a detailed analysis.

Before doing that, Følling asked Borgny to immediately stop giving her children all the herbal remedies she'd been feeding them, to ensure that the signal of whatever was causing this condition was not lost in statistical noise. Only then did he begin his testing. Scans for blood, pus, albumen, and sugar revealed nothing unusual, but then Følling tried adding a few drops of ferric chloride solution to Liv's urine sample. Instead of turning the usual reddish-brown, indicating the presence of ketones, it flashed brightly with an ominous green color that quickly faded. Adding drops of ferric chloride to Dag's sample produced the same unusual result. Never having seen this kind of reaction before, Følling checked his chemistry textbooks but found no useful clues. For two months, he beavered away in the lab, analyzing more than twenty liters of the children's urine in total.

Finally, after evacuating the air from his test tubes with nitrogen, he isolated the crystals of a compound called phenylpyruvic acid that is not normally present in urine. Then he got in touch with mental institutions in the area and asked them to send him samples. Eight out of 430 samples from intellectually disabled children yielded the same odd compound. With more detective work, he discovered that the crystals were a by-product of the children being unable to metabolize a common amino acid called phenylalanine, which is present in cow and breast milk. As a result, the acid slowly built up in their bloodstreams, damaging the children's developing brains and cascading into their urine and producing that musty smell.

Følling named this syndrome "imbecillitas phenypyruvica," which was eventually rechristened phenylketonuria. By studying affected families, he was able to determine that the syndrome was carried on a single recessive gene. If a child inherits copies of the gene from both parents, they are born with PKU. After Buck's book was published, clinicians developed a simple diaper test for PKU that could be administered a few weeks after birth, which was promptly replaced by a blood test that could be given before a newborn left the hospital. Meanwhile, researchers developed a low-phenylalanine diet that could avert PKU's disabling effects if it was started in infancy. In countries where most children have access to good health care, PKU-induced intellectual disability is now a thing of the past. None of these breakthroughs would have happened, Rimland reflected, if Følling had written off Liv and Dag as hopeless cases of a generic disorder called mental retardation.

IV

Rimland's highest hope for his book was that it would kick-start a new era of autism research. To facilitate this process, he came up with a smart idea for soliciting data from his readers by making his book interactive. In the appendix, he included a questionnaire called the "Diagnostic Check List for Behavior-Disturbed Children (Form E-1)," designed as a template for clinicians to copy and give to parents. In keeping with Kanner's notion that autism was a disorder of infancy, most of the seventy-six questions focused on a child's behavior in the first six years of life.

Did (does) the child stare into space for long periods of time as though lost in thought?
Did you ever suspect the child was very nearly deaf?
Does the child ever "look through" or "walk through" people, as though they weren't there?
Did (does) he say phrases over and over in a hollow, parrot-like or echo-like voice, to no purpose?
Did (does) he consistently use the word "You" when he should say "I"?
Did (does) the child seem to want to be liked?

Other sections of the questionnaire were designed to serve Rimland's interest in the biomedical dimensions of autism, featuring questions about the child's eating habits and digestion, skin condition, and temperature regulation. He was delighted when a biochemist read the book and said that he would start searching for signs of a metabolic failure in autism in the hope of developing a nutritional regime similar to the low-phenylalanine diet.

Amazingly, the E-1 was the first standardized clinical tool for autism assessment. Up to that point, the diagnosis was made strictly on the basis of subjective observation by clinicians schooled in Kanner's and Eisenberg's methods. Children who didn't precisely fit Rimland's version of Kanner's model got only a diagnosis of "autistic-like." In this act of winnowing, Rimland was again following in the footsteps of his mentor, who told him in a letter that nine out of ten children sent to his office with an autism diagnosis by other clinicians were not "true cases."

After the book came out, Rimland had no particular plans to do further writing in the field, and he assumed that he would turn his attention back to his day job. But the future of quiet anonymity in Kensington that he imagined for himself and his family was not to be.

Hardly a week had gone by after publication when E-1 forms that had been torn out of the book, filled in by a parent (usually the mother), and sent directly to the address of the U.S. Naval Personnel Research Laboratory listed on the title page—often accompanied by a handwritten letter—started flooding Rimland's mailbox. "That just killed Bernard," Gloria recalls. "He said, 'look what they're doing to my book!'" But he quickly realized that the forms piling up at his door were the most earnest kind of praise he could get from his fellow parents. He opened a file in his office for each child whose mother or father reached out to him directly. In the months to come, hundreds of E-1s would make their way back to Rimland. After scoring the checklists with a proprietary algorithm, he would report the results to parents by mail, typically following up with a personal phone call.

After years of isolation, he and Gloria knew all too well how lonely raising an autistic child could be. His conversations with parents engaged a gregarious and empathetic side of him, and he became "Uncle Bernie" to a generation of families—ready to pick up the phone any time of day or night, and eager to sit down with any distraught mother or father who showed up at his door looking for help.

He also used the notes that parents scribbled in the margins of the E-1 to refine his questionnaire. When a second edition of *Infantile Autism* was published a couple of years later, it featured an updated version of the checklist called the E-2, designed for parents to send to Rimland directly. Persuading parents desperate for information about their children to fill out a form turned out to be a lot easier than persuading other researchers to make use of his data. Studies of the E-1 and E-2 in peer-reviewed journals raised questions about their accuracy. One problem was that the questionnaires depended on parental memories of a child's behavior in infancy, which could be unreliable. Also, the results of his algorithm correlated only moderately well with clinical assessment by other means. This was the inevitable result of his highly selective winnowing process, but it added to doubts about the accuracy of his methods, which hurt his professional pride.

By forging a direct connection with the parents who wrote to him, Rimland ended up taking a much more subversive path that directly challenged the authority of the psychiatric establishment. Instead of becoming the gold standard of autism assessment, Rimland's questionnaires planted the seeds of a revolution.

V

The hardest thing to come by for the parents of children like Mark in the 1960s was hope. Clinicians had little to offer beyond the standard advice to institutionalize the child and quietly remove their pictures from the family album. Parents determined to raise their sons and daughters at home, like Clara Claiborne Park (mother of Jessy Park) and Eustacia Cutler (mother of Temple Grandin), were condemned for endangering their welfare by trapping them in a psychically toxic environment.

Two decades after Asperger wrote his guide to appropriate methods for teaching autistic children, most psychologists in America were still convinced that they were constitutionally incapable of learning. Rimland's book doesn't even touch on the topic of education, instead using the terms *training* and *conditioning,* employed by behaviorists to describe the process of training an animal to respond to certain stimuli in Pavlovian fashion. To his credit, Rimland also noted that "very little has been published relating to true cases of autism grown to maturity," and the few studies available were decidedly discouraging.

In 1956, Eisenberg published a paper called "The Autistic Child in Adolescence" based on his case files from the Harriet Lane. Of the sixty-three teenagers he was able to locate, more than half were confined to institutions. He divided the group into three categories of outcome: *good*, *fair*, and *poor*. A good outcome was defined as "a patient who is functioning well at an academic, social, and community level and who is accepted by his peers, though he may remain a somewhat odd person." A poor outcome described a patient who "has not emerged from autism to any extent and whose present function is markedly maladaptive, characterized by apparent feeble-mindedness and/or grossly disturbed behavior." Only three patients in the group rated a good outcome, while forty-six were classified as poor. The factor most predictive of their outcome, Eisenberg said, was the presence of "useful speech."

Even Bettelheim had offered families a twisted version of hope with his claims that years at the Orthogenic School could unravel the knots tied in a baby's psyche by an icy and domineering mother. It haunted Rimland that, by reframing autism as a genetic disorder instead of a psychogenic one, he had subtracted even that comforting illusion from the equation, contributing to an attitude of "therapeutic hopelessness." With hundreds of parents now looking to him for help and advice, what did he have to offer them?

On an October day in 1964, Rimland found his answer in a blunt-spoken psychologist at the University of California in Los Angeles named Ole Ivar Lovaas. On the surface, the two men were polar opposites: Rimland was a warm, attentive teddy bear from the Midwest, while Lovaas was a ruddy Nordic outdoorsman who would flash his dazzling smile before shaming his colleagues at dinner by saying, "There are more brains in this salad than in the people at this table." But both men were driven and ambitious, disillusioned with the state of psychology, and marginalized by their peers because of their fascination with the same obscure childhood disorder.

Like so many other first-generation autism researchers, Lovaas came of age in Hitler's shadow, the son of a journalist and a farmer's daughter. In 1927, he was born in a village near Oslo called Lier, celebrated for its prolific orchards and fertile fields. As a boy, Ivar would take the train with his family to the mountains, where the snowpack sparkled like diamonds. But everything changed on the morning of April 9, 1940, when he arrived at school to find his teachers in tears. They told him that he must return home immediately because the Nazis had invaded Norway by sea and air to claim it as their own territory. That afternoon, young Ivar saw "green-colored men in their funny helmets" crawling all over his family's valley "like aphids in the Garden of Eden."

By June, the Allied defense forces had been utterly crushed, King Haakon was in exile, and all the radios had been confiscated from the Jewish families in Oslo in preparation for mass deportation to concentration camps. For the next five years, Lovaas and his family were forced to work as migrant laborers, eating only what they could grow themselves, picking cabbages and turnips in the frigid air ten hours a day until their arms and legs felt numb.

When the war ended, Lovaas was allowed to immigrate to the United States on the strength of his violin playing. He got a music scholarship at Luther College in Iowa and earned his bachelor's degree in a year by sleeping three or four hours a night. After seeing a photograph of the snowcapped Olympic mountain range in a newspaper, he hopped on a Greyhound bus to Seattle, knocking on doors until he found a family that would rent him a room in exchange for performing household chores. Then he strolled down to the University of Washington and talked his way into the graduate program in psychology. In another uncanny coincidence of autism history, one of his roommates at UW was Eddie Alf, Gloria Rimland's brother.

Lovaas set out to become a psychoanalyst, like nearly every other psychology student in America at the time. But he didn't have the knack for it: "My clients would ask me, 'Do you mean that by talking to you, I will get better?' I answered 'Yes.' But they often didn't get better; instead, they got worse." Weary of pretending to be interested as his clients free-associated on the couch, he took a post as a psychiatric aide at the Pinel Institute, a private asylum that housed the wayward scions of Seattle's upper crust. One summer, two patients killed themselves by plummeting to the pavement out of second-story windows. "The doctors were all medically oriented, so they called it a 'suicide epidemic,' as if it was a contagious disease," Lovaas recalled in disgust. He quickly lost patience with the tendentious speculations of theory-based psychiatry. After hearing his colleagues droning on in a symposium, he said, "They were like Nero, playing fiddles as the world burned. When you see a war and how horrible it can be to people, you want to be relevant—you want to do something about this world."

Fortunately for Lovaas, many of his professors at UW felt the same way. His advisor was not a psychotherapist but a behaviorist who encouraged him to pursue lab research. One of the stars of the department was Sid Bijou, a former student of B. F. Skinner's who pioneered the use of operant conditioning with intellectually disabled children. The paradigmatic example of operant conditioning was Skinner and his rats. To train a rat to press a bar, he would give the animal a food pellet (the *reward*) if it accidentally approached the bar. If the rat happened to brush the bar with its paw, he would give it another pellet, and then another if it pressed its paw down firmly on the bar. Typically, the end result of this painstaking step-by-step process was the rat frantically punching the bar to get more pellets.

Conversely, to condition the animal to stop pressing the bar, Skinner would quit delivering pellets until the rat stopped emitting the behavior (a process known as *extinction*). Another way to extinguish the behavior would be to zap the rat with an electric shock instead of delivering the pellet (the term of art for this was *punishment*). The use of punishment on animals was controversial among behaviorists but not because it seemed cruel; the animal's internal state—if it had one—was considered completely irrelevant, a black box. In practice, however, punishment turned out to be an inefficient method of training an animal to extinction because it tended to increase the emission of behaviors unrelated to the task at hand. (In other words, the panicked animal would start trying anything to escape the painful shocks.)

To adapt Skinner's model for use with human beings, Bijou analyzed behavior in terms of its antecedents (its triggers in the environment) and its consequences (which could include reward or punishment, depending on whether the experimenter wanted the behavior to increase or decrease). He called the meticulous recording and study of this sequence *behavior analysis*. By experimentally manipulating antecedents and consequences, Bijou found that behavior analysis could be a powerful tool for facilitating change in the responses of human subjects. Furthermore, in these cases, the rewards and punishments available to the experimenter were not limited to food pellets and electric shocks. "That's a good boy!" could be as rewarding to a child as a food pellet to a rat; and a sharp "*No!*" could serve as the equivalent of a punishing jolt. In the lexicon of the field, language was a powerful *discriminative stimulus* in human subjects.

Or rather, in *most* human subjects. After earning his doctorate at UW, Lovaas stayed on in Seattle for three years, teaching and conducting research at the Child Development Institute near the university, where he had two experiences that decisively shaped the course of his career. He saw a girl who could not talk, did not make eye contact, and refused to play with toys, spending whole days rocking back and forth and flapping her hands. He knew that the most likely fate in store for her was to be sent to a state hospital where she would live out the rest of her days on a locked ward. Could nothing more be done for her?

Then he observed an experiment that suggested a more promising possibility. Watching a typically developing boy being conditioned to use speech to obtain a toy trinket—a trivial task at best—it occurred to Lovaas that improving the language skills of children with developmental delays might give them more leverage over their problematic behavior. In 1961, he accepted a position as an assistant professor in the psychology department at UCLA. In children with autism, he felt he had found the ideal pool of subjects for testing his hypothesis—children with severe language deficits whose behavior seemed totally out of control.

A psychologist at Indiana University named Charles Ferster was another critical influence on Lovaas's thinking. Ferster was firmly in the camp of psychologists who believed that Kanner's syndrome was a rare early-onset form of schizophrenia. He felt so confident that it was rare, in fact, that his 1961 paper "Positive Reinforcement and Behavioral Deficits of Autistic Children" begins with an apology for taking up the reader's time with such an arcane subject. Autism "is not important from an epidemiological point of view," he acknowledged, while offering that "the analysis of the autistic child may be of theoretical use, however, since his psychosis may be a prototype of the adult's." Then Ferster goes on to describe the idiosyncratic behavior of autistic children in behaviorist terms as being contingent on *reinforcement*—the receipt of rewards—just like the typical behavior of typical children. A child who repeated the word *candy* over and over would eventually be reinforced for this behavior by getting a piece. If the same child had a violent tantrum, the reward would be seeing their concerned mother rush in to see what was the matter. But what happened if a child gave a tantrum and nobody came?

Ferster described an experiment that involved locking an autistic child in a small room alone every day for a year. Lo and behold, the child's tantrums eventually subsided—which the psychologist took as a clear sign that tantrums are also contingent on reinforcement. He proposed that parents had inadvertently conditioned their children to be more and more autistic by rewarding their misbehavior with doting attention. Ferster extracted a fateful lesson from these experiments: the best way for parents to deal with their children acting out, he said, was for them to ignore their distress entirely until the undesirable behavior extinguished of its own accord.

Though Lovaas had little patience for Freudian psychology, he still suspected that the parents of autistic children somehow played a decisive role in the genesis of their condition, and he was impressed with Ferster's unsentimental analysis. Lovaas would eventually make films of young autistics in institutions like Camarillo State Hospital, located north of Los Angeles—the real-life setting of Olivia de Havilland's noir psycho-thriller *The Snake Pit*—who had broken their noses with their knees and chewed their arms to the bone. Seemingly immune to any drug that the pharmaceutical industry could throw at them, these children struck Lovaas as fundamentally inhuman but with some margin of redemptive potential. "The fascinating part to me was to observe persons with eyes and ears, teeth and toenails, walking around yet presenting few of the behaviors that one would call social or human," he wrote. "Now, I had the chance to build language and other social and intellectual behaviors where none had existed, a good test of how much help a learning-based approach could offer."

He explained to *Psychology Today*, "You see, you start pretty much from scratch when you work with an autistic child. You have a person in the physical sense—they have hair, a nose, and a mouth—but they are not people in the psychological sense. One way to look at the job of helping autistic kids is to see it as a matter of constructing a person. You have the raw materials, but you have to build the person."

VI

To Lovaas's frustration, the clinic referred only one child to his lab at UCLA in his first year on the job: a chubby, blue-eyed nine-year-old brunette named Beth who spoke mostly in echolalia and bore scars all over from banging herself against walls and furniture. To justify his use of laboratory time and the services of a team of grad students, Lovaas began spending entire days with Beth, picking her up at nine in the morning and dropping her off at three, five days a week. He was abashed to admit that he spent more time with Beth than he did with his own children. For a year, she became the subject of an epic experiment with an n of 1. The psychologist outfitted a suite of rooms with one-way mirrors and hidden microphones, along with a push-button device that enabled his assistants to record the frequency and duration of her behaviors. In this state-of-the-art panopticon, Lovaas crafted his lasting legacy: a style of intensive intervention called *applied behavior analysis,* or ABA.

His genius was breaking down complex everyday activities like getting dressed, going to the toilet, and toothbrushing into a sequence of smaller, simpler actions that could be conditioned through sheer repetition. He called his method *discrete-trial training* because each conditioning session was broken up into a series of beats with a distinct beginning and end. In this way, the therapist ensured that each stimulus (called a *prompt*) was strongly associated with a specific behavior, forming a tight loop of cause and effect. While this process might sound mechanical and formulaic, what Lovaas was attempting to do was to teach these children skills that would enable them to stay out of places like Camarillo and lead semi-independent lives. The strapping Nordic psychologist came to regard ABA as an art as well as a science. Some people had an inborn aptitude for it (including, of course, Lovaas himself) and some did not. But most importantly, it was an art that could be taught.

What did this art look like in practice? Here is Lovaas's own description of teaching a child to give a hug. (*Fading* means offering a prompt with decreasing regularity until it is no longer required to elicit the target behavior.)

Step 1: Say, "Hug me," and prompt (e.g., physically move) the child so that his cheek makes momentary contact with yours. Reward him with food the moment his cheek makes contact.

Step 2: Gradually fade the prompt while keeping the instruction ("Hug me") loud and clear.

Step 3: Gradually withhold the reward contingent on longer and longer hugs. Move in slow steps from a 1-second hug to one lasting 5 or 10 seconds. At the same time, require a more complete hug such as placing his arms around your neck, squeezing harder, etc. Prompt these additional behaviors if necessary.

Step 4: Generalize this learning to many behaviors and many persons. Gradually thin the reward schedule so that you get more and more hugs for less and less rewards.

Lovaas used to say that the most important thing to establish at the outset of discrete-trial training is "You are the boss." To make clear that his tough-minded approach was not about being pleasing and supportive, he added, "People whose voices are very tender, who have difficulty asserting themselves, or who are obsessive about right and wrong, just don't make good teachers of developmentally disabled children." He described the ideal ABA therapist as "assertive, confident, and outgoing"—all adjectives that applied readily to Lovaas.

The protocols of ABA, as they were initially developed, were inextricably interwoven with Lovaas's personality, which was both dominating and disarming. Operant conditioning was commonly known as *behavior modification*, but that sounded too mild to him. He called what he was doing with these difficult children *behavioral engineering.* (Most parents would simply refer to ABA as "the Lovaas method.") A lifelong skier who was as competitive on the slopes as he was in a lab, he would charm his students with fractured versions of American idioms, as when he described his critics as "beating up old horses" or chided a graduate assistant, "You're shrinking your responsibilities." Instead of shying away from confrontation, he was energized by criticism and supremely unconcerned with political correctness. When his students voted him the department's biggest "male chauvinist pig," he was delighted.

The deepest impression that Lovaas made on his students, however, was of being a man who never "shrank" his own sense of responsibility to the children in his care. He became a mentor to a generation of psychologists, therapists, and teachers at UCLA and believed so much in the redemptive power of ABA that he once bragged to a reporter from *Los Angeles* magazine, "If I had gotten Hitler here at UCLA at the age of 4 or 5, I could have raised him to be a nice person."

Rimland was skeptical of the Lovaas method when he first heard about it: "The technique seemed much better suited to training dogs or seals than people," he said. But after seeing the psychologist's footage of self-mutilating children before and after ABA, he set his doubts aside and began scheming about ways that the technique could be exported from the lab. If grad students could be schooled in the art, why not parents?

"To my wife's horror, I began to use Lovaas's techniques in training our very difficult eight-year-old autistic son," Rimland recalled in 1987. "I realized that the extremely permissive, indulgent attitude toward autistic children which had been fostered by previous authorities in the field of autism was in fact terribly damaging to the children. I used behavior modification to 'shape up' my son. Self-stimming was no longer tolerated. I used Lovaas' techniques to ensure that Mark paid close attention to what he was told and what was going on around him."

He also brought in one of Lovaas's grad students, David Ryback, who prompted Mark to make eye contact and imitate phonemes with rewards of M&Ms and Coca-Cola. Stimming was punished with a loud "No!" as Ryback slapped himself. "Mark was a very nice kid, very alert, very oriented to his surroundings," Ryback recalls. "He developed very quickly." Soon Mark had learned to distinguish between "Grandma" and "Grandpa."

Lovaas was already thinking about inviting parents into the process to address a weakness in his method that showed up in early studies: the lessons learned in ABA often didn't generalize beyond the highly artificial situation in the lab. (In typical fashion, this was blamed on a global deficit of the children's ability to learn and generalize rather than on any flaw in the method.) The best hope for prompting lasting behavior change was to train the children in their natural environment: at home. A colleague of Lovaas's named Todd Risley had already taught the mother of one of his patients to become her son's ABA therapist, shaping his behavior with bites of ice cream.

At a dinner that Rimland arranged with a few of the couples who wrote to him after reading his book, Lovaas compared behavioral engineering to the techniques employed by Anne Sullivan to teach Helen Keller to talk. Over heaping plates of spaghetti and copious amounts of red wine, he told the parents that ABA was their best chance to rescue their children from being forever trapped behind their "autistic shells." Before the meal was over, they were begging Lovaas to train them in his method. He told Rimland that the dinner was one of the most important nights of his life.

Working alone, both men were vulnerable to the kind of marginalization faced by any researchers who attempt to subvert the dominant paradigms in their field. By forming an alliance and reaching out directly to parents, they gained a level of credibility and influence far beyond what they could have achieved by waiting for confirmation of their theories through the usual peer-reviewed channels. Together, they would build an empire of their own: a shadow infrastructure for autism research in which parents, rather than medical professionals, were the ultimate authorities on their children's well-being.

THE GRAND SCALE OF Rimland's ambitions was apparent in an application he filed for a year's fellowship at the Center for Advanced Study in the Behavioral Sciences at Stanford University in 1964. Each year, the center extended an invitation to fifty distinguished scholars, and he was flattered to receive one.

His top priority for a residency at the prestigious university, he wrote to the center's founder and director, would be expanding on his book's investigation of how the genetic roots of autism cast light on "the nature of perception, motivation, thought, and intelligence." This might have been enough to keep most visiting scholars busy for a year, but Rimland didn't stop there. He took aim squarely at the foundation of psychiatry, aiming to prove that the notion that conditions like autism and schizophrenia could be "caused" (his scare quotes) by psychological factors was "no more than a highly prevalent and tenaciously believed myth—a modern day scientifically sanctioned superstition." He offered to organize a symposium at Stanford called "What's Wrong with Psychology?"

The next item on his agenda was equally lofty: exploring methods of augmenting human intelligence by manipulating maternal hormones and other perinatal factors in the womb. "Man is living in an atomic age with a brain mostly evolved during stone and pre–stone age. Not good enough," Rimland declared.

Needless to say, he got the fellowship. Once Rimland settled into academic life in Palo Alto with his family, he fell under the spell of Linus Pauling, one of the true Renaissance figures of twentieth-century science. Pauling had a quick wit and a photographic memory, and his insatiable curiosity ranged from chemistry to molecular biology, quantum mechanics, immunology, and beyond. He made a series of discoveries about the nature of chemical bonding that won him the Nobel Prize in chemistry in 1954. By applying insights from the physical sciences to biology, he discovered sickle-cell anemia, pioneering the field of molecular medicine. At the height of the cold war, he won a second Nobel for his role in negotiating a global ban on atomic-weapons testing in the atmosphere—the Peace Prize this time.

In 1941, Pauling was embarking on a study of antibodies when he was laid low by a chronic inflammation of the kidneys called Bright's disease (now known as nephritis), which can be triggered by a whole group of ailments including hepatitis C, mononucleosis, and type 2 diabetes. He was referred to a renal specialist named Thomas Addis, who advocated adherence to a strict low-salt, low-protein diet to give the kidneys a chance to "rest" and heal. By following Addis's stringent diet—which included taking supplementary vitamins and minerals while guzzling gallons of water—Pauling was permanently relieved of his debilitating symptoms in just four months.

His consultations with Addis took place in the doctor's bustling clinic at Stanford, where patients could watch him openly performing his experiments. He treated his patients' wives and mothers as his "colleagues" while playing chamber music by Brahms and Beethoven on a phonograph. Each afternoon at the appointed time, all work in the clinic would stop for tea.

Addis's strategy for treating disease struck Pauling with the force of a revelation. Instead of pumping him full of drugs, this wise physician had healed him by manipulating levels of compounds—water, vitamins, minerals, protein, and salt—already present in his body. Pauling dubbed his approach *orthomolecular medicine* (from the Greek root *orthos*, "upright" or "correct") and came to believe that it had potential for curing a broad range of maladies from schizophrenia to cancer.

Pauling became the most prominent advocate of the notion that megadoses of vitamin C could avert the common cold, slow the aging process, and improve mood. He wrote three best-selling books on the subject and received extensive coverage for his theories in the *New York Times* and other prestigious media outlets. A month after publication of his 1970 blockbuster *Vitamin C and the Common Cold*, drugstores across the country reported an unprecedented run on the tablets, and an industry spokesman complained that production was unable to keep up with the demand. Pauling's credibility as one of the few two-time Nobel winners in history helped transform the supplement business from a marginal enterprise serving health food stores into an alt-med powerhouse with annual sales rivaling the pharmaceutical industry—minus the pesky Food and Drug Administration (FDA) regulations.

In placebo-controlled trials, Pauling's extravagant claims for vitamin C received mixed reviews at best. But he had a good reason for believing that vitamins play a role in mental illness. In 1926, his mother, Belle, died in an insane asylum in Oregon, deranged by a type of anemia caused by chronic B-12 deficiency. Just after she died, scientists discovered that the condition that killed her could have been easily averted by eating raw liver. A decade and a half later, two of Pauling's colleagues, Karl Folkers and Alexander Todd, isolated the bright pink crystals of the vitamin in its pure state. Pauling speculated that certain types of intellectual disability were a form of "cerebral scurvy" caused by a general decline of nutrition in the modern era, including the widespread adoption of heavily processed foods.

Pauling's concept of orthomolecular psychiatry meshed perfectly with Rimland's thoughts on PKU and autism. Meanwhile, Rimland had started getting letters from parents who were conducting their own orthomolecular experiments on their children and reporting promising results. A mother from Canada told him that her son's autism had vastly improved after she gave him megadoses of B vitamins inspired by the schizophrenia research of Abram Hoffer and Humphry Osmond at a mental hospital in Saskatchewan. Osmond was no stranger to controversial research: he coined the word *psychedelic* in 1957 after giving Aldous Huxley the dose of mescaline that inspired him to write *The Doors of Perception*. According to the mother, the hospital nurses felt that their patients had made breakthroughs on Hoffer and Osmond's B-vitamin regimen, but the senior psychiatrists on the ward "refused to see what was so clearly evident to everyone else," in Rimland's words.

While Rimland was skeptical at first that anything as innocuous as vitamin tablets could make a significant impact on autism, he saw the same supplements (particularly B vitamins and magnesium) being mentioned over and over by parents. Could it all just be a coincidence?

By the fall of 1965, Rimland was receiving letters and checklists from all over the world. Before attending a Navy conference in Washington, he wrote to parents throughout the New York–D.C. metropolitan area, offering to tell them in person about a new kind of behavioral therapy for autism that offered great promise. One of the mothers on his mailing list was Ruth Christ Sullivan, a young nurse who reached out to him after seeing a reflection of her own son, Joe, in one of the first TV specials about autism.

When Joe was born, Sullivan and her family were living in Lake Charles, Louisiana, near Cajun country. For the first eighteen months of his life, he seemed like an exceptionally bright and engaging boy, but gradually he began putting the world at a distance. In family snapshots, he was often caught in the act of slipping off somebody's lap. After beginning to talk on the usual schedule, he abruptly stopped using words altogether. One day, he parked himself in front of a door to put together a jigsaw puzzle; then his mother accidentally burst through the door from the other side, making a mess of the puzzle. But as Sullivan watched, astonished, he quickly reassembled the puzzle with the pieces upside down, though he could no longer use the pattern they formed as a cue to their proper placement. He soon started drawing maps of the United States while humming "The Star-Spangled Banner."

Then, just as inexplicably as he had stopped, Joe started speaking again and was able to instantly name the day of the week for nearly any date in the past or future. He would startle his mother by recalling things that the family had done years before in photographic detail. He was also extraordinarily agile and fearless and built Tetris-like pyramids of tables and chairs to climb to the tops of bookshelves. One day, a neighbor called to inform Sullivan that her son was crawling around on the roof. A young doctor at a public-health clinic told her that he suspected Joe had autism, but then the doctor died suddenly, and no one else in the area could tell her anything more about her son's condition.

Then the Sullivans moved to upstate New York so that Joe's father, William, could start teaching at a local college. There, Ruth found two child psychiatrists who had worked directly with Kanner at Johns Hopkins, and they confirmed Joe's diagnosis. She was advised to join a therapy group for "overanxious mothers." At the first meeting, the psychologist's assistant asked her to hand out slips of paper so that the other mothers in the room could sign up for future sessions. Instead, she surreptitiously passed around a note inviting everyone to get together in private. Their meetings at each other's houses in Albany marked the birth of the autism parenting movement in the United States.

COMMUNITY ORGANIZING was nothing new to Sullivan. "The first time I held elected office," she laughs, "I was in seventh grade." As a student nurse in the Deep South in the depths of the Jim Crow era, she called for a motion to integrate the Louisiana Nurses' Association, which passed unanimously. She also became active in the League of Women Voters, inspired by her mother, a strong and independent woman for her time. In her correspondence with Rimland, she proposed forming a national group to advocate for the needs of autistic children. He replied that he was already thinking along the same lines.

On November 14, 1965, Sullivan drove down from Albany to Teaneck, New Jersey—a four-hour trip along twisting back roads before the opening of the interstates—where thirty-five mothers and fathers crowded into the living room of a couple named Herbert and Rosalyn Kahn. "We just fell on each other," Sullivan recalls. "It was an incredible experience for us. For the first time, we had hope."

The meeting started at eight p.m. and lasted until midnight. Rimland talked about the need to launch a national organization and touted the potential of the Lovaas method, delivering a talk that he would repeat many times in the coming years. He told the assembly that Lovaas would be willing to send out graduate students from UCLA to offer training sessions and handed out lists of activities that parents could do with their children to improve their behavior in the meantime.

Then a pediatrician named Mary Goodwin from Cooperstown, New York, gave a presentation that was far ahead of its time, like a transmission from thirty years in the future. Goodwin recounted her experiences of teaching dozens of nonspeaking children to use an experimental device called the Edison Responsive Environment Learning System (ERELS), familiarly known as the "talking typewriter." The ERELS was the brainchild of an inventor at the Edison Research Laboratory named Richard Kobler and a sociologist at Yale with the splendid name of Omar Khayyam Moore. Among Kobler's achievements was designing the first telephone to store frequently dialed numbers and a contraption called the Voicewriter that enabled nurses to dictate medical records. Moore theorized that if learning were more like play, children would be able to teach themselves how to read, write, and type at a very young age. Working with Kobler, he developed a device that combined a keyboard, a TV screen, a tape recorder, and an analog processor, like a prototype of the modern computer.

The ERELS interface was designed to be as nonthreatening as possible. When a child sat down at the machine, a color photograph—say, of a sailboat—would flash on the screen. "This is a boat," a soothing recorded voice would say. "*Boat* is spelled *B-O-A-T.* Now type *B.*" Then an onscreen prompt would guide the child's finger to the *B* key—the only key that would work at that moment. Thus it was impossible for the child to make a mistake. When the *B* was pressed, the machine would say, "Very good! Now type *O.*" Typing the whole word correctly prompted the machine to say "Excellent!" and to invite the child to say the word out loud; then it would play the word back in the sound of the child's own voice. Simple games were also available on the ERELS, giving children additional opportunities to become comfortable using the machine. Moore felt there was "no greater deterrent to learning than the fear of making a mistake. So the children discover that when they make an error, nothing happens. The typewriter never scolds; it is never impatient."

Upon seeing one of Moore's talking typewriters in use at a school in New Haven, Goodwin was hopeful that it could provide a valuable learning opportunity for children with autism. With her husband, Campbell, who was also a pediatrician, she raised $35,000 to bring one to the hospital where they worked in Cooperstown and establish a research facility. Over the next two years, they would work on the ERELS with sixty-five autistic children, yielding very positive results. One of the first children to sit down at the machine was a six-year-old boy who had never spoken a word and had been recommended for custodial care because of his violent behavior. After exploring the keyboard for a while, he began typing out brand names he'd heard on TV. Soon he was showing up at the hospital three times a week, and his parents were able to find him a placement at a local school. Other children made similar progress, including a fourteen-year-old boy who had regressed to near catatonia. Unfortunately, the cost of the talking typewriters proved prohibitive, and the Goodwins' far-seeing experiment came to an end in 1966. But Mary's presentation was a preview of the potential of technology for transforming the lives of children who had been written off as incapable of any sort of communication.

Much of the discussion that night in Teaneck was devoted to ways that parents could work together effectively to demand access to education and other services for their children. By the end of the night, the group had a president, a board of advisors, an editor for its newsletter, and a name: the National Society for Autistic Children. "We should weave a cloth so strong," Rimland told the group, "that no one can tear us apart."

Two nights later, he hosted another meeting at the National Institutes of Health in Bethesda. In the coming years, parents would launch hundreds of local NSAC chapters all over the country. "Lifting the burden of shame, guilt, and blame from the parents of autistic children," Rimland wrote, "unleashed an enormous burst of productivity and creativity on behalf of the children." He and Sullivan had raised a mighty army. The battle for their children's future was finally under way.

THE GROUP WAS BOLD and radical from the start, energized by the rage of parents who had been scapegoated for causing their own children's misery. "NSAC was founded because parents of children with autism knew that many things closely affecting their lives were terribly wrong," longtime member Frank Warren said. "[They] knew that their children needed help, that no one understood what was wrong with them, and that leadership in all the helping professions were blaming the parents for their children's disability . . . Naturally the parents were angry. Naturally the fledgling society was a highly charged and scrappy organization."

The fighting spirit and lobbying expertise of parents like Sullivan enabled NSAC to accomplish a great deal in a relatively short time. Sullivan conceived of her fellow parent-activists as "trainers" for alleged experts who often knew little or nothing about their child's condition. In West Virginia, NSAC established a medical lending library promoted with mailings to five hundred pediatricians, psychiatrists, general practitioners, and hearing specialists headlined, "The next child who walks into your office may be autistic. What will you tell the family?" The society established a network of similar libraries throughout the country, offering up-to-date information on education, legislation, and housing.

In 1967, Clarence and Christine Griffith sought in vain through the whole state of Georgia to find a school that would accept their son Joseph.

They realized that only by making common cause with other parents would they be able to get anything done, so they formed an NSAC chapter called the Georgia Society for Autistic Children. Over the course of the next few months, they persuaded the DeKalb County school board to launch a pilot program for autistic children funded by the state. The Women's Club in Sandy Springs set up classes for preschoolers, and the First Baptist Church in Decatur began researching ways of mainstreaming autistic kids in kindergarten. Crucial to these efforts, the Griffiths said, was networking with other groups like the League of Women Voters and the Jaycees. They also stressed the importance of raising public awareness of autism by making contacts at TV and radio stations, parent-teacher associations, and churches. Later that year, when the Georgia House was debating a bill for funding special education called the Exceptional Child Act, a state representative who had seen one of the Griffiths' broadcasts on a local TV station stood up and proposed adding services for autistic children to the bill, saying, "'Autistic' is a label that has been used in the past to deny a child an education; I want it used once *for* an autistic child." The bill passed.

To achieve its legislative goals, NSAC also forged strategic alliances with other disability advocacy groups, including the United Cerebral Palsy Association, the Epilepsy Foundation of America, and the Association for Retarded Citizens (also known as the Arc). By aligning with these groups, NSAC helped reframe autism in the minds of professionals from a form of childhood "emotional disturbance" to an inborn disability that required lifelong care and support. In 1967, the society was a fierce critic of the recommendations of the congressional Joint Commission on the Mental Health of Children, blasting the commission's focus on the role of broken homes and unhappy households as allegedly responsible for conditions like autism.

That same year, NSAC board member Amy Lettick opened a school called Benhaven in Connecticut that embraced an eclectic range of progressive approaches to special education. Housed in a twenty-two-room Tudor mansion on a hillside in New Haven, the school was created as a haven for children like Lettick's son, Ben, who had been excluded and expelled from other schools. At a time when autistic teenagers were still invisible in the clinical literature, students were encouraged to attend the school into adulthood, taking classes, swimming in the pool, and working on the school's thirty-five-acre farm, which featured vegetable gardens, greenhouses, barns, and a chicken coop.

The total environment of Benhaven was shaped with the needs and comfort of the students in mind. Airy classrooms were designed to reduce distracting sights and sounds, and the kitchens, bathrooms, and laundry rooms were extra large so that instruction in self-care skills could take place there also. Along with their academic lessons, students learned to bake bread, build furniture, raise food crops and ornamental flowers, hand-set type, and bind books. Benhaven also offered courses in sex education for teenagers and older students, which was unheard-of in schools for the developmentally disabled.

In 1972, the school enrolled its first students who were both autistic and deaf. To accommodate them, the whole staff learned sign language. Signing turned out to be a popular medium of communication at Benhaven even for hearing students. Lettick realized that too much emphasis was being placed on teaching autistic children to *speak*, when what was truly essential was enabling them to *communicate*. Using sign, students who had previously been unable to learn to read and write were able to do so. "It is fascinating to be able to *watch* the thought processes as the children think aloud in sign language while they do their work," Lettick wrote. "We frequently see these children talking to themselves during the day, getting the same satisfaction from signing that speaking children get from softly talking to themselves in spoken language."

Sullivan was thrilled to see her fellow NSAC parents proudly step out of the shadows and claim their power to change the world. "Though it is a rare parent who is well-informed about this severe, low-incidence disorder at the time of their child's diagnosis, it is *common* to find parents of older children who are highly informed," she wrote. "I believe the sweetest reward of being a parent trainer is seeing a hurt, scared, timid, frustrated, despondent or angry parent blossom into an articulate, well-informed, assertive, energetic, and successful advocate for their child."

After moving to Huntington, West Virginia, she founded state and local NSAC chapters and launched the society's Information and Referral Service out of her house, offering a wide range of services and resources to parents and professionals. Instead of relying on a switchboard operator or answering service, she fielded most of the calls herself. Requests for assistance came in twenty-four hours a day—a mother in New York whose son had been thrown out of school; a father phoning from a motel room in Alabama looking for other parents in the area; a Japanese pediatrician seeking one of the society's professional advisors to talk to parents in Tokyo; a Florida mother trying to get her misunderstood son out of jail. The Information and Referral Service eventually received federal funding and opened its own office in Washington. For years, the society's bimonthly newsletter was the only source of breaking news in the world of autism for families.

Working with Mary Coleman, director of the Children's Brain Research Clinic in Washington, Rimland and other NSAC parents made possible an in-depth study of the biology of autism in 1974 that was as far ahead of its time as the Goodwins' talking typewriters. By conducting thorough examinations of seventy-eight children brought to the clinic by NSAC members from all across the country, the clinic's researchers theorized that autism is not a single clinical entity but is composed of multiple distinct subtypes—a view that has been widely accepted in mainstream science only in recent years.

Rimland also did a groundbreaking study on savant skills based on data from his questionnaires, rediscovering the same clusters of enhanced ability in music, memory, art, mathematics, science, and technology that Asperger dubbed "autistic intelligence." Rimland described very young children who could speak and write in multiple languages, had total recall for various kinds of statistics, could instantly identify a note played on a piano, were able to calculate square roots in their heads, had precocious abilities in drawing, and were so aware of subtle aspects of their environments that they seemed to have ESP. (Meanwhile, nearly all of them had been branded as "profoundly retarded.") One mother's report on her son demonstrated the untapped potential of these children:

> He reads and understands books on electronics and uses the theories to build devices . . . He understands the concepts of electronics, astronomy, music, navigation, and mechanics. He knows an astonishing amount about how things work and is familiar with technical terms. By the age of 12, he could find his way all over the city on his bike with a map and compass. He reads Bowditch on navigation. Joe is supposed to have an IQ of 80. He does assembly work in a Goodwill store.

Based on these accounts, Rimland became more open to the idea of a broader autistic continuum. He theorized that the achievements of geniuses like Einstein, Newton, and world chess champion Bobby Fischer were related to the fact that these men "manifested signs—sometimes several signs—of autism." He ventured, "It may not be too far amiss to suggest that some autistic individuals are incipient geniuses whose eccentricities are so severe and incapacitating that all but minimal participation in the 'normal' world is precluded."

In the midst of a dark age, NSAC laid the foundations of a better future, accomplishing it all with a small but highly committed membership. "So many children . . . needing so much . . . all over the world," Clara Claiborne Park wrote in the society's newsletter. "When the hours (or the money) you devote to NSAC seem too much, reflect that the waves you make may wash shores thousands of miles away, bringing hope to families you will never see."

THIS SCRAPPY MOVEMENT MADE its debut on the national stage at NSAC's First Annual Congress in Washington in July 1969. The theme—reflecting the rebellious spirit of the event and the terminology in use at the time—was "Better *Everything* for Mentally Ill Children."

In the past, inviting patients' families to a conference on autism would have seemed as unthinkable as inviting the "patients" themselves. But this conference, organized by parents, was different: between the formal workshop sessions, speakers and participants commingled in the hallways and the dining room, sharing information on equal terms. Speech therapists, psychologists, and biochemists chatted informally with family members about their research. Most of the participants were too engaged by what was going on around them to pay much attention to the other historical milestone taking place that week: the landing of *Apollo 11* on the moon.

The air in the Sheraton Palace was electric as parents spontaneously formed support groups to address issues that weren't acknowledged in the medical literature, such as the challenges of raising autistic girls, or parenting children who were blind as well as autistic. Rimland and Lovaas were on the speakers list, as was Eric Schopler, a former graduate student of Bettelheim's at the University of Chicago who had gone head-to-head with him for scapegoating parents. Schopler would go on to launch Division TEACCH (Treatment and Education of Autistic and Related Communication Handicapped Children) in North Carolina, the first statewide autism education program in the United States and the model for many other progressive programs since.

The keynote speaker was Kanner himself, who struck his usual note of grandiosity combined with self-effacement. "Ladies and gentlemen, I can't tell you how pleased and touched I am to be spoken of with such affection and respect. Of course there are a few things, which, because of your good feeling toward me, are a bit exaggerated. I never discovered autism. It was there before," he said coyly. (Georg and Anni Frankl could have attested to the truth of that statement, but they weren't invited to the party that night.)

Next, Kanner turned his attention to Bettelheim's *Empty Fortress*. "I need not mention to you *the book*," he said. "An empty book, I call it." (The crowd applauded.) He said that, while reading it, he counted 150 times when the author had used phrases like "'maybe,' 'perhaps,' and 'it may be just mere speculation' . . . One hundred and fifty times!"

Then Kanner spoke the words that everyone in the room desperately wanted to hear, uttered with the formality of a royal proclamation: "And herewith I especially acquit you people as parents." (The grateful audience jumped to its feet and gave him a standing ovation.) In the face of such an enthusiastic response, Kanner couldn't resist acquitting himself also.

"I have been misquoted many times," he went on. "From the very first publication until the last, I spoke of this condition in no uncertain terms as 'innate.' But because I described some of the characteristics of some of the parents as persons, I was misquoted often as having said 'it is all the parents' fault.' Those of you parents who have come to see me with your children know that this isn't what I said . . . Once again, I thank you very, very much. Just keep up the good work."

Far from the cheering crowds, Kanner would continue to refer to autism as a "childhood psychosis" in his work, and in 1973 he reprinted a collection of his essays describing his patients' parents as "cold, humorless perfectionists" lacking "genuine warmth," with no editorial caveats.

But Kanner had already decisively lost his grip on the autism narrative. On her way back to Albany, Sullivan sat down in front of a TV set at the airport to watch Neil Armstrong take his first awkward steps out of the lunar excursion module onto the dusty surface of a new world. She and her fellow NSAC parents had crossed a threshold into a new world too: one in which they would help make the long-silent voices of their sons and daughters heard.

The next NSAC Congress, held in San Francisco in 1970, made good on that promise by inviting a young autistic man to the podium to address an audience of parents and professionals for the first time in history. After a brief introduction by his mother, twenty-one-year-old William Donovan made clear that he was very aware of his environment, even when people assumed he was oblivious. "As an autistic child, I felt very uncomfortable," he began. "I tore up newspapers, pulled bedspreads off the beds, pulled books out of the bookcases, bounced cans and played with spinning tops, and broke every one of them. I would like to take this opportunity to tell you that I destroyed things *because I couldn't talk*. I spun things because I couldn't talk. It also made me feel good, of course."

He was just getting started. "I hated going to school because classrooms were too confining. I didn't like the idea of the other kids making fun of me and I didn't want anyone to pass judgment on me as to how good or bad I was." He described his teachers hitting him with rulers, locking him in a closet, and talking about him as if he weren't there. Someone in the audience asked if he had spoken only in echolalia until he was ten because he "couldn't" or "wouldn't" talk normally. Donovan replied firmly, "*Couldn't.*"

In addition to being autistic, Donovan had severe cataracts, and after getting vocational training at a school for the blind, he had been hired at a packaging company. His first day of work, he said, was the happiest day of his life. He also talked about his love of Charlie Brown and playing music, and concluded by saying, "I feel wonderful here today. I feel like the President. I hope all autistic children could grow up to be socially acceptable."

There were two paths toward achieving that goal, reflected in the two types of sessions on the conference program. One set focused on ways of changing society to make it a more accepting and accommodating place for people like Donovan, with topics like "School Is for All Children," "How to Work with Your State Legislature," and "Help Your Community Help Your Handicapped Child." In her introduction, Donovan's mother talked about how she had finally worked up the courage to take her son everywhere instead of hiding him in the house (or committing him to Bellevue, as she and her husband had been advised to do). She advised her fellow parents:

> Never be embarrassed about taking them places. When Judy Garland was playing in New York, we decided to get a box seat and take Bill to see her in person because he loved her records. God bless Judy, she was wonderful. Bill was directly over her head and acting up as I expected he would and she looked up and said, "What's the matter, darling?" That little bit of recognition from her made all the difference. He calmed down and enjoyed the rest of the show.

The alternate path was trying to change the children themselves to make them more "socially acceptable"—the path that Lovaas had embarked on with ABA and that Rimland was pursuing with his search for an orthomolecular cure for autism. At NSAC meetings, Sullivan would take informal polls asking for a show of hands from those who thought the organization should focus on finding a cure instead of lobbying for services. "Nearly all the parents' hands went up for services," she recalls.

In 1974, West Virginia became the first state in the Union to specifically include autism in its mandatory public education laws, opening the doors of classrooms to hundreds of kids for the first time. Sullivan was one of the chief proponents of the Education for All Handicapped Children Act, Public Law 94-142, which mandated that disabled children in every school district in America have a right to a "free and appropriate" public education and be educated in the "least restrictive environment" possible, encouraging mainstreaming when appropriate. (Before the passage of the law, school districts in most states were allowed to choose whether they were willing to educate a child with disabilities, and more than one million children were locked out of public education.) The act, signed into law by President Gerald Ford in 1975, became the precursor of the Individuals with Disabilities Education Act (IDEA) that is in force today. The law also empowered parents to file grievances if their child's needs weren't being met.

After the passage of the Education for All Handicapped Children Act, Sullivan focused on demanding services for autistic adults. "There was nothing for adults—zip," she recalls. "We had to start from scratch." This was particularly important because the traditional caretakers for autistic adults who were not in institutions were stay-at-home moms, and in the 1960s more and more women were entering the workforce and launching their own careers. Family members that looked to private and public agencies for help were faced with a confusing maze of limited options presided over by underpaid, overworked case managers who often occupied their positions for only a short time. "We cannot allow another generation of our adult children to go without the vital services that any humane society knows is necessary for a life of dignity and worth," Sullivan wrote.

Over time, the two paths represented by NSAC's founders—Sullivan's focus on services and Rimland's search for a cure—would diverge, resulting in Rimland being voted off the board of his own organization. An early sign of this rift was the controversy that broke out in 1965 after a series of articles in the popular press made clear just how far Lovaas was willing to go to make autistic children "socially acceptable."

VII

One of Lovaas's first experiments with Beth was like a music-appreciation class in hell. For months, the psychologist and his assistants played children's songs for her on a guitar while reinforcing proper social behavior by smiling and saying "That's a good girl!" when she clapped or sang along. Lovaas was testing the hypothesis that Beth's self-injurious behavior would decrease as she became more socially aware.

Beth *was* a good girl: within two months, she was clapping her hands in rhythm and joining in rousing choruses of "The children in the bus go 'wiggle-wiggle-wiggle.'" The more she was engaged by the music, the less she banged her head on the furniture and flapped her hands, just as Lovaas predicted.

That was the first *acquisition trial.* Then the first *extinction trial* began. This time, the experimenters withheld their smiles and praise, even when Beth spontaneously broke into song and shimmied her hips at the point in the song when the children went *wiggle-wiggle-wiggle.* At first, she responded to the sudden chill in the air by clapping and singing along even more vigorously. But after more than a week of getting no response, she started beating herself up more than ever. The trials continued in that vein for months with alternating rounds of acquisition and extinction. Lovaas's team varied the parameters of the experimental design methodically, some days reciting the lyrics of the songs to Beth in flat, tuneless voices. During the acquisition trials, her behavior would improve dramatically, but during the extinction trials, she hurt herself so badly that Lovaas aborted the experiment.

A similar pattern emerged when Beth was taught to press a bar as the experimenters urged her on with effusive comments like "I love you very much" and "You're a sweetheart." Then it was extinction time, and Beth was faced once again with a roomful of adults who had inexplicably stopped responding to her. She began battering herself so violently that Lovaas again terminated the experiment.

The psychoanalytical theories of the day held that the source of Beth's self-injurious behavior was her internalized feelings of guilt (a "hostile introject" in Freudian terms). To be on the safe side, Lovaas's assistants would say to Beth "I do not think you are bad" when she injured herself. But their repetition of this stilted phrase only made her flail her limbs more violently. The possibility that Beth was responding in a comprehensible way to the bizarre behavior of the people around her didn't enter Lovaas's mind.

Extinguishing Beth's self-injurious behavior by ignoring her would have been "a slow procedure requiring several sessions or days," Lovaas predicted. He had good reason to fear that his sole experimental subject—on whom his National Institute of Mental Health (NIMH) funding depended—might hurt herself so badly that his experiments could no longer go on. So Lovaas sought a more expeditious solution, which came to him in a flash one day in the lab.

He was talking with a colleague, when Beth began striking her head against the sharp edge of a metal cabinet. Like any good behaviorist, Lovaas rarely ventured to speculate about his subjects' mental states, but in this case he made an exception. He felt that his nearly paternal relationship with her gave him a unique window on the inner being lurking behind her "autistic shell," and what he saw there enraged him: this nine-year-old girl was scheming and plotting against him.

"She would only hit steel cabinets, and she would only hit them on the edge, because, you see, she wanted to draw blood," Lovaas told *Psychology Today*'s Paul Chance. So he "reacted automatically," as he would have with one of his own children—"I reached over and cracked her one right on the rear," he said. The psychologist expressed relief that he didn't have to reach very far, because Beth "was a big fat girl" who offered him "an easy target." Speaking of himself in the third person, he told Chance:

> She stopped hitting herself for about 30 seconds because, you see, she sized up the situation, laid out her strategy and then she hit herself once more. But in those 30 seconds while she was laying out her strategy, Professor Lovaas was laying out his. At first I thought, "God, what have I done," but then I noticed she had stopped hitting herself. I felt guilty, but I felt great. Then she hit herself again, and I really laid it on her . . . So I let her know that there was no question in my mind that I was going to kill her if she hit herself once more, and that was pretty much it. She hit herself a few times more, but we had the problem licked.

Under the laws of the University of California, Lovaas was required to have his research proposals approved by the Human Subjects Board, so explaining that he wanted to "really lay it on" his experimental subjects wouldn't do. But there was an alternate way of saying basically the same thing that was acceptable in the lexicon of behaviorism. He began exploring the use of *aversive stimuli*—otherwise known in the trade as "punishment"—as a less time-consuming way of extinguishing self-injury.

THE USE OF PUNISHMENT on human subjects was controversial among Lovaas's colleagues. In his classic textbook *Science and Human Behavior*, Skinner explained that while aversives may seem to promptly extinguish undesirable behavior, the behavior often returns with a vengeance after the punishment ceases, because the subject has not been taught more adaptive ways to behave. He also pointed out that punishment creates fear, guilt, and shame, resulting in less learning overall. (In other words, a child compelled to practice the piano with threats of spanking does not tend to become a virtuoso but instead learns to hate music.) Skinner also cautioned that the use of aversives has negative effects on the researcher, potentially turning the experimental situation into a sadistic power play. "In the long run," he observed, "punishment, unlike reinforcement, works to the disadvantage of both the punished organism and the punishing agency."

But Lovaas failed to heed this advice, in part because he was convinced that children like Beth would never learn to socially engage unless their self-injurious behavior was extinguished first. Soon he expanded the sphere of behavior targeted for punishment to also include hand flapping, rocking, spinning, and other forms of self-stimulation. On the basis of his own experiments, he concluded that stimming made autistic children less sensitive to auditory input, which interfered with their learning. In the lab, he referred to self-stimulation as "garbage behavior," because if the children were engaged in a more productive activity, they tended to stop stimming.

He also believed that extinguishing this apparently senseless behavior would reduce a major source of stigma for autistic people and their families. "Since the emphasis of our treatment program is to make the child look as neat and appropriate as possible, we attempt to suppress the more severe or grotesque forms of self-stimulatory behavior by the use of aversive stimuli," he explained to NSAC parents. "It is obviously very embarrassing for people to be in the company of a child who jumps up and down and ritualistically slaps his arms in front of his face: such behavior socially isolates the child and embarrasses his parents."

Researchers would eventually discover that autistic people stim to reduce anxiety—and also simply because it feels good. In fact, harmless forms of self-stimulation (like flapping and fidgeting) may *facilitate* learning by freeing up executive-functioning resources in the brain that would otherwise be devoted to suppressing them. For Lovaas, however, self-injury, self-stimulation, and echolalia were all of a piece and equally ripe for extinction. Alone in his lab with his team of devoted grad students and experimental subjects in no position to complain, he began seeking means of punishment that could get past a review board.

After his work with Beth, he conducted a series of experiments on a pair of five-year-old twin boys named Mike and Marty. He estimated that the brothers spent 70 percent of their waking hours "rocking, fondling themselves, and moving hands and arms in repetitive, stereotyped manners" while engaging in "a fair amount of tantrum behaviors, such as screaming, throwing objects, and hitting themselves." They had never spoken or been toilet trained. For one of his first rounds of experiments on Mike and Marty, his punishment of choice was exceptionally loud sound. He aimed blasts of "well over 100" decibels at them—comparable to the roaring of a power saw at close range. His aim was to produce "pain or fear" in the twins as a way of making the presence of adults "meaningful" and "rewarding" by comparison, as typical children might seek safety at their mother's bedside after a bad dream.

The results of these experiments were disappointing. Even when subjected to decibel levels capable of causing physical damage to the eardrum, Mike and Marty "remained unperturbed, particularly after the first two or three presentations." Lovaas doubled down, turning to a method of punishment that had a long track record in behaviorist experiments on animals: electric shock. To head off any criticism for employing such harsh methods on preschool-age children, he added, "It is important to note, in view of the moral and ethical reasons which might preclude the use of electric shock, that their future was certain institutionalization."

He taped strips of metal foil to the floor of a room in his lab and wired these strips to a respectable-sounding device called a Harvard Inductorium—a modified Faraday coil that offered fine-tuning of its electrical output down to zero. The strips were laid across the floor, spaced half an inch apart so that a child who stepped into the room was guaranteed make contact with at least two of them, completing the circuit. To confirm the aversive effect of this apparatus, Lovaas's grad students first tested it on themselves: "The shock was set at a level at which each of the three *Es* (experimenters) standing barefoot on the floor agreed that it was definitely painful and frightening."

In a typical round of trials, Mike or Marty would be placed between researchers standing three feet apart. Then a researcher would say "Come here," beckoning to the boy with outstretched arms. If he didn't approach the researcher within three seconds, he would get a shock. Then the same procedure would be repeated with the other twin, and so on, over and over again, for hundreds of trials. If Mike and Marty tried to escape the shocks by "beginning to sit down, moving toward the window to climb on its ledge, etc.," they would get another jolt from Lovaas's Inductorium.

In contrast to his experiments with sound, Lovaas deemed these experiments a stunning success. In just a handful of sessions, Mike and Marty learned to practically jump into the experimenters' arms to avoid the painful shocks. In a subsequent round of trials, instead of the electrified floor, Lovaas employed a remote-controlled device called a Lee-Lectronic Trainer—a box the size of a cigarette pack used in canine obedience tests—affixed to the boys' buttocks. A researcher would face Mike or Marty, say "Hug me" or "Kiss me," and apply shock if the boy didn't get moving in three seconds. The twins' behavior, Lovaas noted approvingly, "changed markedly toward increased affection." He added that the therapeutic benefits of this procedure exceeded his expectations (*S* and *E* referred to *subject* and *experimenter*, respectively):

> Once *S*s had been trained to avoid shock, they often smiled and laughed, and gave other signs of happiness or comfort. For example, they would "mold" or "cup" to *E*s body as small infants do to parents. Such behaviors were unobserved prior to these experiments.

He ventured that this behavior indicated that the twins' "avoidance of pain generated contentment." It was not an unreasonable speculation.

LOVAAS WAS NOT THE first to employ devices designed for use in kennels and feedlots in the service of demonstrating that autistic children were capable of learning. That distinction belonged to Todd Risley, his colleague at the University of Kansas. In 1963, Risley repurposed "a commercially available device for shocking livestock" from a company called Hot Shot Products in Minneapolis to discourage a nonverbal, seizure-prone six-year-old girl from climbing up a bookshelf. With Skinner, one of the pioneers of the field, in the anti-aversive camp, Lovaas and Risley were at risk of being perceived as outliers. But in 1964, Richard L. Solomon, a leading expert on the lengths to which animals would go to escape pain (technically known as "avoidance learning"), mounted a case for punishment in *American Psychologist* that couldn't have been better timed from Lovaas's perspective.

Even allowing for changing trends in psychology, Solomon's article makes for disquieting reading as he depicts a veritable Noah's ark of starved, shocked, and throttled animals undergoing the torments of the damned in the name of advancing his theories of learning. He reported that appetite can be permanently suppressed in dogs and cats by hotwiring their food dishes. Spider monkeys swore off eating altogether if a researcher surprised them with toy snakes at mealtime, though in some cases only "odd sexual behaviors, tics, and long periods of crying" ensued. Puppies swatted with newspapers while eating horsemeat would go on a permanent hunger strike before ever tasting it again, and rats trained to press a bar for food would freeze in place, breathe heavily, defecate, and urinate if the bar unexpectedly yielded a jolt of electricity instead. Even the most primordial instinct—the urge to mate—could be extinguished with sufficient application of aversive stimuli, Solomon marveled.

He had just one helpful suggestion to make: too many learning theorists were still relying on that old classic, electric shock. "Perhaps a bit of softheartedness is partly responsible for limiting our inventiveness," he mused. "The Inquisitors, the Barbarians, and the Puritans could have given us some good hints!"

Suitably grateful to his distinguished colleague from the University of Pennsylvania, Lovaas characterized Solomon's work as a triumph of rationality over sentimentality. "Psychology and related professions have shied away from, and often condemned, the use of pain for therapeutic purposes," he wrote. "We agree with Solomon that such objections to the use of pain have a moral rather than a scientific basis . . . Punishment can be a very effective tool for behavior change."

Seeking other innovative methods to promote learning, Lovaas tried preventing the children in his lab from eating before an experiment. Immediately after the "Hug me" trials, Lovaas put Mike and Marty on a strict behaviorist diet: no food at all, seven days a week, but the token scraps earned by their acquiring the ability to perform a complex social task while pressing a bar to avoid shock. Water deprivation was also stringently enforced, though he noted that, "to avoid dehydration," water was available to the boys "*ad libidinum*" after six p.m. each day. One of the twins didn't perform well in this round because he would never stop stimming, but the psychologist remained hopeful that hunger could provide a powerful incentive for the subjects of his future experiments.

"Let me tell you, it is a pleasure to work with a child who is on mild food deprivation," Lovaas told a room full of NSAC parents, "particularly if he has a history of being a good eater, because that is a child who is truly motivated to learn."

Concerned that some of his techniques might seem unorthodox, Lovaas invited members of the press down to the lab to watch him in action. As usual, he prefaced his demonstration by showing footage of children who had attempted to chew through their own limbs or bite off their nails with their teeth. (When he exhibited this reel to parents, he explained that the little girl on camera "won't hit her head on round corners. She wants it bloody.") His message was clear: *This is what autism looks like if it is left untreated.*

Even journalists who might normally have been troubled by the sight of a barefoot five-year-old boy recoiling from an electrified floor were persuaded by Lovaas's solemn pronouncements that once you had taken it upon yourself to physically strike a child, you were morally responsible for his fate. "No one punishes who isn't prepared to devote a major part of his life to that child. Nobody punishes a child who doesn't also love that child," he told a reporter. "Once you lay your hand on a child it morally obligates you to work with that child. You see, that is one of the reasons that people stay away from punishment—they don't want to commit themselves. After you hit a kid you can't just get up and leave him; you are hooked to that kid." The reporter was so impressed that he dubbed Lovaas a visionary—a "poet with a cattle prod."

His bid for transparency would prove to be more controversial than he expected. *Life* magazine elevated the psychologist to international fame with a profile that ran under the memorable headline "Screams, Slaps, and Love." Praising Lovaas's work as "a surprising, shocking treatment that helps far-gone mental cripples," the article (and its photo spread, billed as "an appalling gallery of madness") shaped public perceptions of autism for decades to come.

It's hard to imagine a more disturbing introduction to the subject. The first page is dominated by photographs of a graduate student slapping a seven-year-old boy named Billy for not "paying attention during his speech lesson." The boy is in tears on page two as the student bellows at him inches away from his face. Meanwhile, another boy, his back against a wall, stares into space "like a fragile Buddha . . . endlessly contemplating nothing." If there was a conspicuous lack of toys and games in these rooms full of children, it was because "such children do not play."

In a sidebar, *Life* reporter Don Moser described the terrifying existence of Pat, Billy's mother, "at the mercy of a small boy so cunning and so violent that he almost propelled her into a nervous breakdown." Refusing to eat anything but hamburgers from one fast-food chain, he forced his father to buy "cheap, greasy" burgers by the sack every morning at a local franchise. One day, Billy flushed one of his sister's dolls down the toilet. "It was like living with the devil," his mother said. The only thing that put fear into the heart of this possessed child was the dour visage of Alfred Hitchcock, so Pat taped up portraits of the director in various locations throughout the house, including the bathroom door, so she could take her baths in peace. But there was hope. Enter Lovaas, like Max von Sydow in *The Exorcist*, bearing a cattle prod instead of a crucifix. After ninety thousand discrete-trial sessions, *Life* reported, Billy can "ask for any food by name."

Immediately after the article came out, hands started shooting up at NSAC meetings when Rimland gave his usually warmly received talk on operant conditioning. "I saw the article in *Life*," some concerned mother or father would say. "Aren't these kids being treated brutally at UCLA?" To quell this unanticipated uprising, Rimland prepared a snappy comeback: "If you think that the children in the article were mistreated, you should see what they do to the kids only two floors away in that very same building! They don't just yell at them or slap them once in a great while. In that same building, there are people who actually gas children and cut them with sharp knives." The parents in the room would collectively gasp. After a dramatic pause, he would deliver the punch line: "How else are you going to do an appendectomy or tonsillectomy?"

To promote the use of strong aversives at home, Rimland equated the jolts delivered by devices like the Lee-Lectronic Trainer to the harmless static discharges produced by "touching a doorknob or an elevator button on a dry day." He tried to make cattle prods seem less frightening by christening them "tingle sticks."

Thankfully, the lanky, curly-haired, soft-spoken graduate student dispatched from UCLA to NSAC chapters around the country to train parents in Lovaas's method—Mark Rimland's speech coach, David Ryback—focused less on punishment and more on rewarding engagement in the task at hand with praise and M&Ms. Slapping his own thigh while shouting "No!" was as aversive as he was willing to get. Ryback would fly into a town for a week to host presentations at schools that would be piped over the PA system or broadcast on closed-circuit TV, prefacing these sessions with discussion groups for parents so that it was clear from the start that they were going to play a central role in the process as their children's "co-therapists." After years of being treated like pariahs by medical professionals, parents were grateful to finally be recognized as powerful allies in their children's treatment.

Ryback's respectful attitude also extended to the children. Instead of viewing them as barely adequate foundations on which to "build a person," he was in awe of their extraordinary talents and abilities. "They could hear sirens coming from several blocks away, and a phonograph needle clicking two floors below," he recalls. One day, while waiting for a session to begin in a classroom, a neatly dressed, nonspeaking eleven-year-old named

Mickey stood up and drew a meticulously detailed landscape on the blackboard with no preliminary sketching or deliberation. "There was no hesitation, no second-guessing. The image was perfect from the very first line," Ryback says.

Despite Rimland's tireless cheerleading for aversives, many NSAC parents refused to use them, including Ruth Sullivan. "No, I never let anyone do that to Joe," she says. "My gut told me it wasn't a good idea." The president of the Manhattan chapter, Anita Zatlow, also declined to jump on the bandwagon. "Today we are plagued with increased numbers of experimentalists calling themselves 'therapists' who practice a variety of do-it-yourself aversive techniques on vulnerable children," she wrote in response to one of Rimland's pro-shock editorials. "Who will protect them from abusive 'quacks'? What message is really received by the already disoriented autistic child/recipient of aversives? Can aversives create anxiety and, if so, might not the 'treatment' increase the pathological behavior? No one knows for sure." Rimland's response was to call parents like Zatlow "irrational" and "sanctimonious."

A parallel debate was raging among behaviorists. On the basis of his theory that autistic children would never be capable of learning unless their autistic behaviors were extinguished first, Lovaas was able to convince Skinner that they were the exception to the rule of not using punishment on human subjects. By 1988, the senior psychologist felt compelled to issue a statement clarifying his position. "If brief and harmless aversive stimuli," Skinner wrote, "made precisely contingent on the self-destructive or other excessive behavior, suppress the behavior and leave the children free to develop in other ways, I believe it can be justified." But he took care to add: "To remain satisfied with punishment without exploring nonpunitive alternatives is the real mistake."

It was a mistake that overworked hospital administrators and overzealous ward attendants were willing to risk making. Though Lovaas promoted the use of aversives as a way of liberating children from institutions, the harsh techniques he legitimized at UCLA were eagerly embraced in state hospitals across the country as a way of keeping problem patients in line. A rage for "behavior mod" swept the field, hastened by a lack of professional standards and ethics guiding the conduct of behavioral therapists.

In some states, it was possible to hang out a shingle as a "behavior expert" after attending a one-day workshop in a hotel ballroom. Ward attendants were urged to "be creative" in coming up with innovative punishments, and orderlies in newly formed behavior units would arm themselves with bottles of hot sauce to douse the lips and tongues of uncooperative patients.

VIII

In 1966, a young neurologist began working on a residential ward at the Bronx Psychiatric Center after serving an internship at Mt. Zion in San Francisco and a residency at UCLA. He already knew that, in addition to being a doctor, he wanted to be a writer like Freud or Darwin—a precise observer of the world who wrote literarily but with scientific accuracy. He would fill up hundreds of pages in his notebooks (with an occasional boost from methamphetamine), staying up all night in transports of inspiration. In the nocturnal underground of San Francisco where he consorted with Hells Angels, poets, and other members of the bohemian demimonde, this bearded, burly doctor-in-training—who set a state weightlifting record with his six-hundred-pound squat—called himself by his middle name, Wolf. But now that he had moved east and left his druggie days behind him, he resumed using the name he was born with in London: Oliver Sacks.

In the dismal warehouse for hopeless cases known as Ward 23, he met a pair of identical twins named George and Charles Finn who had been variously diagnosed as autistic, schizophrenic, and mentally retarded. But despite the impoverishment of their surroundings, the twins carried a glory of numerical symmetry in their heads. "*Give us a date!*" they would cry in unison, and they were instantly able to calculate the day of the week for any date in a multiple-thousand-year span. As they executed these seemingly impossible cogitations, they would focus their attention inward—their eyes darting back and forth behind thick glasses—as if they were consulting an internal calendar that spanned dozens of millennia or more.

The twins' calendar-calculating abilities were just one aspect of their extraordinary cognitive gifts. The next time that Sacks saw the twins, they were raptly enjoying a conversation that consisted solely of numbers. George would utter a string of digits, and Charles would turn them over in his mind and nod; then Charles would reply in similar fashion, and George would smile approvingly. In a case history published twenty years later in *The Man Who Mistook His Wife for a Hat*, Sacks wrote that the brothers (called John and Michael in the book) looked like "two connoisseurs wine-tasting, sharing rare tastes, rare appreciations." At first, he had no idea what they were doing, but he took notes on these cryptic exchanges anyway. "I was attracted by their uncanny twinship, their twin bonding," he explains, adding that he felt a special kinship with the Finns because he had "a thing for numbers" himself. Upon consulting a book of mathematical tables at home, he was shocked to discover that the twins were instantaneously calculating six-digit prime numbers, a feat that even a computer would have found difficult to pull off at the time. The next time he visited the twins, he made sure to bring his book of tables along, so he could raise the bar by casually dropping an eight-digit prime into the conversation. Surprised and delighted, the Finns invited him to join in their ethereal exchange, seeing him and raising him with even longer primes. Yet George and Charles were incapable of performing simple multiplication, reading, or even tying their own shoes.

Then Sacks met José, a twenty-one-year-old autistic man afflicted by frequent seizures. A ward attendant openly referred to him as an "idiot" and said that he was unable to comprehend language and rudimentary concepts like the passage of time. But when Sacks handed the young man his watch and said, "Draw this," José gazed at it in intense concentration and took up his pencil. The neurologist was astonished by what happened next:

> José had drawn the watch with remarkable fidelity, putting in every feature (at least every essential feature—he did not put in WESTCLOX,

> SHOCK RESISTANT, MADE IN USA), not just "the time" . . . The general grasp of the thing, its "feel," had been strikingly brought out—all the more strikingly if, as the attendant said, José had no idea of time. And otherwise there was an odd mixture of close, even obsessive, accuracy, with curious (and, I felt, droll) elaborations and variations.

"I had never seen such an ability before," Sacks recalls. "José was fond of the non-human world, and especially the botanical world, as I am. Like his drawing of my watch, his images of dandelions and other things had *feeling* as well as great accuracy." Inspired by his experiences with José and the twins, Sacks began exploring other ways of forging connections with the patients on Ward 23. He started taking them for walks in the New York Botanical Garden, invited them to join him at the pool table in the day room, and brought in his own piano to entertain them with music. "They would gather around me when I sat down to play. They might keep time; they would smile; they might dance; they might sing," he says. "Some of them had musical talent and might play a few notes, which meant, 'Can you play that?'"

On one of his walks with patients in the botanical garden, Sacks saw a boy named Steve pick a flower, gaze at it, and say the first word that any of the doctors in the hospital had ever heard him say: "Dandelion."

Using his acute powers of observation, Sacks came to realize that, instead of being incommunicative, his patients were communicating all the time—not in words, but in gestures and other nonverbal forms of utterance, particularly among themselves. He wrote an essay called "Culture and Community among Mental Defectives" for the hospital journal to make his colleagues more aware of the subtle forms of interaction unfolding all around them.

But his days on the ward were numbered once he started raising objections to what was known as "therapeutic punishment" among the staff. "I finally spoke up at one of our Wednesday meetings and said that I thought it was morally reprehensible," Sacks says. "I emphasized that I did not want to be associated with it, and that I was happy to have found other ways of contacting the patients." Looking around the table, he saw a circle of dark faces. A few days later, a hospital administrator transferred him off the ward.

In the weeks that followed, Sacks consoled himself by writing his first book: a collection of case histories that he called *Ward 23*. But in a fit of self-doubt, he tossed his only copy of the manuscript into the fireplace. "Jonathan Swift had thrown *Gulliver's Travels* into the fire, and his friend Alexander Pope pulled it out," he says, wincing at the memory. "But I didn't have a Pope."

That night, he had a vivid dream of hearing passages of melancholy vocal music in German, a language that he didn't understand. These unwelcome melodies continued playing loudly in his mind throughout the following day. After hearing Sacks hum a few bars over the phone, a friend identified the score as Mahler's *Kindertotenlieder*—songs of mourning for dead children.

IX

Lovaas's crusade to "normalize" deviance was not limited to autistic children. In the 1970s, he lent his expertise to a series of experiments called the Feminine Boy Project, the brainchild of UCLA psychologist Richard Green. After interviewing one hundred men and women who applied for gender reassignment surgery, Green became interested in tracing the roots of sexual identity back to childhood. He teamed up with Lovaas to see if operant conditioning could be employed as an early intervention in cases of gender confusion to prevent the need for reassignment surgery in the future.

The project's most celebrated success story was Kirk Andrew Murphy, enrolled at UCLA by his parents at age five. Bright and precocious, Kirk would ask for his favorite snacks by their brand names at the supermarket. But after seeing Green interviewed on TV about "sissy-boy syndrome"—his term for early-onset gender dysphoria—Kirk's parents became concerned that he was exhibiting behavior that was inappropriate for a little boy. One day, his father caught him posing in the kitchen in a long T-shirt and saying, "Isn't my dress pretty?" Children with this syndrome, Green claimed, often grew up to become transsexual or homosexual. Lovaas assigned a young graduate student named George Rekers to become Kirk's behavioral therapist.

In a case report that would go on to become a classic in undergraduate psychology courses, Rekers and Lovaas wrote that Kirk (called "Kraig") possessed "a remarkable ability to mimic all the subtle feminine behaviors of an adult woman." They framed his "offer to 'help mommy' by carrying her purse" as an example of the boy's devious manipulation of his mother to "satisfy his feminine interests." Their descriptions of the little boy's behavior, compared with the transcripts of Green's intake interviews with Kirk's parents, were decidedly more extreme, as if the boy were clearly a world-class drag queen in the making at age five. They claimed that he had an elaborate "history of cross-dressing" that included plundering his grandmother's makeup kit for cosmetics and "swishing around the home and clinic, fully dressed as a woman with a long dress, wig, nail polish, high screechy voice, [and] slovenly seductive eyes." (In family photographs, Kirk more resembles a Mouseketeer.)

Paying lip service to the idea of tolerance at a time when gay liberationists had started marching in the streets, Lovaas and Rekers proposed that "society probably could afford to become more tolerant with individuals with sex-role deviations" but insisted that "the facts remain that it is not tolerant. Realistically speaking, it is potentially more difficult to modify society's behaviors than Kraig's."

To nip the little boy's inappropriate behavior in the bud, they devised a program of total immersion based on Lovaas's work on autism. This time, instead of hand-flapping, gaze aversion, and echolalia, the behaviors targeted for extinction included the "limp wrist," the submissively yielding "hand clasp," the notorious "swishy gait," the girlish "hyperextension" of the limbs in moments of exuberance, and prissy declarations like "goodness gracious" and "oh, dear me."

At home, Kirk's "masculine" behaviors were rewarded with blue chips that could be redeemed for candy and other treats, while his "feminine" behaviors were punished with red chips that were subtracted from the total. In interviews conducted by blogger Jim Burroway, who undertook a thorough investigation of the case in 2011, Kirk's brother, Mark, recalled their father punishing the boy—with Rekers's approval—by converting each red chip into a "swat." Mark broke down sobbing as he confessed to hiding red chips from his brother's pile so that Kirk wouldn't have to endure the abuse.

Meanwhile, at UCLA, Kirk was presented with tables full of things to play with—"right" tables, loaded up with gender-appropriate objects like football helmets, army belts with hatchet holders, plastic handcuffs, dart guns, rubber knives, and electric razors, and "wrong" tables, piled with costume jewelry, cosmetics, Barbie dolls, baby powder, and miniature clotheslines. (In pilot studies, the researchers were dismayed to discover that "normal subjects frequently mixed toys from the two tables in their play, complicating the scoring.") Before leaving the room, the experimenter would instruct Kirk to play with only "right" toys. Then his behavior was scored through one-way mirrors. If he asked questions not directly related to the instructions, they were ignored. Eventually, Kirk's mother was brought in to sit in a chair and reward him by smiling and telling him he was a good boy if he strapped on a football helmet or brandished a rubber knife, and punish him by pretending to read if he sat down with his legs crossed or fancied a pretty bracelet instead. ("Plays with Barbie dolls at five, sleeps with men at 25," Green ominously intoned on TV.)

After sixty sessions in the lab, Rekers and Lovaas declared victory over Kirk's "sissy-boy" behavior. "There is no doubt that our treatment intervention produced a profound change" in the boy, they wrote, offering as evidence the fact that he was "no longer 'fussy' about color-coordinating his clothes," had quit fretting when his hair got mussed, and expressed desire to attend Indian Guide campouts with his father. They argued that the success of their experiments cast doubt on the notion that sexual preference is the product of "irreversible neurological and biochemical determinants" and touted the potential of their model for the treatment of other deviant children.

The Feminine Boy Project turned into a cash cow for the university, attracting six-figure grants from the NIMH and the Playboy Foundation until 1986. Children wore wrist counters to monitor whenever they were tempted to play with the "wrong" toys, and parents were enlisted to surveil their children's closets, steer boys away from the kitchen, and keep girls out of the garage.

Kirk effectively became Rekers's version of Beth—the case that launched a career. The psychologist published nearly twenty papers related to the boy's alleged metamorphosis, several of them co-authored with Lovaas. The case propelled Rekers to teaching positions at the University of Miami, Kansas State University, and other institutions, and he was awarded more than $1 million in grants from the NIMH and the National Science Foundation. He also became a sought-after speaker on the subject of treating sexual deviancy before committees of the U.S. Senate and House of Representatives.

In 1983, he co-founded the Family Research Council, an influential Christian lobbying group that helped craft the plank in the 2012 Republican national platform calling for an amendment to the Constitution defining marriage as the union of one man and one woman. Rekers's ubiquity in courtrooms coast to coast, furnishing expert testimony against gay marriage and gay adoption in pivotal cases, inspired the *New York Times*' Frank Rich to call him "the Zelig of homophobia." In the meantime, his star patient wasn't faring nearly as well. Kirk hanged himself in 2003 at age thirty-eight, following decades of depression.

Rekers's lucrative career as an expert witness came to an abrupt end in 2010 when two photojournalists ambushed him at the Miami International Airport returning from a holiday in Madrid with a young male companion who turned out to be a paid escort from Rentboy.com. In the scandal that followed, he told the press that his handsome "travel assistant" had been hired to lift his luggage as he recuperated from hernia surgery, claiming that they had spent their time together in Spain "sharing scientific information on the desirability of abandoning homosexual intercourse." Informed of Kirk's suicide by CNN's Anderson Cooper, he dismissed the Murphys' assertion that their son's experiences at UCLA contributed to his despair as "a hypothesis" that would require empirical proof.

THOUGH REKERS CREDITED HIM with coming up with the idea of Kirk's treatment in the first place, Lovaas downplayed his own role in the Feminine Boy Project, claiming that he had only served on a committee. In the context of his work on autism, his role in treating "sissy-boy syndrome" was surely a footnote. But both projects were based on the same fundamental view: that it's easier to change a child's behavior than it is to destigmatize that behavior in society—whether it's limp wrists or flapping hands.

Despite Lovaas's unflagging enthusiasm for aversives, an ethical debate raged in the larger ABA community about whether intentionally inflicting pain in the name of treatment is any way to treat young human beings, even if they're autistic and self-injurious. "One could argue, for example, that a locked iron mask would prevent nail biting, but the law and common sense would argue against such an intrusive intervention," wrote ABA expert Gary LaVigna and autism researcher Anne Donnellan in a book called *Alternatives to Punishment*. Two years later, in 1988, the board of directors of the Autism Society of America (ASA) passed a resolution calling for a ban on aversive techniques. Yet the ASA continued to promote the use of aversives well past that, and some ABA practitioners rely on techniques like withholding food and administering physical punishment to modify behavior to the present day. Painful electric shocks are still employed to punish autistic children at an institution called the Judge Rotenberg Educational Center in Massachusetts, even in the face of a public outcry against their use.

By the late 1970s, however, Lovaas had changed his mind about a few things. He was no longer convinced that teaching a child to talk freed up a normal child trapped inside. Inside every "autistic shell" was an autistic *person*. "We were disappointed," he admitted. "There were no sudden awakenings. There seemed to be no large internal reorganizations. Would it not have been nice if the child had said: 'Now that I can speak well, I see how I have been very sick, but now I am well.' No one said that."

But as Sacks had discovered on Ward 23, Lovaas learned that even self-injurious children were communicating in their own ways. Exuberant use of echolalia turned out to be a distinctively autistic way of acquiring language: children who parrot their favorite Disney movies and Pokémon cartoons learn to use expressive language more readily. He also came to recognize that many of the behaviors he had put children through hell to extinguish were attempts to find channels for self-expression. In an unusually candid interview in 1989, Lovaas told psychologist Richard Simpson that he had come to identify with the children who had seemed most resistant to his brutal methods:

> When I think back upon the kids that I tried to treat back in the 1960s, who were so extremely self-injurious, I think, "Boy, they were tough!" What they were really saying is, "You haven't taught me right, you haven't given me the tools whereby I can communicate and control my environment." So the aggression that these kids show, whether it is directed toward themselves or others, is an expression of society's ignorance, and in that sense I think of them as noble demonstrators. I have a great deal of respect for them.

BUT ONE THING THAT LOVAAS never changed his mind about was that the best hope for such children was for them to aspire to become "normal"—purged of all visible traces of autistic behavior.

For most of his career, Lovaas professed that prompting full recovery from autism was beyond the scope of even the most intensive behavior engineering. "The program does not turn out normal children," he cautioned parents at the Second NSAC Congress. "Should a child become normal as we treat him, then that, no doubt, is based on the fact that he had a lot going for him when he first started treatment." In a popular ABA manual called *The ME Book*, he told parents and therapists not to expect a cure:

"Find pleasure in small steps forward. You should be pleased at reaching a set of smaller goals, rather than hoping and struggling for some often unattainable and absolute ideal of normalcy."

But then, in 1987, Lovaas dropped a bombshell by claiming that nearly half of the children in an experimental group at UCLA had achieved "normal intellectual and educational functioning" by undertaking intensive ABA starting at age three. He described a totally immersive program requiring participation from "all significant persons in all significant environments," including parents, teachers, and teams of graduate students working in the home. In essence, Lovaas replaced the world in which the child didn't fit in with one that would train him or her to do so. "One may assume that normal children learn from their everyday environments most of their waking hours," he wrote. "Autistic children, conversely, do not learn from similar environments. We hypothesized that construction of a special, intense, and comprehensive learning environment for very young autistic children would allow some of them to catch up with their normal peers."

Lovaas's study, which was covered in glowing terms in the mainstream press and a special report on CBS, was the breakthrough that many parents had been waiting for: empirical proof that their children could be rendered indistinguishable from their typical peers given enough devotion, effort, and expense. Though he carefully danced around the word *cure*, opting for the more neutral-sounding term *recovery* in his paper, his meaning was never in doubt: "If you met [the children] now . . . you would never know that anything had been wrong with them," Lovaas told the *New York Times*. "I'm positive now that autism need not be chronic."

Part of his strategy for proving that neurology was not destiny was to separate the child from the diagnosis. Some preschool teachers were not told that his experimental subjects were autistic. ("If we had to admit that the child had a problem, we'd say that it was 'language delay,'" Lovaas said.) He took the unusual step of changing the name of his lab at UCLA from the Autism Clinic to the Clinic for the Behavioral Treatment of Children to avoid tipping off school administrators. If a diagnosis leaked out anyway, parents were prompted to move the child to another school. Lovaas also believed it was essential to insulate his subjects from "the detrimental effects of exposure to other autistic children." The mere presence of other such children in a classroom, he declared in the *Times*, was "the kiss of death."

In addition to conducting an average of fourteen thousand hours of discrete-trial sessions for each child, his tireless graduate students helped parents negotiate educational placements and manage household chores, and they went to bat for the children and their families in dozens of other ways. For a boy who had no playmates, they hosted parties at his home for the neighborhood kids, "making him a social star of sorts." Needless to say, Lovaas's program entailed a level of commitment and support that was beyond the reach of most families, but compared to the cost of lifelong institutionalization—which he estimated at $2 million—it was a bargain, he said.

The psychologist's supporters hailed the study as a milestone. "If true, these results are absolutely extraordinary," Leon Eisenberg told the *Times*. Rimland followed suit with a banner headline in his parents' newsletter. The following year, Lovaas's work became the subject of an award-winning documentary that claimed that, without ABA, "more than 95 percent [of autistic children] will require custodial care for the rest of their lives."

Other longtime experts in the field, however, found reasons to be more skeptical. TEACCH founder Eric Schopler accused Lovaas of front-loading his data by excluding "low-functioning" children from his sample while favoring those with unusually high IQs. He also observed that families in Lovaas's experimental group had more resources available to them in general than families in the control group, which Lovaas tried to explain by saying he had an insufficient number of graduate assistants to meet the needs of both. Schopler pointed out that calling autistic children "the kiss of death" in a classroom could result in kids all across the country being denied an education.

Rimland fired back with a full-page defense of Lovaas in his newsletter. "It's not unusual for humanity to treat its pioneers with hostility," he said. But even Lovaas's former colleague Catherine Lord—a pioneer of autism research in her own right—eventually admitted that the psychologist "tried to structure things in a way that . . . did not reflect what really happened and certainly cannot be used as scientific evidence." Independent researchers have never been able to replicate the extraordinary findings reported in his 1987 paper.

The spectacular nature of his claims even created problems for other researchers at UCLA, as their phones began ringing off the hook with calls from parents desperate for a cure for their children. "But we at the Medical School Neuropsychiatric Institute weren't promising a cure," psychiatrist and autism expert Ed Ritvo recalled. "Ivar Lovaas in the Department of Psychology was."

Soon, so was Rimland, though his pathway to recovery was quite different from intensive behavioral engineering.

X

Shortly after publishing *Infantile Autism*, Rimland started getting letters from parents claiming that their sons and daughters had become more calm and engaged after taking megadoses of certain nutrients. In particular, the same two classes of vitamins—B and C—kept popping up.

This wasn't totally surprising: Pauling was touting heroic quantities of ascorbic acid as a panacea in his best-selling books, and Hoffer and Osmond's experiments with B vitamins and schizophrenia were already part of the rapidly burgeoning alt-med lore. Rimland was initially skeptical, but as he came to know the parents in his network at NSAC meetings, they struck him as perceptive, careful, and reliable people. (Indeed, many of them were fellow psychologists.) After talking with doctors convinced of the therapeutic value of the megavitamin regimen, Rimland decided that he "could not in good conscience fail to pursue this lead." Christening his storefront in San Diego the Institute for Child Behavior Research (later renamed the Autism Research Institute), he launched an ambitious study by relying on his parents' network as a source of volunteers.

Rimland started the children on a potent multiple B-vitamin tablet plus several grams of vitamin C per day. After two weeks, more B vitamins (niacinamide and pyridoxine) were added at several hundred times the recommended minimum daily requirement. Then pantothenic acid, another vitamin, was thrown into the mix. (He would eventually supplement the vitamins with magnesium, on the advice of celebrity nutritionist Adelle Davis.) At each stage, a physician enlisted by the parents would rate the child's behavior as parents submitted biweekly reports on the child's speech, eating patterns, tantrums, and alertness. Finally, these data were transferred from printed forms to IBM punched cards for computer analysis.

In the pharmaceutical industry, the gold standard of drug development is the so-called double-blind placebo-controlled trial. Volunteers are randomly assigned to receive either the active drug or an inert placebo, and neither the volunteers nor the experimenters are aware of who is getting the real drug and who is getting the equivalent of sugar pills. Inevitably, both groups of patients will show some improvement because of a phenomenon known as the placebo effect.

At the root of the placebo effect is the fact that the attention of medical professionals, in an environment of care, produces beneficial changes in the mind and body of the patient even in the absence of an active drug. Researchers like Ted Kaptchuk at Harvard and Fabrizio Benedetti at the University of Milan have discovered that the mere act of swallowing a pill triggers cascades of hormones and neurotransmitters that can reduce pain and inflammation, enhance motor coordination, boost brain activity, lift mood, and improve digestion. These effects are pervasive, as if the body contains a self-healing network that is activated by the knowledge that one is receiving care. (Exercise and meditation also prompt this network into action.) While no one has ever cured cancer or dispelled pneumonia with a sugar pill, powerful placebo effects have been observed in an astonishingly broad range of conditions, from Parkinson's and hypertension to chronic depression and Crohn's disease. In placebo-controlled trials, if the volunteers in the placebo group and the experimental group show comparable amounts of benefit, the FDA judges the drug to be ineffective—often at the cost of tens of millions of dollars to the company that spent years developing it.

But Rimland decided not to use this well-established model of drug testing for his study. Instead, he employed his psychometric prowess to develop a home-brewed form of data analysis that he called "computer clustering"—in essence, an algorithmic search for clinically significant ripples in a sea of Big Data. He insisted that standard methods of conducting trials presuppose that the patients under study have a single unified condition, which made them inappropriate for a condition composed of distinct subtypes like autism. His go-to analogy was intellectual disability and PKU. "Until it became possible to fractionate the mass of 'retardates' into smaller groups such as PKU, cretinism, galactosemia, mongolism, etc., it was hopeless to try to devise means of prevention or treatment," he observed. "I believe the children loosely called 'autistic' or 'schizophrenic' actually represent a dozen or more different diseases or disorders, each with its own cause."

With 45 percent of parents reporting that the vitamins "definitely helped" their children, Rimland was thrilled with the results of his experiment. "There is no reasonable explanation for these findings other than that the vitamins do help some children," he wrote in the *Journal of Orthomolecular Psychiatry.* He went on to include accounts from parents testifying to their children's dramatic regression when the vitamins were stopped.

He admitted, though, that his failure to employ a placebo control group had come under fire from other researchers in the field. "Some of our critics have suggested that our findings reflect only wishful thinking," he said. "They assert that our positive results might stem from the fact that many parents would be inclined to over-rate the vitamins because they want so badly to see their child improve." He deflected these criticisms wholesale, claiming that the people making them "did not understand the experimental design," and insisting that the accusations of wishful thinking were "not valid, since parent expectation could not influence the computer grouping."

It was not a scientifically sound argument for him to make, since all of the data tabulated on his punched cards was derived from subjective reports by parents and physicians who were likely to be enthusiastic about his project. Indeed, three independent analyses of his dataset revealed more problems with his design than his claims suggested. A Navy statistician with access to the raw data concluded that no reliable information about the reaction to the vitamins by various subtypes in the sample population could be obtained by using Rimland's computer-clustering scheme.

Furthermore, the design of the experiment—with parents as evaluators of changes in their children's behavior—was anything but "blind" in the statistical sense, and a perfect incubator for placebo effects. Rimland knew that accurately gauging the efficacy of new treatments for autism is tricky because the condition is so mercurial. "These children spurt ahead or fall apart periodically for no discernible reason," he said, "and whatever treatment is being used at the time gets the credit or the blame." Yet even Rimland was not immune to the pitfalls of wishful thinking.

A thinly veiled account of his experiments with Deaner appeared in his book, referencing an unnamed "four-year-old autistic child who unquestionably belonged to the Kanner category." He wrote that Mark's mutism abruptly "disappeared" after taking the drug. For the first time, he said, "simple commands such as 'Bring it here' and 'Close the door' were understood and obeyed. Later, simple tasks such as opening the door for the family cat and placing milk bottles on the porch were performed with obvious pleasure." He reported that the effects of Deaner were so dramatic and immediate that this unnamed boy's sister would tell her parents to slip him another dose when he engaged in "disturbing behavior."

If Rimland's description in the book of Deaner as a "new psychic-energizer" sounded suspiciously like a marketing term from a brochure, that was because it was precisely the phrase that Riker Laboratories used to promote the drug in ads in medical journals. Deaner was aggressively marketed to pediatricians and child psychologists for a wide variety of fuzzily defined symptoms, including "problem" behavior, emotional instability, hyperactivity, and underachievement at school. The drug was allegedly so well tolerated that the company recommended it for children who were already taking tranquilizers to offset their depressant effects.

The American Medical Association (AMA) was decidedly less impressed. Months before Rimland enthused about the drug's salutary effects on his son to Kanner, the AMA's drug council issued a cautionary note about Deaner in its journal. The litany of "vague complaints" for which it was commonly prescribed, the AMA cautioned, "are characterized by the difficulty in their evaluation, their spontaneous fluctuations, and their great susceptibility to suggestion."

In other words, Deaner was the perfect placebo. It was also a gold mine for Riker Laboratories until it was finally taken off the market by the FDA in 1983 after a thorough review of independent studies concluded that the drug didn't even rate as "possibly effective" and also put children with epilepsy at heightened risk for grand mal seizures. Supplement manufacturers quickly stepped into the breach, promoting a "mixed berry flavor" analog of the drug called DMAE, combining it with fatty acids, soy, and other health food staples, and promoting it with the slogan "If yelling, begging, and pleading doesn't get your child to do their homework, maybe this will."

THE DISAPPOINTING RESPONSE OF his peers to his megavitamin experiment bugged Rimland. Though he once had yearned to become a prominent member of the medical establishment, confident that his innovative ideas would be eagerly embraced as clearly superior, he was rapidly turning against it.

The turning point in his thinking was a question that Humphry Osmond asked him after he published two charts in his newsletter. One chart compared the results of giving children megadoses of various vitamins, and the other compared the effects of prescription drugs like Dexedrine and Mellaril. Upon seeing the two charts side by side, Osmond asked Rimland, "Why didn't you compare the drugs with the vitamins directly?" Noting the serious side effects caused by the prescription drugs, Rimland concluded that the future of his work was not to be found in conventional medicine. The charts also further convinced him that he could ignore the role of placebo effects in his studies, because the drugs had performed so badly compared to the vitamins despite equally high parental expectations. Rimland would eventually encourage his growing army of parent-experimenters to try several treatments at once, making it nearly impossible to tease out the benefits and side effects of any single one. "You are not undertaking a scientific experiment in order to publish an article in a professional journal," he advised, "but rather are trying to help your child, and you know time should not be wasted." One of his mottoes was "Help the child first, worry later about exactly what it is that's helping the child."

This try-everything-at-once approach gave the parents in his network a tremendous sense of hope and momentum at a time when the mainstream science of autism was advancing at a snail's pace. But there was irony in the fact that Rimland's quest for a cure for autism in orthomolecular medicine had been inspired by Følling's discovery of PKU. If the cautious doctor hadn't instructed Borgny Egeland to immediately stop giving Liv and Dag all the tonics, herbal teas, and other nostrums they were taking before performing his chemical analyses of their urine, he might never have zeroed in on the crystals of phenylpyruvic acid that provided him with the key to the mystery.

Rimland's disdain for placebo-controlled trials, the process of peer review, and other traditional safeguards also made it hard for other researchers to take his work seriously, even when he was right. As a result, he found himself gradually growing more isolated from his colleagues while being regarded as a lone voice in the wilderness by the parents in his network.

For Ruth Sullivan, Rimland's obsession with finding a cure for autism was a distraction from the enormous challenge of building a better world for their children. "Bernie got very into the vitamins. He was always pushing something," she recalls. "I think that put him off track." Things finally came to a head at NSAC (by then called the Autism Society of America) when Rimland called for a motion requiring all members to put their children on a high-dose vitamin B-12 regimen immediately after diagnosis. Ed Ritvo stood up and said, "This is a parent-run organization. There is no evidence that vitamin B-12 works and we don't want to submit to this regime." Instead of backing down, Rimland went all in: "If you go with Ritvo, I resign."

But he no longer had the clout to make such a power play, and he was voted off the board of his own organization. The once-strong fabric of NSAC had been rent in two.

To plan his next move, Rimland decamped to his office in Kensington, where he forged a productive alliance with the only undergraduate in Lovaas's lab, a nineteen-year old psychology/sociology major named Steve Edelson. Like Rimland, Edelson was religiously agnostic but culturally Jewish—a lanky, curly-haired Ramones fan who might slip away from a lecture on child development to catch an Andy Warhol book signing. When Edelson was growing up in Oregon, his mother and sister converted to Christian Science, a sect founded in 1875 by a self-anointed prophet named Mary Baker Eddy who believed that diseases are healed not by doctoring but by submission to God. Traditionally, Christian Scientists eschew most aspects of modern medicine, including drugs, tests, hospitals, and vaccines. Though Edelson never converted, his mother refused to have him vaccinated as a child, signing the equivalent of a religious conscience waiver to exempt him.

He first heard the word *autism* at UCLA while watching a documentary called *The Invisible Wall* that featured interviews with Rimland, Lovaas, and the Sullivans. Rimland was in top form, delivering a nuanced view of the biology of the condition that was decades ahead of its time. He reiterated his belief in a connection between autism and genius, suggesting that children with the syndrome inherit "a double dose of the extreme ability to concentrate—to narrow their attention to a very fine point, like a searchlight, to illuminate with great intensity a very small matter."

It occurred to Edelson that self-injurious behavior might be an attempt to mediate a barrage of overwhelming sensations from the environment. He wrote a paper on the subject that attracted the attention of Lovaas, who invited Edelson to assist him in data collection at Camarillo State Hospital. While going through records there, Edelson noticed that the autistic patients reacted in unusual ways to anesthesia and started thinking about the role of serotonin in the autistic brain. Lovaas suggested that he pay a visit to his friend Bernie, drawing a map to ARI that Edelson has kept all these years. His curiosity about the neurochemistry of autism meshed perfectly with Rimland's interest in orthomolecular medicine, and he would play a key role in ARI's study of biomedical interventions. Together, they would author a book called *Recovering Autistic Children* that became one of the bibles of the biomed movement, along with books like Jacqueline McCandless's *Children with Starving Brains.*

This effort would culminate in the launch of Defeat Autism Now!—the network of clinicians and alt-med practitioners that Shannon Rosa turned to for advice on the GFCF diet and other treatments after Leo was diagnosed in 2002. At DAN!-sponsored events all over the country, "recovered" children were paraded in front of cheering crowds in an atmosphere befitting tent revival meetings. The fact that some children who displayed all the classic signs of early infantile autism—like Kanner's patients Donald T. and Richard S.—had managed to grow up to become happy and well-adjusted autistic adults without the benefit of elaborate elimination diets and gray-market drugs like secretin (a digestive hormone heavily promoted by Rimland that showed no evidence of benefit in placebo-controlled studies) had been forgotten. So had Kanner's observation that one of the most crucial factors in determining the outcome of his patients was a "sympathetic and tolerant reception" by their teachers.

By then, the estimated prevalence of autism was spiking dramatically. Rimland's decades of work in orthomolecular medicine led him to look beyond genetics for an explanation for the increase hidden somewhere in the toxic modern world. Eventually, he would zero in on vaccines and mercury as the most likely triggers of what appeared to be a rapidly accelerating epidemic of Kanner's once-rare disorder, launching the Autism Wars in earnest.

From his unique perspective at the central hub of a network of parents committed to their children's recovery, Rimland was ideally positioned to track the initial surge of diagnoses in the last decade of the twentieth century. But his alienation from mainstream medicine made other things harder to see, like the behind-the-scenes machinations at the American Psychiatric Association that led to the radical transformation of the diagnostic criteria for autism, prompted by the mother of a little girl in England who was much like his son Mark.

Eight

NATURE'S SMUDGED LINES

Nothing exists until it has a name.

—LORNA WING

For parents of newly diagnosed children like the Rosas, the turn of the millennium was a time of great fear and great hope. The fear was that their children had been stolen away from them by a mysterious and terrifying disorder triggered by routine events like taking a recommended drug during pregnancy or inoculating them against measles. The hope was that intensive interventions like ABA or the DAN! protocol could make their children normal enough that they would lose their diagnoses and could go on to attend mainstream schools. Furthermore, the advent of new technologies like high-throughput DNA sequencing was widely touted in the press as the long-awaited breakthrough that would finally uncover the elusive "autism gene" and make this baffling condition a thing of the past.

Peter Bell had just graduated from Northwestern University when his wife, Liz, became pregnant. It was actually her second pregnancy; her first had ended in a miscarriage, so she followed her obstetrician's advice and took progesterone during the first trimester. By the time their son, Tyler, was born, Peter was working in the marketing division of Johnson & Johnson, located just outside Philadelphia, promoting over-the-counter medications like Motrin and Tylenol.

Tyler was born in January 1993. At first, he seemed like "the perfect baby," Peter recalls. He was highly social, he slept peacefully through the night, and though he didn't talk as much as the other children in his play group, he had an extensive repertoire of animal noises that he loved making, like *moo* and *meow*. A couple of years later, the Bells had a second child, another boy, Derek, who had obvious language delays from the start. But during Tyler's well-baby check at his second birthday, the Bells' pediatrician dismissed their concerns about his not talking much, saying that boys often talk later than girls.

Then both boys got mild cases of the chicken pox. The Bells had decided not to inoculate their children against the disease, because the vaccine had just been introduced in the United States and their friends told them it might be better not to try out a relatively new vaccine on their children.

The effect of chicken pox on Tyler appeared to be catastrophic. He exploded in tantrums, started throwing his toys around, and lost what little spoken language he had, sharply withdrawing into himself. He also suffered terrible bouts of diarrhea. Liz told Peter that it was like their son was possessed.

The Bells put him through the usual round of hearing tests and other evaluations, and in 1996, Tyler was diagnosed with *pervasive developmental disorder not otherwise specified*—one of several shades of the autism spectrum that had been added to the *Diagnostic and Statistical Manual of Mental Disorders* in the preceding years. When the diagnostician delivered the results of Tyler's evaluation, she drew a little X on the left side of a bell curve representing the whole spectrum. She could see that the Bells were upset, because they had never even considered the possibility that Tyler had autism. She tried to reassure them by saying, "I didn't tell you your son has autism. I told you he has PDD-NOS, which is very different." That night, Peter and Liz called their relatives in tears, feeling like they had lost the child they once knew.

Like the Rosas, the Bells found very little information about autism available to parents, and most of it was horrifying, based on the little research that had been done during the Kanner era. Even the medical library at Johnson & Johnson had only a handful of articles on PDD-NOS, Peter discovered. But he eventually found Catherine Maurice's *Let Me Hear Your Voice*, which gave the Bells the hope that if they invested enough time, effort, and expense, Tyler could eventually lose his diagnosis. A month later, they had a team of therapists lined up to give him forty hours a week of one-on-one ABA at home, on top of speech and occupational therapy.

Peter started going to DAN! conferences, and Tyler seemed to benefit from some of the alternative treatments recommended by the members of Rimland's network. But he was nowhere close to being "recovered." In 1997, Peter attended a conference in New York City where he heard Portia Iversen, the co-founder of a new group called Cure Autism Now (CAN), give a presentation on the steps they were taking to eradicate autism in future generations. Peter and Liz formed a local chapter in Philadelphia. After raising a million dollars for the organization by hosting a walk for the cure, along with an equally remunerative golf tournament and corporate breakfast, Peter was asked to join the CAN board. In 2004, he became the executive director.

CAN was one of a number of parents' groups launched in the late 1990s with similar names (Talk About Curing Autism, founded in 2000, was another) that focused primarily on biomedical interventions and genetic research rather than on improving access to services for families. For parents like the Bells, focusing on the need for services seemed like an admission of defeat at a time when the possibility of vanquishing autism permanently seemed to be in the air.

By 2012, when I visited the Bells at their home in Princeton, Peter was the vice president of programs and services at Autism Speaks, the largest autism fund-raising organization in the world. As I spoke with the couple in their sunny living room, Tyler—who had grown into a lanky and handsome teenager—was pivoting gracefully over a canvas, painting in silent immersion as his sister played the piano. The walls of the basement were lined with his art, which often features the cars and motorcycles that fascinate him, rendered in vivid, luminescent hues. There was also an enormous freeform chart on the wall called "Tyler's Map," drawn by his father, featuring signposts on the road to a satisfying adult life: art, education, self-expression, support, employment, and making a positive impact on other people's lives.

Four decades after a young British psychiatrist named Lorna Wing embarked on a quest to discover the kinds of assistance and services that would be most useful to families of children like her daughter, parents are still trying to fill in the holes in the map.

IN THE LATE 1960S, Lorna set out to help her husband, John, a schizophrenia researcher at the University of London, compile a database of case records in a borough called Camberwell to determine if the National Health Service was providing the families of cognitively disabled children with adequate resources. The fact that the Wings' daughter had a classic case of Kanner's syndrome gave them special insight into the challenges that these families faced every day, and a number of historical forces were conspiring to bring the problems of these long-neglected children to the fore.

The emotional difficulties of a generation of boys and girls evacuated from central London during the German air raids, and thus separated from their parents for a time, sparked a wave of interest in the psychology of development in the 1950s, exemplified by the work of John Bowlby on attachment theory. Another impetus for this work was the passage of the Mental Health Act in 1959 in response to a series of scandals about overcrowding and inhumane conditions in the country's mental institutions and homes for the "subnormal."

At Exminster Hospital in Devon, up to 1,400 patients were crowded into a facility built to accommodate 440. The beds had been pushed together so they could be wedged into the available space. More than 80 percent of the patients were "certified," meaning that they had been committed to the hospital against their will. In the exercise yard, patients were chained together in groups of three to discourage escape attempts.

The Mental Health Act dismantled the legal apparatus that oversaw this certification process and turned over the responsibility for the care of many people who would have been destined for institutions to local authorities. Thousands of children who would have been invisible in previous generations were dumped back into communities that had few resources and services prepared for them. Suddenly, understanding the emotional problems and prognosis of these children became a pressing social need.

One of the leaders in this emerging field was Mildred Creak, a psychiatrist at the Great Ormond Hospital in central London. Founded during the Victorian era as the Hospital for Sick Children, it was the first such facility in Britain to offer state-of-the-art medical care to the children of families of limited means. (Meanwhile, an army of servants, nurses, nannies, and visiting physicians doted on the ailing sons and daughters of the wealthy.) In its early days, the venerable institution counted as its most illustrious patron Charles Dickens, who was well acquainted with the hardships of London's least fortunate families.

To raise funds for the purchase of a home for the new facility, the author of *Bleak House* and *Oliver Twist* penned an article called "Drooping Buds" in the popular magazine *Household Words.* He reported that of every hundred children born in the gray city, only sixty-five survived long enough to celebrate their eighth birthday. "Think of it, of all the coffins that are made in London, one in every three is made for a small child, a child that has not yet two figures to its age," he wrote with inimitable pathos. When his posh readers in Knightsbridge and Belgravia finished daubing their cheeks and resurrecting themselves from their fainting couches, they would post a benefaction to Great Ormond Street. The author also gave a benefit reading of *A Christmas Carol* at St. Martin's Hall, raising more than three thousand pounds in one night.

In the late 1800s, a physician at the hospital named William Howship Dickinson described dozens of children with a variety of neurological disorders in meticulous detail. Medical scholar Mitzi Waltz has identified several likely cases of autism in Dickinson's records, including a boy named Ralph Sedgwick who spent his waking hours in endless cycles of repetitive motion, tensing his tiny fists, rubbing and slapping his eyes, arching his neck, jerking his head, and waving his fingers in front of his face. He had spoken only one word in his two and a half years on earth: "Mum."

When Creak established the first department of pediatric psychology in the country at the hospital in 1946, she had to make the case to her colleagues that "psychosis" among children was not rare. The constellation of traits shared by many of these children—a lack of "social awareness," "rigidity" of behavior, and irregularities of speech—could have been lifted directly from Kanner:

> An action, once started, continues indefinitely. Words, phrases, motor behaviour and even reaction patterns such as sleep and appetite tend to become stereotyped. An example of this was given by a psychotic child who liked chocolate but would only take it if cut in squares. Round chocolate croquettes he would reject.

The diagnosis and care of these children was severely hampered by the welter of competing labels in use by various clinicians. It was unclear whether they should be classified as cases of Kanner's syndrome, Despert's childhood schizophrenia, Bowlby's reactive attachment disorder, Margaret Mahler's symbiotic psychosis, or none of the above. The absurdity of this situation was wryly summed up by a child psychotherapist named James Anthony, who wrote in 1958, "The cult of names added chaos to an already confused situation, since there did not seem to be a sufficiency of symptoms to share out among the various prospectors, without a good deal of overlap." Kanner admitted, "We seem to have reached a point where a clinician . . . can say honestly: he is schizophrenic, because in my scheme I must call him so. Another clinician, equally honest, can say: he is not schizophrenic because in my scheme I cannot call him so."

To cut through this muddle, Lauretta Bender prompted Creak to convene a working party of experts and design the first set of standardized criteria for the diagnosis of what she called "schizophrenic syndrome in childhood." These criteria, which became known as the Nine Points, were imported into autism research wholesale:

1. Gross and sustained impairment of emotional relationships with people.
2. Apparent unawareness of his own personal identity to a degree inappropriate to his age.
3. Pathological preoccupation with particular objects or certain characteristics of them, without regard to their accepted functions.
4. Sustained resistance to change in the environment and a striving to maintain or restore sameness.
5. Abnormal perceptual experience (in the absence of discernible organic abnormality).
6. Acute, excessive, and seemingly illogical anxiety as a frequent phenomenon.
7. Speech either lost, or never acquired, or showing failure to develop beyond a level appropriate to an earlier age.
8. Distortion in motility patterns.
9. A background of serious retardation in which islets of normal, near-normal, or exceptional intellectual function or skill may appear.

There were significant departures from Kanner's model in this list, particularly the notion that intellectual disability and organic conditions like tuberous sclerosis could also be part of the clinical picture. Kanner was clearly losing control over the scope of his syndrome, but Creak's Nine Points turned out to be hard to apply in practice. How was a clinician supposed to establish a child's "unawareness of his own personal identity"? It was precisely this type of fog that John Wing was striving to dispel. In the days before computers, he would bring a hand-cranked calculator to meetings at the Institute of Psychiatry so he could crunch the data. For decades psychiatrists had been spinning out theories of childhood psychosis that were never subjected to empirical scrutiny.

Soon, John would change that. In Lorna, he found more than an intellectual equal who operated on the same wavelength as he did. He found a soul mate.

II

Growing up in a little town called Gillingham on the southeastern tip of England in the 1930s, Lorna was bored by cooking and sewing and all the other domestic activities that girls were supposed to care about. Instead, she emulated her father, who was an engineer. When she was six years old, she decided that what she wanted to do for a living was to figure out how things work. Rather than enrolling in art classes, as she was expected to do, she studied biology and chemistry and signed up for physics courses at a local boys' school.

By the time the war began, her family had moved north to Mitcham, a suburb of central London. Her father shipped out with the Navy, and Lorna read his letters eagerly, fascinated by his accounts of life on a ship in the theater of war. She was horrified by the newsreel footage from Germany that started appearing in local cinemas but charmed by the brash young Americans who were suddenly everywhere, carousing in the local pubs and shops. They were so much more outgoing than the people she was used to, and she loved hearing them call out to each other on the high street in their strange and colorful accents.

Lorna was sixteen when she made up her mind to study medicine at the University College London, which placed a heavier emphasis on science than on clinical practice. The teachers there were also known to be more hospitable to female students at a time when the long-standing prejudice against female doctors was finally starting to wane. (Two decades earlier, after Mildred Creak earned her medical degree from the same school, she applied unsuccessfully for more than ninety posts in London, finally taking a job at a mental hospital run by Quakers in York.)

John's childhood years were more difficult by comparison. When he was five, his father, who owned a bookstore, died of pneumonia from the delayed effects of being gassed in World War I. His mother suffered a fatal heart attack a few months later. John and his older sister, Barbara, were placed in a boarding school for orphans, where he pushed himself to excel, enabling him to transfer to a better school. At thirteen, he set his sights on becoming a doctor, but none of his aunts and uncles could afford to send him to university. When World War II began, he enlisted in the Navy, hoping to get a government grant to medical school if he survived combat. He spent most of his military service in Australia, leading bombing runs against enemy shipping lines, and when he returned home, he was awarded a scholarship to the University College London. There he met his future wife in a dissecting room. "It was very romantic," Lorna told me. "We were both assigned the same dead body." She found John dashing and brilliant, and they were married a short time later.

After Lorna had served a year's residency in the university hospital as a general physician, she and John decided to have a child—hopefully the first of many. They were thrilled when Susie was born in 1956, but almost immediately it was clear that she was having problems feeding. She refused to nurse, so Lorna had to place the bottle in her daughter's mouth and squeeze it so that she would swallow. Lorna's breasts ran dry of milk—a memory so painful that it still made her wince describing it to me more than fifty years later. But when she talked to the doctors and nurses at the hospital, they didn't seem to think much of it. Eventually, her daughter moved on to eating solid foods and began gaining weight, so she tried to push her worries out of her mind.

This was not easy. Susie began staying up all night screaming, so Lorna and John started switching off caretaking duties so they could at least sleep every other night. Nothing in their medical education had prepared them for this experience with their daughter. The word *autism* had never been mentioned in any of their classes.

Six months later, Lorna got on a train and took a seat with Susie in her lap. Another young mother, carrying a boy about the same age as her daughter, sat down directly across from her. As the train rolled through the lush countryside, the boy got excited, spotting sheep and cows passing by the window. He kept glancing into his mother's eyes expectantly and smiling, making sure that he had engaged her attention before directing it to what he was seeing by pointing his finger out the window and laughing.

Lorna felt a shiver pass through her and thought: *Susie has never done that.* She had never pointed to direct her mother's attention toward anything. Instead, if Susie wanted something, she would grab Lorna's hand and place it on the thing that she desired.

Susie had a toy panda that she clearly loved—she carried it everywhere and seemingly couldn't be happy without it. She would smell it, rub her cheeks against it, and enjoy the sensation of feeling its fur with her fingers. But what she never did, Lorna noticed, was to play games in which she pretended that the panda was a real bear. She also had a little tea set that Lorna had given her, and she would occasionally stage imaginary tea parties, but she never invited other children. She always sipped her imaginary tea alone.

One day, John came home from work and told Lorna that he thought he knew what was going on with their daughter. He had seen a lecture by Creak about a form of childhood psychosis called early infantile autism, and he felt like she was describing Susie. The Wings arranged for Creak to evaluate her. She confirmed the diagnosis.

It didn't take John and Lorna long to figure out that there were almost no resources in place to support the families of children like their daughter and to ensure that they had any sort of future outside an institution. Psychotic children were considered uneducable, so they were excluded from the school system and shunted into sheltered workshops called Junior Training Centres for the Severely Subnormal, where they were occupied with make-work projects like basket weaving. No one seemed to know what became of these children when they got older. Like the Rimlands after Mark's diagnosis, the Wings felt very much alone. But they were not alone.

IN 1958, A SCHOOL SECRETARY named Sybil Elgar, who was taking a correspondence course to become a Montessori teacher, visited an institution for "severely and emotionally disturbed children" called the Marlborough

Day Hospital near her home in St. John's Wood in London. Though the facility was advertised as progressive and based on psychoanalytic principles, she was deeply shaken by what she saw, and the children were clearly miserable.

Vowing to do better, Elgar started teaching classes for a small group of autistic children in the basement of her house in St. John's Wood in London at the behest of two mothers, Helen Allison and Peggie Everard. In his first two weeks at the school, Helen's son, Joe, smashed all the lightbulbs and nearly tore the place apart. But Elgar persisted in her efforts to find ways of reaching him. Though she knew very little about autism when she started, she was a formidable woman and an extraordinarily perceptive reader of what her students were thinking and feeling. Under her firm but compassionate tutelage, Joe Allison calmed down and learned to speak.

Susie Wing also became one of her early students and would eagerly exclaim "Mrs. Elgar!" when it was time to go to school. As word of Elgar's success spread among parents, it became clear that her basement was not large enough to accommodate all of the children on her waiting list.

In 1961, Joe and Helen Allison were featured on an episode of the BBC's popular *Women's Hour.* Hundreds of calls and letters poured in after the broadcast. The following January, a group of parents—many of whom had heard the BBC segment—met at a private house to form the Society for Psychotic Children, which changed its name to the Autistic Children's Aid Society of North London on Lorna's advice. (It's now known simply as the National Autistic Society.) Like NSAC, founded in the United States two years later, the group saw media outreach as essential to building up its membership so that it could exert pressure on local authorities to achieve its goals. The following year, the society received full-page coverage in the *Evening News* (under the unfortunate headline "Children in Chains"), which produced another influx of letters and phone calls.

The logo adopted by the society—a puzzle piece drawn by a father named Gerald Gasson—would eventually become the universal symbol of autism parents' organizations worldwide.

WHEN THE GROUP HAD raised enough money to convert an old railway hostel in Ealing into the Society School for Autistic Children (later renamed the Sybil Elgar School), even the Beatles got into the act. Though John Lennon promised to drop in for just an hour, he spent the entire afternoon there gleefully rolling on the floor with the children. He became one of the school's first donors and attracted other celebrities to the cause.

As Elgar's initial group of students became teenagers, she turned her attention to the need for the care and support of autistic adults, recognizing that while the children had made tremendous gains, they were not "cured" and would require a living environment suited to their needs for the rest of their lives. "Children need praise and encouragement," she said, "but most of all they need the opportunity to continue their education and training so that they can maintain and extend educational abilities . . . and acquire occupational skills." In 1972, the society launched Somerset Court, the first residential facility and school in Europe for autistic adults. Elgar and her husband moved into a flat on the top floor.

These achievements put Lorna and her professional colleagues light-years ahead of their American peers in their understanding of autism. By 1973, when Kanner finally admitted that autism might manifest itself in varying degrees of severity, this was already common knowledge in London. She was also free of the heavy load of guilt that Kanner, Eisenberg, and Bettelheim laid on American parents. "When I read Kanner's later papers," Lorna told me, "I thought they were bloody stupid. I knew I wasn't a refrigerator mother."

One of the leading lights of the London group was Michael Rutter, also at the Institute of Psychiatry. He conducted the first twin study of autism with a research fellow named Susan Folstein, which provided proof of the genetic basis of the condition for the first time. Rutter's early work also decisively untangled autism from schizophrenia, showing that they were separate conditions that only rarely occur together.

Despite all the anecdotal evidence to the contrary accumulated by parents, the biggest empirical question that remained unanswered into the 1960s was whether autism was as rare as Kanner continued to insist that it was. As the provision of services hinged on this point, the time for examining his claims was long overdue. Settling questions like that was the core mission of the Social Psychiatry Unit of the Medical Research Council (MRC), which was led by John Wing and based in the Maudsley Hospital in Camberwell.

III

In 1964, Guy Wigley, the medical officer of health for the county of Middlesex—encompassing a huge area stretching north of the river Thames and west of the City of London—came to the MRC with a problem. He had no idea how to calculate how many children with autism might live in the county, because a study of its prevalence had never been done.

John put a graduate student named Victor Lotter on the case. By sending out thousands of questionnaires to schoolteachers, training center supervisors, nurses, and parents, he managed to screen nearly the entire population of eight-, nine-, and ten-year-olds in Middlesex. Basing his selection criteria for autism on Creak's Nine Points, Lotter came up with a group of fifty-four children for whom complete medical and social records were available. He calculated a prevalence estimate of 4.5 cases of autism in 10,000—that is, thirty-two children in total, a very small number indeed. After being replicated by other researchers using similarly restrictive criteria, this number became the oft-quoted baseline against which all future autism prevalence estimates would be compared in the coming decades.

A closer look at these numbers, however, reveals a number of problems. Though Kanner insisted at first that early infantile autism was apparent at birth, nearly half of the children identified in the study experienced a "definite and recognizable setback in development" at some point in their early lives. (Antivaccine activists would later claim that "regressive autism" was a novel phenomenon linked to the combination measles-mumps-rubella vaccine, but the MMR wasn't introduced in Britain until 1988.) Nine of the children in the group also displayed evidence of neurological abnormalities that would have likely disqualified them for a diagnosis by Kanner.

Lotter's interviews also revealed the crass attitudes taken by medical professionals toward parents in this era. A pediatrician told the mother of one three-year-old boy, "He's mentally defective. There is no hope for him whatsoever." After asking for further guidance on his care, she was advised to "let him play in the garden with a ball." Nearly half of the children had received no education of any sort. "Services leave a great deal to be desired," Lotter concluded, citing the Elgar School as a rare and promising exception.

FEW RESEARCHERS AT THE MRC were more aware of the consequences of this than Lorna Wing. Suspicious of the empirical validity of Kanner's criteria after a decade of talking with her fellow parents, she decided to take a different approach in following up the Middlesex study in the early 1970s. Rather than using a top-down method as Lotter had done—*starting* with Kanner's definition of autism, and looking for examples of it—she decided to employ a bottom-up approach, searching for aspects of autistic behavior among children in Camberwell who were already identified as cognitively disabled.

Lorna and another MRC researcher named Judith Gould reached out to pediatricians, psychologists, teachers, public-health workers, and clinic directors in the area—anyone whose job might bring them in contact with a child with special needs. To locate the families that most needed help, they included only children with IQs of less than seventy in their sample, screening them for signs of autism with a questionnaire developed by Lorna called the Handicaps, Behaviour and Skills schedule. For months, they made phone calls and wrote letters while visiting hospitals, clinics, group homes, and special schools to dig through dusty cabinets of records.

Though Lorna is usually quite reserved, she wasn't above using whatever means were necessary to get the data she needed.

"I had completely given up with one particular psychiatrist who was being very resistant," Gould recalls. "But Lorna put on all her charm and her feminine wiles because she was determined to get this information, which she did."

Just as the Middlesex study predicted, they found only a handful of children in Camberwell—4.9 in 10,000—who met Kanner's criteria. But Lorna and Judith didn't stop there. As they made their rounds of the neighborhood, they couldn't help but notice a much larger group of children who clearly had traits reminiscent of his syndrome but were not eligible for a diagnosis under his guidelines. These children exhibited the same cluster of social aloofness, repetitive behavior, and insistence on sameness as Kanner's patients in Baltimore, but in a more diverse and colorful range of presentations.

They saw kids who flapped their hands and reversed their pronouns but never lined up their toys in rows. They met teenagers who engaged in elaborate repetitive rituals and were terrified by changes in routine but helped their mothers clear the table before retiring to a corner to play their favorite songs on the phonograph. Some of these children were completely nonverbal, but others were eager to wax on at length about their fascination with astrophysics, dinosaurs, or the genealogy of royalty.

While Lorna was trying to make sense of what she was seeing, she came across Dirk Arn Van Krevelen's paper in the *Journal of Autism and Childhood Schizophrenia* arguing that Kanner's autism and Asperger's syndrome were distinct conditions. As she read it, however, she saw reflections of the children in Camberwell in descriptions of both syndromes. This was despite the fact that her study had specifically excluded kids in mainstream schools and likely left out most of the children likely to fall on the Asperger side of the line. In other words, says Gould, "these children didn't fit into nice, neat boxes."

Because Asperger's paper had still not been translated into English, Lorna asked John to translate it for her. Reading it, Lorna realized that

Asperger had seen the same thing in his Vienna clinic that she was seeing in Camberwell.

THE VALIDITY OF ASPERGER'S MODEL became even more apparent to Lorna once her colleagues started sending her "kids that no one knew what to do with," as she put it. They clearly didn't fit into Kanner's narrow box, so most of them had been diagnosed with schizophrenia. They were also obviously highly intelligent but seemed naïve, as if they couldn't pick up on subtle social signals from the people they were talking to.

One young man had been fished out of the Thames by the police after jumping off a bridge and brought to the Maudsley. Lorna noticed that he was wearing two wristwatches. He explained that he kept one set to Greenwich mean time and the other to local time, even when the two times were the same. He was quite distraught that the time in London had recently changed to the British equivalent of daylight saving time. As a child, he had not learned to speak until he was three, and he had no friends until he was fourteen. He loved reading books on physics and chemistry, and he had memorized a large number of facts related to both. He dressed in old-fashioned clothes and was very particular about keeping his things in order and following a strict daily routine. But he was painfully aware that people generally didn't like him. His father had an intuition that something was different about him, but he had never been able to quite put his finger on it.

He was often ridiculed for being clumsy, rude, and unfashionable, though he went to great effort to be polite. He was very articulate, but he tended to add extraneous details in conversation, as when Lorna asked him about his relationship with his father and he replied, "My father and I get on well. He is a man who likes gardening." After his attempt to commit suicide by leaping from the bridge was defeated by the fact that he was an excellent swimmer, he tried to strangle himself. Clearly, this young man needed help and support in navigating daily life, but there was no diagnostic label on the books that would enable him to access psychiatric services.

Lorna knew that the parents of young people like this were not likely to readily embrace a diagnosis of autism, which was irrevocably linked with nonverbal preschool-aged children. The disabilities of these other young people were just as real and deserving of professional attention, but they were harder to see.

In their 1979 paper on the Camberwell study, Wing and Gould reported, "The behavior pattern described by Kanner could be identified reliably, but the findings of the present study bring into question the usefulness of regarding childhood autism as a specific condition." From the perspective of the MRC's mission of advising the government on guidelines for service provision, this was particularly true because it was obvious that there were more of these people, of all ages, struggling to get by without help or any explanation for their difficulties, than there were children with Kanner's syndrome.

IV

Lorna began a quiet but determined campaign to expand the concept of autism to include the people who had been systematically excluded from Kanner's walled garden. Her strategy was to work on two fronts simultaneously.

First, she would attempt to persuade her colleagues that autism was not a *categorical* diagnosis but a *dimensional* one (not a "yes" or "no" but rather "of what type?"). To replace Kanner's unified syndrome, she proposed the term the *autistic continuum*. While there were clearly many shades and hues along this continuum, all autistic people seemed to benefit from the same highly structured and supportive educational approaches, just as Asperger predicted.

It was equally apparent that a person could occupy one point on the continuum at a given point in their lives and another point later. Some children, like Susie, would remain profoundly disabled into middle age and beyond. But others blossomed in unexpected ways when given an accommodating environment and special consideration by their teachers (like several of Kanner's patients, including Donald T. and Richard S.). A Society School alum named David Braunsberg, for example, went on to earn an art degree at a university and become an accomplished painter and textile artist.

Next, Lorna introduced a new diagnostic label, conscious of the social stigma that the word *autism* carried. This was less a strictly empirical decision on her part and more like smart marketing. She wrote:

> Parents without special experience tend to overlook or reject the idea of autism for their socially gauche, naïve, talkative, clumsy child, or adult, who is intensely interested in the times of tides around the coast of Great Britain, the need for the abolition of British Summer Time, or the names and relationships of all the characters who have ever appeared in a television soap opera, such as *Coronation Street*. The suggestion that their child may have an interesting condition called Asperger's syndrome is more acceptable.

Lorna wasn't the first person to come up with the term *Asperger's syndrome*, which the Viennese pediatrician never used. In 1970, a German psychologist named Gerhard Bosch published a book called *Infantile Autism* in which he referred to "the Asperger and Kanner" syndromes. "From our experience," he concluded, "it is to be assumed that there is an intermediate realm between the two syndromes which cannot easily and clearly be ascribed to this or to that side." As Kanner had done for early infantile autism, Lorna codified the condition by writing a case series of her own called "Asperger's Syndrome: A Clinical Account," which included descriptions of the man with two wristwatches and five other young adults. It was published in 1981.

Resurrecting Asperger's name from a place and time that no one wanted to remember was not easy. When German cognitive psychologist Uta Frith finally made an elegant English translation of Asperger's paper in the late 1980s for a book of her own, her publisher turned down the manuscript.

(Cambridge University Press eventually published it.) Lorna's proposal also came under fire from Eric Schopler for adding yet another label to a field just starting to recover from the confusion between autism and schizophrenia. (He preferred the term *high-functioning autism.*) There were persistent backstage whispers that Asperger had worked for the Nazis—did such a man truly deserve recognition?

Over time, Lorna would lose her taste for the word *continuum*, because it suggested an incremental gradient of severity, from least to most severe, when she was suggesting something more individualized, nuanced, and multidimensional. While she was trying to think of a better term, she heard a phrase of Winston Churchill's echo in her mind: "Nature never draws a line without smudging it." This seemed particularly true of autism. One of the most subversive aspects of Lorna's concept was her suggestion that the continuum shades imperceptibly into garden-variety eccentricity. ("All the features that characterize Asperger's syndrome," she observed, "can be found in varying degrees in the normal population.")

Ultimately, she adopted the term *autism spectrum*. She liked the sound of it, which evoked pleasing images of rainbows and other phenomena that attest to the infinitely various creativity of nature. Clinicians readily adopted the phrase, because it helped explain what they'd been seeing in the real world for decades. It was a meme destined to go viral, so to speak—with assistance from a collusion of cultural forces that Lorna could not have foreseen, including a film that would turn Kanner's formerly obscure disorder into a household word virtually overnight.

Nine

THE *RAIN MAN* EFFECT

He remembers things. Little things.

—Charlie Babbitt

Barry Morrow drove his 1954 Studebaker around the back of the Minikahda Club in Minneapolis to pick up his new bride, Beverly, who was closing out her shift as a cocktail waitress. As he waited in his freezing car, he watched the valets running to fetch the Cadillacs and Lincolns that filled the parking lot in front of the grand plantation-style clubhouse. As a twenty-three-year-old singer in a rock-and-roll band working a variety of odd jobs, Morrow wasn't going to be fixing the busted heater in his jalopy anytime soon. On his second (and last) day as a door-to-door encyclopedia salesman, he persuaded a poor old woman to cancel her order, telling her that a better set was available at the library down the street.

While waiting for his wife to change out of the skimpy French frock that she was required to wear, Morrow caught the eye of a man in an upstairs window, who smiled and waved at him. He waved back. The next night, the same thing happened, and again the night after that. This little ritual went on for months. Morrow started to feel a bit weird about this mysterious figure who seemed to wait for him to appear each night. He christened him "the Waver." Beverly informed her husband that the man's name was Bill and that he scrubbed the club's ovens on the graveyard shift. She also told him that Bill was "retarded"—and that he was also the happiest and friendliest person she'd ever met.

At the Minikahda's Christmas party for staff that year, the Morrows glimpsed Bill sitting at a table by himself across the room. As a roving string quartet played holiday songs and black-tied waiters circulated with trays of canapés, he was bundled up in his winter parka, nursing a glass of water, with a glossy black Beatle wig perched precariously on his head. Unable to contain his curiosity any longer, Morrow strolled over to Bill's table and wished him a merry Christmas. The older man stood up, ceremoniously doffed his wig with his left hand and extended his right. Morrow sat down and they availed themselves of several flutes of complimentary champagne, which swiftly went to their heads.

As they laughed together, Morrow couldn't help but notice that the few teeth that Bill had left in his mouth were brown from smoking and that his neck was swollen with a goiter. He had also doused his wig with so much Aqua Net that it was as stiff and glistening as a bowling ball. Being a naturally inquisitive person, Morrow started asking him questions about his life. Bill wasn't shy, but his conversation ranged over such a broad and random variety of topics that the younger man had a hard time keeping up. "It was as if he had some epic tale he wanted to weave for me," Morrow observed, "but could remember none of the particulars."

Morrow would learn that there was a lengthy period of Bill's life that he never liked to talk much about. This was the forty-four years that he had spent in a place he referred to as "that hellhole"—Faribault State Hospital, fifty miles away. Bill had been committed there in 1920 at age seven. His parents, Sam and Mary Sackter, were Russian-born Jews who owned a corner grocery store. When Sam died suddenly of a heart attack at age thirty-five, the business collapsed, and Bill started doing badly in school because of his "filthy habits," as one teacher's report put it.

The principal insisted that Bill was feebleminded and that there was no place for him in the public school system. His mother fought for her son's right to attend classes as long as she could, but eventually the local mental health authorities deemed that Bill was at risk of becoming a burden to the community. He was declared a ward of the state and shipped off to the asylum, then known as the Faribault State School for the Feebleminded and Epileptic.

During his first five years there, he received letters and care packages of food and clothing from his mother. But as he had been diagnosed as an "imbecile," Bill was never taught to read or write, and Mary's letters were only occasionally answered by a member of the staff, who misspelled his last name in the replies. In 1925, Mary asked the hospital superintendent if her son might be briefly "paroled" (the term in use at Faribault, where the residents were called "inmates") for a weekend visit with his family. When she was informed that he was considered too "subnormal" to leave the hospital grounds, she sent the superintendent one last request: for a photograph of her son.

Fearing that the stigma of mental illness in the family would exert a chilling effect on her daughters' chances of finding husbands, Mary told them that they should consider their brother dead. She remarried, moved to Canada, and never attempted to contact him again.

Bill's ill health and unkempt appearance were the aftermath of nearly half a century of institutional neglect and abuse. He had never been taught how to tell time or handle money, and had never received proper dental care. Like the other inmates, he was paid the equivalent of 30 cents to $1.50 a month—redeemable only in goods from the hospital store—for backbreaking work like pushing food trolleys through the miles of dank tunnels that connected the various areas of the hospital. He also volunteered to help feed and care for fellow residents who were more profoundly disabled than he was. "You know, buddy," Bill (who called everyone "buddy," even his parakeet) told Morrow, "I was there for so long, I didn't even know I was there." The high fences on the outskirts of the facility defined the horizons of his universe.

One night, one of the men on his ward had a seizure. Fearing for the man's life, Bill woke up an orderly who was sleeping off a bout of heavy drinking. The orderly became so enraged that he threw Bill down a flight of stairs while maintaining a tight grip on his hair, scalping him. That was why Bill wore a wig. He also had an ulcer on his leg that had never been adequately treated. In the 1960s, a group of parents from the Minnesota chapter of the Association for Retarded Citizens demanded increased scrutiny of living conditions in the custodial care facilities in the state. (A group of senators' wives had to abort their tour of Faribault when they became too nauseated to go on.) In the wave of liberal reforms that followed, Bill was judged to be a promising candidate for community placement. On his own for the first time, he boarded a train to Minneapolis and found a room in a local boardinghouse, where he lived with other former institutional residents for several years, doing yard work, shoveling snow, and cleaning up in an auto body shop. Eventually, a social worker found him his job at the Minikahda.

In spite of everything he had been through, Bill struck Morrow as a remarkably cheerful man. ("I'm as good as downtown!" he exclaimed often.) He was delighted to be out among people, even if they mostly ignored him. By the end of the night, Bill had stuck his wig in his pocket and pulled out his harmonica—inherited from a friend who died in the institution—and transformed the slightly stuffy affair into a raucous hoedown by blowing dozens of choruses of the "Too Fat Polka." At the end of the night, Morrow scribbled down his number and told Bill that if he ever needed anything, he shouldn't hesitate to give him a call.

Bill didn't hesitate. At six a.m. the following morning, Morrow awoke with a throbbing headache to the sound of the phone ringing. A woman at the other end identified herself as "the dialer" before handing the phone to Bill. He told his new buddy that he needed a lift to the drugstore because he was out of toothpaste. When Morrow pulled up in his Studebaker two hours later, Bill was sitting out on the stoop, covered in inches of snow like a snowman, because after hanging up he had immediately stepped outside to wait for Morrow to arrive. It was the beginning of a beautiful and unlikely friendship that would change the course of autism history.

II

Bill wasn't autistic himself, though childhood schizophrenia was a common diagnosis on the overcrowded wards of Faribault. He was the opposite: a born schmoozer and people-pleaser who said hello to strangers in the street if he sensed that they might be friendly. At Faribault, the staff openly referred to residents like Bill as "crack-minded." They hadn't even tested his IQ until he had already been there for thirteen years.

But instead of taking Bill on as a charity case, Morrow and his wife accepted him as a friend—as eccentric in his own ways as the other members of their circle, a scruffy crowd of artists, writers, and musicians. Soon, the errands for toothpaste and "wig spray" turned into leisurely drives around the city narrated by Bill's unending monologues.

"His head was swiveling every which way as he observed everything happening around us," Morrow recalls, adopting Bill's raspy delivery, the result of decades of smoking Old Rip, the harsh tobacco sold at the hospital store. *Nice buses, yeah. Look at them buses, they're really big, hold a lot of people. The school kids, yeah, they're learning, and the men are working, they gotta work, and a man's gotta have a good job.* Morrow adds, "I only realized later that Bill was describing a world he was seeing for the very first time."

As an undergraduate at the University of Minnesota, Morrow became fascinated by emerging technology like Super 8 and the Sony Portapak, the first portable video system, which he used to start filming Bill and their friends on their odysseys through the city. Bill was twice the age of anyone else in this crowd of midwestern bohemians but fit right in; his perpetual wonder was just another altered state. "Bill was not the elephant in the room," Morrow laughs. "The room was full of elephants, and half of them were high."

When the Morrows had a son, Clay, Bill became his unofficial "grandpa" and a frequent guest at Sunday-night chicken dinners with Clay's actual grandparents. On the nights that Morrow's band, the Blue Sky Boys, played in bars and hotel lounges, "Wild Bill" would get his own moment in the spotlight to bring down the house with his trusty harmonica. At age sixty, for the first time since he was a child, he had a family.

Bill reciprocated Morrow's kindness by admitting him to his own inner sanctum: a little room at the rear of the Minikahda, next to the shed where the lawn mowers were parked, furnished with little more than a bed and a metal locker filled with cans of Aqua Net. In hushed and reverent tones, Bill showed Morrow his wig stand, the centerpiece of a personal shrine of pictures of children playing, dogs leaping, and suns rising that he had cut out of magazines. In the corner of the room was an old black-and-white TV for watching his favorite show, *I Dream of Jeannie.* Bill rarely missed an episode, and he would ask Morrow's friends, "Do you dream of Jeannie too?"

Morrow admits that his deep feeling of connection with Bill was inexplicable to outsiders. Their exchanges had a gently teasing, Zen-like quality:

Bill: See, to be a regular good man, buddy, you need three things in life: You need a good job, that's what I think, and you need a good buddy.
Morrow: That's only two, Bill. What's the third?
Bill: Hair, like what you got. That's why you're a regular good man, see?

After years of constant immersion in Aqua Net, Bill's wig "broke" one day, and Morrow persuaded him to grow a distinguished-looking beard instead. He also arranged for Bill to see a dentist and get fitted for a pair of false teeth. As Bill took more care in his appearance, people treated him with more respect, and his self-confidence increased. It was a virtuous circle. "I wasn't Bill's friend to do him a favor. I don't believe in pure altruism," Morrow says. "If it hadn't been fun to have him around, I wouldn't have done it."

INEVITABLY, THOUGH, the young filmmaker was soon caught up in the necessity of making a living to support his growing family. When he got an offer to become a multimedia specialist for the School of Social Work at the University of Iowa, he decided to take it. He was heartbroken to leave his friend behind, but there was nothing he could do. As a ward of the state, Bill was unable to leave Minnesota without the approval of the mental competency board. In the fall of 1974, the Morrows packed up, said a tearful good-bye, and relocated to a farm in Kalona, not far from the university.

A few months later, Morrow's phone rang again. A social worker was calling because Bill had been found by the side of the road, passed out from the pain of his ulcerous leg, which he had neglected to care for after the Morrows left town. Feeling abandoned, he had reverted to his old ways, vegetating alone in his room while dreaming of Jeannie in reruns. His leg would likely have to be amputated, and the social worker asked for Morrow's help in preparing him for the operation. On the long drive back to Minneapolis, he rehearsed the speech he would deliver when he got there—about how he felt bad about Bill's leg, but after all, he had brought this suffering on himself by not doing the simple things that the doctors had told him to do to keep himself healthy. He had to lose the leg or he'd lose his life.

Upon arriving at the hospital, Morrow consulted with the medical team about Bill's postoperative options, which he assumed would include being fitted with a prosthetic leg and entering a rehab program so he could return to work. Instead, Morrow was informed that, given the patient's mental competency status, he would not be eligible for a prosthesis or rehab and would almost certainly be sent back to Faribault to live out the rest of his days as a bedridden invalid. When Morrow walked into Bill's room, instead of delivering his prepared speech, he said, "We've got to get you out of here, buddy. Do you want to come and live with us in Iowa?" Bill was overjoyed. Together, the two men headed south.

Morrow helped Bill nurse his leg back to health, found him a room in a local boardinghouse, and arranged with a sympathetic advisor at the university, Thomas Walz, to hire Bill as a developmental disabilities consultant and brainstorm about productive things for him to do. But there was an unexpected legal wrinkle. From the point of view of the Minnesota authorities, Morrow had broken the law by taking Bill out of state; he could have been charged with kidnapping. The two men would have to return to Minneapolis and face the mental competency board to make a compelling case for Morrow becoming Bill's legal conservator despite the fact that he was less than half his age.

On the day of the hearing, Morrow tied his long blond hair back into a ponytail and tucked it under his collar. He also put on a sport coat and brought along a briefcase (which was empty) to complete the picture of a supremely competent conservator. To avoid unexpected outbursts during the hearing, he instructed Bill to stay mum: "These people are tricky, buddy, so just let me do all the talking."

Even with Morrow's makeover, however, the hearing did not go well. Sitting around a long table, the members of the board started grilling him with questions that he hadn't prepared for, and he found himself lapsing into legal doublespeak that sounded absurd even to him. The men who would decide Bill's fate didn't seem to be buying any of it. Basically, their questions focused on only one thing: Why was this twentysomething trying to become the legal guardian of this older, blatantly retarded man in ill health?

Suddenly, Bill interrupted the somber proceeding and took matters into his own hands. "Let us pray!" he declared. Instinctively, the members of the board bowed their heads respectfully. "Our Father, who art in Heaven, hollow be thy knee," he began—staying with the cadence of the Lord's Prayer, but substituting his own life story. "And thank you, dear Lord, for bringing me my buddy, Mister Barry, he takes good care o' me. I got a bird named Chubby, I got a *good* life now, and I don't want to ever go back to that hellhole—you know that, Lord." He continued on in that vein until the concluding "amen."

After a brief silence, the man at the head of the table cleared his throat and said, "Well, I think that says it all." He signed an official form and slid it down to the end of the table. Bill christened the form his "on-my-own papers." He was officially a free man.

III

With Morrow's and Walz's help, Bill became the proprietor of his own café at the University of Iowa, Wild Bill's Coffeeshop, which remains open to this day, employing adults with developmental disabilities. He never really figured out how to work the cash register—sometimes a mug of java cost 25 cents and sometimes it cost $250—but it all worked out, and he became a treasured member of the community. In 1978, Bill was named the Handicapped Iowan of the Year, and President Jimmy Carter invited him to the White House. Letters of congratulations poured in from all over, including one from the owner of a local salon who offered to make him a new, stylish salt-and-pepper wig, which he wore proudly for the rest of his life.

Morrow had started making videos for the university on topics like aging and child abuse, and it occurred to him that Bill's story would make a compelling documentary. He started shopping the idea around to funding agencies, but no one was interested in funding a film about the life of an intellectually disabled man. In 1980, however, Morrow was invited to present his show reel to a representative of the Mobil Oil corporation in New York City. Several NBC executives also attended the screening and told him that they were interested in producing a made-for-TV drama based on the story of Bill's journey to independence.

Bill, starring Mickey Rooney, with a handsome unknown named Dennis Quaid playing Morrow, aired in 1981—the year of *Reds, On Golden Pond*, and *Chariots of Fire*. The film went on to win an Emmy award, a Peabody, and two Golden Globes. Rooney turned in a masterful performance that captured Bill's distinctive mixture of childlike wonder and poignant gravitas, shooting scenes during the day while appearing in *Sugar Babies* on Broadway at night. At the Golden Globes ceremony, Bill was invited to accept the Best Actor award in Rooney's stead, preemptively stripped of his harmonica. At the last moment, though, he again took matters into his own hands and whipped a backup mini-harmonica out of his pocket. Jane Fonda started clapping along, and the usually slick event was interrupted by a spontaneous outburst of authenticity.

Two years later, Morrow wrote a sequel, *Bill: On His Own*. By then, he'd moved to Hollywood to try his luck as a screenwriter. "I want to stay here," Bill told him before he left Iowa City. "It's my home." Though he had been written off as incapable of learning at age seven, he developed dramatically in his fifties and sixties, prompted by the respect of those who had made a place for him in their lives. On the morning of June 16, 1983, Bill's landlady found him slumped in his favorite chair, freshly showered and dressed, with his lunch box at his side, ready to take his usual bus to the café. Bill had died peacefully of old age. He was buried with his harmonica and his on-my-own papers in his pocket.

"What Bill taught me," Morrow says, "is that not only do people like Bill need society, society needs people like Bill."

In the years after Bill's death, Morrow was unable to get this lesson off his mind. As he pursued his career in Hollywood, he became active in advocacy organizations like the Arc, the network of parents and disabled adults that had fought for the reforms that led to Bill's liberation from Faribault.

One night in 1984, at an Arc conference in Arlington, Texas, Morrow met a man who had one of the most unusual minds on earth. The bones of Kim Peek's cranium had failed to fuse properly in the womb, so at birth, part of his cortical tissue protruded through a baseball-sized blister at the back of his head. His brain also lacked a corpus callosum, the thick bundle of white matter that usually coordinates communication between the left and right hemispheres. When he was nine months old, a neurologist rushing off to a golf game told his parents that Peek was hopelessly retarded, would never amount to anything, and belonged in an institution. But his father and mother, Fran and Jeanne, refused to abandon him, vowing to care for him at home as best they could.

As an infant, Peek began developing cognitive capacities so extraordinary that they can only be described as uncanny. By eighteen months, he was memorizing every book his parents read to him, word for word, and turning them over on the shelf so they wouldn't waste his time by reading them again. At three, he was able to look up words in the dictionary and sound them out phonetically. He was equally adept with numbers. He would read telephone books for fun and total up the numbers on passing license plates. He was eventually able to read two pages of a book simultaneously—one with his right eye and one with his left—even if they were held upside down or reflected in a mirror.

Permanently excluded from school for being disruptive, he mastered the standard high school curriculum with the help of tutors by the time he was fourteen, though the local school board declined to award him with an equivalency certificate. Taking a job in a sheltered workshop for disabled people, he performed complex payroll calculations without benefit of an adding machine; one of his nicknames was "the Kimputer." Yet he was unable to dress himself or attend to many of his basic needs without help. When he finally learned to shave, he would close his eyes in front of the mirror because he couldn't stand seeing the sides of his face reversed.

Peek was a savant: a modern version of the prodigiously gifted "idiots" described by nineteeth-century clinicians like Édouard Séguin and John Langdon Down, the superintendent of the Royal Earlswood Asylum in Surrey. One of Langdon Down's patients was an intellectually disabled boy who had memorized *The Rise and Fall of the Roman Empire* after reading it once and could recite it word for word—albeit in rote, mechanical fashion. (Having skipped a line in his original reading, he went back and corrected himself, but then every time he reached that passage in his memory, he went through the same cumbersome process.) Another boy could recall the address of every confectioner's shop where he'd eaten sweets in London, along with the dates of all his visits. A third boy was able to instantly multiply two three-digit numbers in his head even before the doctor could jot them down—but was rarely able to recall Down's name, despite the fact that he talked to him nearly every day. Langdon Down also recalled seeing "many examples of children who had spoken well and with understanding, but who lost speech at the period of the second dentition, and had also suspension of mental growth"—a description that anticipated modern parents' accounts of their autistic children's abrupt loss of skills by a century.

Unlike the savants in Earlswood Asylum, however, Peek's special abilities were not restricted to one or two narrow domains. He could also recall classical music scores note for note, would advise conductors about mistakes that the orchestra had made, and once stood up in the middle of a production of Shakespeare yelling, "Stop the play!" When one of the actors asked him what was wrong, Peek informed him that he had omitted some words from a previous line. When the actor remarked that he didn't think anyone would notice or care, Peek countered, "Shakespeare would have cared!"

After seeing the *Bill* films, Peek's father, who was the communications director for the Arc, invited Morrow to Arlington to enlist him in raising public awareness of intellectual disability. Peek introduced himself with the dramatic statement, "Think about yourself, Barry Morrow." Fran explained that when his son got excited, he would lose track of his pronouns; what he had really meant to say was "I think about you, Barry Morrow." The screenwriter couldn't fathom why Peek had been thinking about someone he'd never met, but that became clear when he reeled off the closing credits from *Bill* verbatim. As they went over mailing lists, Peek began correcting erroneous zip codes on the fly and was able to recite step-by-step driving directions between any two points in the United States and Canada. He was also an inexhaustible font of sports trivia. To his family and a small circle of friends, Peek was an eccentric marvel who spent most of his time alone in his room. To Morrow, though, he seemed like an extraordinary protagonist in search of a plot. On the plane back to Los Angeles, he started jotting down ideas for his next film.

Morrow's agent warned him to steer clear of any more projects involving disability, but he couldn't stop thinking about his meeting with Peek—"a man with more information in his brain than the encyclopedias I used to sell," as he puts it. The notion of a Hollywood movie with a "retarded" lead character was unusual, to say the least, but it had been tried successfully once before: Cliff Robertson won an Academy Award in 1969 for his sensitive portrayal of an intellectually disabled baker in *Charly*, an adaptation of Daniel Keyes's heartbreaking novella *Flowers for Algernon*.

That film's broad appeal had benefited from its Pygmalionesque science fiction twist—an experimental operation that temporarily turned the shambling Charlie Gordon into a genius. Only after the operation did his character become fully human, capable of love, lust, ambition, sorrow, and rage. In Peek's case, Nature had already performed the operation that made him a genius, but would moviegoing audiences accept a permanently impaired protagonist as human?

Morrow's original conception for the character he would call Raymond Babbitt was part Peek and part Bill—a man with savant abilities who was "kidnapped" from an institution that was the only world he knew. To ratchet up the dramatic tension, Morrow designed Raymond's younger brother Charlie as his own opposite. Rather than being a naïve and well-intentioned midwesterner, Charlie was an abrasive, egotistical gray-market dealer in luxury sports cars who befriended this awkward brother he didn't know he had to gain control of a $3 million trust fund.

In a scene calculated to thrill mainstream audiences, Morrow had Charlie exploit his brother's savant abilities by bringing him to a casino in Vegas, where Raymond beat the blackjack dealer by counting cards. (Ironically, when the screenwriter brought Peek to Reno to see if this was truly plausible, he declined to go along with the scheme, saying, "This is not fair, Barry Morrow.")

Morrow also flipped the Pygmalion theme on its head. Rather than Raymond becoming human by being cured of his disability, Charlie would learn what was truly important in life by interacting with him—as Morrow himself had learned from Bill. He also put the unlikely pair of brothers on the road for a series of perilous adventures involving loan sharks and survivalists in the desert. At the end of the script, the two brothers decided to live together happily ever after.

Though the *Bill* films had been well received, Morrow still had so little confidence in his ability that he listed his occupation on tax forms as "typist." But in the fall of 1986, he got enormously encouraging feedback from United Artists. "This script is a beautifully written, extremely moving tragi-comedy that depicts a personality type seldom, if ever, explored in a feature film format," a UA production assistant wrote. "This is a remarkable first draft offering two meaty roles that should appeal to a number of big name acting duos . . . this is the kind of gripping, original and emotional script that could evolve into a film classic."

Anticipating a lighthearted, action-packed, buddy comedy appropriate for a Christmas release, UA optioned the script, prevailing upon Morrow to add a "ring of fire" sequence in which the brothers were trapped by survivalists in a barn surrounded by a moat filled with flaming gasoline. To escape, Raymond employed his savant superpowers to assemble a motorcycle from parts stored in a hayrack.

The production assistant's enthusiasm turned out to be prophetic, but not before the script had passed through the hands of several A-list directors, including Martin Brest (*Beverly Hills Cop*), Sydney Pollack (*The Way We Were*), and Steven Spielberg (*E.T.*). Luckily for Morrow, his draft landed on the desk of superagent Michael Ovitz, who forwarded it to one of the hottest marquee names in the business: Dustin Hoffman, who was coming off his *tour de force* performance in *Tootsie* as a male actor who transformed himself into an actress to earn a sought-after role. Ovitz's idea was to have Hoffman play Charlie opposite Bill Murray as Raymond.

Hoffman loved the script. But he didn't want to play Raymond's callow younger brother—he wanted to play Raymond. A few years earlier, he'd seen a *60 Minutes* broadcast profiling three savants: an intellectually disabled black sculptor named Alonzo Clemons who crafted astonishingly lifelike representations of horses with no artistic training; a blind musical savant with cerebral palsy named Leslie Lemke, who spontaneously developed the ability to play complex compositions on the piano after hearing them once; and George Finn, one of the calculating twins that Oliver Sacks met at the Bronx Psychiatric Center and described in his 1985 bestseller, *The Man Who Mistook His Wife for a Hat*. When Morley Safer asked Finn what the weather had been like in his hometown on November 3, 1958, he replied correctly without hesitation, "It was a cloudy day, it was on a Monday. Snow flurries that morning, very cold. Little bits of raindrops too." In a flash, he determined that June 6 in the year 91,360 will fall on a Friday. Yet he was unable to multiply seven and five.

Though Murray could have pulled off the tricky role of Raymond with panache, Hoffman had already proven himself to be an actor of inimitable range, having memorably played an anxious intellectual wooed by an older married woman (*The Graduate*), a jaded Times Square con man (*Midnight Cowboy*), and a driven ad executive (*Kramer vs. Kramer*). What Ovitz didn't know was that long before his breakthrough role in *The Graduate*, Hoffman had been polishing the skills he would need to play the first member of Asperger's forgotten tribe that most people in the world would ever see.

IV

Shortly after arriving in New York City from Los Angeles in 1958, Hoffman moved into a sixth-floor walkup at West 109th Street and Broadway with another actor who would rise to the stratosphere of their profession: Robert Duvall. They teamed up with the equally talented Gene Hackman, and the men became an inseparable trio. They applied themselves to the perfection of their craft with the intensity of religious fanatics. (Their goal, as Duvall once described it, was to be able to "live truthfully in an imaginary set of circumstances . . . in a somewhat effortless way.") Between cold readings into pitch-black, echoing rooms at cattle-call auditions, they took any job they could scrounge up, mining the speech and behavior of the people around them for rhythms and gestures they could use to flesh out their roles onstage. Hoffman checked coats on Broadway, threaded orchids on wires for a company that sold Hawaiian leis, dressed up as Paul Revere to shout out headlines in Times Square, and became a typist for the Yellow Pages. To cultivate his French accent, he waited tables in a bistro, where he passed himself off as a native speaker. (If a customer happened to actually be a native speaker, he would explain that he needed to practice his English.)

But the job that opened up the richest vein of material for him was being a nurse's aide at the New York Psychiatric Institute (NYPI), a short hop on the A train from his apartment. Starting each morning at 6:30 a.m., he worked an eight-hour shift that consisted of playing Ping-Pong, Scrabble, and other games with the patients, accompanying them to hydrotherapy sessions, laundering their soiled bedclothes, and holding them down for shock treatments. (The technique was introduced to America in 1939 with a public demonstration at NYPI on a boy diagnosed with childhood schizophrenia.) "All my life I had wanted to get inside a prison or a mental hospital, like most kids want to go to a zoo," Hoffman recalled. "I wanted to get inside where behavior, human behavior, was so exposed. All the things the rest of us were feeling and stopping up were coming out of these people, as if through their pores."

The patient who made the deepest impression on him was an older man known simply as "the Doctor." He had once been a brilliant pathologist at NYPI but then suffered a series of strokes that left him nearly immobile. His devoted wife, also a doctor, would visit him every day at lunch. By that point, he could speak only in gibberish; the young actor would speak gibberish back to him. As Oliver Sacks was doing at Bronx Psychiatric, Hoffman would play piano to entertain the patients, and the Doctor particularly loved it when he sang "Goodnight, Irene." One day, he began singing along when his wife walked in. Suddenly the Doctor stood up, met his wife in the middle of the room, and began to sob. "What is it?" she asked, adding tenderly, "We'll have lunch, we'll talk." A moment of stark lucidity crossed his face. "*I can't, I caaan't!*" he moaned.

Hoffman broke down crying too, and he quit the institution shortly after that. When he read Morrow's script for *Rain Man*, memories of that moment came flooding back to him.

A meeting was arranged in Hollywood between Hoffman, Peek, Peek's father, Morrow, and Brest, who was still attached to the project. Accompanying the actor was his longtime friend Murray Schisgal, an award-winning playwright and co-author of *Tootsie*, who acted as his consigliere. Jazzed up to meet a famous Hollywood actor, Peek had added knowledge of cinematic history to his memory banks. As he perambulated around the room, flapping his hands excitedly, Hoffman fell in behind him. "I can vividly recall Dustin walking behind Kim, mimicking his walk, his body language, his hand movements, and his head tilt—as if he was trying Kim on like a coat," Morrow says. "I thought everything was going well—how could you not be fascinated meeting a person like Kim? But then Murray sidled up to me and said something like, 'This isn't going to work. Dustin's not going to do Kim. He's too complicated and weird.'"

This unpromising meeting was the first of a long series of setbacks for the project that nearly scuttled it altogether. In the coming years, Hoffman would emerge as *Rain Man*'s most tireless champion, steering it through troubled waters that would have sunk many other films. His unwavering commitment to the project also attracted the interest of a handsome young former seminarian named Tom Cruise, then rising rapidly through the ranks buoyed by lead roles in *Top Gun* and *The Color of Money*. He idolized Hoffman and jumped at the chance to play his smarmy younger brother.

Morrow had never even heard the word *autism* when he wrote the first draft of *Rain Man*. Hoffman was instrumental in making the character of Raymond specifically autistic rather than just intellectually disabled. If it weren't for a chance conversation between Hoffman's associate producer, Gail Mutrux, and a psychotherapist named Bruce Gainsley, the movie that introduced the concept of autistic adults to the world might never have touched on the subject at all.

One day, Mutrux happened to mention to Gainsley that she needed to find out more about savant syndrome. He referred her to two psychologists who agreed to read Morrow's script and offer feedback. One was Peter Tanguay, an NIMH-funded researcher on social communication at UCLA. And the other was Bernie Rimland. The notion of making his son's condition the subject of a Hollywood blockbuster was the golden opportunity that Rimland had been waiting for.

Both Tanguay and Rimland came to the same conclusion: the chances of finding a real-life "idiot savant" who could beat a blackjack dealer in Vegas were statistically slim. But the possibility of an *autistic* savant being capable of such a feat was much more likely. In the files in his office, Rimland had the names of half a dozen young men who could fill the bill. He also felt that the eccentricities of autism (such as the difficulty in expressing emotion) would make the film far more interesting. Tanguay agreed: "I told Gail, this guy's autistic."

For Hoffman, the idea of taking on a role that would deny him the usual ways of connecting with his fellow actors and the audience was an irresistible challenge. But the notion of playing Raymond that way threatened to take the film far out of the realm of feel-good holiday fare. By that point, Brest had brought on screenwriter Ron Bass to rework Morrow's script. Hoffman told Brest and Bass that the essence of the film was a love story between the estranged brothers. "Maybe it's too easy to love this guy, because he's so sweet," he added. "What if the guy was, like, autistic or something, and a real pain in the ass?" Brest changed the subject, telling Bass privately that he would set Hoffman straight about this misguided idea. That conversation evidently didn't go as planned and Brest bailed on the project over "creative differences" shortly thereafter, effectively shelving the film.

But then, a few months later, Ovitz called Bass with good news: Steven Spielberg, fresh off the success of *The Color Purple*, had decided to resurrect *Rain Man*. The first time the director spoke with Bass, he told him bluntly that he was in favor of playing Raymond as autistic: "Dustin Hoffman is right and you're wrong," Spielberg said. "Do you know why?" Bass was already ahead of him: "I know why. The love story is only as good as its obstacle—and it's a much greater obstacle if the guy's autistic. I think it's a cool idea, so let's give it a try." Another reason Bass supported the idea was that his sister worked with autistic people at UCLA. After a few months of brainstorming, though, Spielberg dropped the project to direct *Indiana Jones and the Last Crusade*.

When it looked like *Rain Man* was going to be scrapped for good, Barry Levinson, on a roll after *Diner*, *The Natural*, and *Good Morning, Vietnam*, stepped up and agreed to direct the film. He believed that treating the subject of developmental disability in a lighthearted fashion, instead of the somber tone of an after-school special, would give the audience "greater empathy for it in the end." Finally, all the stars were aligned for autism to make its big-screen debut.

V

In 1986, Bass and Mutrux paid a visit to Rimland's office in Kensington, carting out armfuls of books and papers. Hoffman read Temple Grandin's *Emergence* and sought out the author, who told him that the one thing she wanted more than anything else in life was for someone to hug her—but the moment that anyone did, she couldn't bear it. "That sentence just destroyed me," Hoffman said.

He also made a pilgrimage to Oliver Sacks's house on City Island, a New England–style hamlet on an island in the Bronx. After visiting one of Sacks's patients in the hospital, they headed to the New York Botanical Garden, where Hoffman trailed a few yards behind as the neurologist chatted with a member of the actor's entourage. "Suddenly I thought I heard my patient," Sacks recalled. "I was extremely startled, and turned round—and saw it was Dustin thinking to himself, but thinking with his body, thinking enactively, thinking of the young autistic man he had just seen."

Rimland also put Mutrux in touch with several parents in his network, including Ruth Christ Sullivan, whose son Joe was featured in *Portrait of an Autistic Young Man*. When Ruth and her daughter arrived in California for a much-needed vacation, Mutrux sent a car to bring them to the studio. Sullivan felt a heavy weight of responsibility going into the meeting, as if she had to speak for the mothers of autistic children all over the world. But Hoffman, in jeans and tennis shoes, made her feel at ease while asking her to tell story after story about her son.

An hour into the meeting, the actor seemed to abruptly withdraw from the conversation. He shifted slightly in his chair as a serious expression came over his face. "*Tuh-raaaagedy*," he said—drawing out the vowel, perfectly capturing Joe's mischievous way of saying one of his favorite words. Sullivan was profoundly moved that the actor had studied his behavior so closely. The scenes of Raymond instantly multiplying large numbers, compulsively lining up salt and pepper shakers, and snapping photographs with a little camera in the car were all based on Joe.

Peek went down in history as "the real Rain Man" (the title of a book written by his father), but that was a benign white lie that enabled the filmmakers to keep the identity of a second family in Rimland's network secret. In truth, Raymond was a composite of Joe Sullivan and a young man in New Jersey named Peter Guthrie, whose distinctive shuffling gait, bemused tilt of the head, and verbal tics ("Uh-oh," "Definitely," and "Of course") became central to Hoffman's conception of the character. While Peek reveled in all the attention he got after the film came out, Peter had no interest in becoming a celebrity. When Mutrux contacted his family, he told his parents, "I don't want my name becoming a household word. I definitely don't want my name in *USA Today*." But he agreed to be part of Hoffman's research, and Mutrux lent his brother Kevin a movie camera so he could film Peter at home.

Robert and Becky Guthrie fit Kanner's descriptions of gifted and highly accomplished parents to a T, minus the lack of affection for their children. Robert was a four-star general who served as the Army's project officer for the launching of the first American satellite, *Explorer 1*, in 1958. He went on to oversee the development of the Black Hawk helicopter and the Patriot missile. Becky was a first-generation autism "mother warrior": as president of the northern Virginia chapter of NSAC in the 1970s, she fought for the right of autistic children to a public education at a time when they were ineligible for admittance to mainstream schools. Kevin, a few years younger than Peter, was a college football star who bore more than a passing resemblance to Tom Cruise. After *Rain Man*, he went on to launch JSTOR, a digital archive of journals and other research materials that now services eight thousand institutions in more than 160 countries.

The Guthries suspected that Peter was different from their other kids when he was just a few months old. When he glanced at his mother, she felt that he was looking straight through her. Several doctors diagnosed him as severely retarded, but just before he turned two, as his brothers and sisters unwrapped their gifts on Christmas morning, Peter reached for a magnetic letter board and spelled out *Esso*, *Grecian Bread*, and *Smirnoff Vodka*. Soon he was assembling jigsaw puzzles upside down, drawing maps of the United States to scale freehand, and cutting letters of identical width out of construction paper without a ruler. He communicated with his parents by spelling out words rather than saying them, like "C-h-e-e-r-i-o-s." (For two years, he ate nothing but Cheerios.) A child psychiatrist at Walter Reed Army Medical Center finally diagnosed him with autism.

Instead of treating Peter's passions for letters, numbers, and order as pathological, Becky encouraged them. By age ten, he had taught himself Cyrillic using a pocket dictionary; he was eventually able to read, write, and speak French, Arabic, Hebrew, Spanish, and Old English. When his father was stationed in Tokyo, Peter became fascinated with the statistics of sumo wrestling. For years after the family returned to the States, he kept track of matches in Japanese newspapers, copying the results into the archive of spiral notebooks and manila folders that filled his bedroom. In addition to being a walking database of sports history and an impressive calendar calculator, he memorized *Billboard*'s record-sales charts going back to the 1950s. A decade before most people thought about buying a personal computer, he was using one to cut down the clutter in his room.

Hoffman and Cruise met the Guthrie brothers at the Carlisle Hotel in Manhattan on Valentine's Day, 1987. Though Peter, like Peek, prepped himself for meeting the actors by memorizing every detail of the actors' filmographies, he wasn't good at recognizing faces. When Cruise stuck out his hand, Peter asked him, "What's your first name?" Then he said the same thing to Hoffman. After a stiff two-hour meeting, Kevin said to the actors, "You know, if you really want to see Peter relaxed, you have to go bowling with him. He loves to bowl."

A few days later, the brothers met up with Hoffman and Cruise at Bowlmor Lanes in Union Square. As the actors engaged in a heady discussion of dramatic strategy for their roles, Peter worked the lanes. When it was Cruise's turn, he would shout, "Top Gun, Top Gun, you're up!"

The process of helping Hoffman develop the character, and generally being regarded with respect by people other than his family, had a beneficial effect on Peter. "People began treating him more seriously—as more than just this bizarre guy," Kevin recalls. "He became more willing to be social. I saw him reach inside himself and pull out emotional responses that I didn't know he was capable of. He enjoyed showing off what he could do."

To ensure that the dialogue in the film rang true, Hoffman called Kevin regularly to read him the day's scenes and ask him what his brother would say. Mutrux also kept Ruth Sullivan on speed dial. The climactic scene in which Raymond is freaked out by a blaring smoke detector—the pivotal moment when Charlie realizes that his brother would have to go back to the institution—was based on her description of Joe's reaction to a fire in a wastebasket. "All of that stuff came from me making calls ten minutes before we started shooting," Mutrux recalls.

The one major way that the film departed from real life was that Joe Sullivan and Peter Guthrie—like Bill Sackter and Kim Peek—were fully capable of living outside of institutions with the help of their families. In fact, it's highly unlikely that any of them would have developed their impressive skills and abilities had they been condemned to a place like Wallbrook, the institution depicted in the film. Peter lived in his own apartment in Princeton with a roommate, shopped and cooked for himself, managed a bank account, and regularly took the train to see his parents in Virginia. For the past four decades, he has quietly worked as a reference librarian at the university. Joe had never lived in an institution, because his parents fought hard to make a space for him in the community.

But Mutrux's experts were adamant that few autistic people would be able to survive outside institutions. "The 'happy ending' in the original script is simply not realistic," Wisconsin psychiatrist Darold Treffert, the world's leading expert on savant syndrome, wrote in his book *Islands of Genius*. "There is no six-day cross-country cure for autism." Though Rimland never considered putting his son, Mark, in an institution, he insisted that state homes like Wallbrook were the only appropriate places to house people like Raymond Babbitt.

Ironically, while Raymond was widely referred to in the press as "high-functioning" and "one of the lucky ones" when the film came out, he was portrayed as less capable of living independently than any of the real-life models on which his character was based. Levinson—who made an uncredited appearance in the film as Raymond's psychiatrist—insisted that the poignancy of him going back to Wallbrook would be more dramatically satisfying for the audience. Though Morrow made sure that Sackter never had to go back to Faribault, he has made peace with the ending of *Rain Man*. "I felt betrayed politically, but artistically, it was a triumph," he says.

THE FILM'S SUCCESS was not at all assured in the weeks leading up to its release. Responses at test screenings were mixed because audiences were so unfamiliar with autism. ("Why doesn't the little guy just snap out of it?" one viewer wrote.) Ruth Sullivan talked Hoffman into giving *Rain Man* a sneak preview in Huntington as a benefit for the Autism Services Center (ASC) there two nights before its official New York premiere. This gala event took place in a grand old vaudeville showcase called the Keith-Albee Theater, and tickets sold out far in advance, enabling the ASC to buy its first piece of property—Pelican House, the group home where her son still resides. Hoffman introduced the movie by saying:

> We just made a film that will play for a month or two, or whatever, in cities around the world, and be put out on cassette and put on shelves and seen once. But you people have Joe in your community for the rest of your life, and I would take that any day of the week . . . When I first looked at that footage [of Joe in *Portrait of an Autistic Young Man*] I said, "I love that man." And I love you for making him a part of your community.

Then he took a seat behind Joe to observe his reactions. Ruth recalls, "Joe told me that he especially liked the parts about him, like the scene where Raymond eats cheese puffs with toothpicks." Only on her second viewing did Ruth notice that Charlie ate his cheese puffs with toothpicks too—a subtle tribute to the ways that the families of autistic children learn to adapt to their behavior.

Leading critics took issue with the film in ways that said more about prevailing views of autism than they did about *Rain Man*. Richard Schickel of *Time* compared it favorably to the usual "disease-of-the-month TV movie" while admiring Hoffman's portrayal of a "truly hopeless case" who had only two options: being committed to an institution or becoming "a kind of living pull toy for his brother, flapping and clacking in his wake." Pauline Kael was equally scathing in the *New Yorker*, writing that she left the theater feeling "stupefied."

But audiences embraced the film, which went on to gross nearly $355 million worldwide, making it one of the most financially successful Hollywood releases of all time. In addition to winning Oscars for Best Picture, Best Actor in a Leading Role, Best Director, and Best Screenplay, *Rain Man* earned a slew of other honors and distinctions, including two Golden Globes and a People's Choice award. It even spawned its own fandom. Handmade posters sprang up on walls all over Tokyo when the movie opened there, and when the oak trees in front of the Kentucky convent that served as the Wallbrook exterior set were cut down in 2007, devotees gathered to reenact Raymond's liberation from the hospital.

Morrow got his first glimpse of the phenomenon he had wrought by reading a letter from a mother shortly after the film opened. She explained that taking her son shopping was an ordeal because he almost inevitably had a meltdown, and other mothers would chastise her for having such an out-of-control child. Recently, however, when a woman skewered her with a withering look at the market, she asked her: "Did you see *Rain Man*?"

"Oh yes," the woman replied, "I loved that movie."

"Well, my son Johnnie is like Raymond Babbitt," the mother said.

The other woman's face softened. "Oh, Johnnie," she said. "Do you have autism? I understand."

Phyllis Terri Gold, one of NSAC's co-founders, told Hoffman that her mother had refused to even acknowledge the existence of her son to her friends until she saw the film. The parents of another boy described in a letter how on the way home from the theater their son, who rarely spoke, declared proudly, "I'm autistic!" By putting one autistic person on the screen, the filmmakers had made innumerable others visible—to their loved ones, to their neighbors, to their teachers and doctors, and to themselves.

Rimland's phone began ringing off the hook. One call came from a man in his forties named Jerry Newport who had spent his life wondering why he never felt at home among other people. As a little boy, he discovered that he could add columns of four-digit numbers and factor square roots in his head. At first, he used these skills to impress his classmates, but he ended up feeling like a sideshow freak. Unable to find a job after college, he drove a cab for twenty years, eventually becoming so depressed that he tried to commit suicide. Then he saw *Rain Man* and immediately recognized himself on the screen. Rimland referred him to UCLA for a diagnosis.

The character of Raymond Babbitt made autism recognizable and familiar even to those who had no personal connection to the subject. In his promotional tour, Hoffman made it a point to portray the condition in universal human terms. At a press conference in New York City, the actor broke down crying, saying that the film "touches something in us that I can't explain. We all go through life not hugging quite as much as we'd like to. Something cuts us off . . . We're always keeping a lid on our own autism." Soon, Ruth Sullivan was fielding calls from parents in England, France, Japan, Italy, Sweden, and Australia, seeking practical strategies for getting groups like NSAC off the ground.

An unprecedented surge of interest in autism rippled outward through mainstream media. "It seems that *Rain Man* has stimulated almost every newspaper and magazine in the country to run an article" on the subject, Rimland observed. He was only slightly exaggerating. In the year before the film came out, fewer than a hundred stories on autism had been published in major newspapers in the United States. The following year, that number quadrupled. It would never decline again. After Hoffman thanked Peter Guthrie at the Academy Awards ceremony, the *Washingtonian* ran an in-depth story on him called "Dustin and Me." (He had warmed to the idea of his name becoming a household word.) Inevitably, Peter was presented as the exception to the rule, the rarest of the rare, one of the lucky ones who was able to live a "fairly normal life," which was "virtually unheard of among autistic people."

People ran a spread on Joe Sullivan that described his mother's fight for his education. The handsome, soft-spoken young man went on to make appearances on *Oprah* and *The Larry King Show*, performing feats of lightning calculation for the wide-eyed hosts. In 1993, the Disney Company added a feature on Joe to the multimedia presentation "Frontiers of Medicine" at the Epcot Center, seen by more than a million people a year.

Soon other autistic characters began to infiltrate the popular imagination. Within months of *Rain Man*'s release, Ann Martin published *Kristy and the Secret of Susan*, the thirty-second installment of *The Baby-Sitters Club*, one of the biggest-selling series of young adult books in history. Susan's "secret" was autism, and while she wasn't much of a character—doing little to advance the plot but flap her hands and make life difficult for her mother—the book was notable for portraying autism in terms that even a twelve-year-old could understand.

A FEW MONTHS AFTER the film opened, Ruth Sullivan attended a family wedding in Pittsburgh. Only aunts and uncles of the bride and groom were invited to the rehearsal dinner, so Joe was on his own for supper in a strange city, which normally would have been a cause of great anxiety for her.

Ruth asked the hotel doorman if he could help her son find a place to eat close by, adding that because Joe was autistic, he might not seem to be listening to his directions. The doorman's eyes lit up. "Like *Rain Man*!" he said. She watched as the two men crossed the street into a world that had been transformed in a very short time. "One film did that. One film did more for autism than all of us working together worldwide had been able to do in twenty-five years," she says.

But *Rain Man* was just the beginning.

Ten

PANDORA'S BOX

It's a question of diagnosis.

—Lorna Wing

While autism was rapidly assimilating into mainstream awareness in the wake of *Rain Man*, a strategic series of revisions to the *Diagnostic and Statistical Manual of Mental Disorders*, prompted by Lorna Wing and her colleagues in London, were chipping away at Kanner's monolithic edifice from the inside.

It was only because of these revisions that children like Tyler Bell were able to get their initial diagnoses of PDD-NOS, one of several new flavors of autism spectrum disorder added to the manual in 1994, along with Asperger's syndrome. This was, of course, precisely what Lorna had in mind when she undertook her campaign to recast the *DSM* criteria: to make it possible for children who would have been excluded from support services before to get them. By the end of the decade, however, the startling rise in diagnoses—and the alarms in the media that autism had become an epidemic—took even Lorna by surprise. "Since the publication of my paper on Asperger's work," she admitted, "I have felt like Pandora after she opened the box."

Autism made its debut in the first edition of the bible of psychiatry, the *DSM-I*, in 1952, as "schizophrenic reaction, childhood type." This condition was unhelpfully defined only by what it was not: "The clinical picture may differ from schizophrenic reactions occurring in other age periods because of the immaturity and plasticity of the patient at the time of onset of the reaction." What this clinical picture looked like in human terms was left to the clinician's imagination.

The original impetus for creating a standardized guide of diagnostic nomenclature for psychiatrists was war. Before the 1940s, the only such guide was the *Statistical Manual for the Use of Hospitals for Mental Diseases*, designed for use by the staff of large institutions to aid in the collection of clinical data. But Veterans Administration (VA) psychiatrists found this guide of little help in diagnosing and treating the problems of the young men returning from Europe and Asia traumatized by what they had seen. Veterans unable to shake off memories of bombed-out cities and starved bodies in concentration camps ended up being diagnosed as having "psychopathic" or "psychoneurotic" personalities, because they were the only labels available.

The *DSM-I* added a couple of alternate categories to the list—"gross stress reaction" and "adult situational reaction"—so these young men could receive VA benefits without being branded psychopaths for life. The notion that the successors to this modest 132-page document (crammed with terms like *vagabondage*, *urge to say words*, and *homosexual panic, acute*) would someday be employed to determine a child's access to an education, behavioral therapy, insurance reimbursement, and other essential services would have seemed unlikely.

The description of "schizophrenia, childhood type" in the *DSM-II*, published in 1968, when Bettelheim was the rage, was more specific, but in the wrong direction, citing "autistic, atypical and withdrawn behavior" and "general unevenness" as evidence of a "failure to develop identity separate from the mother's." If this description was still vague, and the theory behind it was nonsense, the *DSM*'s impact was still limited. Few copies of the slim second volume, about the same length as its predecessor, found their way outside the walls of asylums, where it was used to provide convenient labels for patients by superintendents and ward supervisors who—in increasing numbers—often lacked a medical degree themselves.

By contrast, the *DSM-III*, published in 1980, was designed by the APA's Robert Spitzer with a more sweeping mission in mind: saving psychiatry itself from extinction. By that point, the forces amassed against the profession were powerful and various, including disgruntled academic researchers, well-connected insurance lobbyists, and a rising phalanx of "anti-psychiatry" groups like the Insane Liberation Front. (A significant boost to this movement was provided in 1975 by another Hollywood blockbuster: *One Flew over the Cuckoo's Nest.*) The pressures exerted by these groups—and the idiosyncratic mind of Spitzer himself—reframed the *DSM* in a way that reinvented psychiatry as the front end of the pharmaceutical industry rather than the arcane art of soul healing, akin to shamanism, that it had been.

The key word in Spitzer's mind as he undertook the revision in 1974 was *reliability*—the ability to produce consistent, replicable results. It was an open secret that two patients presenting with the same complaints in two psychiatrists' offices might end up diagnosed with different disorders. This flexibility, so to speak, was built into the system, reflecting the enduring influence of Kanner's mentor, Adolf Meyer. For Meyerians, atypical behavior was merely the superficial manifestation of an underlying "reaction" caused by the patient's struggle to adapt to a particular life situation. It was the psychiatrist's job to arrive at an understanding of this situation by interpreting symptoms and probing into the patient's background, using the tools of whatever theoretical school the therapist subscribed to. The first two editions of the *DSM* were designed to sit unobtrusively beside the monumental tomes of Freud, Otto Rank, Alfred Adler, and other master cartographers of the psyche.

But Spitzer was less tolerant than his predecessors of approaches to therapy that promised much and delivered little in the way of practical improvement in patients' lives. As a resident at the Columbia Center for Psychoanalytic Training and Research, Spitzer had an unimpressive experience attempting to treat patients with psychoanalysis. "I was always unsure that I was being helpful," he said. "I don't think I was uncomfortable listening and empathizing—I just didn't know what the hell to do." He became obsessed with the problem of diagnostic unreliability and developed a software program for computer-assisted diagnosis called DIAGNO in 1965, when few psychiatrists had even seen a computer.

By the 1970s, his frustration was widely shared, and much of the blame was put on the *DSM*. Researchers were frustrated by descriptions of conditions like "inadequate personality," "social maladjustment," and "other neurosis" (with symptoms that included writer's cramp) that were so ill-defined and context-dependent that there was little hope of uncovering empirical proof that they even existed. Powerful drugs like chlorpromazine were proving more effective than talk therapy in pacifying "difficult" and "agitated" patients, but pharmaceutical companies saw few blockbuster opportunities in targeting afflictions like "hysterical neurosis" and "adjustment reaction of adolescence" (described as "irritability and depression associated with school failure and manifested by temper outbursts, brooding and discouragement").

Payment for psychotherapy was increasingly becoming the responsibility of insurance companies and the federal Medicaid program, and decision makers were understandably wary of pouring stockholders' and taxpayers' money into fishing expeditions. Time on the couch wasn't easily translatable into spreadsheet terms for cost-benefit analysis; even the traditional bond of confidentiality between client and therapist was seen as a barrier to accountability, the buzzword du jour in discussions of mental health care on Capitol Hill. "Compared to other types of [medical] services there is less clarity and uniformity of terminology concerning mental diagnoses, treatment modalities, and types of facilities providing care," the vice president of Blue Cross, Robert J. Laur, said in 1975. "One dimension of this problem arises from the latent or private nature of many services; only the patient and the therapist have direct knowledge of what services were provided and why." Senator Jacob Javits agreed: "Unfortunately, I share a congressional consensus that our existing mental health care delivery system does not provide clear lines of clinical accountability."

For decades, psychoanalytic pundits like Bettelheim had occupied an exalted place in American culture akin to secular priests, but psychologists and social workers were making significant inroads into the APA's client base. What value did a medical degree add if psychiatry wasn't really medicine?

Meanwhile, the very raison d'être of the *DSM* was under attack by apostates and heretics like Thomas Szasz, psychiatrist-author of such popular books as *The Manufacture of Madness*, who declared that mental illness was a myth, brutally employed to police the bounds of socially acceptable behavior. "Our adversaries are not demons, witches, fate, or mental illness," he wrote in 1960. "We have no enemy whom we can fight, exorcise, or dispel by 'cure.' What we do have are *problems in living*—whether these be biologic, economic, political, or sociopsychological." These critics found an unexpectedly sympathetic ear in Spitzer, who had written about the stigmatizing effect of labels in reference to schizophrenia and played a key role in eroding psychiatry's aura of infallibility by leading the task force behind the abrupt "delisting" of homosexuality as a mental illness in the *DSM-II*'s seventh printing in 1974.

Spitzer's strategy was to ground his revamped field guide to mental illness in as much empirical research as possible. He formed twenty-five committees to develop detailed descriptions of disorders in each category, favoring psychiatrists who saw themselves primarily as scientists rather than clinicians. These committee members came to be known as DOPs: "data-oriented people." Clinicians with nonmedical backgrounds were included only after the basic framework had been established. (An APA oversight committee had to step in and insist that he engage more psychoanalysts in the process.) Spitzer's overall goal was to finally "operationalize" the *DSM* criteria—to make them mission-critical for clinical practitioners and researchers while aligning them with the standards of the *International Classification of Diseases* (*ICD*), the diagnostic manual used in most of the world.

Not surprisingly, Spitzer was a confirmed DOP himself. He labored over the *DSM-III* for six years, often working seventy or eighty hours a week in relative isolation even when he was sitting in a crowded conference room.

His uncanny ability to glide above the fray was associated with a certain personal remoteness. Around Columbia, where Spitzer was a professor of psychiatry, he became infamous for never saying hello to anyone, for failing to recognize colleagues' faces, for sometimes not even acknowledging the presence of those speaking directly to him, and for striding down busy corridors paying no heed to anyone. For a man who spearheaded the creation of the most detailed map of psychological states ever created, he didn't seem to pick up on other people's internal states very well. He found it difficult to adopt their perspectives, even in relatively trivial matters like buying a gift for a colleague.

His primary criterion for signing off on the adoption of a new diagnosis was that it worked in the context of the whole: "Whether it fit in. The main thing was that it had to make sense. It had to be logical." This Spock-like approach won Spitzer few friends but enabled him to unburden psychiatry of baggage it had been lugging around since turn-of-the-century Vienna.

In short, while Spitzer's eccentricities may have fallen short of meeting the criteria for Asperger's syndrome, the *DSM-III* was the product of a mind that exhibited many classic qualities of autistic intelligence. These traits enabled Spitzer to get the job done with a minimum of fretting about offending various sectors of the profession. Calling him an "idiot savant of diagnosis," Spitzer's colleague Allen Frances, who went on to chair the task force that created the *DSM-IV*, observed, "He doesn't understand people's emotions. He knows he doesn't. But that's actually helpful in labeling symptoms. It provides less noise."

The inclusion of "infantile autism" in the *DSM-III*, published in 1980, marked Kanner's moment of triumph. At last, his "unique syndrome" was lifted out of the swamp of schizophrenia, establishing it as the core of a new category of "pervasive developmental disorders." Autism was framed narrowly in terms of his two cardinal signs: "pervasive lack of responsiveness to other people" coupled with "resistance to change." The age of onset was specified as "before 30 months," in keeping with his theory that his syndrome was present from the start, which ruled out virtually all the kids who would later be diagnosed with Asperger's syndrome.

Most importantly, the checklist of clinical features that had to be present before making the diagnosis—including "gross deficits of language development" and "bizarre responses to the environment"—was nonnegotiable. Every single feature was required, as Kanner would have demanded. (In technical terms, the checklist was *monothetic*, describing a class alleged to be identical in every salient aspect.) The description of autism also noted that it was "apparently more common in the upper socioeconomic classes"—an accurate description of the families in Kanner's referral network, if nothing else.

Each of these qualifications increased the likelihood that autism would forever remain as Kanner had described it: a rare disorder. Furthermore, the word *infantile* guaranteed that it would continue to be viewed primarily as a condition of early childhood. For the mature Temple Grandins of the world, the only diagnosis on offer was "Infantile Autism, Residual State"—an awkward kluge invented to describe people who met the criteria for the full syndrome in infancy and still manifested "oddities of communication and social awkwardness."

To accommodate kids who suffered a loss of skills after thirty months, there was "Childhood Onset Pervasive Developmental Disorder" (COPDD) marked by "lack of appropriate social responsivity" (which was vague enough), "inappropriate clinging" (along with "asociality"—clearly a mixed bag), "hyper- or hypo-sensitivity to sensory stimuli" (covering all the bases), and "insistence on doing things in the same manner every time." COPDD was described as being even rarer than autism, which was not surprising, considering that it was *also* characterized by "bizarre" fantasizing and preoccupation with "morbid" thoughts and interests. (Can calendar dates, multiplication, chemistry, and the weather be considered morbid?) In actual practice, few clinicians bothered with the ill-conceived diagnosis.

One clinic reported only a single child meeting the criteria for COPDD in five years.

On the whole, however, Spitzer's reinvention of the *DSM* was a hit that succeeded far beyond the APA's expectations. Compared to its svelte, spiral-bound predecessors, it was a gargantuan tome, with descriptions of 265 mental disorders (as opposed to *DSM-II*'s 182) sprawling across 494 pages—nearly four times longer than the previous edition. Its very heft communicated authority. *DSM-III* "looks very scientific," Spitzer recalled. "If you open it up, it looks like they know something."

Soon, everyone would know something. The readership of the new edition went far beyond the usual crew of hospital superintendents and nosological data wonks. Psychiatrists who never thought about giving the *DSM* a second glance became very interested, glimpsing in it a road map to their own economically viable futures (which led straight to Big Pharma). It became de rigueur reading for psychologists, educators, social workers, prison administrators, drug developers, judges, insurance underwriters, government officials, service providers, and virtually everyone involved in health care and research.

Spitzer had done more than revise a manual. He had elevated psychiatry to new prominence in the national conversation, academia, and the research enterprise. The *DSM-III* became an international best seller, making "an unbelievable amount of money for the APA," said Spitzer. In the coming years, sales of the supersized *DSM*—and a whole cottage industry of related merchandise, including "pocket guides"—would become a cash cow for the formerly struggling organization.

THOUGH FEW PEOPLE OUTSIDE the APA knew it at the time, the *DSM-III* had a dark secret. For a document created by DOPs, much of the data behind it was sketchy and provisional. Allen Frances later admitted that "there was very little scientific evidence available to guide" the decision making of Spitzer's committees. Nowhere was that more evident than in the description of the pervasive developmental disorders, with its weird hodgepodge of vagueness ("music of all kinds may hold a special interest for the child") and overspecificity (the arbitrary cutoff point between infantile autism and COPDD).

The popularity of the *DSM-III*—particularly with regard to autism—was brief and distinguished by a chorus of complaints from clinicians who found the criteria difficult to apply in practice. To prepare for the next revision, Spitzer appointed three of the smartest clinician-scientists in the field to review the literature and draft an improved set of criteria: Lorna Wing and two American psychologists, Lynn Waterhouse and Bryna Siegel. A task force was formed to refine their drafts and conduct field tests. The fruits of this labor were published in 1987, in the next major revision of the manual, the *DSM-III-R*.

This edition was even longer and more ambitious than its predecessor, adding twenty-seven new disorders and seventy-three pages of description to its taxonomy of misery. The changes in the criteria for the pervasive developmental disorders were bold and comprehensive, reflecting the depth of cognitive research that had been going on in London while Bettelheim blathered on about Nazi mothers on American talk shows.

The word *infantile* was finally gone for good, and Kanner's syndrome was rechristened "autistic disorder," which was understood to persist from the cradle (or shortly thereafter) to the grave. The age-of-onset cutoff was modified to a suggestion that the clinician take note of when the signs first appeared, while the notion of a "residual state" was dispensed with entirely. The COPDD diagnosis was also dropped.

Crucially, the nonnegotiable checklist had been replaced by a veritable banquet of options for the diagnostician to pick and choose from: "At least eight of the following sixteen items are present, these to include at least two items from A, one from B, and one from C." This ensured that fewer children would slip through the diagnostic net because they failed to exhibit one behavior or another on evaluation day. The descriptions of these behaviors were also made less absolute. In the A list, for example, Kanner's "pervasive lack of responsiveness to other people" became Wing's "qualitative impairment in reciprocal social interaction." It was left to the clinician to decide whether the degree of impairment was sufficient to make the diagnosis. Items on the B list encompassed a similarly vast expanse of terrain, from having "no mode of communication" whatsoever (including an utter absence of facial expression and gesturing) to making "frequent irrelevant remarks (for example, starts talking about train schedules during a conversation about ports)." Likewise, C-list items—describing a "restricted repertoire of activities"—ranged from "hand flicking or twisting, spinning, [or] head-banging" to "amassing facts about meteorology." It's hard to imagine another disorder composed of such seemingly oxymoronic extremes.

One thing that is immediately obvious is that the new criteria could be applied to a much larger and more diverse population than the criteria in the *DSM-III*. A nonspeaking boy of six who rocked in a corner all day would fill the bill, as would a woman in her late twenties who reflexively averted her eyes when speaking and calmed herself by knitting while inwardly fancying herself the real-life equivalent of Sarah Jane Smith on *Doctor Who*. The potential for the *DSM-III-R* triggering a significant rise in diagnoses was not lost on Wing and her colleagues. Indeed, their field trials had already shown this to be the case. Later studies confirmed that the revised criteria were better at picking up cases of autism at every level of ability, including children who would have been diagnosed only with "mental retardation" in previous generations. Wing and company had done their job well.

But there was a sleeper in the new criteria that refused to behave the way they anticipated: "Pervasive Developmental Disorder—Not Otherwise Specified." Basically, PDD-NOS was subthreshold autism, but with the rituals, intense focus, and repetitive behavior à la carte. ("Some people with this diagnosis," the *DSM* advised, "will exhibit a markedly restricted repertoire of activities and interests, but others will not.") Based on their field trials and additional research, the task force made the reasonable assumption that PDD-NOS would remain a humble footnote to the primary label. Instead, it turned out to be wildly popular, quickly eclipsing autistic disorder to become the most commonly used PDD diagnosis. Like Asperger's syndrome, it was an autism diagnosis that didn't contain the word *autism* and thus was more readily accepted by parents and health care workers.

On the front lines, clinicians played fast and loose with the labels anyway. Judy Rapoport, former chief of child psychiatry at the NIMH, told anthropologist Roy Richard Grinker, "I am incredibly disciplined in the diagnostic classifications in my research, but in my private practice, I'll call a kid a zebra if it will get him the educational services I think he needs."

The *DSM-III-R* was an even bigger hit than the previous edition. Over the course of six years and eighteen printings, half a million copies of *DSM-III* were sold—an unheard-of number by *DSM* standards—but the *DSM-III-R* sold 280,000 copies in its first two years alone.

There was some hemming and hawing at the APA about the "fuzzy boundaries" of Wing's criteria, but they were clearly an improvement over the last batch, so these concerns were deferred until the next edition. By the end of the process, autism had been transformed into something that Kanner would have barely recognized. And Wing wasn't finished yet.

II

Estimates of autism prevalence began to increase worldwide after the publication of the *DSM-III* and *DSM-III-R*. To Wing and her Swedish colleague Christopher Gillberg, this was no surprise: awareness of autism among professionals was dramatically increasing at the same time that the boundaries of the condition were expanded. The new numbers reflected the estimates realigning themselves with the reality of the spectrum.

Support for this theory was emerging in a handful of studies undertaken in the wake of Wing and Gould's survey in Camberwell. The resulting estimates varied widely, depending on the scope of the survey, but the overall trend was clear: the more recent the criteria employed, the higher the estimate turned out to be. "Autism spectrum disorders (i.e., autism and autistic-like conditions) might be as prevalent as 1 in 100 children," Wing and Gillberg ventured. "Autism should no longer be conceptualized as an extremely rare disorder . . . The higher prevalence rate needs to be communicated to administrators, service providers and boards of research funds so that appropriate resources may be allocated." But many medical professionals and childcare specialists didn't get the memo.

One of the first clinicians in the world to raise the alarm about the rising numbers was Martin Bax, an unusually colorful pediatrician in London who founded a magazine of avant-garde art, poetry, and erotica called *Ambit*. (J. G. Ballard, Ralph Steadman, and David Hockney were regular contributors.) In the 1970s he had written a dystopian novel called *The Hospital Ship* about a global outbreak of psychosis that resulted in scores of children becoming autistic. By 1994, he became fearful that his apocalyptic vision was coming true.

"Rates of autism appear to be rising in the Western world," Bax alerted the readers of *Developmental Medicine and Child Neurology*. How did he know this? Because he had been "wandering around both in Europe and in North America asking colleagues whether they are seeing more cases; anecdotally the answer has always been 'yes.'" As further evidence of a frightening increase, Bax noted that registration of cases of autism with the Family Fund—a provider of grants to low-income families raising disabled children in the United Kingdom—"have recently gone up year by year."

On that point, Bax was entirely correct. Between 1990 and 2000, cases of autism in the Family Fund database went up by an astonishing 22 percent on average each year. By the end of the decade, autism-related conditions accounted for a quarter of the disabilities among families of children age sixteen and younger receiving grants—up from a mere 5 percent in 1990. What the devil was going on? Referring to himself as an "outsider" to autism research, Bax didn't get into subtle issues of nosology and epidemiology in his editorial, turning his attention instead to a colleague's theory that, in some cases, autism is "wholly or partly the expression of early-life onset" of bipolar disorder, another condition allegedly on the rise.

In fact, what was going on was precisely what Wing and Gillberg said was going on, concluded PricewaterhouseCoopers, the auditing giant that undertook a comprehensive analysis of the Family Fund database for the

U.K. Department of Education and Skills. The apparent increase in autism and related conditions among U.K. schoolchildren receiving grants was almost certainly the "result of better recognition," they said, while "improved diagnosis and recognition have resulted in increased numbers of children reporting specific disabilities."

A major change in referral patterns was also under way in England that was guaranteed to produce a spike in autism diagnoses that would never level off again. Before the 1970s, most kids with learning disabilities were admitted to special schools, vocational training centers, and institutions without being referred to a specialist for a specific diagnosis. By the 1990s, however, referral to a specialist before applying for services had become the rule rather than the exception. Contrary to Bax's framing of his anecdata as "depressing," the uptick in the numbers at the Family Fund was a sign that the system was finally working.

A similar evolution was taking place in the United States, prompted by a set of amendments to the Individuals with Disabilities Education Act—the new name for the Education for All Handicapped Children Act that Ruth Sullivan, Becky Guthrie, and other NSAC parents had fought so hard for fifteen years earlier. In 1991, autism was included in IDEA as its own category of disability for the first time, which enabled children with a diagnosis to gain access to individualized instruction and other services. The effects of this change rippled outward nationally, motivating clinicians to apply the diagnosis more readily and increasing awareness of autism among schoolteachers and staff. The new IDEA rules also required schools to comply by reporting an annual count of the number of children being served to the Department of Education. Autism was finally coming out of the statistical shadows at the federal level.

In tandem with IDEA's promise of a "free and appropriate public education" for all, state legislators passed laws making public funds available to families for early-intervention therapy, under pressure from parents encouraged by Lovaas's claims that forty hours of ABA a week could prompt full recovery. Only the wealthiest families could afford forty hours a week of one-on-one intervention without financial assistance, and widespread fears that parents could "miss the window" in their child's development when behavioral training would be effective suggested that there was no time to waste. In an era when the standard prognosis for autism was life in an institution, clinicians felt an ethical obligation to provide a diagnosis as early in their young patients' lives as possible.

Simultaneously, the first standardized clinical instruments to screen for autism were becoming widely available. Before the 1980s, autistic kids were generally considered "untestable" in America. Psychiatrists diagnosed them on the basis of whatever concepts were in vogue in their school of psychiatry. The same child might be diagnosed with early infantile autism by one clinician, by another with schizophrenia, and by a third with minimal brain damage. (And children who were black or poor were likely to end up classified as mentally retarded.) This was precisely the problem Spitzer set out to solve by "operationalizing" the *DSM*, but without a set of tools for diagnosis and assessment, the revised criteria provided just another outline of behavior framed in terms of deficits and impairments.

The first attempt to develop and popularize such a tool was Rimland's E-1 behavioral checklist and its successor, the E-2. While his lists were effective in encouraging parents that their son's or daughter's condition could finally be understood by a compassionate clinician, they had serious methodological flaws in practice. They were entirely dependent on parental recall rather than direct clinical observation, and a child's score could vary widely depending on which parent filled in the checklist. Independent analyses of the validity of the data produced highly uneven results. This work was hampered by the fact that Rimland refused to publish his scoring key; as far as other researchers were concerned, his algorithm was a black box.

There were several attempts over the years to come up with assessment tools that were more reliable and versatile than Rimland's checklists, but the big breakthrough didn't come until 1980, when Eric Schopler and his TEACCH colleagues introduced the Child Autism Rating Scale (CARS), which was particularly good at distinguishing autism from other forms of developmental delay, such as intellectual disability. After observing the child engage in a structured interaction through a one-way mirror, the rater scored the child on a seven-point continuum along several dimensions, including verbal and nonverbal communication, interaction with people and objects, sensory responsiveness, intellectual functioning, bodily movement, adaptation to change, and so on. By rating behaviors along a scale of severity, CARS anticipated the spectrum model of autism in the *DSM-III-R*. Independent analyses demonstrated that the scale was highly reliable and consistent, and that its scores matched well with assessment by other means. Best of all, new raters could be trained in a single one-hour session.

CARS also provided an accurate picture of the child's strengths, which was crucial for developing an appropriate plan for his or her education. Schopler believed that an approach to autism that took into account strong rote-memory capabilities and enhanced visual-processing skills would result in not only more effective teaching but more accurate neurological research. In 1988, Schopler and his colleagues issued a second edition of CARS that was even easier to use. After reading the manual and watching a thirty-minute video, medical students, speech-language pathologists, and special-education teachers could produce ratings that were nearly as accurate as those of seasoned clinical observers. Additionally, the new version of CARS could be employed to diagnose teenagers and adults. As a result, it became wildly popular, far beyond what Schopler and his colleagues expected.

Diagnosing autism was no longer the exclusive domain of a small, elite network of specialists. At the historical moment that autism was poised to enter mainstream awareness, reliable tools to screen for it—and to distinguish it from other forms of disability—were made available on a mass scale. The demand for diagnoses and the clinical means of meeting that demand were perfectly calibrated.

Then, six months after *Rain Man* opened, an international team of researchers led by Catherine Lord and Michael Rutter introduced a comprehensive tool for assessing problems with communication, social interaction, and play in children between ages five and twelve called the Autism

Diagnostic Observation Schedule (ADOS). Based on the criteria that would appear in the upcoming *DSM-IV*—which stretched the spectrum even more broadly—the ADOS and a companion tool called the Autism Diagnostic Interview were instantly embraced as the long-awaited gold standard of autism assessment. A series of revisions to both were introduced shortly thereafter to extend their reach to infants, teenagers, and adults. As word got around, parents began showing up for their appointments carrying voluminous notebooks of observations—the equivalent of Beamon Triplett's thirty-three-page letter to Kanner about Donald. But this time, clinicians welcomed parents' input; collaboration was now seen as essential to the process.

The clinical population was changing enormously, but clinicians' estimations of what their young patients would be capable of in the future had barely changed at all. "Fifty percent of the autistic population are mute and remain that way all of their lives," one author declared in a 1994 anthology for professionals called *Autism in Children and Adults*. "Even high-IQ autistic adolescents sustain only rudimentary social relationships and seem to retain the characteristic lack of empathy and the shallow affect," another author claimed.

The clinical definition of autism was mutating, ramifying, spreading out into a rainbow of a million colors. But the outlook on the lives and potential of autistic people remained relentlessly monochrome.

III

The head of the APA subcommittee charged with developing a new set of criteria for the *DSM-IV* was an affable, rumpled man with a Captain Kangaroo mustache named Fred Volkmar, chairman of the autism research program at the Yale Child Study Center. Among the items on his to-do list was considering Wing's proposal to include Asperger's syndrome as a separate diagnosis in the next revision. Her successful lobbying for its inclusion in the tenth edition of the *ICD*, published by the World Health

Organization (WHO) in 1990, made it nearly inevitable that the diagnosis would also appear in the *DSM*. But the study of the condition was still in its infancy. The first international conference on Asperger's wasn't held until 1988, once the revision process was already under way, and the first draft of a set of criteria to define it didn't emerge for another year.

The fact that the syndrome shaded into subclinical eccentricity raised a question that cut to the core of the entire psychiatric enterprise: Was Asperger's syndrome truly a mental disorder or a common personality type in its most extreme form? Asperger's 1944 description suggested a more holistic view: it was a personality type that could become profoundly disabling in the absence of adequate adaptation by the patient and the people in his or her environment. Volkmar cautioned his colleagues, "Odd and unusual behaviors do not, in and of themselves, constitute a 'disorder' unless they are related to a manifestation of serious dysfunction within the individual." Yet, even in Volkmar's clinic at Yale, the nature of what constituted "serious dysfunction" was much more open to interpretation than an elevated level on a blood test or an anomalous waveform on an EEG.

Consider Robert Edwards, an eleven-year-old boy profiled by Volkmar and his colleague Ami Klin as a "relatively classic" case of Asperger's disorder. Robert said his first words by his first birthday and breezed through C. S. Lewis's seven-volume fantasy epic *The Chronicles of Narnia* while still in kindergarten. Despite his prodigious verbal abilities, by the time he was three, he had become "a major source of concern" to his parents—who were both doctors—because he didn't seem to be making friends in preschool.

Klin and Volkmar attributed Robert's "social problems" to his precocious fascination with astronomy. "He would pursue this interest at any opportunity," they reported. "The interest intruded on essentially all aspects of his life. For example, in any conversation with peers, he inevitably brought the conversation or play around to stars and planets or time and its measurement." His "eccentric" interests also included "computer games—their rules, programmers, and the companies that produce them." (Within a few years, such interests on the part of an eleven-year-old boy wouldn't be considered odd or eccentric at all.)

By the time Klin and Volkmar saw Robert, the boy had already spent nearly all of his life under the clinical gaze. When he was five, his parents had him evaluated by an occupational therapist for his "low motor tone." Three years later, they sent him to a psychiatrist, who diagnosed him with an anxiety disorder. At ten, he was put through a battery of tests because of his poor handwriting and "social isolation." Once his teacher "started to make some accommodations" for him (never described by Klin and Volkmar), Robert was accepted into an accelerated math program. But he was still regarded as profoundly ill.

Klin and Volkmar were disturbed by his "rather formal and pedantic communication style." When they asked Robert to provide another word for *call*, he said "beckon," which might not have sounded out of place in the world of *The Lion, the Witch, and the Wardrobe.* Asked to produce a synonym for *thin*, he replied "dimensionally challenged," but this witticism was lost on his examiners. They noted that Robert's friendships appeared to be "based almost exclusively on their common interest in computers," as if the idea of friendships based on shared interests was clinically suspicious. Klin and Volkmar were equally unimpressed by an autobiographical statement that they asked Robert to bring to their office, which they cited as another example of his special interests "intruding" into other areas of his life.

> My name is Robert Edwards. I am an intelligent, unsociable, but adaptable person. I would like to dispel any untrue rumors about me. I am not edible. I cannot fly. I cannot use telekinesis. My brain is not large enough to destroy the entire world when unfolded. I did not teach my long-haired guinea pig Chronos to eat everything in sight (that is the nature of the long-haired guinea pig).

Absent the context of a psychiatric case history, the story of a boy who reads the *Narnia* books in kindergarten, cracks jokes about being "dimensionally challenged," and spends his grade school years hanging out with his fellow geeks could be the biography of practically anyone destined to become a successful entrepreneur in Silicon Valley. Thus, clinical accounts of Asperger's syndrome tended to reframe neutral or even positive aspects of behavior as manifestations of deficit and impairment. Intense curiosity became *perseveration*. Precociously articulate speech became *hyperlexia*. An average score on a test became a *relative deficit*—evidence of an *uneven cognitive profile*.

If Robert represented a classic case of Asperger's syndrome, it was clearly a disorder of degree, and gauging the degree of social impairment is highly subject to social context. "As I explain to parents, the cure for Asperger's syndrome is very simple—it is not surgery, medication or intensive therapy," says Tony Attwood, one of the world's leading authorities on the subject. "It is taking your son or daughter to their bedroom, leaving the bedroom, and closing the door. You cannot have a social deficit when you are alone. You cannot have a communication problem when you are alone. Your repetitive behavior does not annoy anyone when you are alone. All the diagnostic criteria dissolve in solitude. That's why teenagers with Asperger's are reluctant to leave their bedroom for school: the signs of autism, and the degrees of stress and withdrawal, are proportional to the number of people present."

Left to his own devices, Robert might not have experienced himself as mentally ill at all, though he certainly could have developed an anxiety disorder from being perpetually grilled by men with clipboards. Given a technology that enabled him to communicate with other like-minded young people, he might have encouraged them to feel that their problems originated not in themselves, but in the system that had branded them diseased and inferior.

Considerations like this in psychiatry are usually left to sociologists, but they would come back to haunt the editors of the *DSM-IV* once the criteria for Asperger's syndrome were set loose in the wild. Few members of Volkmar's subcommittee could have predicted that the term *Aspie* would become a badge of honor and defiant pride within a decade, even for those without an official diagnosis. The genie of autistic intelligence was poised to escape the bottle in which it had been trapped for fifty years.

The chair of the *DSM-IV* task force, Allen Frances, was wary of the rampant proliferation of labels and disturbed by his colleagues' apparent willingness to pathologize eccentricity. But seeing his job as that of being a "consensus scholar," he deferred on the subject of autism to the expertise of Volkmar and his colleagues, who reassured him that the changes planned for the fourth edition would not result in any major upheaval. In the end, Wing's pragmatic argument that the addition of the diagnosis would result in more families gaining access to services won the day. Of ninety-four new diagnoses proposed for the fourth edition of the manual, only two—Asperger's and type II bipolar disorder—would make the cut.

There was just one bit of unfinished business to attend to: those rumors that Asperger, who had died in 1980, was a Nazi. "It was a crazy problem. It took me weeks to figure it out," Volkmar confessed. Finally, he decided to phone up Wing and bluntly ask her if there was any truth to the rumors. She came up with the perfect answer—one that was utterly irrelevant but virtually guaranteed to persuade Volkmar to sign off on the new diagnosis. "Oh, dear no," she reassured him from London. "Asperger was a deeply religious man."

If the *DSM-III* turned Spitzer and his data geeks into "rock stars" (as his wife, Janet Williams, put it), the fourth edition was Michael Jackson's *Thriller*. *DSM-IV* was an international smash that earned $18 million in its first ten months in print alone and $100 million altogether while launching a thriving industry of branded tie-ins and lucrative subsidiaries. *DSM-IV* casebooks, study guides, videotapes, and software poured onto the market, and readers interested in the making-of backstory could browse through a four-volume *DSM-IV Sourcebook*. Spotting the signs of autism—once the arcane skill of the initiated few—became the job of nearly everyone involved in pediatric medicine, psychology, and education.

In fourteen years and a handful of revisions, the *DSM* had gone from a slim volume that sat unread on dusty shelves in institutions to a nine-hundred-page behemoth that found its way into classrooms, courtrooms, community clinics, research labs, congressional hearings, pharma stockholders' meetings, social service agencies, and guidance counselors' offices. The entire clinical infrastructure of autism had been transformed from a channel for optional reporting of isolated cases to a network for active surveillance of the general population. Inevitably, the more that clinicians and educators looked for a condition, the more they found it. The upward trend that began in the wake of the *DSM-III-R* began to snowball after the publication of the *DSM-IV.*

In fact, the numbers were rising a little *too* steeply, because the *DSM-IV* editors had made a small but crucial error in the final run-up to publication. Instead of requiring that a child display impairments in social interaction, communication, and behavior before getting a diagnosis of PDD-NOS, the criteria substituted the word *or* for *and.* (In other words, a clinician could deliver the whole banquet by choosing one from column A.) This fateful typo went uncorrected for six years and was unacknowledged in the literature until the editor of the *DSM-IV Text Revision*, Michael First, finally copped to it in a notably understated article in an obscure journal in 2002.

This certainly didn't mean that every child diagnosed with PDD-NOS in the years between 1994 and 2000 was misdiagnosed, but the impact of the botched language was potentially significant. By reanalyzing the field-test data using the erroneous wording, Volkmar found that "about 75 percent of children identified by clinicians as not having the disorder (true negatives) were incorrectly identified as having it according to DSM-IV." For epidemiologists gauging the *DSM-IV*'s impact in the crucial period that would go down in history as the years a mysterious "autism epidemic" took hold, it was a statistical nightmare. Yet, until author Roy Richard Grinker called attention to the typo in his 2008 book *Unstrange Minds*, hardly anyone outside the usual tiny circle of experts was aware of it.

IV

Far from the APA subcommittees debating issues of nosology over pastrami sandwiches and cream soda, an explanation for the rising numbers was taking shape that had nothing to do with diagnostic criteria, screening instruments, or the rise of medicalized psychiatry. Instead, it was a terrifying story of the poisoning of innocent children by heartless corporations.

Nestled among apple orchards forty-five miles northwest of Boston, Leominster is a classic New England factory town, with austere white steeples and sprawling strip malls juxtaposed around a central common. Celebrated as the birthplace of Johnny Appleseed, Leominster earned another distinction in the 1940s, when one in five residents was working for plastics manufacturers like Foster Grant, the company that turned sunglasses—a product formerly associated with invalids—into a fashion accessory for strolling on the Atlantic City boardwalk. To manufacture its stylish frames, Foster Grant built a giant plastic-injection plant along the Nashua River. The proud town fathers posted signs along the highway christening Leominster "the Plastic City."

Soon it became the Polluted City. A green haze hung in the air that smelled alternately like rotten eggs and paint thinner. The locals used to say that you could tell which shade of sunglasses was being made that day depending on the color of the clouds belching out of the plant's smokestacks. The waters of the Nashua flowed red, white, and blue. Local gardeners got used to PVC particles frosting their vegetable beds like sugar, and housewives sucked on Vicks cough drops to numb the burning sensation in their throats. Then an international conglomerate acquired Foster Grant and outsourced its frame manufacturing to Mexico. The defunct plant was declared a hazardous-waste site by state authorities.

A couple of years after the plant closed, a couple in Leominster named Lori and Larry Altobelli had their second child, Joshua. It soon became apparent that he had profound developmental delays. His parents were unable to toilet-train him, and he learned to speak only a handful of words.

He would spin endlessly in circles and run laps around the living room while maintaining a tight grip on his favorite toy. When he was three, he was diagnosed with PDD-NOS, which his mother dubbed "junior autism." His younger brother, Jay, was also eventually diagnosed with PDD-NOS.

Joshua's speech therapist asked Lori and Larry if they would be willing to offer tips about local services and resources to another couple whose son had recently been diagnosed with PDD-NOS, Melanie and Ralph Palotta. As the couples swapped stories, Ralph couldn't shake the feeling that Larry looked familiar; then he remembered seeing his face on the school bus in the morning when they were in fifth grade together. A few months later, at a meeting of the Association for Retarded Citizens, Ralph met Rich Frenette, the father of another newly diagnosed boy on the spectrum. Ralph recalled that they had played on the same Little League team and lived one block apart. The fact that all three men were from the same neighborhood seemed too suggestive to be merely a coincidence, as did their shared memories of growing up in the poisonous penumbra of Foster Grant.

The Altobellis were haunted by a similar chain of events that had unfolded a decade earlier forty miles up the highway, in a working-class town called Woburn. Jimmy Anderson was just four years old when he was diagnosed with a rare form of cancer called acute lymphocytic leukemia. As his mother, Anne, glanced around a waiting room at Massachusetts General in Boston, she recognized the faces of women that she'd seen at her neighborhood supermarket. Then she began to hear about other neighborhood kids who had also contracted this rare disease. What was going on?

Anne had a flash of mother's intuition. It was the water—the stinky, acrid-tasting, perpetually discolored Woburn water. But doctors and city officials pooh-poohed her concerns, and even her friends thought she was a little crazy. No one could deny, however, that the residents of East Woburn seemed increasingly unwell, with headaches, blurred vision, and awful rashes that wouldn't go away. Was it really normal for this many young women to have miscarriages? Eventually, Anne didn't seem so crazy. She organized the neighborhood parents into a united front to demand answers from city officials. A local newspaper reporter uncovered the fact that barrels of industrial chemicals known to be carcinogenic and neuro-toxic had been buried near two of East Woburn's wells. Anne's investigation became the basis for a best-selling book by Jonathan Harr called *A Civil Action*, which was turned into an Oscar-winning film.

Lori, who had a master's degree in health care administration, started asking parents at autism support group meetings if they had ever lived in her husband's old neighborhood. She was shocked by how many said yes. She pinned a map of the neighborhood up on her wall, marking with an X the places where the mother or father of an autistic child had lived. Soon dozens of X's had accumulated on the map.

On March 25, 1990, Lori sent a letter to the CDC headquarters in Atlanta demanding an investigation. She also sent a copy to the mayor. CDC officials forwarded her letter to the Massachusetts Department of Public Health (MDPH), and a couple of months later an epidemiologist arrived in town to begin collecting data. To avert mass panic, MDPH officials asked Lori to keep the investigation a secret until a definitive connection to the plant was found. She was willing to play along until she heard that the city was planning to build a playground adjacent to the location of the old factory. Furious, Lori called up the mayor, Steve Perla, and said, "You can't build a kids' playground two hundred feet from a toxic waste dump!"

Perla postponed the opening of the playground by releasing a phony story about a missing bolt in a swing set, but an anonymous caller tipped off local reporters. The Altobellis and an environmental activist named Matt Wilson responded by holding a press conference in the shadow of the old plant and launching an organization called Leominster Citizens for a Safe Environment. The Altobellis were inundated with phone calls from frightened parents. The link to the Foster Grant plant seemed undeniable; at least one study in the literature suggested that a disproportionate number of the parents of autistic children—one in four—had suffered occupational exposure to toxic chemicals. (It was Mary Coleman's study conducted in 1974 with the help of Rimland and other NSAC parents.) Exposure to thalidomide, an over-the-counter drug used in the 1960s to relieve morning sickness in pregnant women that resulted in ten thousand cases of babies being born with serious malformation of the limbs, had been linked to autism in numerous studies over the years.

The Altobellis decided to go national. They contacted *ABC News*'s chief medical editor, Timothy Johnson, who had previously worked as a reporter for Channel 5 in Boston and was already familiar with the story. On March 13, 1992, veteran news anchor Hugh Downs prepared millions of viewers of the award-winning show *20/20* for a landmark broadcast. "We begin with a report we believe will surprise the medical world. Indeed, the information offered tonight is groundbreaking," said Downs. "Along with you, many experts will hear it here for the first time."

The ABC segment, "The Street Where They Lived," became a sensation. "Consider this," Johnson said. "Only fifteen children in every ten thousand have symptoms of autism or PDD and yet, so far, Lori has connected forty-two cases of autism and PDD to the small neighborhood of about six hundred homes which circle the Foster Grant plant." Firm evidence of the role of toxicity, he acknowledged, was frustratingly elusive: "Scientists don't know what causes autism, although they have many theories, from head trauma to upbringing to heredity." Barbara Walters praised Lori for embarking on a "lonely crusade" to expose the ignorance of the medical establishment.

Then it was the parents' turn to testify. "We were a completely normal family, doing completely normal things, and we were so looking forward to the baby," one father said. "Our children look perfectly normal," Lori added. "They all look perfect." Another mother compared Leominster to the Twilight Zone.

Larry reminisced about playing ice hockey as a boy on the river, which froze unevenly because of the sheer volume of industrial toxins that had been pumped into it. A former Foster Grant employee was brought on to admit to dumping "several thousands of gallons of styrene . . . where all the kids play down there." Johnson painted a vivid picture of "twenty-seven smokestacks belching out a potent derivative of vinyl chloride, which is known to cause cancer and other serious problems." Including autism? The show's producers finessed the absence of any known link by turning their cameras onto a terrified mother who said she was convinced of the connection because the rates of autism were "blown out of the water" in Leominster.

But anecdotes are not statistics, and *20/20*'s producers didn't mention that there were no statistics for the historical prevalence of autism in Leominster, because studies to establish the normal baseline rates had never been done. Indeed, the PDD-NOS diagnosis was too new to determine if the incidence was rising at all. ABC's cameras cut back to Johnson, who made the chilling claim that "spontaneous abortions" and "certain cancers associated with environmental exposure" were rampant in Plastic City. He appended a halfhearted caveat—"It's a long road from coincidence to proving causation, but it's certainly a theory worth pursuing"—before moving on to the next story.

The Altobellis' phone rang continuously in the wake of the broadcast, and the map on their wall grew dark with X's. The story was picked up by the *Sally Jessy Raphael* show, and a week later *20/20* aired an even more sensationalistic follow-up. Johnson declared that parents all over the country had contacted the network, expressing "relief at finding out that they're part of a larger picture, they're not alone, that maybe they're not responsible for what happened" (as if anyone had implied that they *were* responsible). Lori was defiant: "This morning, as Larry left for work, he said, 'You really opened Pandora's box, didn't you?' I said, 'And now that it's open enough, I'm not going to let anybody close it.'" She predicted that she and her fellow parents would "rewrite the book on autism."

A team of geneticists had arrived from Stanford to take blood samples and analyze them for potentially damaging mutations. A toxicology unit from MDPH tested the soil near the defunct plant for solvents, heavy metals, and other lingering contaminants. A graduate student named Martha Lang spent three years working with the Altobellis and the other families of Leominster for her graduate thesis at Brown University on the leadership of mothers in community struggles against powerful polluters.

Lang's research was hampered by another lingering contaminant: the social stigma of having a child with autism. Many families declined to participate in her data-gathering process. But an examination of the medical records of the kids in Lori's files indicated that the number of confirmed cases of autism in town was lower than she had been led to believe. Of the twenty-four kids whose records were analyzed by the MDPH, six "quite clearly did not meet the criteria" for either autism or PDD-NOS, while the data for seven more proved inconclusive. In several cases, the parents' proximity to the Foster Grant plant was tenuous at best; indeed, some parents in Lori's files had never lived in Leominster at all. After failing to find evidence of chromosomal abnormalities in the community, the Stanford team suggested that "secular changes in the definition of autism" rather than a true increase in prevalence were driving the rising numbers. Lang concluded that the tale of the "Leominster autism cluster" was much less clear-cut than she thought. But the media circus had long ago moved on.

One of the reporters who broke the story for a local newspaper, David Ropeik, is now a consultant on the science of risk perception. After watching the events in Plastic City unfold firsthand, he says he understands why so many people there—and in the viewing audience of *20/20*—were drawn to the explanation that their children had been poisoned by the town's toxic legacy.

"As a parent, your one job in life is to take care of your kid. When you feel powerless over a serious risk, you have a deep emotional need to find answers," he says. "Your mind is open to suggestion—*could it be the plastics?*—because in those suggestions, there is a kind of hope. Lori, who is a very reasonable person, grudgingly accepted the fact that the real story was more complicated. But you could also see that it hurt her to do that, because she was desperate for some sense of control over her children's plight."

V

In the aftermath of the Leominster scandal, other "autism clusters" started popping up all over the country—notably one in Brick Township, New Jersey, where sixty-three million gallons of septic waste had been dumped into a landfill between 1969 and 1979. No one was tracking these events more closely than Bernard Rimland, who started covering the Leominster story in his newsletter two years before the *20/20* broadcasts.

At first, he seemed resistant to the idea that the rates of diagnosis were changing rapidly on his watch. When the *DSM-IV* was published in 1994, Rimland said bluntly, "It is not reasonable to believe that the population of [autistic] children has changed much" in the years between the 1920s and the 1990s. But soon his position changed dramatically, and his position as the most trusted authority in the autism parents' community gave him enormous influence.

At the same time, his alienation from mainstream medicine was increasing. The 1990s were a frustrating time for Rimland as the center of gravity in autism research tilted away from his storefront in Kensington and toward Wing and the London group. He barely addressed the potentially enormous impact of Wing's *DSM* revisions in his newsletter, focusing instead on an inside-baseball controversy over the APA's use of the word *pervasive*. (He called the PDD-NOS label "pseudoscientific" and predicted that it was too cumbersome to catch on.) ARI was also struggling financially. In a bizarre turn of events, a $75,000 check intended for Rimland from the producers of *Rain Man* ended up going to the Autism Society of America; even a letter from Dustin Hoffman and a lawsuit by Rimland failed to convince the organization to yield.

In 1995—after a torrent of inquiries from parents—Rimland ran a banner headline in his newsletter, "Is There an Autism Epidemic?" His answer was yes: "I believe that the increase is real, and not merely an increase in awareness." To prove his point, he provided a chart showing that, in the years from 1965 to 1969, only 1 percent of the parents in his network sought a diagnosis for a child younger than three. In the 1980s (following the publication of the *DSM-III* and *DSM-III-R*), that number increased to 5 percent. After the release of the *DSM-IV*, it spiked to 17 percent. But instead of focusing on the changes in the diagnostic criteria, he raised the terrifying possibility that pollution, antibiotics, and vaccines were triggering a tsunami of new cases, citing the Leominster "cluster" as a dramatic example.

Rimland's version of the events in the town took hold permanently in the autism parents' community, becoming part of the growing lore of the epidemic.

Considering the potential impact of environmental factors on autism was nothing new for Rimland. Back in 1967, after receiving a number of reports from parents that their children had been adversely affected by the diphtheria-pertussis-tetanus vaccine, he added a question about it to ARI's evaluation forms. He had good reason to: in the annals of public health, the original form of the DPT vaccine—the only inoculation based on killed whole bacterial cells widely distributed in the United States—was the most "reactogenic" vaccine in the country's history. Adverse events like seizures, fainting, fevers, swelling, shock, and high-pitched crying for hours were not uncommon. The whole-cell DPT was also bedeviled by quality control failures, unreliable potency, and other serious problems, includings individual batches (known as "hot lots") that triggered higher-than-usual incidences of side effects before being removed from distribution by the CDC. The whole-cell DPT was eventually scrapped in the United States in favor of the much safer "acellular" form of the inoculation.

One of the key factors in Rimland's turnabout on the question of the rising rates was a book called *DPT: A Shot in the Dark*, written by Harris Coulter and Barbara Loe Fisher. In the early 1980s, Fisher was working as a PR consultant in Virginia when her two-and-a-half-year-old son, Christian, received his fourth DPT shot and oral polio inoculation. Until that day, according to Fisher, he was a cheerful and sociable child who spoke in full sentences, read avidly, and could count up to twenty. After his third DPT injection, however, a hard, red lump had appeared on his arm, which a nurse attributed to a "bad lot" of vaccine.

Within hours of Christian getting his fourth shot, according to Fisher, she found him in a chair staring vacantly, his face pale and his lips blue. When she called out his name, his eyes fluttered and rolled back, and he seemed to fall asleep. She carried him to bed, where he slept for six hours. Fisher woke him, but he was disoriented, and he fell asleep again for another half a day. She would later describe these events as a classic vaccine reaction. In the days and weeks that followed, "Chris became a totally different child," she testified to a congressional committee in 1999. He never smiled, seemed to have trouble focusing, lost interest in his beloved books, and suffered a series of debilitating infections. He was eventually diagnosed with multiple learning disabilities, including ADHD.

Two years later, Fisher saw an NBC special called "DPT: Vaccine Roulette," and the pieces fell into place. The broadcast featured a parade of experts who played down the risks of pertussis (which had killed 7,500 children in 1934 alone, out of 265,000 cases) while highlighting the risks of the vaccine, intercut with wrenching footage of brain-damaged children being cared for by their parents. Gordon Stewart, identified as a member of the United Kingdom's Committee on the Safety of Medicines, described the vaccine as a "crude brew, literally, of all the bacteria and their gross products." Bobby Young, billed as a former FDA vaccine researcher, warned that DPT shots were capable of turning a healthy child into "a vegetable," while producer Lea Thompson hinted that the plummeting death rates from diseases like pertussis after the widespread adoption of vaccines was a coincidence caused by better sanitation. Thompson also suggested that savvy British mothers, armed with the knowledge that "the vaccine is worse than the disease," were opting not to immunize their children. As the daughter of a nurse, Fisher, watching the broadcast, "felt betrayed by a medical profession I had revered all my life."

In truth, Thompson, who was awarded an Emmy for "DPT: Vaccine Roulette," had consistently exaggerated or distorted the credentials of her cherry-picked "experts." Young, for example, had never researched bacterial vaccines for the FDA, while Stewart had only provided data to the committee and was well-known in the United Kingdom as a prominent antivaccine activist.

After airing on WRC-TV in Washington, "DPT: Vaccine Roulette" was rebroadcast on local affiliates coast-to-coast and excerpted at length on the *Today* show. Pediatricians reported levels of fear among parents unseen since the polio scare of the 1950s, and members of Congress were besieged by constituents demanding immediate changes in national vaccine policy.

WRC-TV capitalized on the growing scandal by providing viewers who called the station with the numbers of other callers. Fisher was one of the parents who phoned in, and another was Kathi Williams, whose son also experienced a reaction to a DPT shot. With another parent, Jeff Schwartz, they founded a group called Dissatisfied Parents Together, later renamed the National Vaccine Information Center (NVIC), which became the organizational powerhouse of the movement. (The NVIC is careful not to identify itself as "antivaccine" in its PR materials, instead calling itself "the oldest and largest consumer led organization advocating for the institution of vaccine safety and informed consent protections in the public health system.")

To write *DPT: A Shot in the Dark*, Fisher teamed up with a man named Harris Coulter, a longtime foe of government-mandated vaccination programs with a complex past. Though he is often described on antivaccine websites as a Yale-educated medical historian, he did not study medicine at Yale. In fact, he never took a single course in biology, physiology, or chemistry, and he had no intention of becoming a historian of the field as an undergraduate. Instead, his focus was Russian studies.

At the height of the cold war in the early 1960s, Coulter was working in Moscow, translating the Kremlin's official pronouncements for the U.S. State Department. (During the Warren Commission hearings into the assassination of John F. Kennedy, he served as the official interpreter for Marina Oswald, wife of accused assassin Lee Harvey Oswald.) While vacationing in Paris, Coulter's wife, Catherine, suffered an allergy attack. Instead of going to see a doctor, they decided to visit a homeopath, because traditional doctoring had never done her much good. The homeopath gave her a remedy that "worked like magic," Coulter recalled. After a single dose, she was able to eat fish, which had always provoked hives in her before.

Coulter returned to the United States fascinated by homeopathy. When his thesis on Russian studies at Columbia fell through, he persuaded his graduate advisor to let him write a dissertation on the history of homeopathy instead. He became convinced that homeopathy was superior to mainstream ("allopathic") medicine but had lost out as the dominant paradigm in the nineteenth century because of widespread corruption in the American Medical Association. His dissertation became the third volume of a series of books called *Divided Legacy*, which he self-published.

While researching *DPT: A Shot in the Dark*, Fisher interviewed families while Coulter filled in the historical background. It's a terrifying book, depicting pediatric medicine as a horror show of heedless doctors, craven vaccine manufacturers, opportunistic researchers, sleazy government officials, grieving parents, and desperately sick kids who have allegedly been rendered mute, incontinent, and permanently disabled by the inoculations that were supposed to keep them safe. Throughout the book, infants recoil from their doctors' overeager needles, shrieking in primal terror as the shots wreak havoc in their brains.

DPT: A Shot in the Dark was much more than an exposé of the risks of a vaccine—it was a scathing critique of the whole apparatus of mainstream medicine, including the process of peer review and the use of placebo-controlled trials in drug testing. Clearly, for Coulter, the book was homeopathy's long-overdue revenge against the AMA and a call to arms against an inhumane society that puts the good of the many over the fate of the vulnerable few who suffer violent reactions to vaccines. "I do know that God gave me a perfect child. I was so happy when he was born," says one mother. "He was so beautiful, with ten toes and ten fingers. God gave me a perfect child, and man, with his own ways, damaged God's perfect work."

The notion that children with learning disabilities are damaged goods runs through the book; the authors refer to them as "vaccine-injured" instead of as dyslexic or autistic and portray them as helplessly entombed inside their own bodies. "She understands everything, but she can't get it out," another mother says. "You can see it in her little eyes. It's all there, but she can't get it out the way she wants to. Sometimes her little voice quavers because she tries so hard. You can see she's got it but it's trapped."

The book's publication inspired a public uproar that culminated in a series of congressional hearings and a wave of reforms. The National Childhood Vaccine Injury Act, passed in 1986, set up a federal vaccine injury compensation program and created a federal Vaccine Adverse Events Reporting System (VAERS) to enable public-health authorities and consumers to track emerging problems with immunization programs nationwide. In that sense, the book accomplished what it had set out to do. Coulter, however, was not nearly through with his life's work. In the years following the publication of *A Shot in the Dark*, his views became even more extreme.

At the height of the AIDS epidemic, Coulter theorized that human immunodeficiency virus (HIV) was not responsible for the illness, which he believed was a form of syphilis that specifically targets drug users and people living "the gay lifestyle . . . which involves very heavy consumption of medications." Though autism was barely mentioned in *A Shot in the Dark*, it was the central subject of his next book, *Vaccination, Social Violence, and Criminality*, in which he proposed that rising rates of autism, homosexuality, obesity, dyslexia, ADHD, drug abuse, epilepsy, juvenile delinquency, and spree killings were all expressions of an epidemic of encephalitis caused by mandatory vaccine programs. Furthermore, he claimed that these facts were well-known in the medical community but were being covered up by a vast conspiracy. Indeed, he claimed that this conspiracy was so vast that "it is not easy to discern the outlines of the incubus which the vaccination program has loosed upon us."

One night in February 1995, Rimland was at home watching a talk show about the risks of vaccination when he noticed that several of the mothers interviewed for the broadcast referred to Coulter and his work. After looking into it, he came to believe that Coulter had found the elusive solution to the puzzle of the rising autism rates. That fall, he published his full-page editorial declaring his belief in an autism epidemic.

Rimland's endorsement gave Coulter's fringe theories about autism, encephalitis, and vaccines a reach they would never have had otherwise while effectively laundering them of their more unsavory aspects, such as his association of autism and criminal behavior. By then, Coulter had already moved on to the next stage of his career, which was helping a Russian immunologist to develop a vaccine derived from human placenta that would treat cancer. The outcome of the experimental trials, conducted on patients in Moscow and the Bahamas, was decidedly mixed—several of the patients died anyway. But Coulter was undaunted, seeing in the patients' responses to the vaccine (including fevers, headaches, and increased pain at sites of previous surgical operations) vivid demonstrations of homeopathic principles.

VI

While Rimland was instrumental in spreading Coulter's ideas within the autism parents' community, a young gastroenterologist in England named Andrew Wakefield was responsible for introducing them into the mainstream by claiming to have discovered a potential mechanism by which the combination measles-mumps-rubella (MMR) vaccine causes brain injury.

On February 28, 1998, Wakefield held a press conference at Royal Free Hospital in Hampstead, North London. The occasion was the publication of his new case series in the *Lancet*, one of Britain's most prestigious medical journals. To ensure that the press conference would be a major event, the hospital's public relations staff had taken the unusual step of sending out a twenty-minute promotional video to journalists beforehand, featuring graphic footage of children who were obviously in agony. The video was accompanied by a press release, which read in part, "Researchers at the Royal Free Hospital School of Medicine may have discovered a new syndrome involving a new inflammatory bowel disease and autism." As a result, the room was packed with reporters.

Wakefield seemed well positioned to make a breakthrough in pediatric gastroenterology. In 1987, he took a post as the head of the Royal Free Hospital's Inflammatory Bowel Disease (IBD) Study Group, where the major focus of his work became investigating links between viruses and Crohn's disease. In a series of studies published in the 1990s, Wakefield and his colleagues zeroed in on the measles virus as potentially contributing to Crohn's and IBD. These studies were considered groundbreaking when they were first published and attracted media attention to the Royal Free

Hospital's medical school, which was trying to shed its image as a backwater of inconsequential research. But they eventually came under fire as other researchers either failed to replicate Wakefield's results or directly refuted them.

Undaunted, Wakefield continued to search for a measles-Crohn's connection, eventually publishing a study in the *Lancet* that seemed to validate his theory. After reviewing twenty-five thousand patient records taken at the University Hospital in Uppsala, Sweden, in the 1940s, Wakefield and co-author Anders Ekbom found three cases of children born of measles-infected mothers who developed Crohn's later in life. On the basis of these cases, Wakefield and Ekbom drew a sweeping and dramatic conclusion: "Our study suggests that exposure to measles virus in utero is a major risk factor for the development of Crohn's disease later in life; such early exposure appears to incur a risk of extensive, aggressive disease."

Wakefield then turned his focus of his investigations toward the MMR vaccine, which is formulated with live viruses in a weakened state to activate the body's immune response. It was at this point that his work began to attract pointed criticism from British public-health officials who were well aware of the potentially catastrophic danger of shaking public confidence in the safety of a vaccine that prevents millions of deaths worldwide every year. (The World Health Organization estimates that, in 2000 alone, thirty to forty million people developed measles, resulting in 777,000 deaths, most of them in sub-Saharan Africa, where rates of inoculation and standards of medical care are lower.) Eventually, Wakefield's dean at the medical school, Arie Zuckerman, privately expressed concern about the "unwelcome controversy" gathering around Wakefield's work on Crohn's and the MMR to the United Kingdom's chief medical officer, Kenneth Calman. In retrospect, that controversy was a teapot-tempest compared to the storm on the horizon.

In 1995, Wakefield got a call from the mother of an autistic boy that left him profoundly distressed. At first, he didn't know why she was calling him, a gastroenterologist. "I didn't know anything about autism," he later admitted. According to Wakefield, the mother explained that her son had serious bowel problems, including diarrhea and incontinence up to twelve times a day. He also seemed to be in pain and was violent and self-injurious. She said that he had been developing "perfectly normally" until he received an MMR vaccine. Shortly after getting the shot, the mother said, he suffered a high fever, after which point he deteriorated rapidly and lost the ability to speak. Wakefield would later claim that he was compelled to undertake further research on autism after receiving "five calls in two days" like this. It turns out that his controversial work on Crohn's disease had already made him a respected figure among antivaccine activists, and the mothers who called him were members of the same antivaccine network.

Like the Uppsala study, Wakefield's 1998 case series hinged on a small sample of patients; in this case, a dozen children. In cautious and qualified language, his team reported that the onset of the "behavioral symptoms" of autism had been "associated by the parents" with administration of the MMR vaccine in eight of the twelve cases. The researchers claimed that all of the children showed evidence of intestinal abnormalities, ranging from "patchy chronic inflammation" to "ulceration." In most of these cases, they reported, "after a period of apparent normality," the children had dramatically regressed in the wake of receiving the vaccine.

Building on Wakefield's earlier investigations of viruses, vaccines, and intestinal inflammation, as well as the work of other scientists, the researchers postulated that partially digested proteins from grains and dairy products were leaking into the children's bloodstreams through the walls of their damaged intestines. Once there, they theorized, these proteins—known as opioid peptides—were carried to the developing brain, where they caused disruption of neural regulation and growth, causing a sudden and dramatic loss of skills. Wakefield eventually christened this syndrome "autistic enterocolitis."

The concept of opioid peptides disrupting brain development was not new, particularly among the clinicians and science-savvy parents in Rimland's network, who had dubbed the same phenomenon "leaky gut syndrome." They had been frustrated for years that their observations of their children's gastrointestinal distress and fussy food preferences were generally dismissed by doctors as just another inexplicable aspect of a mysterious condition. Many parents, following the advice in Karyn Seroussi's book, had found that removing grains and milk (sources of gluten and casein respectively) from the child's diet not only relieved cramping, diarrhea, and bloating but also seemed to improve the child's level of social engagement. It is perhaps not surprising that children who would be happier to persist in eating only a single dish at every meal (like Henry Cavendish's leg of mutton, Joseph Sullivan's cheese curls, and Leo Rosa's naan) would eventually develop GI issues.

In addition, episodes of fever, rashes, convulsions, and other usually transitory reactions to vaccines (understandably terrifying to parents) are well documented in the annals of immunology, as Coulter and Fisher had documented extensively in their book. Very rarely, these negative reactions are neither mild nor transitory, resulting in lifelong incapacity or death. The fact that modern medicine is built on trade-offs of socially acceptable risks (most lifesaving drugs have serious side effects, and every major surgery or anesthesia is potentially fatal) is precisely why Coulter favored homeopathy. While it may never cure, it also never kills directly. The most novel aspect of Wakefield's paper was the supreme confidence with which he turned this confluence of disparate phenomena into a theory of autism causation.

After peer reviewers of an early draft expressed concerns about the study's language and potential impact, the *Lancet*'s editor requested a rewrite and slapped an "Early Report" slug on the article in print, emphasizing its speculative nature. The researchers took care to note in the discussion section, "We did not prove an association between measles, mumps, and rubella vaccine and the syndrome described. Virological studies are under way that may help to resolve this issue. If there is a causal link between measles, mumps, and rubella vaccine and this syndrome, a rising incidence might be anticipated after the introduction of this vaccine in the UK in 1988. Published evidence is inadequate to show whether there is a change in incidence or a link with measles, mumps, and rubella vaccine."

In the promotional video and the press conference itself, however,

Wakefield was not nearly so tentative or cautious. Instead, he suggested that his study was just the latest evidence challenging the safety of the MMR. A formidably built man with deep-set blue eyes and a crisp, no-nonsense manner, Wakefield carried himself like a man who was above the fray. At the press conference, he used every ounce of this gravitas to cast a pall of doubt over the MMR vaccine, venturing much further into the realm of conjecture than the wording of his paper suggested.

"This is a moral issue for me," Wakefield intoned gravely. "With the debate over MMR that has started, I cannot support the continued use of the three vaccines given together." He struck a similarly ominous tone in the promotional video, insisting that the study "certainly raises a question mark" over the vaccine while acknowledging that "there is no proven link as such," but then adding, "It is our suspicion that there may well be . . . I have to say that there is sufficient anxiety in my own mind of the safety."

Predictably, most of the reporters assembled in the room downplayed or ignored the caveats of Wakefield's colleagues and kicked into horror-movie mode. "Scientists' Warning Prompts Fears over Measles Vaccine," blared the headline on the *London Evening Standard*. "Doctors Warn of a New Child Vaccine Danger," screamed the *Independent*. "Undetected Bowel Illness Led to Baby's Misery," wailed the *Guardian*. "Measles Jab Turned My Son into an Autistic Child," howled the *Daily Record*. The dependably hyperbolic *Daily Mail*—which had been sowing the seeds of mass panic for months with headlines like "Both of My Little Boys Are Autistic and My Wonderful Marriage Is in Tatters, Our Lives Have Been Ruined by a Vaccine"—ran with "Ban Three-in-One Jab Urge Doctors after New Fears," as if the Royal College of Paediatrics had issued an emergency alert.

This press coverage sent shock waves through the autism parents' community and far beyond. For Rimland, the Wakefield study was the smoking gun he'd been waiting for. In the coming years, many members of his network would become convinced that autism was the product of multiple insults to a child's developing brain from vaccines, vaccine preservatives, or both. Activists like Fisher set their sights on eliminating the use of a specific vaccine preservative, thimerosal, which became the subject of a raging worldwide debate. As public health authorities rushed to reassure terrified parents that the vaccine was safe, Rimland thundered in a press release, "It is ludicrous to claim that the link between many cases of autism and vaccination is just coincidental. Dr. Wakefield's group has greatly expanded our understanding of one possible mechanism."

After an outcry from organizations like Fisher's National Vaccine Information Center, the Centers for Disease Control in Atlanta and the American Academy of Pediatrics asked vaccine manufacturers to remove thimerosal from their products, and the preservative was quickly phased out of most vaccines in the United States and Europe. While later studies would show that this had no impact on rising rates of autism diagnosis, this precautionary step had the unintended effect of appearing to provide an official imprimatur to parental anxieties about mercury. News of the link between autism and vaccines spread through the parent-run e-mail lists and websites proliferating across the Internet, stoked by an endless stream of "balanced" stories in major media outlets by journalists who found the David-and-Goliath angle—a visionary doctor backed by an army of warrior moms going up against a conspiracy between Big Pharma and government officials—irresistible. In November 2000, Wakefield appeared on *60 Minutes* to blame the MMR for triggering an epidemic of autism, framed by frightening before-and-after footage of a boy who he claimed was made autistic by a vaccine.

Rates of immunization for measles, mumps, and pertussis began to fall worldwide. For parents in countries where these communicable diseases were rare, nursing a kid through a week of the measles seemed like a small price to pay for dodging the bullet of a lifelong developmental disorder. Self-published books started popping up like *Melanie's Marvelous Measles*, described by its author, Stephanie Messenger, as a story that "takes children aged 4–10 years on a journey of discovering about the ineffectiveness of vaccinations, while teaching them to embrace childhood disease." Similarly, some parents began hosting "pox parties"—promoted in members-only online networks—where their children were intentionally exposed to diseases like chicken pox.

Wakefield's case series became one of the most influential journal articles in the history of public health—a considerable accomplishment for someone who admits that he knew nothing about autism before he undertook the study. But it would also become one of the most widely and thoroughly refuted. Investigations and inquiries launched in the years following its publication by journalist Brian Deer, the General Medical Council, the *British Medical Journal*, and other watchdogs uncovered numerous problems with its methodology, ethics, and reporting.

Children described in the study as "normal" before receiving the vaccine had actually been flagged for developmental issues such as hand flapping and language delay. Two children who were reported to have suffered from autistic enterocolitis after the MMR had never been diagnosed with autism at all. Wakefield had also been creative in calculating the time between administration of the vaccine and the onset of regression, making it appear as if the children had suffered symptoms within days of receiving the MMR, when his own records showed that weeks or months had elapsed. The father of one boy in the study told Deer, "If my son really is Patient 11, then the *Lancet* article is simply an outright fabrication."

Even more damningly, Deer discovered that Wakefield had failed to disclose to the *Lancet* editors a substantial financial agreement with lawyers planning to mount a class-action suit against vaccine manufacturers. As these and other irregularities came to light, ten of the study's co-authors took their names off the paper, and the study itself was finally retracted by the *Lancet* in 2004. Wakefield was stripped of his medical license in England by the General Medical Council in 2010, and the editors of the *British Medical Journal* denounced his study as "an elaborate fraud" in 2011.

Multiple attempts by independent researchers to confirm a link between autism and the MMR vaccine have failed. In 2003, researchers writing for the *Archives of Pediatrics and Adolescent Medicine* performed a systematic meta-analysis of a dozen epidemiological studies and concluded, "The current literature does not suggest an association between ASD and the MMR vaccine. While the risk of autism from MMR remains theoretical, the consequences of not vaccinating are real."

FROM THEIR OFFICE AT the Lorna Wing Centre for Autism a few miles outside London, Lorna and Judith regarded the vaccine controversy with a sense of tragic inevitability. There was no question in their minds that the changes they wrought to the *DSM* criteria were the primary factor responsible for rising numbers. Chatting over tea with the two senior researchers in 2011, overlooking the quiet garden they had planted for the benefit of the children at the center, was like sitting in the calm eye of a hurricane that was blowing all over the world.

"It's a question of diagnosis," Lorna said firmly. By expanding Kanner's narrow definition of his syndrome to include more mildly impaired children and adults, she had expected estimates of autism prevalence to rise. That was precisely the point: making the diagnosis available to more people, so that they and their families wouldn't have to struggle along without help as they had in the 1960s. "These people have always existed," she said.

Judith agreed. "We were not surprised when people started saying it was an epidemic," she said. "Obviously, by broadening the spectrum, you're going to get higher numbers. We've been saying this all along, but people were just pooh-poohing us."

Lorna suggested that blurring the boundaries between autism and eccentricity has also inevitably contributed to the widespread perception that the condition is on the rise. After their development of the concept of Asperger's syndrome, Lorna and Judith began to see traits of the syndrome as common in the people around them, particularly in the families of children brought to the center for evaluation and workers in technical fields. "It's very difficult to draw the lines, certainly between Kanner's and Asperger's," Lorna said, "but also between Asperger's and normality."

Another reason that autistic people have become more visible, Judith proposed, is that gender roles have become more fluid in recent decades.

"In traditional British life, men worked, and were cared for by their wives, who didn't work. They were the caregivers and men were the breadwinners," she said. "I see many, many men who refer themselves here for diagnosis who would never have even thought they had a problem in times gone by because they were protected by the family and society." Lorna added that if a "dash of autism" is essential for success in science and art, as Asperger suggested, perhaps the advent of the Internet has accelerated "an evolutionary tendency in that direction."

But she had no illusions about how disabling the core features of autism can be, even with the best kinds of care. By the time I spoke with her, Lorna and her husband, John, had buried their beloved Susie, who died in 2005 at age forty-nine after the hormonal storms of menopause gave her a compulsion to drink excessive quantities of water. She finally died of a heart attack. John died of Alzheimer's disease five years later, after Lorna nursed him faithfully at home through the final stages of his illness. She would pass away herself in 2014 at age eighty-five.

The day I visited her clinic, Lorna seemed remarkably youthful and cheerful in a bright floral-print dress, reminiscing about having tea with Asperger one afternoon in the Maudsley Hospital cafeteria just before he died in 1980. (She described him as "charming, polite, and a man who listened well.") With the help of his paper, she and the other parents who launched the National Autistic Society in the 1960s had changed the world to make it a better place for their children.

THE MOST INSIDIOUS EFFECT of Wakefield's case study and the firestorm of controversy that followed it was hijacking the movement created by parents like Lorna and Ruth Sullivan, diverting it from its original mission of demanding services and accommodations in education into a rancorous debate about vaccines. In the heat of the Autism Wars, virtually every other issue—such as the pressing need for programs to help autistic teenagers prepare for employment—was swept off the table.

Fears of an epidemic have also skewed the direction of autism research.

Most studies backed by the NIMH and other federal agencies and private organizations like Autism Speaks are committed to an endless search for potential causes and risk factors, while projects devoted to improving the quality of autistic people's lives are perpetually underfunded.

But now that's starting to change. By leveraging the technology passed down to them by their predecessors in previous generations, autistic people are taking control of their own destinities, with the help of parents who no longer believe that what their children need most is a cure.

Eleven

IN AUTISTIC SPACE

> All our lives we've been alone in a world of alien men. To find kindred at last is a special joy.
>
> —A. E. van Vogt, *Slan*

In May 1989, a lanky, sandy-haired industrial designer sporting a Western suit and Texas tie stepped up to the podium at a conference of autism professionals and educators in Chapel Hill, North Carolina. The focus of the gathering, prompted by the release of *Rain Man* five months earlier, was "high-functioning individuals with autism," and the featured speaker certainly filled the bill. "I am a 44-year-old autistic woman who has a successful international career designing livestock equipment," she began. "I completed my PhD in Animal Science at the University of Illinois in Urbana and I am now an Assistant Professor of Animal Science at Colorado State University." Her name was Temple Grandin, and she was not yet widely known outside autism circles.

A few years earlier, Ruth Sullivan had spotted Grandin in a terminal at the St. Louis Airport en route to a conference, eavesdropping from the sidelines as parents swapped stories about raising their children. Though NSAC was two decades old by that point, Sullivan had never seen a mature woman who called herself autistic; the thought didn't even cross her mind as they rode on the bus to their hotel. "If I'd known then what I know now, I would have seen it," Sullivan recalls. "But Temple was just kind of shy, nicely dressed, and spoke very well. After she went to her room, all of a sudden it hit me." By inviting the industrial designer to moderate a roundtable discussion, she effectively launched Grandin's career as a public speaker.

"There were about twenty roundtables going on in this big banquet hall, but when I started talking, suddenly the whole room got quiet," Grandin says. "Everybody at the other tables started turning around so they could listen to me." (Two decades later, the scene was re-created for the Emmy-winning HBO biopic *Temple Grandin* starring Clare Danes.) "You could ask Temple questions, and it was like speaking to all of our kids," Sullivan recalls. "None of them could tell us what she could tell us."

Recounting the story of her life for the audience of professionals in Chapel Hill in her inimitably gruff and blunt-spoken way, Grandin cast more light on the day-to-day reality of autism than decades of clinical observation and speculation had managed to produce. The fact that this accomplished and articulate industrial designer was unable to speak until age three and struggled with severe behavioral issues through her teens suggested that labels like *high-functioning* and *low-functioning* were too simplistic. She had managed to avoid being institutionalized only because the neurologist who initially examined her diagnosed her with brain damage rather than autism.

First Grandin characterized descriptions of nonverbal children as willfully oblivious to the people around them as terribly misguided. "If adults spoke directly to me I could understand everything they said, but I could not get my words out," she said. "My mother and teachers wondered why I screamed. Screaming was the only way I could communicate." Then she pointed out the inadequacy of existing empirical methods for capturing the sensory sensitivities at the core of autistic experience. The auditory tests she was given as a child revealed nothing unusual about her hearing, but Grandin described being bombarded with certain sounds as like "having a hearing aid stuck on 'super loud.'" The reason that she misbehaved in church so often as a little girl, she explained, was that the unfamiliar petticoats, skirts, and stockings she was forced to wear on Sundays felt scratchy against her skin.

She pointedly referred to her autism as a "handicap" rather than a mental illness, invoking the humanizing language of disability over the stigmatizing lexicon of psychiatry. But in addition to shedding light on the challenges faced by people with autism, she also described the ways that the visual nature of her thought processes and memory had given her practical advantages in her career. "If somebody says the word *cat*," she said, "my images are of individualized cats I have known or read about. I do not think of a generalized cat. My career as a designer of livestock facilities maximizes my talent areas and minimizes my deficits . . . Visual thinking is an asset for an equipment designer. I am able to 'see' how all the parts of a project fit together and see potential problems." She cited the infamous case of a catwalk that collapsed in the lobby of a Hyatt Regency in 1981, killing more than a hundred people, as a catastrophe that could have been averted by having a visual thinker like her on the design team.

Then she traced the roots of her creative gifts through the branches of her family tree, describing her paternal great-grandfather as a maverick who launched the biggest corporate wheat farm in the world and her maternal grandfather as a shy engineer who helped invent the automatic pilot for airplanes. She pointed out that all three of her siblings think visually and that one of her sisters, a gifted interior designer, is dyslexic. Her emphasis on the virtues of atypical minds marked a significant departure from the view of most psychologists, who framed the areas of strength in their patients' cognitive profiles as mere "splinter skills"—islands of conserved ability in seas of general incompetence. Instead, Grandin proposed that people with autism, dyslexia, and other cognitive differences could make contributions to society that so-called normal people are incapable of making.

She ended her talk by paying tribute to her mentors, starting with her mother, Eustacia Cutler, who never lost faith in her potential and fought many battles to ensure that Temple got an education. She also thanked William Carlock, the high school science teacher who channeled her teenage fascination with cows into a career in animal science. She explained that the turning point in her young life occurred one summer at her aunt

Ann's ranch, when she noticed that fearful calves calmed down when they were herded into a device called a squeeze chute that held them securely in place. Like many autistic people, Grandin struggles with chronic anxiety, and she wondered if she, too, might gain peace of mind if she placed herself in the chute. With her aunt's help, she did just that, and the feeling of deep pressure from the device pressing against her sides alleviated her "nerve attacks." Later, with Carlock's encouragement, she devised a similar apparatus for herself out of scrap wood.

Predictably, the school psychologist wasn't pleased with her invention, telling her that he couldn't decide if it was "a prototype of a womb or a casket." ("*We* don't think we're a cow or something, do *we*?" he asked Grandin, who shot back, "Do you think *you're* a cow?") School officials tried to persuade Eustacia that her daughter's device represented a "sick" fixation that should be taken away from her. But Grandin sensed that she was on the right track. Safely ensconced in the arms of her squeeze machine, she not only became less anxious, she felt more emotionally connected to the people around her. "For the first time in my life," she said, "I felt a purpose for learning."

As ONE OF THE first adults to publicly identify as autistic, Grandin helped break down decades of shame and stigma. One nearly forgotten aspect of her "coming out," though, shows how quickly the ground was shifting under her feet. To most clinicians at the time, the notion of an autistic adult with a doctorate and a successful career seemed implausible at best. So Grandin presented herself in Chapel Hill as someone who had "recovered" from autism, encouraged by Rimland, who introduced her 1986 memoir, *Emergence*, as "the first book written by a recovered autistic individual."

It soon became obvious to her, however, that she had not recovered but had learned, with great effort, to adapt to the social norms of the people around her. "When I said that early stuff, I didn't realize how different my thinking was," Grandin says. "I was doing a lot of construction projects in the early nineties, and I could draw something and test-run that piece of equipment in my mind. I started asking other designers to describe how they think, and they told me they could draw the layout for a meat-cutting line but couldn't make the conveyors move. I could make the conveyors move."

She had a similar revelation when she asked a speech therapist what came into her mind after hearing the phrase *church steeple*. "I was shocked when she said 'vague pointy thing,'" Grandin recalls. "I saw pictures of specific steeples." She began to think of herself as having a powerful digital workstation in her head, capable of running instantaneous searches through a massive library of stored images and generating 3-D videos from the sketches on her drafting table.

Grandin also noticed how many parents at autism conferences were gifted in technical fields. "Early on I met a family with two severely autistic nonverbal kids. Dad was a computer programmer and Mom was a chemist. Both super-smart," she says. "I saw lots and lots of cases like this. I started to think of autistic traits as being on a continuum. The more traits you had on both sides, the more you concentrated the genetics. Having a little bit of the traits gave you an advantage, but if you had too much, you ended up with very severe autism." She warned that efforts to eradicate autism from the gene pool could put humankind's future at risk by purging the same qualities that had advanced culture, science, and technological innovation for millennia. The maker of the first stone spear, she observed, was likely a lone autistic at the back of the cave, perseverating over the subtle differences between various types of rocks—not one of the "yakkity yaks" chattering away in the firelight.

> Aware adults with autism and their parents are often angry about autism. They may ask why nature or God created such horrible conditions as autism, manic depression, and schizophrenia. However, if the genes that caused these conditions were eliminated there might be a terrible price to pay. It is possible that persons with bits of these traits are more creative, or possibly even geniuses. If science eliminated these genes, maybe the whole world would be taken over by accountants.

Two years later, a distinguished visitor arrived in Grandin's office in the animal sciences department at Colorado State University: Oliver Sacks, who had flown in from New York City while researching a profile of the young savant artist Stephen Wiltshire. His own views of autism were evolving swiftly, informed by the insights of Lorna Wing, Uta Frith, and the others in the London group. When he first read *Emergence*, he suspected that Grandin's co-author, Margaret Scariano, must have ghostwritten it. "The autistic mind, it was supposed at that time, was incapable of self-understanding and understanding others and therefore of authentic introspection and retrospection," he explained. "How could an autistic person write an autobiography? It seemed a contradiction in terms." After reading dozens of her papers, however, he found that Grandin's distinctive persona—that of an irrepressibly curious observer of society from the outside, an "anthropologist on Mars," as she put it—was consistent throughout. She was clearly writing in her own voice.

After decades in the shadows, Asperger's forgotten tribe was finally making its way toward the light. Before meeting Grandin, Sacks had spent the summer visiting camps for autistic kids and acquainting himself with a California couple he called the B.'s, who had turned their home into a haven for expat extraterrestrials. Upon meeting in college, Mr. and Mrs. B. felt like they had known each other for a million years. As fellow *Star Trek* fans, they liked to say that they had beamed down on the transporter together. Both of their sons turned out to be autistic—one nonverbal and one with Asperger's syndrome—so they put up a trampoline in their backyard where the whole family could jump and flap to their hearts' content. Their walls were emblazoned with surrealistic cartoons, their bookshelves were laden with science fiction, and notes posted in the kitchen offered meticulously explicit directions for cooking and setting the table. Sacks initially assumed that these detailed directives were an expression of the B.'s need for order and routine, but he eventually realized they were a family in-joke at the expense of those who thought that autistic people were incapable of "getting" humor.

The B.'s were well aware that the protocols and conventions of non-autistic society were opaque to them, and that they were required to "ape human behavior" at work, as Mr. B. put it, to avoid alarming their professional colleagues. But Sacks reported that they had come to feel that their autism, "while it may be seen as a medical condition, and pathologized as a syndrome, must also be seen as a whole mode of being, a deeply different mode or identity, one that needs to be conscious (and proud) of itself." At home with other members of their tribe, in an environment designed for their comfort, they didn't feel disabled; they just felt different from their neighbors.

Eager to observe Grandin in her native element, Sacks spent several days touring cattle farms and meatpacking plants that she helped design, sharing a meal of ribs and beer with her in a cowboy-themed restaurant, and visiting her at home, where he gamely climbed into her squeeze machine to try it out himself, finding a "sweet, calming" feeling in its mechanical embrace. They also took hikes together in the mountains, where he was impressed by her knowledge of the names of the local birds, plants, and rock formations, even if she seemed unimpressed by the feelings of sublimity and awe that they evoked in him. In turn, Grandin was amused to discover that the eminent neurologist was nearly as eccentric as she was. "He was like a kindly absentminded professor who zoned out a lot," she recalls. "When he had to pee in the woods, he announced that he was going to 'fertilize the ground.' He had me stop the car so he could go swimming in a lake, but he didn't notice that the current would have carried him right over a dam. I probably saved his life."

Their interactions made such a profound impression on Sacks that he turned his planned footnote to the Wiltshire story into an in-depth profile that became the centerpiece of his next bestseller, *An Anthropologist on Mars*. After fifty years of case reports describing autistic people in terms befitting robots or "imbeciles," Sacks presented Grandin in the full breadth of her humanity—capable of joy, whimsy, tenderness, passion about her work, exuberance, longing, philosophical musing on her legacy, and sly subterfuge (she smuggled him into a plant by giving him a hard hat and telling him to act like a sanitary engineer). He acknowledged the prevailing theory that autism is "foremost a disorder of affect, of empathy," but also explored her deep sense of kinship with other disabled people and with animals, whose fates she saw as intertwined in a society that views them both as less than human.

In one study for the university, Grandin analyzed the social and environmental factors that influence the attitudes of livestock industry employees toward cattle in feedlots, auction markets, and slaughterhouses. In badly designed facilities where animals routinely slipped on slick floors or were trapped by slamming gates, she observed, workers tended to become desensitized to their plight and used whips and electric prods on them with abandon. She noted that in states where cattle are routinely treated badly, disabled people face high levels of abuse and discrimination.

She came to see her profound emotional connection with animals as essentially autistic, and crucial for her work. "If I could snap my fingers and be non-autistic, I would not, because then I wouldn't be me," she told Sacks. "Autism is part of who I am." By then, she was on her way to becoming the most widely recognized autistic person on earth. After the publication of *An Anthropologist on Mars*, Sacks's office was deluged with letters from readers who saw aspects of themselves, their relatives, or their coworkers in his descriptions of a mature person on the spectrum with a complex inner life. "It was overwhelming, like opening a floodgate," recalls Kate Edgar, the neurologist's longtime assistant and editor. "There was such a pent-up desire to have a name for this cluster of traits in older people and to hear someone talk about autism from the perspective of acceptance."

The chances of Grandin's perspective taking root among autism professionals or traditional advocacy organizations, however, were slim. The notion that an autism diagnosis was a fate worse than death proved hard to dispel even in sectors of the medical profession. As late as 2001, one of the most respected figures in modern epidemiology, Walter Spitzer of McGill University, described autism as "a terminal illness . . . a dead soul in a live body."

In fact, the expansion of the diagnosis inspired the creation of a whole new set of dehumanizing stereotypes in the media. The first mention of

Asperger's syndrome in an English-language newspaper, in the *Toronto Star* in 1989, described "strange" and "clumsy" nerds who read books compulsively without understanding them, were incapable of friendship, and burst into tears and laughter for no reason "like stroke patients who have suffered brain damage." The second mention, in the *Sydney Morning Herald*, led off with the sentence, "It is the plague of those unable to feel."

Even within the autism community, there were problems. When parent-run advocacy organizations got online in the 1990s, they continued to feature images of children exclusively on their websites, as if autistic adults didn't exist. The presentations at conferences inevitably dwelled on the usual deficits and impairments, rather than on exploring the atypical gifts that Grandin found so useful in her work.

One young man sitting in the room in Chapel Hill on the day that Grandin gave her presentation became determined to change that. By doing so, he laid the foundation of something that would have been unimaginable in previous generations: a sanctuary where people on the spectrum could just relax and be themselves, celebrating their distinctive ways of being, without feeling pressure to socialize, suppress their autistic behavior, or otherwise "act normal."

II

Jim Sinclair had driven twelve hundred miles to North Carolina in the hope of meeting other people like him after receiving his diagnosis. He had never had the luxury of feeling in the majority: in addition to being on the spectrum, he was born neuter, lacking physical characteristics of either gender. His parents had raised him as female on the advice of their doctor, but he had never felt female. His first act of self-definition was to jump off his father's lap and shout "No!" when his father sang to him about being "Daddy's little girl."

In third grade, Sinclair read a book on worms. Upon discovering that they, too, are hermaphroditic, he made a point of carrying them to safety when they got stranded on the sidewalk after a rain. "Earthworms were the first living creatures that I could identify with," he says.

At a very young age, he also began identifying with other disabled people. One day, Sinclair saw a blind man with a cane striding down the street. "I was just amazed to see him walking so confidently," he says. "It wasn't at all like I had thought it would be to walk as a blind person." Discovering a cane in his grandparents' basement, he closed his eyes and used it to navigate around the room. But his grandmother caught him in the act and started shouting that he had done a very shameful thing. He didn't understand what he had done to make her so angry. Then when he was six, he and his brother got a set of Johnny West action figures. If the arm of one of these plastic cowboy figurines came loose, he would secure it by turning its "lasso" into an improvised sling; when another figurine lost its leg, he fashioned a little wheelchair for it. "From very early on," he explains, "I had the concept that you don't throw people away for being broken."

A year later, he saw a movie called *Run Wild, Run Free*, starring Mark Lester as a boy named Philip who suddenly stopped talking at age three as a result of being traumatized by his dominant mother—a typical view of autism at the time. Sinclair felt a deep sense of connection with Philip, who was eventually brought out of his solitude by the patient mentorship of an older man and his affection for a wild white colt.

Meanwhile, Sinclair's parents were taking him to a series of doctors and therapists to determine why he was having so much trouble getting his ideas across. He was clearly bright and articulate—*too* bright and articulate for an autism diagnosis, they were told repeatedly. Yet, when he became tense or overwhelmed and began flapping his hands or rocking, they would yell, "Stop acting so autistic!" He learned to suppress those behaviors, which only made him more anxious. His teachers suggested that gifted children often stand on the sidelines, watching their peers interacting and gauging the right moment to jump in. But he wasn't waiting to jump in—instead, he preferred to be off somewhere else, doing his own thing.

What only Sinclair knew was that, until he was twelve, he was speaking primarily in echolalia. "I had to be given the words first," he recalls; "then

I could pick which ones I needed in a particular context. I could take words that were in a textbook, or that a teacher had said, and parrot them back, so I got good grades. But what I couldn't do well was put new words together on my own." One of the first original ideas he articulated to his parents was "I am not a girl," which only succeeded in upsetting them further. He refused to undergo a bat mitzvah—the female coming-of-age ceremony in Judaism—precipitating a major breach with his family. "There was no ceremony because I was not willing to do it under false pretenses," he says. "I stood my ground."

As Sinclair and his peers became teenagers, the increasingly complex rules of the social world seemed incomprehensible to him. When other kids bullied him, which happened often, his mother would say, "Be nice to them and they'll be friends with you." But he couldn't figure out why he was expected to want to be friends with people who treated him so cruelly.

By the time Sinclair was in graduate school, his efforts to pass as non-autistic began falling apart. Once he was stripped of the reassuringly familiar structures and routines of his life at home, he felt the behaviors he had worked so hard to keep under wraps returning. "I was stimming a lot more in public, which was something I had made a point of stopping when I was eleven years old, because I realized I was going to be institutionalized if I didn't stop rocking in class," he says. "When I had to go to school, hold down a part-time job, have my own apartment, do my own grocery shopping, laundry, and everything, I had to choose between suppressing the stims in the supermarket or buying groceries. And I found I couldn't do both. For a while, my doctors thought I was having seizures, because I would push myself and push myself to do all these things, and I would finally shut down and be unable to respond."

Eventually, he lost his job at the university and became homeless for a time. Trying to make sense of why his life was imploding, he read an information packet on autism from UCLA, but the description didn't seem to apply to him. "I didn't consider myself to be someone who didn't have empathy, lacked the ability to form emotional bonds, and wasn't interested in relating to others," Sinclair says. But then he saw *Portrait of an Autistic Young Man*. Watching Joseph Sullivan interact with other people, he had a profound sense of recognition. "For the first time in my life, I could understand the body language of someone I was watching," he recalls. Furthermore, he felt that he could see what Rimland and the other experts in the film could not: that Joseph was trying to communicate through his behavior. "They kept saying things like, 'You see, he's totally oblivious.' But Joseph didn't seem oblivious to me. It seemed like he was listening and asking for clarification because he didn't understand the terms."

Sinclair began seeking out other autistic adults, but they were not easy to find in the years before the widespread adoption of the Internet. He subscribed to a quarterly publication originally called the *Residual Autism Newsletter*, later rechristened the *MAAP* (for "more able autistic people"), and began submitting poems and letters to the editor in the hopes that his peers would contact him.

The newsletter was launched in 1984 by Susan Moreno, the mother of a girl named Beth, along with a group of parents she had met at an Autism Society of America conference two years earlier. Like many parents of so-called high-functioning children, Susan and her husband, Marco, struggled for years to find a clinician willing to diagnose their daughter. Most of the psychologists they'd seen had immediately ruled out autism because Beth was able to speak, though her expressive vocabulary was extremely limited. "She couldn't say things like 'My throat is sore,' 'I'm scared,' or 'The babysitter was mean to me,'" Susan recalls. She would usually just repeat nouns.

The Morenos didn't even realize that their daughter was able to read until one day she blurted out, "Chicago, merge left!" as they passed a sign on the highway. When Susan told one of Beth's teachers that her daughter could read, she replied coolly, "Now, Mrs. Moreno, sometimes we love our children so much that we begin to delude ourselves as to the real world and our kids' real capabilities. It doesn't help the child, and it doesn't help the parent." Two weeks later, the teacher called to apologize after Beth read the captions on a set of slides aloud for the whole class. Beth was eventually diagnosed at UCLA by Lovaas and Ed Ritvo after spending three months on a waiting list for an evaluation.

But even with a diagnosis in hand, Susan faced further skepticism from the community she had hoped would provide her with support: the other parents and professionals in the Autism Society of America. "At conferences, I would take notes and try to adapt the material to my daughter's learning style and needs," she recalls. "When I dared to ask a question, if I made any reference to the fact that Beth could talk, people would say immediately, 'You don't have a child with autism. I don't know what your daughter's problem is, but it's not autism.'" One expert in the field, she recalls, "would follow me out of rooms saying, 'I want to explain to you why your daughter does not have autism.' I learned to sit at the back and hide."

Finally, at an ASA meeting in Omaha in 1982, she saw a note on a bulletin board inviting parents of other "high-functioning" children to chat. Susan expected to walk in and see the authors of the note sitting in an empty room. Instead, a couple of dozen couples showed up who were so eager to connect with other parents that they were eventually kicked out of the room for running overtime. Susan launched the newsletter two years later, doing all the typing, copying, and mailing herself.

The *MAAP* broke new ground by featuring essays and poems from autistic contributors. But the fact that they were run anonymously prevented the authors from reaching out to each other—a fact that Sinclair pointed out to Moreno. A poem that he submitted to Moreno attracted the attention of TEACCH co-founder Gary Mesibov, who offered him a scholarship to attend the Chapel Hill conference and write an essay about his experiences. Along with Grandin, the presenters included Lorna Wing, who introduced the concept of the autistic continuum to American clinicians there.

Sinclair found the bustling and noisy atmosphere of the conference overwhelming. One mother told him that she wanted to introduce him to her son, but she felt frustrated because he was "hiding" in their hotel room. Sinclair confessed that he felt like hiding too. Another mother explained that her son was in the honors society for history, but a psychologist had decided that he didn't have the social skills to become a historian and should instead pursue a career as a librarian. How could she explain this to him? Sinclair replied that her son was an adult and that he should be allowed to make his own decisions.

He also made a friend at the conference named Anne Carpenter. Nonverbal until she was five, she had run the usual gamut of misdiagnoses, including mental retardation, but had gone on to get a graduate degree. After being fired from a series of increasingly menial jobs (including data entry, cleaning circuit boards, and weaving belts) for such infractions as asking too many questions, she was turned down for disability benefits because she didn't fit any of the available categories. Not until reading Grandin's *Emergence* did she have a name for what was happening to her: "It was as if my whole personality were contained in the pages of that book."

Sinclair also met two other autistic adults who taught him a valuable lesson. They were housemates who shared a passionate interest in maps despite the fact that they were unable to drive. When they asked him about the route he'd taken to Chapel Hill from Lawrence, he replied that he'd ordered a TripTik from AAA and followed the instructions. "They started asking me questions about which highways I chose, did I take this road or that, and I realized they knew more about the route than I did," he recalls. The following day, one of them recited a list of counties in North Carolina and Kansas that had the same names. It dawned on Sinclair that the man was using his special interest to try to make a connection with him, in a distinctively autistic medium of cultural exchange.

Sinclair's essay on the conference was reprinted in a TEACCH anthology alongside contributions from Lorna Wing and Catherine Lord. It was gratifying to be asked to offer his "inside-out" view of autism to the experts who had been defining the terms of autistic lives for half a century. "Being autistic does not mean being inhuman. But it means that what is normal for other people is not normal for me, and what is normal for me is not normal for other people," he wrote. He compared himself to "an extraterrestrial stranded without an orientation manual."

A YEAR AFTER his trip to Chapel Hill, Sinclair was invited to sit on a panel in California by the Autism Society of America. As he sat there fielding questions, he didn't feel like an inside-out autism expert; instead, he felt like a "self-narrating zoo exhibit," he says—sharing the intimate details of his biography with an audience trained to view every aspect of his life through the prism of pathology. It was not an experience that he was eager to repeat.

Rather than being the token autistic on a panel at a conference in Indianapolis, Sinclair conspired with other members of the *MAAP* list to make their presence visible throughout the proceedings. "I came up with the idea that we should try to get at least one of us into the audience of as many presentations as possible," he says. "Each of us would make a point of raising our hands during the question-and-answer sessions, identify ourselves as autistic people, and then ask some question or make a relevant comment so that people would notice we were there."

At a presentation on sexuality—a topic that would have been considered irrelevant at an autism conference just a few years earlier—one mother raised her hand and said that a psychologist had told her that her son would never need sex education because autistic people can't stand to be touched. Anne Carpenter rose from her seat, took the microphone, and said, "That's not true. I'm a thirty-four-year-old autistic woman and I hope to get married and have children someday."

The fact that Carpenter was female was itself unusual, as women on the spectrum had been virtually invisible to clinicians since the days of Asperger. When another woman in the group, Kathy Lissner, was an infant, her parents were told that her IQ was in the "imbecilic" range, and that she would probably never be able to read, write, or speak. By the time she was twenty-four, she was going to college, living in her own apartment, and dreaming up science fiction stories about aliens with names like "1945 minus 19." Instead of being ashamed of her eccentricities, she reveled in them. "If normal is being selfish, being dishonest, killing, having guns, and waging war," she said, "I do not want any of it."

III

In 1992, a member of the *MAAP* list named Donna Williams came to the United States from Australia to promote her autobiography, *Nobody Nowhere.* Like Grandin, she had felt all her life like an anthropologist observing human interactions from a distance, straining to make meaning out of a confusing barrage of jumbled sensory impressions. The book, which began as a private journal, became a best seller. The *New York Times* described its author as a "mentally ill" woman whose autism had "subsided with time."

Taking a few days off from the stress of her book tour, Williams flew to St. Louis to meet Lissner and Sinclair. None of them had ever spent time with other autistic adults outside the context of a conference, and the experience proved to be a revelation in ways that they couldn't have predicted.

Viewed from the outside, not all that much happened. They brewed up cups of tea that would still be sitting there hours later, cold on the floor, because they suddenly forgot what to do with tea, or got distracted doing something more interesting. Hardly any food got cooked or eaten, and other routine chores fell by the wayside. They shared the playful private terms they'd developed to map their subjective experiences, finding a surprising amount of overlap, and took Sinclair's three dogs out for walks. But the most fun thing that they did was stimming together.

In her letters to members of the *MAAP* list, Williams would often include some little shiny or brightly colored thing as a kind of visual offering. As she sat on Lissner's floor in St. Louis, she would arrange glittering objects in pleasing patterns on the floor, gaze at them through a kaleidoscope, and go into ecstasy. Then she would insist that her companions look at them too. "Being autistic, I'm not supposed to understand things like this,"

Sinclair reflected, "but to me that looked suspiciously like a person wanting to share a pleasurable activity with her friends." Seeing the thrill that Williams got from the lights playing off a Coke can, he later sent her a belt covered in red sequins from Kmart as a gift. He realized that the same behaviors that had been viewed for so long as inherently antisocial could become social in a group of autistic adults, particularly if there were no clinicians around to pronounce them pathological.

In her next book, *Somebody Somewhere*, Williams compared her visit to St. Louis to finally coming home. "Together we felt like a lost tribe. 'Normal' is to be in the company of one like one's self," she wrote. "We all had a sense of belonging, of being understood . . . all the things we could not get from others in general. It was so sad to have to leave."

For Sinclair, the relaxed environment of their interactions marked his first experience of being in "autistic space," as he put it. Soon he would begin building safe space for autistics on a frontier so new that most people were barely aware that it existed: the Internet.

SINCLAIR BECAME one of the first openly autistic adults online, joining a digital mailing list run out of St. John's University in New York frequented primarily by parents and professionals. Its founder, Ray Kopp, was the father of a legally blind girl named Shawna who had sought unsuccessfully for years to get a more specific diagnosis for her than "developmentally delayed." Kopp launched the list in 1992 with a dyslexia expert at St. John's named Robert Zenhausern. On the threshold of the addition of Asperger's syndrome to the *DSM*, one of the most frequently asked questions on the list was whether Kanner's syndrome could persist into adulthood.

With Williams and Lissner, Sinclair also launched the first autistic-run organization in history, calling it Autism Network International. Early on, its founders decided that ANI would stand up for the civil rights and self-determination of people all across the spectrum, not just those considered high-functioning like the members of the *MAAP* list. All of ANI's original founders had been branded low-functioning as children and had gone on to earn university degrees. They understood that functioning levels change not only in the course of the life span but also day to day. Even a chatty "more able" adult could temporarily lose speech, and the term *low-functioning* often obscured talents and skills that could be brought out by providing a more suitable environment or an alternate means of communication.

Like any nascent subculture, this emerging community gave birth to its own in-group slang. The most enduring ANI neologism was the term *neurotypical*, used as a label for nonautistic people for the first time in the group's newsletter. With its distinctly clinical air, the term (sometimes shortened to *NT*) turned the diagnostic gaze back on the psychiatric establishment and registered the fact that people on the spectrum were fully capable of irony and sarcasm at a time when it was widely assumed that they didn't "get" humor.

Carrying the meme to its logical extreme, an autistic woman named Laura Tisoncik launched an official-looking website in 1998 credited to the Institute for the Study of the Neurologically Typical. "Neurotypical syndrome is a neurobiological disorder characterized by preoccupation with social concerns, delusions of superiority, and obsession with conformity," the site's FAQ declared. "There is no known cure."

Taking a cue from the radical Deaf community, ANI members began to refer to themselves as "Autistic" instead of saying that they were people *with autism*. "Saying 'person with autism' suggests that autism is something bad—so bad that it isn't even consistent with being a person," Sinclair observed. "We talk about left-handed people, not 'people with left-handedness,' and about athletic or musical people, not about 'people with athleticism' or 'people with musicality' . . . It is only when someone has decided that the characteristic being referred to is negative that suddenly people want to separate it from the person."

THE EMERGENCE OF E-MAIL, electronic bulletin boards, Usenet newsgroups, Internet Relay Chat, America Online, and ultimately the World

Wide Web provided a natural home for the growing community of newly diagnosed teenagers and adults, where they could interact at their own pace in a language that often felt more native to them than the spoken word. Carolyn Baird, a mother of four who took over management of the St. John's list, spoke for many of her peers when she told a Dutch journalist:

> Autistic people seem to have an affinity with computers and many of them were already working in computer-related fields prior to the advent of the Internet. The appeal of a computer is that there is only one right way to tell it to do something—it doesn't misinterpret what you tell it and do something else as people do.
>
> For many of us, this medium has given us the opportunity to be accepted for the first time in our lives as being just like everyone else, and gives us our first hint at what it feels like to be accepted on the quality of our thoughts rather than the quality of our speech.

The ANI posse began making regular appearances at conferences, where they set up booths and handed out newsletters and buttons emblazoned with slogans like "I'm not just WEIRD, I'm AUTISTIC" and "I survived behavior modification." Their information tables became little oases of autistic space where people could take a break from the probing stares, the swirl of perfumes, the press of flesh, the unpredictable outbreaks of applause, and the constant reminders that their existence was a tragic puzzle. While the NT attendees lined up for lavish banquets and celebrity-studded comedy showcases, the Autistics would pair off to chat and stim in quiet hallways and coatrooms, camping out on the floors of each other's hotel rooms at night, or sleeping in their cars like impoverished science fiction fans crashing worldcons in the 1940s.

At a conference in St. Louis, one parent-ally of the group managed to get access to the whole vacant upper floor of an office building under renovation near the convention center. Amid dusty heaps of plaster and drywall, the Autistics unfurled their mats and sleeping bags, brought in a couple of floor lamps, and set up empty refrigerator cartons for anyone who needed to retreat to an enclosed space for a while. After fielding questions from parents and psychologists all day, it was a relief to return to a place with the fellow members of their tribe that felt like an enchanted cave after dark. When someone pointed out the window at an old radio tower and said that it was for sale, Sinclair replied that, since the aliens were all gathered in one place now, they could transmit the request to the mothership to come take them home at last.

EVERY ASPIRING MOVEMENT requires a manifesto, and Sinclair delivered one at the first international conference on autism in 1993 that would change the course of history. A couple of years earlier, he had heard Susan Moreno give a presentation on the challenges of raising her daughter, Beth. These included finding the right school, classroom, and teacher for her—an ordeal she compared to the quest for the Holy Grail.

Then she talked about the impact of a child's diagnosis on parents, based on the work of psychologist Kenneth Moses, a featured speaker at NSAC conferences, who was a prominent advocate of the notion that the parents of a disabled child need to grieve for the perfect son or daughter they didn't have. "It is as if the child they have dreamed about suddenly is missing, replaced by a child with a very different future," Moreno said. "I definitely feel that this was the case for Marco and me. Our hearts broke; we felt angry, guilty, and afraid. This unique mourning is not an experience that goes in exact stages and then goes away. It stays with parents on and off and in varying degrees for the rest of their lives."

Feelings of grief and confusion are not uncommon among parents of disabled children, particularly in the child's first years, but Moses took this notion to an extreme, echoing in modern psychological terms medieval superstitions that disabled children were changelings, left in place of human children that had been stolen out of the cradle by demons. In an influential article called "The Impact of Childhood Disability: The Parent's Struggle," published in 1987, he probed the feelings of disappointment, depression, and anger among the parents in his practice. For these clients, he said, the birth of an "impaired" child represents the death of their own hope for their family's future.

> Parents, all parents, attach to their children through dreams, fantasies, illusions, and projections into the future. Children are our second chance, our ultimate "life products," the reflection and extension of our very being.
>
> Disability dashes these cherished dreams.

As part of this process, Moses encouraged parents in his workshops to voice their feelings of rage and disappointment toward the child. He described parents who try to have a positive attitude toward their disabled sons and daughters as engaging in a "magnificent" form of denial, touting these views as the hard-won fruits of his own experience. His second child, a son, was born with cerebral palsy, and Moses experienced his arrival as a crushing disappointment. This was "supposed" to be the child, he told his colleagues, who was going to teach him to slow down and stop working so hard. "After 10 years in the field, I had an impaired child . . . I had a dream that this child was going to do something for me that was central to my life, but instead we got an impaired child and it was the opposite."

Moses was not alone in promoting the theory that disabled children could be psychologically toxic to their parents. "There is a limit," wrote Mary A. Slater, the assistant director of a center for the study of intellectual disability at the University of Wisconsin, "beyond which parents cannot healthfully involve themselves emotionally with a handicapped child."

At the conclusion of her talk, Moreno suggested a more nuanced truth: that her life had been enriched in ways that she could never have predicted by coping with the challenges of raising Beth. By wholly investing herself in her daughter's well-being, she said, her heart had been opened in ways that most parents of typical children would never know.

> I waited five years before my daughter ever looked at me. That moment, in April of 1977, was absolutely miraculous. It was at bedtime, during her

> nightly bedtime story, right at the part when I would say, "and Beth went to sleep knowing that her mommy and daddy loved her." Then I said, "Oh Beth, I wish that just once you'd tell me you loved me!" Suddenly she opened her eyes, looked right into mine, and said, "love Mama." It was the most intensely joyous and miraculous experience that I have ever known in my life. For the first time in her young life, I knew that "someone was home." Only those who have lived with or worked closely with autistic people will know exactly what I mean by that. I will never, ever take it for granted when she looks at me, and she does it a lot now.
>
> I will never take for granted my daughter washing her hands. It took me six years to teach her that. Now I think that hand washing is the most amazing and wonderful thing . . . What I am trying to say is that I have learned an exquisite joy in very, very small things.

For Sinclair, who was sitting in the audience taking notes, Moreno's suggestion that the birth of an autistic child was an occasion for mourning felt like a betrayal by someone that he considered an ally. He kept a copy of his notes and developed them into a presentation of his own, which he submitted to the ASA committee planning the next national conference. The committee rejected it, telling him that Grandin had submitted a similar proposal. But a year later, Sinclair sent the text of his talk, called "Don't Mourn for Us," to the Autism Society of Canada for inclusion at an autism conference in Toronto, and it was accepted.

By then, public awareness of autism was increasing rapidly, as were the number of diagnoses. That spring, Lorna Wing published an article on the potential impact of the spectrum on research, concluding that traditional prevalence estimates based on variations of Kanner's criteria—five children in ten thousand—would have to be revised upward to nearly ten times that.

ANI was also growing fast, and the word *international* wasn't a conceit—one of its early members was Sola Shelly, a researcher and mother of an autistic son who would go on to launch the Autistic Community of Israel. In July, a caravan of vehicles headed north for the conference, which attracted 2,300 delegates from forty-seven countries, including Norway and Australia. Sinclair was traveling with an autistic teenager he had been mentoring. Now, for the first time, he found himself in the role of a parent, solely responsible for the boy's safety. "That experience really gave me insight into what parents are going through," he says. "I can remember looking at this kid and being terrified of what was going to happen to him in this world."

As he stood on the podium, Sinclair aimed to dispel several long-standing myths, starting with Lovaas's notion that there was a normal child trapped within the "autistic shell," waiting to be rescued. Sinclair described autism instead as "a way of being . . . [that] colors every experience, every sensation, perception, thought, emotion, and encounter, every aspect of existence."

He acknowledged that some amount of grief was natural but stressed the importance of parents separating their expectations of an idealized child from the child in front of them who desperately needs their love and support. He pointed out that if grief goes on too long, it transmits a dangerous message to the child: that they are inadequate as they are.

> This is what we hear when you mourn over our existence. This is what we hear when you pray for a cure. This is what we know, when you tell us of your fondest hopes and dreams for us: that your greatest wish is that one day we will cease to be, and strangers you can love will move in behind our faces.

He admitted that autism presents a particularly difficult challenge for parents, because the child inhabits a different world of subjective experience from the one that they take for granted. But he emphasized the fact that much of the suffering associated with autism is the result of the ways that autistic people and their families are habitually denied the services they need. He encouraged parents to get mad about *that*, and to use their collective power to change it. "We need you. We need your help and your understanding," he said. "Yes, there is tragedy that comes with autism: not because of what we are, but because of the things that happen to us . . . Grieve if you must, for your own lost dreams. But don't mourn for *us*. We are alive. We are real. And we're here waiting for you."

Sinclair's talk was warmly received, and parents clustered around the ANI booth for the remainder of the conference, including a singer-songwriter named Connie Deming who dropped by to give him a copy of a song called "Butterflies" that she had written for her son David. "I learned more about my son by talking to those people for an hour than I learned talking to everyone else," she says. "They were more compassionate, more accurate, and more understanding."

IN THE DAYS TO COME, however, there was a wave of backlash from parents on the St. John's list about Autistics "wasting bandwidth" by excitedly perseverating about the conference. These flame wars intensified over the next few months, leaving Autistics who had been happy to be of service by answering parents' questions feeling betrayed.

ANI decided to launch its own online list, ANI-L, in 1994. Parents and professionals were welcome to join, but a set of principles and policies were developed in order to ensure that the list remained safe space for Autistics. "We are here to affirm that autistic lives are meaningful and worthwhile," the FAQ advised. "Discussions about ways to make autistic people 'less autistic,' to 'cure' autism, to render autistic people indistinguishable from non-autistic people, or to prevent the births of future autistic people, demean and devalue our lives as autistic people. These topics are not appropriate for this list."

Like a specialized ecological niche, ANI-L acted as an incubator for Autistic culture, accelerating its evolution. In 1995, an organization for parents of "high-functioning" children asked Sinclair to organize a series of presentations at an upcoming conference. He opened up the process to the members of ANI-L, who explored ways of making the event as a whole more accessible and comfortable for people on the spectrum. They requested that a special quiet room be set aside for people who needed to chill out or totally shut down for a while. They also devised an ingeniously low-tech solution to a complex problem. Even highly verbal autistic adults occasionally struggle with processing and producing speech, particularly in the chaotic and generally overwhelming atmosphere of a conference. By providing attendees with name-tag holders and pieces of paper that were red on one side and yellow on the other, they enabled Autistics to communicate their needs and desires without having to articulate them in the pressure of the moment. The red side facing out signified, "Nobody should try to interact with me," while the yellow side meant, "Only people I already know should interact with me, not strangers." (Green badges were added later to signify, "I want to interact but am having trouble initiating, so please initiate an interaction with me.") These color-coded "interaction signal badges" turned out to be so useful that they have since been widely adopted at autistic-run events all over the world, and name-tag labels similar to Autreat ("autistic retreat") green badges have recently been employed at conferences for Perl programmers to indicate that the wearer is open to spontaneous social approaches.

ANI's involvement resulted in a new level of Autistic representation at an event for parents and professionals. But numerous problems arose behind the scenes. One of the organizers told Sinclair to instruct "low-functioning" Autistics not to attend the conference, even accompanied by their parents—a directive he ignored. It was becoming clear that trying to create little islands of autistic space at NT-run conferences had built-in limitations that could never be remedied by huddling in coatrooms and passing out color-coded badges. It was time for the Autistics to hold a conference of their own.

THE FIRST AUTREAT was held at Camp Bristol Hills in Canandaigua, New York, in late July 1996. Quiet and remote, situated in the natural splendor of the Finger Lakes region, the camp offered ANI an opportunity to create an environment that was relatively free of the sensory assaults that were unavoidable in most urban conference centers.

The theme of the conference was "Celebrating Autistic Culture," and nearly sixty people came. The group was as diverse as the spectrum itself, including nonspeaking adults who used letterboards to communicate, an urban planner who worked at the Los Angeles International Airport, and the late photographer Dan Asher, who chronicled the early days of punk and reggae in New York City while hanging out with novelist William Burroughs in his bunker on the Lower East Side. The program included presentations on "self-advocacy" (a term borrowed from the disability rights movement), educating law-enforcement personnel, and the history of Deaf culture, which offered instructive parallels for the culture being born at Autreat.

The conference began with an orientation session in the main lodge led by Sinclair, who explained the guidelines that had been established to maintain and preserve the environment as autistic space. Photographs and videos could only be taken after asking for permission, and only outdoors, so that the flash didn't trigger seizures. Cigarette smoking and perfumes were banned. Respect for each person's solitude and personal space was essential, and the interaction badges allowed everyone to know at a glance who was open to talking. All of the conference events were optional, including the orientation itself; the overriding principle was "opportunity but not pressure."

For a Bard College professor named Valerie Paradiz, attending the first Autreat with her six-year-old son Elijah was a crucial milestone in her journey toward understanding both her son and herself. As they made the drive from Woodstock, they listened to the soundtrack from Elijah's favorite movie, *Pinocchio*, four times in a row, which kept him calm as they ventured down unfamiliar roads to an unfamiliar place. Valerie decided at orientation that she would let her son take the lead: "It was immediately clear to me that Elijah and I were involved in a grand experiment. I would walk where he wished to walk. I would play whatever games he wished to play for as long as he liked. I would lie around with him in our cabin for hours, listening to *Pinocchio*. There were no other responsibilities."

As Valerie and Elijah strolled around the campground, they saw people of all ages who seemed perfectly content whether alone or in a group. Some read books in the sun while others played musical instruments. Some strode briskly along the paths while others walked beside service animals or navigated in wheelchairs. Some talked loudly, flapping their hands, as others tapped silently on letterboards. Of necessity, autistic space was tolerant of a wide range of behavior, because autistics are even more different from one another than they are from NTs. Each person who came to Autreat had their own unique set of abilities and intense interests, which they had been pursuing for years in solitude with monastic devotion. "Each was a star in the sky," Valerie reflected, "and Elijah was a part of that universe."

Autreat became an annual event and provided a template for similar conferences in other countries, including Autscape in England and Projekt Empowerment in Sweden. The most commonly reported experience at these gatherings was that the participants didn't *feel* disabled, though their neurology had not changed.

IV

A new idea was brewing at events like Autreat and in the myriad of autistic spaces taking root online. It turned out to be an idea as old as Asperger's notion that people with the traits of his syndrome have always been part of the human community, standing apart, quietly making the world that mocks and shuns them a better place. In the late 1990s, a student of anthropology and sociology in Australia named Judy Singer, who possesses many of those traits herself, gave that idea a name: *neurodiversity.*

A few years earlier, she had been given a thought-provoking assignment by her rabbi: to develop a version of the Ten Commandments that were better than God's. The occasion was the annual commemoration of the giving of the Torah to Moses and the Jewish people on Mount Sinai, Shavuot. Singer—who considers herself culturally Jewish but is no fan of organized religion—says that she was a bit hesitant to accept the rabbi's challenge because she feared that it "would be rigged in favor of Omniscience." But she marshaled enough chutzpah to come up with a First Commandment that reflected her commitment to the health of the environment: *Honor diversity, lest thou endeth up like unto the cactus of the desert.*

The rabbi ignored her suggestion, Singer says. Such failures of communication were common in her life and always had been. Her mother's odd behavior had been a continuous source of confusion and vexation when she was growing up. Even her body language struck Singer as inexplicably strange, yet when she begged her father to take her mother to see a psychiatrist, he denied that there was any sort of problem, saying, "Everybody's just different, you've got to accept people the way they are." Yet even he regularly became exasperated with his wife's failure to pick up on other people's feelings. Nearly every day, someone in the family would snap at her, "Why can't you be normal for once in your life?"

The eccentricities of Singer's mother were usually chalked up to external factors, primarily the fact that she had managed to survive Auschwitz, an overbearing fact about which even her own daughter was not supposed to ask questions. As Singer got older, she began poring through psychology textbooks in attempts to crack her mother's "case."

Then Singer had a daughter of her own. By the time she was two, it was obvious that she was not developing in the typical way. Singer read an article on early infantile autism that described her daughter's behavior accurately in many respects, but there was also a crucial difference. Kanner's first cardinal sign of his syndrome was a total lack of "affective contact" with others, but her daughter was a loving and affectionate little girl. Still, the parallels were inescapable. Singer confided her suspicions to a friend. It was much more likely, the friend said, that Singer was passing the maladaptations of her own family on to the next generation. The only way to break this cycle was for Singer to confess her own guilt, she advised. But Singer knew she was a warm and attentive mother, and she soon found herself exiled from her circle of friends.

As her daughter got older, the traits she shared with her grandmother became more apparent. But instead of thinking in terms of neuroses and dysfunctions, Singer thought in terms of heredity. She had always been slow of speech and often felt alienated from her peers and from society in general. Perhaps some kind of organic difference was being passed down through the branches of her family tree.

THE TURNING POINT IN Singer's understanding was reading a book called *Disability: Whose Handicap?* by Ann Shearer, a Jungian analyst in London who probed the ways that people with physical and cognitive differences are systematically disabled, excluded, and demonized by society. Singer wept as she read accounts of disabled people being brutalized over the centuries while acknowledging her own participation in such marginalization, even in her own family. Shearer observed, "Just how handicapping the limitations of disability become depends either on how well the environment is adapted to the range of people who use it, or on the opportunities they have had to learn to cope with it, or both." Singer was helped along in this process by a peer counselor who had survived polio and encouraged her to see her conflicts with her mother in light of broader social dynamics rather than as a kind of family curse.

After her daughter's diagnosis of Asperger's syndrome at age nine, Singer began to recognize autistic traits in herself. By reading Williams's *Nobody Nowhere* and Sacks's profile of Grandin, she understood that being autistic does not mean being devoid of empathy, and that the spectrum spans a broad range of intellectual ability. She felt like she had finally found "her people."

Singer joined a mailing list called Independent Living on the Autism Spectrum (InLv), run by a computer programmer in the Netherlands named Martijn Dekker. The exchanges on the list ran the gamut from questions about employment to musing on how NTs gauge the right moment to look one another in the eye during conversation. (The list members concluded that it was obligatory at the beginning and the end, but optional in between.) Many of the regular posters were women. InLv was another nutrient-rich tide pool that accelerated the evolution of Autistic culture.

People with dyslexia, ADHD, dyscalculia, and a myriad of other conditions (christened "Cousins" in the early days of ANI) were also welcome to join the list. The collective ethos of InLv, said writer and list member Harvey Blume in the *New York Times* in 1997, was "neurological pluralism." He was the first mainstream journalist to pick up on the significance of online communities for people with neurological differences. "The impact of the Internet on autistics," Blume predicted, "may one day be compared in magnitude to the spread of sign language among the deaf."

In telephone conversations sparked by their exchanges on the list, Blume and Singer elaborated on the concept of neurological pluralism, which was an apt but cumbersome phrase. Singer, too, was thinking about parallels between Autistics and the Deaf community, and how both groups were empowering themselves by emphasizing their differences from the dominant culture rather than by trying to pass as normal. It was in these talks with Blume that she came up with the term *neurodiversity.*

Singer hoped that the concept of honoring neurodiversity would spread through the disability rights community as a rallying cry, as phrases like "Black is beautiful," "Gay is good," and "Sisterhood is powerful" had helped mobilize mass movements in the 1960s and 1970s. "I was interested in the liberatory, activist aspects of it," Singer explained to author Andrew Solomon in 2008, "to do for neurologically different people what feminism and gay rights had done for their constituencies." In her undergraduate thesis at the University of Technology in Sydney, *Odd People In*, she claimed that the "hidden" constituency for a rebellion of the neurodivergent was much more vast than traditional estimates of autism prevalence would suggest:

> Think back over all those "odd people out," the people who "seem to come from another planet," "march to a different drum." They are the brainy but socially inept nerds at school, the pedants who defy all attempts to divert them from their special interests. Think of those people who hover frozen and blinking at the edges of conversations, unsure when to break in, seemingly operating on a different timescale from everyone else.

Blume was the first person to use the term in the press, writing in the *Atlantic* in 1998, "NT is only one kind of brain wiring, and, when it comes to working with hi-tech, quite possibly an inferior one . . . Neurodiversity may be every bit as crucial for the human race as biodiversity is for life in general. Who can say what form of wiring will prove best at any given moment?"

In his view, it wasn't just that more autistics were becoming visible in the world, but the world itself was becoming more autistic—and this was a good thing. The revenge of the nerds was taking shape as a society in which anyone who had access to a computer and a modem could feel less disabled by the limitations of space and time.

Autism had come a long way since the days when Kanner could pronounce from his papal seat at Johns Hopkins that he had seen only 150 true cases in his career. It was Asperger's world now.

In 2004, two teenagers named Alex Plank and Dan Grover launched Wrong Planet, one of the first autistic spaces on the World Wide Web. They were both digital natives, fluent in the use of the tools that their neurological cousins in previous generations had built for them. A Linux developer while still in high school, Plank contributed dozens of articles and more than ten thousand edits to Wikipedia by the time he was sixteen, writing on Catholic saints, African American abolitionists, Oregon missionaries, fictional species, the Scottsboro Boys, women's suffrage, Banana Yoshimoto, the Articles of the Confederacy, nudibranchs, Greek mythology, Thoreau, Kabbalah, and cryptozoology, among a host of other subjects. He had also suffered the same kinds of bullying, ridicule, and exclusion as many of his atypical peers.

Growing up, Plank had felt confident that his social status as a dork was the inevitable side effect of being highly gifted. He found out he had been diagnosed with Asperger's only by rifling through his parents' drawers. "I had always been told I was special and awesome," Plank says, "then I got this label that made me feel like a loser. So I decided to prove everyone wrong."

Plastering his walls with Apple "Think Different" posters featuring personal heroes like Einstein, Jim Henson, and Miles Davis, he cruised through cyberspace in search of other young autistics but found very few hangouts for them among the many resources for parents. But then he stumbled on a website called Aspergia that was supposed to be like an enchanted island for people with autism. "I met a kid there my age who lived in Vermont. I was like, 'This site sucks.' And he was like, 'Yeah, we could do better.' That was Dan. We decided we would make a new website."

Collaborating via instant messaging, they used open-source tools to whip up community forums on social skills, bullying, and anxiety, with opportunities for members to contribute their own stories and poetry. After poaching Aspergia's best moderators and seeding its forums with buzz about the new website (which instantly made Aspergia obsolete), they blasted out an online press release highlighting the fact that Wrong Planet's creators were fifteen and seventeen years old (Grover and Plank respectively). "The goal is to alleviate those with Asperger's from this pressure that they need to conform," Grover said in the press release. "What is best is to learn how to use your uniqueness to your advantage and find your place in the world." (He later became a successful software entrepreneur, selling his interactive sheet music app, Etude, to Steinway & Sons, the venerable piano company, while Plank became a consultant for the popular TV series *The Bridge*, helping actress Diane Kruger develop the character of Sonya Cross, a detective with Asperger's syndrome.)

For two young men generally too shy to ask a girl out to the local multiplex on Saturday night, they proved adept at promoting their creation in social media, buying placement in Google's AdSense and AdWords so a reporter new to the autism beat would inevitably be directed to Wrong Planet while generating a healthy income stream for the site. The community grew slowly and steadily until Slashdot, the preeminent tech news aggregator, linked to Plank's interview with Bram Cohen, the autistic creator of BitTorrent, a peer-to-peer file-sharing protocol estimated to account for a third of all Internet traffic in the United States. New members poured in by the thousands.

Young people on the spectrum flocked to online communities like

Wrong Planet to announce their diagnoses as cause for celebration rather than as occasions for mourning, because their lives had at last come into focus. It remained to be seen, however, whether a bunch of brainy kids tapping away at their keyboards could evolve into a social force formidable enough to oppose the rhetoric of disease and disorder that had intensified after the publication of Wakefield's study. Could an aggregation of loners become a movement?

V

In December 2007, a series of ominous billboards appeared on street corners and telephone kiosks in Manhattan. Looking like a ransom note, one of the ads read, "We have your son. We will make sure he will not be able to care for himself or interact socially as long as he lives. This is only the beginning." Another warned: "We have your son. We are destroying his ability for social interaction and driving him into a life of complete isolation. It's up to you now." The first was signed "Autism," and the second, "Asperger's syndrome." The ads—produced on a pro bono basis by BBDO, the PR powerhouse that inspired *Mad Men*—were no more histrionic or stigmatizing than the messages that fund-raising organizations like Autism Speaks had been pumping out for years, comparing autism to cancer, cystic fibrosis, and other potentially fatal diseases. (Indeed, BBDO had done similar work for Autism Speaks.) In this case, however, the ads' sponsor was NYU's prestigious Child Study Center, launching a new campaign to alert the public to the "silent public health epidemic" of childhood mental illness. In the words of the center's press release, twelve million children in America were being "held hostage by a psychiatric disorder." "It's like with AIDS," the center's director, Harold Koplewicz, told the *New York Times*. "Everyone needs to be concerned and informed."

But then something unexpected happened. A fledgling organization called the Autistic Self-Advocacy Network (ASAN), along with equally outraged parents, launched a firestorm of e-mails and blogs in NYU's direction objecting to the demeaning wording of the ads, joined by prominent disability rights groups. This well-coordinated offensive seemed to surge out of nowhere, and at first Koplewicz felt confident that he could brush it off. He boasted to reporters that traffic to the Child Study Center's website had doubled in the first ten days of the campaign. After consulting with his colleagues, he told reporters that he had no plans to back down and that the ads would soon be running in other cities, along with print ads in *Newsweek* and other national publications. "I thought we'd be fighting ignorance," he said. "I didn't think we'd be fighting adult patients."

In fact, what had happened was that, for the first time in history, autistics were challenging a conversation about autism in mainstream media without the help of a parent-run organization that claimed to speak for them. The architect of the protest was not a child, a parent, or an "adult patient," but a smart, savvy, and determined policy wonk named Ari Ne'eman, the nineteen-year-old co-founder of the Autistic Self-Advocacy Network.

A burly, handsome young man who looked like a rabbi in training, Ne'eman had come a long way from the days when he was forced to ride in a van for an hour and a half in both directions every day to attend classes at a segregated school for special-needs children rather than being able to walk to the school located five minutes from his family's house in New Jersey.

The first word Ne'eman said as a baby was *Abba*, the Hebrew word for "Father." His mother moved to Israel when she was a teenager to become a paratrooper in the army. There, she met her husband-to-be, a designer of smart-card technology who fought in the Yom Kippur War. When Ne'eman was two and a half years old, he fell in love with dinosaurs, like many children; but, unlike most kids at that age, he could correctly identify an enormous winged skeleton to a guard at the American Museum of Natural History as a pterodactyl. When he and his friend Aryeh (the similarity of their names was pleasing to both of them) were still in grade school, they decided they would become the world's youngest defense contractors. They ordered a microwave-emitting vacuum tube online, which was luckily delivered to the wrong address, and Ne'eman was grounded for months. (In the coming years, he and Aryeh would refer to this as "the Magnetron Incident.")

A story on tape that his father used to listen to while driving made a deep impression on Ne'eman. A young man who renounces his Judaism is warned by his grandfather, "Don't waste time, don't waste time." In Jewish day school, Ne'eman learned the phrase *tikkun olam*, which means living in a way that helps heal the broken world.

After his Asperger's diagnosis at age twelve, he had to leave that school, which he loved. He hadn't changed, but the attitudes of everyone around him seemed to be transformed overnight. "Suddenly I went from being someone that people believed had a lot of potential," Ne'eman recalls, "to someone who surprised people by any positive attribute that I might display. Before, everyone focused on the things that I was good at, the things that I wanted out of life, and the subjects I was interested in. After I was diagnosed, everybody focused on the things I struggled with, and the things that made me different, which were often the same things that people had framed as positive before. All of a sudden, the kinds of opportunities that I was offered changed tremendously."

Struggling to make sense of what was happening to him, he got online, where he read Sinclair's "Don't Mourn for Us" and other writings by the first wave of neurodiversity activists. He also began researching the history of the disability rights movement, because it struck him that many of his difficulties were not "symptoms" of his autism, but problems built into the ways that society treats people who don't meet the standard expectations of "normal."

He read about disability rights pioneers like Ed Roberts, who contracted polio as a teenager in 1953. Paralyzed from the neck down, he had to sleep in an iron lung. He was accepted into UC Berkeley over the objections of a dean who told him, "We've tried cripples before and it doesn't work." The school administrators eventually consented to allowing Roberts to move his iron lung into a wing of Cowell Hospital, where a dozen other quadriplegics eventually took up residence, christening themselves "the Rolling Quads"—the first on-campus self-advocacy group for disabled students. The advocacy work of Roberts and the Rolling Quads became the foundation of the independent living movement, based on the principles that the real disability experts are people with disabilities, because they can offer practical guidance to their peers.

Ne'eman was also inspired by the story of another polio survivor, Judy Heumann, who successfully sued the New York City Board of Education after it denied her a teaching certificate by claiming that she would not be able to shepherd her students out of a building in case of fire. She founded a self-advocacy group called Disabled in Action, one of the key organizations that mounted public protests to pressure President Nixon into signing the Rehabilitation Act of 1973, the seminal law that banned discrimination on the basis of disability in programs conducted by federal agencies or receiving federal funding, and in employment by federal contractors. The act became the model for dozens of civil rights laws worldwide, including the Americans with Disabilities Act passed by Congress in 1990. Under President Obama, Heumann serves as the State Department's special envoy for disability rights.

To Ne'eman, people like Roberts and Heumann were clearly national heroes of the stature of Martin Luther King Jr., but he felt that there was a strange disconnect between the autistic community and the broader disability rights movement. Outside of a few references to Deaf culture in the early ANI literature, autism was still discussed almost exclusively in medical rather than social terms. This was particularly true at the height of the Autism Wars, when virtually all the media coverage revolved around the vaccine controversy.

"I reached out to find writing about the neurodiversity movement in large part because I felt what was happening to me was wrong, but I didn't have a framework for understanding why, or what 'right' might be," Ne'eman recalls. "I always felt that these things were wrong—not just for me, but for a lot of people. And I didn't just want to get out, I wanted to end the fact that there was an 'in.'"

For people with Asperger's syndrome, "in" and "out" turned out to be even more complex and multilayered than he thought. One day in high school, Ne'eman told a friend, "I'm thinking about getting involved in activism, because autistic people are really discriminated against as a minority, and we have to do something about this. We have to organize." His friend looked at him and said, "Ari, you don't even know, you're so unusual. There's no way you have anything in common with other autistic people." The diversity of the spectrum made organizing difficult by opening up wedge issues that drove various factions of the community apart. Some "high-functioning" people went out of their way to distance themselves from "low-functioning" people, and didn't want anything to do with the word *disability*. But Ne'eman rejected this approach, as Jim Sinclair had done before him, because all autistic people would benefit from destigmatizing the condition and improving access to services and education.

Ne'eman managed to get himself readmitted to the mainstream school in his neighborhood for one period a day in the afternoon, which opened up a world of extracurricular activities to him. He signed up for anything that had to do with policy and politics: Model UN, Model Congress, Debate Club, Mock Trial, and the Future Business Leaders of America. By the summer of 2006, he had started attending autism conferences. He was disappointed in how little interest there seemed to be in issues of public policy among the celebrities in the autism world, whom he started thinking of as "professional autistics." Discussions of policy at these events rarely went beyond talk of launching online petitions and sending e-mails to Congress. Sitting in an atrium in Manhattan one day, he found himself reading two letters back-to-back. One was from New Jersey governor Jon Corzine, appointing him as the student representative to the state's Special Education Commission, and the other was from the University of Medicine and Dentistry, inviting Ne'eman to help plan an autism program for adults. It occurred to him, "When I go to these things, I shouldn't just be Ari. I should be representing a larger group of people and acting as a conduit for their access."

He decided that he would help found an organization that would represent autistics in discussions of public policy. One of the first people he called for help was Scott Robertson, a graduate student he'd met a few months earlier. "I brought the politics and the policy and Scott brought the research. We made a great team. We both talked about our personal experience, but we used it as punctuation on the talk about the issues. I really respected that. He was someone who was clearly an autistic professional, not a professional autistic." ASAN was founded in 2006 and soon attracted other members, including Paula Durbin-Westby, who began sitting in on meetings of the Interagency Autism Coordinating Committee in Washington, which coordinates policy within the Department of Health and Human Services and helps set the federal research agenda.

The ransom notes campaign was ASAN's collective initiation: proof that the people formerly known as "patients" could redefine the terms of a public discussion of autism by a powerful institution.

On December 6, the day after the Child Study Center's ad campaign made its debut at a gala dinner for eight hundred people featuring appearances by Hillary Clinton and *CBS Evening News* anchor Katie Couric, messages started pouring into ASAN's inbox demanding a response. Ne'eman e-mailed the Child Study Center politely expressing his concerns and left phone messages, but got no reply. Two days later, ASAN blasted out an action alert with contact numbers and e-mail addresses for the Child Study Center, the director of the NYU Medical Center, BBDO, and the two donors who provided funding for the university's Asperger Institute.

Parents offended by the ads were starting to light up the blogosphere. After reading the ad signed "Autism," a blogger who called herself MOM-NOS replied:

Dear Autism,

You don't have my son; I do.

I will make sure that he is never defined by his autism alone, and I will help him to recognize that, although his autism makes some things incredibly challenging, it also brings with it remarkable gifts. I will make sure that we work on his challenges. I will make sure that we celebrate his gifts.

This is only the beginning.

Kristina Chew, the former classics professor whose acceptance of her son Charlie helped Shannon Rosa come to terms with Leo's autism, wrote on her blog *Autism Vox*:

> This is a "public awareness" campaign that makes the public aware only of one very dark aspect of being an autistic person and of raising an autistic child. Spend a day in our household and, while you will witness more than a few moments of anxiety, fretfulness, and a bit of noise, I hope you might most of all sense my son's limitless desire to do his best, to struggle through his worries, and to smile and speak in half-echoed snatches of phrases—his patience and his constant efforts to try and try harder. It is not a household that Charlie, or Jim or I, feel at all in need of being rescued from.

Ne'eman spent all twenty-four hours of his twentieth birthday, on December 10, coordinating ASAN's response. The group's chances of success seemed slim. NYU was powerful, and BBDO's campaign represented hundreds of thousands of dollars in pro bono work. By contrast, ASAN hadn't yet rented an office or opened a bank account. To persuade other disability advocacy groups to sign a letter of protest, Ne'eman cold-called Bob Kafka, the national director of ADAPT, one of the leading disability rights organizations in the country, with chapters in thirty states. Kafka agreed to sign the letter immediately, and thirteen other organizations quickly added their names to the list. Since Ne'eman had not yet gotten a response from NYU, an ASAN representative hand-delivered it to the receptionist at the Child Study Center, who looked haggard as phones rang in the background. By then, the *Wall Street Journal*, the *New York Times*, the *Daily News*, and other major media outlets were running stories on the controversy. After receiving thousands of calls, letters, and e-mails from across the country, the Child Study Center finally agreed to pull the ads.

It was the first of many victories for ASAN. In 2010, after being nominated by President Obama, Ne'eman took a seat on the National Council on Disability (NCD). In recent years, ASAN has played a significant role in influencing the formulation of federal disability policy. In 2014, when Obama issued an executive order raising the minimum wage for federal contractors, the Secretary of Labor announced that tens of thousands of workers with disabilities making subminimum wages—sometimes as low as a few cents an hour—would be exempt from the new higher wage. In response, ASAN assembled a diverse coalition of organizations—including the American Civil Liberties Union, the AFL-CIO, and the National Association for the Deaf—that persuaded the White House to reverse its decision and include disabled workers in the order, a bridge-building effort that paid off with a historical achievement at the highest level of policy-making.

When the APA drafted its new set of criteria for the *DSM-5*, ASAN staffers worked with the subcommittee to ensure that the coping skills employed by autistic teenagers and adults to fit in would not be used to exclude them from a diagnosis, while other revisions they suggested highlighted the needs of historically underdiagnosed populations, including women and people of color. Nearly eighty years after the discovery of the autistic continuum by Asperger's team at the Heilpädagogik Station, its full breadth was finally reflected in the APA's criteria.

Ironically, the syndrome that made Asperger's name a household word in the 1990s after decades of obscurity also disappeared from the same edition of the manual, folded into the umbrella of autism spectrum disorder. But the fact that the APA included autistic people in the decision-making process was a fitting tribute to a man who collaborated with "uneducable" students like Harro to develop his innovative teaching methods.

As the concept of neurodiversity takes root on college campuses, ASAN has developed into an incubator for the next generation of disability rights activists, many of whom are women. Lydia Brown, an alum of the organization's summer leadership training program, provided testimony to the United Nations Special Rapporteur on Torture that increased public pressure on the Judge Rotenberg Educational Center's continued use of electric shock on autistic children. Brown was named a White House Champion for change in 2013. Another alum, Kris Guin, went on to launch an organization called Queerability to explore the intersection between disability and LGBT issues.

ASAN's Julia Bascom published a groundbreaking anthology of essays by people on the spectrum called *Loud Hands*, which offered a broad range of autistic perspectives on such issues as being labeled "low-functioning" and the harm inflicted by organizations like Autism Speaks that frame autistic people as a tragedy and a burden to society. "One of the cruelest tricks our culture plays on autistic people is that it makes us strangers to ourselves," Bascom wrote, adding that autistics are no longer willing to be "spectators in our own stories."

VI

For parents like Craig and Shannon Rosa, the emergence of the neurodiversity movement has offered ways of fighting for a better future for their children that don't depend on hopes of recovery. It has also made something available to young people on the spectrum that previous generations of autistic people never had: role models of happy, creative, and socially engaged autistic lives.

At a conference in May 2011, Shannon met a professor from Adelphi University named Stephen Shore. When Shore was eighteen months old, he suddenly lost the ability to speak. A year later, he was diagnosed with "atypical development with strong autistic tendencies," and his doctors recommended institutionalization. His parents refused to give up on him and instead created a comprehensive intervention program for him emphasizing music, movement, and techniques to help him integrate the confusing barrage of information from his senses. At four, his spoken language returned, and he went on to earn a PhD in special education at Boston University.

At the conference, Shannon told him that she wished she could find a music teacher for Leo. That October, he arrived at the Rosas' house to give Leo his first lesson. Now in his fifties, Shore is a witty and affable man with a neatly trimmed beard who revels in his autistic eccentricities. (He praises things that he likes by calling them "very stimmy.") At first, Leo didn't seem to notice that Shore had entered the room, but he quickly warmed up to him. For kids with limited expressive language like Leo, Shore has found that music can serve as a more natural medium of communication than speech.

First, Shore sat down at a table with a pen, a piece of paper, a ruler, and a stack of Post-its, and indicated that Leo was welcome to sit with him. He didn't become impatient as Leo orbited around the room, gradually coming to rest in the chair next to Shore. Then Shore asked Leo to draw a straight line on the paper, using the ruler, and then three more perpendicular lines, creating a grid. Shore asked Leo to name the first letter of the alphabet and he said "A!" He prompted Leo to draw an *A* in the first box on the grid, which he did successfully. Eventually, Leo had filled in the grid with the first seven letters of the alphabet, corresponding to the range of keys on his sister Zelly's electronic keyboard. Then Shore took a stack of Post-its that had been labeled with these letters and began laying them across the tops of the appropriate keys. Leo quickly picked up on the pattern and completed it himself, earning praise from Shore.

At no point did Shore compel Leo to do something he didn't want to do. If Leo jumped up and hopped up and down for a minute because he got excited, that was okay. Shore acted like there was all the time in the world. The little tasks he gave Leo quickly became self-rewarding, because they played to a classic autistic strength: pattern recognition. Together, they turned the eighty-eight keys on the keyboard into a map that Leo could then explore by playing the notes. Shannon had never seen anyone "get" Leo so quickly. (Shore confesses that he finds neurotypical kids harder to teach, because he doesn't understand how their minds work.) By the end of the hourlong lesson, Leo could play a simple, pleasing sequence of notes—and he had also learned that he could be good at doing something he had never tried before.

One of the most important lessons that Shannon and Craig have learned on their journey with Leo is patience. Instead of comparing his arc of development to an idealized set of milestones, they have come to accept that he is unfolding at his own pace. Two steps forward and three steps back—and then, one day, a hurtling leap into his own future, as if he'd been saving it up.

So that parents just starting out on the journey with their own children don't have to go through the ordeal that the Rosas did, Shannon and her circle of friends launched a website called Thinking Person's Guide to Autism. The range of subjects covered on the site is broad (from "Outings, Travel, and Autism" to "When Is Medication the Right Choice for Your Child?") and there's no whitewashing or promotion of dubious treatments. Just the facts, from people a little further down the road.

Some of the site's regular contributors are on the spectrum themselves, and some are autistic parents of autistic children, like Carol Greenburg. I visited Carol; her husband, John Ordover; and their son Arren at their home in Brooklyn, which was decorated with artifacts reflecting their shared love of science fiction, including a replica of a brain in a bubbling aquarium. They met at a *Star Trek* convention as teenagers, married years later, and eventually became the editors of the *Star Trek* book franchise.

As a young girl, Carol was drawn to *Star Trek* because she saw a metaphor for an inclusive society in the multiracial, multispecies crew of the *Enterprise*. "There was no one who was left out in the *Star Trek* universe, no one who was ostracized, no one who was too weird. In fact, the weirder you were, the cooler you were, because you had more to bring to the table," she says. "That was a lifesaving message for a kid who got bullied for being different. Look at Geordi, who had a visual impairment but had access to technology that enabled him to turn it into a gift and made it possible for him to see things that other people couldn't see. I wanted to live on the *Enterprise*."

Predictably, the member of the crew that Carol related to most was Mr. Spock, who seemed much cooler than the conniving and chronically intemperate humans around him. (When her peers ridiculed her in school, she would ask herself, "What would Spock do?") When Arren was diagnosed, she began researching autism online and kept seeing messages for parents like "Prepare to have to enter a totally different world to understand your child." But reading the descriptions she kept thinking, "Different how?"

Carol was diagnosed two years later, at age forty-four. Now she works as a special-education advocate for families, helping them through the process of having their children evaluated, developing an individualized education program, and accompanying them to IEP meetings.

As we wrapped up our interview, night was falling in Brooklyn. Arren came downstairs and said, "Light candles, light candles." When he first started doing this, Carol and John became concerned about his sudden interest in fire. But then they heard him whisper "*Baruch*," the first word of the Hebrew blessing for the Sabbath. Though it wasn't actually the Sabbath, Carol and Arren went into the kitchen, lit candles at the stove, and sang the old prayers together anyway. "When I look at my son," she says, "I think, 'He's not broken. He's just neurologically outnumbered, like me.'"

On a drizzly, windswept afternoon in 2012—a typical spring day in San Francisco—Shannon and Leo visited the California Academy of Sciences with Julia Bascom and Zoe Gross of ASAN. The Cal Academy, located in Golden Gate Park, is one of Leo's favorite places to go, because it boasts an aquarium that wraps around overhead (allowing Leo to lie flat on a bench looking up through schools of glittering fish) and a planetarium ("I want to go to *space*!" he says).

Friends like Julia and Zoe are able to translate Leo's world into terms that Shannon can understand. After she posted a video of her son furiously pacing in a circle at the top level of an elaborate jungle gym in a playground, Zoe commented:

> Oh wow, what a great video. That pacing looks delicious (delicious is a food word, but acceptable here because I refer to a pleasurable and nutritious component of one's sensory diet). There's a certain size of circle you can pace—the one Leo's doing here looks about perfect for his height—

> that gives you a sensation of pressure in your body, when you find yourself leaning inward to stay on course.

Leo also clearly enjoys being around people who are on the same wavelength. When Zoe sits down in the wraparound aquarium, Leo sits down too. (She's wearing headphones to limit the confusing barrage of noise in public spaces.) He gently slides his fingertips down her forearm while twiddling one of his ever-present straws between his lips, and she brushes his forearm in return. Then he lies down on the bench in a comfortable tilde shape to stare up at the fish while resting his head in the softness of her lap, and she's okay with that. After a while, he flips over on his belly and looks at the floor through the narrow slats in the bench, enjoying a quiet moment to himself. She's okay with that too. Finally he gathers himself up so that he's facing Zoe and gently interlaces his fingers with hers and commences rocking back and forth, making a kind of human seesaw. Only when a loud group of children comes bustling through their little sanctuary do they decide it's time to move on.

Leo gets a little upset when his mother decides that there's not enough time to "go to space" today, but soon he's blissed out in front of the main window of the aquarium, pacing back and forth along its full length, gently resting himself or pressing against the glass periodically, as if this invisible boundary is somehow reassuring. (Later, as Leo, Zoe, and Julia walk down a hall, they each nonchalantly tap the same spot on the wall as they pass, as if it provides a useful coordinate for situating their bodies in space.)

On our way out of the museum, Leo spots a big, white puffy dinosaur wearing a striped orange scarf, which exerts an irresistible attraction upon him. He puts his face right up to the face of this improbable creature (really a guide in a dinosaur suit), gazing at it intently from a couple of inches away. The employees at the Cal Academy are well aware of the fact that kids like Leo love dinosaurs, and no one bats an eye. As we walk out into the soft rain, Shannon bends her head down, kisses the crown of her son's head, and says, "You did good, friend."

Twelve

BUILDING THE *ENTERPRISE*: DESIGNS FOR A NEURODIVERSE WORLD

We need all hands on deck to right the ship of humanity.

—Zosia Zaks

What is autism?

Eight decades after Gottfried's grandmother brought him to the door of Asperger's clinic seeking to understand his behavior, many aspects of this question are still open. But there are a few points on which clinicians, parents, and neurodiversity advocates agree.

Most researchers now believe that autism is not a single unified entity but a cluster of underlying conditions. These conditions produce a distinctive constellation of behavior and needs that manifests in different ways at various stages of an individual's development. Adequately addressing these needs requires a lifetime of support from parents, educators, and the community, as Asperger predicted back in 1938. He was equally prescient in insisting that the traits of autism are "not at all rare." In fact, given current estimates of prevalence, autistic people constitute one of the largest minorities in the world. There are roughly as many people on the spectrum in America as there are Jews.

A thorough review of history also vindicates Asperger's notion that autistic people have always been part of the human community, though they have often been relegated to the margins of society. For most of the twentieth century, they were hidden behind a welter of competing labels—Sukhareva's "schizoid personality disorder," Despert and Bender's "childhood schizophrenia," Robinson and Vitale's "children with circumscribed interests," Grandin's initial diagnosis of "minimal brain damage," and many other labels not mentioned in this book, such as "multiplex personality disorder," which have fallen out of use. In the wake of the vaccine controversy, however, society continues to insist on framing autism as a contemporary aberration—the unique disorder of our uniquely disordered times—caused by some tragic convergence of genetic predisposition and risk factors hidden somewhere in the toxic modern world, such as air pollution, an overdose of video games, and highly processed foods.

Our DNA tells a different story. In recent years, researchers have determined that most cases of autism are not rooted in rare de novo mutations but in very old genes that are shared widely in the general population while being concentrated more in certain families than others. Whatever autism is, it is not a unique product of modern civilization. It is a strange gift from our deep past, passed down through millions of years of evolution.

Neurodiversity advocates propose that instead of viewing this gift as an error of nature—a puzzle to be solved and eliminated with techniques like prenatal testing and selective abortion—society should regard it as a valuable part of humanity's genetic legacy while ameliorating the aspects of autism that can be profoundly disabling without adequate forms of support. They suggest that, instead of investing millions of dollars a year to uncover the causes of autism in the future, we should be helping autistic people and their families live happier, healthier, more productive, and more secure lives in the present.

This process has barely begun. Imagine if society had put off the issue of civil rights until the genetics of race were sorted out, or denied wheelchair users access to public buildings while insisting that someday, with the help of science, everyone will be able to walk. Viewed as a form of disability that is relatively common rather than as a baffling enigma, autism is not so baffling after all. Designing appropriate forms of support and accommodation is not beyond our capabilities as a society, as the history of the disability rights movement proves. But first we have to learn to think more intelligently about people who think differently.

One way to understand neurodiversity is to think in terms of *human operating systems* instead of diagnostic labels like *dyslexia* and *ADHD*. The brain is, above all, a marvelously adaptive organism, adept at maximizing its chances of success even in the face of daunting limitations.

Just because a computer is not running Windows doesn't mean that it's broken. Not all the features of atypical human operating systems are bugs. By autistic standards, the "normal" brain is easily distractible, is obsessively social, and suffers from a deficit of attention to detail and routine. Thus people on the spectrum experience the neurotypical world as relentlessly unpredictable and chaotic, perpetually turned up too loud, and full of people who have little respect for personal space.

The main reason why the Internet was able to transform the world in a single generation is that it was specifically built to be "platform agnostic." The Internet doesn't care if your home computer or mobile device is running Windows, Linux, or the latest version of Apple's iOS. Its protocols and standards were designed to work with them all to maximize the potential for innovation at the edges.

In recent years, a growing alliance of autistic self-advocates, parents, and educators who have embraced the concept of neurodiversity have suggested a number of innovations that could provide the foundation for an open world designed to work with a broad range of human operating systems.

The physical layout of such a world would offer a variety of *sensory-friendly environments* based on principles developed in autistic spaces like Autreat. An inclusive school, for example, would feature designated quiet areas where a student who felt temporarily overwhelmed could avoid a meltdown. In classrooms, distracting sensory input—such as the buzzing of fluorescent lights—would be kept to a minimum. Students would also be allowed to customize their personal sensory space by wearing noise-reducing headphones, sunglasses to avoid glare, and other easily affordable and minimally disruptive accommodations.

In 2011, a nonprofit corporation called the Theatre Development Fund in New York City launched an initiative to encourage Broadway producers to offer "autism-friendly" performances of hit shows like *Mary Poppins* and *The Lion King*. At these events, the use of strobe lights and pyrotechnics onstage was limited, quiet areas were set aside in the theater lobby, and social stories were made available to parents beforehand so that their children could know what to expect. These events were so successful that major cinema chains like AMC have begun offering sensory-friendly showings of movies like Disney's *Frozen* in theaters all over the country. This is not only a humane idea, it's smart marketing too, because the families of autistic children are often hesitant to bring them to movies and restaurants for fear of disrupting the experience of the other patrons. These special showings are invariably in high demand.

The advent of digital technology has opened up new horizons in education for adapting teaching materials to suit learners with a diverse range of learning styles. Some students learn best by reading, while others benefit most from oral instruction; with tablet devices and customizable software, the same core curriculum can support both. The leader in this area has been the National Center on Universal Design for Learning, which offers free guidelines and resources to help teachers adapt their curricula for students with learning differences.

Educators like Thomas Armstrong, author of *Neurodiversity in the Classroom*, suggest that more emphasis should be placed on early childhood education, when a child's individual learning style first comes to light, because a child's experiences in school can set him or her up for success or failure in later life. Armstrong points out that, too often, the process of negotiating an Individualized Education Program focuses exclusively on addressing a child's deficits at the expense of focusing on strengths that teachers could employ to engage the child's interests and help build confidence.

Many autistic people benefit from hands-on learning. The rise of the

Maker movement—which hosts events called Maker Faires, where garage inventors of all ages are encouraged to show off their latest projects—has been a boon to young people on the spectrum. At the White House Science Fair in 2012, President Obama was featured shooting off an "Extreme Marshmallow Cannon," which a fourteen-year-old autistic boy named Joey Hudy had designed and built himself.

Neurodiversity is also being embraced in the workplace by companies like Specialisterne, founded in Denmark, which employs people on the spectrum to put their autistic intelligence to work in the technology industry. Specialisterne has been so successful that it has opened satellite offices in the United Kingdom and the United States and recently forged a strategic alliance with the German software company SAP to serve the needs of the rapidly growing technology industry in India. Instead of putting potential candidates through grueling face-to-face interviews, Specialisterne lets them cut loose with a table full of Lego Mindstorm Robots, little machines that can be programmed to perform simple tasks. Thus, candidates can just show off their skills rather than have to explain them.

Neurodiversity activists have also pushed for more autistic representation in policy making, using the slogan "Nothing about us, without us." Fund-raising organizations like Autism Speaks have been resistant to the input of autistic adults, who are arguably in the best position to decide what kinds of research would benefit autistic people and their families most.

"Nothing about us, without us" also extends to the process of doing science itself. In recent years, a psychiatrist at the University of Montréal, Laurent Mottron, has produced a series of groundbreaking studies on autism with the help of his principal collaborator, an autistic researcher named Michelle Dawson. She fulfills a number of essential functions in the lab, including keeping Mottron up-to-date with the state of the research in the field ("She reads everything and forgets nothing," he says), vetting experimental designs for errors and subtle forms of bias, and advocating for higher scientific standards in the field overall. "Many autistics, I believe, are suited for academic science," Mottron wrote in *Nature* in 2011. "I believe that they contribute to science because of their autism, not in spite of it."

A group called the Academic Autistic Spectrum Partnership in Research and Education (AASPIRE) is collaborating with self-advocates to set their agenda for research. In 2014, AASPIRE released a comprehensive toolkit designed to inform patients and providers of the unique needs of autistic people in the health care system. ASAN's leadership training program has demonstrated the potential of peer mentoring for young people on the spectrum. Zoe Gross has recently completed a term of service as a disability policy staffer for the Senate Health, Education, Labor and Pensions Committee, and is now working in the HHS Administration on Community Living. Like Lydia Brown, she was named a White House Champion for Change in 2013. ASAN has also launched an internship program with the Federal Home Loan Mortgage Corporation.

The process of building a world suited to the needs and special abilities of all kinds of minds is just starting, but unlike long-range projects like teasing out the genetics and environmental factors that contribute to complex conditions like autism, the returns for autistic people and their families are practical and immediate. These innovations are also often much less expensive than projects requiring millions of dollars in federal funding.

With the generation of autistic people diagnosed in the 1990s now coming of age, society can no longer afford to pretend that autism suddenly loomed up out of nowhere, like the black monolith in *2001: A Space Odyssey*. There is much work to be done.

Epilogue

THE MAYOR OF KENSINGTON

Bernie Rimland's desk is much as he left it, buried under stacks of file folders and letters from parents all over the world. The room that once resonated with the sound of his voice instilling confidence in a mother or father who dialed a number in the middle of the night is eerily quiet, as if he had just stepped away for a moment. The headquarters of the Autism Research Institute feels a bit sleepy these days, with its autographed *Rain Man* memorabilia and racks of dusty brochures.

But suddenly the door swings open and a fit, boyishly handsome man with hair graying at the temples walks in and shakes my hand. It's Mark, Bernie's son, who has come down to the office to make the final preparations for his art opening in the gallery next door. Before he does that, we sit down to chat on his favorite bench in a sunny park. Even locals who have no idea of the roles that Mark and his father played in autism history smile and wave to the man they call the Mayor of Kensington.

Despite the dire prognostications about Mark's future when he was a child, his life in middle age is creative and rewarding. Although his father was a vocal opponent of removing autistic children from institutions, Mark has never lived in one. He resides in a house near the office with his mother, Gloria; his younger brother, Paul; and his two beloved cats. On weekdays, he attends a day program for adults at St. Madeleine Sophie's Center in El

Cajon, founded in 1966 by nuns and families who rejected the conventional wisdom that developmentally disabled children were uneducable. When Mark was twenty-one, he surprised his mother one day by coming home from the center with a luminous watercolor of an eagle. "Where did you get it?" Gloria asked him. "I'm an artist now," he replied.

After seeing one of his paintings, his sister Helen was inspired to write a children's book called *The Secret Night World of Cats*, about a tabby that slips out a bedroom window and has a series of adventures in the urban wilderness, trailed by her curious owner, a little girl named Amanda. Mark worked with his art teacher for a year to develop illustrations using traditional and digital media and to learn how to sprinkle salt on wet watercolors to simulate stars in the night sky. The figures in Mark's art blaze with an otherworldly radiance, as if he has captured not just their forms and outlines but their inner life force.

In the pool at St. Madeleine Sophie's, he learned to channel his inner jock, competing in five sports (swimming, skiing, basketball, volleyball, and floor hockey) and earning blue ribbons in the Special Olympics. He also got a job at the center's gift shop and gallery, where people often drop by just to hang out with him. At night, he listens to music and reads about the bands he loves (mostly sixties groups like the Beatles, the Beach Boys, and the Doors) before heading down to the Kensington Café, where the waitresses pour his iced tea when they see him coming in the door. A young painter named Ryan Dean who met Mark at the café helps him manage his day-to-day affairs and keeps a notebook at hand to capture his observations of life, which are often amusingly profound—a sort of *Tao According to Mark Rimland*, with rules of thumb like "Create with laziness."

As we chat on the bench about his cat, Sierra ("She cries like a baby when we don't pet her, because she doesn't know there are other things to do besides petting"), his love of *The Simpsons* and the San Diego Zoo ("The zoo just gives me the feeling there aren't as many spider monkeys as there used to be"), and his indelible memory of riding in an elevator in Beverly Hills to meet Dustin Hoffman ("It was on March 17, 1988, a Thursday"), it's obvious that Mark is still profoundly autistic, but he is also at ease in his own skin. He knows precisely how many steps it will take to get from the door of his house to the café, and occasionally, when he's not sure if you're being as sincere as he is, he'll say, "Oh, you're teasing me"—as when I accidentally refer to *Sleepless in Seattle* as *Sleepless in San Diego*. When I ask him if he ever gets anxious before giving a presentation at a conference, he says, "I don't ever let nervousness get in the way of my happiness."

Exhausted by all the infighting in the autism community, his mother rarely grants interviews anymore, but Gloria agrees to meet me at the Kensington Café for breakfast with Steve Edelson. In her eighties, she is still spry and sharp, with sparkling blue eyes and a salty laugh. Over bagels and tea, I ask her if there's anything that she wished she'd known when Mark was young.

"How well he'd turn out!" Gloria says proudly. "One of the most important things I learned from his teachers was to work with his strengths rather than trying to correct his deficits. Bernard and I were always so focused on what Mark *couldn't* do—'If only he could talk!' Then he'd learn to talk and we'd move on to 'If only he could read!' But once he figured out that he loves art, everything else came along with it, because it feels good to do something you're good at doing."

After helping Rimland launch Defeat Autism Now! in the 1990s, Edelson now advises parents to "run in the other direction" if a biomedical practitioner promises a cure. For years, he was married to Valerie Paradiz, who brought her son Elijah to the first Autreat. Now she designs curricula for teaching young people how to become effective self-advocates at school.

Shortly before Rimland died in 2006, he told a reporter from a local newspaper that his fondest wish was to make his son "normal." But he and Gloria had already given him something better than normal: a community that celebrates him for being exactly who he is. Midway through the journey of his life, Mark has the most precious and elusive thing that anyone can hope for. He is completely at home on earth.

Afterword

The night that *NeuroTribes* was published, my local independent bookstore in San Francisco hosted a reading. It was an emotional experience for me, in part because I had seen several of my literary heroes at the Booksmith over the years, and in part because I had spent the previous five years barely leaving the house, reconstructing decades of lost autism history. During the writing of the chapter on the prescient work of Hans Asperger and his colleagues, I would often listen to Steve Reich compositions like *The Daniel Variations* to restore my faith in humanity in the face of unspeakable Nazi atrocities against disabled children.

I didn't know who, if anyone, would be interested enough in my book to show up for such an event. Parents and relatives of kids on the spectrum? Teachers, doctors? General-science readers? People simply curious about a perennially controversial subject? Autistic people themselves?

Happily, the answer turned out to be "all of the above" and more. I was thrilled to see a group of autistic adults sitting to the left of the podium that night, contentedly rocking with expectation, feeling confident that they were in a space where they wouldn't be mocked or stigmatized for their behavior. During the question-and-answer period, a man in his forties asked me, "What are the virtues of getting an autism diagnosis in mid-life?" It took me only a moment to realize that instead of me responding to that question, there were some real experts in the room. I asked an autistic friend named Rina if she would feel comfortable answering instead. She stood up and said, "For me, getting a diagnosis in mid-life was like finding the Rosetta Stone to myself."

The signing at my neighborhood bookstore proved to be an auspicious foreshadowing of the future, and in the months to come, I would give talks to neurologically diverse audiences all over the world. I was interviewed by the autistic artist Jon Adams at the headquarters of the National Autistic Society in London, with Uta Frith, the cognitive psychologist who first made Asperger's 1944 paper available to the English-speaking world, sitting in the audience. (Parents also brought their children to the event, which was advertised as "autism friendly.") I've spoken with student neurodiversity activists at the College of William and Mary and Columbia University, and was honored to receive an Ally of the Year award at the Autistic Self Advocacy Network's annual gala in Washington, where I announced the creation of a prize for young autistic writers, named for disability-rights pioneer Harriet McBryde Johnson. I also received an email from the director of an autism society in Africa who told me that the first neurodiversity conference ever to be hosted on the continent would be held in the spring, inspired by my book. A few weeks later, I gave the keynote speech at the United Nations in observance of World Autism Awareness Day.

Many people who lived through the difficult history I describe in this book have reached out to me to tell me their stories. One of the pioneers of autism research, Ed Ritvo at UCLA, told me he faced widespread skepticism from his peers when he began studying the neurobiology of autism at a time when the psychiatric establishment was still blaming it on "refrigerator" parenting. He was also mocked for suggesting in 1988 that when some autistic children reach adulthood, they would be capable of getting married, having kids, and working regular jobs. Mothers who raised their kids during the era of parent-blaming recalled being shunned by their former friends and neighbors, the pain still visible in their faces. Psychologist Stine Levy, who began working just after Leo Kanner introduced the autism diagnosis to the world, told me that as late as the 1980s, by the time she saw a child, the family had usually visited ten specialists searching for someone who had any idea what autism looked like. No wonder autism was considered so rare for most of the twentieth century.

Hans Asperger's daughter, Maria, who continues her father's work in Vienna, sent me precious photographs of the original roundtable discussions during which her father and his associates developed the concept that Lorna Wing would christen the "autism spectrum" forty years later. I also heard from the granddaughter of a Jewish man hidden as a child from the Nazis by Asperger's colleague Josef Feldner in his Vienna apartment. After the war, Feldner adopted him and raised him as his stepson.

When I began writing *NeuroTribes*, autistic adults were invisible in most news stories about autism, and almost never quoted. I was heartened by the fact that several of the journalists who have written about the book—including Dylan Matthews of *Vox* and Eric Michael Garcia of the *National Journal*—are on the spectrum themselves. Now an autism story that doesn't include autistic voices feels as incomplete as a story about women in the workplace that quotes only men.

IN THE PAST YEAR, however, there have also been sobering reminders of how much work is left to be done to build a humane world for autistic people and their families. A report released in the spring of 2016 by Autistica, a major autism research organization in England, made this clear in the starkest possible terms.

Adults on the spectrum who aren't also intellectually disabled (i.e., those who are often referred to as "high-functioning") are nine times more likely to commit suicide than neurotypical people. Suicidality is no more a "symptom" of autism than incarceration is a symptom of being black. This shocking statistic represents the cumulative emotional cost of a lifetime of bullying, unemployment, lack of access to mental health care, and exclusion from society.

Meanwhile, for autistic people who are intellectually disabled, the second leading cause of death (after heart disease) is epilepsy. We know that epilepsy manifests very differently in the brains of autistic people than in neurotypical brains, with the period of highest risk of seizures starting at puberty rather than in the first year of infancy. Yet the report pointed out that no research has been done to specifically examine the effects of seizure-controlling drugs in the autistic population. This is just one of many areas of research that have gone underfunded and overlooked as the scientific community has focused on identifying potential risk factors for autism in the genome and the environment.

We still know so little about how the condition manifests itself in women, who often pass under the radar, at great emotional expense to themselves, into adulthood. Kevin Pelphrey, a neuroscientist at the Yale Child Study Center, recently admitted to *Scientific American*, "Everything we thought was true of autism seems to only be true for boys." Autism also remains underdiagnosed among people of color—a lingering effect of the era when Kanner framed autism as primarily a disorder of upper-middle-class academic families, like the ones that came to his office. All in all, the insidious illusion that autism is a historical aberration—a by-product of the toxic modern world—has contributed to an astonishing neglect of the needs of autistic adults and their families.

But now, at last, things are starting to change. A growing coalition of educators, clinicians, and disability-rights advocates are embracing the concept of neurodiversity, and refusing to view autistic people only in light of what they can't do. ("The thing about being autistic," a young woman once told me, "is that you spend your life looking for something you're good at, and then everyone tells you to shut up about it.") And the horizon of what they *can* do is expanding all the time, as more schools, workplaces, and service providers learn about the kinds of accommodations that enable people on the spectrum to express their full potential. Inclusion is not about doing something nice for disabled people; it's about making sure that everyone has the best chance to succeed.

I recently attended an "Autism at Work" summit conference hosted by SAP, the global software company mentioned in this book, which has committed to hiring thousands of autistic employees in the coming years. Its pilot program in India turned out to be so successful that the company has launched similar initiatives in seven countries, including Canada, Germany, and the United States. The employees are recruited in a five-week program that enables candidates to demonstrate their potential by solving problems with Lego Mindstorms robots rather than by having to charm an interviewer across a desk; the company also provides training in basic life skills and builds a "support circle" around each candidate to help him or her navigate the corporate environment.

The project's director in the United States, José Velasco—who is the father of two autistic children himself—explained that because tech employees are generally so hard to retain and expensive to replace, the company benefits from the fierce loyalty and intense focus of its employees on the spectrum. Many had been unemployed for years before SAP hired them. "This is not about charity," Velasco told an auditorium packed with executives from Microsoft, Hewlett-Packard, IBM, and other tech giants. "It's about increasing our profits and building value for SAP stockholders."

There have also been promising developments for autistic people with higher support needs. A new set of Medicaid guidelines, crafted with the input of the Autistic Self Advocacy Network, ensures that people with disabilities have the opportunity to live and work in truly integrated settings, instead of in group homes and segregated day programs. A number of states have passed laws or regulations to eliminate sheltered workshops (segregated settings where exploitation and abuse are rampant) and ban the payment of subminimum wages to disabled workers.

As schoolteachers say in Finland, "We can't afford to waste a brain." To meet the unforeseeable challenges racing toward us in the twenty-first century, we will need many kinds of minds working together. My hope is that this book has helped move the world a millionth of an inch toward that goal.

Ultimately, however, the most important changes are happening in the hearts of those on the front lines: the autistic people who are demanding that they be included in decisions that affect their lives, and the people who help them achieve their fullest potential. After a reprise of my TED talk,

"The Forgotten History of Autism," a young father in Los Angeles told me, "It never occurred to me to see my beautiful boy as diseased, damaged, or inferior. But your talk gave me permission to love him as he is."

The importance of loving autistic people as they are is a truth that parents have been coming to on their own for decades, even when they got little support for it from the most trusted experts in the field. The more hopeful future for their children that mothers like Lorna Wing, Ruth Christ Sullivan, and Clara Claiborne Park worked so hard for is finally arriving, one day at a time.

Steve Silberman
March 2016

Acknowledgments

This book would not have been written without the encouragement, support, and patience of my husband, Keith Karraker; my editor, Megan Newman; my agent, Beth Vesel; and my mother, sister, and late father, Leslie, Hillary, and Donald Silberman. Special thanks to the autistic people and their loved ones and allies who allowed me deep glimpses into their lives, including Shannon, Craig, Leo, Zelly, and India Rosa; the staff and members of the Asperger/Autism Network; Alysia Abbott, Jeff Howe, and Finn; Julia Bascom; Peter, Liz, and Tyler Bell; Samantha Bodwell; Lydia Brown; Michael Buckholtz; Laura Butler; Matt Carey; Kerima Cevik; Kristina Chew; Rachel Cohen-Rottenberg; Liz Ditz; Todd, Erika, and Sam Drezner; Adam Feinstein; Lee Felsenstein; Chen Gershuni; Temple Grandin; Dan Grover; Carol Greenburg, John Ordover, and Arren; Zoe and Rob Gross; Scott Holman; Janet Lawson and Autistry Studios; Russell Lehmann; Karla McLaren; Colin Meloy, Carson Ellis, and Hank; Ari Ne'eman and the ASAN membership; Jennifer Byde Myers; Alex Plank; Barbara Platt; Dora Raymaker; Mark and Gloria Rimland; Scott Robertson; John Elder and Jack Robison; Marc Rosen; Jason Ross; Jim St. Leger; Ralph and DJ Savarese; Kathleen Seidel and neurodiversity.com; Sola Shelly; Rudy Simone; Jim Sinclair; Lynne Soraya; Ruth Christ Sullivan; Emily Titon; Nick Walker; Michael Forbes Wilcox; and Emily Willingham.

I'm also grateful to the clinicians, researchers, educators, writers, and professionals who generously shared their time and knowledge to inform this book, including Thomas Armstrong; Tony Attwood; Simon Baron-Cohen; Jon

Brock; Geraldine Dawson; Steve Edelson and the Autism Research Institute; Brock and Fernette Eide; Graham Farmelo; Al Filreis; Uta Frith; Morton Ann Gernsbacher; Judith Gould; Roy Richard Grinker; Bennett Leventhal; Susan Moreno; Barry Morrow; Laurent Mottron; Christina Nicolaidis; Sally Ozonoff; Valerie Paradiz; Samantha Pierce; David Ropeik; Mark Roithmayr; Oliver Sacks; Marc Sirkin; Darold Treffert; Garret Westlake; the staff of the Willliams Syndrome Association and the campers at Whispering Trails; and Lorna Wing. Thanks also to those who provided assistance by transcribing interviews and translating texts, including Abby Royle and Eric Jarosinski.

In memory of Lorna Wing (1928–2014).

Notes

For a full bibliography, see the author's website at stevesilberman.com.

INTRODUCTION: BEYOND THE GEEK SYNDROME

to cover the maiden voyage for *Wired* magazine: "Scripting on the Lido Deck," Steve Silberman. *Wired*, 8.10, Oct. 2000.

"Swiss Army chainsaw": "Beginner's Introduction to Perl," Doug Sheppard. Perl.com, 2000. http://www.perl.com/pub/2000/10/begperl1.html

he derived it from the parable of the "pearl of great price": Larry Wall, interview with the author, 2000.

laziness, impatience, and hubris: *Programming Perl*, Larry Wall, Jon Orwant, and Tom Christiansen. O'Reilly Media, 3rd ed., 2000, p. xix.

she helped Vint Cerf develop the TCP/IP protocols: *Closing the Innovation Gap: Reigniting the Spark of Creativity in a Global Economy*, Judy Estrin. McGraw-Hill, 2008.

"No two people with autism are the same": *An Anthropologist on Mars*, Oliver Sacks. Knopf, 1995.

twice as likely to be engineers: "Is There a Link between Engineering and Autism?" Simon Baron-Cohen, Sally Wheelwright, et al. *Autism*, Vol. 1, No. 1, July 1997, pp. 101–109.

grants in the field climbed each year by an average of $51 million: "Which Neurodevelopmental Disorders Get Researched and Why?" Dorothy Bishop. *PLoS ONE*, Vol. 5, No. 11, 2010.

Private funding groups like the Simons Foundation: "About Us," Simons Foundation. https://www.simonsfoundation.org/about-us/

Autism Speaks: "Partnership Aims to Sequence 10,000 Autistic Genomes." Press release, Autism Speaks, Oct. 13, 2011.

"This Just In . . . Being Alive Linked to Autism": "This Just In . . . Being Alive Linked to Autism," Emily Willingham. The Biology Files, Oct. 27, 2011. http://biologyfiles.fieldofscience.com/2011/10/this-just-in-being-alive-linked-to.html

"Most individuals with autism are probably genetically quite unique": "Functional Impact of Global Rare Copy Number Variation in Autism Spectrum Disorders," Stephen Scherer, Dalila Pinto et al. *Nature*, Vol. 466, July 2010, pp. 368–72.

Stanley Nelson: "Researchers Find Genes Related to Autism," Liz Szabo. *USA Today*, June 10, 2010.

an extraordinary video: "In My Language," Amanda (Amelia) Baggs. YouTube. https://www.youtube.com/watch?v=JnylM1hI2jc

CHAPTER 1. THE WIZARD OF CLAPHAM COMMON

never hailing those who recognized him: *The Life of the Hon. Henry Cavendish: Including Abstracts of His More Important Scientific Papers, and a Critical Inquiry into the Claims of All the Alleged Discoverers of the Composition of Water*, George Wilson. Printed for the Cavendish Society, Jan. 1, 1851.

making an undignified but effective escape: *Sketches of the Royal Society and the Royal Society Club*, Sir John Barrow. Murray, 1849.

A maid wielding a broom: *Cavendish: The Experimental Life*, Christa Jungnickel and Russell McCormmach. Bucknell, 2001.

a perfect simulation of the fish's electrical organs: *Draw the Lightning Down: Benjamin Franklin and Electrical Technology in the Age of Enlightenment*, Michael Brian Schiffer. University of California Press, 2006, p. 119.

knocking one sixth of the city flat: *On the Nature of Thunderstorms; and on the Means of Protecting Buildings and Shipping against the Destructive Effects of Lightning*, W. S. Harris. Parker, 1743.

The lightning committee devised a crafty plan: *The Electrical Researches of the Honourable Henry Cavendish, F.R.S.: Written between 1771 and 1781*, Henry Cavendish. Ulan Press, repr. ed., 2011.

"the most rigid and satisfactory explanation": *Cavendish (Memoirs of the American Philosophical Society)*, Christa Jungnickel and Russell McCormmach. American Philosophical Society, Dec. 1996.

his experimental methods made that revolution possible: "Henry Cavendish: The Catalyst for the Chemical Revolution," Frederick Seitz. *Notes and Records of the Royal Society*, 2005, p. 59.

Lord Henry Brougham: *Lives of Men of Letters and Science Who Flourished in the Time of George III*, Henry, Lord Brougham. Philadelphia, 1845.

"the expression could hardly be called calm": *The Life of the Hon. Henry Cavendish*, p. 167.

On one such occasion: Ibid., p. 166.

"even to articulate with difficulty": Ibid., p. 167.

if anyone tried to catch his eye: Ibid.

"He did not love; he did not hate . . .": Ibid., p. 185.

"Wisely, therefore, he dwelt apart": Ibid., p. 186.

"a great man, with extraordinary singularities": Ibid., p. 167.

Christa Jungnickel and Russell McCormmach: *Cavendish: The Experimental Life*, Christa Jungnickel and Russell McCormmach. Bucknell, 2001.

another socially inept genius: "The Legend of the Dull-Witted Child Who Grew Up to Be a Genius," Barbara Wolff and Hananya Goodman. Albert Einstein Archives. http://www.albert-einstein.org/article_handicap.html

"His theory of the universe": *The Life of the Hon. Henry Cavendish*, p. 186.

His final instructions to his servants: *The Personality of Henry Cavendish*, Russell McCormmach. Archimedes, Vol. 36. Springer, 2014, p. 100.

a "true anchor": Ibid., p. 8.

replaced in 1905: Ibid., p. 270.

Wilson alluded to "talk about Mr. Cavendish": Ibid., p. 75.

"These many years later, I still look for a fuller understanding": Ibid., p. 7.

"Pshaw!": *English Eccentrics and Eccentricities: Volume 1*, John Timbs. Bentley, 1866.

the Duchess Georgiana of Devonshire . . . was one of the few people: "Henry Cavendish: The Catalyst for the Chemical Revolution," p. 59.

"Hundreds of youths . . .": *The Life of the Hon. Henry Cavendish*, p. 172.

"his habits had, from early life, been secluded": *The Personality of Henry Cavendish*, p. 100.

the regimen of cold baths: *The History of Bethlem*, Jonathan Andrews. Psychology Press, 1997, p. 272.

Raised in humbler circumstances: *The Strangest Man: The Hidden Life of Paul Dirac, Mystic of the Atom*, Graham Farmelo. Basic Books, 2009, pp. 10–19.

"the stuff of legend": *The Strangest Man*, p. 58.

"metronomic" stride: Ibid., p. 60.

a title for his biography: Ibid.

In 2001: "Henry Cavendish: An Early Case of Asperger Syndrome?" Oliver Sacks. *Neurology*, Vol. 57, No. 7, Oct. 9, 2001, p. 1347.

neighbors who thought they'd said their son or daughter was "artistic": Ruth Christ Sullivan, interview with the author, 2012.

"Nearly all" of the Dirac stories: *The Strangest Man*, p. 422.

he had no intention of venturing a diagnosis: Graham Farmelo, personal communication, March 4, 2013.

"If Dirac was autistic": "Silent Quantum Genius," Freeman Dyson. *New York Review of Books*, Feb. 25, 2010.

the virtues of having an "autistic cognitive style": *Create Your Own Economy*, Tyler Cowen. Dutton, 2009.

coming out in midlife about her diagnosis: "Daryl Hannah Breaks Her Silence about Her Autism Struggle," Rebecca Macatee. E! Online, Sept. 27, 2013. http://www.eonline.com/news/464173/daryl-hannah-breaks-her-silence-on-autism-struggle

musing about his autistic traits: "Interview with Richard Borcherds," Simon Singh. *Guardian*, Aug. 28, 1998.

"On a very drawn-out scale, I think I'm on the spectrum": "Jerry Seinfeld to Brian Williams: 'I Think I'm on the Spectrum.'" NBC News, Nov. 6, 2014. After a storm of media attention, Seinfeld would eventually walk those comments back, saying that he "related" to a dramatized account of the lives of people on the spectrum. http://www.nbcnews.com/nightly-news/jerry-seinfeld-brian-williams-i-think-im-spectrum-n242941

CHAPTER 2. THE BOY WHO LOVES GREEN STRAWS

On a good day: "Language Development," Amanda C. Brandone et al. *Children's Needs III: Development, Prevention, and Intervention.* National Association of School Psychologists, 2006.

"The agents of L.U.S.T. are dedicated and sneaky": "The Agents of L.U.S.T.," Shannon Des Roches Rosa. BlogHer, May 19, 2009. http://www.blogher.com/agents-l-u-s-t-1

divorce rates are no higher for families like the Rosas: "80 Percent Autism Divorce Rate Debunked in First-of-Its Kind Scientific Study," Kennedy Krieger Institute, May 19, 2010.

"The odor has finally made its way down the hall": "Planet Autism," Scot Sea. Salon.com, Sept. 27, 2003. http://www.salon.com/2003/09/27/autism_8/

shunting him into a series of temporary jobs: "Stress Pushed Man to Kill Son, Himself, Family Says," Mai Tran and Mike Anton. *Los Angeles Times,* July 31, 2002.

"Her activities were becoming stranger": *Let Me Hear Your Voice,* Catherine Maurice. Ballantine Books, repr. ed., 1994.

based on ornithologist Nikolaas Tinbergen's observations of birds: *"Autistic" Children: New Hope for a Cure,* N. Tinbergen and E. A. Tinbergen. Allen & Unwin, 1983, pp. 52–53.

"We are not *blaming* these unfortunate parents": "Ethology and Stress Diseases," Nikolaas Tinbergen. Nobel lecture, Dec. 12, 1973.

by force, if necessary: *"Autistic" Children: New Hope for a Cure,* p. 229.

Tinbergen promoted as a "new hope": *"Autistic" Children: New Hope for a Cure.*

"How does that make you feel?": "Introduction to Welch Method Attachment Therapy," Martha Welch. YouTube. http://www.youtube.com/watch?v=OdWhcyz6KbY&feature=player_embedded#!

"indistinguishable" from their nonautistic peers: "Behavioral Treatment and Normal Intellectual and Educational Functioning in Children with Autism," O. I. Lovaas. *Journal of Consulting and Clinical Psychology,* Vol. 55, 1987, pp. 3–9.

the peptide test "has not been cleared or approved": *Urinary Peptides Final Report.* Great Plains Laboratory, revised form, Oct. 24, 2001.

The consequences of yeast overgrowth: "What Is Yeast Overgrowth?" Holly Bortfield. Talk About Curing Autism. http://www.tacanow.org/family-resources/what-is-yeast-overgrowth/

a way of clearing "dissonant" energy blockages: "The BioSET System: Three Basic Treatments. Organ-Specific Detoxification, Enzyme Therapy, and Desensitization," Ellen Cutler. http://www.drellencutler.com/pages/articles/?ArticleID=215

(A voice-over briefly mentions . . . therapy.): "Mom: Son Recovers from Autism," Amy Lester. News 9. http://www.news9.com/story/8341532/mom-son-recovers-from-autism

sales topping $33 billion: "The Use of Complementary and Alternative Medicine in the United States: Cost Data," National Center for Complementary and Alternative Medicine, Department of Health and Human Services, 2007. http://nccam.nih.gov/news/camstats/costs/costdatafs.htm

Americans now consult: "Complementary and Alternative Medicine in the United States," Tonya Passarelli. Case Western Reserve University, Apr. 2008.

Up to three quarters of all autistic children in the United States: "Complementary and

Alternative Medicine Treatments for Children with Autism Spectrum Disorders," Susan E. Levy and Susan L. Hyman. *Journal of Child and Adolescent Psychiatry*, Vol. 17, No. 4, 2008.

A study in Japan: "No Effect of MMR Withdrawal on the Incidence of Autism: A Total Population Study," Hideo Honda, Yasuo Shimizu, and Michael Rutter. *Journal of Child Psychology and Psychiatry*, Vol. 46, No. 6, June 2005.

Another study in Hong Kong: "Mercury Exposure in Children with Autistic Spectrum Disorder: Case-Control Study," P. Ip, V. Wong, et al. *Journal of Child Neurology*, June 2004.

Measles would eventually be declared endemic: "MMR—Autism Scare: So, Farewell Then, Dr. Andrew Wakefield," Tom Chivers. *Telegraph*, May 24, 2010.

the DAN! consensus: *Treatment Options for Mercury/Metal Toxicity in Autism and Related Developmental Disabilities: Consensus Position Paper.* Autism Research Institute, Feb. 2005.

being able to dress and undress himself: *Leo Rosa: Summary Progress Report*, June 3, 2004.

One day it occurred to Kristina: Kristina Chew, interview with the author, 2014.

a "unique 'syndrome,' heretofore unreported": "Autistic Disturbances of Affective Contact," Leo Kanner. *Nervous Child*, Vol. 2, 1943, pp. 217–50.

"saving" her son Evan from autism: *Healing and Preventing Autism: A Complete Guide*, Jenny McCarthy and Jerry Kartzinel. Dutton, 2009.

"It's all now": "Jenny McCarthy on Healing Her Son's Autism and Discovering Her Life's Mission," Allison Kugel. PR.com, Oct. 9, 2007. http://www.pr.com/article/1076

CHAPTER 3. WHAT SISTER VIKTORINE KNEW

"Once one has learnt to pay attention": "Autistic Psychopathy in Childhood," Hans Asperger. Translated by Uta Frith. *Autism and Asperger Syndrome.* Cambridge University Press, 1991, p. 39.

"feeble-minded": "Qualitative Intelligence Testing as a Means of Diagnosis in the Examination of Psychopathic Children," Anni Weiss. *American Journal of Orthopsychiatry*, Vol. 5, No. 2, Apr. 1935, pp. 154–79.

He had been encouraged to do his postgraduate work: "Hans Asperger (1906–1980): His Life and Work," Maria Asperger-Felder. Translated for the author by Kenneth Kronenberg.

Hamburger offered a popular course in children's diseases: "News and Comment." *American Journal of the Diseases of Children*, Vol. 52, No. 3, 1936, p. 674.

Nicknamed "Red Vienna": *Red Vienna: Experiment in Working Class Culture, 1919–1934*, Helmut Gruber. Oxford University Press, 1991.

dozens of ongoing salons: "I See Psychoanalysis, Art and Biology Coming Together: An Interview with Eric Kandel." *Der Spiegel*, Oct. 11, 2012.

Gustav Mahler's music: "Vienna: Trapped in a Golden Age," Alexandra Starr. *American Scholar*, Winter 2008.

"His names for the various types were always quite incisive": *Erwin Lazar und sein Wirken*, Valerie Bruck, George Frankl, Anni Weiss, and Viktorine Zak. Translated for the author by Eric Jarosinski. Springer, 1932.

"It must give every child a chance": "Mellansjö School-Home: Psychopathic Children Admitted

1928–1940, Their Social Adaptation over 30 Years: A Longitudinal Prospective Follow-up," Ingegärd Fried. *Acta Paediatrica*, Vol. 84, Suppl. s408, 1995.

"It had never occurred to any of us to see [the children] as delinquents": *Wayward Youth*, August Aichhorn. Penguin Books, repr. ed., 1965.

Each morning, a procession: "Clemens Pirquet and His Work: Director of the Vienna University Kinder-Klinik, 1911–1929," Harriette Chick. *Lancet*, Vol. 213, No. 5508, March 1929.

Erwin Jekelius: See the reference to the 1936 paper by Jekelius in "Encopresis," *Acta Paediatrica*, Vol. 55, Suppl. s169, 1966.

the "true genius" of his clinic: "Asperger and His Syndrome," Uta Frith. *Autism and Asperger Syndrome*. Cambridge University Press, 1991.

started working at the clinic in 1927: George Frankl's biographical file, Alan Mason Chesney Medical Archives, Johns Hopkins University.

Asperger would often just sit with the children: "Hans Asperger: His Life and Work."

a report published in 1991: "Asperger and His Syndrome."

an overlooked paper: "The Heilpedägogical Station of the Children's Clinic at the University of Vienna," Joseph J. Michaels. *American Journal of Orthopsychiatry*, 1935.

"fixed in numbered seats": Ibid.

"In this 'age of technocracy'": Ibid.

provided by Weiss in a paper: "Play Interviews with Nursery School Children," Anni Weiss-Frankl. *American Journal of Orthopsychiatry*, Vol. 11, No. 1, Jan. 1941, pp. 33–39.

one boy's fascination: "The Importance of Symbol-Formation in the Development of the Ego," Melanie Klein. *International Journal of Psychoanalysis*, Vol. 9, 1930, p. 5.

"Some children frequently volunteered for play turns": "Play Interviews with Nursery School Children," Anni Weiss-Frankl. *American Journal of Orthopsychiatry*, Vol. 11, No. 1, Jan. 1941, p. 35.

Weiss's play sessions: Ibid., p. 34.

"to determine the innate capacities of the child": "The Heilpedägogical Station of the Children's Clinic at the University of Vienna."

Even the physical layout: "Asperger and His Syndrome."

"We cannot be interested so much in the concrete result": "Qualitative Intelligence Testing as a Means of Diagnosis in the Examination of Psychopathic Children," p. 165.

"G. is not able to escape from his logical attitude": Ibid., p. 168.

more than two hundred children: "Autistic Psychopathy in Childhood," p. 84.

("If something was only slightly different"): Ibid., p. 61.

a thousand matchboxes: Ibid., p. 82.

"If one lays one's head": Ibid., p. 73.

"a particularly interesting and highly recognizable type of child": Ibid., p. 37.

these odd young ducks: "Die schizoiden Psychopathien im Kindesalter," G. E. Sukhareva. Translated by Sula Wolff. *Monatsschrift für Psychiatrie und Neurologie*, 1926.

"autistic thinking": *Dementia Praecox oder Gruppe der Schizophrenien*, Eugen Bleuler. Deuticke, 1911.

the hazy borderland between mental health and illness: "Mellansjö School-Home."

"all levels of ability": "Autistic Psychopathy in Childhood," p. 74.

"we have never met a girl with the fully fledged picture of autism": Ibid., p. 85.

"an extreme variant of male intelligence": *Prenatal Testosterone in Mind: Amniotic Fluid Studies*, Simon Baron-Cohen et al. MIT Press, 2004.

underestimation of the prevalence of autism in women: "The Extreme Male Brain Theory of Autism and the Potential Adverse Effects for Boys and Girls with Autism," Timothy M. Krahn, Andrew Fenton. *Journal of Bioethical Inquiry*, Vol. 9, No. 1, March 2012.

the Asperger FAQ: "Asperger Syndrome Fact Sheet," National Institutes of Health. http://www.ninds.nih.gov/disorders/asperger/detail_asperger.htm

Weiss's in-depth case study of Gottfried: "Qualitative Intelligence Testing as a Means of Diagnosis in the Examination of Psychopathic Children."

"We know an autistic child": "Autistic Psychopathy in Childhood," p. 72.

the designers of spaceships themselves were autistic: See Uta Frith's footnote in "Autistic Psychopathy in Childhood," p. 72.

"Autistic children have the ability": "Autistic Psychopathy in Childhood," p. 71.

"a dash of autism is essential": "Problems of Infantile Autism," Hans Asperger. *Communication: Journal of the National Autistic Society*, Vol. 13, 1979.

"the useless protrusion of a single faculty": "New Facts and Remarks Concerning Idiocy: Being a Lecture Delivered Before the New York Medical Journal Association, October 15, 1869," Édouard Séguin. *American Journal of the Medical Sciences*, Vol. 59, No. 120, 1870.

"In the case of learning difficulties, the question is": "Qualitative Intelligence Testing as a Means of Diagnosis in the Examination of Psychopathic Children."

"The teacher must at all costs be calm and collected": "Autistic Psychopathy in Childhood," p. 47.

"the teacher has to become somehow 'autistic'": *Heilpädagogik*, Hans Asperger. Excerpts translated for the author by Uta Frith. Springer, 1953.

Who was this man: "Hans Asperger (1906–1980): His Life and Work," Maria Asperger-Felder. Translated for the author by Kenneth Kronenberg.

"Reading is bound up with one's fate and destiny": Ibid.

"one of the noblest flowerings of the German spirit": Ibid.

The second turning point in his early life: Ibid.

their replacements were bumbling fanatics: "A Leading Medical School Seriously Damaged: Vienna 1938," Edzard Ernst. *Annals of Internal Medicine*, Vol. 122, No. 10, May 1995.

a gala weeklong event: *War Against the Weak: Eugenics and America's Campaign to Create a Master Race*, Edwin Black. Four Walls Eight Windows, 2003.

promoted in journals: *Scientific Monthly*, Vol. 13, No. 2, Aug. 1921.

Museum officials devoted two floors of the building to the event: Floor plan of the exhibit of the Second International Congress of Eugenics, from Cold Spring Harbor eugenics archive.

Papers were presented: "The Second International Congress of Eugenics," C. C. Little. Carnegie Institution of Washington, 1921.

At one end of Eugenics Hall: Floor plan of the exhibit of the Second International Congress of Eugenics, from Cold Spring Harbor eugenics archive.

he refused to believe that any creature as noble as *Homo sapiens*: "Biographical Memoir of Henry Fairfield Osborn (1857–1935)," William K. Gregory. Presented to the autumn meeting of the National Academy of Sciences, 1937.

Piltdown Man: "Piltdown Man: British Archaeology's Greatest Hoax," Robin McKie. *Observer*, Feb. 4, 2012.

it was the duty of his fellow scientists: "The Second International Congress of Eugenics Address of Welcome," Henry Fairfield Osborn. *Science*, New Series, Vol. 54, No. 1397, Oct. 7, 1921.

Of the fifty-three papers presented at the conference: *War Against the Weak*.

in 1883, he warned the National Academy of Sciences: "Upon the Formation of a Deaf Variety of the Human Race," Alexander Graham Bell. Presented to the National Academy of Sciences, Nov. 13, 1883.

"random flavors of chaos": *War Against the Weak*.

On the last day of the congress: "The Second International Congress of Eugenics."

They also mapped the pedigrees: Eugenics Record Office Records, 1670–1964. American Philosophical Society.

"Indeed they are so crooked": "Some Notes on Asexualization," Martin W. Barr. *Journal of Nervous and Mental Disease*, Vol. 1, 1920.

"While we have some laws for the protection of the feeble-minded": Ibid.

sent out a survey: *The Third Reich: A New History*, Michael Burleigh. Hill & Wang, 2000.

Meltzer concluded: *Cleansing the Fatherland: Nazi Medicine and Racial Hygiene*, Götz Aly, Peter Chroust, and Christian Pross. Johns Hopkins University Press, 1994.

"Their life is absolutely pointless": "Useless Eaters: Disability as a Genocidal Marker in Nazi Germany," Mark P. Mostert. *Journal of Special Education*, Vol. 36, No. 3, 2002.

a crash course in eugenics: *War Against the Weak*.

The thrust of his argument: *The Passing of the Great Race: or, the Racial Basis of European History*, Madison Grant. Scribner, 4th rev. ed., 1922.

"A rigid system of selection": Ibid.

the seminal guide to applied eugenics: *Die Rassenhygiene in den Vereinigten Staaten von Nordamerika*, Géza Hoffman. Lehmann, 1913.

"We will not allow ourselves to be turned into niggers": *Unmasked: Two Confidential Interviews with Hitler*, Edouard Calic. Translated by R. H. Barry. Chatto & Windus, 1971.

In July 1933: Law for the Prevention of Hereditarily Diseased Offspring. Enacted on July 14, 1933. Reichsdruckerei, 1935.

The law also mandated the creation of Genetic Health Courts: *IBM and the Holocaust*, Edwin Black. Crown, 2001.

more than four hundred thousand men, women, and children: *Racial Hygiene: Medicine under the Nazis*, Robert Proctor. Harvard University Press, 1988.

"An entire people goes in a single direction": "Hans Asperger: His Life and Work."

"talk about autistic!": Ibid.

The Italian dictator received word of Dolfuss's assassination: "Austria: Death for Freedom," *Time*, Aug. 6, 1934.

The official newspaper of the NSDAP: "From Eugenic Euthanasia to Habilitation of 'Disabled' Children: Andreas Rett's Contribution," Gabriel M. Ronen et al. *Journal of Child Neurology*, Vol. 24, No. 1, Jan. 2009.

Asperger did not join: "Hans Asperger: His Life and Work."

The network of Catholic youth organizations: *The Resistance in Austria: 1938–1945*, Radomír Luža. University of Minnesota Press, 1984.

Signs appeared on park benches throughout the city: *Hotel Bolivia: The Culture of Memory in a Refuge from Nazism*, Leo Spitzer. Hill & Wang, 1998.

Hundreds of families: Ibid.

Of the nearly 5,000 physicians practicing in the city, 3,200 were Jews: "A Leading Medical School Seriously Damaged."

***paradoxal obstipation*:** "Encopresis." *Acta Paediatrica*, Vol. 55, 1966.

Society of Physicians: "The Medical Club—Billrothhaus: Epoch-Making Lectures in Medical History." American-Austrian Foundation. http://www.aaf-online.org/

"Now we must face the fact": "National Socialism and Medicine: Address by Dr. F. Hamburger to the German Medical Profession." *Wiener Klinische Wochenschrift*, No. 6, 1939.

thousands of Austrians huddled: Eric Kandel's biographical memoir, delivered on the occasion of receiving the Nobel Prize in medicine, 2000.

The final strains of the national anthem barely had faded from the airwaves: *Fallen Bastions*, G. E. R. Gedye. Faber & Faber, 1939.

Cheering Austrians lined the streets: "*Mit den deutschen Soldaten im befreiten Österreich*," *Die Wehrmacht*, Vol. 2, No. 6, 1938.

"Everywhere and without exception": Ibid.

"the Brown flood was sweeping through the streets": *Fallen Bastions.*

As a crowd chanted, "We have found work for the Jews at last": Ibid.

Vienna neurologist Walter Birkmeyer told his colleagues: "From Eugenic Euthanasia to Habilitation of 'Disabled' Children."

the newly installed dean of medicine, anatomist Eduard Pernkopf, delivered a rousing speech: Photograph of Eduard Pernkopf's lecture to the medical faculty, University of Vienna. *The War against the Inferior: On the History of Nazi Medicine in Vienna.* http://gedenkstaettesteinhof.at/en/exibition/04-persecuted-and-expelled

"the greatest son of our home country": "Racial Hygiene in Vienna 1938," Wolfgang Neugebauer. *Wiener Klinische Wochenschrift*, March 1998.

80 percent of the medical faculty had been dismissed: "A Leading Medical School Seriously Damaged."

Swastika flags flew from the university's main building: "University of the 'Reich' (1938–1945)." An Historical Tour of the University of Vienna. http://www.univie.ac.at/archiv/tour/19.htm

Many former professors at the university: Ibid.

The zealots who took their places: "A Leading Medical School Seriously Damaged."

Only in 1996, when a Jewish surgeon working with a Holocaust scholar: "How the Pernkopf Controversy Facilitated a Historical and Ethical Analysis of the Anatomical Sciences in Austria and Germany: A Recommendation for the Continued Use of the Pernkopf Atlas," Sabine Hildebrandt. *Clinical Anatomy*, Vol. 19, No. 2, 2006, pp. 91–100.

the first public talk on autism in history: *A History of Autism: Conversations with the Pioneers*, Adam Feinstein. Wiley, 2010.

the Vienna Psychiatric and Neurological Association issued a decree: Ibid.

"We are standing in the midst of an enormous change": "The Mentally Abnormal Child," Hans Asperger. *Wiener klinische Wochenzeitschrift*, No. 49, 1938. Translation provided by Tony Atwood, adapted by the author.

"a bit too Nazistic for your reputation": "Hans Asperger: His Life and Work."
"not at all rare": "Autistic Psychopathy in Childhood," p. 39.
deserted sidewalk cafés: *Fallen Bastions.*
"put him to sleep": *The Nazi Doctors: Medical Killing and the Psychology of Genocide*, Robert J. Lifton. Da Capo Press, 1988.
"If the facts given by the father were correct": Ibid.
euthanasia was already standard practice on the maternity wards: Ibid.
one of his subordinates murdered the baby with an injection: *Forgotten Crimes: The Holocaust and People with Disabilities*, Susanne E. Evans. Dee, 2004.
"5,000 idiots": Ibid.
"specialist children's wards": Ibid.
The institution had 640 beds when he arrived, and he added 240 more: *Medicine and Medical Ethics in Nazi Germany: Origins, Practice, Legacies*, Francis R. Nicosia and Jonathan Huener, eds. Berghahn Books, 2002.
children who were "simply annoying": *The Origins of Nazi Genocide: From Euthanasia to the Final Solution*, Henry Friedlander. University of North Carolina Press, 1995.
The lesson of Meltzer's 1920 survey: *Cleansing the Fatherland.*
One doctor at the Maria Gugging Psychiatric Clinic: *The Origins of Nazi Genocide.*
Ugo Cerletti, who was inspired by seeing a butcher: "Electroconvulsive Shock in a Rural Setting," George R. Martin. PowerPoint presentation, James A. Quillen VA Medical Center, Mountain Home, TN.
hundreds of brains harvested during the program: "Unquiet Grave for Nazi Child Victims," Kate Connolly. *Guardian*, Apr. 29, 2002.
"special diet": *Forgotten Crimes.*
As clinics, hospitals, and schools: For example, Kalmenhof, a former *Idiotenanstalt* ("Facility for Idiots") in the German province of Hesse-Nassau. "Child Murder in Nazi Germany: The Memory of Nazi Medical Crimes and Commemoration of 'Children's Euthanasia' Victims at Two Facilities (Eichberg, Kalmenhof)," Lutz Kaelber. *Societies*, Vol. 2, No. 3, 2012.
improvised furnaces on wheels: *Century of Genocide: Eyewitness Accounts and Critical Views*, Samuel Totten, William S. Parsons, and Israel W. Charny, eds. Garland, 1997.
they told her that they were in favor of euthanasia: Ibid.
it was obvious that he had died in agony: *Nazi Medical Crimes at the Psychiatric Hospital Gugging*, Herwig Czech. Executive Committee of the Institute of Science and Technology, Austria, 2007.
Pernkopf's 1938 decree: "A Leading Medical School Seriously Damaged."
"a truly dangerous situation": *A History of Autism: Conversations with the Pioneers*, Adam Feinstein. Wiley, 2010.
the White Rose resistance group: *The Nazi Doctors: Medical Killing and the Psychology of Genocide*, Robert Jay Lifton. Basic Books, 1986, pp. 39–40.
Franz Hamburger used his power: Ibid.
superior code breakers: Author's interview with Tony Atwood, who confirmed the anecdote with Maria Asperger-Felder.
the gray zone: *The Drowned and the Saved*, Primo Levi. Summit Books, 1986.
a letter of referral: *Die ermordeten Kinder vom Spiegelgrund*, Waltraud Häupl. Böhlau, 2006.
served on a committee: *In a Different Key: The Story of Autism*, John Donvan and Caren Zucker. Crown, 2016, p. 340.

His thesis was published the following June: "Die 'Autistischen Psychopathen' im Kindesalter," Hans Asperger. *Archiv für Psychiatrie und Nervenkrankheiten*, Vol. 117, 1944, pp. 76–136.
"a great gift of fate": "Hans Asperger: His Life and Work."
They were buried together: *A History of Autism.*

CHAPTER 4. FASCINATING PECULIARITIES

a bitter war of words for priority: *The Road to Reality*, Roger Penrose. Vintage Books, 2005.
***Listing strips*:** *Vorstudien zur Topologie*, Johann Benedict Listing. *Göttinger Studien*, 1847.
"When the time is ripe": *An Introduction to Kolmogorov Complexity and Its Applications*, Ming Li. Springer, 3rd ed., 2008.
Kanner compared himself to the legendary Persian prince Serendip: "Early Infantile Autism: S. Spafford Ackerly Lecture," Leo Kanner. University of Louisville, May 16, 1972.
The mellifluous sounds of Yiddish: *Freedom from Within*, unpublished memoir of Leo Kanner, Melvin Sabshin Library and Archives, American Psychiatric Association, Arlington, VA.
his "way of playing solitaire": Ibid.
Historian Adam Feinstein speculates: *A History of Autism*, p. 19.
"Klara the Cossack": *Freedom from Within.*
"a sort of mechanical toy": Ibid.
So he began calling himself Leo: Ibid.
"Obviously, there is nothing like an established reputation": Ibid.
Kanner enrolled at the University of Berlin in 1913: "Leo Kanner (1894–1981): The Man and the Scientist," Victor Sanua. *Child Psychiatry and Human Development*, Vol. 21, No. 1, Fall 1990.
En route to his deployment: *Freedom from Within.*
"on a sleety winter evening": Ibid.
Karl Bonhoeffer, a pioneering neurologist: "Karl Bonhoeffer (1868–1948)," Andreas Ströhle et al. *American Journal of Psychiatry*, 2008.
Bonhoeffer gave Kanner only a passing grade: "Leo Kanner: His Years in Berlin, 1906–24. The Roots of Autistic Disorder," K. J. Neumärker. *History of Psychiatry*, Vol. 14, 2003.
"I felt a bit as John D. Rockefeller may have felt": *Freedom from Within.*
"collector of people": Ibid.
Jewish doctors had to work much harder than their colleagues: "Leo Kanner: His Years in Berlin, 1906–24."
"Everything was drenched in beauty": *Freedom from Within.*
the global epidemic of encephalitis lethargica: "What Caused the 1918–30 Epidemic of Encephalitis Lethargica?" R. R. Dourmashkin. *Journal of the Royal Society of Medicine*, Vol. 90, Sept. 1997.
"I was embarrassed at the thought of my diagnostic blunder": *Freedom from Within.*
Kanner was appalled by the spectacle: Ibid.
a farmer named Charlie Miller: Ibid., p. 269.
On his first Christmas Eve at the hospital: Ibid., p. 296.
In 1925, Kanner made his professional debut: "A Psychiatric Study of Ibsen's *Peer Gynt*," Leo Kanner. *Journal of Abnormal Psychology and Social Psychology*, Vol. 19, No. 4, Jan. 1925, pp. 373–82.

the imminent arrival of Emil Kraepelin: "General Paralysis in Primitive Races," *British Medical Journal*, Vol. 2, No. 3439, 1926, p. 1064.

Kanner asked Adams: *Freedom from Within*, p. 300.

Kanner and Adams published a paper: "General Paralysis among the North American Indians: A Contribution to Racial Psychiatry," G. S. Adams and Leo Kanner. *American Journal of Psychiatry*, 1926.

Kanner's bold notion that syphilis is of New World origin: "On the Origin of the Treponematoses: A Phylogenetic Approach," K. N. Harper et al. *PLoS Neglected Tropical Diseases*, Vol. 2, No. 1, p. e148. http://www.plosntds.org/article/info%3Adoi%2F10.1371%2Fjournal.pntd.0000148

Subsequent inspections: "The Canton Asylum for Insane Indians: An Example of Institutional Neglect," John M. Spaulding. *Journal of Hospital and Community Psychiatry*, Vol. 37, No. 10, 1986, pp. 1007–1011.

Diagnosed as insane: Ibid.

Silk described conditions at the asylum: Ibid., p. 1009.

"come see the crazy Indians": "Hiawatha Diary." http://hiawathadiary.com/hiawatha-asylum-for-insane-indians/

Perkins specifically called out Hummer: "Psychoses of the American Indians Admitted to Gowanda State Hospital," Anne Perkins. *Psychiatric Quarterly*, Vol. 1, No. 3, 1927, pp. 335–43.

"my efforts lacked consistency and direction": *Freedom from Within.*

"as natural a phenomenon as the rising and setting of the sun": Ibid.

a scathing indictment of his colleagues: *Medical America in the Nineteenth Century: Readings from the Literature*, Gert H. Brieger, ed. Johns Hopkins University Press, 1970.

his students hadn't even been schooled: "Psychobiology, Psychiatry, and Psychoanalysis: The Intersecting Careers of Adolf Meyer, Phyllis Greenacre, and Curt Richter." *Medical History*, 2009.

he pioneered the modern form of psychiatric history taking: Ibid.

a school of psychiatry that was dubbed Meyerian: "Adolf Meyer's Contribution to Psychiatric Education," Frank G. Ebaugh. *Bulletin of the Johns Hopkins Hospital*, 1951.

the albino rat: "The Altered Rationale for the Choice of a Standard Animal in Experimental Psychology: Henry H. Donaldson, Adolf Meyer, and 'the' Albino Rat," Cheryl A. Logan. *History of Psychology*, Vol. 2, No. 1, Feb. 1999.

Visiting Meyer's office for the first time: *Freedom from Within.*

skepticism for psychoanalysis: "Psychobiology, Psychiatry, and Psychoanalysis."

"quiet, epic grandeur": *Psychobiology and Psychiatry*, W. Muncie. Mosby, 2nd ed., 1948.

the woebegone countenance of a sad beagle: Virtually every image of Kanner captured during his lifetime—in photographs, film, and art—attests to his disconsolate appearance. See, for example, the footage of Kanner archived on YouTube: http://www.youtube.com/watch?v=Hr1HF6a0w40

"I knew you folks were Jewish right away": *Freedom from Within.*

Meyer quietly instructed the stenographer: Ibid.

a new child-behavior clinic: "A Child Psychiatric Clinic in a Paediatric Department," Edward A. Park. *Canadian Medical Association Journal*, Vol. 38, No. 1, Jan. 1938, pp. 74–78.

By the end of Kanner's first year: *Freedom from Within*, p. 363.

"I was free to proceed according to my own convictions": *Freedom from Within.*

he committed suicide with his wife: *Allergy: The History of a Modern Malady*, Mark Jackson. Reaktion Books, 2007, p. 35.

psychiatry, pediatrics, and even a dash of *Heilpädagogik*: "Outline of the History of Child Psychiatry," Leo Kanner. *Victor Robinson Memorial Volume: Essays on the History of Medicine*, Solomon R. Kagan, ed. Froeben Press, 1948, p. 171.

(Meyer did his best teaching with his eyes . . .): *Freedom from Within.*

"Work with the child": *Child Psychiatry*, Leo Kanner. Thomas, 1947.

"a remarkable achievement": "*Child Psychiatry* by Leo Kanner," book review by Virginia Kirk, RN. *American Journal of Nursing*, Vol. 36, No. 5, May 1936, p. 545.

straightforward headings: *Child Psychiatry*, Leo Kanner. Thomas, 3rd ed., 1966.

stayed in print for an astonishing sixty-seven years: Charles C. Thomas Publisher, personal communication.

"How can we blame the children for being afraid of thunderstorms": "Spare the Rod, but Don't Spoil the Child: Psychiatrist's Advice," *Washington Post*, Dec. 4, 1935.

"virtual middle managers": *Babes in Tomorrowland: Walt Disney and the Making of the American Child, 1930–1960*, Nicholas Sammond. Duke University Press, 2005, p. 109.

When behaviorist John B. Watson: *Psychological Care of Infant and Child*, John B. Watson. Norton, 1928.

Kanner responded by writing a soothing, chatty book: *In Defense of Mothers*, Leo Kanner. Thomas, 1941, p. 7.

He expressed hope: *Freedom from Within*, p. 387.

"Nature's mistakes": "The 1942 'Euthanasia' Debate in the American Journal of Psychiatry," Jay Joseph. *History of Psychiatry*, Vol. 16, No. 171, 2005.

"Sewage disposal, ditch digging, potato peeling": Ibid.

the State Department instructed consular officials: "The Voyage of the St. Louis" (supplementary reading materials), United States Holocaust Memorial Museum. http://www.ushmm.org/museum/exhibit/online/stlouis/teach/

"Emma Lazarus' heartwarming words of invitation": *Freedom from Within*, part V.

rumors that they were spies: "The Emigré Physician in America, 1941," David L. Edsall and Tracy Putnam. *Journal of the American Medical Association*, Vol. 117, No. 22, Nov. 29, 1941, pp. 1881–1888.

Furthermore, they graciously opened their home in Baltimore: *Freedom from Within*, part V.

hiding under a truckload of coal: Ibid., p. 378.

After the war, only eighty-eight Jews were left alive: "The Rise and Fall of Brody." Ukraine.com. http://www.ukraine.com/lviv-oblast/brody/

The economy of the region was suffering through its own sequel to the Great Depression: "Growth of the Lumber Industry (1840 to 1930)," *Mississippi History Now*, Mississippi Historical Society. http://mshistorynow.mdah.state.ms.us/articles/171/growth-of-the-lumber-industry-1840-to-1930

The couple lived in a cozy house: *The Age of Autism*, Dan Olmsted and Mark Blaxill. St. Martin's Press, 2010.

Even the sight of a man dressed as Santa Claus failed to impress him: "Autistic Disturbances of Affective Contact."

he could hum and sing many of his favorite tunes accurately: *The Age of Autism.*

At age two, he could count to one hundred: "Early Infantile Autism: S. Spafford Ackerly Lecture."

"Donnie, do you want your milk?": Ibid.

The Tripletts' family doctor suggested: "Autism's First Child," John Donvan and Caryn Zucker. *Atlantic*, Oct. 2010.

renowned for the compassionate ministrations of its nursing staff: *Mississippi State Sanatorium: Tuberculosis Hospital, 1916–1976*, Marvin R. Calder. Messenger Press, 1986.

his parents visited him only twice a month: "Autism's First Child."

"paying no attention to anything": Ibid.

He told them to leave him alone: "Follow-up Study of Eleven Autistic Children First Reported in 1943," Leo Kanner. *Childhood Psychosis: Initial Studies and New Insights.* Winston, 1973, p. 162.

"hopelessly insane child": "Autism's First Child."

In October, they boarded a train: *The Age of Autism*, p. 170.

the full-time psychiatrist-pediatrician at the Child Study Home: Letter to Adolf Meyer from Leo Kanner, March 3, 1939. Alan Chesney Medical Archives, Johns Hopkins University.

Kanner's colleagues maintained that he was simply unfamiliar with the parallel work: For example, "We can take it for granted that neither was then aware of the other's work." "Early Infantile Autism and Autistic Psychopathy," D. Arn Van Krevelen. *Journal of Autism and Childhood Schizophrenia*, Vol. 1, No. 1, Jan.–March 1971, pp. 82–86. Kanner was the editor of the *Journal of Autism and Childhood Schizophrenia.*

a quaint shingled house: The Frankls lived at 5793 Clearspring Road, according to a letter to Anni Weiss-Frankl from Adolf Meyer in the Alan Chesney Medical Archives dated Dec. 5, 1940. The Child Study Home was located at 721 Woodbourne Avenue.

Kanner and Frankl hosted "mental clinics" together: For example, "Mental Clinic Held at Winchester Hall." *Frederick Post*, May 18, 1939.

Weiss (now Weiss-Frankl) became an enthusiastic participant in Meyer's seminars: Letter from Anni Weiss-Frankl to Adolf Meyer, Dec. 4, 1940. Alan Chesney Medical Archives, Johns Hopkins University.

In a letter to Meyer: Letter from Leo Kanner to Adolf Meyer, March 3, 1939. Alan Chesney Medical Archives, Johns Hopkins University.

the Child Study Home was as close to the Heilpädagogik Station as America had to offer: "News and Notes." *American Journal of Psychiatry*, Vol. 96, No. 3, 1939, pp. 736–46.

"fascinating peculiarities": "Autistic Disturbances of Affective Contact."

"[Donald] wandered about smiling": Ibid.

Only later did Kanner figure out: *Child Psychiatry*, Leo Kanner. Thomas, 3rd ed., 1966, p. 537.

Donald performed better: "Early Infantile Autism: S. Spafford Ackerly Lecture."

"He paid no attention to persons": "Autistic Disturbances of Affective Contact."

"a fellow the expert does not want to be bothered with": *In Defense of Mothers*, p. 104.

"*?schizophrenia*": "Autism's First Child."

The first account of "childhood schizophrenia" in America: "Schizophrenia in Children," Howard Potter. *American Journal of Psychiatry*, Vol. 89, Issue 6, May 1933, pp. 1253–70.

One boy in this group, S.K.: Despert discusses S.K.'s case in "Schizophrenia in Children," *Schizophrenia in Children*, J. Louise Despert, Robert Brunner, 1968, pp. 1–7, and also in "Prophylactic Aspect of Schizophrenia in Childhood" in the same volume, pp. 54–87.

"Schizophrenia in children is probably not so rare": "Schizophrenia in Children," p. 1.

the concept of the schizophrenogenic mother bloomed in a hothouse of cultural anxieties: "The Schizophrenogenic Mother Concept in American Psychiatry," Carol Eadie Hartwell. *Psychiatry*, Vol. 59, No. 3, Fall 1996, pp. 274–97.

but admitted that this was speculation on her part: "Schizophrenia in Children," p. 4.

a seven-year-old girl named Elaine C.: "Autistic Disturbances of Affective Contact."

"Nobody realizes more than I do myself": "Autism's First Child."

someone in his office asked the mother of a boy called Alfred L.: *The Age of Autism*, p. 173.

his daughter Bridget: Ibid., pp. 173–74.

The cracks in the old ceiling of Kanner's office: "The Conception of Wholes and Parts in Early Infantile Autism," Leo Kanner. Originally published in 1953, reprinted in *Childhood Psychosis: Initial Studies and New Insights*, Leo Kanner. Winston, 1973, pp. 63–68.

a diagnosis historically associated with the working class, immigrants, and people of color: *The Autism Matrix*, Gil Eyal et al. Polity Press, 2010, p. 85.

pointing to the development of mercury-containing fungicides and vaccine preservatives like Merthiolate: *The Age of Autism*, pp. 147–49.

eighteenth-century account by the Swiss poet: From "Der grüne Heinrich," by Gottfried Keller. Quoted by Leo Kanner in "Emotionally Disturbed Children: A Historical Review," *Child Development*, Vol. 33, No. 1, March 1962, pp. 97–102.

"I have followed a number of children": *The Age of Autism*, pp. 173–74.

Despert published a paper in the debut issue of Harms's journal: "Prophylactic Aspect of Schizophrenia in Childhood," Louise Despert. *Nervous Child*, No. 1, 1942, pp. 199–231.

"The outstanding, 'pathognomonic,' fundamental disorder": "Autistic Disturbances of Affective Contact."

"Their world must seem to them to be made up of elements": Ibid.

the name that stuck: *early infantile autism*: "Early Infantile Autism," Leo Kanner. *Journal of Pediatrics*, Vol. 25, No. 3, Sept. 1944, pp. 211–217.

"The major part of his 'conversation'": "Autistic Disturbances of Affective Contact."

a "*lack of contact with persons* in its most extreme form": "Language and Affective Contact," George Frankl. *Nervous Child*, Vol. 2, No. 3, 1943.

"There were things he wanted to do and did regularly": Ibid.

Epilepsy is now considered one of the most common comorbidities: "Risk of Epilepsy in Autism Tied to Age, Intelligence," Laura Geggel. SFARI.org, Aug. 19, 2013. http://sfari.org/news-and-opinion/news/2013/risk-of-epilepsy-in-autism-tied-to-age-intelligence

the "most important" article in the field: "Review of *The 1944 Year Book of Neurology, Psychiatry and Endocrinology*," Wendell Muncie. *Quarterly Review of Biology*, Vol. 21, No. 2, June 1946, pp. 205–6.

the father of Kanner's patient Barbara K.: *The Age of Autism*.

CHAPTER 5. THE INVENTION OF TOXIC PARENTING

"One is struck again and again": "Problems of Nosology and Psychodynamics of Early Infantile Autism," Leo Kanner. *American Journal of Orthopsychiatry*, Vol. 19, No. 3, July 1949, pp. 416–26.

"I am extremely sorry about that": Letter from Anni Weiss-Frankl to Adolf Meyer, Dec. 4, 1940. Alan Chesney Medical Archives, Johns Hopkins University.

Meanwhile, Kanner was enlisting Meyer's help: Letter from Leo Kanner to Adolf Meyer, March 3, 1939. Alan Chesney Medical Archives, Johns Hopkins University.

focused exclusively on the "serendipity" of the Tripletts' arrival: "The Birth of Early Infantile Autism," Leo Kanner. *Journal of Autism and Childhood Schizophrenia*, Vol. 3, No. 2, Apr.–June 1973, pp. 93–95.

the "social value of this personality type": "Autistic Psychopathy in Childhood."

No less than four of the fathers: *The Age of Autism.*

less than one in four women: *Census Atlas of the United States*, U.S. Census Bureau, 2000, p. 158.

Meyer was also mentoring Theodore and Ruth Lidz: "Dr. Theodore Lidz, a Noted Specialist on Schizophrenia, Dies." *Yale Bulletin and Calendar*, Vol. 29, No. 21, March 2, 2001.

the schizophrenogenic mother hypothesis: *The Pathological Family: Postwar America and the Rise of Family Therapy*, Deborah Weinstein. Cornell University Press, 2013, p. 31.

"To a child 2 or 3 years old": "Autistic Disturbances of Affective Contact."

"His interview with parents is remarkable": "Preface," Leon Eisenberg. *Childhood Psychosis: Initial Studies and New Insights*, Leo Kanner. Winston, 1973, p. ix.

"His mother brought with her copious notes": "Autistic Disturbances of Affective Contact."

a Johns Hopkins nurse named Rachel Cary: *The Age of Autism*, p. 182.

a rave review: "Review of *The 1944 Year Book of Neurology, Psychiatry and Endocrinology.*"

"rare enough": "Autistic Disturbances of Affective Contact."

he would soon see seven more: "Early Infantile Autism."

only one in ten children examined at the Harriet Lane: "A Child Psychiatric Clinic in a Paediatric Department."

a barbed letter from Louise Despert: *The Age of Autism*, p. 186.

"previous difficulty in adaptation": "Schizophrenia in Children," p. 4.

"The case material has been expanded": "Early Infantile Autism (1943–1955)," Leo Kanner and Leon Eisenberg. *Childhood Psychosis: Initial Studies and New Insights*, Leo Kanner. Winston, 1973, p. 93.

"the earliest reactions to the issue": *Childhood Psychosis*, pp. 77–90.

its own book-length annotated bibliography: *Annotated Bibliography of Childhood Schizophrenia*, W. Goldfarb and M. M. Dorsen. Basic Books, 1956.

one hundred children diagnosed with early-onset schizophrenia: "Childhood Schizophrenia: Clinical Study of One Hundred Schizophrenic Children," Lauretta Bender. *American Journal of Orthopsychiatry*, Vol. 17, No. 1, Jan. 1947, pp. 40–56.

850 young patients with that diagnosis at Bellevue alone: "Infantile Autism and the Schizophrenias," Leo Kanner. *Behavioral Science*, Vol. 10, No. 4, 1965, p. 418.

from 1946 to 1961, one in seven children: "A Statistical Study of a Group of Psychotic

Children," Dorothy Bomberg, S. A. Szurek, and Jacqueline Etemad. *Clinical Studies in Childhood Psychoses.* Brunner/Mazel, 1973, pp. 303–45.

"The concept of a *gradient* of severity": Ibid.

Hilde Mosse of the Lafargue Clinic in Harlem: "The Misuse of the Diagnosis Childhood Schizophrenia," Hilde L. Mosse. *American Journal of Psychiatry*, Vol. 114, March 1958, pp. 791–94.

"the earliest possible manifestation of childhood schizophrenia": "Problems of Nosology and Psychodynamics of Early Infantile Autism."

(subtitle: "Diaper-Age Schizoids"): "Frosted Children," *Time*, Apr. 26, 1948.

Leon Eisenberg published his own case series: "The Fathers of Autistic Children," Leon Eisenberg. *American Journal of Orthopsychiatry*, Vol. 27, Issue 4, Oct. 1957, pp. 715–24.

kibbutzim "in reverse": "Early Infantile Autism (1943–1955)," Leo Kanner and Leon Eisenberg. *American Journal of Orthopsychiatry*, Vol. 26, 1956, pp. 55–65.

Bettelheim first heard about psychoanalysis: "Bruno Bettelheim and the Concentration Camps," Christian Fleck and Albert Müller. *Journal of the History of the Behavioral Sciences*, Vol. 33, No. 1, Winter 1997, pp. 1–37.

Bettelheim would go out of his way to walk down the steep slope of Bergasse: "Bergasse 19." *Freud's Vienna*, Bruno Bettelheim. Vintage Books, 1991, p. 21.

When his father died of syphilis in 1926: *Bettelheim: A Life and a Legacy*, Nina Sutton. Westview Press, 1996, p. 80.

Gina came to despise: Ibid., p. 85.

a Jew and an advocate of Austrian independence: "Bruno Bettelheim and the Concentration Camps."

Meyer Schapiro, Theodor Adorno, and Dwight D. Eisenhower: "The Man He Always Wanted to Be," Sarah Boxer. *New York Times*, Jan. 26, 1997.

"The prisoners developed types of behavior": "Individual and Mass Behavior in Extreme Situations," Bruno Bettelheim. *The Journal of Abnormal and Social Psychology*, Vol. 38, No. 4, Oct. 1943, pp. 417–52.

"We believed that autistic children were usually attractive: "Autism at the Orthogenic School and in the Field at Large (1951–1985)," Jacqueline Seevak Sanders. *Residential Treatment for Children & Youth*, Vol. 14, No. 2, 1996.

Research that suggested an organic etiology: Ibid.

He had the locks on the doors changed: *Bettelheim: A Life and a Legacy*, p. 265.

Instead of institutional bunk beds: *The Creation of Dr. B*, Richard Pollak. Touchstone, 1997, p. 332.

"in abject, animal terror": "Who, Really, Was Bruno Bettelheim?" Ronald Angres. *Commentary*, Oct. 1990.

"The precipitating factor in infantile autism": *The Empty Fortress: Infantile Autism and the Birth of the Self*, Bruno Bettelheim. Free Press, 1967, pp. 125, 348.

"None of them were 'successful'": "Autism at the Orthogenic School and in the Field at Large (1951–1985)."

Bender's preferred method of treatment: "Theory and Treatment of Childhood Schizophrenia," Lauretta Bender. *Acta Paedopsychiatrica*, Vol. 34, 1968, pp. 298–307.

Another drug that Bender felt showed great promise was LSD: Ibid.

children who displayed many traits: For example: "Until the late 1970s, children with autism were often labeled as having 'childhood schizophrenia.'" "Multiplex Developmental Disorder." Autism Program at Yale. http://childstudycenter.yale.edu/autism/information/mdd.aspx

"the Space Child": "The Space Child: A Note on the Psychotherapeutic Treatment of a 'Schizophrenoid' Child," Rudolf Ekstein and Dorothy Wright. *Bulletin of the Menninger Clinic*, 1952.

with a lookout on the roof: Note on a 2011 photograph of the abandoned facility, Patrick Emerson. http://www.flickr.com/photos/kansasphoto/7341230726/

"a mixture of Freud and friendliness": Kansapedia. Kansas Historical Society. http://www.kshs.org/portal_kansapedia.

"the company of lower class colored people": "Freedom and Authority in Adolescence," Frederick J. Hacker and Elisabeth R. Geleerd. *American Journal of Orthopsychiatry*. Vol. 15, No. 4, Oct. 1945.

"circumscribed interest patterns": "Children with Circumscribed Interest Patterns," J. Franklin Robinson and Louis J. Vitale. *American Journal of Orthopsychiatry*, Vol. 24, No. 4, Oct. 1954, pp. 755–66.

a particularly disheartening roundtable: "Childhood Schizophrenia: Round Table, 1953," Herbert Herskovitz, chairman. *American Journal of Orthopsychiatry*, Vol. 24, No. 3, July 1954, pp. 484–528.

a draft for a paper he never published: "Autism in Childhood: An Attempt of an Analysis," George Frankl. Courtesy of Spencer Library, University of Kansas Archives.

***kvelling* like a proud father:** "Notes on the Follow-up Studies of Autistic Children." Leo Kanner and Leon Eisenberg. Originally published in 1955; reprinted in *Childhood Psychosis: Initial Studies and New Insights*, Leo Kanner. Winston, 1973, pp. 77–90.

"Jay S., now almost 15 years old": Ibid., p. 86

"I was amazed at the wisdom of the couple who took care of him": "Follow-up Study of Eleven Autistic Children Originally Reported in 1943," Leo Kanner. *Journal of Autism and Childhood Schizophrenia*, Vol. 1, No. 2, 1971, p. 163.

"If one factor is significantly useful, it is a sympathetic and tolerant reception by the school": "Early Infantile Autism (1943–1955)," Leo Kanner and Leon Eisenberg. *American Journal of Orthopsychiatry*, Vol. 26, Issue 3, July 1956, pp. 55–65.

four thousand boys and girls: "Thiells Journal: Graves without Names for the Forgotten Mentally Retarded," David Corcoran. *New York Times*, Dec. 9, 1991.

"One cannot help but gain the impression": "Follow-up Study of Eleven Autistic Children Originally Reported in 1943," Leo Kanner. *Journal of Autism and Childhood Schizophrenia*, Vol. 1, No. 2, 1971, pp. 119–145.

"Richard M., Barbara K., Virginia S., and Charles N.": Ibid., p. 185.

***forme fruste*:** Ibid., p. 187.

"New discoveries are period-bound rather than time-bound": "Early Infantile Autism and Autistic Psychopathy."

"The name is Asperger": "Review: *The Autistic Child*, by Isaac Kugelmass," Leo Kanner. *Journal of Nervous and Mental Disease*, Vol. 152, No. 5, 1971, pp. 370–71.

only 150 true cases: "Childhood Problems in Relation to the Family: Summary of a Seminar," Leo Kanner and Leon Eisenberg. *Pediatrics*, Vol. 20, No. 1, 1957, pp. 155–64.

nine out of ten children: *A History of Autism*, p. 47.

CHAPTER 6. PRINCES OF THE AIR

forcing him to amend: See Uta Frith's footnote in "Autistic Psychopathy in Childhood," p. 72.

the son of a Jewish wine merchant in Luxembourg: *The Gernsback Days*, Mike Ashley and Robert A. W. Lowndes. Wildside Press, 2004, p. 16.

the bell rang amid a shower of sparks: "The Gernsback Story," Ed Raser. Reprinted in *QST*, Apr. 2008.

(a prediction confirmed in 2009 by the Phoenix Mars Lander): "The Dirt on Mars Lander Soil Findings," Andrea Thompson. Space.com, July 2, 2009. http://www.space.com/6918-dirt-mars-lander-soil-findings.html

first spotted by Giovanni Schiaparelli in 1877: "Lunar Bat-men, the Planet Vulcan and Martian Canals," Erik Washam. *Smithsonian*, Dec. 2010.

"of an order whose acquaintance was worth the making": *Mars as the Abode of Life*, Percival Lowell. Macmillan, 1908.

"The concept that intelligent life might exist on other worlds": *Explorers of the Infinite: Shapers of Science Fiction*, Sam Moskowitz. World, 1963.

an attempt to use solar energy to roast coffee beans: *The Gernsback Days*, p. 17.

One icy-cold winter's day: Ibid., p. 18.

a thousand a day: "The Gernsback Story."

instead of the $50,000 cost of a standard commercial rig: *The Gernsback Days*, p. 20.

A policeman burst into Gernsback's office: Ibid.

Gernsback's kits flew off the shelves: "A Dreamer Who Made Us Fall in Love with the Future," Daniel Stashower. *Smithsonian*, 1984, reprinted Aug. 1, 1990.

"We feel sure": Electro Importing Company: *Catalogue No. 7*, 1st ed., 1910, foreword.

If a ringing telephone interrupted him: "A Dreamer Who Made Us Fall in Love with the Future."

"I vowed to change the situation if I could": *The Gernsback Days*, p. 20.

the navigational abilities of homing pigeons: Ibid.

He christened this genre "scientifiction": *Science-Fiction: The Gernsback Years*, Everett Franklin Bleiler. Kent State University Press, 1998.

"One to foresee for more than one": "Hugo Gernsback Is Dead at 83; Author, Publisher, and Inventor." *New York Times*, Aug. 20, 1967.

Telautomata: "My Inventions," Nikola Tesla. *The Electrical Experimenter*. Experimenter Publishing, 1919.

"the whole earth will be converted into a huge brain": "When Woman Is Boss: An Interview with Nikola Tesla," John B. Kennedy. *Collier's*, Jan. 30, 1926.

one was "not as ugly as the other": "My Inventions."

"I needed no models, drawings, or experiments": *My Inventions*, Nikola Tesla. Martino Fine Books, repr. ed. 2011, p. 13.

"Before I attempt any construction, I test-run the equipment in my imagination": *Thinking in Pictures*, Temple Grandin. Vintage Books, 1996, p. 4.

printing his readers' names and addresses along with their letters: *Science-Fiction: The Gernsback Years.*

more fervent discussion of Einstein's theory of relativity in the letters column of *Amazing Stories*: *The Gernsback Days*, p. 117.

a group of New York City teens: *Astrofuturism: Science, Race, and Visions of Utopia in Space*, De Witt Douglas Kilgore. University of Pennsylvania Press, 2003.

an African American space buff named Warren Fitzgerald: "Without You, There's No Future," Paul Malmont. Tor.com. http://www.tor.com/blogs/2011/07/without-you-theres-no-future

(Sam Moskowitz's 1954 chronicle . . .): *All Our Yesterdays*, Harry Warner. Advent, 1969.

Clarke himself circulated copies of *Thrilling Wonder Stories*: "British Scientists Now Read Wonder." *Fantasy Review*, Vol. 2, No. 9, June–July 1948.

"cognitive estrangement": "Introduction," Victor Wallis. *Socialism and Democracy Journal*, Apr. 6, 2011.

"gadget fiction": *The Detached Retina: Aspects of SF and Fantasy*, Brian W. Aldiss. Syracuse University Press, 1995.

When a reader objected to *Wonder Stories* publishing translations from the German: *Science-Fiction: The Gernsback Years*, p. xiv.

According to a dossier: "Investigation in Newcastle," Jack Speer, 1944.

mandating his forced sterilization: Ibid.

"a fannish island in a sea of mundania": *All Our Yesterdays.*

"Our planning included a fanzine room": "The Legendary Slan Shack," Dal Coger. *Mimosa* 22, June 1998.

"Our children shall inherit not only this earth": *All Our Yesterdays.*

"Looking back at the science fiction of the 1930s pulp magazines": "*Homo aspergerus*: Evolution Stumbles Forward," Gary Westfahl. *Locus Online*, March 6, 2006.

most fans were "handicapped": *All Our Yesterdays.*

celebrated episode: "The City at the Edge of Forever," Harlan Ellison. *Star Trek*, season 1, episode 28.

"Fans today can't imagine the threadbare existence": "Looking for Degler," David B. Williams. *Mimosa* 30, Aug. 2003.

(. . . "an addiction to obscure lingo for its own sake"): *All Our Yesterdays.*

fandom was a community that was unusually accepting of individual quirks: "Those Fabulous 'Handicapped' Fans," Arnie Katz. *Fanstuff*, No. 33, March 17, 2013.

"reading and conjecturing about worlds in which customs might differ from ours": *Rough News, Daring Views*, Jim Kepner. Haworth Press, 1998.

"reasonable to assume": Gary Westfahl, personal communication, 2013.

crying out for a high-tech solution: "The Future: Electronic Mating," Hugo Gernsback. *Sexology*, Feb. 1964.

"a well-known optical law": "How to Write 'Science' Stories," Hugo Gernsback. *Writer's Digest*, Feb. 1930. Reprinted in *Science Fiction Studies*, July 1994.

thirty mistakes commonly made by writers: *The Mechanics of Wonder: The Creation of the Idea of Science Fiction*, Gary Westfahl. Liverpool University Press, 1998, p. 131.

"think room": *Hugo Gernsback: A Man Well Ahead of His Time*, Larry Steckler, ed. BookSurge, 2007, p. 191.

"an air of ducal authority": "Barnum of the Space Age: The Amazing Hugo Gernsback, Prophet of Science," Paul O'Neil. *Life*, Sept. 9, 1963.

"carrying the world on his shoulders": Ibid.

impoverished and emaciated in his room at the Hotel New Yorker: "Nikola Tesla, 86, Prolific Inventor." *New York Times*, Jan. 8, 1943.

death mask: "About New York," Meyer Berger. *New York Times*, Jan. 6, 1958.

a "radio mind": "Your Boy and Radio," Hugo Gernsback. *Radio News*, Dec. 1924.

"The neophyte does not metamorphose easily": *Calling CQ*, Clinton DeSoto. Doubleday, Doran, 1941.

One of the radio-minded boys who answered DeSoto's call: "Bob Hedin to Be Awarded the 2013 GRASP Distinguished Spectrumite Medal." GRASP website. http://grasp.org/profiles/blogs/bob-hedin-to-be-awarded-the-2013-grasp-distinguished-spectrumite

He was drawn to amateur radio: Robert Hedin, personal communication, 2013.

"Through amateur radio . . . I've learned so much: "From a Female Viewpoint," Judith C. Gorski. *QST*, Jan. 1978.

she learned to conduct herself in social situations gracefully: "Lenore Jensen; Actress, Ham Radio Operator," *Los Angeles Times*, May 8, 1993.

"That sonorous hulk of varnished wood": "I Am a Survivor," Mark Morris Goodman. Asperger's Association of New England. http://www.aane.org/asperger_resources/articles/adults/i_am_a_survivor.html

"Sometimes I tuned in episodes crafted for those my age": Ibid.

the story of a young ham named Walter Stiles who became a hero: *Calling CQ*, Clinton DeSoto. Doubleday, Doran, 1941.

"like coming ashore after a life of bobbing up and down": "I Am a Survivor," Mark Morris Goodman. Asperger's Association of New England, http://www.aane.org/asperger_resources/articles/adults/i_am_a_survivor.html

172 spacecraft: National Space Science Data Center. http://nssdc.gsfc.nasa.gov/nmc/spacecraftSearch.do?launchDate=1967&discipline=All

the first undergraduate course in computer programming: *Hackers: Heroes of the Computer Revolution*, Steven Levy. O'Reilly Media, 2010, p. 11.

he coined the term *artificial intelligence*: "A Proposal for the Dartmouth Summer Research Project on Artificial Intelligence," J. McCarthy, M. L. Minsky, N. Rochester, and C. E. Shannon. Aug. 31, 1955.

If his colleagues wanted him to read a paper: *Scientific Temperaments*, Philip Hilts. Simon & Schuster, 1982, p. 203.

"His greeting consisted of an expectant stare": Ibid.

A fellow pilot recalled McCarthy coaching himself: Ibid.

Gernsbackian how-to guides: *The Project Gutenberg EBook of Electricity for Boys*, J. S. Zerbe. http://www.gutenberg.org/files/22766/22766-h/22766-h.htm

He advocated installing a terminal in every home: "The Home Information Utility," John McCarthy. *Man and Computer: Proceedings of the International Conference, Bordeaux, France, 1970. Basel.* S. Karger, 1972, pp. 48–57.

habitually unwashed, Coke-guzzling, Chinese-takeout-eating obsessives: See the descriptions of TMRC hackers in *Hackers: Heroes of the Computer Revolution*, Steven Levy. O'Reilly Media, 2010.

As hard-core fans of science fiction, ham radio, and Japanese monster movies: "Spacewars and Beyond: How the Tech Model Railroad Club Changed the World," Henry Jenkins. http://henryjenkins.org/2007/10/spacewars_and_beyond_how_the_t.html#sthash.vNI7iDoK.dpuf

equal parts of "science, fiction, and science fiction": *Scientific Temperaments*, p. 266.

"Do the arithmetic or be doomed to talk nonsense": "John McCarthy, 84, Dies; Computer Design Pioneer," John Markoff. *New York Times*, Oct. 25, 2011.

François Mitterrand, the president of France, visited her office: Jean Hollands, personal communication.

Homebrew Computer Club: Ibid.

a combination of Sherlock Holmes and A. J. Raffles: *The Senior Class Book*, compiled by the class of 1906, Cornell University, 1906, p. 147.

he embarked on a bike tour of Europe: Lee Felsenstein, personal communication.

"I'm not daydreaming, I'm inventing": "Oral History of Lee Felsenstein," Kip Crosby. Edited by Dag Spicer. May 7, 2008. Computer History Museum, p. 2. http://www.computerhistory.org/collections/catalog/102702231

He began to think of the basement as a holy sanctuary: Lee Felsenstein, personal communication.

"I realized that I had made a mistake": Lee Felsenstein, interview with the author, 2014.

While McCarthy wanted to design machines: "An Interview with John Markoff: What the Dormouse Said." *Ubiquity*, Aug. 2005.

tools that would facilitate "conviviality": *Tools for Conviviality*, Ivan Illich. Harper & Row, 1973.

a programmer at a bustling commune: "Spacewar: Fanatic Life and Symbolic Death among the Computer Bums," Stewart Brand. *Rolling Stone*, Dec. 7, 1972.

which was twenty-four feet long: "Convivial Cybernetic Devices: An Interview with Lee Felsenstein," Kip Crosby. *Analytical Engine* (newsletter of the Computer History Association of California), Vol. 3, No. 1, Nov. 1995.

a "communication device between humans": "Spacewar."

Emoticons like :-)—originally proposed by Lisp hacker Scott Fahlman: "Smiley Lore," Scott Fahlman. https://www.cs.cmu.edu/~sef/sefSmiley.htm

On August 8, 1973: "Convivial Cybernetic Devices."

"We invite your participation and suggestions": Community Memory flyer, courtesy of Mark Szpakowski and Loving Grace Cybernetics. http://www.well.com/~szpak/cm/cmflyer.html

via an Oakland telephone exchange: "The First Community Memory," interview with Lee Felsenstein, Jon Plutte. Computer History Museum, 2011. http://www.computerhistory.org/revolution/the-web/20/377/2328

"As a kid, I had a feeling": Lee Felsenstein, interview with the author, 2014.

CHAPTER 7. FIGHTING THE MONSTER

"'this is heaven. I'm never leaving'": "Dr. Bernard Rimland Is Autism's Worst Enemy," Patricia Morris Buckley. *San Diego Jewish Journal*, Oct. 2002.

"how one determines what is true, or what might be true": "The Modern History of Autism: A Personal Perspective," Bernard Rimland. *Autism in Children and Adults*, Johnny L. Matson, ed. Brooks/Cole, 1994, p. 1.

who loved to go down to the park: Gloria Rimland, interview with the author, 2012.

Impressed by his chutzpah: Ibid.

Rimland was third in line at the viewing window: *Madness on the Couch*, Edward Dolnick. Simon & Schuster, 1998, p. 219.

"We thought we were really living": Ibid., p. 219.

"like a fish out of water": Gloria Rimland, interview with the author, 2012.

The Rimlands began meeting twice a week: "A World unto Himself: One Family's Agonizing Fight to Help Their Autistic Child," Lloyd Grove. *Washington Post*, Aug. 5, 1984.

"Tell me, why do you hate your son?": Gloria Rimland, interview with the author, 2012.

a team of Navy translators: "Bernard Rimland's *Infantile Autism*: The Book That Changed Autism," Steve Edelson. Autism Research Institute, 2014.

When the Navy sent him to New Orleans: "The Modern History of Autism."

"This was war": Ibid.

"Only Churchill comes to mind": Undated letter (early 1960s) from Bernard Rimland to Leo Kanner. Courtesy of the Autism Research Institute.

"We feel that there is real progress": Ibid.

"We think it is mostly due to Deaner": Ibid.

"since Mark's taking of Deaner has resulted in such striking improvement": Ibid.

He began compiling his observations: "Apparent" not because he questioned Kanner's diagnostic acumen but because Rimland was using the word *autism* in the old sense, as a description of behavior rather than the name of a disorder.

teaching courses on abnormal psychology: "Application for Fellowship at the Center for Advanced Study in the Behavioral Sciences," Bernard Rimland. Stanford University, July 23, 1964.

a bit dull by comparison: In a July 23, 1964, letter to Ralph W. Tyler, director of the Center for Advanced Study in the Behavioral Sciences at Stanford University, Rimland said that the forty technical papers and journal articles he'd written on psychometrics for the Navy "would not be considered important outside their immediate context."

His moonlighting as an autism researcher: "Preface," *Infantile Autism: The Syndrome and Its Implications for a Neural Theory of Behavior*, Bernard Rimland. Appleton-Century-Crofts, 1964.

"if you study an object of nature intently enough": Ibid.

on the strength of the writing alone: Gloria Rimland, interview with the author, 2012.

"It is interesting to conjecture that the silent, unreachable autistic child": *Infantile Autism*, p. 13.

"Imagine the child's reaction to the futility of living in an incomprehensible world": Ibid., p. 108.

He said only that Kanner and Eisenberg had "subscribed" to the notion of psychogenic causation: Ibid., p. 43.

autism is primarily a product of genetic inheritance: "The Genetics of Autistic Disorders and Its Clinical Relevance: A Review of the Literature," C. M. Freitag. *Molecular Psychiatry*, Vol. 12, Issue 1, Jan. 2007, pp. 2–22.

"We must give serious consideration": *Infantile Autism*, p. 127.

"The conclusion I reached then, and by which I stand today": "The Modern History of Autism," p. 6.

a significantly higher number of fathers working in the technical professions: "A Retrospective Analysis of the Clinical Case Records of 'Autistic Psychopaths' Diagnosed by Hans Asperger and His Team at the University Children's Hospital, Vienna," Kathrin Hippler and Christian Klicpera. *Philosophical Transactions: Biological Sciences*, Vol. 358, No. 1430, *Autism: Mind and Brain* (Feb. 28, 2003), pp. 291–301.

Researchers at the University of Edinburgh discovered in 2015: "Common Polygenic Risk for Autism Spectrum Disorder (ASD) is Associated with Cognitive Ability in the General Population," T. K. Clarke, M. K. Lupton, et al. *Molecular Psychiatry*, advance online publication, March 10, 2015.

"If autism is solely determined by organic factors": *Infantile Autism*, p. 40.

"from clinic to clinic": Ibid., p. 57.

continuing underdiagnosis of autism in minority communities: "Race Differences in the Age at Diagnosis among Medicaid-Eligible Children with Autism," D. S. Mandell, J. Listerud, et al. *Journal of the American Academy of Child and Adolescent Psychiatry*, Vol. 41, No. 12, Dec. 2002, pp. 1447–53.

"It may be that some of the cases the present writer cites": *Infantile Autism*, p. 19.

In the 1920s, a young couple in Oslo named Harry and Borgny Egeland: Details in this section are from "The Discovery of Phenylketonuria: The Story of a Young Couple, Two Retarded Children, and a Scientist," Siegfried A. Centerwall and Willard R. Centerwall. *Pediatrics*, Vol. 105, No. 1, Jan. 1, 2000, pp. 89–103.

a multiple-choice questionnaire: "Diagnostic Check List for Behavior-Disturbed Children (Form E-1)." Provided by Steve Edelson of the Autism Research Institute.

not "true cases": *Infantile Autism*, p. 18.

Rimland had no particular plans to do further writing in the field: Steve Edelson, personal communication.

sent directly to the address of the U.S. Naval Personnel Research Laboratory: Steve Edelson, personal communication, based on a conversation with Gloria Rimland.

He also used the notes: Steve Edelson, personal communication.

"very little has been published": *Infantile Autism*, p. 16.

In 1956, Eisenberg published a paper: "The Autistic Child in Adolescence," Leon Eisenberg. *American Journal of Psychiatry*, Vol. 112, Issue 8, Feb. 1956, pp. 607–12.

"therapeutic hopelessness": *Infantile Autism*, p. 64.

"There are more brains in this salad": "Poet with a Cattle Prod," Paul Chance. *Psychology Today*, Jan. 1974.

"like aphids in the Garden of Eden": Ibid.

forced to work as migrant laborers: "The Phantom Chaser," Robert Ito. *Los Angeles Magazine*, Apr. 2004.

earned his bachelor's degree in a year: "In Memoriam: O. Ivar Lovaas (1927–2010)," Eric V. Larsson and Scott Wright. *Behavior Analyst*, Vol. 34, No. 1, Spring 2011, pp. 111–14.

talked his way into the graduate program in psychology: "Poet with a Cattle Prod."

one of his roommates at UW was Eddie Alf: Gloria Rimland, interview with the author.

"instead, they got worse": "An Interview with O. Ivar Lovaas," Richard Simpson. *Focus on Autistic Behavior*, Vol. 4, No. 4, Oct. 1989.

"they called it a 'suicide epidemic'": "The Phantom Chaser."

"They were like Nero, playing fiddles as the world burned": "Poet with a Cattle Prod."

One of the stars of the department was Sid Bijou: "Pioneer Profiles: A Few Minutes with Sid Bijou," Michael D. Wesolowski. *Behavior Analyst*, Vol. 25, No. 1, Spring 2002, pp. 15–27.

Lovaas stayed on in Seattle for three years: "O. Ivar Lovaas: Pioneer of Applied Behavior Analysis and Intervention for Children with Autism," Tristram Smith and Svein Eikeseth. *Journal of Autism and Developmental Disorders*, Vol. 41, Issue 3, March 2011, pp. 375–78.

Watching a typically developing boy: "The Development of a Treatment-Research Project for Developmentally Disabled and Autistic Children," O. Ivar Lovaas. *Journal of Applied Behavior Analysis*, Vol. 26, Issue 4, Winter 1993, pp. 617–30.

"the analysis of the autistic child may be of theoretical use": "Positive Reinforcement and Behavioral Deficits of Autistic Children," Charles B. Ferster. *Conditioning Techniques in Clinical Practice and Research*, Springer, 1964, pp. 255–74.

the best way for parents to deal with their children acting out: "Strengths and Weaknesses of Operant Conditioning Techniques for the Treatment of Autism," O. Ivar Lovaas. *Research and Education: Top Priorities for Mentally Ill Children. Proceedings of the Second Annual Meeting and Conference of the National Society for Autistic Children*, 1971.

Lovaas would eventually make films: Ibid.

"The fascinating part to me": "The Development of a Treatment-Research Project for Developmentally Disabled and Autistic Children," p. 620.

"you have to build the person": "Poet with a Cattle Prod."

a chubby, blue-eyed nine-year-old brunette named Beth: *Behavioral Treatment of Autism.* Documentary by Edward L. Anderson and Robert Aller. Focus International, 1988.

To justify his use of laboratory time: "O. Ivar Lovaas."

more time with Beth: "Poet with a Cattle Prod."

(including, of course, Lovaas himself): Lorna Wing, interview with the author, 2011.

"Say, 'Hug me'": *The ME Book: Teaching Developmentally Disabled Children*, O. Ivar Lovaas. PRO-ED, 1981.

the department's biggest "male chauvinist pig": "Memories of Ole Ivar Lovaas. http://www.psychologicalscience.org/index.php/publications/observer/2010/november-10/memories-of-ole-ivar-lovaas.html

"the technique seemed much better suited to training dogs": "In Defense of Ivar Lovaas," Bernard Rimland. Autism Research Institute International newsletter, Vol. 1, No. 1, 1987.

"To my wife's horror": Ibid.

"Mark was a very nice kid": David Ryback, interview with the author, 2013.

between "Grandma" and "Grandpa": Gloria Rimland, interview with the author, 2012.

Todd Risley had already taught the mother of one of his patients: "Experimental Manipulation of Autistic Behaviors and Generalization into the Home," Todd Risley and Montrose M. Wolf. Paper presented at the American Psychological Association, Los Angeles, Sept. 1964.

Over heaping plates of spaghetti and copious amounts of red wine: "Strengths and Weaknesses of Operant Conditioning Techniques for the Treatment of Autism."

"autistic shells": "An Interview with O. Ivar Lovaas."

one of the most important nights of his life: "The Modern History of Autism."

a strict low-salt, low-protein diet: "Thomas Addis (1881–1949): A Biographical Memoir," Kevin B. Lemley and Linus S. Pauling. National Academy of Sciences, 1994.

all work in the clinic would stop for tea: Ibid.

He wrote three best-selling books: *Vitamin C and the Common Cold* (1970), *Vitamin C and Cancer* (1979), and *How to Feel Better and Live Longer* (1986).

production was unable to keep up with the demand: "Vitamin C Sales Booming Despite Skepticism on Pauling," Jane E. Brody. *New York Times*, Dec. 5, 1970.

Pauling's extravagant claims for vitamin C: "Vitamin C for Preventing and Treating the Common Cold," H. Hemilä and E. Chalker. The Cochrane Collaboration, May 31, 2013.

Karl Folkers and Alexander Todd: "Linus Pauling and the Advent of Orthomolecular Medicine," Stephen Lawson. *Journal of Orthomolecular Medicine*, Vol. 23, 2nd Quarter, 2008. Folkers shared the credit for isolating B-12 with his colleague Mary Shaw Shorb.

"cerebral scurvy": "Orthomolecular Psychiatry," Linus Pauling. *Science*, Vol. 160, No. 3825, Apr. 1968. *Journal of Orthomolecular Medicine*, Vol. 23, No. 2, 2008, pp. 265–271.

"refused to see what was so clearly evident to everyone else": *Recovering Autistic Children*, Stephen M. Edelson and Bernard Rimland, eds. Autism Research Institute, 2nd ed., 2006.

Before attending a Navy conference in Washington: "The Modern History of Autism."

Sullivan and her family were living in Lake Charles, Louisiana: Ruth Christ Sullivan, interview with the author, 2012.

On November 14, 1965: "The Role of the National Society in Working with Families," Frank Warren. *The Effects of Autism on the Family*, Eric Schopler and Gary B. Mesibov, eds. Plenum Press, 1984.

a pediatrician named Mary Goodwin: Ruth Christ Sullivan, interview with the author, 2012.

a contraption called the Voicewriter: *The World of Typewriters (1714–2014)*, Robert Messenger. Australian Typewriter Museum. http://oztypewriter.blogspot.com/

"The typewriter never scolds": "How to Teach Infants to Read," *Saturday Evening Post*, Nov. 20, 1965.

sixty-five autistic children: "Autism, Brain Damage, Mental Retardation: Observations with the Talking Typewriter," Mary Goodwin. *Research and Education: Top Priorities for Mentally Ill Children. Proceedings of the Second Annual Meeting and Conference of the National Society for Autistic Children*, 1971.

"We should weave a cloth so strong": Ruth Christ Sullivan, interview with the author.

"unleased an enormous burst of productivity and creativity": "The Modern History of Autism."

"parents of children with autism knew that many things closely affecting their lives were terribly wrong": "The Role of the National Society in Working with Families."

a network of similar libraries throughout the country: "Parents as Trainers of Legislators, Other Parents, and Researchers," Ruth Christ Sullivan. *The Effects of Autism on the Family*, Eric Schopler and Gary B. Mesibov, eds. Plenum Press, 1984.

Over the course of the next few months: "How to Work with Your State Legislature," S. Clarence Griffith and Christine Griffith. *Proceedings of the Second Annual Meeting and Conference of the National Society for Autistic Children*, 1971.

NSAC board member Amy Lettick opened a school called Benhaven: "Benhaven: A School That Works for the Autistic," Stephen Rudley and Cynthia Lynes. *New York*, Oct. 8, 1969.
students were encouraged to attend the school into adulthood: Ibid.
The total environment of Benhaven: "Benhaven," Amy Lettick. *Autism in Adolescents and Adults*, Eric Schloper and Gary Mesibov, eds. Plenum Press, 1983, pp. 355–79.
Signing turned out to be a popular medium of communication: "Pre-Vocational Training Program at Benhaven," Amy Lettick. *Proceedings of the Fourth Annual NSAC Congress*, 1972.
Sullivan was thrilled to see her fellow NSAC parents: "Parents as Trainers of Legislators, Other Parents, and Researchers."
the society's bimonthly newsletter: Based on accounts in "The Role of the National Society in Working with Families.
an in-depth study of the biology of autism in 1974: *The Autistic Syndromes*, Mary Coleman, ed. North-Holland, 1976.
"He reads and understands books on electronics": "Savant Capabilities of Autistic Children and Their Cognitive Implications," Bernard Rimland. *Cognitive Defects in the Development of Mental Illness*, George Serban, ed., Brunner/Mazel, 1978, p. 44.
"It may not be too far amiss": Ibid, p. 44.
small but highly committed membership: NSAC had just two thousand members in 1970. *The Autism Matrix*, Gil Eyal et al. Polity Press, 2010, p. 186.
"So many children . . .": Ibid.
"Better *Everything* for Mentally Ill Children": "Special Report on the First NSAC Congress," Clara Claiborne Park. Quoted in *Research and Education: Top Priorities for Mentally Ill Children. Proceedings of the Second Annual Meeting and Conference of the National Society for Autistic Children*, 1971.
sharing information on equal terms: "The Role of the National Society in Working with Families."
The air in the Sheraton Palace was electric: "Special Report on the First NSAC Congress."
a former graduate student of Bettelheim's: A Tribute to Eric Schopler (1927–2006). http://www.youtube.com/watch?v=D_THeWH0ox4
"herewith I especially acquit you people as parents": Transcript of Kanner's address to the First Annual NSAC Congress provided by Ruth Christ Sullivan.
a collection of his essays: *Childhood Psychosis.*
Never be embarrassed about taking them places: *Research and Education: Top Priorities for Mentally Ill Children. Proceedings of the Second Annual Meeting and Conference of the National Society for Autistic Children*, 1971.
"We cannot allow another generation of our adult children": "Autism Society of America Position Paper on the National Crisis in Adult Services for Individuals with Autism," ASA Board of Directors, adopted July 17, 2001, updated May 2007.
"That's a good girl!": "Experimental Studies in Childhood Schizophrenia: Analysis of Self-Destructive Behavior," O. Ivar Lovaas et al. *Journal of Experimental Child Psychology*, Vol. 2, 1965, pp. 67–84.
"a slow procedure": Ibid.
"She stopped hitting herself for about 30 seconds": "Poet with a Cattle Prod."

less sensitive to auditory input: "Response Latencies to Auditory Stimuli in Autistic Children Engaged in Self-Stimulatory Behavior," O. Ivar Lovaas, Alan Litrownik, and Ronald Mann. *Behaviour Research and Therapy*, Vol. 9, No. 1, Feb. 1971, pp. 39–49.

"garbage behavior": "Strengths and Weaknesses of Operant Conditioning in the Treatment of Autistic Children."

"It is obviously very embarrassing": Ibid.

may *facilitate* learning: "A Cognitive Defense of Stimming," Cynthia Kim. http://musingsofanaspie.com/2013/06/18/a-cognitive-defense-of-stimming-or-why-quiet-hands-makes-math-harder/

Mike and Marty: Lovaas never names the twins in his published studies, but his dedication for *The ME Book* appears to be a list of the first experimental subjects at the Young Autism Project at UCLA, beginning with Beth. *Teaching Developmentally Disabled Children: The ME Book*, O. Ivar Lovaas. PRO-ED, 1981.

"rocking, fondling themselves, and moving hands and arms": "Building Social Behavior in Autistic Children Using Electric Shock," O. Ivar Lovaas, Benson Schaeffer, and James Q. Simmons. *Journal of Experimental Research in Personality*, Vol. 1, 1956, pp. 99–109.

blasts of "well over 100" decibels: Ibid.

capable of causing physical damage to the eardrum: "About Hearing Loss." Centers for Disease Control and Prevention. http://www.cdc.gov/healthyyouth/noise/signs.htm#3

Harvard Inductorium: "The First Stimulators—Reviewing the History of Electrical Stimulation and the Devices Crucial to Its Development," L. A. Geddes. *Engineering in Medicine and Biology Magazine*, No. 4, Vol. 13, Aug.–Sept. 1994.

used in canine obedience tests: *Mansfield News Journal*, March 31, 1963.

"a commercially available device for shocking livestock": "The Effects and Side Effects of Punishing the Autistic Behaviors of a Deviant Child," Todd R. Risley. *Journal of Applied Behavioral Analysis*, No. 1, 1968. (Note: Risley says in the paper that the experiments described commenced in 1963.)

a case for punishment: "Punishment," Richard L. Solomon. *American Psychologist*, Vol. 19, No. 4, Apr. 1964, pp. 239–53.

"Punishment can be a very effective tool for behavior change": "Building Social Behavior in Autistic Children by Use of Electric Shock," O. Ivar Lovaas, Benson Schaeffer, James Q. Simmons. *Journal of Experimental Research in Personality*, Vol 1, No. 2, 1965, pp. 99–109.

Lovaas tried preventing the children in his lab from eating: "Establishment of Social Reinforcers in Two Schizophrenic Children on the Basis of Food," O. Ivar Lovaas, Gilbert Freitag, et al. *Journal of Experimental Child Psychology*, Vol. 4, No. 2, Oct. 1966, pp. 109–125.

"it is a pleasure to work with a child who is on mild food deprivation": "Strengths and Weaknesses of Operant Conditioning in the Treatment of Autistic Children."

"She wants it bloody": Ibid.

he dubbed Lovaas a visionary: "Poet with a Cattle Prod."

the dour visage of Alfred Hitchcock: "The Nightmare of Life with Billy," Don Moser, *Life*, May 7, 1965.

"If you think that the children in the article were mistreated": "Risks and Benefits in the Treatment of Autistic Children," Ruth Christ Sullivan, *Journal of Autism and Childhood Schizophrenia*, Vol. 8, No. 1, March 1978.

"tingle sticks": Ibid.

focused less on punishment and more on rewarding engagement: David Ryback, interview with the author, 2012.

"There was no hesitation": Ibid.

"I never let anyone do that to Joe": Ruth Christ Sullivan, interview with the author, 2012.

"Today we are plagued with increased numbers of experimentalists calling themselves 'therapists'": "Risks and Benefits in the Treatment of Autistic Children," Ruth Christ Sullivan.

"irrational" and "sanctimonious": Ibid., p. 101.

"To remain satisfied with punishment": "B. F. Skinner's Position on Aversive Treatment," James C. Griffin et al. *American Journal of Mental Retardation*, Vol. 93, No. 1, 1988, 104–105.

innovative punishments: *Ethics for Behavior Analysts*, Jon Bailey and Mary Burch. Taylor & Francis, 2011.

"two connoisseurs wine-tasting, sharing rare tastes": "The Twins." *The Man Who Mistook His Wife for a Hat, and Other Clinical Tales*, Oliver Sacks. Summit Books, 1985, p. 202.

a special kinship with the Finns: Oliver Sacks, interview with the author, 2013.

"José had drawn the watch with remarkable fidelity": "The Autist Artist," *The Man Who Mistook His Wife for a Hat and Other Clinical Tales*, Oliver Sacks. Summit Books, 1985, pp. 214–33.

"I had never seen such an ability before": Oliver Sacks, interview with the author, 2013.

These unwelcome melodies: Without identifying the contents of the book, Sacks wrote about this dream in *Musicophilia: Tales of Music and the Brain*. Knopf, 2007, p. 280.

He teamed up with Lovaas: *The "Sissy-Boy Syndrome" and the Development of Homosexuality*, Richard Green. Yale University Press, 1987.

"a remarkable ability": "Behavioral Treatment of Deviant Sex-Role Behaviors in a Male Child," George Rekers and O. Ivar Lovaas. *Journal of Applied Behavior Analysis*, Vol. 7, No. 2, Summer 1974, pp. 173–90.

Their descriptions of the little boy's behavior: *The "Sissy-Boy Syndrome" and the Development of Homosexuality.*

Mark broke down sobbing: "What Are Little Boys Made Of?" Jim Burroway. *Box Turtle Bulletin*, 2011. http://www.boxturtlebulletin.com/what-are-little-boys-made-of-main

("Plays with Barbie dolls at five, sleeps with men at 25 . . ."): "The Feminine Boy Project Still Threatens Gender Expression," Cynthya BrianKate. Stony Book Press, March 30, 2010. http://sbpress.com/2010/03/feminine-boy-project/

six-figure grants from NIMH and the Playboy Foundation: *The "Sissy-Boy Syndrome" and the Development of Homosexuality.*

"the Zelig of homophobia": "A Heaven-Sent Rent Boy," Frank Rich. *New York Times*, May 16, 2010.

Informed of Kirk's suicide: "The 'Sissy Boy' Experiment: Uncovering the Truth." *AC 360*, Anderson Cooper, June 2011. http://www.youtube.com/watch?v=A-irAT0viF0

Though Rekers credited him: "Treatment of Gender Identity Confusion in Children: Research Findings and Theoretical Implications for Preventing Sexual Identity Confusion and Unwanted Homosexual Attractions in Teenagers and Adults," George Rekers. Keynote address, 2009 NARTH Convention, West Palm Beach, FL.

"a locked iron mask would prevent nail biting": *Alternatives to Punishment: Solving Behavior*

Problems with Non-aversive Strategies, Gary W. LaVigna and Anne M. Donnellan. Ardent Media, 1986, p. 6.

the board of directors of the Autism Society of America (ASA) passed a resolution: *Understanding Autism*, Chloe Silverman. Princeton University Press, 2012, p. 111.

some ABA practitioners: "Personal Paradigm Shifts Among ABA and PBS Experts: Comparisons in Treatment Acceptability," Fredda Brown, Craig Michaels, et al. *Journal of Positive Behavioral Interventions*, Vol. 10, No. 4, Oct. 2008, pp. 212–27.

Painful electric shocks are still employed: "Sending $30 Million a Year to a School with a History of Giving Kids Electric Shocks," Heather Vogell and Annie Waldman. *Pacific Standard*, Jan. 5, 2015. http://www.psmag.com/politics-and-law/sending-30-million-year-school-history-giving-kids-electric-shocks-97501

"We were disappointed," he admitted: "The Autistic Child: Language Development through Behavior Modification," O. Ivar Lovaas. Irvington, 1977, p. 119.

"When I think back": "An Interview with O. Ivar Lovaas."

"The program does not turn out normal children": "Strengths and Weaknesses of Operant Conditioning in the Treatment of Autistic Children."

"Find pleasure in small steps forward": *Teaching Developmentally Disabled Children: The ME Book*, p. 4.

"normal intellectual and educational functioning": "Behavioral Treatment and Normal Educational and Intellectual Functioning in Young Autistic Children," O. Ivar Lovaas. *Journal of Consulting and Clinical Psychology*, Vol. 55, No. 1, Feb. 1987, pp. 3–9.

"I'm positive now that autism need not be chronic": "Research Reports Progress against Autism," Daniel Goleman. *New York Times*, March 10, 1987.

an award-winning documentary: *Behavioral Treatment of Autism.*

"It's not unusual for humanity": "In Defense of Ivar Lovaas."

the psychologist "tried to structure things": *A History of Autism*, p. 134.

Independent researchers: Ibid., p. 135.

"But we at the Medical School Neuropsychiatric Institute weren't promising a cure": Ibid.

"could not in good conscience fail to pursue this lead": "An Orthomolecular Study of Psychotic Children," Bernard Rimland. *Journal of Orthomolecular Psychiatry*, Vol. 3, 1974, pp. 371–77.

often at the cost of tens of millions of dollars: "The Placebo Problem," Steve Silberman. *Wired*, Sept. 2009.

"computer clustering": "The Modern History of Autism."

a dozen or more different diseases: "An Orthomolecular Study of Psychotic Children."

no reliable information: Earnest Wells Richardson. "A Hierarchical Clustering Technique," master's thesis, United States Naval Postgraduate School, 1971, p. 58.

ads in medical journals: Deaner advertisement. *Canadian Medical Association Journal*, Vol. 80, No. 12, June 1959, p. 73.

The litany of "vague complaints": "Council on Drugs: New and Nonofficial Drugs," *JAMA*, Vol. 172, No. 14, Apr. 2, 1960, pp. 1518–19.

it was finally taken off the market: *Natural Organics, Inc. v. Gerald A. Kessler*, Docket No. 9294, 2001.

heightened risk for grand mal seizures: "Clinical Uses of Deanol (Deaner): A New Type of

Psychotropic Drug," J. D. Moriarty and J. D. Mebane. *American Journal of Psychiatry*, Vol. 115, No. 10, 1959, pp. 941–42.

"If yelling, begging, and pleading:" *Natural Organics, Inc. v. Gerald A. Kessler.*

"Why didn't you compare the drugs with the vitamins directly?": "Progress in Research," Bernard Rimland. *Proceedings of the 4th Annual Meeting of the National Society for Autistic Children*, 1972.

"You are not undertaking a scientific experiment": *Recovering Autistic Children*, Stephen Edelson and Bernard Rimland. Autism Research Institute, 2006, p. 23.

the key to the mystery: "The Discovery of Phenylketonuria: The Story of a Young Couple, Two Retarded Children, and a Scientist," Siegried A. Centerwall and Willard R. Centerwall. *Pediatrics*, Vol. 105, No. 1, Jan. 1, 2000, pp. 89–103.

"If you go with Ritvo, I resign": *A History of Autism.*

a lanky, curly-haired Ramones fan: Steve Edelson, interview with the author.

Lovaas suggested that he pay a visit: Ibid.

no evidence of benefit: "A Systematic Review of Secretin for Children with Autism Spectrum Disorders," S. Krishnaswami, M. L. McPheeters, and J. Veenstra-VanderWeele. *Pediatrics*, Vol. 127, No. 5, May 1, 2011, pp. e1322–25.

a "sympathetic and tolerant reception" by their teachers: "Early Infantile Autism (1943–1955)," Leo Kanner and Leon Eisenberg. *American Journal of Orthopsychiatry*, Vol. 26, Issue 3, July 1956, pp. 55–65.

CHAPTER 8. NATURE'S SMUDGED LINES

Peter Bell had just graduated from Northwestern University: Peter Bell, interview with the author, 2012.

More than 80 percent of the patients were "certified": *Moving On from Mental Hospitals to Community Care: A Case Study of Change in Exeter*, David King. Nuffield Trust, 1991.

the Mental Health Act: "How Autism Became Autism: The Radical Transformation of a Central Concept of Child Development in Britain," Bonnie Evans. *History of the Human Sciences*, Vol. 26, No. 3, July 2013, pp. 3–31.

raising more than three thousand pounds in one night: "Heart and Soul: Charles Dickens on the Passion and Power of Fundraising," Aline Reed. SOFII. http://www.sofii.org/node/829

several likely cases of autism: *Autism: A Social and Medical History*, Mitzi Waltz. Palgrave Macmillan, 2013.

"An action, once started, continues indefinitely": "Discussion: Psychoses in Childhood," Mildred Creak et al. *Proceedings of the Royal Society of Medicine*, Vol. 45, No. 11, 1952.

"The cult of names added chaos": "An Experimental Approach to the Psychopathology of Childhood Autism," E. J. Anthony. *British Journal of Medical Psychology*, Vol. 21, 1958, pp. 211–25.

"he is schizophrenic, because in my scheme I must call him so": "Infantile Autism and the Schizophrenias," Leo Kanner. *Behavioral Science*, Vol. 10, No. 4, 1965.

the Nine Points: *A History of Autism*, p. 168.

Creak's Nine Points turned out to be hard to apply in practice: "The History of Ideas on

Autism: Legends, Myths, and Reality," Lorna Wing. *Autism*, Vol. 1, No. 13, July 1997, pp. 13–23.

Growing up in a little town called Gillingham: Lorna Wing and Judith Gould, interview with the author, 2011.

she applied unsuccessfully for more than ninety posts in London: "Obituary: Dr. Mildred Creak," Philip Graham. *Independent*, Nov. 6, 1993.

John's childhood years were more difficult by comparison: "Contribution and Legacy of John Wing (1923–2010)," *British Journal of Psychiatry*, Vol. 198, 2011, pp. 176–78.

In 1958, a school secretary named Sybil Elgar: *Oxford Dictionary of National Biography 2005–2008*, Lawrence Goldman, ed. Oxford University Press, 2013, pp. 344–46.

at the behest of two mothers: *A History of Autism*, p. 88.

But Elgar persisted in her efforts: "Perspectives on a Puzzle Piece," Helen Allison. National Autistic Society, 1987.

gleefully rolling on the floor with the children: *A History of Autism*, p. 89.

"Children need praise and encouragement": *Oxford Dictionary of National Biography, 2005–2008*, p. 344.

Somerset Court: *A History of Autism*, p. 162.

Rutter's early work also decisively untangled autism from schizophrenia: "Today's Neuroscience, Tomorrow's History: A Video Interview with Sir Michael Rutter," Richard Thomas. History of Modern Biomedicine Research Group, 2007.

a prevalence estimate of 4.5 cases of autism in 10,000: "Autistic Conditions in Early Childhood: A Survey in Middlesex," J. K. Wing, N. O'Connor, and V. Lotter. *British Medical Journal*, Vol. 3, 1967, pp. 389–92.

They saw kids who flapped their hands: "The Continuum of Autistic Characteristics," Lorna Wing, *Diagnosis and Assessment in Autism*, Eric Schopler and Gary B. Mesibov, eds. Plenum Press, 1988.

"Parents without special experience tend to overlook or reject the idea of autism": "Asperger's Syndrome and Kanner's autism," Lorna Wing. *Autism and Asperger Syndrome*. Cambridge University Press, 1991.

images of rainbows: Lorna Wing and Judith Gould, interview with the author, 2011.

CHAPTER 9. THE *RAIN MAN* EFFECT

Barry Morrow drove his 1954 Studebaker: Barry Morrow, interview with the author, 2013.

"It was as if he had some epic tale he wanted to weave for me": "Everybody's Bill," Barry Morrow. *School of Social Work Newsletter*, University of Iowa, Summer 1977.

Mary told them: Sackter's family background and years at Faribault are chronicled in *The Unlikely Celebrity: Bill Sackter's Triumph over Disability*, Thomas Walz. Southern Illinois University Press, 1998.

he was paid the equivalent of 30 cents to $1.50 a month: Questionnaire returned by Faribault staff member to Southbury Training School, Connecticut State Department of Health, Aug. 15, 1966.

(A group of senators' wives . . .): "Parents Fight for Children with Developmental Disabilities," Jane Birks. Minnesota Historical Society Library, 1999.

protruded through a baseball-sized blister at the back of his head: *Islands of Genius*, Darold Treffert. Kingsley, 2010, pp. 120–22.

rushing off to a golf game: *The Real Rain Man.* Documentary by Focus Productions. Bristol, England, 2006.

John Langdon Down, the superintendent of the Royal Earlswood Asylum: *Mental Disability in Victorian England: The Earlswood Asylum, 1847–1901*, David Wright, Oxford, Oxford University Press, 2000.

"many examples of children who had spoken well and with understanding but who lost speech": "Dr. J. Langdon Down and 'Developmental' Disorders," Darold Treffert, Wisconsin Medical Society, https://www.wisconsinmedicalsociety.org/professional/savant-syndrome/resources/articles/dr-j-landon-down-and-developmental-disorders/

"Shakespeare would have cared!": *Islands of Genius*, p. 126.

he listed his occupation on tax forms as "typist": Barry Morrow, personal communication.

"could evolve into a film classic": UA-Project "coverage" of the original *Rain Man* script, Anne Brand. Courtesy of Barry Morrow, Sept. 18, 1986.

to "live truthfully": "Before They Were Kings," Richard Meryman, *Vanity Fair*, March 2004.

To cultivate his French accent: Ibid.

(The technique was introduced to America . . .): "Electric Shock, a New Treatment," Marjorie Van de Water. *Science News-Letter*, Vol. 38, No. 3, July 20, 1940, pp. 42–44.

"All my life I had wanted to get inside a prison or a mental hospital": "Playboy Interview: Dustin Hoffman," Richard Meryman. *Playboy*, Vol. 22, No. 4, 1975.

"I can't, I caaan't!": "Tales of Hoffman," Hendrik Hertzberg. *New Yorker*, Jan. 21, 2013.

He believed that treating the subject of developmental disability: "Barry Levinson: Making Out Like Bandits," Alex Simon. *Venice*, Oct. 2001.

as his brothers and sisters unwrapped their gifts: "Dustin and Me," Sherri Dalfonse. *Washingtonian*, July 1992.

A decade before most people thought about buying a personal computer: Ibid.

"People began treating him more seriously": Kevin Guthrie, interview with the author, 2014.

"All of that stuff came from me": Gail Mutrux, interview with the author, 2014.

"We just made a film that will play for a month or two": "*Rain Man*, the Movie/*Rain Man*, Real Life," Darold Treffert. https://www.wisconsinmedicalsociety.org/professional/savant-syndrome/resources/articles/rain-man-the-movie-rain-man-real-life/

one of NSAC's co-founders: "'Rain Man' validates the feelings of many touched by autism," Sue Reilly. *Los Angeles Daily News*, Jan. 15, 1989.

"We're always keeping a lid on our own autism": "The Real Press Junket," Edward Guthmann. *San Francisco Chronicle*, July 15, 2001.

"It seems that *Rain Man* has stimulated almost every newspaper and magazine in the country": "*Rain Man* and the Savants' Secrets," Bernard Rimland. *Autism Research Review International*, Vol. 2 No. 3, 1988.

"virtually unheard of among autistic people": "Dustin and Me."

more than a million people a year: "Joseph's Story." Autism Services Center. http://www.autismservicescenter.org/about/josephs_story

CHAPTER 10. PANDORA'S BOX

"I have felt like Pandora": "Past and Future Research on Asperger Syndrome," Lorna Wing. *Asperger Syndrome*, A. Klin, F. Volkmar, and S. Sparrow, eds. Guildford Press, 2000, p. 418.

"I just didn't know what the hell to do": "The Dictionary of Disorder," Alix Spiegel. *New Yorker*, Jan. 3, 2005.

"Compared to other types of [medical] services there is less clarity": *The Making of DSM-III: A Diagnostic Manual's Conquest of American Psychiatry*, Hannah S. Decker. Oxford University Press, 2013, p. 27.

"I share a congressional consensus": "DSM-III and the Transformation of American Psychiatry: A History," M. Wilson. *American Journal of Psychiatry*, Vol. 150, No. 3, March 1993, pp. 399–410.

"Our adversaries are not demons, witches, fate, or mental illness": *The Myth of Mental Illness*, Thomas Szasz. Harper & Row, 1961.

"data-oriented people": "The Dictionary of Disorder."

"He doesn't understand people's emotions": Ibid.

One clinic reported only a single child: "A Comparison of Schizophrenic and Autistic Children," W. H. Green, M. Campbell, et al. *Journal of the American Academy of Child and Adolescent Psychiatry*, Vol. 23, No. 4, July 1984, 399–409.

***DSM-III* "looks very scientific":** Robert Spitzer, quoted in *The Book of Woe: The DSM and the Unmaking of Psychiatry*, Gary Greenberg. Blue Rider Press, 2013, p. 41.

"I'll call a kid a zebra": *Unstrange Minds*, Roy Richard Grinker. Basic Books, 2008, p. 131.

280,000 copies in its first two years alone: *The Physiology of Psychological Disorders*, James G. Hollandworth. Springer, 1990, p. 17.

"Autism should no longer be conceptualized as an extremely rare disorder": "Autism: Not an Extremely Rare Disorder," Christopher Gillberg, Lorna Wing. *Acta Psychiatrica Scandinavica*, Vol. 99, 1999, pp. 399–406.

an unusually colorful pediatrician in London who founded a magazine: "Ambitious Outsider: An Interview with *Ambit* Editor Martin Bax," *3 A.M.*, 2002.

In the 1970s he had written a dystopian novel: *The Hospital Ship*, Martin Bax. New Directions, 1976.

a comprehensive analysis of the Family Fund database: "Market for Disabled Children's Services—A Review." PricewaterhouseCoopers LLP, 2006.

By the 1990s, however, referral to a specialist: "Autistic Spectrum Disorders," Lorna Wing. *British Medical Journal*, Feb. 10, 1996.

The new IDEA rules also required schools to comply: "Three Reasons Not to Believe in an Autism Epidemic," Morton Ann Gernsbacher, Michelle Dawson, and H. Hill Goldsmith. *Current Directions in Psychological Science*, Vol. 14, No. 2, Apr. 2005.

Simultaneously, the first standardized clinical instruments: "Psychometric Instruments Available for the Assessment of Autistic Children," Susan L. Parks. *Diagnosis and Assessment of Autism*, Eric Schopler and Gary Mesibov, eds. Plenum Press, 1988, pp. 123–36.

Before the 1980s, autistic kids were generally considered "untestable": "The Anatomy of a Negative Role Model," Eric Schopler. *The Undaunted Psychiatrist: Adventures in Research*, Gary Brannagan and Matthew Merrens. McGraw-Hill, 1993, p. 182.

a child's score could vary widely depending on which parent filled in the checklist: "An Experience with the Rimland Checklist for Autism," Aubrey W. Metcalfe. *Clinical Studies in Childhood Psychoses*, S. A. Szurek and I. N. Berlin, eds. Brunner/Mazel, 1973, pp. 469–70.

Rimland refused to publish his scoring key: "Psychometric Instruments Available for the Assessment of Autistic Children," Susan L. Parks. *Diagnosis and Assessment of Autism*, Eric Schopler and Gary Mesibov, eds. Plenum Press: New York and London, 1988, pp. 123–36.

which was particularly good at distinguishing autism: *A History of Autism*, p. 177.

Schopler believed that an approach to autism that took into account: "The Anatomy of a Negative Role Model," p. 183.

After reading the manual and watching a thirty-minute video: *The Autism Matrix*, p. 235.

As a result, it became wildly popular: *A History of Autism*, p. 177.

"Fifty percent of the autistic population are mute": "Speech and Language Acquisition and Intervention: Behavioral Approaches," Marjorie Charlop and Linda Haymes. *Autism in Children and Adults*, Johnny Matson, ed. Brooks/Cole, 1994, p. 213.

The first international conference on Asperger's: *The Complete Guide to Asperger's Syndrome*, Tony Attwood. Kingsley, 2006, p. 36.

"Odd and unusual behaviors do not, in and of themselves, constitute a 'disorder'": "Clinical Case Conference: Asperger's Disorder," Fred R. Volkmar and Ami Klin. *American Journal of Psychiatry*, Vol. 157, 2000, pp. 262–67.

Consider Robert Edwards, an eleven-year-old boy: Ibid.

"As I explain to parents, the cure for Asperger's syndrome is very simple": Tony Attwood, personal communication, 2014.

"It was a crazy problem": Unpublished segment of Volkmar interview with Gary Greenberg for *The Book of Woe*, March 1, 2012.

***DSM-IV* casebooks, study guides, videotapes, and software:** For example, *DSM-IV Videotaped Clinical Vignettes*, Vols. 1 and 2, William Reed, Michael Wise. Brunner/Mazel Studios.

a small but crucial error: *Unstrange Minds*, Roy Richard Grinker. Basic Books, 2008, p. 140.

a notably understated article in an obscure journal: "The *DSM-IV* Text Revision: Rationale and Potential Impact on Clinical Practice," Michael B. First and Harold Alan Pincus. *Psychiatric Services*, Vol. 53, No. 3, March 2002.

By reanalyzing the field-test data: Ibid.

a fashion accessory for strolling on the Atlantic City boardwalk: "Foster Grant, Inc. History," Funding Universe. http://www.fundinguniverse.com/company-histories/fostergrant-inc-history/

a giant plastic-injection plant along the Nashua River: "Welcome to the Plastic City: Community Responses to the Leominster Autism Cluster," dissertation by Martha E. Lang. Guilford College, Brown University, May 1998.

"the Plastic City": *Combing through Leominster's History*, Gilbert P. Tremblay. Leominster Historical Commission Book Committee, Office of the Mayor, 2006, pp. 145–74.

Local gardeners got used to PVC particles frosting their vegetable beds: Martha E. Lang.

"Welcome to the Plastic City: Community Responses to the Leominster Autism Cluster," dissertation, Guilford College, Brown University, May 1998.

The Altobellis were haunted: "Welcome to the Plastic City."

Jimmy Anderson was just four years old when he was diagnosed with a rare form of cancer: *Anderson v. W. R. Grace: Background/About the Case*, Seattle University School of Law. http://www.law.seattleu.edu/centers-and-institutes/films-for-justice-institute/lessons-from-woburn/about-the-case

at least one study in the literature: *The Autistic Syndromes.*

thalidomide: "Autism in Thalidomide Embryopathy: A Population Study," C. Gillberg et al. *Developmental Medicine and Child Neurology*, Vol. 36, Issue 4, No. 4, April 1994, pp. 351–56.

Timothy Johnson, who had previously worked as a reporter for Channel 5 in Boston: David Ropeik, interview with the author.

"We begin with a report we believe will surprise the medical world": "The Street Where They Lived." *20/20*, ABC News, March 13, 1992.

Parents all over the country had contacted the network: "The Street Where They Lived," Part 2. *20/20*, ABC News, March 20, 1992.

Lori was defiant: Ibid.

her graduate thesis at Brown University on the leadership of mothers: "Welcome to the Plastic City."

six "quite clearly did not meet the criteria" for either autism or PDD-NOS: "Panel: Half of Leominster Autism Claims Verifiable," Ralph Ranalli. *Boston Herald*, May 15, 1992.

"As a parent, your one job in life": David Ropeik, interview with the author, 2013.

"It is not reasonable to believe that the population of [autistic] children has changed much": "The Modern History of Autism," p. 5.

(He called the PDD-NOS label "pseudoscientific" . . .): "Plain Talk About PDD and the Diagnosis of Autism," Bernard Rimland. *Autism Research Review International*, Vol. 7, No. 2, 1993, p. 3.

a $75,000 check intended for Rimland from the producers of *Rain Man*: "Hoffman Couldn't Retrieve Donation," *Rome News-Tribune*, Aug. 13, 1997.

Rimland's version of the events in the town: See, for example, *Healing the New Childhood Epidemics: Autism, ADHD, Asthma, and Allergies*, Kenneth Bock and Cameron Stauth. Ballantine Books, 2008.

the most "reactogenic" vaccine in the country's history: *The Panic Virus*, Seth Mnookin. Simon & Schuster, 2011, p. 69.

her two-and-a-half-year-old son, Christian: Testimony of Barbara Loe Fisher, U.S. House Government Reform Committee, Washington D.C., Aug, 3, 1999.

a "bad lot" of vaccine: Statement by Barbara Loe Fisher, Institute of Medicine Immunization Safety Committee, National Academy of Sciences, Washington, D.C., Jan. 11, 2001.

the risks of pertussis (which had killed 7,500 children in 1934 alone, out of 265,000 cases): "Junk Science in the Courtroom," Peter Huber. *Forbes*, July 8, 1991, p. 68.

Fisher, watching the broadcast, "felt betrayed": Statement by Barbara Loe Fisher, Institute of Medicine Immunization Safety Committee, National Academy of Sciences, Washington, D.C., Jan. 11, 2001.

In truth, Thompson, who was awarded an Emmy for *DPT: Vaccine Roulette*: Excerpt, *DPT: Vaccine Roulette*, WRC-TV, producer Lea Thompson, 1982.

Young, for example: "TV Report on DTP Galvanizes US Pediatricians," Elizabeth Rasche Gonzales. *JAMA*, Vol. 248, No. 1, July 2, 1982.

Pediatricians reported levels of fear: Ibid.

members of Congress were besieged: "State Defends Vaccine," Elsa Walsh. *Washington Post*, June 30, 1982.

never took a single course in biology, physiology, or chemistry: "Coincidental Man: An Interview with Harris Livermore Coulter." Greg Bedayn and Julian Winston. *The American Homeopath*, Vol. 2, 1995.

translating the Kremlin's official pronouncements: "Review: *On Resolutions: Soviet Communist Party History and Politics as Reflected in Official Documents,* edited by Harris Coulter and Robert Ehlers," John S. Reshetar, Jr. *Slavic Review*, Vol. 35, No. 2, June 1976, pp. 321–25.

"worked like magic": "Harris Coulter Interview: History, Vaccinations, and 'Mongrel Prescribing,'" William Berno. Conducted on the Homeopathy at Sea cruise, Oct. 1995.

persuaded his graduate advisor: "An Interview with Harris Livermore Coulter."

"the gay lifestyle": *AIDS and Syphilis: The Hidden Link*, Harris L. Coulter. North Atlantic Books, 1987.

Rimland was at home watching a talk show: "Children's Shots: No Longer a Simple Decision," Bernard Rimland. *ARRI Newsletter*, Vol. 9, No. 1, 1995.

several of the patients died anyway: "VG-1000—A Therapeutic Vaccine for Cancer," Harris Coulter, Valentin Govallo, et al. *Potentiating Health and the Crisis of the Immune System*, Springer, 1997, pp. 199–205.

trying to shed its image as a backwater: In his book *Callous Disregard*, Wakefield described the medical school as having been "becalmed in the academic doldrums for some years." *Callous Disregard*, Andrew Wakefield. Skyhorse, 2010.

"Our study suggests that exposure to measles virus in utero": "Crohn's Disease After In-Utero Measles Virus Exposure," Dr Anders Ekbom, Peter Daszak, Wolfgang Kraaz, Andrew J. Wakefield. *Lancet*, Vol. 348, No. 9026, Aug. 1996, pp. 515–17.

(The World Health Organization estimates that in 2000 alone . . .): "The Clinical Significance of Measles: A Review," Walter A. Orenstein. *Journal of Infectious Diseases*, Vol. 189, Suppl. 1, 2004, pp. S4–S16.

Wakefield's dean at the medical school, Arie Zuckerman: *Vaccine: The Debate in Modern America*, Mark A. Largent. Johns Hopkins University Press, 2012, pp. 102–103.

"I didn't know anything about autism": "Dr. Andrew Wakefield—In His Own Words," Alan Golding, Apr. 2010.

The mother explained that her son had serious bowel problems: "Dr. Andrew Wakefield on the Autism/Vaccine Controversy and His Ongoing Professional Persecution," Anthony Wile. *Daily Bell*, May 30, 2010.

In cautious and qualified language, his team reported: "Ileal-Lymphoid-Nodular Hyperplasia, Non-Specific Colitis, and Pervasive Developmental Disorder in Children," Andrew Wakefield et al. *Lancet*, Vol. 351, No. 9103, Feb. 28, 1998.

After peer reviewers of an early draft expressed concerns: "The Vaccine-Autism Fraud's Surprising History," Seth Mnookin. *Daily Beast*, Jan. 13, 2011. http://www.thedailybeast.com/articles/2011/01/13/mmr-vaccine-scare-andrew-wakefields-fraudulent-study.html

"We did not prove an association between measles, mumps, and rubella vaccine": "Ileal-

Lymphoid-Nodular Hyperplasia, Non-Specific Colitis, and Pervasive Developmental Disorder in Children."

A formidably built man with deep-set blue eyes and a crisp, no-nonsense manner: "The Crash and Burn of an Autism Guru," Susan Dominus. *New York Times,* Apr. 20, 2011.

He struck a similarly ominous tone in the promotional video: Transcript via "Royal Free Facilitates Attack on MMR in Medical School Single Shots Videotape," Brian Deer. http://briandeer.com/wakefield/royal-video.htm

Rimland thundered in a press release: "Parent Groups and Vaccine Policymakers Clash over Research into Vaccines, Autism and Intestinal Disorders," *PR Newswire*, March 3, 1998.

no impact on rising rates of autism diagnosis: "Thimerosal and the Occurrence of Autism: Negative Ecological Evidence from Danish Population-Based Data," K. M. Madsen et al. *Pediatrics*, Vol. 112, 2003, pp. 604–606.

News of the link between autism and vaccines spread: "Anti-Vaccine Activists, Web 2.0, and the Postmodern Paradigm—An Overview of Tactics and Tropes Used Online by the Anti-Vaccination Movement," Anna Kata. *Vaccine*, 2011.

stoked by an endless stream of "balanced" stories: "Sticking with the Truth," Curtis Brainard. *Columbia Journalism Review*, May 1, 2013.

Similarly, some parents began hosting "pox parties": "What to Do if You Get Invited to a Chickenpox Party," Melinda Wenner Moyer. *Slate*, Nov. 15, 2013. http://www.slate.com/articles/double_x/the_kids/2013/11/chickenpox_vaccine_is_it_really_necessary.html

one of the most widely and thoroughly refuted: "The Crash and Burn of an Autism Guru."

"If my son really is Patient 11": "Exposed: Andrew Wakefield and the MMR-Autism Fraud," Brian Deer. http://briandeer.com/mmr/lancet-summary.htm

ten of the study's co-authors took their names off the paper: "Controversial MMR and Autism Study Retracted," Maggie McKee. *New Scientist*, March 4, 2004.

Wakefield was stripped of his medical license: "Retracted Autism Study an 'Elaborate Fraud,' British Journal Finds," CNN Wire Staff. http://www.cnn.com/2011/HEALTH/01/05/autism.vaccines/

a systematic meta-analysis of a dozen epidemiological studies: "Association of Autistic Spectrum Disorder and the Measles, Mumps, and Rubella Vaccine: A Systematic Review of Current Epidemiological Evidence," Kumanan Wilson et al. *Archives of Pediatric and Adolescent Medicine*, Vol. 157, No. 7, July 2003, pp. 628–63.

"It's a question of diagnosis": Lorna Wing and Judith Gould, interview with the author, 2011.

CHAPTER 11. IN AUTISTIC SPACE

"I am a 44-year-old autistic woman": "An Inside View of Autism," Temple Grandin. *High-Functioning Individuals with Autism*, Eric Schopler and Gary Mesibov, eds. Plenum Press, 1992, pp. 105–125.

"If I'd known then what I know now": Ruth Christ Sullivan, interview with the author, 2013.

"suddenly the whole room got quiet": Temple Grandin, interview with the author, 2014.

a shy engineer: "In the Spotlight: Tony and Temple," Tony Attwood. *Autism Asperger's Digest*, Jan.–Feb. 2000. http://www.fenichel.com/Temple-Tony.html

("*We* don't think we're a cow or something, do *we*?" . . .): *Emergence: Labeled Autistic*, Temple Grandin. Arena Press, 1986, p. 91.

"For the first time in my life": Ibid.

"the first book written by a recovered autistic individual": "Foreword," Bernard Rimland. *Emergence*, p. 3.

"I was doing a lot of construction projects": Temple Grandin, interview with the author, 2014.

"Aware adults with autism": "An Anthropologist on Mars," Oliver Sacks. *New Yorker*, Dec. 27, 1993.

"The autistic mind, it was supposed at that time": Ibid.

they had come to feel that their autism, "while it may be seen as a medical condition": Ibid.

a "sweet, calming" feeling: Ibid.

in states where cattle are routinely treated badly: "Commentary: Behavior of Slaughter Plant and Auction Employees toward the Animals," Temple Grandin. *Anthrozoos*, Vol. 1, No. 4, 1998, pp. 205–213.

"If I could snap my fingers and be non-autistic, I would not": "An Anthropologist on Mars."

"a dead soul in a live body": "The Real Scandal of the MMR Debate," Walter Spitzer. *Daily Mail*, Dec. 20, 2001.

"like stroke patients who have suffered brain damage": "'Odd Duck' Behavior in Families Perhaps Caused by Brain Disorder," Marilyn Dunlop. *Toronto Star*, Feb. 17, 1989.

"It is the plague of those unable to feel": "The Cruel, Heartless Victims of Asperger's; Only Human," Stephen Juan. *Sydney Morning Herald*, July 19, 1990.

"Earthworms were the first living creatures that I could identify with": Jim Sinclair, interview with the author, 2013.

a boy named Philip who suddenly stopped talking at age three: *Run Wild, Run Free*, David Rook. Dutton, 1967.

Susan and her husband, Marco, struggled for years: Susan Moreno, interview with the author, 2013.

introduced the concept of the autistic continuum and Asperger's syndrome: "Manifestations of Social Problems in High-Functioning Autistic People," Lorna Wing. *High-Functioning Individuals with Autism*, Eric Schopler and Gary Mesibov, eds. Plenum Press, 1992, pp. 129–41.

she was turned down for disability benefits: "Autistic Adulthood: A Challenging Journey," Anne Carpenter. *High-Functioning Individuals with Autism*, Eric Schopler and Gary Mesibov, eds. Plenum Press, 1992, pp. 289–94.

"Being autistic does not mean being inhuman": "Bridging the Gaps: An Inside-Out View of Autism (Or, Do You Know What I Don't Know?)," Jim Sinclair. *High-Functioning Individuals with Autism*, Eric Schopler and Gary Mesibov, eds. Plenum Press, 1992, pp. 289–94.

"If normal is being selfish, being dishonest": "Insider's Point of View," Kathy Lissner. *High-Functioning Individuals with Autism*, Eric Schopler and Gary Mesibov, eds. Plenum Press, 1992, pp. 303–6.

"subsided with time": "A World of Her Own," Daniel Goleman. *New York Times*, Feb. 21, 1993.

"Being autistic, I'm not supposed to understand things like this": "Social Uses of Fixations," Jim Sinclair. *Our Voice*, Vol. 1, No. 1, 1992.

"Together we felt like a lost tribe": *Somebody Somewhere*, Donna Williams. Three Rivers Press, 1994, p. 186.

"autistic space": "Autism Network International: The Development of a Community and Its Culture," Jim Sinclair. 2005. http://www.autreat.com/History_of_ANI.html

Its founder, Ray Kopp, was the father of a legally blind girl named Shawna: "My Affiliation with Autism," Ray Kopp. http://www.syr.edu/~rjkopp/data/history.html, accessed through archive.org

Kopp launched the list in 1992: Autism List FAQ. Archived at http://kildall.apana.org.au/autism/autismlistfaq.html

***neurotypical*:** "Neural connections in Toronto," Steve Cousins. *Our Voice*, Vol. 1, No. 3, 1993.

"Neurotypical syndrome is a neurobiological disorder": Institute for the Study of the Neurologically Typical. Muskie, 1998. http://isnt.autistics.org/

"Saying 'person with autism' suggests that autism is something bad": "Why I Dislike Person-First Language," Jim Sinclair. Autism Network International, 1999.

"Autistic people seem to have an affinity with computers": Carolyn Baird, interviewed by Wouter Schenk, Jan. 8, 1998. https://web.archive.org/web/19990128120401/http://web.syr.edu/~rjkopp/data/casinter.html

At a conference in St. Louis: "Autism Network International: The Development of a Community and Its Culture."

a presentation on the challenges of raising her daughter, Beth: "A Parent's View of More Able Individuals with Autism," Susan Moreno. *High-Functioning Individuals with Autism*, Gary Mesibov and Eric Schopler, eds., Plenum Press, 1992.

"It is as if the child they have dreamed about suddenly is missing": Ibid.

"Parents, all parents, attach to their children through dreams": "The Impact of Childhood Disability: The Parents' Struggle," Kenneth Moses. *Ways Magazine*, Spring 1987.

"After 10 years in the field, I had an impaired child": "Handicapping Conditions, Family Dynamics, and Grief Counseling," Kenneth Moses. *Family Support Services: A Parent/Professional Partnership*, Mary A. Slater and Patricia Mitchell, eds. National Clearinghouse of Rehabilitation Training Materials, 1984, p. 22.

"There is a limit": "Handicapping Conditions and the Interplay of the Family, Professionals, and Community," Mary A Slater. In *Family Support Services: A Parent/Professional Partnership*, p. 9.

"I waited five years before my daughter ever looked at me": "A Parent's View of More Able Individuals with Autism."

Lorna Wing published an article on the potential impact of the spectrum: "The Definition and Prevalence of Autism: A Review," Lorna Wing. *European Child and Adolescent Psychiatry*, Vol. 2, No. 2, Jan. 1993, pp. 61–74.

Sola Shelly, a researcher and mother of an autistic son: "Who Says Autism's a Disease?" Limor Gal. *Haaretz*, June 28, 2007.

"a way of being": "Don't Mourn for Us," Jim Sinclair. *Our Voice*, Vol. 1, No. 3, 1993.

"This is what we hear when you mourn over our existence": Ibid.

"I learned more about my son by talking to those people for an hour": Connie Deming, interview with the author, 2014.

name-tag labels similar to Autreat's green badges: "My Pro-Tips for YAPC First-Comers." http://techblog.babyl.ca/entry/yapc-tips

the late photographer Dan Asher: Dan Asher's attendance at Autreat 1996 is mentioned in *Elijah's Cup: A Family's Journey into the Community and Culture of High-Functioning Autism and Asperger's Syndrome*, Valerie Paradiz. Kingsley, 2005. His art and history are discussed in "Dan Asher by Ben Berlow," Ben Berlow. *BOMB*, No. 112, Summer 2010.

"It was immediately clear to me": *Elijah's Cup*, p. 137.

"Each was a star in the sky": Ibid., p. 138.

Projekt Empowerment in Sweden: "Mapping the Social Geographies of Autism—Online and Off-Line Narratives of Neuro-Shared and Separate Spaces," Hanna Bertilsdotter Rosqvist, Charlotte Brownlow, and Lindsay O'Dell. *Disability & Society*, Vol. 28, Issue 3, 2013.

she had been given a thought-provoking assignment by her rabbi: Judy Singer, personal communication, 2013.

"rigged in favor of Omniscience": Ibid.

Her mother's odd behavior: "Why Can't You Be Normal for Once in Your Life?" Judy Singer. *Disability Discourse*, Marian Corker and Sally French, eds. Open University Press, 1999.

"Just how handicapping the limitations of disability become": *Disability: Whose Handicap?* Ann Shearer. Blackwell, 1981, p. 61.

Many of the regular posters were women: "On Our Own Terms: Emerging Autistic Culture," Martijn Dekker. Self-published, 2000. http://web.archive.org/web/20000928205753/http://trainland.tripod.com/martijn.htm

"The impact of the Internet on autistics": "Autistics Are Communicating in Cyberspace," Harvey Blume. *New York Times*, June 30, 1997.

"I was interested in the liberatory, activist aspects of it": "The Autism Rights Movement," Andrew Solomon. *New York*, May 25, 2008.

Think back over all those "odd people out": "Odd People In: The Birth of Community amongst People on the 'Autistic Spectrum,'" Judy Singer. Bachelor's thesis, Faculty of Humanities and Social Science, University of Technology, Sydney, 1998.

"NT is only one kind of brain wiring": "Neurodiversity: On the Neurological Underpinnings of Geekdom," Harvey Blume. *Atlantic*, Sept. 1998.

They were both digital natives: Alex Plank and Dan Grover, interviews with the author, 2012.

Plank contributed dozens of articles: http://en.wikipedia.org/wiki/User:AlexPlank

"I met a kid there my age": Alex Plank, interview with the author, 2012.

an online press release: "Autistic Teens Create Website for People with Asperger's Syndrome," Alex Plank and Dan Grover, *PRWeb*, July 1, 2004.

his interactive sheet music app, Etude: "Steinway & Sons Debuts Etude 2.0 iPad App for Learning and Playing Piano." Press release, Sept. 15, 2011.

Plank's interview with Bram Cohen: "Asperger's Interviews: The Creator of BitTorrent," Alex Plank. http://wrongplanet.net/new-wrongplanet-net-aspergers-interviews-the-creator-of-bittorrent/

a third of all Internet traffic in the United States: "The 'One Third of All Internet Traffic' Myth," Ernesto. TorrentFreak. http://torrentfreak.com/bittorrent-the-one-third-of-all-internet-traffic-myth/

"We have your son": "The Autism Rights Movement," Andrew Solomon. *New York*, May 25, 2008.

the PR powerhouse that inspired *Mad Men*: "Matthew Weiner's No Madman," Kamau High. *AdWeek*, July 30, 2007. http://www.adweek.com/news/advertising/matthew-weiners-no-madman-89728

(Indeed, BBDO had done similar pro bono work for Autism Speaks): "When PSAs Work: Autism Speaks," Suzanne and Bob Wright. *Advertising Age*, June 17, 2009.

In the words of the center's press release: "Millions of Children Held Hostage by Psychiatric Disorders." *Business Wire*, Dec. 3, 2007.

"It's like with AIDS": "Campaign on Childhood Mental Illness Succeeds at Being Provocative," Joanne Kaufman. *New York Times*, Dec. 14, 2007.

He boasted to reporters that traffic to the Child Study Center's website had doubled: "Ads about Kids' Mental Health Problems Draw Fire," Shirley Wang. *Wall Street Journal*, Dec. 14, 2007.

the ads would soon be running in other cities: "Ads Anger Parents of Autistic Children." UPI. Dec. 14, 2007.

"Suddenly I went from being someone that people believed had a lot of potential": Ari Ne'eman, interview with the author, 2012.

"We've tried cripples before and it doesn't work": "An Elegant Tribute," Eve Kushner. *Monthly*, March 2009. http://themonthly.com/feature-03-09.html

the first on-campus self-advocacy group for disabled students: "The Rolling Quads," Rebecca Klumpp. *Disability Bible*, Apr. 2013. http://www.disabilitybible.com/disability-bible-listing/the-rolling-quads

the seminal law that banned discrimination: "Fact Sheet: Your Rights Under Section 504 of the Rehabilitation Act," U.S. Department of Health and Human Services, revised June 2006. http://www.hhs.gov/ocr/civilrights/resources/factsheets/504.pdf

didn't want anything to do with the word *disability*: "'It Is Not a Disease, It Is a Way of Life,'" Emine Saner. *Guardian*, Aug. 6, 2007.

appearances by Hillary Clinton and *CBS Evening News* anchor Katie Couric: "NYU Child Study Center Raises $9 Million and Celebrates 10th Anniversary." Press release, NYU Child Study Center, Dec. 5, 2007.

ASAN blasted out an action alert: "An Urgent Call to Action: Tell NYU Child Study Center to Abandon Stereotypes against People with Disabilities." Press release, ASAN, Dec. 8, 2007.

"This is a 'public awareness' campaign": "Rescue Me: The NYU Child Study Center's Ransom Notes Ad Campaign," Kristina Chew. Blisstree. Dec. 11, 2007. http://www.blisstree.com/2007/12/11/mental-health-well-being/rescue-me-the-nyu-child-study-centers-ransom-notes-ad-campaign/#ixzz3AgpNrbMn

In 2014, when Obama issued an executive order: "Obama's Wage Hike For Federal Contractors Won't Apply to Disabled Workers," Mike Elk. *In These Times*, Jan. 30, 2014. http://inthesetimes.com/working/entry/16205/obamas_wage_hike_for_federal_contractors_wont_apply_to_disabled_workers

ASAN assembled a diverse coalition of organizations: "After Outcry, White House Extends $10.10 Minimum Wage to Some Disabled Workers," Mike Elk. *In These Times*, Feb. 12, 2014. http://inthesetimes.com/working/entry/16263/in_a_reversal_white_house_extends_10.10_minimum_wage_boost_to_some_disabled.

provided testimony to the United Nations Special Rapporteur on Torture: "Compliance is Unreasonable: The Human Rights Implications of Compliance-Based Behavioral

Interventions under the Convention Against Torture and Convention on the Rights of Persons with Disabilities," Lydia Brown, *Torture in Healthcare Settings: Reflections on the Special Rapporteur on Torture's Thematic Report*, Center for Human Rights and Humanitarian Law, Washington College of Law, 2013.

"One of the cruelest tricks": "Foreword," Julia Bascom. *Loud Hands: Autistic People, Speaking*, Julia Bascom, ed. Autistic Self-Advocacy Network, 2012.

Zoe commented: Zoe Gross's comment on "Identifying and Accepting Happy Autistic Kids on the Playground," Shannon Rosa. Squidalicious. http://www.squidalicious.com/2012/04/identifying
-accepting-happy-autistic.html

CHAPTER 12. BUILDING THE *ENTERPRISE*: DESIGNS FOR A NEURODIVERSE WORLD

There are roughly as many people on the spectrum: John Elder Robison, interview with the author, 2014.

very old genes that are shared widely in the general population: "Most Genetic Risk for Autism Resides with Common Variation," Trent Gaugler, Lambertus Klei, Stephan J. Sanders, et al. *Nature Genetics*, Vol. 46, 2014, pp. 881–85.

"Many autistics, I believe, are suited for academic science": "The Power of Autism," Laurent Mottron. *Nature*, Vol. 479, Nov. 3, 2011.

EPILOGUE: THE MAYOR OF KENSINGTON

Although his father was a vocal opponent: "Beware the Advozealots: Mindless Good Intentions Injure the Handicapped," Bernard Rimland. *Autism Research Review International*, Vol. 7, No. 4, 1993, p. 7.

"run in the other direction": "Biomedical Treatments for Autism from the Autism Research Institute: Interview with Steve Edelson," Lisa Jo Rudy. About.com, Sept. 23, 2011. http:// http://autism.about.com/od/treatmentoptions/a/DANQandA.htm

Index